2000

BASIC READINGS
IN ANGLO-SAXON ENGLAND
VOL. 7

THE ARCHAEOLOGY OF ANGLO-SAXON ENGLAND: BASIC READINGS

GARLAND REFERENCE LIBRARY
OF THE HUMANITIES
VOL. 2086

BASIC READINGS IN ANGLO-SAXON ENGLAND

CARL T. BERKHOUT, PAUL E. SZARMACH,
AND JOSEPH B. TRAHERN, JR., *General Editors*

OLD ENGLISH SHORTER POEMS
Basic Readings
edited by Katherine O'Brien O'Keeffe

ANGLO-SAXON MANUSCRIPTS
Basic Readings
edited by Mary P. Richards

BEOWULF
Basic Readings
edited by Peter S. Baker

CYNEWULF
Basic Readings
Robert E. Bjork

THE ARCHAEOLOGY OF ANGLO-SAXON
ENGLAND
Basic Readings
edited by Catherine E. Karkov

THE ARCHAEOLOGY OF ANGLO-SAXON ENGLAND: BASIC READINGS

edited by

Catherine E. Karkov

GARLAND PUBLISHING, INC.
A MEMBER OF THE TAYLOR & FRANCIS GROUP
New York & London / 1999

Published in 1999 by
Garland Publishing Inc.
A Member of the Taylor & Francis Group
19 Union Square West
New York, NY 10003

10 9 8 7 6 5 4 3 2 1

Library of Congress Cataloging-in-Publication Data
Basic Readings in Anglo-Saxon Archaeology / [compiled] by Catherine E. Karkov.
        p.   cm. -- (Garland reference library of the humanities :
H2086. Basic readings in Anglo-Saxon England : #7)
        Includes bibliographical references and index.
        ISBN 0-8153-2916-4 (acid-free paper)
        1. England--Antiquities.   2. Great Britain--History--Anglo-Saxon
period, 449-1066.   3. Excavations (Archaeology)--England.
4. Archaeology, Medieval--England.   5. England--Civilization--To
1066. 6. Anglo-Saxons.   I. Karkov, Catherine. II. Series:
Garland reference library of the humanities. Basic readings in
Anglo-Saxon England: vol. 7.
DA155.B37   1999   99-30865
942.01--dc21   CIP

Printed on acid-free, 250 -year-life paper
Manufactured in the United States of America

Contents

Preface of the General Editors

Basic Readings in Anglo-Saxon England (BRASE) is a series of volumes that collect classic, exemplary, or ground-breaking essays in the fields of Anglo-Saxon Studies generally written in the 1960s or later, or commissioned by a volume editor to fulfill the purpose of the given volume. The General Editors impose no prior restraint of "correctness" of ideology, method, or critical position. Each volume editor has editorial autonomy to select essays that sketch the achievement in a given area of study or point to the potential for future study. The liveliness and diversity of the interdisciplinary field, manifest in the Annual Bibliography of the *Old English Newsletter* and in the review of that Bibliography in the Year's Work in Old English Studies, can lead only to editorial choices that reflect intellectual openness. BRASE volumes must be true to their premises, complete within their articulated limits, and accesible to a multiple readership. Each collection may serve as a "first book" on the delimited subject, where students and teachers alike may find a convienent starting point. The term *nus a quo*, approximately the 1960s, may be associated with the general rise of Anglo-Saxon Studies and a renewed, interdisciplinary professionalism therein; other collections, particularly in literature, represent the earlier period. Changes in publications patterns and in serials acquisitions policies, moreover, suggest that convenient collections can still assist the growth and development of Anglo-Saxon Studies.

In this seventh volume of the series, *Anglo-Saxon Archaeology*, Catherine E. Karkov seeks to bring to the broad scholarly audience interested in Anglo-Saxon England the major developments, larger issues, and potentialities of perhaps the most exciting subfield in the grand inter-disciplinary enterprise. Yet archaeology and the pursuit of material culture present a special difficulty to the Anglo-Saxonist who is at home in North America, not to mention to the nonspecialist. Without the *realia* of Anglo-Saxon England at hand to give daily confrontation, the North American student and scholar creates a phantasm of time and place and occasionally person, derived from illustrated books, slides, posters, and the odd summer or sabbatical visit. Shadowy as this image can be, it can lead to overinterpretation, as facile comparisons between Sutton Hoo and *Beowulf* have demonstrated this past generation. The safe and easy passage to the real Anglo-Saxon England from the merely imagined has few experienced guides who recognize the epistemological trolls lurking beneath.

By virtue of her professional training and her field experience Karkov is well placed to direct the general Anglo-Saxonist and, indeed, to fulfill the BRASE series mandate to offer classic, exemplary, and ground-breaking essays in the field. The general reader, and specifically the North American who is typically a student of literature, must begin with Kelley Wickham-Crowley's synthesizing essay on the history and methods of Anglo-Saxon archaeology over the last century and continue on with Martin Carver's complementary paper on the treatment of terminology and techniques, with special reference to a cross-section of sites and objects. Roberta Frank's witty essay on *Beowulf* and Sutton Hoo as odd couple, which has quickly attained classic status, might be the next stop for the literary student, but a joint trip with a history student to Eric Cambridge's consideration of the cult of Oswald might prove equally fruitful. The last four essays reflect the interest of the current decade in women's issues, thus providing another metalink between material culture and other disciplines pursuing these issues. Most of the other essays focus on specific sites, such as Rosemary Cramp on Wearmouth-Jarrow, or specific topics, such as David Hinton on the transition from the late Roman Empire to Anglo-Saxon England—all helping to fill out the general context for the Anglo-Saxon achievement. When Alfred wrote in his Preface to the *Pastoral Care* that there were books most needful to know, he did not anticipate that for our day and time there would be sites most needful to know.

The General Editors would like to thank Professor Karkov for taking on the special challenges that a book on Anglo-Saxon archaeology poses for a likely nonspecialist audience, whether those challenges were the specific ones of negotiating a heavily illustrated volume or locating or commisioning essays that bridge the gap between nonspecialists and archaeologists. Accordingly, the General Editors very warmly welcome this volume to BRASE.

Carl T. Berkhout
Paul E. Szarmach
Joseph B. Trahern

Introduction

An understanding of the material culture of Anglo-Saxon England is essential to the study of the Anglo-Saxon period in general. It is impossible to understand truly any aspect of the world of the Anglo-Saxons without an awareness of the people and techniques that produced the artifacts and monuments that have come down to us, as well as the landscapes and functions for which they were originally produced. The essays collected in this volume are intended to provide a basic guide to the breadth, history, terminology and types of site common in the field. Exhaustive coverage is impossible; there are simply too many different site types and too many different ways of excavating, mapping and analyzing them. The essays were chosen and commissioned to provide a balance between the general survey and analyses of specific sites or monuments, the world of the living and the world of the dead, straightforward archaeology and the intersection of archaeological theory and practice with other scholarly fields.

The volume opens with an essay by Kelley Wickham-Crowley that offers an introduction to the history and methods of Anglo-Saxon archaeology from the nineteenth century to the 1990s. The list of works cited at the end of her paper provides a basic research tool for further study of archaeological history and methods, as well as individual sites or object types. Martin Carver's paper is complementary to Wickham-Crowley's, presenting an overview of the period with clear definitions of terminology and techniques, and a discussion of the problems inherent in each. Carver both analyzes and illustrates a representative cross-section of sites and objects. The paper moves chronologically through the early, middle and late Saxon periods, charting developments and changes from one period to the next, and relating the archaeological material to art historical sources and historical events.

Beginning with David Hinton's essay "The Fifth and Sixth Centuries: Reorganization Among the Ruins," the papers are more specialized in focus. Hinton's paper covers the problematic period of transition from post-Roman Britain to what we now identify as Anglo-Saxon England. Bringing together a wide range of sources, from excavation reports to numismatic evidence, Hinton sets the archaeology of the period firmly within its cultural context. Simon James, Anne Marshall and Martin Millett consider the types of buildings found on Anglo-Saxon settlements during the sixth through eighth centuries, as well as the cultural sources and affinities these buildings exhibit. The authors define an early medieval building tradition with identifiable characteristics and roots in both Germanic and Romano-British architecture. First published in 1984, their essay remains a classic example of systematic analysis and the synthesis of an impressive range of evidence. For more recent information on some of the sites surveyed the reader is directed to the annual bibliographies and reports published in *Anglo-Saxon England*, the *Old English Newsletter,* and *Medieval Archaeology*.

In "York 700–1050," Richard Hall takes up chronologically where David Hinton left off. In contrast to James, Marshall, and Millet's analysis of a geographical range of sites, Hall focuses on the evolution over several centuries of one of the most important and extensively excavated Anglo-Saxon cities, providing a clear sense of the development of and difference between Anglo-Saxon *Eoforwic* and Anglo-Scandinavian *Jorvik*.

Rosemary Cramp's study of the twin monastic foundations of Monkwearmouth and Jarrow is the latest report on an important pair of sites still awaiting definitive publication. In this essay Cramp gives a thorough introduction to the plan and remains of the Anglo-Saxon monasteries, and then goes on to examine the crucial question of just how we can distinguish ecclesiastical from secular settlements. In so doing she situates Anglo-Saxon monasticism and the Anglo-Saxon church within a broader consideration of early medieval monasticism on the Continent. Harold Taylor's "The Anglo-Saxon Cathedral Church at Canterbury," also explores the continental influence on the Anglo-Saxon church, in this case the very specific influence of St. Peter's, Rome. Taylor uses early documentary sources describing the church at Canterbury combined with analysis of the cathedral plan and fabric to reconstruct the plan and structure of the original church. The passages reproduced from the writings of

Eadmer and Osbern also provide us with a good sense of how the spaces of the church were actually used by the Anglo-Saxons. Since Taylor's paper was written, excavations at Canterbury have proven his suggested reconstruction to be basically correct.

"Anglo-Saxon Church Building: Aspects of Design and Construction" remains the most succinct and detailed study of Anglo-Saxon building techniques. Warwick Rodwell musters evidence from surviving churches across England to elucidate the ways in which the Anglo-Saxons went about constructing everything from window frames to scaffolding. His paper, written originally for H. M. Taylor's festschrift, answers Taylor's plea in the inaugural issue of *Anglo-Saxon England* (1972) for a more systematic approach to the study of Anglo-Saxon architecture, and also provides an ecclesiastical parallel to James, Marshall and Millet's study of vernacular architecture.

Place-names are one area in which linguistics and the study of settlement and land use come together. Eric Cambridge's paper on "Archaeology and the Cult of St. Oswald in pre-Conquest Northumbria" uses analysis of place-names and church dedications to set both church and saint's cult within the larger religious and political landscape. Like Hinton, Cambridge highlights the need to consider all available forms of evidence, particularly when it comes to identifying and defining early ecclesiastical sites—an issue also raised by Rosemary Cramp. In addition, Cambridge explores the interrelation of important ecclesiastical and royal centers and the variety of contexts in which Oswald dedications might have originated in pre-Viking Northumbria.

Techniques of excavation and questions asked of the material record changed enormously between 1938 and 1992, the years that mark the beginning and end of field-work at Sutton Hoo. The history of excavation at the site, the nature of the cemetery and the finds, as well as an agenda for the future are the subject of Martin Carver's "The Anglo-Saxon Cemetery at Sutton Hoo: An Interim Report." Arguably the most fascinating and controversial of Anglo-Saxon archaeological sites, Sutton Hoo is also important as a lesson in the changing politics of archaeology. What began as an amateur rescue excavation sparked by an interested landowner became the first site in British history to be excavated according to a pre-established research agenda. Carver and the members of the Sutton Hoo Research Project demonstrated to both the scholarly community and the general public the need to question how much of a site we are justified in digging and how much should be left for future generations with different concerns, questions, and technologies. As well-known and important as Sutton Hoo may be, Roberta Frank demonstrates the all too powerful influence it has had on *Beowulf* (that most famous of Anglo-Saxon poems), and vice versa. Carver has described Sutton Hoo as a poem in need of interpretation; Frank shows that *Beowulf* has been interpreting it all along, while Sutton Hoo has, in turn, revealed the concrete archaeological evidence that proves the "truth" of the poem.

Sally Crawford's paper on "Children, Death and the Afterlife in Anglo-Saxon England" introduces a very new subject in the field of early medieval archaeology: childhood. Crawford's main interest is in childhood and the death of children as manifested in the material record of Anglo-Saxon England; however, she enriches our understanding of that subject by drawing on evidence from myth, medical practices surrounding birth and the care of children, literary sources and the beliefs and traditions of other cultures in addition to the archaeological evidence. While Crawford presents an overview based on study of a number of cemeteries and burials, Tania Dickinson focuses on a single fascinating and ambiguous burial. In "An Anglo-Saxon 'Cunning Woman' from Bidford-on-Avon," she identifies and describes the contents of the grave, reconstructs its probable original appearance, and locates it within its cultural and historical context. The study also has a larger purpose: enhancing the "agenda for studying Anglo-Saxon burials and society."

Carol Farr and Jane Hawkes both deal with Anglo-Saxon sculpture, what it has to tell us about the past, and how the ways in which we examine the evidence influence our interpretation of the period. In "Questioning the Monuments: Approaches to Anglo-Saxon Sculpture through Gender Studies," Farr examines the relevance of gender and discourse theory as tools for shedding light on Anglo-Saxon women and material culture. This is a field that has until *very* recently received little attention, but one that she demonstrates has the potential of offering much. Jane Hawkes's "Statements in Stone: Anglo-Saxon Sculpture, Whitby and the Christianization of the North," focuses on one of the most important and enigmatic of all early Anglo-Saxon sites. Her specific interest is in the role played by sculpture from Whitby in the process of christianization in the north of England. However, because Whitby was a double house under the care of abbess Hild and her successors, the subject is automatically one that is crucial to the study of Anglo-Saxon women and their role in the conversion process. Citing sculpture from a number of Northumbrian monasteries, Hawkes shows exactly how the Whitby monuments fit into the larger corpus of Anglo-Saxon stone sculpture, and what role that sculpture is likely to have played in the eyes of the church.

The volume closes with two chapters reprinted from Gale Owen-Crocker's book *Dress in Anglo-Saxon England*, again, a subject that has gained relatively little attention. The selections reprinted here deal with both women's dress in late Anglo-Saxon England, and textile production, a field apparently dominated by women in the early Middle Ages. We see, in other words, women as both products and producers of culture. Owen-Crocker's detailed and fully illustrated discussion of exactly what Anglo-Saxon women wore in the tenth and eleventh centuries allows us a glimpse of some of the people who inhabited this archaeological landscape.

The archaeology of Anglo-Saxon England is a diverse and ever-changing field. New discoveries and the development of new techniques and methodologies have required, and will continue to require new interpretations and reinterpretations, as well as new ways of practicing and thinking about the "science" of archaeology.

Acknowledgments

I would like to thank to all those who have helped in the preparation of this volume over the past two years, particularly Paul E. Szarmach, George H. Brown, David Pelteret, Linnea Dietrich, and Kristi Long. Special thanks go to the authors who contributed new essays: Kelley M. Wickham-Crowley, Martin O. H. Carver, Carol Farr and Jane Hawkes. I am also indebted to all the authors who have given permission to reprint their papers, most especially to David A. Hinton and Gale R. Owen-Crocker, both of whom provided help beyond the call of duty.

The following journals, publishers and institutions have provided permission to reprint papers and illustrations:

Figure 2.3: (a) Heinrich Härke, (b) Aarhus University Press.
Figure 2.4: Suffolk County Council.
Plate 2.1: Dr. Jane Hawkes.
Figure 2.6: The British Academy

David A. Hinton, "The Fifth and Sixth Centuries: Reorganization among the Ruins." Reprinted from *Archaeology, Economy and Society: England from the Fifth to the Fifteenth Century*, pp. 1–20. By permission of the author and Routledge. Copyright ©1990 The Author. Figure 3.1: by permission of the British Library. Figure 3.2: by permission of the Council for British Archaeology. Figure 3.3: by permission of the Ashmolean Museum, Oxford.

Simon James, Anne Marshall and Martin Millet, "An Early Medieval Building Tradition." Reprinted from *Archaeological Journal* 141 (1984), 182–215, by permission of the Royal Archaeological Institute and Society of Antiquaries of London. Copyright ©1984 Royal Archaeological Institute.

Richard A. Hall, "York 700–1050." Reprinted from *The Rebirth of Towns in the West*, eds. Richard Hodges and Brian Hobley (C.B.A. Research Rep. 68), 125–32, by permission of the author. Copyright ©1988 The Author.

Rosemary Cramp, "Monkwearmouth and Jarrow in their Continental Context." Reprinted from *Churches Built in Ancient Times*, 279–94, by permission of the Society of Antiquaries of London and Accordia Research Institute, University of London. Copyright ©1994 Society of Antiquaries and Accordia Research Institute.

H. M. Taylor, "The Anglo-Saxon Cathedral Church at Canterbury." Reprinted from *Archaeological Journal* 126 (1969), 101–30, by permission of the Royal Archaeological Institute and Society of Antiquaries of London. Copyright ©1969 Royal Archaeological Institute.

Warwick Rodwell, "Anglo-Saxon Church Building: Aspects of Design and Construction." Reprinted from *The Anglo-Saxon Church: Papers on History, Architecture, and Archaeology in Honour of Dr. H. M. Taylor*, eds. L. A. S. Butler and R. K. Morris (C.B.A. Research Rep. 60). Copyright ©1986 The Author.

Eric Cambridge, "Archaeology and the Cult of St. Oswald in pre-Conquest Northumbria." Reprinted from *Oswald: Northumbrian King to European Saint*, eds. Clare Stancliffe and Eric Cambridge, 128–63, by permission of the author and Paul Watkins Publishing. Copyright ©1995 The Author. A second edition of *Oswald* with additional references (included in this volume) was published by Paul Watkins in 1996.

Martin O. H. Carver, "The Anglo-Saxon Cemetery at Sutton Hoo." Reprinted from *The Age of Sutton Hoo*, ed. Martin Carver, 343–71, by permission of the author. Copyright ©1992 The Author.

Roberta Frank, "Beowulf and Sutton Hoo: The Odd Couple." Reprinted from *Voyage to the Other World: The Legacy of Sutton Hoo*, eds. Calvin B. Kendall and Peter S. Wells, 47–64, by permission of the publisher. Copyright ©1992 The Regents of the University of Minnesota.

Sally Crawford, "Children, Death and the Afterlife in Anglo-Saxon England." Reprinted from *Anglo-Saxon Studies in Archaeology and History* 6, ed. William Filmer-Sankey, 83–91, by permission of Oxford University Committee for Archaeology. Copyright ©1993 Oxford University Committee for Archaeology and the author.

Tania Dickinson, "An Anglo-Saxon 'Cunning Woman'" from Bidford-on-Avon." Reprinted from *In Search of Cult: Archaeological Investigations in Honour of Philip Rahtz*, ed. Martin Carver, 45–54, by permission of the author. Copyright ©1993 The Author and *University of York Archaeological Papers*.

Gale R. Owen-Crocker, "Women's Costume in the Tenth and Eleventh Centuries and Textile Production in Anglo-Saxon England." Reprinted from Gale R. Owen Crocker, *Dress in Anglo-Saxon England*, 131–148, 175–95. Copyright ©1986 The Author. All figures by Christine Wetherell except: figs. 16.33–16.34 (Kathleen Wood), fig. 16.37 (John Hines), figs. 16.42–16.46, 16.48–16.53, 16.55 (author).

Abbreviations

A.S.E.	*Anglo-Saxon England*
Archaeol. J.	*Archaeological Journal*
A.S.P.R.	Anglo-Saxon Poetic Records
A.S.S.A.H.	*Anglo-Saxon Studies in Archaeology and History*
B.A.R.	British Archaeological Reports
C.B.A.	Council for British Archaeology
C.C.S.L.	*Corpus Christianorum Series Latina*
E.E.M.F.	Early English Manuscripts in Facsimile
E.E.T.S.	Early English Texts Society
E.H.	*Bede's Ecclesiastical History of the English Church and People*, ed. B. Colgrave and R. Mynors (Oxford, 1969).
J.B.A.A.	*Journal of the British Archaeological Association*
M.A.	*Medieval Archaeology*
M.G.H.	Monumenta Germaniae Historica
O.E.D.	*Oxford English Dictionary*
P.B.A.	*Proceedings of the British Academy*
R.C.A.H.M.	Royal Commission on Ancient and Historic Monuments
R.C.A.H.M.S.	Royal Commission on Ancient and Historic Monuments of Scotland

CHAPTER 1

Looking Forward, Looking Back
Excavating the Field of Anglo-Saxon Archaeology

KELLEY M. WICKHAM-CROWLEY

> *The very obscurity that enshrouds the period ren-*
> *ders it certain that some of its truths must still have*
> *escaped detection, and that only examination on*
> *yet more intensive lines will bring them to the light.*
> —E. T. LEEDS, INTRODUCTION TO *EARLY ANGLO-*
> *SAXON ART AND ARCHAEOLOGY (1936), xi.*

Things from the past: the initial urge that created the field of archaeology arose when the desire for objects compelled people to search for them. For Anglo-Saxon archaeology, should that be the discovery and retrieval of bones for a saint, as C. J. Arnold suggests in mentioning the account of Roger of Wendover, and the invention (discovery) of Saint Amphiboles, as perhaps the first mention of Anglo-Saxon graves? The thirteenth-century historian describes in his *Flowers of History* how the monks of St. Albans excavated ten skeletons at Redbourne, Herts., mentioning the swords and knives found, and the signs of violence on the bones.[1] For Roger, they were proof of martyrdom; for Arnold, they suggest Anglo-Saxon burials discovered in 1178. Right away, we face the problem of interpretation of evidence, an issue that has become increasingly central to what archaeology sees itself as doing, but important, too, to a field where so much of it is without documentation; indeed, as Patrick Wormald puts it, "as Anglo-Saxonists, we cultivate the borders of prehistory."[2] Do science and history give us the facts? Is there a place for intuition or reasonable speculation? What is the relationship of texts, historical and literary, to material culture? How do we compare finds and sites without excessive assumptions? As should be clear, Anglo-Saxon archaeology and its history as a field both need some excavation of their own to clarify their origins and potential.

Objects are most quickly found, for Anglo-Saxons, in early pre-Christian graves, so it is no surprise that the early history of the field, in the eighteenth and nineteenth centuries, has so much to do with burials.

The Reverend Bryan Faussett energetically excavated over 700 graves in twenty years in East Kent, though he thought he was excavating material of Roman Britain. Arnold comments on his notorious speed: "it was he who managed the now-famous and hurried disinterment of twenty-eight graves in one day, and nine barrows before breakfast to avoid the disturbance of spectators" (unremarked is that his avoidance of an audience speaks for a degree of focus in his work). Welch, among many, comments that most of what he found is in the Liverpool Museum "together with his excellent notebooks which record each grave in considerable detail."[3] His work was not published in his lifetime, but instead was edited and published in 1856 by Charles Roach Smith, who considered his findings to be of British (Celtic) remains.

So the first to recognize Anglo-Saxon material for what it was, Reverend James Douglas, published in 1793 his *Nenia Britannica* ("funeral dirge of the British"), with its characteristically long but entertainingly informative eighteenth-century subtitles. To read them in their entirety gives a sense of how encyclopedic and systematic he wished his account to be:

> *A SEPULCHRAL HISTORY OF GREAT BRITAIN; FROM THE EARLIEST PERIOD TO ITS GENERAL CONVERSION TO CHRISTIANITY. INCLUDING A COMPLETE SERIES OF THE BRITISH, ROMAN AND SAXON SEPULCHRAL RITES AND CEREMONIES, WITH THE CONTENTS OF SEVERAL HUNDRED BURIAL PLACES, opened under a careful inspection of the AUTHOR. THE BARROWS CONTAINING URNS, SWORDS, SPEARHEADS, DAGGERS, KNIVES, BATTLE-AXES, SHIELDS AND ARMILLÆ:—Decorations of Women; consisting of GEMS, PENSILE ORNAMENTS, BRACELETS, BEADS, GOLD and SILVER BUCKLES, BROACHES ornamented with Precious Stones; several MAGICAL INSTRUMENTS; some very scarce and unpublished coins; and a Variety of other curious Relics deposited with the Dead. TENDING TO ILLUSTRATE THE EARLY PART OF And to fix on a more unquestionable Criterion for the Study of ANTIQUITY: TO WHICH ARE ADDED, OBSERVATIONS ON THE CELTIC, BRITISH, ROMAN, and DANISH BARROWS, discovered in BRITAIN.[4]*

Douglas was the first antiquarian to recognize that the small barrows found were Saxon in date, and though he too was clearly fascinated by objects, as the emphatic typesetting of his title indicates, he attempted far in advance of others a more systematic approach to excavation and to comparative study. His modern biographer, R. F. Jessup, entitled his work on Douglas *Man of Many Talents*.[5]

The Reverends Faussett and Douglas, as churchmen, point to a connection between clergy and Anglo-Saxon archaeology that would hold true through the nineteenth century, not least perhaps because of the 1817 publication of another landmark study. Thomas Rickman applied the principle of stratigraphy to standing churches as buildings likely to have survived for centuries and to have recorded a sequence of changes during their existence. (In doing so he was a pioneer of theoretical models, for, as Rodwell notes, his "enunciation of the principles of archaeological stratification in buildings was not effectively extended to buried remains for more than half a century."[6]) He observed fabric and decorative differences, creating relative chronologies that allowed him to periodize English architecture. He was the first to recognize that Anglo-Saxon churches survived, with his most famous example that of the tower of St. Peter's at Barton-on-Humber, Lincs., an example he then used to compare with other possible surviving churches. His book went on to many editions, a testament to its hold on the imagination and scientific interest of the time.

The latter half of the nineteenth century began a greater upsurge in interest in things identified as Anglo-Saxon. As noted, Smith published Faussett's findings in 1856, but increased attention to detail as well as to finds produced studies of both individual cemeteries and larger areas. Early studies of Oxfordshire and Yorkshire in 1852 were followed by Thomas Bateman's daily accounts of his work in three counties: *Ten Years' Diggings in Celtic and Saxon Grave Hills in the Counties of Derby, Stafford and York, from 1848 to 1858,* published in 1861. Web pages of Nottingham University reproduce sizable excerpts from this work as important even now to understanding the Peak district, and include Bateman's account of finding the first Anglo-Saxon helmet at Benty Grange, still only one of four known:

> About the centre and upon the natural soil, had been laid the only body the barrow ever contained, of which not a vestige besides the hair could be distinguished. Near the place which, from the presence of hair, was judged to have been the situation of the head, was a curious assemblage of ornaments. . . . Proceeding westward from the head for about six feet, we arrived at . . . the frame of a helmet.
>
> The latter consists of a skeleton former [sic] of iron bands, radiating from the crown of the head, and riveted to a circle of the same metal

which encompassed the brow: from the impression on the metal it is evident that the outside was covered with plates of horn disposed diagonally so as to produce a herringbone pattern, the ends of these plates were secured beneath with strips of horn corresponding with the iron framework, and attached to it by ornamental rivets of silver at intervals of about an inch and a half from each other; on the bottom of the front rib, which projects so as to form a nasal, is a small silver cross slightly ornamented round the edges by a beaded moulding; and on the crown of the helmet is an elliptical bronze plate supporting the figure of an animal carved in iron, with bronze eyes, now much corroded, but perfectly distinct as there [sic] presentation of a hog [that is, a boar].[7]

With such finds, it is not difficult to see why artifacts, then and now, are still a fascination as well as a distortion, as Arnold says. Typology, the classification of objects according to perceived evolution of forms and their details, was accepted as determining the relative dating of pieces for which stratigraphy and absolute dates were lacking, a common problem with Anglo-Saxon material. It paralleled theories of Darwinian evolution and progress current at the time, as well as the anthropological concept of "culture," introduced in the 1860s.[8] As more material was found, early typological study and excavations in Germany by J. M. Kemble showed continental connections (1863), and surveys were attempted, such as J. Y. Akerman's *Remains of Pagan Saxondom* (1855) and the Baron De Baye's *Industrie Anglo-Saxonne,* translated and published in English in 1893 as *The Industrial Arts of the Anglo-Saxons* (and panned by Leeds twenty years later). The early twentieth century continued the interest in objects because of the museum careers of many of the distinguished British scholars writing about the period, most notable among them Edward Thurlow Leeds and Thomas Downing Kendrick. In 1910, Leeds published *Two Types of Brooches from the Island of Gotland, Sweden,* and then in 1912, a study of Anglo-Saxon saucer brooches; brooches and the comparison between northwest European and British material would form the basis of his future contributions. Serving as Assistant Keeper and then Keeper in the Ashmolean Museum of Oxford, Leeds also carried on an active career as excavator, acquiring an important collection for the museum and publishing cemeteries and the site of "a Saxon village" near Sutton Courtenay, Berkshire, through the twenties.

Leeds's most notable early contribution in terms of the development of the field, however, is his 1913 volume, *The Archaeology of the Anglo-*

Saxon Settlements. It was the first attempt to synthesize the available settlement information and as such, went beyond the mere amassing of objects and data to consider historical aspects. The book was described as "still an indispensable tool for all who interest themselves in this subject," by J. N. L. Myres in his introduction to the reprint in 1970. Leeds drew on his knowledge of comparative material from the Frankish Rhineland, and "was the first to show the relevance to our Anglo-Saxon antiquities of such fundamental concepts as the distinction drawn by Salin [*Die Altgermanische Thierornamentik,* 1904, a stylistic study] between the different styles of animal ornament, or the typological analysis of cruciform brooches devised by Shetelig in Norway [*The Cruciform Brooches of Norway,* 1908]."[9]

Leeds's 1936 volume, *Early Anglo-Saxon Art and Archaeology,* continued his attempt to synthesize known information to advance historical knowledge. His chapters, based on the Rhind Lectures he gave at Edinburgh in 1935, cover "Invaders," "The Kentish Problem," and "Cultural Relations of East Anglia," as well as a chapter on the native art already present before the Anglo-Saxons came, a notable addition and one perhaps included on consideration of the site of his lectures. The politics of the nineteenth century, which denied "that the native population of England or of the other parts of the British Isles [i.e., the Celtic peoples] had made any major contribution to post-Roman society,"[10] continued into the early twentieth, as did the tensions, and had its impact on scholarship. Leeds's work was not simply notable for its art historical connections, however. Leeds was interested in what artifacts could tell us about the people who made and used them; by comparing English and continental evidence, he hoped to illuminate the progress of migration and settlement of the various tribes Bede had described as Angles, Saxons, and Jutes. As Dark notes, his interpretation of the distribution of artifacts and the patterns of burial "in terms of both population groups and political units . . . [anticipated] Childe's famous definition of an archaeological culture . . . by sixteen years."[11] Later scholars would use the identification of artifacts with ethnic identities to map the dominance of Anglo-Saxons, as in the study of *Anglo-Saxon Pottery and the Settlement of England* published by J. N. L. Myres (1969), who was noted earlier for hailing the reprint of Leeds's work and clearly following his approach. At times it could be seen to be misguided, as with Myres's mapping of stamped panel-style pottery alongside battles cited in the *Anglo-Saxon Chronicles*; the reliance on texts as a kind of grid into which to fit constructed typologies was a crucial limitation on the field, until the 1960s introduced more independent means of dating materials and later decades called those very texts to account. The relative conservatism of early Anglo-Saxon archaeology, even compared to other archaeological investigations at the same time, seems directly related to the early focus on amassing objects combined with the difficulty of dating them and therefore of making links to what little was known from texts.

Leeds's admiration for Salin was shared by R. A. Smith, another museum scholar, who in 1923 published *A Guide to the Anglo-Saxon and Foreign Teutonic Antiquities*. This guide became a handbook for scholars and excavators in the field alike, and stands as a further example of how closely related art history and artifactual study in archaeology were at the time. Influential Scandinavian interest in Anglo-Saxon studies also looked at art style, most notably in the work by Shetelig already cited, and in another work which influenced English scholars, Niels Åberg's 1926 publication of *The Anglo-Saxons in England During the Early Centuries after the Invasion*.[12] Another great reference work was in production at the same time: Gerard Baldwin Brown began publishing his great multi-volume study, *The Arts in Early England,* in 1903, and volumes continued to come out through 1937. Even after the work was superseded in various areas, it remained a landmark synthesis and much admired; Leslie Webster of the British Museum commented in 1986 that it was a "monumental work, unlike that of any of his contemporaries, [which] covered the entire Anglo-Saxon period, [and] surveyed the social aspects of the material over a wide range, attempting to define social custom and usage."[13]

The period of the 1930s through the 1950s continued along much the same lines as described, with additional studies on artifact types such as pottery and metalwork giving little new information on the economy or social aspects of the Anglo-Saxons. To be sure, the spectacular finds of Mound 1 at Sutton Hoo, on the eve of World War II, put Anglo-Saxon archaeology on the map for the public, with all the old lure of objects focused on the find as treasure. But it was not published in its entirety until much later (1975–83) and then in a quite traditional way, and certainly the rescue excavation did nothing to advance excavation methodology, though it was a marvel of care and professionalism under pressure. A spectacular find, Sutton Hoo nevertheless kept the focus on *things,* while hinting at problems of interpretation in its silence on who was buried there, whether he was buried at all, if he were royal or even Anglo-Saxon, where he lived and traded, and with whom. The site as known early on serves as a touchstone for the tremendous changes about to occur in the field and in how the field's practitioners and interpreters viewed it. The seeds of change were present in the physics of the time, but not until the discovery by American Willard F. Libby of radiocarbon dating in 1949 did the "first universal clock of archaeology" exist.[14] Therefore, while the publication of typologies and further descriptions of sites did not break new ground (as it were) in terms of advancing methodology or overall knowledge, such publications did provide a strong relative chronology for a period in need of dates. In addition, for the Anglo-Saxon period, as Arnold notes, the use of radiocarbon dates is not as conclusive as it is in periods of longer duration, such as the Iron Age: "If the development of theoretical archaeology became possible within prehistoric studies in the 1960s because of the development of scientific dating techniques, the difficulties of using those techniques within the early Anglo-Saxon period might, in part, explain the desire to retain traditional methodologies. The degrees of confidence that can be applied to scientific dates are inadequate for a period that can be viewed in terms of generations. . . ."[15] The 1950s and 1960s saw the rescue excavation of large numbers of cemetery sites, the excavation of major religious, royal and secular settlements such as Monkwearmouth/Jarrow, Winchester, Yeavering and Mucking, the publication of H. M. and Joan Taylor's first two volumes in the seminal *Anglo-Saxon Architecture* (1965), and the introduction of what was called the New Archaeology (in 1959),[16] which changed the shape of the field immeasurably.

The attraction of science, part of the field from the beginning with its links to geology and the radiocarbon dating breakthrough, reached its critical mass in the 1960s. But along with the new scientific approaches came accompanying philosophies and theories, at least as important as the new methods themselves, because the differences from the older cultural-history approach caused a distinct break. Arnold comments on the shift:

> The 'New Archaeology' of the 1960s onwards had as its main aim the explanation of societal change rather than the description of the data. It viewed societies as systems whose workings could be understood by examining the inter-relationship between its components. In keeping with the contemporary philosophy of science, theories should be explicit and conclusions should be testable. The result was a very functional, scientific approach to society that viewed it in a mechanistic manner.[17]

Much of what would be familiar in scientific method (testing a hypothesis) was thus considered logically part of the field, and suddenly, the science that had always lurked at the periphery of the field's history became central to its identity; the great debate became whether archaeology was a discipline in the sciences or in the humanities. Dark, in his handbook on theoretical archaeology, notes that this led to "some spectacular conflicts and virulent debates," and contrasts "articles in the archaeological journal *Antiquity* during the 1960s and early 1970s, notably Hawkes's (1968) 'The proper study of mankind' and Clarke's (1973) 'Archaeology: the loss of innocence.' "[18] What is also notable, however, is how little Anglo-Saxon archaeologists involved themselves in this controversy; Arnold comments on "resistance to the application of such new theories within early Anglo-Saxon archaeology" with "little explicit criticism of the theories from within the specialisation. . . . For many, the New Archaeology passed by like a skirmishing army on a distant ridge."[19] It took a new generation of students become specialists to absorb and apply the advances through computer modeling, social analysis, and the increasingly complex assortment of theoretical approaches borrowed and adapted from the humanities and social sciences. Eventually, three important or major "camps" of thought were referred to as culture-historians, processualists, and post-processualists, discussed below.

As stated, in Anglo-Saxon studies, however, the New Archaeology of the 1960s and early 1970s took a while to have an impact. The journal *Anglo-Saxon England,* begun in 1972, could publish studies in history, literature and archaeology alongside one another as if all were humanities. In the late 1970s, publications important in the field still included traditional site and artifact reports on the Mound 1 ship burial at Sutton Hoo (Bruce-Mitford's first two volumes, 1975 and 1978), the massive ongoing excavation of the rural settlement of Mucking (Jones and Jones 1975), the beginning of many volumes on the total excavation of the cemetery at Spong Hill (Hills 1977), the delayed publication of the British/Anglo-Saxon royal site of Yeavering (Hope-Taylor 1977), Taylor's two volumes of Repton studies (1977 and 1979) and the third, analytical volume of his *Anglo-Saxon Architecture* (1978), Myres's *Corpus of Anglo-Saxon Pottery of the Pagan Period* (1977), and the publication of Saxon and later palaces at Cheddar (Rahtz 1979). Excavations which would be fully published later were of course also going on, as at Winchester. Another new journal, founded in 1979, continued the long British association of history and archaeology, *Anglo-Saxon Studies in Archaeology and History* (as opposed to the American pairing of archaeology with anthropology, which did not become part of any British programs until about this time). Overviews of aspects of the period were published in Hall's collection on *Viking Age York and the North* (1978),

Lang's *Anglo-Saxon and Viking Age Sculpture* (1978), and Taylor's important third volume on Anglo-Saxon church architecture (1978), among others. The most widely available text was also an overview, Wilson's *Archaeology of Anglo-Saxon England* (written ca. 1972, published 1976), a book which, as Dickinson puts it diplomatically,

> made a much more deliberate attempt at synthesis and was designed for a more general readership, though in fact its range was less extensive and there was no overall summary bringing together the new nature of Anglo-Saxon archaeology. It was, however designed to reflect the present state and interests of the subject. . . . On the whole, method played a minor role in discussions. D. M. Wilson made some general points: Anglo-Saxon archaeology was firmly rooted in the empirical traditions of historical scholarship and should not be separated from it. In particular, he argued that empirical evidence ('facts') gave rise to hypotheses, which then had to be critically tested, and, in denying any role to the ideas of so-called New Archaeology, he somewhat alarmingly referred to the often more appropriate 'loose methods of induction.' (Wilson 1976: 2–3)[20]

She goes on to note the strengths of the book, including its acknowledgment of "the expanding horizons and capabilities in excavation" when including ecclesiastical sites in consideration of settlement types, along with rural and urban, and a shift to crediting pottery rather than metalwork as the key to relative chronologies, which also ushered in consideration of larger economic and social issues.[21] The text is oddly unbalanced, however. Wilson avoided the older categories of discussion such as artistic styles, but the chapter headings show major gaps and revaluings. "Agriculture and rural settlement," "Buildings and rural settlement," "Towns," "Ecclesiastical architecture," "Monastic sites," "Craft and industry" all seem important and reasonable divisions, but the next four are more haphazard: "The pottery," "The coins," "The animal-resources," "The Scandinavians in England" (Wilson's own interest). The older focus on cemeteries is banished entirely, and while a great deal of new work was being done at the time, not even a cursory overview is offered of past work. Metalwork is consigned briefly to "Craft and industry," which would be fair enough if pottery had been there too (but again, pottery replaces metalwork as "reliable" in dating, and so it was separate and parallel to "Coins"). It is of course easy to carp from a distance, and the book was certainly an appreciated compendium, as no one else had

tried any such overview. It was mainly conservative and old-fashioned in
its own time if not in its field, however, and did not reflect the changes
going on in archaeological thought.

The "history" and "facts" which Wilson and others had held to be
fundamental were already under attack by historians and manuscript specialists as well as those who espoused a more self-critical and theorized
awareness. David Dumville's writings, most crucially "Sub-Roman
Britain: History and Legend" (1977), re-examined texts long relied on in
the light of new scepticism about the contexts of their recording and the
uninformed use of such texts by scholars in fields other than those primarily concerned with texts. Dickinson commented, ". . . historians like
Dumville . . . have most thoroughly cut away the ground from under those
who indiscriminately combine written and archaeological evidence," and
in the same volume, Philip Rahtz comments that Dumville "has warned
archaeologists of the danger of even attempting to explain their evidence
in terms of that of the early written sources, since these are themselves in
such urgent need of a critical and rigorous approach."[22] Of course, Wilson was too careful a scholar to rely "indiscriminately" on historical
writings, but faith in them was countered at the time by such writers as
Addyman, who stressed the prehistoric aspect of Anglo-Saxon studies,
and in the next decades by theorists who rejected laws and hypotheses in
favor of paradigms which explained science and other systems of knowledge as coming out of particular historical contexts. As Dark notes:

> This alternative view [in archaeology] underpinned post-processualist
> thought. . . . Post processualists thus defined archaeology in general
> terms not as a way of obtaining truth about the past, but in order to gen-
> erate potential 'useful' interpretations for understanding it. . . . it is a
> characteristic of this school that it sees archaeology always in
> artistic . . . or social science terms. . . . Conversely, processualists al-
> ways see archaeology in scientific terms, whether as a 'natural sci-
> ence', a 'social science' . . . [or] a 'human science'. . . .[23]

The crucial difference here is the emphasis on the subjective aspect,
which post-processualists of most persuasions consider an important
component of both past thought and current thought; thus, any archaeological interpretation or theory, while it usually depends upon accepting
a logical reasoning, itself remains a product of or reflection of contemporary structures, thought, and historical context, just as what is found in
the field reflects such settings.

But we are getting ahead of the story. Chronologically, the New Archaeology gave way to processual thought in the late 1970s and 1980s, though of course not all adherents converted to the new approaches, and Anglo-Saxon archaeology gave its first fruits of the shift to increased use of computers and development of theoretical awareness. The first computerized classifications of artifacts were published, systems theory and social and economic analysis increased, practical science applied to fieldwork yielded new forms of evaluating sites. A great belief in the value of quantification and in the study of processes paralleled the enthusiasm for "hard" or quantitative science which characterizes processualism. As Tania Dickinson put it in her survey of Anglo-Saxon archaeology 1957–1982, "our traditional classificatory and chronological concerns are other obvious beneficiaries of the new methodology with its emphasis on explicitness and quantification. After all, why do we produce corpora of artifacts if it is not because we believe more can be gained from documented numbers than imperfectly known individuals?"[24] Counting or weighing or testing items such as potsherds or pollen grains or bones, looking for their relationship to environment, trade and larger settlement and political concerns, all yielded invigorating new ways to argue about the past. Philip Rahtz supported the changes, as evidenced by his inaugural lecture as the first Professor of Archaeology at York (also Dickinson's institution), entitled "The New Medieval Archaeology" (1980), though the critics' initial, dismissive reception of work such as Randsborg's *Viking Age in Denmark* (1980), later more respected, shows that Rahtz was in the forefront of such acceptance. Hodges' prodigious work on trade, pottery and the economy of Anglo-Saxon England showed the potential for interdisciplinary approaches using economics, history and archaeology for reconstructing the economic and political past without reliance on texts alone (1981, 1982, 1983, culminating in his synthetic work, *The Anglo-Saxon Achievement: Archaeology & the Beginnings of English Society*, 1989). Hill's *Atlas of Anglo-Saxon England* similarly crossed disciplinary boundaries to synthesize maps detailing resources, textual evidence, distributions, and charter evidence, from many sources. Fieldwalking as a non-invasive and cost-effective way to evaluate sites was championed, dowsing was similarly evaluated, and underwater and waterlogged site archaeology benefited from the interest in science, though the deaths of several promising young archaeologists in underwater archaeology set back the pursuit of this area of exploration. Carver's publication of *Underneath English Towns* also showed the value of a longer and broader theoretical perspective, following up on an earlier much praised article using New Archaeology's systems theory, "Three Saxo-Norman tenements in Durham city."[25]

More traditional approaches also thrived, and projects which began
to synthesize the increasingly large bodies of information appeared.
Alongside Carver's excavations of a larger portion of Sutton Hoo and his
use and creation of new approaches to excavation and its problems, the
final volume of the original excavation was published in two parts
(1983), the end of Bruce-Mitford's magisterial survey of material in a
unique find. The ambitious *Corpus of Anglo-Saxon Stone Sculpture* published its first volumes (1984, 1988), initiated and propelled forward by
Rosemary Cramp of Durham. The 1980s also saw an increased interest
in things Scandinavian, with major exhibits at New York's Metropolitan
Museum ("The Vikings," 1980–81) and at the Yorkshire Museum, York
("The Vikings in England and in their Danish Homeland," 1982). Wilson
and Klindt-Jensen's *Viking Art* was reissued in 1980, and new publications included Bailey's on *Viking Age Sculpture in Northern England,*
coverage of Scandinavians in Cumbria and Scandinavian settlement
names in the northwest, and continued publications on excavations of
Viking York. Two major exhibits at the British Museum also featured
Anglo-Saxon culture: "The Golden Age of Anglo-Saxon Art" in 1984,
and its counterpart in 1991, "The Making of England: Anglo-Saxon Art
and Culture A.D. 600–900." Both owed much to the leadership of David
Wilson as Director, and to Leslie Webster and Janet Backhouse, all specialists working in this period at the museum and so carrying on a long-
standing tradition in the field. Though both exhibits did so, the latter
especially showed the great debt owed to archaeology for its recovery of
material culture in a period with scarce surviving documentation.

Church archaeology saw increased publication and discussion of issues affecting church excavation and recording due to the number of
sites declared redundant. Rodwell's *English Heritage Book of Church
Archaeology* (1981, revised 1989), Morris's *The Church in British Archaeology* (1983), Ryder's *Saxon Churches in South Yorkshire* (1983),
Fernie's *Architecture of the Anglo-Saxons* (1983), Cambridge's prize-
winning essay on "The Early Church in Durham: A Reassessment"
(1984),[26] and Butler and Morris's *The Anglo-Saxon church: papers on
history, architecture, and archaeology in honour of Dr. H. M. Taylor*
(1986), which included a fine summary article by Rodwell on "Anglo-
Saxon church building: aspects of design and construction,"[27] all testify
to the revitalization of church archaeology after the combination of re-
dundancies and new approaches.

Study of buildings did not simply include those still standing, however. Work at Cowdery's Down, Basingstoke, Hants., generated discus-

sion about building traditions after the publication of the site and then a subsequent article by James, Marshall and Millett on the origins of halls and various possible reconstructions (1984). Excavation allowed a reconstruction to be drawn of the watermill at Tamworth, Staffs., with its horizontal wheel. In fact, reconstructions and visual representations appeared more and more, with accompanying controversy. The reconstruction of colored window glass fragments as figural at Jarrow caused initial heated debate, though the model in nearby Jarrow Hall museum of the monastic buildings excavated there was well received. More life-size reproductions, such as are found in experimental archaeology at West Stow, again caused debate, though a variety of reconstructions of SFBs (sunken-featured buildings, also known as *grubenhäuser*) were tried. The late-1980s reconstruction of the Viking levels at Coppergate, York, as an educational ride through "Jorvik" has evoked extremes of rejection and approval: for some, it is a perfect blend of exacting reproduction, entertaining and educational creativity, and fund-raising, while to others it reeks of commercialism and the "dumbing down" of scholarly work for popular consumption, or worse, a misrepresentation of the many possibilities as resolved. Similar misgivings were voiced over the current project of Bede's World, a 1990s project that reconstructs a variety of buildings, experimenting with craft, the growing of ancient crops and the keeping of breeds of animals as close as possible to those known from the Anglo-Saxon period. One side claims there is no point; the other argues that such experiments make us aware of details and aspects we otherwise could not test (how particular joists fit and support, or which crops thrive). A recent book in the Theoretical Archaeology Group (TAG) series epitomizes the more self-aware theorizing discussed earlier, here in the area of reconstruction: *The Cultural Life of Images; Visual Representation in Archaeology* (1997) discusses the contexts of decisions about representation, from photographs to drawings and charts to three-dimensional attempts. James, for example, writes about facing Cowdery's Down and

> the problem of representing the varying degrees of knowledge and conjecture in a single drawing . . . [the representations of buildings] were more and more conjectural the further they were from the ground. How could we indicate what we knew, and where we were guessing? Our solution was to produce three drawings . . . to express the range of plausible variation possible on the same evidence. . . . We had hoped that this approach would encourage discussion of these alternatives in

print, but we were disappointed. . . . Despite (or perhaps because of)
the lack of effective critique, these drawings have been much reproduced, sometimes without the variants, and ironically are in danger of
becoming exactly the *idées fixes* we tried to avoid.[28]

The 1980s and early 1990s were also a period in which Anglo-Saxon archaeologists took stock of the field in light of changes in method, fund-
ing, publication expectations and planning, and the next wave of new
approaches, namely post-processual theories and debate. Back in 1983,
Dickinson, already cited under the discussion of processualism, took as
her starting point the founding of the Society for Medieval Archaeology
in 1956 and its journal, *Medieval Archaeology* (begun in 1957), and
ended with suggestions for more work on rural settlements, sites of
"pagan ritual and worship . . . and of early Saxon metalworking," and
full excavation and publication of the "very large cemeteries now under
examination." More importantly, however, she called for synthesis,
something much neglected since earlier in the century, and argued that

> the inability to offer broad synthesis reflects our lack of a good theoret-
> ical framework. . . . The issue has been raised, and rightly so, whether
> archaeology . . . should operate within an historical framework or ac-
> cording to some other discipline or paradigm, be it modern prehistoric
> archaeology, linguistics, the sciences, or a multidisciplinary combina-
> tion of them all. This may rather depend on our understanding of the
> term 'history'. . . . Why tie ourselves to the political, ethnic and
> chronological vision that the early sources have preserved for us? . . .
> We should not then ignore the potential of historical tie-ups, but we
> *must* take the *best* from the historian's armoury in so doing—notably
> critical evaluation of our data.[29]

Her comments therefore open the door for new theoretical approaches,
especially from other disciplines than archaeology, which do indeed become a rich source for post-processualism. Similarly, in a 1986 volume
entitled *Archaeology in Britain Since 1945,* Leslie Webster of the British
Museum wrote an excellent overview of how our knowledge of the
Anglo-Saxons changed in those forty years, and cheered on the "recent
trends towards fully integrated and wide-ranging area studies" which
"offer tremendous potential for our understanding of the Anglo-Saxon
landscape and how, in the widest sense, people used it. In other words,
any given unit—field systems, villages, cemeteries, churches, palaces,
towns, and so on—is ideally studied in its context; indeed, the context is
the goal." She cited two urgent needs: excavation of more waterlogged

sites, for their preservation of the organic, and "more armchair archaeology," "for more overall synthesis" along with "a need for a revised philosophy of the subject." She went on:

> Much recent debate has centred around the question of whether Anglo-Saxon archaeology needs to be liberated from what has been described as 'the historical strait-jacket'. . . . History is a unified discipline; what is required is a new theoretical and methodological framework in which documentary and archaeological evidence are scrupulously assessed in tandem.[30]

The Society for Medieval Archaeology also published its recommendations, in 1987, echoing, "any excavation should be considered as a detailed investigation of a small part of the landscape, that is, a 'site' needs to be seen in its widest possible context. The most worthwhile sites are those which produce the greatest amount of evidence that can be used to reconstruct the total environment of their period." Again, context and larger issues emerge as concerns, and in addition, there is a desire to see less focus on the "elite" sites: "The Society urges that the Commission should adopt policies that lead to the furtherance of our knowledge and understanding of the entire landscape and all who peopled it, not just of the great monuments and the aristocracy. Medieval archaeology is the study of the record of human activity contained within the physical evidence, of every kind, that survives from the Middle Ages."[31] Thus, the main concerns of post-processual theory seeded and grew: the focus on a larger context, on the subjective human choices made in the past and in the present, on the need to theorize those positions from many angles and approaches rather than assuming a fixed, authoritative given. A manifesto published in the collection *Pragmatic Archaeology: Theory in Crisis?* (1987) makes these changes explicit:

> . . . a pragmatic archaeology should have the following characteristics:
> it should be humanistic
> it should accept the context-dependence of knowledge
> it should be free in its use of hypotheses
> it should use theory as a 'leading principle'. . . .
> It is too easy for theoreticians to become so engrossed in their statistics and systems theory that they forget the human side: the individuals who fashioned the societies and artifacts they study, as well as the individuals who extract those artifacts from the soil.[32]

Post-processual thought continues to influence the interpretations and growth of Anglo-Saxon archaeology. Areas such as social archaeology and economic archaeology, and considerations of cultural change, are approached from a variety of stances within the three groups of culture-historians, processualists, and post-processualists, too numerous to detail here. Literary and cultural theory, sociology, and anthropology have all expanded the directions from which to approach archaeological problems. The 1987 publication of Julian Richards's work on seventeen cemeteries, *The Significance of Form and Decoration of Anglo-Saxon Cremation Urns,* constitutes a fine and suggestive post-processualist example of the marriage of computerized databases with an exploration of the subjective. Richards attempted to uncover patterns which would indicate conscious choices on the part of those burying the dead, clues that would tell us something of what status looked like, what markers (age, sex, wealth) mattered to them, what rituals repeated or varied. Another specialty, that of cognitive archaeology, practiced by processualists but more so by post-processualists, has also thrived (though not without frequent criticism), and encompasses "all that is concerned with belief, thought, perception and decision-making. Religion and ritual can be considered here, as can symbolism and categorisation, and issues requiring the application of rules or concepts such as law, literacy, measurement and planning." Cognitive-processualism works from a recognition of human perception, reasoning and intuition as relevant to the testing of hypotheses, while a post-processualist would reject generalizations, seeing "all cognition as specific to its time and place, and to the individual, rather than ascribing cognitive similarities across cultures on any level above the conceptual structure of the mind. Consequently, an observation such as 'all people think alike' is said to be untrue by post-processualist writers . . . , whereas the observation or hypothesis that 'we do not think like Romans' would be considered to be true."[33]

The 1990s have continued to provide publications and excavations both traditional and innovative, which is as it should be in a field where openness to potential avenues of examination should be cultivated. Only a fraction of what has been done could be discussed here, and certainly important work has been slighted or omitted due to constraints of length for this essay. Science in the form of paleopathology, zooarchaeology, DNA research, petrography of pottery and stone quarrying, dendrochronological analysis by area or region, and archaeomagnetic dating tests what we can learn of daily life. The new interest in ethnicity has introduced questions about the construction and stability of the categories

"Anglo-Saxon" and "English."[34] Webster's call for more sites of water-logged areas has been partially answered by venues such as the Fenland Project and the journal *Fenland Research* (begun in the 1980s), as well as the increased interest in waterfront archaeology at such sites as London and York. The annual bibliography of *Anglo-Saxon England* has a full section on rural settlements being excavated and published, and the beginning of synthetic discussions can be seen in works such as Astill's "Towns and Town Hierarchies in Saxon England" (1991) or Carver's collection of wide-ranging articles in *The Age of Sutton Hoo*.[35] Syntheses of large amounts of data have begun to appear, such as the Marshalls's "Survey and Analysis of Buildings of Early and Middle Anglo-Saxon England" (1991) and "Differentiation, Change and Continuity in Anglo-Saxon Buildings" (1993). Owen-Crocker's work on Anglo-Saxon dress pulls together both textile study and study of archaeological contexts for reconstructing how clothes and accessories were worn, with the Manchester Textiles Project database located at Manchester University.[36] Härke's work on warrior graves and weapon burials, begun in the late 1980s, continues to develop, with his fullest synthetic discussion appearing in his book *Angelsächsische Waffengräber des 5. bis 7. Jahrhunderts* (1992). Crawford's work on Anglo-Saxon children considers a part of the population too long neglected,[37] though surprisingly, work on women and on gender studies in archaeological findings is still rare.

The future for Anglo-Saxon archaeology looks to manage the increasing number of sites and amounts of information. Computers will continue to play a large part in areas needing work, such as regional and gender studies, but more than that, the potential of hypertexts and the World Wide Web should be examined as a solution to an old problem, the quick and accessible publication of excavation reports and data. A group such as the Society for Medieval Archaeology stands in perfect position to sponsor and maintain a website or its future incarnation, where full reports and illustrations could be scanned in at a fraction of the cost of current publications. Instead of complaints about inaccessible archives or misleading reports, researchers would be able to download data and manipulate it for their own analyses, and a full visual documentation would be possible as well. Such a website could also provide a forum for ongoing discussions of theory and application (though discussion groups do exist, of course) and perhaps more appositely, of particular sites or of aspects of planning national goals. While the obscurity Leeds wrote about at the beginning of this essay will never entirely vanish, the explosion of archaeological debate and thought in the field promises that a passionate interest in this past will continue to be interrogated and explored.

NOTES

[1] The Latin text is found in Roger de Wendover, *The Flowers of History (Flores Historiarum), vol.* 1, ed. Henry G. Hewlett (London, 1886), 114–15. Mentioned in C. J. Arnold, *An Archaeology of the Early Anglo-Saxon Kingdoms* (London, 1988), 3; new edition (London, 1997), 2–3. Arnold's account of the early history of the field in his first chapter (1997 ed.) is quite good, and I also benefitted greatly from reading Leslie Webster's 1986 overview as well as Tania Dickinson's (1983)—see references below in notes 13 and 20.

[2] P. Wormald, *How do We Know so Much About Anglo-Saxon Deerhurst?,* Deerhurst Lecture 1991 (Deerhurst, 1993), 1.

[3] Arnold, *Archaeology* (1997), 3. M. Welch, *Discovering Anglo-Saxon England* (University Park, 1992), 12. S. C. Hawkes and M. Rhodes wrote about Faussett and his collection in E. Southworth, *Anglo-Saxon Cemeteries: A Reappraisal* (Stroud, 1990), 1–64.

[4] Copied from the facsimile included as Figure 1.1 in Arnold, *Archaeology* (1997), 4.

[5] R. F. Jessup, *Man of Many Talents: An Informal Biography of James Douglas, 1753–1819* (London, 1975).

[6] W. Rodwell, *The Archaeology of Religious Places: Churches and Cemeteries in Britain* (Philadelphia, 1989), 25.

[7] The Bateman excerpts on Benty Grange, as well as a large number of other sites of the author's excavations are found on the Trent & Peak Archaeological Unit site of the University of Nottingham at http://www.ccc.nottingham.ac.uk/~aczkdc/tenyrs/benty.html (June 25, 1999). For those interested in the full original publication, it was published in 1861, in London, by J. R. Smith.

[8] For a brief discussion of archaeological concepts between 1850 and 1918, see K. R. Dark, *Theoretical Archaeology* (Ithaca, 1995), 4–5. This period was the first to begin to understand the true age of the world through the new science of geology, which reinforced Darwin's biological observations and caused furious debate with Christians who used the Bible to date and describe the planet and its inhabitants. Yet Darwin's ideas found echoes in the industrial progress so admired by most Victorians, and science was increasingly seen as a sign of such progress, so that the young fields of archaeology and anthropology were very much a part of the great issues of the day.

[9] E. T. Leeds, *The Archaeology of the Anglo-Saxon Settlements,* with an introduction by J. N. L. Myres (Oxford, reprint 1970). There is no pagination for the introduction.

[10] Arnold, *Archaeology* (1997), 21.

[11] Dark, *Theoretical Archaeology*, 6.

[12] Åberg's work was published in Uppsala by Almqvist & Wiksells. The Scandinavians were instrumental in the development of early Anglo-Saxon studies, but a problematic relationship between English and Scandinavian perspectives emerged: while the Scandinavians saw Old English and its culture as linked to their own heritage, the English tended to side with the Germans, except perhaps for George Stephens, "an Englishman turned Dane," who called Old English "'de Danskes Modersmaal' (the Danish mother tongue)" (Bjork, "Nineteenth-Century Scandinavia," 119–120). A recent article by R. E. Bjork documents the importance of Scandinavian scholarship, here mainly in literary and linguistic study: "Nineteenth-Century Scandinavia and the Birth of Anglo-Saxon Studies," in A. J. Frantzen and J. D. Niles, eds., *Anglo-Saxonism and the Construction of Social Identity* (Gainesville, 1997), 111–32.

[13] L. Webster, "Anglo-Saxon England A.D. 400–1100," in I. Longworth and J. Cherry, eds., *Archaeology in Britain Since 1945* (London, 1986), 119–59, at p. 123.

[14] From journalist D. Wilson's account, *The New Archaeology* (New York, 1975), 67. Even with the discovery of C_{14} dating, it needed refinements; assessments had to be "reset" and recalibrated to accommodate miscalculations and omissions.

[15] Arnold, *Archaeology* (1997), 15.

[16] The term was used in fact of American archaeology, and adopted a bit later once the scope of the impact of these new approaches was appreciated. For the introduction of the term, see J. R. Caldwell, "The New American Archaeology," *Science* 129/3345 (1959), 303–07.

[17] Arnold, *Archaeology* (1997), 14.

[18] Dark, *Theoretical Archaeology*, 22.

[19] Arnold, *Archaeology* (1997), 14.

[20] T. M. Dickinson, "Anglo-Saxon Archaeology; Twenty-Five Years On," in D. Hinton, ed., *25 Years of Medieval Archaeology* (Sheffield, 1983), 33–43, at pp. 35–6.

[21] Ibid.

[22] Ibid., 39, and P. Rahtz, "New Approaches to Medieval Archaeology, Part 1," in Hinton, *25 Years of Medieval Archaeology*, 12–23, at p. 15.

[23] Dark, *Theoretical Archaeology*, 23.

[24] Dickinson, "Anglo-Saxon Archaeology," 40.

[25] *M.A.* 23 (1979), 1–80. Dickinson praised it in her survey article as "the clearest—most systematic—*and* most exciting urban excavation report that I have yet read . . . !" Dickinson, "Anglo-Saxon Archaeology," 39–40. Carver's interest in and use of new theoretical perspectives doubtless was a factor in his ap-

pointment as Rahtz's successor in the Professorship at York, and he has continued to use new approaches in his excavations, notably of Sutton Hoo and now Tarbat.

[26] E. Cambridge, *J.B.A.A.* 137 (1984), 65–85.

[27] Reprinted in this volume.

[28] S. James, "Drawing Inferences: Visual Reconstructions in Theory and Practice," in B. L. Molyneaux, ed., *The Cultural Life of Images: Visual Representation in Archaeology* (London, 1997), 27–48, at pp. 31–33.

[29] Dickinson, "Anglo-Saxon Archaeology," 40–41.

[30] Webster, "Anglo-Saxon England," 156.

[31] "Archaeology and the Middle Ages: Recommendations by the Society for Medieval Archaeology to the Historic Buildings and Monuments Commission for England," *M.A.* 31 (1987), 1–12, at p. 2.

[32] R. Yorston, C. F. and V. L. Gaffney, "A Manifesto for Pragmatic Archaeology," in C. F. and V. L. Gaffney, eds., *Pragmatic Archaeology: Theory in Crisis?*, B.A.R. Brit. ser. 167 (Oxford, 1987), 107–13, at p. 109.

[33] Dark, *Theoretical Archaeology,* 143.

[34] See, for example, J. Hines, ed., *The Anglo-Saxons from the Migration Period to the Eighth Century: An Ethnographic Perspective,* Studies in Historical Archaeoethnology 2 (San Marino, 1997). Ethnicity and identity are not irrelevant to presentations of the past in contemporary exhibits either, as witnessed by the mixed reaction to the title of the otherwise spectacular 1991 exhibit "The Making of England," where Nicholas Brooks's "Historical Introduction" unfortunately began "The Anglo-Saxons…were the true ancestors of the English of today (L. Webster and J. Backhouse, eds., *The Making of England: Anglo-Saxon Art and Culture* A.D. *600–900* [London, 1991], 9.)

[35] Carver's own, "The Anglo-Saxon Cemetery at Sutton Hoo: An Interim Report," from *The Age of Sutton Hoo* (Woodbridge & Rochester, 1992) is reprinted in this volume.

[36] A section from her book *Dress in Anglo-Saxon England* (Manchester, 1986) is reprinted below.

[37] Crawford's paper "Children, Death and the Afterlife in Anglo-Saxon England" is reprinted in this volume.

REFERENCES

Åberg, Niels. *The Anglo-Saxons in England during the Early Centuries after the Invasion.* Uppsala, 1926.

Ackerman, John Yonge. *Remains of Pagan Saxendom.* London, 1855.

Astill, Grenville. "Towns and Town Hierarchies in Saxon England." *Oxford J. of Archaeol.* 10.1 (March 1991), 95–117.

Backhouse, Janet, D. H. Turner and Leslie Webster, eds. *The Golden Age of Anglo-Saxon Art 966–1066.* London, 1984.

Bailey, Richard. *Viking Age Sculpture in Northern England.* London, 1980.

Bateman, Thomas. *Ten Years' Digging in Celtic and Saxon Grave Hills.* London, 1861.

Baye, Joseph, baron de. *Études archéologiques; époques des invasions barbares; industrie anglo-saxonne.* Paris, 1889.

Baye, Joseph baron de. *The Industrial arts of the Anglo-Saxons.* Trans. T. B. Harbottle. London & New York, 1893.

Brown, G. Baldwin. *The Arts in Early England.* Vol. 1, *The Life of Saxon England in its Relation to the Arts.* London & New York, 1903. Vol. 2, *Ecclesiastical Architecture in England from the Conversion of the Saxons to the Norman Conquest.* London & New York, 1903. Vols. 3 & 4, *Saxon Art and Industry in the Pagan Period.* New York, 1915. Vol. 5, *The Ruthwell and Bewcastle Crosses, The Gospels of Lindisfarne, and Other Christian Monuments of Northumbria, with Philological Chapters by A. Blyth Webster.* London & New York, 1921. Vol. 6, pt. 1, *Completion of the Study of the Monuments of the Great Period of the Art of Anglian Northumbria;* vol. 6, pt. 2, *Anglo-Saxon Sculpture,* prepared for press by E. H. L. Sexton. London, 1937.

Bruce-Mitford, R. L. S. *The Sutton Hoo Ship Burial.* Vol. 1. London, 1975.

Bruce-Mitford, R. L. S. *The Sutton Hoo Ship Burial.* Vol. 2. London, 1978.

Butler, L. A. S. and R. K. Morris. *The Anglo-Saxon Church: Papers on History, Architecture and Archaeology in Honour of Dr. H. M. Taylor.* C.B.A. Research Rep. 60. London, 1986.

Carver, M. O. H. *The Age of Sutton Hoo.* Woodbridge & Rochester, 1992.

Carver, M. O. H. *Underneath English Towns: Interpreting Urban Archaeology.* London, 1987.

Clarke, David L. "Archaeology: The Loss of Innocence." *Antiquity* 47 (1973), 6–18.

Corpus of Anglo-Saxon Stone Sculpture: Cramp, Rosemary. *County Durham and Northumberland.* Vol. 1, two parts. Oxford, 1984; Bailey, Richard N. and Rosemary Cramp. *Cumberland, Westmorland and Lancashire North-of-the-Sands.* Vol. 2. Oxford, 1988; Lang, James. *York and Eastern Yorkshire.* Vol. 3. Oxford, 1991; Tweddle, Dominic, Martin Biddle and Birthe Kjølbye-Biddle. *South-East England.* Vol. 4. Oxford, 1995.

Dumville, David. "Sub-Roman Britain: History and Legend," *History* 62 (1977), 173–92.

Fernie, Eric. *The Architecture of the Anglo-Saxons.* New York, 1983.

Hall, Richard A. *Viking Age York and the North.* C.B.A. Research Rep. 27. London, 1978.

Härke, H . *Angelsächsische Waffengräber des 5. bis 7. Jahrhunderts.* Cologne & Bonn, 1992.

Hawkes, J. "The Proper Study of Mankind." *Antiquity* 42 (1968), 255–62.

Hill, David. *An Atlas of Anglo-Saxon England.* Toronto & Buffalo, 1981.

Hills, Catherine. *The Anglo-Saxon Cemetery at Spong Hill, North Elmham, Part 1.* East Anglian Archaeol. Rep. 6. Dereham, 1977.

Hodges, Richard. *The Hamwih Pottery: The Local and Imported Wares from 30 Years' Excavations at Middle Saxon Southampton and their European Context.* C.B.A. Research Rep. 37. London, 1981.

Hodges, Richard. *Dark Age Economics: the Origins of Towns and Trade* A.D. *600–1000.* New York & London, 1989.

Hodges, Richard. *The Anglo-Saxon Achievement: Archaeology and the Beginnings of English Society.* London, 1989.

Hodges, Richard and David Whitehouse. *Mohammed, Charlemagne and the Origins of Europe: Archaeology and the Pirenne Thesis.* London & Ithaca, 1983.

Hope-Taylor, Brian. *Yeavering: An Anglo-British Centre of Early Northumbria.* London, 1977.

James, Simon, Anne Marshall and Martin Millett. "An Early Medieval Building Tradition," *Archaeol. J.* 141 (1984), 182–215.

Jones, M. U. and W. T. Jones, "Crop-mark Sites at Mucking, Essex, England." In R. L. S. Bruce-Mitford, ed., *Recent Archaeological Excavations in Europe.* London & Boston, 1975, 133–87.

Kemble, J. M. *Horae Ferales; or, Studies in the Archaeology of the Northern Nations.* London, 1863.

Lang, James, ed. *Anglo-Saxon and Viking Sculpture and its Context: Papers from the Collingwood Symposium on Insular Sculpture from 800 to 1066.* B.A.R. Brit. ser. 49. Oxford, 1978.

Leeds, E. T. *Early Anglo-Saxon Art and Archaeology.* Oxford, 1936.

Leeds, E. T. *The Archaeology of the Anglo-Saxon Settlements.* Oxford, 1913. Repr. 1970 with an introduction by J. N. L. Myres.

Leeds, E. T. "The Distribution of the Anglo-Saxon Saucer Brooch in Relation to the Battle of Bedford A.D. 571." *Archaeologia* 63 (1912), 159–202.

Leeds, E. T. *Two Types of Brooches from the Island of Gotland Sweden.* London & Aylesbury, 1910.

Marshall, Anne and Garry Marshall. "A Survey and Analysis of the Buildings of Early and Middle Saxon England." *M. A.* 35 (1991), 29–43.

Marshall, Anne and Garry Marshall, "Differentiation, Change and Continuity in Anglo-Saxon Buildings." *Archaeol. J.* 150 (1993), 366–402.

Morris, Richard. *The Church in British Archaeology.* C.B.A. Research Rep. 47. London, 1983.

Myres, J. N. L. *Corpus of Anglo-Saxon Pottery of the Pagan Period.* Cambridge, 1977.

Randsborg, Klaus. *The Viking Age in Denmark: The Formation of a State.* London & New York, 1980.

Richards. J. D. *The Significance of Form and Decoration of Anglo-Saxon Cremation Urns.* B.A.R. Brit. ser. 166. Oxford, 1987.

Rickman, Thomas. *An Attempt to Discriminate the Styles of Architecture in England from the Conquest to the Reformation.* 5th ed. London, 1848.

Rodwell, Warwick. *The Archaeology of Religious Places; Churches and Cemeteries in Britain.* Rev. ed. Philadelphia, 1980.

Ryder, P. F. *Saxon Churches in South Yorkshire.* Barnsley, 1983.

Salin, Bernhard. *Die altgermanische Thierornamentik: typologische Studie über germanische Metallgegenstände aus dem IV. bis IX. Jährhundert.* Berlin, 1904; Stockholm, 1935.

Schetelig, Hakon. *The Cruciform Brooches of Norway.* Bergen, 1908.

Smith, Charles Roach. *Inventorium Sepulchrale: An Account of Some Antiquities Dug up at Gilton, Kingston, Sibertswold, Barfriston, Beakesborne, Chartham, and Crundale, in the County of Kent, from* A.D. *1757 to* A.D. *1773 by the Rev. Bryan Faussett.* London, 1856.

Smith, Reginald A. *A Guide to the Anglo-Saxon and Foreign Teutonic Antiquities in the Department of British and Medieval Antiquities.* London, 1993.

Taylor, H. M. *Anglo-Saxon Architecture.* Vol. 3. Cambridge, 1978.

Taylor, H. M. *Repton Studies 1.* Cambridge, 1977.

Taylor, H. M. *Repton Studies 2.* Cambridge, 1979.

Taylor, H. M. and Joan Taylor. *Anglo-Saxon Architecture.* 2 vols. Cambridge, 1965.

Webster, Leslie and Janet Backhouse, eds. *The Making of England: Anglo-Saxon Art and Culture* A.D. *600–900.* London, 1991.

Wilson, David M., ed. *The Archaeology of Anglo-Saxon England.* London, 1976; pbk. edition, Cambridge, 1981.

Wilson, David M. and Ole Klindt-Jensen. *Viking Art.* Ithaca, 1966.

Wilson, David M. and Ole Klindt-Jensen. *Viking Art.* Trans. of *Vikingetidens kunst.* The Nordic Series, vol. 6. Minneapolis, 1980.

CHAPTER 2

Exploring, Explaining, Imagining
Anglo-Saxon Archaeology 1998

MARTIN O. H. CARVER

THE EVIDENCE

Anglo-Saxon archaeology refers to the material culture of the people who lived in the more southerly part of eastern Britain, between the Channel and the Forth in the period from the fifth to the eleventh century A.D. This culture shows considerable variety, but can be conventionally organized into three regions and three periods of time. Geographically we can define three principal zones: "Saxon" areas in the south, Anglian areas in Yorkshire, Humberside, and the Midlands and "Northumbria" the coastal area north of York, which is an amalgam of Anglo-Saxon and British culture. These zones are most visible and distinguishable in the sixth century, and largely disappear with grave goods in the seventh, but they persisted in some form throughout the Anglo-Saxon period and beyond it; they are remembered and palpable today; for example, in place-names, shire names and regional accents of speech.

The three periods in which Anglo-Saxon culture is studied are defined as "Early" (400–600 A.D.), "Middle" (600–800 A.D.) and "Late" (800–1100 A.D.). The early period covers the end of Roman Britain up to the conversion of the English to Christianity, the middle period the conversion to the coming of the Vikings and the late period from the Vikings to the Norman Conquest in 1066. Anglo-Saxon culture is held to have continued up to the end of the eleventh century, and to include such works of art as the Bayeux Tapestry. The transition period between the Roman and the Saxon is called "sub-Roman" and refers to cultures prevalent, mainly in the west, between 400 and 600 A.D. The period around 600 in the east is becoming increasingly referred to as the "Conversion Period." The culture prevalent around the ninth century in the "Danelaw," the area of northeast England occupied by Danes, is known as "Anglo-Scandinavian." The transition period in the eleventh century is called "Saxo-Norman." Authors also use the term "English" somewhat randomly to refer to any Anglo-Saxon activity, but its application is inhibited by the capture of the term "early English" for an architectural style of the thirteenth century. The term "Anglo-Saxon" is most properly applied to a language (otherwise Old English). Archaeologists try to use the term "early medieval" to avoid begging the question of ethnic attribution; but in general "Anglo-Saxon" has long been understood to refer to a range of cultural practices rather than a genus of people.

The archaeological evidence is very variable over these regions and over these periods, making it difficult to compare like with like. The sub-Roman period is notoriously difficult to see at all; the early period is dominated by cemeteries, with a few small settlements; the middle period now has a notable cemetery archaeology too, and a wide variety of settlement types, together with a new range of media—churches, sculpture and illuminated manuscripts—in which Christianity was expressed. The late period sees a plethora of churches, manuscripts, and sculpture, and the new type of settlement known as the *burh,* a forerunner of the medieval town. Less well known are late-period villages and cemeteries.

Anglo-Saxon England is among the most extensively explored of ancient cultures.[1] So although there will always be surprises in store, this uneven distribution of evidence is thought to be representative; in other words the differences in material culture between regions and periods represent real differences in investment in the Anglo-Saxon period. If accepted as real, these differences throw a great deal of light on political priorities. In practice this means that the examples cited in this paper will be unevenly distributed, too: for the early and conversion periods, the evidence is most plentiful and synthesis has been taken furthest in East Anglia. For the middle Saxon period, the evidence is most vivid in Northumbria and Kent; and for the late Saxon period, the most useful results so far have come from Wessex and the Midlands.

ITS INTERPRETATION

Bede's *History of the English Church and People* has been the biggest single influence on archaeological interpretation of the Anglo-Saxon period to 700, with the *Anglo-Saxon Chronicle,* Asser's *Life of Alfred,* Aelfric's *Colloquy,* and the *Sagacious Reeve,* performing similarly inspiring roles for the late period. New recruits to the subject continue to find their way into Anglo-Saxon archaeology through a love of art, literature and history. These sources encourage the view that the English were ethnically distinct immigrants from northern Germany and southern Scandinavia, who had kings, were divided into social classes, converted to Christianity as a result of a mission from Rome, and eventually conquered a large part of the island in response to Scandinavian disruption, creating a highly individual and sophisticated artistic and commercial culture. The role of archaeology has often been seen as providing illustrations and endorsement of this basic structure.

Scholars who approach from an archaeological background may start from a different set of premises and have different agenda. "Processualists" are most interested in the processes that formed communities and changed them from one formation and economic base to another, and particularly in the symbiosis between people and their resources. Change is induced not by leaders but by a changing ecology and access to resources. Each community is the expression of one or more "systems," ecological, economic and social, which can be discovered analytically using the techniques of social science applied to modern communities. "Post-processualists" have been influenced by structural anthropology to apply a much more rigorous criticism of the source material, recognizing that the evidence has already been "constructed" by its creators. Rather than revealing its secrets by analysis, material culture has to be "read" and the ulterior motives of its makers discovered by "deconstruction." "Post-structuralists" apply this source criticism to themselves, too, seeing in their own interpretations special pleading for a desired outcome, which must be countered "reflexively."

In Anglo-Saxon studies, this archaeological theorizing has led to a widespread scepticism for historical models, which had already had their credibility reduced by rigorous source criticism by historians.[2] Archaeological analysis of settlement and cemetery evidence has suggested that most communities were tribal and did not acquire kings until the eve of conversion in the late sixth century.[3] Considerable doubts have been expressed about the degree to which Anglo-Saxon culture can be regarded as rooted in a particular people which migrated to England. The "Anglo-Saxon" mode of burial could have been exercised by native Britons as a form of political expression, allowing the number of actual immigrants to be seen as minimal.[4] The questions asked are now less concerned with causation via artistic influence, or force of arms, but with why a particular form of expression was used at a particular place and time.

In my view these different approaches should not be regarded as following an itinerary of progress, and they have not in practice superseded one another, however much their proponents may protest to the contrary. Good students have always been aware that the historical, the analytical, the deductive, the intuitive and the self-critical each have a role in any successful model of the past,[5] and archaeologists working in the Middle Ages, with its pilgrim routes and monastic fishponds, could perhaps recognize the degree to which material culture was used actively and symbolically more readily than their prehistorian colleagues.[6] It should also be noted that archaeological evidence is not theoretically homogenous; so that while a midden heap is suitable for processualist analysis, to determine the economic system through discarded animal bones, a furnished grave or an illuminated manuscript is clearly expressive and demands interpretation with structuralist principles: what did the burial party or the scriptorial authority intend by what they chose to highlight? Different kinds of question draw on different kinds of archaeological evidence, which must be manipulated using different theoretical bases (fig. 2.1).

A multi-disciplinary and a multi-theoretical approach is the most difficult for an archaeologist, and the risks of superficiality and half-knowledge are perilous. For all that, it is still the best, and the one most likely to minimize the ill-effects of special pleading which form the basis

Fig. 2.1. Using Archaeological Evidence in the Anglo-Saxon Period.

Theory	Objective	Early	Middle	Late
Scientific [measurable]	Ecology	pollen agriculture	pollen agriculture	pollen mss. illustrations
Processual [statistically assessible systems]	Economy	settlement form animal bones	settlement forms animal bones	burh assemblages pottery industry
Processual [statistically assessible systems]	Social structure	burial	burial settlement hierarchy	burh plans sculpture
Post-processual [read by analogy]	Ideology	burial	burial sculpture illuminated mss	Church architecture illuminated mss. Anglo-Scandinavian sculpture

of post-structuralist anxiety. The agenda for Anglo-Saxon archaeologists is now quite varied: the changing ecology, economy, and social organization, deduced analytically from cemeteries, pollen sequences, assemblages of animal bones, settlement plans and settlement distributions in the landscape.[7] The formation of kingdoms is still a hot topic, on which different theoretical procedures have been brought to bear.[8] My own particular interest, which will be inevitably and unfairly reflected in this paper, is in the way that cemeteries, sculpture and other kinds of investment were used to reflect the ideological preferences, and by implication the political programs (real or intended), of Anglo-Saxon communities throughout the period.

The way that Anglo-Saxon people lived, the way they related to each other, the beliefs and aspirations they expressed corporately, their interactions with neighbors inland and across the seas, and the significance of the Anglo-Saxon experience for modern Europe—all these ideally form a legitimate part of the modern archaeological quest, one supported and tested by daily interaction with partners exploring the fields of Old English literature, history and art history.

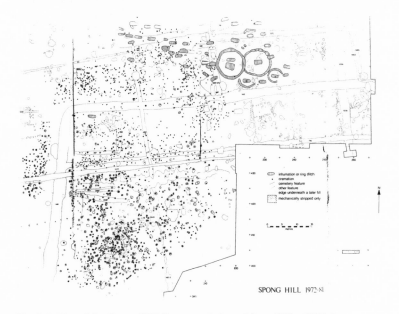

SPONG HILL 1972-81

Fig. 2.2. Plan of the Spong Hill Cemetery (adapted from Hills, 1977–).

WORK IN PROGRESS: A PARTICULAR SYNTHESIS

The Early Period

The early period 400–600 A.D. in East Anglia is characterized by large folk cemeteries containing many cremations or inhumations, and dispersed settlements. Both kinds of site are imperfectly known, from a handful of examples. The cemetery type-site is Spong Hill in Norfolk, since it is the only one that has been completely excavated and completely published, although it awaits a synthesis by its excavator. Spong Hill has around 2000 cremations in pottery vessels and fifty-eight inhumations, of which four are surrounded by ring ditches implying barrows (fig. 2.2).[9] Both types of burials were usually accompanied by grave goods, highly characteristic in both the choice and the style of the object. The cemetery at Schmalstede in Schleswig-Holstein has cremation urns which are nearly identical to some examples from Spong Hill.[10] Richards[11] found signals of unequal rank among the urns and Böhme[12] has put the earliest chamber grave in the fifth century, allowing Carver[13] to suggest that Spong Hill served a community of about 400 persons which at the time of its initiation already knew some family or tribal hierarchy, its more senior members being remembered with investment in chambers and mounds. The social and ethnic identity of the people buried in the cremation urns remains uncertain. Among Anglo-Saxon inhumations Härke has shown that 48 percent of the males bear arms and has found a correlation between weapon bearers and males of greater than average stature.[14] These he proposes as representatives of immigrant families whose arms signal their ethnic origin, the other half of the inhumed population by inference being the less privileged Britons. However, roughly the same proportion (half the male graves contained weapons) is found in Scandinavia too, where no immigration is suspected, suggesting that the weapon carriers may represent the leading rank in a relatively flat hierarchy, rather than an intrusive group.[15] For both males and females grave goods defined as Anglo-Saxon are at their most distinctive in the sixth century (fig. 2.3). The ideology of the early period is thought to be expressed by claiming identity through grave goods and communing with nature, rather than directed to deities at formal structures, although it has been proposed that the Anglo-Saxons used quadrilateral shrines adapted from British exemplars.[16]

The picture of immigrant land-claiming in East Anglia is reinforced by the settlement evidence of which the type-site is West Stow[17] (fig. 2.4). Here a settlement of fourteen houses and sixty-nine sunken-floored

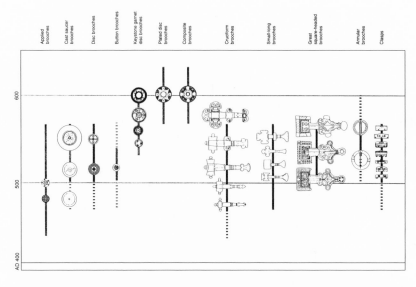

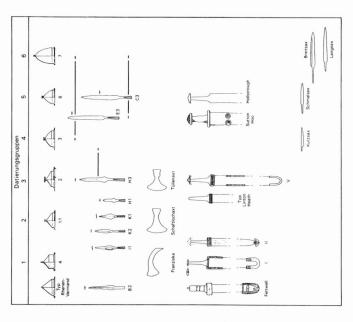

Fig. 2.3. Anglo-Saxon Burial "Kit" for (a) men and (b) Women (after Härke 1992, Abb. 6; Høilund-Nielsen 1997, fig. 28).

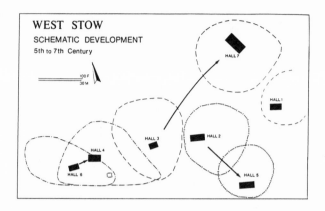

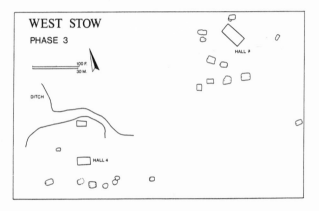

Fig. 2.4. West Stow (after West, 1985).

buildings was shown by its excavator, Stanley West, to have been not one big settlement, but an overlapping sequence of seven smallholdings. Each of these consisted of one or two houses and a number of workshops making cloth, wooden vessels and other objects; West showed that the huts had suspended floors, beneath which rubbish and abandoned stores had accumulated. The livestock is the same as that in use in Roman Britain,[18] but the agricultural practice quite different: self-sufficient mixed farming as opposed to producer or consumer establishments of the late Roman period. The occupation is dated fifth–seventh century, and the village has a final phase in which the principal dwelling is demarcated by a fence. Using a similar analysis to West, Helena Hamerow showed that Mucking in Essex supported a population of around 100 persons distributed among around ten contemporary farmsteads.[19]

Landscape and environmental studies also endorse the picture of a community of networked families taking over defunct imperial estates. Roman alignments, such as roads, remain functional as boundaries, but the size, siting and distribution of settlements are quite new. In his Deben valley survey Newman showed that all early Anglo-Saxon settlements were sited within a kilometer of running water, while middle Saxon settlements were larger and differently sited, making use of the claylands.[20] In the Witton survey, Keith Wade and others used abraded sherds from surface collection as an indication of the location of ancient arable fields, while freshly broken sherds were deemed to come from settlements.[21] On this basis, early Anglo-Saxon Witton was a small homestead with 40 ha of land under cultivation. In the middle Saxon period, the settlement had moved and expanded and the land under cultivation had doubled to 80 ha. In the later period, the settlement had expanded again and the land under arable cultivation was now 150 ha. Environmental studies by Rackham, Murphy and others imply that such an expansion is not necessarily an indication of land clearance. Rackham has shown that the ancient woodland of England had been cleared from East Anglia by the Roman period if not the Iron Age.[22] Cleared land, once cultivated and abandoned can regenerate as secondary woodland, and then be cleared again. It is the choice of each generation how much land is ploughed and how much is pasture or woodland, and this choice is as much about social formation or taxation as about natural resources themselves.

The East Anglian model is thus of a tribal community living in dispersed homesteads, farming arable, pasture and woodland and burying their dead in folk cemeteries, in which gender, rank and membership of the folk is signaled by distinctively patterned pottery, brooches and other artifacts. Some contrasts to this model have been suggested from elsewhere in the Anglo-Saxon cultural zone. Cemetery studies by Lucy in Northumbria show a major "British" component, reinforced in the sixth and seventh century.[23] For her this implies that the intrusive elements were never numerous, which may, of course, be true for Northumbria. A major excavation at West Heslerton in the Vale of Pickering has uncovered seventy-five possible houses and 115 sunken floored huts, but in contrast to West Stow or Mucking the excavator Dominic Powlesland prefers to see his buildings as largely contemporary and the whole to represent a vast settlement zoned into industrial, residential and agricultural areas.[24] In Wessex, the major settlement excavation is that at Chalton on the chalk downs near Petersfield. Here, too, patterning has been seen in the overall plan; but Chalton and West Heslerton are still unpublished and it is not impossible that they, too, will conform to the West Stow model: a shifting homestead, which towards the end of its life in the seventh century begins to acquire the characteristics of a nucleated village or high-status "manorial" place.

The Middle Period A.D. 600–800

Major changes in both settlement and cemetery form herald the arrival of the middle period in about 600 A.D. In East Anglia the new settlement types are exemplified by Wicken Bonhunt where the buildings are laid out in an ordered way and include a granary indicated by an array of posts;[25] Brandon, a planned village of houses with a church and cemetery;[26] and North Elmham, a documented early Bishop's palace.[27] In these settlements, the main buildings are houses or "halls" constructed on earth-fast posts or posts set in trenches with wattle and daub or plank fillings. The sunken-floored building is infrequent. In Northumbria, the site of Yeavering near Wooler continues to provide the model for the middle-period palace, with its large halls and outbuildings (see fig. 3.1, this volume). Hope-Taylor saw the place as a British (sub-Roman) foundation, built in imitation of Roman ways and later adopted by the Anglian kings of Northumbria.[28] The monastery is a fifth new type of settlement for the middle period, much sought after but still poorly defined. Bede's establishment at Wearmouth-Jarrow has been partially excavated and can be seen to feature timber halls of secular type as well as stone churches.[29]

The middle period has three types of burial practice: princely burial, "Roman" burial, and church burial, each representing an important change from the period before. Small burial mounds occurred in early-period East Anglian cemeteries, for example at Spong Hill, and provide a common and notable feature of Kentish cemeteries such as Finglesham.[30] The Kentish mound cemeteries suggest a sizeable aristocracy with (from grave goods) Frankish connections. But from the late sixth/early seventh century, the burial mound appears mainly outside Kent in the form of large isolated mounds covering a variety of wealthy graves, such as at Taplow,[31] Asthall,[32] and Swallowcliffe Down,[33] which collectively can be termed "princely burials" (fig. 2.5).[34] Most famously, the burial mounds at Sutton Hoo begin and end in this transition period around 600, as the recent major campaign of excavation has demonstrated.[35] It was a burial ground of about eighteen mounds reserved for

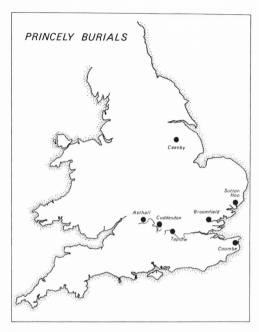

Fig. 2.5. Princely burials.

the elite, and featured cremations in bronze bowls, chamber graves, a horse-burial and two ship burials. Of these, the most prominent, viz the cremations and the ship-burials, represent departures that are new to Britain and common in Scandinavia. The grave goods included locally made polychrome jewelry, and a number of high-status objects from all over Europe. At an early date the site became a place of execution, the victims being placed around Mound 5 and around a gallows sited at the edge of the cemetery. Radiocarbon dating shows that these executions were taking place between the seventh century and the tenth. Recent work by Reynolds has shown that the practice of execution was known, to a limited extent, in the folk cemeteries during the early period, and became established around the princely burial-mounds after 600.[36] In the later Saxon period, the number and size of these sites, known as *cwealm-stow* (killing ground), expanded greatly as the Anglo-Saxon kings increased their demands for conformity.

In her study of conversion-period burial, Geake discovered over 7000 furnished graves of the later seventh/early eighth century.[37] Originally termed "final phase," Geake showed that they were not so much the end of early-period practice as a new wave of expression in which female and to a lesser extent male graves were investing in grave goods which were initially Roman and later Byzantine in style. The alignment here was not with the Germanic folk, but with a new "British" or "Roman-type" revival, or, to use her word, "renaissance." It has proved difficult to date this material before 675, thus reinforcing the idea that this represents a new form of expression, not the lingering of an old practice. Even more severe dating problems beset the third type of middle-period burial, unfurnished graves which appear in open cemeteries with radiocarbon dates from the seventh century.[38] Some of these were or may have been associated with churches, but the elusive churchyards may be expected in general to begin at the same time as private or parish churches which blossom from the ninth century.[39] As in Scandinavia,[40] burial in a church-yard is expected to be a sign of conversion to Christianity, with only so-cial rejects (including execution victims) being laid to rest beyond its limits.

West's survey of Anglo-Saxon Suffolk has shown that other sites like Sutton Hoo probably existed, although perhaps not on such a grand scale.[41] The implication is that a new hierarchy is expressing itself in both nucleated settlements or manor sites (above) and in separated elite family cemeteries, resulting in both cases in a drastic reorganization of the landscape. This social revolution was coincident with the conversion of the English to Christianity, but the relationship between the two is not necessarily direct. The proliferation of burial in small mounds in sixth-century Kent and their disappearance by the early seventh century is consistent with the formation of an aristocracy there in first a pagan Frankish and then a Christian Frankish idiom.[42] The emergence of the princely burials in East Anglia in the early seventh century showed a strong Scandinavian alignment, which Carver suggested was not so much ancestral as intentionally created, the adoption (or construction) of pagan Scandinavian ideas in order to keep Christianity at bay.[43] The break-up of folk society into manorial networks run by aristocratic families headed by a king was therefore either consequent on conversion or provoked by the conversion of a neighbor. It is likely that kings and kingdoms only existed as a reality from this point. Once converted, the Anglo-Saxons experienced not only a fundamental change in the way that society was organized—under a single leader supported by law codes—but a change in the axis of exchange from the North Sea and Scandinavia to the Channel, France, and the southern Continent and Mediterranean.[44] A sixth type of new settlement, the *wic,* appears in the late seventh or early eighth century. Hamwic was an ordered community engaged in both trade and manufacture,[45] and there is reason to believe that Ipswich was similar in function.[46] For Hodges these were creations of the (new) monarchs,[47] and it is likely that the formation of the *wics* (and their archaeological detection) is owed to the need to canalize trade in order to tax it.[48] A seventh settlement type connected with exchange functions is currently being defined; these are concentrated patches of coins and metalwork found from surface collection.[49] When excavated they produce no buildings, and are likely to represent fairs or more informal rendezvous for making exchanges or paying dues. These sites have been (temporarily one can only hope) given the misleading name "productive sites" (i.e., they "produce" finds of metalwork for treasure-hunters: a better term would be "exchange sites"). In the midlands and the north, the *wics* are hard to tell from monasteries and may have performed a very similar function. Flixborough in Lincolnshire and Brandon in Suffolk are not mentioned by Bede but have produced "ecclestiastical" metalwork such as styli which encourage the monastic attribution. On the other hand, they may belong to a period (late seventh–eighth century) when the monasteries were otherwise being secularized.[50]

The seventh-century political revolution is evident, too, in monuments, which represent the tangible remains of political investment and expression. In the early seventh century, at least in East Anglia and Wessex, the principal monument is the large burial mound, often sited on a scarp or ridge as though to dominate land. In contemporary Kent, churches of Roman style were constructed at Canterbury, Rochester, and elsewhere. These are rectangular stone buildings with a small square or apsidal chancel, sometimes accompanied by a number of small rooms, or *porticus* attached to the outside of the nave, and are assumed to be based on Roman examplars from France or Italy.[51] Rectangular churches of similar build are sparsely distributed in the Anglo-Saxon cultural zone, at Bradwell-on-Sea in Essex, Escomb (Du), and at Jarrow.[52] In the further north and the west, a stronger advocacy for Christianity of a different kind was received from Iona, founded by the Irish missionary Columba in ca. 563 A.D. Columba died in 597, the year that Augustine arrived as England's official emissary from Rome, and the contrasting and often competing influence of both men and the political solutions they stood for has lasted for more than a millennium in the British Isles. In spite of decades of investigation at Iona,[53] and other documented sites, the form of a Columban monastery is largely inferential, and may not have differed much from contemporary secular settlement. They were undoubtedly major political centers in north Britain, as in Ireland.

Monumental investment in the north may have been primarily in monastic sites of this kind, and has survived best in the arts of sculpture and manuscript production. The earliest sculpture in stone takes the form of grave-markers carrying the names of those commemorated incised in Latin (or sometimes in runes). The earliest illuminated books that have survived which are likely to have been made in Britain are Durham A.II.10, the Book of Durrow, and Durham A.II.17, all of the later seventh century, and made (if not in Ireland) at Iona or one of its daughter houses.[54] The earliest manuscript to have survived from an Anglo-Saxon context is Cotton Nero Civ, otherwise the Lindisfarne Gospels, made on Lindisfarne probably before 698 A.D.[55] It carries a wonderful composition of geometric art and portraiture drawing on Irish, British, English, Roman and Byzantine ideas. In its elements and meaning, as Bruce-Mitford showed, the animal ornament is the art of the Sutton Hoo jewelry translated to a gospel book.[56] The lacertine animals on the Sutton Hoo jewelry may be seen as performing a protective role as the guardians of treasure, a role which may have been simply transferred to the carpet pages of manuscripts, themselves skeuomorphs of decorated metal book-covers and shrines such as that from Lough Kinale.[57] This style of art is known as insular ornament, since it is found in both Britain and Ireland and difficult to locate more precisely.

Almost contemporary with the Lindisfarne Gospels but made in quite a different idiom is the Codex'Amiatinus, made for Abbot Ceolfrid at Jarrow and taken by him as a present for the Pope, but abandoned when Ceolfrid died at Langres. The enormous codex, which required the skins of 500 calves, has virtually no insular ornament (there is a tiny scrap of interlace on f. 802) and contains illustrations of neo-Classical type with references to the holy places in Jerusalem.[58] The productions of Lindisfarne and Jarrow represent a real Northumbrian dilemma between the Roman Christian empire and what Columba called the "western churches," that is, those of Cornwall, Wales, Ireland, and the Irish of Scotland, the Scots. Bede reported this ideological conflict in terms of rival liturgies, and deemed it solved in favor of the Roman party at the Synod of Whitby in 664. But there is little doubt, from the archaeology at least, that the conflict remained a live issue to the end of the Anglo-Saxon period.

From the eighth century the sculpture of the western churches becomes notably more monumental, but it is less clear that high crosses at Ruthwell (pl. 2.1) or Bewcastle or the Pictish sites need be sited at monasteries. The period 750–800 is not well documented, but it is possi-

Pl. 2.1. The Ruthwell Cross (photo Jane Hawkes).

ble that the secular reaction against monasticism, so marked after 800, had already begun in the previous fifty years, in England as in Pictland.[59]

The Late Period A.D. 800–1050

The two strongly opposed trends towards, on the one hand a centralized kingdom supported by orthodox Christianity, and on the other, a deregulated secular aristocracy (even if Christian), may be observed in settlements and monuments over the next two-and-a-half centuries, first one side and then the other having ascendancy. The best known exponents of deregulated (or indeed unregulated) aristocracy were the Vikings, whose documented attacks on monasteries were probably provoked as much by their objection to commercial restrictive practice as to Christianity as such. Although the Vikings, as Danes or Norse, are recorded as having settled in a number of regions on the island of Britain, characteristic settlement and burial is best seen in the northern and western coastlands and islands. In the Anglo-Saxon cultural zone, Viking settlement is documented through references and place-names in Yorkshire and the North Midlands—the "Danelaw." Mound-burial is known in the area of Repton and Ingleby;[60] but in Yorkshire, where Scandinavian place-names are thickest, the Viking element appears at first sight to have been subsumed in English Christian society. However, the political impact of Scandinavian interest in the area was determinant, as shown by their main medium of expression, the carved stone crosses and grave-markers. In his survey of East Riding, James Lang shows dramatic changes in both the type and distribution of sculpture around 800.[61] In the seventh and eighth centuries, sculpture carrying Latin inscriptions is distributed in sites known or likely to have been monastic; but in the ninth century, the sculpture is more numerous, secular in theme and distributed widely in what are deemed to be estate centers (fig. 2.6). Scandinavian policy, it seems, was not anti-Christian, but anti-centralization. The monasteries are "suppressed," and investment by secular lords shifts to monuments erected at their own estate headquarters carrying, among others, messages of Christian alignment. To quote Rosemary Cramp, "the Vikings introduced a secularization of taste in art, as they also secularized landholdings."[62]

In contrast, and in reaction, from the later ninth century many of the Anglo-Saxon aristocratic families in the south were urging a program of centralized Christian kingship, and this emerged in the documentation as a successful policy in the hands of the royal family of Wessex, finding political expression in Alfred's wars with the Danes. In material culture

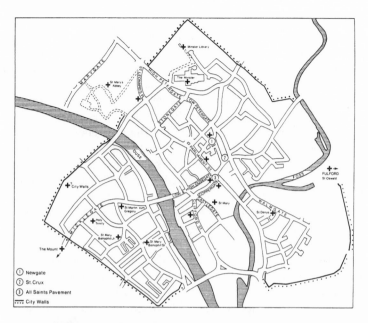

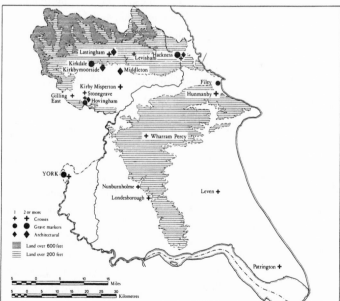

Fig. 2.6. (a) Sites with Sculpture in York, (b) Early Sculpture (after Lang, *Corpus* 3, figs. 2, 3).

it has become increasingly clear that this policy was expressed in imitation of all things Roman. The principal marker is a new type of settlement, the *burh,* which imitated Rome in its shape, its distribution, and its pottery. Two major archaeological programs have defined the cycle of the *burh.* When first applied in late-ninth century Wessex, the *burh* is effectively a fort, a rectangular enclosure which may have contained only tents, as at Cricklade,[63] or a reused Roman defense as at Winchester.[64] These were the *burhs* documented in the "Burghal Hideage" which effectively records the manpower required to defend them, and by a given formula, their length of wall.[65] Fieldwork by David Hill and others has confirmed that the formula was applied to peninsula sites and old Iron Age fortifications as wells as Roman forts and greenfield sites. The *burhs* of Wessex were distributed at intervals throughout the kingdom, apparently offering army bases and refuge in reach of all. Alfred's children and heirs, Edward and Æthelflæd, carried on the war of conquest against the Danes, building a chain of *burhs* in the East and West Midlands respectively in imitation of the manner in which Britain was conquered by the Romans. At Stafford,[66] the *burh* built by Æthelflæd was found to overlie a seventh–eighth-century center in which surplus grain was collected, and it is likely that many *burh* sites represent pre-existing manorial or royal tax-collection points as predicted by Chadwick.[67]

The *burhs* thereafter displayed an evolution which also resembled that of their Roman predecessors and (probably) exemplars. In a second phase, the *burh* might be planned and was used to site supply industries within the enclosure,[68] as at London and York,[69] or in suburbs outside the defenses. At Stafford, bread ovens in the central area and heaps of animal bones dumped outside it suggested that grain and carcasses were being processed for redistribution. Also in Stafford, as in other second-phase *burhs,* a standardized form of pottery makes its appearance: orange wheel-thrown jars, mass produced and distributed in this case around the *burhs* of West Mercia. In separate instances, human skulls had been discarded within heaps of broken pottery wasters from an unsuccessful firing. "Stafford Ware" is distinctly Roman in appearance, and moreover resembles the Roman pottery which had been made (800 years earlier) in the area of Stafford itself (Trent Vale Ware), suggesting a conscious emulation of a recognized Roman past. Stafford Ware is paralleled by a number of similar industries: Thetford Ware, York Ware, St. Neots Ware, Cheddar Ware, all designating areas or dioceses in which the *burh* system held sway.

In a third stage of development, in the decades before the Norman Conquest, the *burh* became less of a garrison and more of a residential and manufacturing center, in which goods were made, exchanged and taxed under the eye of a reeve. This production took place in "tenements," which were long narrow properties with the house at the street end, and the ovens, hearths, wells and pits of the light industrial processes at the back. The tenements established in Anglo-Saxon towns often endured through the Middle Ages and even in some cases to the present day (e.g., Durham[70]). The changes in the occupation and function of *burhs* are being graphically chronicled through animal bones. To take an example from York, at Fishergate, or *Eoforwic,* and in the early phases at Coppergate (Viking *Jorvik*), the meat supply seems to have been highly regulated,[71] while in the later phases there are clear signs in the rubbish pits that the inhabitants had a wide choice of foodstuffs; a regulated community fed by an authority has been superseded by a market economy.[72] In eleventh-century Durham, leather workers had access to sea fish, lobsters, and mollusks as well as the usual domestic meats. There was also game: ptarmigan, salmon and red deer, which became notably absent from the leather-workers' successors in the Norman period.[73] In York, there is some sign of the town acquiring a dual purpose and of the street plan being altered to serve it. The *burh* was sited in the old legionary fortress and using its derelict street plan, while the *wic* of Jorvik developed down by the confluence of the Rivers Ouse and Foss— a series of closely arrayed tenements rich in manufacturing activity.[74]

Ideological investment in the politics manifested by the *burh* was extensive and varied. A new silver penny was developed from the *sceatta.* It had an experimental phase in Offa's Mercia, as part of this king's Romanizing policy. The kings of Wessex introduced standardized size and weight and stamped the head and name of the monarch, the name of the moneyer, and eventually the mint, which was officially restricted to *burh* sites. The coins were presumably used to register receipts of surplus concentrated in the *burh* and turned into silver for the exchequer. The Christian church was redesigned and promoted as an astute combination of the episcopal, the monastic and the secular systems. Churches, known as "Minsters" (abbreviated from the Latin for monastery) made their appearance in *burhs.*[75] In the mid-tenth century, a major reform, which was mainly episcopal in application, was known, confusingly, as the "Benedictine Revival." It was master-minded by Bishops Æthelwold, Oswald and Dunstan who set up episcopal centers in Winchester, Glastonbury, Worcester and York, at the same time staffing them with dedicated non-secular clergy, who were highly regulated by the Benedictine rule (thus the name of the revival). The effect was a centralized Christian network driven by a dedicated bureaucracy, closely associated with the monarch. Traditionally, the inspiration for the culture in which the Benedictine revival was expressed came from Carolingian France, which had promoted a similar revival of a centralized Christian empire in the Roman style, and also invented a version of Benedictine monasticism to administer it. The extravagant westwork of the Old Minster at Winchester is thought to have had Frankish antecedents.[76] The movement also inspired a revival of manuscript illumination, applied not to gospels but to a revised repertoire of sacred books: prayer books, sacramentaries, psalters and the *Liber Vitae,* all of them suitable for the service of a Christian secular aristocracy as well as aristocratic colleges of clergy.

The history of illumination in the late period is a window on the Anglo-Saxon mind at a surprisingly diverse number of social levels, featuring both heavy ceremonial and appealing informality. In Alfred's formative years, the ribbon animals and heavy geometric repertoire of the insular styles (the Book of Kells of about 800 is considered by some to be a last brilliant masterpiece in this genre) had been succeeded in the mid-ninth century by more individual and endearingly playful creatures that appear in margins and pose for initials (Oxford, Bodl. Lib. Junius 27; Oxford, Bodl. Lib. Tanner 10).[77] The first generation of the new orthodox manuscript art begins with London, B. L., Cotton Galba Axviii of ca. 930, developing with London, B. L. Cotton, Vespasian Aviii and the Benedictional of St Æthelwold.[78] This "first style," as Wormald termed it, is heavily ornamented with acanthus and features ceremonial figures, mainly clerics and kings.[79] The form of the human figures is a little stilted in the "First Style," but became greatly animated after the appearance in Canterbury of the Utrecht Psalter, an illustrated book made in Hautvilliers about 820. The figures of Wormald's "Utrecht style" beginning in A.D.1000 are lively enactments of the text of the psalter (e.g., London, B. L. Harley 603, which is based closely on Utrecht), or of the *Psychomachia* of Prudentius (e.g., London, B. L., Cotton Cleopatra Cviii) or the Old Testament, (e.g., London, B. L., Cotton Claudius Biv, or Oxford, Bodl. Lib., Junius 11), and seem to feature people from every walk of life. The artists who made these books generally copied from exemplars—but not always. In many cases it can be shown that the Anglo-Saxon illustrator departed from his model and introduced scenes, people and objects from contemporary Anglo-Saxon life (fig. 2.7).[80] These rare and evocative scenes reveal a busy countryside of farmworkers clad in smocks, carrying sticks, plowing the land, tending sheep and cattle, and cutting wood. In these bucolic scenes, there is a remarkable lack of emphasis on kings and bishops.

Two kinds of investment in burial have been detected that are particular to the late period: under York Minster unfurnished graves radiocarbon-dated to the ninth–eleventh-century cemetery were covered by carved grave slabs,[81] including the house-shaped "hog-backs,"[82] a burial

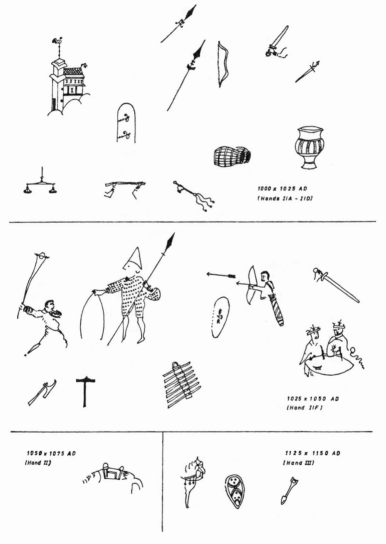

Fig. 2.7. Details from London, B. L. Harley 603 (after Carver, "Contemporary Artefacts," fig. 16.)

practice which becomes widespread in contemporary rural churches too, now apparently in equilibrium with the centralized Christian authority.[83] The second type of burial practice is "charcoal burial," which involved placing the corpse on a bed of charcoal. It appears to be confined to important minsters in the tenth–twelfth century. It is not impossible that the use of grave-slabs (particularly hog-backs) and charcoal burial owe something to Scandinavian adaptions of Christian practice.[84]

Outside the *burhs* it is thought that the majority of the population lived in villages which resembled those of the later Middle Ages, had the same names, and often occupied the same sites. These villages were based on manorial sites like Goltho or Wharram Percy, where a large house was accompanied by a number of simpler dwellings,[85] as well as sites of higher status, of which Cheddar is the best studied.[86] The small manor sites might be fortified, anticipating the motte and bailey castle which was to follow.[87] Relatively quickly, by the example of surviving structures (90 percent of which are from the tenth–eleventh centuries), the villages acquire churches presumably as a result of either private or episcopal sponsorship, depending on which political system was in the ascendancy. The expectation for the late Saxon era is that the churches of Wessex and the Midlands would belong to a phase of state-driven parish-making, while those of the Danelaw would be privately owned (*eigenkirche*). Archaeology has not succeed in distinguishing the two, though current work on the churches themselves is investigating a regional variety long observed, but little understood. The round towers of East Anglia, for example, provide a well-known specialty, which must have begun in the late period, even if many surviving examples can be shown to have been built later still. Their particular affiliation with Schleswig-Holstein no doubt owes something to targeted commerce and the influence of the German Empire.[88] But this was not the first time that East Anglia and Schelswig-Holstein enjoyed a special cultural relationship; in the early period the same two areas shared a common type of cremation urn (see above).

Such persistent tendencies, or perhaps one might say valencies, whether due to kith and kin, favorable winds and currents, terrestrial resources, enemies or chance, show that Anglo-Saxon politics were driven by more than a marketplace. Their changing viewpoints and creative energies (like ours) were the result of continually marrying new convictions with old loyalties.

NOTES

[1] D. M. Wilson, *The Archaeology of Anglo-Saxon England* (London, 1976); J. Campbell, ed., *The Anglo-Saxons* (London, 1991); M. Welch, *Anglo-Saxon England* (London, 1992).

[2] D. N. Dumville, "Kingship, Genealogies and Regnal Lists," in P. Sawyer and I. Wood, eds. *Early Medieval Kingship* (Leeds, 1977), 72–104; P. Wormald, "Bede, the Bretwaldas and the Origins of the gens Anglorum," in P. Wormald, D. Bullogh and R. Collins, eds., *Ideal and Reality in Frankish and Anglo-Saxon Society: Studies Presented to J. M. Wallace-Hadrill* (Oxford, 1983), 99–129.

[3] C. J. Arnold, *An Archaeology of the Early Anglo-Saxon Kingdoms* (London & New York, 1988); M. O. H. Carver, "Kingship and Material Culture in Early Anglo-Saxon East Anglia," in S. Bassett, ed., *The Origins of Anglo-Saxon Kingdoms* (London & New York, 1989), 141–58.

[4] E.g., N. Higham, *Rome, Britain and the Anglo-Saxons* (London, 1992); N. Higham, *The English Conquest: Gildas and Britain in the Fifth Century* (Manchester, 1994); R. Hodges, *The Anglo-Saxon Achievement* (London, 1989); M. C. Whyman, "Invisible People? Material Culture in 'Dark Age' Yorkshire," in M. O. H. Carver, ed., *In Search of Cult: Archaeological Investigations in Honour of Phillip Rahtz* (Woodbridge & Rochester, 1993), 61–68; S. Lucy, "The Anglo-Saxon Cemeteries of East Yorkshire," unpub. Ph.D. thesis, Cambridge University, 1995; cf S. J. P. Trafford, "Theoretical Approaches to Early Medieval Migration," unpub. Ph.D. thesis, University of York, 1997, but see H. Härke, "Material Culture as Myth. Weapons in Anglo-Saxon Graves," in C. K. Jensen and K. Høilund-Nielsen, eds., *The Chronological and Social Analysis of Archaeological Burial Data* (Aarhus, 1997), 119–27; H. Härke, "Early Anglo-Saxon Social Structure," in J. Hines, ed., *The Anglo-Saxons from the Migration Period to the 8th Century: An Ethnographic Perspective* (San Marino, 1997), 125–60.

[5] See for example S. Piggott, *Ancient Europe* (Edinburgh, 1965), chapter 1.

[6] M. O. H. Carver, "Digging for Ideas," *Antiquity* 63 (1989), 666–74.

[7] E.g., P. Rahtz, T. Dickinson, and L. Watts, eds., *Anglo-Saxon Cemeteries 1979,* B.A.R. Brit. ser. 82 (Oxford, 1980); H. Härke, *Angelsächsische Waffengräber des 5. bis 7. Jahrhunderts* (Cologne & Bonn, 1992), Härke, "Material Culture"; J. Rackham, ed., *Environment and Economy in Anglo-Saxon England,* C.B.A. Research Rep. (London, 1994); Hodges, *Anglo-Saxon Achievement*; C. Scull, "Archaeology, Early Anglo-Saxon Society and the Origins of the Anglo-Saxon Kingdoms," *A.S.S.A.H.* 6 (1993), 65–82; J. Bourne, ed., *Anglo-Saxon Landscapes in the East Midlands* (Leicester, 1995).

[8] B. Burnam and J. Kingsbury, eds., *Space, Hierarchy and Society: Interdisciplinary Studies in Social Area Analysis,* B.A.R. Int. ser. 59 (Oxford, 1979); C.

Renfrew and J. Cherry, eds., *Peer Polity Interaction and Socio-political Change* (Cambridge, 1986); Arnold, *Archaeology*; S. Bassett, ed., *The Origins of the Anglo-Saxon Kingdoms* (London & New York, 1989); Hodges, *Anglo-Saxon Achievement*; Scull, "Archaeology."

[9] C. M. Hills et al., *The Anglo-Saxon Cemetery at Spong Hill, Norfolk,* East Anglian Archaeol. Rep. 6, 11, 21, 24 and continuing (1977–).

[10] M-J. Bode, Schmalstede. *Ein Urnengräberfeld der Kaiser- und Volker-wanderungszeit,* Offa-Bucher 8 (Neumunster, 1998).

[11] J. D. Richards, *The Significance of Form and Decoration of Anglo-Saxon Cremation Urns,* B.A.R. Brit. ser. 82 (Oxford, 1987), 24.

[12] H. W. Böhme, "Das Ende der Römerherrschaft in Britannien und die an-gelsächsische Besiedlung Englands im 5. Jahrhundert," *Jahrbuch der Römisch-Germanischen Zentralmuseums Mainz* 33 (1986), 469–574.

[13] Carver, "Kingship and Material Culture," 150.

[14] Härke, "Material Culture"; "Early Anglo-Saxon."

[15] A. Nørgård-Jørgensen, "Scandinavian Military Equipment and the Weapon Burial Rite, A.D. 530–800," in Jensen and Høilund-Nielsen, *Burial and Society,* 149–63, at p. 161.

[16] J. Blair, "Anglo-Saxon Pagan Shrines and their Prototypes," *A.S.S.A.H* 8 (1995), 1–28.

[17] S. E. West, *West Stow: The Anglo-Saxon Village,* East Anglian Archaeol. Rep. 24 (Ipswich, 1985), fig. 4 a, b.

[18] P. J. Crabtree, "Animal Exploitation in East Anglian Villages," in Rack-ham, *Environment and Economy,* 40–54.

[19] H. Hamerow, "Settlement Mobility and the Middle Saxon 'Shift': Rural Settlements and Settlement Patterns in Anglo-Saxon England," *A.S.E.* 20 (1991), 1–17; H. Hamerow, *Excavations at Mucking, Essex Volume 2: The Anglo-Saxon Settlement* (London, 1993).

[20] J. Newman, "The Late Roman and Anglo-Saxon Settlement Pattern in the Sandlings of Suffolk," in M. O. H. Carver, ed., *The Age of Sutton Hoo* (Wood-bridge & Rochester, 1992), 25–38.

[21] In A. Lawson, *The Archaeology of Witton near North Walsham, Norfolk,* East Anglian Archaeol. Rep. 18 (Norfolk, 1983).

[22] O. Rackham, *The History of the Countryside* (London, 1986); *idem,* "Trees and Woodland in Anglo-Saxon England: the Documentary Evidence," in Rackham, *Environment and Economy,* 7–11.

[23] Lucy, "Anglo-Saxon Cemeteries."

[24] D. Powlesland, C. Haughton and J. Hanson, "Excavations at Heslerton, North Yorkshire, 1978–1982," *Archaeol. J.* 143 (1986), 53–173; D. Powlesland, "Early Anglo-Saxon Settlements, Structures, Form and Layout," in Hines, *Anglo-Saxons,* 101–24.

[25] Unpublished: see K. Wade, " Settlement Site at Bonhunt Farm, Wicken Bonhunt, Essex," in D. G. Buckley, ed., *Archaeology in Essex to 1500 A.D.: In Memory of Ken Newton,* C.B.A. Research Rep. 55 (London, 1980), 96–102; Crabtree, "Animal Exploitation."

[26] Unpublished: see R. D. Carr, A. Tester and P. Murphy, "The Middle Saxon Settlement at Staunch Meadow, Brandon," *Antiquity* 62 (1988), 371–77.

[27] P. Wade-Martins, *Excavations in North Elmham Park 1967–72,* East Anglian Archaeol. Report 9 (Norfolk, 1980).

[28] B. Hope Taylor, *Yeavering: An Anglo-British Centre of Early Northumbria* (London, 1977).

[29] Unpublished: see R. J. Cramp, "Excavations at the Saxon Monastic Sites of Wearmouth and Jarrow: An Interim Report," *M.A.* 13 (1969), 24–66; Cramp, this volume.

[30] S. C. Hawkes, "Anglo-Saxon Kent, c. 425–725," in P. E. Leach, ed., *Archaeology in Kent to A.D. 1500: In Memory of Stuart Eborall Rigold,* C.B.A. Research Rep. 48 (London, 1982), 64–78.

[31] G. Speake, *Anglo-Saxon Animal Art and its Germanic Background* (Oxford, 1980).

[32] T. M. Dickinson and G. Speake, "The Seventh Century Cremation Burial in Asthall Barrow, Oxfordshire: A Re-assessment," in Carver, *Age of Sutton Hoo,* 95–130.

[33] G. Speake, *A Saxon Bed-Burial on Swallowcliffe Down* (London, 1989).

[34] J. Shepherd, "The Social Identity of the Individual in Isolated Barrows and Barrow-Cemeteries in Anglo-Saxon England," in Burnham and Kingsbury, *Space, Hierarchy and Society,* 47–79.

[35] M. O. H. Carver, *Sutton Hoo Burial Ground of Kings?* (London, 1998), chaps. 6 and 7.

[36] A. J. Reynolds, "Anglo-Saxon Law in the Landscape. An Archaeological Study of the Old English Judicial System," unpub. Ph.D. thesis, University College London, 1998.

[37] H. Geake, *The Use of Grave-Goods in Conversion Period England c. 600–c. 850,* B.A.R. Brit. ser. 261 (Oxford, 1997).

[38] Ibid., 127, Table 6.2

[39] R. K. Morris, *Churches in the Landscape* (London, 1989), chapter 4.

[40] J. Kieffer-Olsen, "Christianity and Christian Burial. The Religious Background and the Transition from Paganism to Christianity from the Perspective of Churchyard Archaeology," in Jensen and Høilund-Nielsen, *Burial and Society,* 185–89.

[41] S. E. West, *A Corpus of Anglo-Saxon Material from Suffolk,* (in press); see also, J. Newman, "New Light on Old Finds—Bloodmoor Hill, Gisleham, Suffolk," *A.S.S.A.H.* 9 (1996), 75–79.

[42] Cf. I. Wood, *The Merovingian North Sea* (Alsingas,1983).

[43] M. O. H. Carver, "Sutton Hoo in Context," *Settimane di Studio del Centro Italiano di Studi sull'Altro Medioevo* 32 (Spoleto, 1986), 77–123; M. O. H. Carver, "Ideology and Allegiance in East Anglia," in R. Farrell and C. Neuman de Vegvar, eds., *Sutton Hoo: Fifty Years After,* American Early Medieval Studies 2 (Oxford, OH, 1992), 173–82.

[44] J. Hines, *The Scandinavian Character of Anglian England in the pre-Viking Period,* B.A.R. Brit. ser. 124 (Oxford,1984); U. Näsman, "Vendel Period Glass from Eketorp-II, Oland, Sweden," *Acta Archaeologica* 55 (1986), 55–116, at figs 9, 10.

[45] A. D. Morton, *Excavations at Hamwic, Vol. 1,* C.B.A. Research Rep. 84 (London, 1992).

[46] Unpublished: see K. Wade, "Ipswich," in R. Hodges and B. Hobley, eds., *The Rebirth of Towns in the West A.D. 700–1050,* C.B.A. Research Rep. 68 (London, 1988), 93–100.

[47] Hodges, *Anglo-Saxon Achievement.*

[48] M. O. H. Carver, "Pre-Viking Traffic in the North Sea," in S. McGrail, ed., *Maritime Celts, Frisians and Saxons,* C.B.A. Research Rep. 71 (London, 1990), 117–25; M. O. H. Carver, *Arguments in Stone: Archaeological Research and the European Town in the First Millennium A.D.* (Oxford, 1993); C. Scull, "Urban Centers in pre-Viking Europe," in Hines, *Anglo-Saxons* 269–98.

[49] M. A. S. Blackburn and D. M. Metcalf, eds., *Productive Sites of the Middle Saxon Period,* 12th Oxford Coin Symposium (forthcoming).

[50] L. Webster and J. Backhouse, eds., *The Making of England: Anglo-Saxon Art and Culture A.D. 600–900* (London, 1991); Carr, Tester and Murphy, "Middle Saxon Settlement"; Morris, *Churches in the Landscape*; J. Blair, "Churches in the Early English Landscape: Social and Cultural Contexts," in J. Blair and C. Pyrah, eds., *Church Archaeology: Research Directions for the Future,* C.B.A. Research Rep. 104 (York, 1996), 6–18; M. O. H. Carver, "Conversion and Politics on the Eastern Seaboard of Britain: Some Archaeological Indicators," in B. Crawford, ed., *Conversion and Christianity in the North Sea Region* (St. Andrews, in press).

[51] A. Clapham, *English Romanesque Architecture before the Conquest* (Oxford, 1930).

[52] H. M. Taylor and J. Taylor, *Anglo-Saxon Architecture* (Cambridge, 1965).

[53] R. Sharpe, ed., *Adomnan's Life of Columba* (Harmondsworth, 1995), introduction.

[54] J. J. G. Alexander, ed., *Insular Manuscripts 6th to 9th Century* (London, 1978); G. Henderson, *From Durrow to Kells: The Insular Gospel Book 650–800* (Oxford, 1987).

[55] J. Backhouse, *The Lindisfarne Gospels* (Oxford, 1987).

[56] In T. D. Kendrick, T. J. Brown, and R. L. S. Bruce-Mitford, eds., *Evangeliorum Quattuor Codex Lindisfarnensis,* vol. 2 (Olten & Lusanne, 1960); R. L. S. Bruce-Mitford, *The Sutton Hoo Ship Burial,* 3 vols. (London 1975, 1978, 1983), see especially vol. 2, pp. 432–611.

[57] E. P. Kelly, "The Lough Kinale Book-Shrine," in R. M. Spearman and J. Higgitt, eds., *The Age of Migrating Ideas: Early Medieval Art in Northern Britain and Ireland* (Edinburgh, 1993), 168–74.

[58] R. L. S. Bruce-Mitford, "The Art of the Codex Amiatinus," *J.B.B.A.,* 3rd ser. 32 (1969), 1–25.

[59] M. O. H. Carver, "Conversion and Politics."

[60] J. D. Richards, *Viking Age England* (London, 1991).

[61] J. Lang, "The Hogback: A Viking Colonial Monument," *A.S.S.A.H.* 3 (1984), 85–176; J. Lang, *York and Eastern Yorkshire, Corpus of Anglo-Saxon Stone Sculpture,* vol. 3 (London, 1991). (Hereafter *Corpus* 3.)

[62] R.J. Cramp, "The Viking Image," in R. T. Farrell, ed., *The Vikings* (London, 1982), 18; see also, Morris, *Churches in the Landscape,* chap. 4.

[63] J. Haslam, *Anglo-Saxon Towns in Southern England* (Chichester, 1984), 107.

[64] M. Biddle, "Excavations at Winchester 1971. Tenth and Final Interim Report," *Antiquaries J.* 55 (1975), 96–126, 295–337; *idem,* "Felix Urbs Winthonia: Winchester in the Age of Monastic Reform," in D. Parsons, ed., *Tenth Century Studies* (London, 1975), 123–40; *idem,* "Towns," in Wilson, *Archaeology of Anglo-Saxon England,* 99–150.

[65] D. H. Hill, "The Burghal Hideage: The Establishment of a Text," *M.A.* 13 (1969), 84–92.

[66] M. O. H. Carver, *Underneath English Towns* (London, 1987).

[67] H. M. Chadwick, *Studies in Anglo-Saxon Institutions* (Cambridge, 1905), 255.

[68] M. Biddle and D. Hill, "Late Saxon Planned Towns," *Antiquaries J.* 51 (1971), 70–85.

[69] A. G. Vince, *Saxon London: An Archaeological Investigation* (London, 1990); R. A. Hall, this volume.

[70] M. O. H. Carver, "Three Saxo-Norman Tenements in Durham City," *M.A.* 23 (1979), 1–80.

[71] T. O'Connor, "8th–11th Century Economy and Environment in York," in Rackham, *Environment and Economy,* 136–47.

[72] Ibid.; A. G. Vince, "Saxon Urban Economies: An Archaeological Perspective," in Rackham, *Environment and Economy,* 108–19.

[73] Carver, "Saxo-Norman Tenements."

[74] R. K. Hall, *The Viking Dig* (London, 1986); M. O. H. Carver, "Roman to Norman at York Minster," in A. D. Phillips and B. Heywood, *Excavations at York Minster,* vol. 1 (London, 1995), 177–221.

[75] J. Blair, ed., *Minsters and Parish Churches. The Local Church in Transition 950–1200* (Oxford, 1988).

[76] Biddle, "Felix Urbs Winthonia"; *idem,* "Archaeology, Architecture and the Cult of Saints," in L. A. S. Butler and R. K. Morris, *The Anglo-Saxon Church: Papers on History, Architecture, and Archaeology in Honour of Dr. H. M. Taylor,* C.B.A. Research Report 60 (London, 1986). 70–85.

[77] T. D. Kendrick, *Late Saxon and Viking Art* (London, 1949).

[78] E. Temple, ed., *Anglo-Saxon Manuscripts 900–1066* (London, 1976), nos. 5, 16, 23; J. Backhouse, D. H. Turner and L. E. Webster, eds., *The Golden Age of Anglo-Saxon Art, 966–1066* (London, 1984).

[79] F. Wormald, *English Drawings of the Tenth and Eleventh Centuries* (London, 1952).

[80] M. O. H. Carver, "Contemporary Artefacts Illustrated in Late Saxon Manuscripts," *Archaeologia* 108 (1976), 117–46.

[81] Phillips and Heywood, *Excavations at York Minster.*

[82] Lang, "Hogback"; *Corpus 3.*

[83] Morris, *Churches in the Landscape,* 163.

[84] M. O. H. Carver, "Early Medieval Durham. The Archaeological Evidence," in *Medieval Art and Architecture at Durham Cathedral* (London, 1980), 11–19.

[85] P. A. Rahtz, "Buildings and Rural Settlements," in Wilson, *Archaeology of Anglo-Saxon England,* 49–98.

[86] P. A. Rahtz, *The Saxon and Medieval Palaces at Cheddar,* B.A.R. Brit. ser. 65 (Oxford, 1979).

[87] Hodges, *Anglo-Saxon Achievement,* 169.

[88] S. Heywood, "The Round Towers of East Anglia," in Blair, *Minster and Parish Churches,* 169–78.

CHAPTER 3

The Fifth and Sixth Centuries
Reorganization Among the Ruins

DAVID A. HINTON

Two of the most informative categories of archaeological evidence are pot sherds and coins, and nothing shows more clearly the extent to which the economic system of the fourth century had changed by the middle of the fifth than that mass-produced vessels ceased to be made in the British Isles, and that there were not enough coins to sustain the circulation of an officially recognized currency.

Coins had been used to pay the Roman army and to maintain the Empire's bureaucracy, to collect tax and to facilitate the exchange of goods; without them, no large-scale organization could operate. Early fifth-century coins are found at various sites, but there were no new supplies to maintain a coin-using economy—although the extent to which coins were used in Britain even in the fourth century for marketing rather than for paying the army is not clear. In the same way, the army had created a substantial demand for pottery; without the troops, long-distance transport of pottery was not economic. It was probably also increasingly difficult to carry goods as roads and waterways became overgrown or silted up without the regular maintenance that a central authority could insist upon; consequently production centers could only hope to supply their own immediate hinterlands. Such restricted circulation was unable to justify the scale of production of earlier periods, so the industries came to an end, their workforces presumably merging into the general population. The coarse, hand-made pots of the fifth and sixth centuries, many tempered with farmyard dung, seem to owe nothing to the wheel-thrown products of the specialist late Roman industries.[1]

Within the span of what for some could have been a single life-time, the structure of the economy and society in those parts of the British Isles which had been under the governmental control of the Roman Empire greatly changed. The nature of the changes was not necessarily uniform: differences in soil types, ease of access to other regions, possession of natural resources, the weight of inherited traditions and external pressures would all have been factors creating wide diversity. Some contrasts between the fourth and fifth centuries can be exaggerated by modern values; that stone buildings were widely in use in the former may hinder proper appreciation of the quality of timber buildings that can be inferred from post-holes and beam-slots in the latter. It may, however, have been a contrast in standards of which contemporaries were themselves well aware. Timber buildings erected within the walled area of Wroxeter, Shropshire, were solid and substantial, but were they regarded as highly as the partly still-standing stone baths alongside, or were they seen as a feeble attempt to keep up appearances?[2] Those who had enjoyed the trappings of power, wealth and luxury would not willingly have given up all pretense of them or have lost hope that revival might occur. Even those who had not shared in them could still aspire to what they had offered.

Few agricultural workers or artisans need have felt much sense of loss. For producers, as opposed to entrepreneurs and merchants dealing in finished articles, the breakdown of the market and taxation systems, and of the social structure which went with them, probably meant some relaxation of ties that forced dependence. A family might have the opportunity to take up land, perhaps keeping up a craft skill as a limited part-time activity. Those who worked the land could expect to benefit from the weakening of the state's support for land owners in their exploitation of the production capacity of their slaves and tenants, just as state-imposed tax burdens were reduced, removing some of the pressures on land owners in areas where they managed to remain in possession of some vestiges of their former rights. If there were slaves, their legal servility might be relaxed, equating them with other producers whose role was to support their own families and to create some surplus for their lords.[3]

One of the problems in this period is to assess the extent to which a landowning class continued to exist, a problem exacerbated by the difficulty of reconstructing the complete settlement pattern in any area, and of recognizing any hierarchy both within individual settlements and within the overall pattern. In the south and east, excavations of rural domestic sites have not produced evidence that much social differentiation was physically expressed in the fifth and sixth centuries, but this may be because settlement sites are still far from common, and the most fully excavated and published site, West Stow in Suffolk, may not be typical. But there was at any rate no house-complex there which, from the size of its buildings or from the quality of the contents of the rubbish deposits closest to it, can be claimed as that of a "headman" surrounded by his dependents.[4]

West Stow was practicing a mixed agricultural economy. There was evidence for a range of cereals: wheat, barley, rye and oats. Because pollen samples could not be obtained from the site, evidence of the use of peas and beans is all but absent, but animal and bird bones survived well, and are further evidence of mixed farming: cattle, sheep, pigs, a few goats, and domestic fowl and geese.[5] A small number of horses were kept. The bones of some red and roe deer, and of wild birds, were so few that they show plainly that domestic stock was what mattered; anything hunted was an incidental addition to the basic diet. Bones from all parts of the animals were found, so carcasses were not brought to the site already partly jointed, an indication, if any were needed, that they had been locally produced. The quality of the stock is a reflection of agricultural standards; the animals were in general not noticeably smaller or scrawnier than animals from earlier sites. Although changes in the economic pattern destroyed the potteries and took money out of circulation, they did not also cause a collapse of the rural base. Meadowland must have been maintained, with a hay crop that could sustain cattle through the winter, since about half the animals were allowed to live until fully grown. Many cows were five years old or more when slaughtered, an indication that they were kept largely for their milk. The pigs on the other hand were nearly all slaughtered while still young, which is good husbandry: only a few breeding sows were allowed to continue to live and feed, since the only point of a pig is its pork. A site with the bones of old pigs is often one with woodland near it, where the swine could range freely and were difficult to recapture. If there were no great woods close to West Stow, however, it was still possible for its inhabitants to acquire timber plentifully, as they used it liberally in their buildings. They may therefore have had gathering rights in woodland quite distant from their homes.

The sheep at West Stow were being killed at an earlier average age than on most later sites, which implies that their main function was to supply meat and milk rather than wool. This suggests that wool was not being produced in quantity for commercial reasons, as it was to be in the rest of the Middle Ages. Weaving was certainly taking place, as clay loom-weights and bone tools attest the use of vertical looms (see fig. 16.41, this volume)—as indeed they do on most residential sites before about 1100. This was probably basic domestic production, with each household supplying its own needs; certainly the evidence for weaving was not concentrated in particular zones of the site, which would have suggested specialized craft workshop areas. There may have been some production of a surplus, but the sheep bones do not indicate pressure to concentrate upon wool at the expense of other crops.

Other evidence of craft activity that a self-reliant settlement site might produce includes pottery. Over 50,000 sherds were recovered from West Stow, a huge quantity in comparison to most contemporary sites, even though no more than two or three farms may have been operating there at any one time. All the fifth- and sixth-century pottery was made in the locality, since none of the fabrics contained minerals other than what can be found within a ten-mile radius. None was made on a wheel, none was glazed, and all could have been fired in bonfires which would usually leave no trace in the ground. No structural evidence of pot-making can therefore be expected. There was, however, a "reserve" of raw clay found on the site, although this could have been intended for use in wall-building. There were also, near the clay, five antler tools cut so that their ends could be used as stamps, possibly on leather, but more probably on pots. The sheer quantity of pottery found at West Stow, and the care that went into the burnishing and other decoration of at least some of it, suggest a high demand, and perhaps therefore production by people for whom it was a special activity, albeit part-time or seasonal, rather than production by each household just for its own immediate needs. Presumably therefore the pot-makers were turning out a surplus which they could exchange with their neighbors, perhaps in other settlements.

The direct evidence of other crafts is no less scanty. Fragments of worked bone and antler can be assumed to be the waste discarded during the production of some of the tools, such as the five antler dies, and combs. Again, these could all have been produced on the site, but both the quantities and the decoration suggest that those making them had particular skills. Similarly, iron could have been smelted, in small bowl hearths difficult to locate archaeologically, as superficial ore deposits probably existed locally; but only someone with a blacksmith's skills could have produced knives, reaping-hooks and other tools and weapons, and a little slag indicates that at least some smithing did take place. Some raw materials, such as glass, could have been scavenged from earlier, abandoned sites, but the iron objects are too numerous all to have been made from such scrap, nor were any distinctively pre-fifth-century iron objects found awaiting recycling at West Stow, whereas earlier glass rings, and copper-alloy coins, brooches, spoons and other miscellanea were quite common. The glass beads found there may well have been made by melting down such detritus, as could the copper-alloy and silver objects, although no crucibles or moulds were found. Analyses at other sites are showing that considerable care went into the selection of metal for the alloys used in particular objects, although scrap was certainly utilized.[6] Amber, used like glass for making beads, could have been collected on occasional forays to the coast, just as shed antlers could have been found in the woods. The West Stow dwellers could therefore have been very self-reliant in producing objects for their everyday needs, just as they were in food; but the range of materials in use, and the variety of skills needed to produce the objects made from them, suggests a more complex system than one in which each household consumed only what it produced, and indicates a greater range of expertise than the known size of West Stow seems likely to have been able to accommodate.

Some of what was found at West Stow cannot have come from the immediate area. Fragments of lava quern-stone could only have come from the Rhineland. Four fragments of glass claw-beakers datable to the sixth century would almost certainly have been made either in Kent or in the Rhineland. West Stow must, therefore, have been involved in some exchange transactions, many of which, such as the need to acquire salt to preserve foodstuffs, would not have left any archaeological trace. Such exchanges may have been fairly infrequent, perhaps little more than annual. Nevertheless, despite the absence of evidence that the site's economy was geared to producing an exportable wool surplus, there was an ability to acquire objects that were status-supporting as well as life-supporting. Even the apparently prosaic Rhenish quern-stones should perhaps be thought of in status terms, for it would have been possible to use local "pudding stones" for grinding, and a few examples were indeed found. Lava may have been more efficient, but it was also more eye-catching.

The range of objects recovered from the West Stow settlement can be compared to that from a cemetery half a mile away. Certain types of object were found at both sites, but whereas some, such as beads, are directly comparable, others, such as brooches, seem far grander at the cemetery and were presumably specially selected for burial. Because it is so elaborate, the ornament on many of the brooches can be likened to that on brooches from a myriad of other sites, in England and abroad. They probably arrived in a variety of ways—such as with spouses from other communities, as spoils of war, or in exchange for other goods or services. Some may have been made on the spot by an itinerant bronzesmith, who did not stay long enough to have to replace his moulds, leaving his old ones or his broken crucibles behind him. Some were probably new when buried, others heirlooms. Although they are not paralleled at the settlement, they are not really discordant with what was found there in terms of wealth, allowing for the inevitable discrepancy between accidental loss and deliberate deposit. The only silver pin, for example, was from the settlement, where there were also a silver-gilt buckle fragment and a silver pendant; in terms of precious metal, the settlement site holds its own against the cemetery.

Nowhere near to West Stow has been recognized as a local market center where such goods were regularly available; only a mile away is a site at Icklingham which was large enough to have functioned as a small town in the fourth century, and where coins show use into the early fifth, but no later material such as pottery is recorded from there, nor was West Stow acquiring goods of types recognizable as developing out of the traditions of the fourth century, which would have been the case if there had been trade between two co-existing communities. Instead, the reused scraps at West Stow are of all centuries from the first onwards, which suggests that they were collected randomly from abandoned places. The local fifth-century economy must have functioned without the use of established market centers such as Icklingham, nor is there evidence that new ones were created; instead, exchanges in basic materials must have been effected by visits to or from producers, or during occasional assemblies held for religious, administrative or social reasons. Family and personal relationships may have been the modes by which many goods went from one person to another, and barter must have played an important part where no such interdependence existed. But the Rhenish quernstones and the glass claw-beakers had to come from too far away for a system relying on face-to-face negotiations between producer and user, and promises of future requital. Any merchant bringing such things— and their provenances suggest that wine may have been coming in as well—would not have been satisfied with three dozen eggs and a day's hay-making next summer. Similarly, the objects could not have been sent directly as presents to a family member or to someone whose friendship or service was sought, for personal alliances can only operate over such a long distance amongst the rich and powerful, not at the social level of West Stow farmers. It may be significant that the claw-beakers all date from the later part of the sixth century—the quern-stones cannot be so precisely dated—by which time it may be that a system of exchange was developing in the area between an elite group of merchants, supplementing an existing, local system based on personal knowledge and contact. Some imported and other goods may then have been passed on by the elite to their dependents.

Icklingham has not been excavated, so the history of its abandonment is not fully known. It may have been a gradual process, as it was in a comparable small town at Heybridge, Essex, in which buildings have been found with pottery of various fifth-century types; initially some of this was coming from Oxfordshire and from the Nene valley some eighty miles away, but those supplies had dried up by the middle of the fifth century and only locally-made wares were available. Occupation in Heybridge did not last until the end of the century, although the site was on the coast and potentially a port. There are very few fourth-century towns of this scale which are likely to have had a very different history, even if they survived at all into the fifth century; the reemergence of some of them as sites of markets later in the Middle Ages could simply be because they were well-placed on communication lines, or it might possibly be because in a few cases they continued as occasional meeting-places, even if not as occupation sites. Exodus from them in the fifth century was inevitable if they were not to be market or production centers—building debris would have hindered their use even for agricultural purposes.[7]

A rather different picture is emerging from excavations within the walled towns. The extent to which these had operated as market places and artisan centers in the fourth century, as well as administrative, religious, defensive and leisure foci, is not well understood. Wroxeter is not the only one with standing buildings surviving into the fifth century, and in York and Gloucester collapsed tiles sealing later levels show that some structures at least remained partly roofed for several generations.[8] This is not proof of continuous use, however, any more than is topographical evidence that gates or certain street lines were kept open or were re-opened. In many such towns, thick deposits of soil have been found, the compositions of which suggest that they did not accumulate slowly from rotting timbers and other inert debris, and were not washed in as flood silts, but occasionally result from rubbish dumping sometimes from deliberate attempts to level up uneven ground. In either case, they indicate a lot of abandoned building space, but paradoxically also a considerable human involvement in their accumulation, although many seem insufficiently humic to have been cultivated.[9]

One possibility is that some at least of the walled towns were being used into the fifth century as centers for the collection of agricultural products. Grain driers in Exeter, Devon, and in Dorchester, Dorset, could indicate large-scale processing, just as a building in Verulamium, Hertfordshire, interpreted as a barn, may indicate a need for storage of large quantities of agricultural supplies. A function of this sort for the towns could have lasted only for so long as there was an authority which could enforce the collection of the produce, and so it is symptomatic of the changing nature of that authority that there is no sign of storage and processing after the end of the fifth century, and in most towns much earlier. It is as though a system initiated during a period of strong government operating a complex structure of control and distribution was temporarily sustained by a few opportunists who were able to usurp authority locally despite the disintegration of centralized state power.[10] Their inability to redistribute large volumes of produce into a wide market might cause them only to seek to maintain that part of the system which brought them what they required for their own consumption. For this, direct supply from the producers to the residences of the powerful was more effective than collection in and redistribution from some formerly urban center.

The loss of central authority inevitably affected different areas in different ways, as a unified state broke down into discordant parts. In Suffolk's Lark Valley, for instance, there is no known site which would seem to be "superior" in status to West Stow. If Caistor-by-Norwich had been the center of the local area in the fourth century, its decline in the fifth seems to have left a vacuum, or it may be that it is difficult to locate the aristocratic site or sites that succeeded it. At Gloucester, by contrast, there are fifth-century timber buildings inside the walls, and the town may have remained as a focal point in the area. Authority, however, probably resided just outside in the Roman fort at Kingsholm, where the burial of a man within an already existing small stone structure, and the objects buried with him, mark him out as someone of distinction who died early in the fifth century. Although there is nothing else of that date from Kingsholm, it was later to be the site of the royal palace, of which substantial timber buildings identified in excavations may have formed part.[11]

The precise status of the Kingsholm man is not indicated by the objects buried with him, but it may be significant that nothing about the grave suggests an intention to denote that he had been a warrior. He had a small iron knife, but it is not a weapon distinctively for use in battle, as a sword would have been. The man appears to have been wearing shoes with silver strap-ends, rather than boots, and the rest of his surviving costume fittings are not associated with specifically military dress. It was obviously not considered important to associate him in death with a warrior's life. His accoutrements and his place of burial suggest however that he was at least an aristocrat, if not an autocrat.

A site which shows how an aristocrat's life-style might have been maintained in the fifth and sixth centuries is in the far north at Yeavering, Northumberland, an inland promontory—though not hill-top—site. Timber buildings, some very large and using very solid posts and planks, were replaced at various times in a period of occupation which ended during the seventh century (fig. 3.1).[12] The site's initial use was in the Bronze Age as a cemetery, and recognition of this religious use in the past may have been a reason for reoccupation, if association with such antiquities was considered to give some claim to ancestral links, and rights of inheritance to land and authority. The reuse probably started in the fifth century as no mass-produced pottery or other fourth-century artifacts were found. The very few objects that were recovered included an elaborate bronze-bound wooden staff in a grave aligned on the largest building; its purpose is unknown, but its importance must have been clear to those who deposited it in such a prominently-placed grave.[13]

Ceremonial and ritual at Yeavering are also suggested by a timber structure, the fan-like ground-plan of which has generally been accepted as the remains of wooden staging, for use during assemblies. These occasions were presumably enlivened by feasts and sacrifices, which the ox skulls overflowing from a pit alongside one building seem to attest. Before their slaughter, the animals were probably kept in a great enclosure on one side of the site. Sheep were also taken to Yeavering, and at least one building may have been used specifically for weaving since loom-weights were found in it.

Yeavering suggests a site to which large numbers of animals came, presumably brought as tribute owed from the surrounding area to its chieftain. The feasts that were held after their slaughter would have confirmed this leader's status as one whose authority brought wealth which could be conspicuously, even recklessly, consumed; the high proportion of young calf bones suggest a profligate disregard for the need to maintain breeding herds. The meeting-place was where decisions were announced and agreed; the biggest of the buildings is interpreted as a hall where the feasts took place and oaths were sworn. These occasions were used to reinforce social ties that bound people together, as lord and

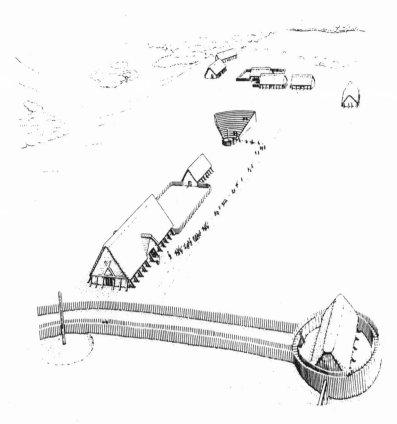

Fig. 3.1. Reconstruction drawing by S. James of one of the phases of the use of Yeavering, Northumberland. In the foreground is part of the "great enclosure" and one side of its entrance, a fenced circle enclosing a building. If animals were brought here as tribute to the palace's owner, it is difficult to see how they could have been prevented from trampling the barrow mound (emphasized here by a totem-like post). The great hall, joined by an open enclosure to a small annex building, would have been the focus of feasts and entertainment. Beyond, the reconstruction of the post-holes and slots as staging suggests a setting for decision-making by the leader and his people. One of the buildings in the background may have been used as a temple, as human burials and deposits of ox bones and skulls were found associated with it.

dependent. Nor is Yeavering unique, since there is a site not far from it at Sprouston which seems to have most of the same features, except for the assembly-place, and at Thirlings, also in Northumberland, a complex of rectangular buildings, one some twelve meters long, has been investi-gated.[14] Dating is not precise at any of these, but that the Yeavering staging was enlarged from its original size could be an indication that a larger group of people was becoming involved in the affairs conducted there as time passed, as though the authority of the ruler was becoming extended over a wider area.

Nowhere that has been excavated in the south of England has shown evidence comparable to Yeavering's. In the south-west, and possibly further east in a few cases, hill-top sites may have been used by the aristocracy, but it is difficult to establish the precise functions of those places where some evidence of activity has been found. Glastonbury Tor, Somerset, was initially interpreted as a chieftain's residence, on the basis that animal bones suggested food inappropriate to the religious life, but that is now seen as too exclusive an interpretation.[15] Activities there included metal-working; crucibles were found, and copper-alloy residues and a fine little head. Dating depends upon Mediterranean and Gaulish pottery imported into the south-west in the fifth, sixth and seventh centuries, bowls and dishes being recognizable as having been made in the East Mediterranean and North Africa between ca. 450 and 550.[16] Most such sherds are from amphorae, which were probably reaching the south-west as wine containers, so their presence at Glastonbury Tor suggests drinking of an exotic rarity at the feasts of those who managed to obtain it. But the bones found there do not suggest such high-quality consumption; most of the beef and mutton came from elderly animals, not young stock which would have provided the most succulent joints, as at Yeavering.

The meat consumed on Glastonbury Tor was nearly all brought there already butchered and prepared, which is hardly surprising on such a small site where there would have been no room to do the slaughtering. At Yeavering, the great enclosure and the ox skulls suggest that animals were brought on the hoof; only one quern-stone was found, however, which could indicate that most of the grain arrived already ground into flour. A good standard of agriculture would have been necessary to supply Yeavering and the other residences used by a chief and his entourage as they progressed round their territory. Various pollen studies from the north of England show no decrease in meadowland and cereal plants in the fifth century, though some show regeneration of scrub and bog during the later sixth; but these analyses have to be made on sites which, being prone to wetness, have low agricultural potential and are inevitably therefore marginal and not necessarily representative of what was happening everywhere. It is even possible that poorer land was being farmed in preference to better, because the latter tended to be in less remote areas and was therefore more vulnerable in troubled times to slave raiders and other disrupting agents.[17] Nevertheless the evidence from the north seems to support that from West Stow in the east, of reasonable standards being kept up.

The extent to which actual fields and field systems were maintained, abandoned, or allowed to revert from arable to grazing land is not easy to evaluate. On the one hand, there are areas like the high chalk downs in Hampshire, where field boundaries of the fourth century or earlier have been found in what is now thick woodland, and so may never have been used again. In north Nottinghamshire, field boundaries can be seen to have grown over, and to have had no later use. The opposite has happened elsewhere, however; from Wharram Percy, in the Yorkshire wolds, and other sites has come evidence of ditches which were filled up during the third and fourth centuries, but which remained as boundary lines into the Middle Ages and are identifiable as furlong boundaries in strip-field systems. Such cases may only mean that the ditch created a conveniently visible line for later farmers to follow—or one which still affected drainage so that it could not be ignored—and there may have been an intervening period of disuse.[18] There is also Nature to consider; flooding and raised sea-levels certainly affected parts of northern Europe, such as the Low Countries, and some low-lying land was probably lost in England as well, creating the Isles of Scilly, for instance, though some of the fens and marshes may have resulted as much from failure to maintain drainage systems. Certainly flood deposits recorded in some towns are more plausibly attributed to the collapse of sewers than to increased rainfall or rising sea-levels.

It is proving very difficult to find field systems that can be directly associated with the rural settlements that have been located. Around West Stow, for instance, there are no surviving field boundaries or scatters of pottery resulting from manure spreading to indicate whether an infield/outfield system was operated, with arable fields adjacent to the site and rough grazing further away, or with all the land available to the settlement being ploughed at least periodically. It is now established that strip-fields with their ridge and furrow, characteristic of many areas later in the Middle Ages, were not yet introduced, as no such strips and furlongs underlie sites that came into use in the seventh century as they do under some sites of the eleventh, nor can they be seen to radiate out from any fifth- or sixth-century settlements later abandoned. It can also be assumed, from the locations of most of these last, that light soils such as river-gravel terraces, sands and chalks were in use: place-names attributed to the fifth, sixth and seventh centuries show a strong sense of terrain and topography. That leaves unresolved the problem of whether heavier soils such as clays were still ploughed, perhaps from existing sites, or were allowed to revert to rough grazing or scrub or woodland. The Lark Valley again provides an example of the problem: if people were still living in the fifth century at sites where pottery scatters suggest that they had been in the fourth, they have left no trace of themselves, which is not impossible if they did not adopt new burial customs, were no longer acquiring the types of objects available to them before, and eschewed the use of crude, hand-made pottery in favor of wood and leather. Such an aceramic situation can arise: in Gloucester, various sites had been excavated and little pottery found, yet a previously unknown ware was discovered in some quantity in a recent excavation close to the wall of the Roman town. In the Lark Valley, re-emergence of enameling on metalwork in the sixth century could be evidence for the survival of knowledge of that craft among people for whom its use was traditional, unlike those buried in the cemetery near West Stow.[19] Nevertheless, abandonment of many settlement sites in favor of those on lighter soils does seem the most likely pattern in most areas, and would have been facilitated by any weakening of the legal restrictions that tied people to their homesteads. Decline in population, through plague, migration, or falling birth-rates—often a demographic response to adversity—may have been another factor, but one extremely difficult to measure in a period of rapidly fluctuating change. There seem to have been fewer large cemeteries in the sixth century than the fifth, but there are also more smaller ones, so that the change may reflect changes in ideas about appropriate burial-places, not in population totals.

Some rural sites used in the fourth century were also used in the fifth. Although the stone buildings at Barton Court Farm, Oxfordshire, were demolished, activity in and around them continued into the sixth century, with timber buildings and burials, the latter not necessarily of people who had lived on the site, since the objects with them suggest a mid sixth-century context, by which time the timber buildings may have been abandoned (fig. 3.2).[20] Connections between the fourth and fifth centuries are hard to evaluate, but nearly all the latter's buildings were outside the former's enclosure, and the pottery and other objects used were very different in kind. The culture was different, even if the land area utilized may have been the same. Other sites have reported a comparable pattern, such as Orton Hall Farm in Cambridgeshire. At Rivenhall, Essex, a stone complex had a timber structure built over it, and there were then burials before the area was used for a Christian church and cemetery. Although the dating is uncertain, this could indicate an elite site remaining in use through from the fourth century so that its owners

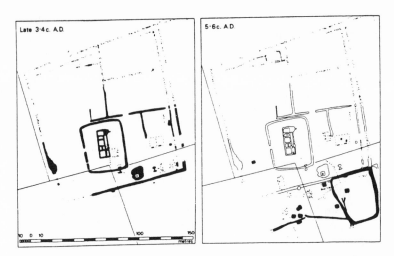

Fig. 3.2. Romano-British and later phases at Barton Court Farm, Oxfordshire, excavated by D. Miles. An eight-roomed stone house was demolished after ca. 370, other buildings surviving a little longer. Sunken-featured structures, fence-lines and burials followed, but not in arrangements which suggest that they had any direct connection with the previous use of the site. The new enclosure emphasizes the break: it is almost as though for most purposes the earlier lay-out's effect was a negative one, and its structures were avoided except for burials—which could be later than the sunken-featured buildings.

eventually became the owners and builders of the church, a sequence that could be more common than has been realized.[21] Field patterns in Essex also suggest the continuing importance of existing boundaries.[22]

Cultural differences seem to be even more clearly revealed in studies of burial practices. In Essex, there are considerably fewer cemeteries in which people were buried with grave goods than there are in other eastern counties. Yet even in areas in which objects are found in quantity, there is little uniformity. An analysis of two cemeteries some twelve miles apart has shown the subtlety of variation that can occur. The artifacts in the graves at the two sites were not significantly different in type, but there were differences in the ways in which they were deposited. In Holywell Row, near Mildenhall, Cambridgeshire, knives were found in most of the graves of both males and females, as though they were primarily a symbol of adulthood, whereas in Westgarth Gardens, near Bury St. Edmunds, Suffolk, knives were found much more frequently in men's than women's graves, as though there they usually signified specifically male adulthood. There were also differences in the way that the cemeteries were arranged—children were kept more separate from adults at Westgarth Gardens, but male and female adults were more intermingled.[23] Differences like these are at least as important as differences between the objects, particularly since they held good for several generations, which suggests surprisingly stable communities retaining variations in their burial customs despite the intermingling with neighbors through marriage and other social alliances that must surely have taken place. In times of stress, even quite small groups of people may be tenacious of their customs, to emphasize their sense of community.[24] With localized differences like these, it becomes difficult to put too much weight upon grave goods as an indication of wealth. A cemetery in which there are many elaborate brooches may be the burial-place of people richer than those in a cemetery with few such exotica: or it may just be that one group thought it appropriate to festoon their dead, while another did not.

In many parts of the south and east, cremation as well as inhumation was practiced. Only a mile from West Stow and its adjacent cemetery, though separated from it by the River Lark, is a totally contrasting cemetery which contained, so far as is known, nothing but cremations. Was Lackford for people of particular distinction, or particular infamy, or race, or family? At another predominantly cremation cemetery, Spong Hill, Norfolk, excavations are making it possible to observe variations in the contents, fabrics, sizes, shapes and locations of burial urns. From this it may be possible to suggest that particular kin-groups can be identified, and to reveal attitudes to age and gender. Children were often distinguished from adults by placing them in smaller pots, as though to acknowledge that they had not attained full membership of the community; women usually have more accompanying objects than men, as they do in contemporary inhumations; taller pots with what seem to be "higher status" objects such as playing-pieces may notify the resting place of those higher in the social hierarchy.[25]

Identification of the sex of cremated bones is usually very difficult, but even bone from inhumation does not always survive in good enough condition to be fully analyzed. At Sewerby, East Yorkshire, the sex of several adults could not be recognized, and some uncertainty is created amongst the rest by two identifications of bones as being those of males although they were accompanied by objects normally associated with females, which may indicate aberrant behavior if it does not indicate the limitations of sexing criteria.[26] No one seems to have been buried in this small assemblage who was aged less than seven or over forty-five; presumably the former were disposed of elsewhere—but did the community have no venerable elders, or were they also given special burial treatment?[27] One man had had a bad injury or wound which had damaged his forehead, but it had partly healed, and other bones did not have the sort of breaks and cuts that a violent society, or one regularly engaged in warfare, might be expected to show. Similarly at Portway, near Andover, Hampshire, only a single wound could be recognized.[28] At that site, infants as well as youths and adults were buried, though baby bones had mostly rotted away if they were ever present. Childhood and youth were vulnerable periods, with a one-in-three chance of dying before the age of fifteen; the three years from fifteen to eighteen were relatively safe; the death-rate then rose steadily to the end of about the fortieth year, reached by fewer than a quarter of the population. A small number of people older than forty-five were buried at Portway, however, which shows that some reached a greater age than Sewerby would have suggested possible.

The approximate age-at-death of a reasonably well-preserved skeleton is not difficult to estimate; nor is the average height. Some graves have produced "giants" over 6ft. 6ins., but Portway produced no one over 5ft. 11ins. and Sewerby's tallest was only 5ft. 8ins; 5ft. 1in. was the smallest recorded there even for a female, however. The heights measured in these cemeteries are of well-grown people, which is some indication that adequate food supplies were available for the whole population. There are occasional signs of deficiency-related problems in the bones, such as *cribra orbitalia* which can result from insufficient iron in the food, but this was recognized in only two of the Portway skeletons. Many more such investigations are needed before the population's true profile can be established, but there is at present no evidence that some people were consistently deprived of access to a sufficient share of the food resources, or were particularly protected from the strains of manual labor. This is not quite in keeping with what might have been expected from the quantities of objects in cemeteries where grave goods occur; the number of objects varies from grave to grave, with many having nothing at all in them. This could be taken to suggest a wide range of status variation, even within small communities, but it may actually reflect differences in ideas about goods-deposition during the time that a cemetery was in use; there seems to be an increase in quantities generally in the sixth century.

Grave goods are usually taken to indicate that the people responsible for providing them believed in some sort of after-life, or perhaps a world of gods and spirits running concurrently with the human world. Since tools are infrequent, goods do not seem to have been meant for "use" but may have been symbols—weapons to identify the status, or brooches the family, of their possessor. Occasionally, it is possible to go further; some of the designs are recognizable as being the same as symbols associated with particular gods whose names and deeds are recorded in north European sagas written down in later centuries, and the use of other motifs on both pots and brooches may signify that they are family emblems. In the west, both a hill-top site at Cadbury-Congresbury, Somerset,[29] and Wroxeter have had finds that may indicate a skull or head cult, which could have Celtic antecedents. Is the Glastonbury Tor copper-alloy head another example? Several western temples or shrines have produced evidence that a site was still used in at least some way after the fourth century; near that at Brean Down, Somerset, burial seems to have continued into the seventh century, and at Uley, Gloucestershire, there is evidence of a shrine completely remodeled at the end of the fourth century that remained active for a long time thereafter, possibly converted to Christian usage.[30] There is no archaeological, as opposed to documentary, evidence that Christianity, which had been widely though not exclusively practiced in the fourth century, was still practiced anywhere in the fifth, until the appearance of memorial stones. The earliest of these, such as one from Wroxeter of the late fifth to mid sixth century, may not be Christian, as they record simply the names of fathers and sons; distinctively Christian formulae such as *"Hic iacet"* do not occur until the sixth century. Their distribution in England is then confined to Cornwall and Devon, with outliers in the extreme south-west of Somerset and at Wareham, Dorset.[31]

Also exclusive in its distribution is the imported Mediterranean and south Gaulish pottery, found at various sites in Cornwall, Devon and Somerset, but nowhere further east. Some of the "A" ware bowls of ca. 450 to 550 have incised crosses, and so were at first thought to have been for use in the Christian Mass with the wine that would also have been needed at such services, but the quantity of this imported pottery that has now been found at a variety of sites indicates that it did not have exclusively religious use. The difficulty of establishing the real nature of those sites has already been referred to in relation to Glastonbury Tor, and is well illustrated by Tintagel, Cornwall, where excavations on the peninsula in the 1930s produced evidence then interpreted as identifying a Celtic monastery. More recent work has recognized that that part of Tintagel has no burials or other proof of Christian use. The quantity of imported pottery could be because there was a landing place, and the goods arriving there may not have been consumed at Tintagel. There are, however, timber structures and hearths which show that there was occupation, and mounds in the graveyard of the present church on the mainland suggest the possibility of barrow-burials of people of high status. It therefore seems that Tintagel was a residential complex, perhaps visited seasonally by a wealthy element who controlled the resources of the local territory.[32]

Tintagel is not apparently a very good harbor, though usable; an example of a site which may have been more inviting as a coastal trading-station is at Bantham, South Devon, where middens, rubbish pits, hearths and traces of structures have been found. A variety of objects, including a number of knives and other iron and bone tools, suggests crafts being practiced, and animal as well as fish bones were found in some quantity, indicating that this was not simply a site specializing in the exploitation of marine resources for food. There were also imported pottery sherds, mostly "B" wares, particularly handles of amphorae, suggesting breakages. Bantham may well have been a landing place, therefore, perhaps a "beach market" only used seasonally, as it is too exposed to make a comfortable winter residence.[33] Goods landed there were probably passed on to consumers elsewhere. That Devon and Cornwall possessed an aristocracy able to command such things is suggested by the memorial stones with their formulae stressing the male line of family descent, which presumably enhanced claims to inherited rights and property. They were in a good position to control the peninsula's trade, particularly perhaps the production and export of its valuable metals, notably tin; ingots at Praa Sands, Cornwall, where radiocarbon dates centering on the seventh century have been obtained, may indicate the whereabouts of another landing place like that at Bantham. Gwithian, Cornwall, may be another, but it also served as an agricultural site, since there are traces of scratch-ploughing associated with it. Its small, drystone-footed huts do not suggest high-status use, but there is a quantity of imported pottery from it. If that was not being passed on up the line to a superior site, it suggests a remarkably high standard of living for ordinary farmers.[34]

Pottery found at some south-western sites indicates where the local aristocrats were probably living. In Cornwall there are enclosures called "rounds" such as Trethurgy, where much "A" ware has been found. These "rounds" were not necessarily new sites in the fifth century, and suggest less disruption to settlement patterns than occurred further east. Their surrounding banks would have distinguished them and thus their owners, from their neighbors. Such sites have not been identified in any other county, even Devon; the best candidate there for a place of comparable status is High Peak, on the coast near Sidmouth, where "B" ware has been found, but in circumstances that do not explain its context. The site is a prehistoric hill-fort, with a stone wall revetting the banks, but it is unlikely that this was contemporary with the pottery. In Somerset, the Iron-Age hill-fort at South Cadbury was certainly given a stone and timber wall on its existing top rampart, and there is evidence for timber gates and wall-walks. "B" wares were among the finds from it.[35]

The cultural differences between the four most south-westerly of England's later counties are worth stressing because they illustrate how divergent were different areas: only Cornwall has "rounds"; it also has stone-lined cist graves, unknown in Devon, whereas both Dorset, at a cemetery at Ulwell, and Somerset at Cannington, have them.[36] Devon and Cornwall have memorial stones, otherwise found only in the extreme south-west of Somerset, and in Dorset only at Wareham, where there is a group of five, none necessarily earlier than the later seventh century. At Poundbury, outside Dorchester, is a cemetery which probably had some use after the fourth century. There is no trace at Maiden Castle or at any of Dorset's other hill-forts of the sort of reuse found at South Cadbury in Somerset. All that is firmly datable to the sixth century is a small cemetery excavated at Hardown Hill, near Bridport, where the objects are like those found in counties to the east.[37]

No "A" or other such imported wares have yet been found in Dorset, or anywhere east of Somerset. Their distribution is clearly owed to contacts that some, but not all, parts of the south-west had with the Mediterranean and, into the seventh century, southern Gaul. Further east, different overseas contacts can be demonstrated; there are sufficient objects that must have originated in the areas on the Continent controlled by the Franks for it to be possible to argue that they signify not only importing of prestigious material, but actual immigration of Frankish people.[38] So similar to cremation urns in the area of north Germany around the rivers Elbe and Weser are some in certain cemeteries in Norfolk that it seems impossible that they should not have been made by potters from that area who had settled in East Anglia.[39] There are bracteates, brooches and other objects which suggest strong contacts between Kent and modern Denmark. Further north in Humberside and East Anglia, wrist-clasps indicate contact with Norway. But some of the wrist-clasps were buried in England in positions which suggest that they were not all worn on the ends of sleeves, and almost all were worn by women, whereas in Norway a significant proportion were also worn by men.[40] Slight though these differences may be, they underline the difficulty in knowing how far objects can be used to measure direct migrations of people, rather than links created through trade, through formation of family and political alliances, or through exchanges created by the unknown demands of some religious cult. Similarly, to trace the internal distribution of a particular type of brooch or pot may be to trace the settlement progress of immigrants who used it, but is as likely to be to identify a particular local custom not directly associated with an ethnic group, and the appearance of the object may owe more to burial rites and any changes to them than to an actual spread of the object's use.

Many objects in use in the fifth century, such as the distinctive quoit-brooches, cannot be associated with any particular continental area, because they are heavily influenced by styles of costume and decoration that originated in the fourth century in the Roman provinces.[41] Contacts between those who lived on the two sides of the formal frontier led to a fusion of "classical" Imperial and "barbarian" Germanic tastes. Consequently objects cannot usually be used to indicate the precise origins of those who made or owned them. Some brooches, such as simple discs with ring-and-dot ornament, are common to a number of areas in England, whereas some, like square-headed brooches, can be grouped into sub-divisions which are geographically confined. These may not indicate significant cultural divisions, however, so much as the area in which a particular family dominated, or even where a single craftsman's output circulated. They do not even make clear-cut frontiers between "British" of native descent and "English" immigrants; penannular brooches were certainly made by the former, but are frequently found deposited as grave goods in the manner assumed to be characteristic of the latter.[42] Such things suggest a great deal of interaction between peoples of different origins, and much acceptance of others' fashions and modes of behavior. It is likely that it was not just superficialities that were accepted; many burials in the cemeteries of eastern England may be predominantly indigenous people who had accepted new customs, willingly or not. Similarly there may well be English stock in at least the latest phases of unfurnished cemeteries like Cannington, which had come into use long before migration is likely to have reached so far west. In some areas, distinctions may have been carefully retained if co-existence was uneasy. The upper Thames Valley has many cemeteries with fifth- and sixth-century grave goods, yet outside Dorchester and at Beacon Hill, Lewknor, Oxfordshire, are large graveyards with virtually no objects but fifth- and sixth-century radiocarbon dates show that they were in contemporaneous use.[43]

It is not only objects used and funerary rites practiced which are studied to try to distinguish between peoples of different origins. As an increasing number of buildings is revealed, they too can be considered. The most distinctive fifth-century and later structure has a sunken area, sometimes apparently floored over, as can be demonstrated in one or two of the seventy-odd examples at West Stow, but more usually using the lowered ground surface as the floor. Because they would have been cool and moist inside, they are thought especially suitable for craft activities such as spinning and weaving, as thread and yarn must not become dry and brittle. They have been found as far apart as Yorkshire and Hampshire; there are even a couple as far west as Poundbury at a late, probably seventh-century stage in that site's use, after it had ceased to be a cemetery.[44] There are also examples on the Continent, in the Low Countries and Germany. Many larger, rectangular timber buildings are now known. Their origin is uncertain, for whereas their plan is like that of Roman buildings, such details of their construction as can be postulated from the traces of timbers in the ground suggest that they were not built in the Roman manner, but had external buttresses, ridge-beams and pairs of opposed doors. They suggest a fusion of "British" and "Germanic" modes, widely spread; building styles seem less geographically confined than many artifacts.[45] It is also worth noting the absence of any features in the buildings at Yeavering to mark any point at which ownership passed from one cultural group to another. Either fusion there was complete, or the place was owned by "Germanic" people from the start, even though it is an area well to the north of those in which fifth- and sixth-century "Germanic" cemeteries are found.

Certain types of buckle and strap-end of the later fourth and the first half of the fifth centuries are thought originally to have been issued by the Roman authorities to barbarian warriors brought over for defense against pirates, and later by those "British" who were trying to maintain Romanized authority. One British writer, Gildas, knew the word *foederati* that had been applied in the Roman Empire to barbarian troops used on the frontiers in the hope that they would defend it against other barbarians.[46] The claim that examples found in England in fifth-century contexts must have been associated with "mercenary" soldiers assumes a continuity of practice that runs counter to the general evidence of the speed of fifth-century change; a buckle type originally issued as military wear might quickly become an item of dress not specific to a soldier. Furthermore, as organization broke down, specialization of that sort would have disappeared, as defense became a preoccupation of all holders of land. It is also sobering that the best-known graves in which early "Germanic" objects were found, outside Dorchester, Oxfordshire, did not certainly have weapons with what is thought to have been the one male burial; but iron objects were reportedly thrown away, so he may have had at least a knife or spear.[47] Those graves are the only ones of their kind known, so they do not establish a pattern.

Because so much of the *Anglo-Saxon Chronicle* and other sources are written in terms of warfare, it has usually been assumed that confrontation between different groups of people, particularly natives and immigrants, was the norm. Archaeological material is used to try to prove or to disprove the conquest of a particular area by a particular group at a particular time (e.g. pl. 3.1). But most of the dates in the documents are no less problematical than those that can be attributed to the archaeological record, and it is not until the end of the sixth century that a clear narrative

Pl. 3.1 Old Sarum, Wiltshire. The Iron-Age ramparts might have sheltered an army when "Cynric fought against the Britons at the place which is called Salisbury" in 552—but even if the *Anglo-Saxon Chronicle* is correct about site and date, the record need not mean more than that Sarum was a landmark close to where the battle took place. Cemetery evidence suggests that people using English burial customs were already established in the area: a victory for Cynric may have been a stepping-stone in the progress of his dynasty, but not in that of the Saxon settlement. In the early eleventh century, Sarum became a place defended against Viking raiders, but the castle ruins and the outline of the cathedral attest its Norman use. As a town, Sarum was replaced by Salisbury in the early thirteenth century: its numerous inhabitants, intra- and extra-mural, have left no visible trace, a reminder of the difficulty of recognizing many sites even from the air (photo, Ashmolean Museum, Oxford).

framework begins to emerge. As the end of the formal administration of *Britannia* by the Roman Empire removed from the province the stability of an imperial system based on taxation and a standing army, so the economic system of big estates, perhaps associated with "plantations" of slaves, and the wide distribution of bulk products and of money could not be maintained. The eastern side of the island was both closer to the Continent and had been more Romanized than the west; consequently its social and economic structures were more complex and more liable to collapse, and it was more open to migrant peoples. Yet even Essex and Kent, on the two sides of the Thames, seem to have varied in their patterns of settlement. Some areas retained more ability to resist change than others, but the unity of *Britannia* broke down into parcels of separate elements, in some of which more signs of elites and power structures are recognizable than in others. Some of these separate elements may be thought of as no more than bands of kin-groups in loose alliance with or actively hostile towards their neighbors; others may be classified as tribal confederacies, though probably ethnically mixed; and others, in the north and west at least, may have evidence of chieftains. What the lack of uniformity shows certainly to have been lacking in this plethora of human conditions was the overriding authority of a centralized state.

NOTES

[1] P. J. Casey, ed., *The End of Roman Britain,* B.A.R. Brit. ser. 71 (Oxford, 1979) still seems to contain the best discussions—see especially the essays by J. P. C. Kent, J. P. Gillam and M. Fulford.

[2] P. A. Barker, "The Latest Occupation of the Site of the Baths Basilica at Wroxeter," ibid., 175–81.

[3] Issues like these are considered by C. J. Arnold, *Roman Britain to Saxon England* (London & Sydney, 1984). See also C. Wickham, "The Other Transition: From the Ancient World to Feudalism," *Past and Present* 103 (May 1984), 3–36.

[4] S. West, *West Stow. The Anglo-Saxon Village,* East Anglian Archaeol. Rep. 24 (Ipswich, 1985), including the specialist reports in it by P. Crabtree, A. Russel, V. I. Evison et al.

[5] In addition to her summary on the bones in ibid., see P. Crabtree, "The Archaeozoology of the Anglo-Saxon Site at West Stow, Suffolk," in K. Biddick, ed., *Archaeological Approaches to Medieval Europe* (Kalamazoo, 1985), 223–35.

[6] L. Mortimer, "Anglo-Saxon Copper Alloys from Lechlade, Gloucestershire," *Oxford J. of Archaeol.* 7.2 (1988), 227–34.

[7] P. J. Drury and N. P. Wickenden, "An Early Saxon Settlement within the Romano-British Small Town at Heybridge, Essex," *M.A.* 25 (1982), 1–40. For

the evidence of towns generally, D. A. Brooks, "A Review of the Evidence for Continuity in British Towns in the 5th and 6th Centuries," *Oxford J. of Archaeol.* 5.1 (March, 1986), 77–102.

[8] York: R. Hall, *The Viking Dig* (London, 1984); *idem*, "The Making of Domesday York," 233–47 in D. Hooke, ed., *Anglo-Saxon Settlements* (Oxford, 1988) Gloucester: T. Darvill, "Excavations on the Site of the Early Norman Castle at Gloucester, 1983–84," *M.A.* 32 (1988), 1–49 and C. Heighway, "Saxon Gloucester," 359–83 in J. Haslam, ed., *Anglo-Saxon Towns in Southern England* (Chichester, 1984).

[9] R. MacPhail, "Soil and Botanical Studies of the 'Dark Earth'," 309–32 in M. Jones and G. Dimbleby, eds., *The Environment of Man: The Iron Age to the Anglo-Saxon Period,* B.A.R. Brit. ser. 87 (Oxford, 1981).

[10] For "opportunism," see C. Thomas, *Celtic Britain* (London, 1988), chapter 3.

[11] H. Hurst, "Excavations at Gloucester: Third Interim Report—Kingsholm 1966–75," *Antiquaries J.* 55.2 (1975), 267–94, especially the specialist section by D. Brown, 290–94.

[12] B. Hope-Taylor, *Yeavering: an Anglo-British Centre of Early Northumbria* (London, 1977).

[13] C. J. Arnold, *An Archaeology of the Early Anglo-Saxon Kingdoms* (London & New York, 1988), chapter 5, discusses this further.

[14] N. Higham, *The Northern Counties to AD 1000* (London, 1986).

[15] P. Rahtz, "Celtic Society in Somerset AD 400–700," *Bul. of the Board of Celtic Studies* 30.1 and 30.2 (Nov., 1982), 176–200.

[16] For dates see Thomas, *Celtic Britain,* 58–60.

[17] Higham, *Northern Counties,* note 14, 243 *seq.,* summarizes recent work and makes the interesting point about slave raids.

[18] Hampshire: P. J. Fasham, "Fieldwork in Micheldever Wood, 1973–80," *Proc. of the Hampshire Field Club and Archaeol. Soc.* 39 (1983), 5–45, at p. 33. Nottinghamshire: T. Unwin, "Townships and Early Fields in North Nottinghamshire," *J. of Historical Geography* 9.4 (1983), 341–46; Wharram Percy: C. C. Taylor and P. J. Fowler, "Roman Fields into Medieval Furlongs," in H. C. Bowen and P. J. Fowler, eds., *Early Land Allotment,* B.A.R. Brit. ser. 48 (Oxford, 1978), 159–62. See also contributions by P. Warner, T. Unwin and T. Williamson in Hooke, ed., *Anglo-Saxon Settlements.*

[19] C. Scull, "Further Evidence from East Anglia for Enamelling on Early Anglo-Saxon Metalworking," *A.S.S.A.H.* 4 (1985), 117–24.

[20] D. Miles, *Archaeology at Barton Court Farm, Abingdon, Oxfordshire,* C.B.A. Research Rep. 50 (London, 1984).

[21] W. J. and K. A. Rodwell, *Rivenhall: Investigations of a Villa, Church and Village 1950–1977,* C.B.A. Research Rep. 55 (London, 1985) and dating caveats

by M. Millett, "The Question of Continuity: Rivenall Reviewed," *Archaeol. J.* 144 (1987), 434–44.

[22] P. Drury and W. Rodwell, "Settlement in the Later Iron Age and Roman Periods," in D. G. Buckley, ed., *Archaeology in Essex to A.D. 1500,* C.B.A. Research Rep. 34 (London, 1980), 59–75; T. Williamson, "Settlement Chronology and Regional Landscapes: The Evidence from the Claylands of East Anglia," in Hooke, ed., *Anglo-Saxon Settlements,* 153–75.

[23] E.-J. Pader, *Symbolism, Social Relations and the Interpretation of Mortuary Remains,* B.A.R. Int. ser. 130 (Oxford, 1982).

[24] J. D. Richards, *The Significance of Form and Decoration of Anglo-Saxon Cremation Urns,* B.A.R. Brit. ser. 166 (Oxford, 1987).

[25] Ibid.

[26] S. M. Hirst, *An Anglo-Saxon Inhumation Cemetery at Sewerby, East Yorkshire,* University of York Archaeol. Publications 4 (York, 1985).

[27] Precise aging of older skeletons is difficult, however.

[28] A. M. Cook and M. W. Dacre, *Excavations at Portway, Andover, 1973–75,* University Com. for Archaeol. Monograph 4 (Oxford, 1985).

[29] Rahtz, "Celtic Society in Somerset."

[30] A. Ellison, "Natives, Romans and Christians on West Hill, Uley: An Interim Report on the Excavation of a Ritual Complex of the First Millennium A.D.," in W. Rodwell, ed., *Temples, Churches and Religion in Roman Britain,* B.A.R. Brit. ser. 77 (Oxford, 1980), 305–28.

[31] S. Foster, "Early Medieval Inscription at Holcombe, Somerset," *M.A.* 32 (1988), 208–11 for west Somerset and bibliography.

[32] Thomas, *Celtic Britain,* 71–76; work by Cornwall Archaeological unit summarized in S. M. Youngs, J. Clark and T. Barry, "Medieval Britain and Ireland in 1986," *M.A.* 31 (1987), 110–91, entry 19. M. Fulford, "Byzantium and Britain: A Mediterranean Perspective on Post-Roman Mediterranean Imports in Western Britain and Ireland," *M.A.* 33 (1989), 1–6 emphasizes the direct contact between Britain and the eastern Mediterranean which can be implied from the nature and range of the imported pottery.

[33] R. J. Silvester, "An Excavation on the post-Roman site at Bantham, North Devon," *Devon Archaeol. Soc. Proc.* 39 (1981), 89–118; F. M. Griffith, "Salvage Operations at the Dark Age Site at Bantham Ham, Thurlestone, 1982," *Devon Archaeol. Soc. Proc.,* 44 (1986), 39–58.

[34] A. Preston-Jones and P. Rose, "Medieval Cornwall," *Cornish Archaeol.* 25 (1986), 135–85.

[35] L. Alcock, "Cadbury-Camelot: A Fifteen-year Perspective," *P.B.A.* 68 (1982), 356–88.

[36] Ulwell: work by Wessex Archaeological Committee (now Trust for Wessex Archaeology) summarized in S. M. Youngs, J. Clark and T. B. Barry, "Me-

dieval Britain and Ireland in 1982," *M.A.* 27 (1983), 161–229, entry 36 (and also P. W. Cox, "A Seventh-Century Inhumation Cemetery at Shepherd's Farm, Ulwell near Swanage, Dorset," *Proc. of the Dorset Natural Hist. And Archaeol. Soc.* 110 [1988], 37–47); Cannington: Rahtz, "Celtic Society in Somerset."

[37] V. I. Evison, "The Anglo-Saxon Finds from Hardown Hill," *Dorset Natural Hist. and Archaeol. Soc. Proc.* 90 (1968), 232–40.

[38] V. I. Evison, *The Fifth-Century Invasions South of the Thames* (London, 1965).

[39] T. Capelle, "Animal Stamps and Animal Figures on Anglo-Saxon and Anglian Pottery," *M.A.* 31 (1987), 94–96 and references.

[40] J. Hines, *The Scandinavian Character of Anglian England in the pre-Viking Period* B.A.R. Brit. ser. 124 (Oxford, 1984) and review by G. Speake, *M.A.* 30 (1986), 203–04.

[41] B. M. Ager, "The Smaller Variants of the Anglo-Saxon Quoit Brooch," *A.A.S.A.H.* 4 (1985), 1–58.

[42] T. M. Dickinson, "Fowler's Type G Penannular Brooches Reconsidered," *M.A.* 26 (1982), 41–68.

[43] R. A. Chambers, "The Late and sub-Roman Cemetery at Queenford Farm, Dorchester-on-Thames, Oxfordshire," *Oxoniensia* 52 (1987), 35–70.

[44] C. Sparey Green, *Excavations at Poundbury 1964–1980. Volume 1: The Settlements,* Dorset Natural Hist. and Archaeol. Soc. Monograph 7 (Dorchester, 1987).

[45] A point of debate—see S. James, A. Marshall and M. Millett, "An Early Medieval Building Tradition," *Archaeol. J.* 141 (1984), 182–215. Reproduced as Chapter 4, this volume.

[46] D. Dumville, ed., *Gildas: New Approaches* (Woodbridge, 1984) shows that Gildas's work should not be thought to establish a precise chronology to this period.

[47] J. R. Kirk and E. T. Leeds, "Three Early Saxon Graves from Dorchester, Oxfordshire," *Oxoniensia* 17–18 (1952/53), 63–76.

An Early Medieval Building Tradition

SIMON JAMES, ANNE MARSHALL
AND MARTIN MILLETT

*Excavations have recently produced valuable
new evidence for the structural types used in the
vernacular architecture of lowland and eastern
Britain during the sixth–eighth centuries A.D.
The evidence from a number of contemporaneous sites suggests that a highly characteristic
building tradition was in widespread use. The
identifying features of this building tradition are
defined and its affinities discussed.*

INTRODUCTION

Recent excavations at Cowdery's Down, Basingstoke have revealed exceptionally well preserved details of the buildings of a sixth–seventh-
century settlement. The buildings, which are closely similar to others
excavated elsewhere, possessed substantial foundations of post-holes or
wall trenches cut into the subsoil. Within these foundations remarkably
well-defined timber ghosts provided extremely detailed information
about the construction of the buildings. These features, published in detail in the *Archaeological Journal* in 1983,[1] can be used to interpret less
well-defined remains on the related sites. The common features of both
groundplan and structure indicate that the buildings on these settlements
were constructed with a limited and definable repertoire of techniques
which may be identified as an early medieval building tradition of national
importance, comparable in significance with the cruck and box frame tra-

Note: Throughout this paper references to sites and buildings are made by citing
the site name and structure number, thus Chalton AZ1. Full references to the sites
and the specific buildings within them are collected in Appendix 1 for Britain and
Appendix 2 for the Continent.

ditions of the later Middle Ages. This paper reviews this evidence and discusses the affinities and likely origins of this building tradition.

A considerable number of stylistically similar settlements in lowland and north-east Britain are now known through excavation and air photography. These are generally dated to the fifth to eighth centuries, although there is only independent evidence to confirm this for a few sites (Cowdery's Down, Yeavering, Chalton). These settlements have been the subject of previous synthetic studies by Radford, Addyman, and Rahtz.[2] A major landmark was the publication of Yeavering in which Hope-Taylor was the first to formulate some of the ideas developed in this paper. Most recently Dixon has challenged the supposed Germanic pedigree of the buildings on such sites.[3]

An examination of the characteristics of this tradition leads to a reappraisal of the cultural affinities of the buildings, which should not be given ethnic labels such as Anglo-Saxon on grounds of date alone.

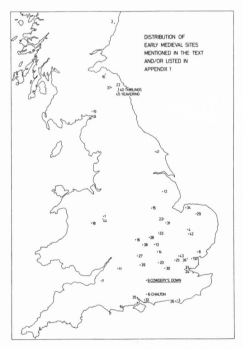

Fig. 4.1. Distribution map showing sites mentioned in the text and those listed in the gazetteer (Appendix 1). Sites are identified by the numbers used in the gazetteer.

This study is not designed to be exhaustive, although a gazetteer of the sites referred to, or discovered since that compiled by Rahtz was published in 1976, is presented in Appendix 1. No comprehensive gazetteer of comparable Romano-British and continental sites is presented as work on these is currently being undertaken by one of the authors (A. M.). Appendix 2 lists only the continental sites mentioned in the text. For reasons of brevity it is also assumed that the reader has consulted the Cowdery's Down report.

DEFINITION OF THE AREA OF STUDY

There are several distinctive characteristics which Cowdery's Down shares with other sites. These are summarized in Tables 4.1–4.3 and figures 4.4–4.9. The buildings are rectangular, precisely laid-out and constructed in substantial earth-fast foundations. Their plans frequently employ simple geometric forms or length-width ratios: the square is very common and often occurs in pairs. Most buildings have a door exactly in the center of each long wall, and some have an annex at one or both ends. Most of the structures stand within, or abut palisaded enclosures, and *grubenhäuser* are present. These and other features, such as ridge top location, appear at other of the sites (Chalton, Yeavering). Few sites pos-

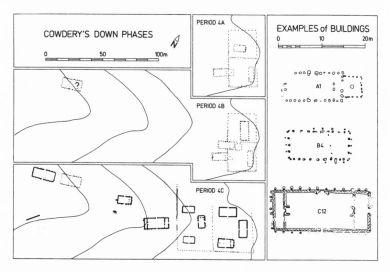

Fig. 4.2. Plans of the phases of the Cowdery's Down settlement, with examples of the buildings of each phase.

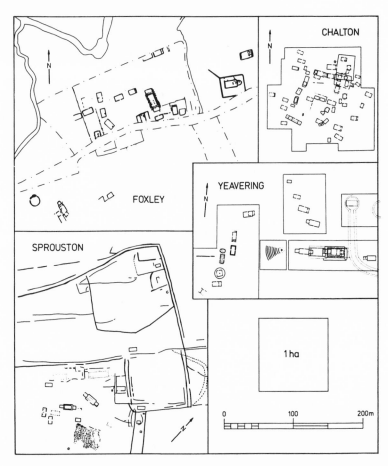

Fig. 4.3. Ground plans of selected settlements (Table 4.1). The sources of the plans are given in Appendix 1.

sess all these characteristics, but all possess most. Two sites present espe-cially obvious parallels: Yeavering with all the features, and Chalton which lacks only the end wall annexes. A number of similar sites have re-cently been identified from the air (Table 4.1).

The common features show that these settlements are clearly re-lated, although other evidence (fig. 4.5) suggests that there are two im-portant subdivisions which may correlate with the status of the sites. Thus one group has predominantly large buildings, whilst the other has mostly small buildings. The largest structures in the latter group are comparable in size to the smaller buildings in the former. It is of significance that the settlements with large buildings show clearer signs of planning and are often focused on a major central building (Cowdery's Down, Milfield, Foxley, Yeavering). For the purpose of this paper, we need only note that most elements of the building traditions discussed are common to buildings of both settlement types. It may therefore be seen as a style of building which is not demonstrably related to a site's status.

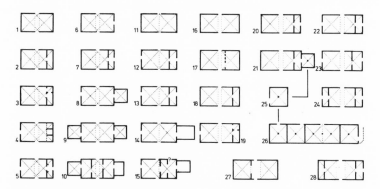

Fig. 4.4. Schematic plans of the currently known groundplans of early medieval buildings, interpreted in terms of combinations of square modules. 11–15 are simple double-squares; 16–24 double-square plus door width; 1–10 are double-squares minus the door width (i.e. they are laid-out from the opposite door posts); 27–28 are not readily interpreted on this module although both are large, and may thus have reached the maximum possible timber span; 25 is the simple, single square with central post-hole, also used as an annex (no. 21) or to form a composite long building (no. 26). The following are examples of the types shown:

1. Yeavering D2	11. Yeavering D3	21. Cowdery's Down A1
2. Chalton A10	12. Yeavering C3	22. Yeavering A4
3. Cowdery's Down C9	13. Yeavering C2	23. Yeavering D4
4. Chalton A1	14. Yeavering C4a	24. Yeavering A2
5. Chalton A2	15. Doon Hill B	25. New Wintles
6. Yeavering A1a	16. Cowdery's Down C10	26. Chalton, unnumbered
7. Chalton A20	17. Cowdery's Down B4	27. Cowdery's Down C14
8. Yeavering A1c	18. Cowdery's Down C8	28. Cowdery's Down C12
9. Yeavering A1b	19. Cowdery's Down C13	
10. Yeavering A3b	20. Chalton AZ1	

(For sources see Appendix 1. Drawings are not to scale)

DEFINITION OF THE TRADITION

The defining characteristics discussed below are summarized in Tables 4.1–4.3, and illustrated in figures 4.4 and 4.7.

Groundplans: (figs. 4.2 and 4.3)

The shape and arrangement of groundplans in this building tradition show a consistent pattern. While the great majority of the buildings are fairly precise rectangles, with a pair of central long wall doors, the proportions of the rectangle vary. The presence and disposition of internal partitions, additional doors in the end walls, and the provision of an annex at one or both ends allows for considerable variation on the basic theme.

Table 4.1: Defining Characteristics of Settlements (for references see Appendix 1)

		Rectangular earthfast structures, doors mid way along side walls	*Grubenhäuser*	Centralized layout	Decentralized layout	Palisaded enclosures.	Ridge top location	Number of identified structures. (excluding *grubenhäuser*)
EXCAVATED DATA	Cowdery's Down	p	p	p	–	p	p	16
	Yeavering	p	p	p	–	p	p	28
	Thirlings	p	–	p	–	p	–	9
	Chalton	p	p	–	p	p	p	25
	Wickham Bonhunt	p	–	–	p	u	–	12
	Mucking	p	p	–	p	e	p	15
	West Stow	p	p	–	p	e	–	3
	Catholme	p	p	–	p	p	p	63
	Bishopstone	p	p	–	p	e	p	13
	Doon Hill	p	d	p	–	p	p	1
	Northampton	p	–	d	d	d	–	1
	Springfield Lyons	p	–	u	u	u	p	1
	Raunds	p	p	p	–	–	–	3
AIR PHOTOGRAPHIC	Hatton Rock	p	d	p	–	d	p	6
	Sprouston	p	p	p	–	p	p	16
	Foxley	p	d	p	–	p	p	17
	Milfield	p	p	p	–	p	p	6

KEY:
p = present
– = absent
e = indeterminate due to erosion
d = indeterminate due to scale or nature of investigation
u = information unavailable

The shape of the main structure can vary from a short, broad rectangle (Cowdery's Down C9), to an elongated form (Cowdery's Down C12). However, simple ratios between the two dimensions are usually detectable. The vexed question of metrology is not here discussed.[4] The most common shape is the two-square module in which the groundplan consists of a square on either side of the central long-wall doors. This module has been commented upon by several excatators.[5]

An additional external door is sometimes found in one end wall, usually placed centrally (figs. 4.2, 4.4, and 4.7). External doors in both end walls are rare except at Yeavering whilst external doors in other positions are virtually unknown (Yeavering BC is an exception) although the positions of entrances in many less well preserved buildings are uncertain.

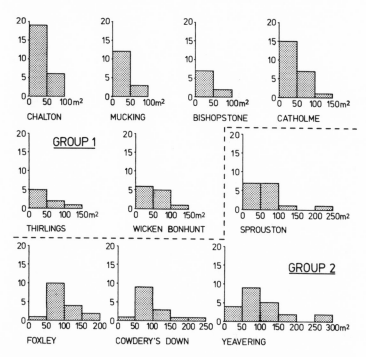

Fig. 4.5. Histograms to illustrate the numbers of buildings of various size categories on selected, extensively known sites. The horizontal axis represents the size categories (floor area) for each structure, the vertical axis gives the number of examples of each category. Data are derived from published plans, the sources given in Appendix 1. Note that the Sprouston measurements are from a small scale plan.

How common internal partitions were is difficult to establish, as these features often had shallow foundations, prone to erosion. Consequently, many excavated buildings apparently lacking them may originally have possessed them. However, a variety of internal wall dispositions is known. In the most common pattern one end of the building is divided-off, generally less than a quarter of the total floor area. The division is usually at the north or eastern end depending on the orientation of the structure. The partitioned area was reached by a door commonly placed in the middle of the dividing wall. This room was sometimes subdivided by further partitions and doors, on one or both sides of the entrance

Table 4.2. General characteristics of building plans (for references see Appendix 1)

		2-square module	opposed mid long wall doors	central end wall doors	off-set end wall doors	single internal partition	two internal partitions	sub-division of partitioned area	annex, one end	annexes both ends	external raking timbers	number of structures for which information available
EXCAVATED DATA	Cowdery's Down	p	p	p	p	p	p	p	p	–	p	15
	Yeavering	p	p	p	p	p	p	p	p	p	p	23
	Thirlings	p	p	p	–	p	–	–	p	–	p	8
	Chalton	p	p	p	u	p	–	p	–	–	p	29
	Wickham Bonhunt	p	p	e	e	p	–	–	–	–	e	12
	Mucking	p	p	e	e	p	e	e	e	e	e	15
	West Stow	p	p	p	u	p	–	–	–	–	p	3
	Catholme	p	p	u	u	p	u	u	–	–	e	41
	Bishopstone	p	p	p	–	p	e	e	–	–	e	13
	Doon Hill	p	p	d	–	–	p	p	p	–	u	1
	Northampton	p	p	p	–	u	–	–	–	p	u	1
	Springfield Lyons	p	u	u	u	u	u	u	p	–	p	1
	Raunds	p	p	–	–	–	p	–	–	–	p	5
AIR PHOTOGRAPHIC	Hatton Rock	p	d	d	d	d	d	d	–	–	d	6
	Sprouston	p	p	p	d	p	d	d	p	p	d	16
	Foxley	p	p	d	d	p	p	d	p	p	p	17
	Milfield	p	d	d	d	d	d	d	–	p	d	6

KEY:

p = present

– = absent

e = indeterminate due to erosion

d = indeterminate due to scale or nature of investigation

u = information unavailable

(Chalton A1, Cowdery's Down C9 and C13). That these end rooms may have had a variety of functions is suggested by the fact that some were built by end-wall doors (Chalton AZ1) or access doors into annexes (Cowdery's Down A1). Some larger buildings had such rooms at both ends, with or without external doors (Yeavering A2, Cowdery's Down C12).

A less common position for partitions was close to the transverse door axis. Examples with both one partition (Cowdery's Down B4) and two (Yeavering A3a, A3b) are known. The doorways, where discernible, are sometimes off-center, perhaps because one of the door posts had been used to support the ridge.

A quite common element in the groundplan is the annex. These occur only on the end walls, and are generally placed axially although off-set examples are known from the North (Doon Hill B, Yeavering C4, Thirlings B). Annexes have been referred to as porches[6] but as most certainly or probably lack external doors this identification is untenable (the exception is Thirlings B). A number of examples are rectangular and of similar construction to the main part of the building, sometimes with their own external raking timbers (Yeavering B and A3a; Northampton). A semicircular one has been claimed at Foxley on the basis of air photographs although this shape has yet to be confirmed by excavation. Square annexes are common (Cowdery's Down A1), and some have a central post-hole (Cowdery's Down A1, Thirlings C). This square with a central post seems to be a constructional unit which could stand independently (New Wintles; Yeavering "rectangular mortuary enclosure"?), or could be joined into chains (Chalton, unnumbered). Annexes appear at one or both ends of buildings (Table 4.2). It may be significant that they occur only on the larger buildings and are generally confined to those of the common two square module (fig. 4.6). There is no reason to think that they were secondary additions. In most cases access through the main walls was provided from the start as foundations were interrupted to provide doorways.

It must also be emphasized that the presence of an annex is insufficient reason for the identification of buildings as churches as some have suggested.[7] Firstly, at least one example dates to before the conversion (Cowdery's Down A1). Secondly, in an architectural repertoire where the variety of forms is so limited it is unlikely that any form was used for one purpose alone. Indeed, a comparison with the conversion of the Roman Empire would suggest that existing architectural forms were simply adopted for ecclesiastical use.[8]

Structure and Technique (Table 4.3, figs. 4.7, 4.8, and 4.9)

While all the sites under discussion provide information about ground plans and settlement layout, data concerning constructional methods and the assembly of the superstructure are much rarer, because of poor preservation, erosion, and inadequate excavation techniques. The only sites for which we have clear published evidence of well preserved timber ghosts are Yeavering, Cowdery's Down and Thirlings. The timber by timber plans recovered from these sites were not only detailed and largely complete, but complex, permitting progress to be made in understanding their construction as the presence of some features rules out the presence of others. This detailed evidence, in particular that from Cowdery's Down, can be used to define the characteristics of the building tradition. These features are first summarized for that site, and then examined in the sites where the evidence is less clear.

The superstructures were based on substantial, deeply-founded but low timber walls. The wall plates were below head height, on the basis of the interception height of the external raking timbers placed against them. The employment of tie beams is thus ruled out, and the wall plates are unlikely to have been continuous across the doorways. Whilst the joists of the raised timber floors in Cowdery's Down C12 could have

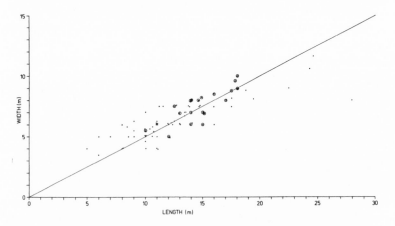

Fig. 4.6. Scattergram showing the size and proportions of structures on sites which have annexed buildings. Each building is shown as a dot; those with annexes are circled. The two-square module is represented by the diagonal line. Note that measurements are accurate to ± 0.5m, and were measured to the nearest meter on some small scale plans.

acted as anchor beams, such floors are not envisaged in all the buildings, so the generalized structural model proposed here ignores them.

Aisle posts were absent, but gable posts were definitely present in some structures, and could be inferred in others. Free-standing internal ridge supports were also present in some buildings but were not typical, and in the case of Cowdery's Down C8 are thought to be secondary. It is thus inferred that the roofs had tall gables, and were based on ridge pieces. The end-wall trenches of several buildings were less substantial than those for the side walls suggesting that they did not carry the roof load and implying gabled rather than hipped roofs. Where there were partitions and axial doors in end walls it is envisaged that the ridge piece was carried on a short kingpost standing on a lintel which was supported on either the tops of the doorposts or on the assembly of additional timbers often seen flanking these doors (figs. 4.7 and 4.8). Similar assemblies which occurred on either one or both sides of the long wall doors are also explained as ridge supports. They were always paired across the building and are seen as evidence for transverse frames supporting the ridge. The form envisaged for this is a simple cruck with the blades supporting a lintel on which stood a kingpost. This assembly is analogous to those over the short-wall doors, and equates with J. T. Smith's crux apex type F1, which he has suggested is amongst the earliest cruck forms.[9]

The problem with this interpretation is that the two putative crucks in Cowdery's Down C12 are not, as one might expect, positioned to divide the length of the ridge to be supported into equal thirds. It may thus be that their exact positions were influenced by other factors such as the need to avoid, or pass directly over the hearth. Hearths, whether originally on the ground, or placed on clay pads (Cheddar, 103) are rarely located on these sites due to erosion, but the great Sutton Hoo cauldron chain, some 3.45m long certainly calls for a firm anchor-point in the roof above the fire.[10]

The positions of these frames do however respect the door positions. As reconstructed, without the tie-beams or wall plates continuous along the length of the building, the lengths of walls flanking the side doors would be prone to spread outwards under the roof thrust. Since the external raking timbers are too steep to counter such thrust, we suggest that they were to counter the torsion motion in the wall plate. The position of transverse frames suggests that the wall panels were attached to them allowing them also to function as ties across the middle of the building.

Although a cruck form is envisaged there are major differences between this and the crucks of later buildings. In the latter, massive cruck

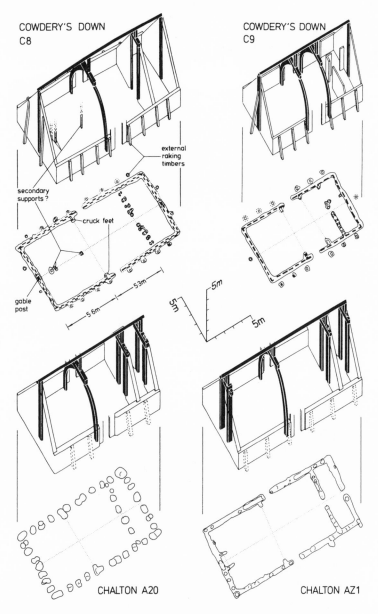

Fig. 4.7. Reconstruction of the principal roof timbers of some buildings from Cowdery's Down and Chalton according to the model proposed. For source of plans see Appendix 1.

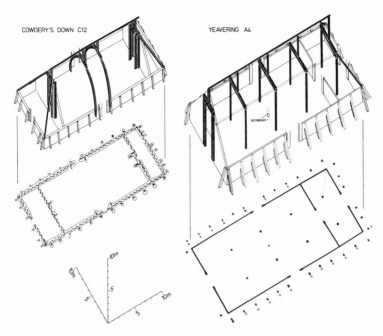

Fig. 4.8. Reconstruction of the principal roof timbers of some buildings from Cowdery's Down and Yeavering according to the model proposed. For source plans see Appendix 1.

blades support a ridge piece and purlins on which the rafters are hung. The roof load is transmitted to the ground via the crucks. In the buildings of the earlier tradition it is clear from the massive construction of the walls, and the provision of external raking timbers, that most of the roof load was transmitted via the walls. This is confirmed by the relatively light scantling of the cruck blades. These features are explained if the rafters stood on the wall plates and leant on, rather than hung from, the ridge-piece. The function of the assembly was the provision of longitudinal stability rather than load transmission, and it may also have carried purlins to prevent rafter sag, as proposed on the reconstruction drawings.

This model is applicable to the bulk of the well-preserved buildings at Cowdery's Down. Those which do not conform (B/C15 and C14) are equally difficult to understand in terms of any other roof type. Considerable variety is to be seen in the various elements employed, such as wall-panels where several alternative constructions were employed. The simplest (*C9 type*) consisted of a single, well-spaced row of rectangular

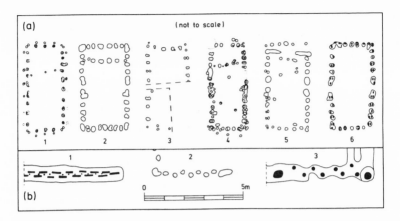

Fig. 4.9. *a* Buildings with walls of paired uprights (Cowdery's Down B4-type):
1. Cowdery's Down B4, 2. Chalton A20, 3. Bishopstone XXVIII, 4. West Stow
2, 5. Mucking (no number), 6. Thirlings G. *b* Buildings with walls containing
two staggered rows of uprights (Cowdery's Down C12-type): 1. Cowdery's
Down C12, 1. Nazeingbury (no number) 3. Thirlings N (For references to
specific buildings see Appendix 1.)

baulks, standing in either discrete post-holes or continuous trenches. The
infill between the baulks seems to have been of wattle and daub. A variant of this form is seen at Yeavering and Foxley where the infill consisted
of staves slotted between the vertical baulks. The *B4 type* consisted of
pairs of baulks in post-holes, with the gaps between aligned along the
wall so that the uprights could clasp horizontals running through the panels. This seems confirmed by the pairs of timbers at the corners, with
which these horizontals would have been intermeshed to form a rigid
box structure (Cowdery's Down, fig. 59). The particular form of this corner assembly at Cowdery's Down is not certainly seen elsewhere and
it seems likely that there was considerable variation on this basic idea
(fig. 4.9).

The *C12 type* had a wattle core, as a line of stake-holes was observed
in the floor of the wall trenches. This core is thought to have had one
or two horizontals in it above ground-level, sandwiched between the
two rows of baulks which were staggered to produce a zig-zag pattern
in plan.

The evidence of the end wall of Cowdery's Down A2 combines elements from the *B4 type* and *C12 type* of panel, and may be an intermediate form not otherwise certainly attested.

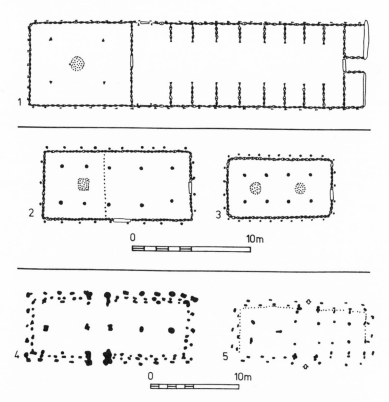

Fig. 4.10. Continental buildings with walls of continuous wattling flanked by timbering. 1. Feddersen Wierde, 2–3. Ezinge, 4. Haps, 5. Hijken. Note that timbering in nos 4–5 is similar to the Cowdery's Down B4 and C12-type panels (fig. 4.9). For sources of plans see Appendix 2.

A DISTINCTIVE BUILDING TRADITION

These characteristics represent a highly distinctive early medieval building tradition in Britain, as the sites listed in Appendix 1 possess buildings which are not only similar, but where the evidence is preserved, show the same repertoire of constructional techniques (Table 4.3). The identification of these techniques on the less well preserved sites is hard to demonstrate, but the more general characteristics such as the absence of sill-beams, and the employment of closely-spaced uprights evidenced by deep post-holes and wall trenches are clear. The detailed evidence for the

Table 4.3. Detailed characteristics of buildings on well preserved sites (for references see Appendix 1)

	COWDERY'S DOWN	CHALTON	YEAVERING*	THIRLINGS	OTHERS
GABLE AND/OR RIDGE POSTS	A2‡, B4‡, C8, C9‡, C10, C14‡, B/C15‡	AZ1?†, AZ2? AZ3, AZ6, A2?†, A10, A20?	A3a, A3b, C2, C4a	G?, H?, I?, P	Bishopstone 35, and 43 Catholme 62 Doon Hill A West Stow 2
CRUCK FOOTINGS single pair	C8, C14?, B/C15?	AZ1, AZ2, AZ6, AZ3, A1?, A10, A20	e	e	
two pairs	A1, C9, C12	AZ3?, A1?, A2	A3b?, C4a	e	
multiple	–	e	C3, C4b?, D4	e	
PAIRS OF UPRIGHTS AGAINST END WALLS OR PARTITIONS	A1, C12, C13	AZ1, A1, A2	A4?, C3, C4b?, D5	e	
OTHER INTERNAL TIMBERS aisle posts	–	A1?, A11?	A2, A4, D1b, D2, D3	A, B, N?	Sprouston?
single pair	C14, B/C15	unnumbered	C4a?, D5		Doon Hill B
WALL PANEL C9 type	C9, C10, C11, C13?, C14, B/15	i	variant in most buildings	L	Catholme 2d, 3d Foxley Doon Hill A
B4 type	A1?, B4, B5?, B6	A1?, A20, AZ2, AZ3, AZ6, A2? unnumbered	–	A?, B?, G, H, I	Bishopstone 1, 28, 37, 43 Catholme 1, 16 Maxey A? West Stow 1, 2
C12 type	C7, C8, C12	unnumbered	–	N	Nazeingbury
A2 type	A2	i	–	H?	Maxey A?— south wall
EXTERNAL RAKING TIMBERS: 1 row	B4, B6?, C7?, C8, C9, C10? C11, C12, C13, C14, B/C15	AZ1?, A10?, A12	most buildings	B, N?, P	Foxley
2 rows	C13?	A10?	C3	A, L	

KEY

– = absent

e = indeterminate due to erosion

i = indeterminate due to insufficiently detailed preservation

Notes

* Many plans incomplete or uncertain due to rebuilding and the absence of individual building plans in report.

† Probably secondary additions.

‡ Timber in end wall, gable post position, but no larger than other wall timbers.

occurrence of the characteristics described is assembled in Table 4.3, showing its widespread uniformity. In this table, we have attempted to distinguish between the absence of features caused by erosion, and genuine absence. This is particularly difficult to assess in the less deeply founded features, the external raking timbers, partitions, and internal post-settings for the roof supports. At sites such as Chalton and Mucking it seems clear that erosion has removed many of these detailed elements, although the weight of the evidence from all the sites suggests that they were originally standard.

A crucial test of the model presented, with its central assumption that roofs depended upon a ridge-piece and heavy walling with external raking timbers, is provided by Yeavering and Thirlings where a number of buildings appear to possess aisle posts (Yeavering A2, A4, D1, D2, D3; Thirlings A, B). J. T. Smith has recently argued that these are difficult to interpret as true aisled buildings as there is little or no provision for the support of the ends of the supposed arcade plates and poor longitudinal alignment of the post rows.[11] Furthermore, a number of the structures provide unequivocal evidence for ridge posts (see Table 4.3). It is therefore suggested that the internal posts probably supported the ridge, with a lintel and kingpost assembly similar to that proposed above. Several buildings at Yeavering also had traces of "cruck" footings by the side doors (Table 4.3), and in no case do these features and rows of internal posts occur together. All the Yeavering examples are therefore explicable in terms of ridge roofs. Furthermore, in all the buildings there are external raking timbers.

Given the fact that the proposed model is applicable to all the well preserved sites, it seems reasonable to propose that it represents a distinctive, and geographically widespread tradition of the sixth to eighth centuries A.D.

When *grubenhäuser* occur alongside the earthfast buildings so far described, there appears to be a regular relationship between the two types of structure, with a *grubenhaus* parallel with the main building just offset from the main door axis. This arrangement is best seen at Chalton (AZ1 and *grubenhaus* A25) and Cowdery's Down (C12 and C18).

ORIGINS OF THE TRADITION

The Germanic Background (figs. 4.10 and 4.11)

The derivation of the tradition described is not clear as it is not obviously identical with the predominant building type of either the Germanic homelands or Roman Britain. A Germanic pedigree is usually assumed although this has recently been questioned by Hope-Taylor and Dixon.[12] The latter has characterized the insular examples as "wall post houses"

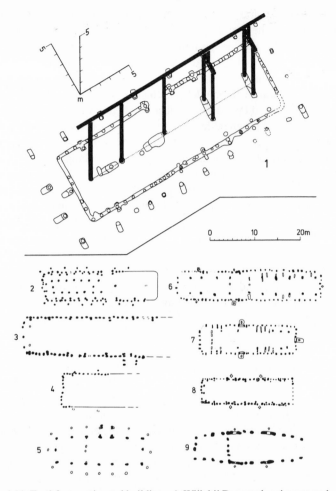

Fig. 4.11. Earthfast continental buildings. 1. Wijk bij Duurstede reinterpreted according to the model presented (cf. fig. 4.8). Note also the external timbers. 2–5. Development of buildings in Westphalia from the early Roman Iron Age to the eighth century. Note that the later structures lack "aisle posts" which have been pushed back to the walls—as crucks? 6–9. Development of buildings in Drenthe from the early Roman Iron Age to the high Middle Ages, showing the same sequence. Note that the latest buildings in both sequences are bow-shaped. 2. Vreden, 3–4. Soest-Ardey, 5. Warendorf, 6. Peeloo, 7. Wijster, 8. Odoorn, 9. Gasselte. For references see Appendix 2.

whose diagnostic features are given as stout, earthfast timber walls, sometimes with external braces, and lack of internal roof supports. He argues that while buildings of this construction are known in Germany, they are atypical and always rare.[13] He emphasizes that the majority of Free German houses of the late Roman Iron Age and Migration period were bipartite byre-houses with aisle posts and less substantial walls. Such long-houses are unknown in early medieval Britain. He contends that these objections raise serious obstacles to the idea of a Germanic origin.

We would challenge Dixon's characterization of both the insular and continental building types. Firstly, as we have shown, the British buildings do often have internal roof supports, generally "pushed out" to the walls, but sometimes either as free standing ridge posts or paired posts which supported the ridge via a lintel and kingpost. In the latter form the long axis of the building was kept clear of uprights. In many of the cases where internal roof supports are apparently absent it seems likely that they have been eroded. The same applies to the external raking timbers, which it is suggested were far more common than Dixon allows. It is virtually impossible to prove that any building lacked them; indeed they could have been universally employed.

Buildings of approximately the size and proportions of the insular types are not particularly unusual on the Continent from the Iron Age onwards. Some settlements consisted almost entirely of them, rather than the bigger long-houses (Grøntoft; Sleen; Dorestad; Rijnsburg; Grubbenvorst; Den Burg; Vreden).

It is also far from the case that all houses in north-west Germany and the Low Countries in the Roman Iron Age and Migration periods were weak-walled and aisled. A preliminary survey of the recent literature indicates that this period is marked by a widespread movement towards first reducing and then eliminating the number of internal posts, thereby putting the roof load on to the walls, at least in the examples with external timbers. Lack of detailed publications makes it difficult to establish whether the provision of the latter was general, and whether they were vertical or raking. The process may be seen in Westphalia[14] and in Drenthe.[15]

The sort of roof structure seen at Cowdery's Down cannot yet be paralleled directly on the Continent, although that of the Yeavering "aisled" type building can. It has been argued above that the latter were not aisled, but possessed a ridge-piece supported on a lintel and kingpost (fig. 4.8). This contrasts with the Romano-British aisled buildings (fig. 4.13), which were probably true aisled structures, with the rows of posts supporting arcade plates rather than a ridge-piece. The difference is also

visible in plan; Yeavering A4, for instance, has an asymmetrical arrangement of its post pairs. They are displaced towards one end of the building, so that one pair of posts is by the door passage, and one end-pair is
excessively close to the end wall. This is not seen in the Romano-British
buildings, where the post-pairs usually maintain a regular spacing along
the length of the building. However, the pattern is paralleled in the continental buildings (e.g. Feddersen Wierde; Flögeln). Furthermore, there is
evidence that at least some, and perhaps all the three-aisled buildings actually had ridge-roofs rather than arcade plates. Some structures actually
possessed both aisle posts and ridge posts (e.g. Wijk bij Duurstede). The
roof in the aisled end of such a building is identical in structure to the
Yeavering type (fig. 4.11). The example also possesses substantial walls
and external raking timbers. It dates to the Roman Iron Age. Prototypes
for the Yeavering roof structure were thus already known in the Low
Countries in the Roman period. The Yeavering type, it is suggested, was
then developed in Britain into the Cowdery's Down roof form.

Other characteristics of the British tradition point towards Germanic
origins, especially the wattle cored wall panels. Earthfast walls made of a
continuous screen of wattle with uprights added to one or both faces are
common in the Low Countries, at well known sites like Ezinge and Feddersen Wierde. Buildings in which pairs of uprights sandwich the wattle
core (like the Cowdery's Down *B4 type*) are known from the Iron Age
onwards at, for instance Hijken and Kablow. A building at Haps has
walls partly of *B4 type,* and partly of the *C12 type.* None of the wattle
cored forms are paralleled in Roman Britain. The *C9 type* is seen at Wijk
bij Duurstede and earlier at Grøntoft.

The most obvious feature of the vast majority of the Germanic
buildings, aisled or otherwise, is the opposed, usually centrally positioned pair of doors in the long walls. Such doors, which are equally typical of the tradition we have described, are virtually unparalleled in
Roman Britain. The writers know of a single parallel in an aisled farm at
Exning (fig. 4.13).[16] These doors and the wall panel types are the clearest
evidence that there was indeed strong Germanic influence on the development of the insular tradition.

The Romano-British Background (figs. 4.12 and 4.13)

Very large numbers of Romano-British buildings are known through excavation, from a variety of sites. The early medieval buildings under discussion come mainly from individual farmsteads and small nucleated
rural settlements, so to compare like with like we should look at the

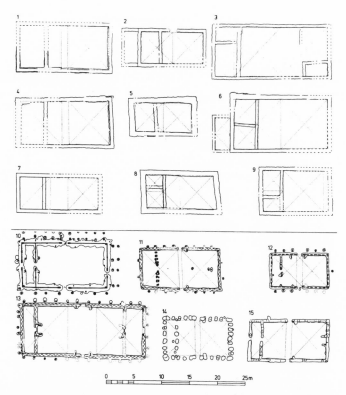

Fig. 4.12. Comparison of the size and groundplans of small late Roman rural buildings (1–9) with early medieval buildings (10–15). Note the similarities of size, shape, and internal layout, and the use of the two-square module in some buildings of each period. 1. Gatecombe 5, 2. Bradley Hill 1, period 2, 3. Hibald-stow, 4. Cirencester, 5 and 6. Catsgore 2.3 and 3.2, 7. Gatecombe 6, 8. Catsgore 2.1, 9. Bradley Hill 2, period 2, 10. Yeavering C3, 11. Cowdery's Down C8, 12. Cowdery's Down C9, 13. Cowdery's Down C12, 14. Chalton A20, 15. Chalton AZ1.[17] (For references to 10–15 see Appendix 1.)

equivalent later Romano-British settlements. Excavated examples of such sites are strikingly rare although they are being identified in increasing numbers (e.g. Chalton[18]; the Fenland[19]; south-west England[20]). The few examples with timber buildings which have been excavated, have been examined on a very small scale and have not therefore produced much evidence for building types. Cunliffe's excavations on one of the Chalton villages located regular floor plans, but little sign of timbering.[21]

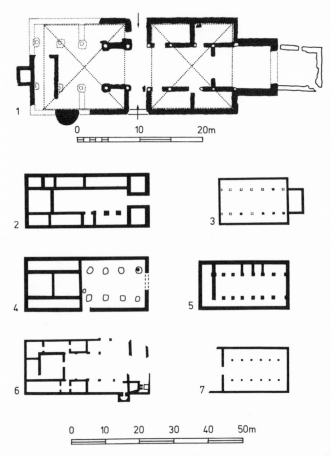

Fig. 4.13. Romano-British aisled buildings including two with annexes, and several divided by partitions. 1. Landwade (Hope-Taylor, *Yeavering,* fig. 105b) is similar in layout to the early medieval structures (cf. Fig. 4.4) although it is much larger. The room on the end shown in outline is a later addition. 2. Norton Disney, 3. Castlefield, 4. West Blatchington, 5. Ickleton, 6. Carisbrooke, 7. Spoonley Wood (2–7 after J. T. Smith, "Romano-British Aisled House," *Archaeol. J.* 120 [1963], 1–30.)

The hamlet excavated at Park Brow was poorly recorded, but the rectangular buildings produced evidence most consistent with the use of sill beams.[22]

It is likely that another reason for our general ignorance of late Romano-British vernacular timber architecture is that fully framed, surface built structures were in general use. There is good evidence for such structures at Wanborough,[23] Chelmsford,[24] and Wroxeter.[25] At the Romano-British small town of Neatham, a sequence of building types culminating in sill beam structures has been observed,[26] although it cannot be claimed that the abandonment of earthfast foundations was universal in late Roman Britain. Indeed an earthfast rectangular building of apparently late Roman date has been found at Dunstan's Clump, and its excavator has followed Dixon in suggesting that post-in-trench walling was of Romano-British origin.[27] Nevertheless, in view of the evidence available it seems highly unlikely that post-in-trench structures were widespread in the fourth century.

No late Romano-British buildings have yet been found to possess the characteristics described in this paper. Nevertheless, a large number of buildings is known which belong to a class which has marked similarities of groundplan (fig. 4.12). These consist of a simple rectangular stone foundation designed to support either stone or timber-framed walls. They are in the same size range as the post-Roman buildings described, and are thus small by the standards of Romano-British masonry structures. They seem to have been open halls, and unlike the larger Romano-British aisled buildings, lacked free-standing roof supports. This, and the common practice of partitioning off one end, and sometimes subdividing the room so defined, make the plans reminiscent of those of the sixth–eighth century. They usually possess a single door in one of the long walls, contrasting with the later structures.

The majority of the examples occur on rural sites, on small farmsteads (e.g. Bradley Hill[28]) and nucleated settlements (e.g. Catsgore[29]). They may also be found on villa sites as outbuildings (e.g. Gadebridge Park[30]), while on some rural sites they appear as simple villas (e.g. Whitton[31]). They also occur in urban contexts (e.g. Cirencester;[32] Silchester[33]) where they form part of the range of urban strip buildings, although the majority of the known examples remain rural.

It must be emphasized that these buildings show a considerable degree of variation, both of proportion and internal arrangement. However, most are fairly short rectangles, with some possessing the "two square" plan when measured internally. The positioning of the partition may also reflect this simple geometry (fig. 4.12). Such basic proportions may of course have been used independently in the fourth and sixth centuries, but there are signs that the "two square" module was favored in Roman Britain. It was, for example, long ago recognized that aisled buildings tended to have 2:1 proportions.[34] This alone is not enough to suggest a direct connection between the Romano-British and early medieval structures. As we have shown, buildings of these proportions are far from unknown in the Low Countries.

The suggestion of a connection between the Romano-British and early medieval structures rests on a combination of characteristics, not only proportions, but size, lack of free standing roof supports, and the common partitioning of one end. This combination is very hard to match on the Continent, there being few parallels for such partitions (e.g. Rijnsburg).

These stone-founded buildings, which where dated to the third and fourth centuries, occur in small identifiable groups comprising individual farms within larger settlements at, for example, Catsgore[35] making a further parallel with the later settlements (e.g. Chalton). However, the distribution of such buildings, although wide (from Somerset to the Humber) is limited to sites either where stone was readily available (e.g. the Oolitic limestone escarpment) or which were wealthy enough to import it (e.g. towns). Given our current state of ignorance of the poorer rural settlements in the timber using areas of the south-east, it is at least possible that similar timber structures lacking stone foundations, were becoming the standard Romano-British farmhouse throughout the lowland zone by the fourth century.

One further feature of the medieval tradition, the end wall annex, deserves special mention as the writers know of no parallels for this on the Continent before the high Middle Ages[36] with the possible exception of Soest-Ardey which had no direct access from the main area of the building. Romano-British parallels are however known, although rare. They occur on aisled buildings (fig. 4.13[37]) and possibly one of the smaller stone buildings at Nettleton Shrub.[38] The earthfast buildings at Dunston's Clump may have had an annex at each end, but this is far from certain.[39] Superficially, the aisled building at Landwade is a striking parallel for the early medieval buildings. Not only is it of the two-square proportions, but it also has opposed doors in the long walls, and an annex. However, its size and the employment of true aisle posts underline its differences with the later buildings.

AFFINITIES OF THE TRADITION

These summaries have sought to demonstrate that the origins of this tradition are not wholly to be found in either Roman Britain or the Germanic homelands. Certain features are extremely rare in Roman Britain, for example, opposed long wall doors. Others are completely unknown, including the characteristic wall panel types, the external raking timbers and indeed the association with *grubenhäuser.* These are all common in Free Germany.

On the other hand, we have features including the groundplan, which are probably of Romano-British inspiration. A major pointer in this direction may perhaps be the uniformity in style over such a wide area. Dixon has contrasted this with the great regional diversity in Anglo-Saxon artifacts, and suggested that it is only explicable in terms of a Romano-British origin.[40] Against this should be weighed the dichotomy between funerary and settlement data, with the probability that the former are more susceptible to local variation and may give an exaggerated picture of regionalism in the post-Roman centuries.

On architectural grounds, we suggest that this early medieval building tradition is a hybrid. There is, of course, considerable variation amongst buildings of the period. This is seen in Bishopstone XXXVII where there is a bow sided building which owes nothing to British forerunners. On the other hand, sill-built structures of presumably Romano-British influence also exist in the early medieval period (apparently Bishopstone XLVII). The overall impression is of a continuum, from pure Germanic, to pure Romano-British, with the majority represented by Cowdery's Down and the related sites holding the middle ground.

This picture of the fusing of two traditions should perhaps occasion no surprise, as there is increasing awareness of the survival of large numbers of Britons in emergent England.[41] This idea has already been suggested for Yeavering on a local scale.[42] It is probably not possible to identify the ethnic origins of the people living in the settlements we have discussed, for although Yeavering or Cowdery's Down correspond closely to the sort of settlement depicted in *Beowulf,* with its great hall, hallyard and ancillary buildings[43] sub-Roman Celtic society was apparently similar, equally heroic and addicted to feasting halls.[44]

Perhaps we are seeing, as Dixon suggests,[45] Germanic immigrants adopting British buildings from their indigenous neighbors, but still using their own constructional techniques developed, as perhaps at Yeavering to imitate the fine stone buildings of earlier times,[46] an echo of the barbarian yearning for *Romanitas* seen so strongly in Europe, most notably in Ostrogothic Italy.

The alternative possibility is perhaps more intriguing, namely that the population of, for example, Cowdery's Down were Romano-British by descent, building houses which were native in plan, but structurally and externally imitating the fashions of the new, politically ascendant elite, the Germans. There is an obvious parallel for this process of acculturation in the Romanization of British architecture in the first centuries A.D., with the adoption of the house-styles of the conquerors, and subsequent development of insular styles. The medieval tradition described could then be evidence for a parallel process of Germanization of the sub-Romano-British.[47] This process could well have included the adoption of other trappings of German culture, such as pots and brooches, rapidly making the native population indistinguishable from newcomers in archaeological terms.[48] It now seems Britain was largely sub-Roman rather than Anglo-Saxon for most of the fifth century,[49] but there seem to be virtually no identifiable cultural markers save possibly for grass-tempered pottery.[50] Perhaps significantly Cunliffe has found this material on the late Romano-British nucleated settlement at Chalton, and on the Saxon village site there.[51] He suggested that the latter was actually populated by Britons moving up from one to the other.

Whatever the ethnic origins of the peoples who occupied these settlements it is clear that by A.D. 800 the building tradition we have described was starting to change and was becoming less unified. Later buildings, which may be labeled Anglo-Saxon with greater certainty, tend to be less precisely laid-out, with different shapes and different techniques, as for example, North Elmham, Sulgrave, and Portchester. It is not clear whether this was due to social change, technical developments (perhaps allowing sound structures to be built from irregular timbers), shortage of timber or the increased use of sill beams and a gradual move towards the familiar fully framed architecture of the later period. By the ninth century the picture is complicated by Norse settlement, and then Norman invasion. How much influence the early medieval tradition had on later architecture is hard to assess, although later echoes are to be found. For example, the ninth-century bow-sided "long-hall" at Cheddar may be interpreted as a double annex, two-square building of the old tradition (fig. 4.14).

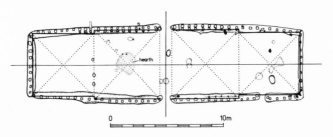

Fig. 4.14. The ninth–tenth-century Cheddar "Long Hall" reinterpreted as a double-annexed two-square building. For references see Appendix 1.

APPENDIX 1

Gazetteer of British sites referred to in the text, together with those discovered or published since the compilation of Rahtz's gazetteer.[52]

1. ATCHAM
   1. Rahtz, P. A. "Atcham Timber Halls, Salop." *West Midlands Archaeol. News Sheet. Group 8,* 18 (1975), 58.
   2. St. Joseph, J. K. "Air Reconnaissance: Recent Results." *Antiquity* 49 (1975), 293.

2. BALBRIDIE
   1. Reynolds, N. "Dark Age Timber Halls." *Scottish Archaeol. Forum* 10 (1978), 41.
   2. Selkirk, A. "Balbridie." *Current Archaeol.* 70 (1980), 326–28.

3. BISHOPSTONE
   1. Bell, M. *Excavations at Bishopstone. Sussex Archaeol. Collect.* 115. Lewes, 1977.
   2. Bell, M. "Saxon Settlement and Buildings in Sussex." In P. Brandon, ed., *The South Saxons.* London, 1978, 36–53
   Structure I Bell 1977, pp. 206–09, fig. 90
   Structure XXVIII Bell 1977, pp. 209–11, fig. 94
   Structure XXXV Bell 1977, p. 215, fig. 96
   Structure XXXVII Bell 1977, pp. 202–06, fig. 92
   Structure XLIII Bell 1977, pp. 213–14, fig. 92
   Structure XLVII Bell 1977, pp. 219–20, fig. 98

4. BRANDON
   1. Carr, R. D. "Brandon, Staunch Meadow." *M.A.* 24 (1980), 232
   2. Carr, R. D. "Brandon, Staunch Meadow." *M.A.* 26 (1982), 207

5. CATHOLME
   1. Losco-Bradley, S. "The Anglo-Saxon Settlement at Catholme, Staffs." *Trent Valley Archaeol. Com. Rep.* 8 (1974)
   2. Losco-Bradley, S. "Catholme." *Current Archaeol.* 59 (1977), 358–64
   Building 1 Losco-Bradley 1977, p. 360
   Building 2d Losco-Bradley 1974, pp. 24–25, figs. 15 and 18
   Building 3d Losco-Bradley 1977, p. 360
   Building 16 Losco-Bradley 1974, p. 12, fig. 6
   Building 62 Losco-Bradley 1977, p. 360

6. CHALTON
    1. Addyman, P. V., D. Leigh and M. J. Hughes, "Anglo-Saxon Houses at Chalton." *M.A.* 16 (1972), 13–31
    2. Addyman, P. V., D. Leigh and M. J. Hughes. "The Anglo-Saxon Village at Chalton, Hants." *M.A.* 17 (1973), 1–25
    3. Champion, T. C. "Chalton." *Current Archaeol.* 59 (1977), 364–69
    4. Champion, T. C. "Strategies for Sampling a Saxon Settlement: A Retrospective View of Chalton." In J. F. Cherry, C. Gamble and S. Shennan, eds., *Sampling in Contemporary British Archaeology.* B.A.R. Brit. ser. 50 (Oxford, 1978), 207–25

    Structures A1, A2, A3 Addyman, et al. 1972, fig. 9
    Structures A6, A7 Addyman, et al. 1973, fig. 5
    Structure A10 Addyman, et al. 1973, fig. 16
    Structure A11 Addyman, et al. 1973, fig. 7
    Structure A12 Addyman, et al. 1973, fig. 11
    Structure A20 Addyman, et al. 1972, fig. 8
    Structure AZ1 Addyman, et al. 1973, fig. 9
    Structures AZ2, AZ3, AZ6 unpublished info. P. Addyman
    Structure B2 Addyman, et al. 1972, figs. 9 and 11
    Unnumbered buildings Champion 1977, pp. 367–68

7. CHEDDAR
    Rahtz, P. A. *The Saxon and Medieval Palaces at Cheddar.* B.A.R. Brit. ser. 65. Oxford, 1979. *Long hall* figs. 30, 31, 32, pp. 99–107

8. COLCHESTER
    Crummy, P. *Aspects of Saxon and Norman Colchester.* London, 1981.

9. COWDERY'S DOWN
    Millett, M. "Excavations at Cowdery's Down, Basingstoke, 1978–1981," *Archaeol. J.* 140 (1983), 151–279.
    Structure A1, pp. 201–02, fig. 30
    Structure A2, pp. 203–04, fig. 34
    Structure B4, pp. 205–07, fig. 37
    Structure B5, p. 207, fig. 36
    Structure B6, p. 207, fig. 44
    Structure C7, pp. 209–10, fig. 44
    Structure C8, pp. 210–12, fig. 39
    Structure C9, pp. 212–13, fig. 40
    Structure C10, pp. 213–15, fig. 41

Structure C11, p. 215, fig. 43
Structure C12, pp. 215–17, fig. 46
Structure C13, pp. 218–21, fig. 49
Structure C14, pp. 221–22, fig. 51
Structure B/C15, pp. 222–24, fig. 54
Structure C18, pp. 217–18, fig. 48

10. DOON HILL
    1. Hope-Taylor, B. "Doon Hill and Dunbar." *M.A.* 10 (1966), 175–76
    2. Hope-Taylor, B. "Balbridie and Doon Hill." *Current Archaeol.* 72 (1980), 18–19
    Structures A and *B* Hope-Taylor 1980, p. 19

11. FOXLEY (Malmesbury)
    Hinchcliffe, J. *Cowage Farm, Foxley, Wilts. Interim Report on Recent Excavations.* Portsmouth, 1983

12. GOLTHO
    1. Selkirk, A. "Goltho." *Current Archaeol.* 56 (1976), 262–70
    2. Beresford G. "The Reconstruction of Some Saxon Buildings at Goltho, Lincs." In P. J. Drury, ed., *Structural Reconstruction.* B.A.R. Brit. ser. 110. Oxford, 1982, 113–23

13. GREAT LINFORD
    1. *M.A.* 25 (1981), 166
    2. *C.B.A. Newsletter, Group 9,* 11 (1981), 52–54
    3. *M.A.* 26 (1982), 173

14. GROVE PRIORY (Leighton Buzzard)
    1. *M.A.* 25 (1981), 166 and 187
    2. *M.A.* 26 (1982), 171

15. HARSTON
    Wilson, D. R. *Air Photo Interpretation for Archaeologists.* London, 1982, pl. 63

16. HATTON ROCK
    1. Rahtz, P. A. "A Possible Saxon Palace Site near Stratford-upon-Avon." *Antiquity* 44 (1970), 137–43
    2. Hirst, S. and P. A. Rahtz. "Hatton Rock." *Trans. Birmingham and Warwickshire Archaeol. Soc.* 85 (1971), 160–77

17. HEYBRIDGE

Drury, P. J. and N. P. Wickenden. "An Early Saxon Settlement within the Romano-British Small Town at Heybridge, Essex." *M.A.* 26 (1982), 1–40

18. HEN DOMEN
    1. Barker, P. A. "Excavations at Hen Domen." *Archaeol. J.* 126 (1969), 177–78
    2. Barker, P. A. "Some Aspects of the Excavation of Timber Buildings," *World Archaeol.* 1 (1969), 220–35
    3. Barker, P. A. "Excavations at Hen Domen." *Archaeol. J.* 127 (1970), 222
    4. Barker, P. A. "Hen Domen." *M.A.* 14 (1970), 165
    5. Barker, P. A. "Hen Domen." *M.A.* 15 (1971), 137
    6. Barker, P. A. and R. Higham. Hen Domen, Montgomery, Vol. 1. London, 1982

19. KIRKCONNEL

McClough, T. H. and L. R. Laing. "Excavations at Kirkconnel Waterbeck, Dumfriesshire, 1968." *Trans. Dumfries. and Galloway Natur. Hist. and Antiq. Soc.* 66 (1968), 128–39

20. LATIMER

Branigan, K. *Latimer.* Dorchester, 1971

21. LINFORD

Barton, K. J. "Settlements of the Iron Age and Pagan Saxon Periods at Linford, Essex." *Trans. Essex Archaeol. Soc.* Ser. 3, 1 (1962), 57–104

22. MAXEY

Addyman, P. V. "A Dark Age Settlement at Maxey, Northants." *M.A.* 8 (1964), 20–73
Building A, pp. 23–25

23. MILFIELD
    1. Hope-Taylor, B. *Yeavering: An Anglo-Saxon Centre of Early Northumbria.* London, 1977, p. 15, fig. 7
    2. Gates, T. "Saxon Settlement Evaluations," C. O'Brien, *Archaeol. Unit for NE England: Rural Excavation and Survey Projects.* 1982, pp. 11–13, fig. 6.

24. MUCKING
   1. Jones, M. U. "Excavations at Mucking, Essex." *Antiquaries J.* 54 (1974), 193–99
   2. Jones, M. U. and W. T. Jones. "The Crop-Mark Sites at Mucking, Essex." In R. Bruce-Mitford, ed., *Recent Archaeological Excavations in Europe* London, 1975, 133–87
   3. Jones, M. U. "Saxon Mucking—a Post-Excavation Note." *A.S.S.A.H.* 1 (1979), 21–28
   4. Jones, M. U. "Early Saxon Settlement Finds." *M.A.* 27 (1983), 141–42

25. NAZEINGBURY
   1. Huggins, P. J. "Excavations of Belgic and Romano-British Farm with Middle Saxon Cemetery and Churches at Nazeingbury, Essex 1975–76." *Essex Archaeol. Hist.* 10 (1978), 29–117
   2. Huggins, P. J., K. Rodwell and W. Rodwell. "Anglo-Saxon and Scandinavian Building Measurements." In P. J. Drury, ed., *Structural Reconstruction.* B.A.R. Brit. ser. 110. Oxford, 1982, 21–65

26. NEWHAVEN
   Bell, M. "The Excavation at an Early Romano-British Site and Pleistocene Landforms at Newhaven, Sussex." *Sussex Archaeol. Collect.* 114 (1976), 218–305

27. NEW WINTLES
   Hawkes, S. C. and M. Gray. "Preliminary Note on the Early Anglo-Saxon Settlements at New Wintles Farm, Eynsham." *Oxoniensia* 34 (1969), 1–4

28. NORTHAMPTON
   Williams, J. H. and M. Shaw. "Middle-Saxon Palaces at Northampton." *Current Archaeol.* 85 (1982), 38–41

29. NORTH ELMHAM
   1. Wade-Martins, P. "Excavations at North Elmham, 1967–8." *Norfolk Archaeol.* 34 (1969), 352–97
   2. Wade-Martins, P. "Excavations at North Elmham." *Norfolk Archaeol.* 35 (1970–72), 25–78, 263–68, 416–28
   3. Wade-Martins, P. *North Elmham Vols. I and II.* Norwich, 1980

30. NORTHOLT
   1. Hurst, J. G. "The Kitchen Area at Northolt Manor, Middlesex." *M.A.* 5 (1961), 211–99
   2. Hurst, J. G. "Northolt." *M.A.* 6 (1962–63), 309

31. ORTON LONGUEVILLE
Mackreth, D. "Orton Hall Farm, the Saxon Connection." *Durobrivae*
5 (1977), 20–21

32. PORTCHESTER
1. Cunliffe, B.W. "Excavations at Portchester Castle, Hants.,
   1966–68." *Antiquaries J.* 49 (1969), 62–74
2. Cunliffe, B. W. *Excavations at Portchester Castle.* Vol. 2 *Saxon.*
   London, 1976

33. RAUNDS
1. Boddington, A. and G. Cadman. "Raunds, an Interim Report on
   Excavations 1977–80." *A.S.S.A.H.* 2 (1981), 103–22
2. Cadman, G. "Raunds, Excavations 1981–82: An Interim Note."
   Northants. Archaeol. 17 (1982), 93–98
3. *M.A.* 26 (1982), 199
4. *C.B.A. Newsletter, Group 9* 12 (1982), 34
5. Cadman, G. "Raunds 1977–1983." *M.A.* 27 (1983), 107–22

34. SEDGEFORD
M.A. 3 (1959), 298

35. SOUTHAMPTON
1. Holdworth, P. "Saxon Southampton: A New Review." *M.A.* 20
   (1976), 26–61
2. Davies, S. M. and J. W. Hawkes. "Southampton, St. Mary's."
   M.A. 23 (1983), 177

36. SPRINGFIELD LYONS
Hodges, J. D. and D. G. Buckley. "Springfield Lyons." *M.A.* 27
(1983), 176

37. SPROUSTON
1. St. Joseph, J. K. "Sprouston, Roxburghshire: An Anglo-Saxon
   Settlement Discovered by Air Reconnaissance." *A.S.E.* 10 (1982),
   191–99
2. Smith, I. M. "Brito-Romans and Anglo-Saxons." In P. Clack and
   J. Ivy, eds., *The Borders.* Durham, 1983, 9–48

38. SULGRAVE
Davison, B. K. "Excavations at Sulgrave, Northants., 1960–1976: An
Interim Report." *Archaeol. J.* 125 (1968), 305–07

39. SUTTON COURTNEY
1. Leeds, E. T. "A Saxon Village near Sutton Courtney, Berkshire (third report)." *Archaeologia* 92 (1947), 79–93
2. Benson, D. and D. Miles. "Cropmarks near the Sutton Courtney Saxon Site." *Antiquity* 48 (1974), 223–26

40. THIRLINGS
1. *M.A.* 18 (1974), 182
2. *M.A.* 19 (1975), 168
3. *M.A.* 20 (1976), 226
4. *M.A.* 26 (1982), 201
5. O'Brien, C. *Excavations at Thirlings 1981, Interim Report.* Newcastle, 1981
Structures A, B, C, G, H, I, L, N and *P.* O'Brien 1981 and unpublished, information from C. O'Brien

41. WEST HESLERTON
Powlesland, D. J. *The Archaeology of Heslerton, Rescue Excavations 1977–1982.* Heslerton, 1982

42. WEST STOW
1. West, S. E. "Anglo-Saxon Village at West Stow: An Interim Report of the Excavations 1965–68." *M.A.* 13 (1969), 1–20
2. Selkirk, A. "West Stow." *Current Archaeol.* 40 (1973), 151–58
3. West S. E. "Die Siedlung West Stow in Suffolk." In C. Ahrens, ed., *Sachsen und Angelsachsen.* Hamburg, 1978, 345–412
Buildings 1 and *2* West 1969, p. 9, figs. 6 and 7

43. WICKEN BONHUNT
Wade, K. "A Settlement Site at Wicken Bonhunt, Essex." In D.G. Buckley, ed., *Archaeology in Essex to A.D. 1500.* London, 1980, 96–102

44. WROXETER
1. Webster, G. "Wroxeter." *Current Archaeol.* 2 (1969), 82–86
2. Barker, P. A. "Some Aspects of the Excavation of Timber Buildings." *World Archaeol.* 1 (1969), 220–33
3. Selkirk, A. "Wroxeter." *Current Archaeol.* 3 (1971), 45–49
4. Selkirk, A. "Wroxeter." *Current Archaeol.* 4 (1973), 111–16
5. Barker, P. A. "Excavations on the Site of the Baths Basilica at Wroxeter." *Britannia* 6 (1975), 106–17
6. Barker, P. A. "The Latest Occupation of the Site of the Baths Basilica at Wroxeter." In P. J. Casey, ed., *The End of Roman*

Britain: Papers Arising from a Conference in Durham, 1978. B.A.R. Brit. ser. 71, Oxford, 1979, 175–81

7. Barker, P. A., ed., *Wroxeter Roman City: Excavations 1966–1980.* London, 1981.

45. YEAVERING

Hope-Taylor, B. *Yeavering: An Anglo-Saxon Centre of Early Northumbria.* London, 1977

Structure A1a, pp. 50–51, fig. 13
Structure A1b, pp. 49–50, fig. 13
Structure A1c, p. 49, fig. 13
Structure A2, pp. 51–53, fig. 15
Structure A3a, pp. 55–58, fig. 17
Structure A3b, pp. 55–58, fig. 17
Structure A4, pp. 58–62, fig. 17
Structure B, pp. 73–78, fig. 33
Structure BC, pp. 86–88, fig. 36
Structure C2, p. 91, fig. 38
Structure C3, pp. 91–92, fig. 38
Structure C4a, pp. 92–95, fig. 39
Structure C4b, pp. 92–95, fig. 38
Structure D1a, pp. 95–96, fig. 42
Structure D1b, p. 96, fig. 42
Structure D2, pp. 97–102, fig. 43
Structure D3, pp. 103–06, fig. 48
Structure D4, p. 117, fig. 53
Structure D5, pp. 117–18, fig. 54
"Rectangular mortuary structure," pp. 108–16, fig. 52

APPENDIX 2

Gazetteer of Continental sites referred to in the text

DEN BURG

> Woltering, P. J. "Occupation History of Texel 1: The Excavation at Den Burg: Preliminary Report." *Berichten van de Rijksdienst voor het Oudheidkundig Bodemonderzeok* 25 (1975), 7–36

DORESTAD

> Es, W. A. van "Excavations at Dorestad: A Pre-Preliminary Report, 1967–68." *Berichten van de Rijksdienst voor het Oudheidkundig Bodemonderzeok* 19 (1969), 183–207

EZINGE

> Giffen, A. E. van "Der Warf in Ezinge, Provinz Groningen, Holland, und seine Westgermanischen Häuser." *Germania* 20 (1936), 40–47

FEDDERSEN WIERDE

> Schmid, P. "Ländliche Siedlungen der Vorrömischen Eisenzeit bis Völkerwanderungszeit im Niedersächsen Küstengebiet." *Offa* 39 (1982), 73–96

FLÖGELN

> Schmid, P. "Ländliche Siedlungen der Vorrömischen Eisenzeit bis Völkerwanderungszeit im Niedersächsen Küstengebeit." *Offa* 39 (1982), 73–96

GASSELTE

> Waterbolk, H. T. "Mobilität van Dorf, Ackerflur, und Gräberfeld in Drenthe seit der Latènezeit." *Offa* 39 (1982), 97–137

GRØNTOFT

> 1. Becker, C. J. "Früheisenzeitliche Dörfer bei Grøntoft, West Jütland." *Acta Archaeologica* 42 (1971), 79–112
> 2. Becker, C. J. "Siedlungen der Bronzezeit und der Vorrömischen Eisenzeit in Dänemark." *Offa* 39 (1982), 53, Abb. 10

GRUBBENVORST

> Es, W. A. van "Early Medieval Settlements." *Berichten van de Rijksdienst voor het Oudheidkundig Bodemonderzeok* 23 (1973), 281–87, at pp. 285–87

HAPS

> Es, W. A. van "Ländliche Siedlungen der Kaiserzeit in die Nederlanden." *Offa* 39 (1982), 144, Abb. 4

HIJKEN
Harsema, O. H. "Structural Reconstruction of Iron Age Houses in the Netherlands." In P. J. Drury, ed., *Structural Reconstruction.* B.A.R. Brit. ser. 110 (Oxford, 1982), 199–222, fig. 11.4

KABLOW
Schlette, F. *Germanen.* Leipzig, 1980, 158–59

ODOORN
Waterbolk, H. T. "Odoorn im frühen Mittelalter: Bericht uber Grabung 1966." *Neue Ausgrabungen und Forschungen* 8 (1973), 25–89

PEELOO
Waterbolk, H. T. "Mobilität von Dorf, Ackerflur, und Gräberfeld in Drenthe seit der Latènezeit." *Offa* 39 (1982), 97–137

RIJNSBURG
Es, W. A. van "Early Medieval Settlements." *Berichten van de Rijksdienst voor het Oudheidkundig Bodemonderzeok* 23 (1973), 281–87

SLEEN
Bruijn, A. and W. A. van Es. "Early Medieval Settlement near Sleen, Drenthe." *Berichten van de Rijksdienst voor het Oudheidkundig Bodemonderzeok* 17 (1967), 129–39

SOEST-ARDEY
Reichmann, C. "Siedlungsreste der vorrömischen Eisenzeit, jüngern römischen Kaiserzeit and Merowingerzeit in Soest-Ardey." *Germania* 59 (1981), 51–77

VREDEN
Reichmann, C. "Ländliche Siedlungen der Eisenzeit und des Mittelalters in Westfalen." *Offa* 39 (1982), 163–82

WARENDORF
Reichmann, C. "Ländliche Siedlungen der Eisenzeit und des Mittelalters in Westfalen." *Offa* 39 (1982), 163–82

WIJK BIJ DUURSTEDE
1. Verwers, W. J. "Roman Period Settlement Traces and Cemetery at Wijk bij Duurstede." *Berichten van de Rijksdienst het voor Outheidkundig Bodemonderzeok* 25–26 (1975–76), 93–132
2. Es, W. A. van "Ländliche Siedlungen der Kaiserzeit in die Niederlanden." *Offa* 39 (1982), 139, Abb. 6 and 8.

WIJSTER
> Es, W. A. van *Wijster: A Native Village Beyond the Imperial Frontier. Paleaohistoria* 11. Groningen, 1967.

ACKNOWLEDGEMENTS

We would like to thank D. Buckley, C. O'Brien, T. Gates, J. Hinchcliffe, and I. M. Smith for providing us with unpublished information about their respective sites. C. O'Brien, R. J. Cramp, J. T. Smith and V. Snetterton-Lewis have all kindly discussed aspects of our work with us, although they do not necessarily agree with our conclusions. Tim Schadla-Hall has encouraged and incited us throughout.

NOTES

[1] M. Millett, "Excavations at Cowdery's Down, Basingstoke, Hants, 1978–1981," *Archaeol. J.* 140 (1983), 151–279.

[2] C. A. R. Radford, "The Saxon House: A Review and Some Parallels," *M.A.* 1 (1957), 27–38; P. V. Addyman, "The Anglo-Saxon House: A New Review," *A.S.E.* 1 (1972), 273–307; P. A. Rahtz, "Buildings and Rural Settlement," in D. Wilson, ed., *The Archaeology of Anglo-Saxon England* (London, 1976), 49–98.

[3] P. Dixon, "How Saxon is a Saxon House?" in P. J. Drury, ed., *Structural Reconstruction,* B.A.R. Brit. ser. (Oxford, 1982), 275–88.

[4] Contrast B. Hope-Taylor, *Yeavering: An Anglo-Saxon Centre of Early Northumbria* (London, 1977) and P. Huggins, K. Rodwell and W. Rodwell, "Anglo-Saxon and Scandinavian Building Measurements," in Drury, *Structural Reconstruction,* 21–66, with M. Millett, "Distinguishing between the *Pes Monetalis* and the *Pes Drusianus*: Some Problems," *Britannia* 13 (1982), 315–20, and M. Millet, review of Drury's, *Structural Reconstruction,* in *Antiquaries J.* 64 (1984), 114–15.

[5] Hope-Taylor, *Yeavering,* 213; M. Bell, *Excavations at Bishopstone, Sussex Archaeol. Collect.* 115 (Lewes, 1977); M. U. Jones, "Saxon Mucking—a post-Excavation Note," *A.S.S.A.H.* 1 (1979), 21–37, at p. 33.

[6] R. J. Cramp, "Anglo-Saxon Settlement," in J. C. Chapman and H. C. Mytum, eds., *Settlement in Northern Britain 1000 B.C.–A.D. 1000: Papers Presented to George Joby, Newcastle upon Tyne, December 1982,* B.A.R. Brit ser. 118 (Oxford, 1983), 263–97, at p. 275.

[7] Huggins, Rodwell and Rodwell, "Building Measurements"; J. Hinchcliffe, *Cowage Farm, Foxley, Wilts., an Interim Report* (Portsmouth, 1983).

[8] R. Krautheimer, *Early Christian and Byzantine Architecture,* 2nd ed. (Harmondsworth, 1975), 39–70.

[9] J. T. Smith, "The Problems of Cruck Construction and the Evidence of Distribution Maps," in N. W. Alcock, ed., *Cruck Construction,* C.B.A. Research Rep. 42 (London, 1981), 5–24, at p. 8.

[10] R. Bruce-Mitford, *The Sutton Hoo Ship Burial,* vol. 1 (London, 1975), 444.

[11] Lecture, Durham, November 1983.

[12] Hope-Taylor, *Yeavering;* Dixon, "How Saxon is a Saxon House?"

[13] Dixon, "How Saxon is a Saxon House," 277.

[14] C. Reichmann, "Siedlungsreste der vorrömischen Eizenzeit und des Mittelalters in Westfalen," *Offa* 39 (1982), 163–82. Compare Abb. 2 with Abb. 11 and 12.

[15] H. T. Waterbolk, "Mobilität von Dorf Ackerflur, und Gräberfeld in Drenthe seit der Latènezeit," *Offa* 39 (1982), 97–137 at p. 104, Abb. 6–8.

[16] Hope-Taylor, *Yeavering,* fig. 105b; Fig. 7.13 this volume.

[17] Gatecombe 5, see K. Branigan, *Gatecombe Roman Villa,* B.A.R. Brit. ser. 44 (Oxford, 1977), fig. 6; Bradley Hill 1, period 2, see R. H. Leech, "The Excavations of a Romano-British Farmstead and Cemetery on Bradley Hill, Somerton, Somerset," *Britannia* 12 (1981), 177–252, fig. 5; Hibaldstow, see R. Goodburn, ed., "Roman Britain in 1975," *Britannia* 7 (1976), 291–377, fig. 13; Cirencester, see A. D. McWhirr, L. Viner and C. Wells, *Romano-British Cemeteries at Cirencester* (Cirencester, 1982), fig. 26; Catsgore 2.3 and 3.2, see R. H. Leech, *Excavations at Catsgore, 1970–73* (Bristol, 1982), figs. 35 and 42; Gatecombe 6, see Branigan, *Gatecombe,* fig. 7; Catsgore 2.1, see Leech, *Catsgore,* fig. 29; Bradley Hill 2, period 2, see Leech, "Excavations of a Romano-British Farmstead," fig. 7.

[18] B. W. Cunliffe, "Chalton, Evolution of a Landscape," *Antiquaries J.* 53 (1973), 173–90.

[19] C. W. Phillips, ed., *The Fenland in Roman Times* (London, 1970).

[20] R. H. Leech, "Larger Agricultural Settlements in the West Country," in K. Branigan and P. J. Fowler, eds., *The Roman West Country* (Newton Abbot, 1976), 142–61.

[21] B. W. Cunliffe, "A Romano-British Village at Chalton," *Proc. of the Hants. Fld. Club and Archaeol. Soc.* 33 (1976), 45–68.

[22] G. R. Wolseley, R. A. Smith and W. Hawley, "Prehistoric and Roman Settlements on Park Brow," *Archaeologia* 76 (1927), 1–40, at p. 8.

[23] S. Anderson and J. S. Wacher, "Excavations at Wanborough, Wilts. An Interim Report," *Britannia* 11 (1980), 115–26, at p. 119.

[24] P. J. Drury, "Chelmsford," in W. Rodwell and T. Rowley, eds., *The Small Towns of Roman Britain,* B.A.R. Brit. ser. 15 (Oxford, 1975), 159–73, at p. 165.

[25] P. A. Barker, ed., *Wroxeter Roman City: Excavations 1966–80* (London, 1981), fig. 4.

[26] M. Millet and D. Graham, *Excavations on the Romano-British Small Town at Neatham, Hants., 1969–79,* Hampshire Field Club Monograph 3 (Hampshire, 1986).

[27] D. Garton and D. Riley, "Dunston's Clump," *Current Archaeol.* 8 (1982), 43–48.

[28] Leech, "Excavations of a Romano-British Farmstead."

[29] Leech, *Catsgore.*

[30] D. A. Neal, *The Excavation of the Roman Villa in Gadebridge Park, Hemel Hempstead 1963–8* (London, 1974), figs. 4 and 32.

[31] M. Jarrett, *Whitton, an Iron Age and Roman Farmstead in South Glamorgan* (Cardiff, 1981).

[32] McWhirr, Viner and Wells, *Cirencester,* 50.

[33] G. C. Boon, *Silchester: The Roman Town of Calleva* (London, 1974).

[34] C. A. F. Berry, "The Dating of Romano-British Houses," *J. Roman Studies* 41 (1951), 25–31, at p. 25.

[35] Leech, *Catsgore.*

[36] E.g. Waterbolk, "Mobilität von Dorf," Abb. 8, 5.

[37] Landwade, Exning, Hope-Taylor, *Yeavering,* fig. 105; Castlefield, J. T. Smith, "Romano-British Aisled House," *Archaeol. J.* 120 (1963), 1–30, fig. 1.

[38] W. J. Wedlake, *The Excavation of the Shrine of Apollo at Nettleton, Wilts. 1956–1971* (London, 1982), 32, fig. 2.

[39] Garton and Riley, "Dunston's Clump."

[40] Dixon, "How Saxon is a Saxon House?"

[41] M. Faull, "British Survival in Anglo-Saxon Northumbria," in L. Laing, ed., *Studies in Celtic Survival,* B.A.R. Brit. ser. 37 (Oxford, 1977), 1–23; B. N. Eagles, *The Anglo-Saxon Settlement of Humberside,* B.A.R. Brit. ser. 68 (Oxford, 1979), 242.

[42] Hope-Taylor, *Yeavering,* 237.

[43] R. J. Cramp, "Beowulf and Archaeology," *M.A.* 1 (1957), 57–77, at 71–7.

[44] L. Alcock, *Arthur's Britain* (London, 1971), 319–27; I. Williams, "The Gododdin Poem," *Trans. Anglesey Antiq. Soc. and Fld. Club* (1935), 25–39.

[45] Dixon, "How Saxon is a Saxon House?"

[46] Hope-Taylor, *Yeavering,* 140.

[47] For "Germanization" see S. E. van der Leeuw, "Acculturation as Information Processing," in R. Brandt and J. Slofstra, eds., *Roman and Native in the Low Countries: Spheres of Interaction,* B.A.R. Int. ser. 184 (Oxford, 1983), 11–42, at p. 12.

[48] R. M. Reece, "The End of Roman Britain Revisited," *Scottish Archaeol. Rev.* 2 (1983), 149–53

[49] C. C. Taylor, "The Nature of Romano-British Settlement Studies—What are the Boundaries?" in D. Miles, ed., *The Romano-British Countryside,* B.A.R. Brit. ser. 103 (Oxford, 1982), 1–16, at p. 8.

[50] Cf. D. Brown, "Problems of Continuity," in T. Rowley, ed., *Anglo-Saxon Settlement and Landscape,* B.A.R. Brit. ser. 6 (Oxford, 1974), 16–20, at p. 18.

[51] B. W. Cunliffe, *The Regni* (London, 1973), 139.

[52] Rahtz, "Buildings and Rural Settlement."

CHAPTER 5

York 700–1050

RICHARD A. HALL

In both 700 and 1050 York could claim to be the premier settlement in north-east England in political, ecclesiastical and economic terms. There was, however, so far as the very limited evidence available allows us to judge, a considerable difference between Anglian *Eoforwic* and Anglo-Scandinavian *Jorvik*. This paper will attempt some definition and exploration of these differences, but two limiting factors should be made clear at the start. Firstly, York's archaeology is usually a palimpsest of inter-cutting features, with the attendant problems of residuality and intrusion affecting the clarity of the picture and further complicating problems of dating. It is often difficult to date a given context or phase within ± 25 or even ± 50 years with much conviction, and this of course may make it uncertain whether a particular development should be attributed, for example, to a late Anglian or an early Anglo-Scandinavian inspiration. Secondly, the sample of pre-Conquest York yet available is unreliably small, and may well exhibit unusual features. Taking Domesday Book's *mansiones* as a guide, only approximately 0.025% of the mid eleventh century city has been archaeologically investigated, and an overwhelming part of this sample is represented by a single excavation at 16–22 Coppergate.

Within these restraints the main concern of this paper will be topographic, with little consideration of artifact studies or of environmental analysis. Both these aspects are being studied at present in York, and a series of detailed studies has been and continues to be published in the series *The Archaeology of York*.

York's regional pre-eminence is a reflection of its chorographic setting. It commands the southern end of the Vale of York, part of the main north–south route up the eastern side of Britain, at a point where a band of glacial moraine traverses the Vale, providing an east–west route-way. Here the moraine is cut by the River Ouse, which flows on for some 50 km. to a junction with the Trent river system in the Humber Estuary, and thence on to the North Sea. The river was tidal to York and beyond, allowing access from the Humber mouth on two tides. The Ouse is joined at York by its tributary the Foss, and in the naturally defended tongue of land at their confluence Roman military surveyors laid out a le-gionary fortress ca. A.D. 71. This 20 ha. fortification was to remain the headquarters of the Romans' northern military command until their with-drawal ca. 400. Off the north-west side of the fortress there was a sub-sidiary walled enclosure of unknown date, size and function.

Across the Ouse civilian settlement developed in the mid to late sec-ond century, and the site was granted *colonia* status by the early third century, eventually becoming the capital of *Britannia Inferior*. It is pre-sumed that a walled circuit enclosed an area of some 27 ha., within which, as well as town houses, there may have been an imperial palace and, perhaps, a church of the Bishop Eborius who attended the Council of Arles in 314.

So far as is known, all elements of the Roman town continued in oc-cupation or use until the end of the fourth century, although there are some signs of change in the *colonia* in the later fourth century[1] and in the extramural zone south-east of the fortress, where at 16–22 Coppergate a fourth century cemetery in an area previously occupied by buildings may suggest contraction.

There is no firm archaeological evidence for what happened in the city after the Roman military withdrawal, and the fifth and sixth cen-turies are at present a "dark age." It has been suggested that Anglo-Sax-ons, either the descendants of German troops in the late Roman army or recently arrived immigrants, took over in the fifth century,[2] although an-other view holds that there is very little fifth century Anglo-Saxon mater-ial in Yorkshire at all.[3] It is more likely that the city remained a British settlement, perhaps ultimately within the "Celtic" kingdom of Elmet, until the later sixth century.[4] It has also been suggested that a large part of the city was flooded in the fifth and sixth centuries in the wake of marine transgression in the Humber estuary.[5] Here at least archaeology has something positive to offer, even though its evidence negates what has been proposed in support of the flood theory, for at several sites where traces of the putative flooding should have been found, there was no sign of it. In all, it may be suggested that some elements of the Romano-

British population and their descendants probably continued to use part of the city into the fifth and perhaps even sixth centuries for political, social or religious purposes, but it can have had no substantial economic role except conceivably as a place of limited exchange at a political level.

As late as 600, when it seems that much of northern and eastern Yorkshire was in Anglo-Saxon hands, evidence for pagan Anglo-Saxon activity in York remains virtually absent—even the well known Anglo-Saxon cremation cemeteries at the Mount and Heworth, 1–2 km. south and north respectively, do not necessarily reflect a population based in York, but could reflect agricultural communities based in the former *territorium*.

In 627 the Northumbrian king Edwin was baptized in a church built for the occasion and dedicated to St. Peter which, it is generally believed was the direct predecessor of York Minster. There has been no trace of any pre-Norman church building in Derek Phillips's Minster excavations, but various eighth to ninth century sculptured stones indicate that there was a contemporary church thereabouts, perhaps in the courtyard of the *principia* which was still, in part at least, standing roofed until that time.[6] If it was in this position it mirrors the position of St. Paul-in-the-Bail at Lincoln; Phillips, however, favors a position to the north of the present Minster.[7] Wherever precisely it stood in this area, there may be a comparison to be drawn with the position of the early seventh century foundation of St. Paul's in London, inside the Roman walls with a probable palace site nearby.[8] The imposing standing remains of the York *principia* may have been incorporated in a prestigious Northumbrian royal palace.

It is also possible to detect the power of the Northumbrian kings in the refortifications of the Roman military *enceinte* detected by Radley[9] at the excavation of the "Anglian Tower" ((1) on fig. 5.1) and by Davison in his observations during the destruction in 1970 of an adjacent stretch of rampart.[10] The earliest element in the refurbishment is the "Anglian Tower" itself, plugging a breach in the fortress walls which, Davison speculated, might have been caused by the collapse of an external tower or postern not otherwise attested.[11] However there is no archaeological confirmation for this hypothetical feature. Buckland has recently summarized the evidence for the tower's date concentrating on its geological composition, exclusively of oolitic limestone.[12] He suggests that the structure would not have been out of place in a late Roman context, but allows that it may have been built from reused Roman building stone at a later date, since it shares one of the geological characteristics of the eleventh century tower of St. Mary Bishophill Junior church.

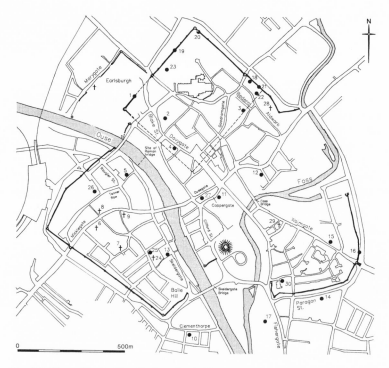

Fig. 5.1. Map of York: Sites Referred to in Text.

Radley demonstrated that the south-west corner of the tower had collapsed before the first phase of rampart refurbishment took place, with a rebuilding of the wall-head in stone and a revetted stone pathway laid behind.[13] He believed on historical grounds that this addition should be attributed to the Vikings in 867. Davison collected a little dating evidence for the southern extension of this work, including an Anglian sherd. Unfortunately two other sherds, of the period 850–950, may also be attributed either to this or to the second phase of strengthening the rampart, leaving the date of this first phase uncertain. It is at least possible, however, that the earliest post-Roman rampart was constructed in the Anglian period before the mid ninth century; the "Anglian Tower" precedes this by the indefinable length of time represented by its partial collapse.

If there was a defended area here that had its fortifications refurbished in the Anglian period, it is unusual in British urban archaeology.

However, there is as yet little evidence for what—apart from the metropolitan church and the putative royal palace—was being defended. The street pattern shows that within the Roman fortress the *insulae* were in some cases disregarded and direct routes between adjacent gateways were created; although there is no clear-cut evidence for when this took place, a date in the fifth–late ninth century bracket seems most likely. These new routes include Goodramgate, running from the *porta principalis sinistra* to the *porta decumana,* but diverted when the latter was replaced by Monk Bar ca. 1300; also Blake Street, which ran from just within the *porta praetoria* to High Petergate near the *porta principalis dextra,* its northern part being enclosed by St. Leonard's hospital in 1299.[14] These routes indicate movement through the fortress but, apart from whatever evidence there may be from Phillips's Minster excavations, no certain intramural occupation site has yet been recognized within the fortress, although possible Anglian structures have been seen in York Archaeological Trust excavations at 9 Blake Street (2)[15] and the Bedern (3).[16] Although individual pieces are of intrinsic interest,[17] there are correspondingly few casual finds of Anglian material. Thus there is little to add here to Cramp's distribution map,[18] although this partly reflects the limited number of opportunities that have presented themselves to excavate in this area.

A single sherd of Roman pottery was found by Wenham at 6–14 Davygate (4),[19] which has an accretion adhering to it that closely resembles glass-making residues identified on similar Roman vessels found at 16–22 Coppergate, reused for glass-working in the mid ninth century. This is all that can be even tentatively adduced to indicate Anglian manufacturing here, and there is no evidence for trading or commercial activities.

Across the River Ouse within the former *colonia* there is a virtual absence of fifth–seventh century artifacts but a greater concentration of eighth and ninth century material, all of a domestic nature. Their distribution is fairly evenly spread across the *colonia*; the apparent density to the north of Micklegate largely mirrors the pattern of deep and substantial redevelopment projects.[20] However discoveries around the Roman bridgehead, notably in Tanner Row[21] and at 5 Rougier Street (5),[22] may perhaps suggest that a crossing-point there remained in use into the ninth century.

As in the fortress, Anglian occupation levels and structures have not yet been recognized in the *colonia,* but recently two commentators have independently suggested, although with different emphases, that there may have been a sizable and important ecclesiastical complex in the Bishophill area. Palliser's general points about archiepiscopal holdings here,[23] which could have been initiated as early as the seventh century, have been refined by Morris who proposes a monastic dimension to the Anglian church in York based within a church complex represented by the sites of Holy Trinity Priory (6), St. Mary Bishophill Junior (7), St. Gregory (8) and St. Martin (9).[24] Only excavation will now advance this argument—the discovery of Archbishop Albert's (767–80) church of Holy Wisdom would indeed be of considerable importance.

Turning to the immediately extramural areas beside both the fortress and the *colonia,* evidence for Anglian activity or occupation is again negligible. South-east of the *colonia* at Clementhorpe (10) a large cobble-raft foundation on the site of the twelfth century Benedictine nunnery of St. Clement is thought to represent a pre-Conquest church, and two mid ninth century coins recovered from later contexts, together with a residual ninth century lead weight, may suggest an origin for the building at that time.[25] Across the river the collection of unstratified material amassed when Clifford Street was constructed in the 1870s includes at least one ostensibly mid ninth century object.[26] The significance of the find spot of the mid eighth century helmet from 16–22 Coppergate (11) is unclear.[27] It was clearly well worn when buried, and there are indications that the wood-lined shaft in which it was discovered was of Anglo-Scandinavian date, but the reason for its deposition is uncertain.

The recognition that several hundred fragments of pottery produced using the hand-made technique associated with the Anglian period were found in the earliest Viking Age layers on this site suggests that there was a tradition of ceramic production in the pre-Viking town, which continued a short time after the Viking takeover.[28] This is an important discovery, controverting as it does the previous supposition that the absence of such pottery from excavations in the city pointed to a largely aceramic Anglian urban culture.[29] It gives weight to the argument that sites where not even isolated pottery sherds of this sort have been recovered were indeed unused in the later Anglian period. Nonetheless this excavation close to the banks of the River Foss did not produce any evidence for Anglian occupation or for the commercial or industrial use of the river in the Anglian period—a repetition of the negative evidence recovered in earlier excavations at Hungate (12).[30] With the exception of a few sherds of Tating ware from within the *colonia* at 58–9 Skeldergate (13) which seem, however, to be in an early Anglo-Scandinavian context,[31] the same is true of the Ouse frontages of the fortress and *colonia.*

Yet there should be evidence for commercial activities. Altfrid's *Life of St. Luidgar* contains a passage that infers the presence of a Frisian trading community in late eighth century York,[32] and York was presumably the gateway through which such imports as the Tating and northern French wares found at Wharram Percy in the East Riding reached Northumbria.[33] A Frisian *sceat* has been found in excavations at 16–22 Coppergate,[34] confirming contact between the two areas. It should be noted, however, that the site of North Ferriby on the Humber shore has produced rather more Frisian coins,[35] and there is a possibility that this site, on a land and ferry route linking Lindsey and Northumbria, also served as an international port of entry in the early eighth century.[36]

Additionally the Northumbrian coinage itself is an indication of economic activity. For long regarded as forgeries, three gold *tremisses* found in York in the mid nineteenth century are now regarded as genuine coins, perhaps of the 640s.[37] They and a fourth, unprovenanced, but apparently related coin, recently rediscovered, were presumably struck by a king, and it may be that they were produced in York; they do not seem to belong to any of the southern mints operating at this time. Even if there is room for doubt as to the commercial role of these gold issues which may have been struck primarily from political motives as a manifestation of royal power, there can be few such reservations about the later, silver coins. Silver coins may have been issued from as early as Aldfrith's reign,[38] and according to the limited number of analyses undertaken, these *sceattas* and *stycas* continued to have a high silver content to the end of the eighth century, becoming debased only in the ninth.[39] Although none of these coins bears a mint signature, it is at least possible and indeed very likely that some of them were minted at York, the most important center in Anglian Northumbria.

The existence of a trading center which stimulated the need for coinage has also been proposed from a consideration of placename elements. The element *wic* in *Eoforwic,* it has been pointed out, occurs in the early name forms of a number of south and east coast sites that are otherwise known as trading centers.[40] Palliser has suggested that the tenth–eleventh century *wic* may be equated with the *colonia* area but,[41] as noted above, there is no archaeological confirmation of such a commercial settlement here in the Anglian period. There is, however, new evidence for settlement of this date from the Fishergate area, north of the Ouse.

Limited excavations were undertaken in 1973–4 in Paragon Street, beyond the medieval city walls, on the site of the new Barbican Baths

and old Cattle Market (14), which had destroyed much of the earlier levels. Nonetheless a single Anglian feature was encountered containing,
among other things, a copper alloy cross-brooch with enameled decoration, and two coins of Eadberht (737–58).[42] Some 250m to the north
within the city walls at 118–26 Walmgate (15), excavations in 1978–9
that were extremely limited in their earliest levels nevertheless revealed
below Anglo-Scandinavian deposits a series of features that may be of
Anglian date,[43] although as at Paragon Street no Anglian pottery was recognized in association. More recently features probably of the Anglian
period, dated by the presence of a small quantity of contemporary pottery, have again been recognized, albeit within a very restricted area (16),
in cuttings through the city rampart just to the north of Walmgate Bar
which have proved that there was not a defensive line here before the
Norman period.[44] Together these three investigations within a radius of
about 120m suggest that there may have been Anglian settlement
throughout this vicinity, although the scale, density and more precise
chronology of that occupation is uncertain.

To their rather limited evidence may now be added the more comprehensive data being produced by an excavation at 46–54 Fishergate, a
riparian site some 250m south-west of the Paragon Street excavation, at
the confluence of the Ouse and Foss (17). Here, in the early thirteenth
century, the Gilbertine Priory of St. Andrew was established, perhaps on
the site of the church of St. Andrew referred to in *Domesday Book.* The
site is already known to students of the pre-Conquest period through a
gold ring, perhaps of the ninth or tenth century, found by chance earlier
this century.[45] Although the river margins of the Anglian period have not
been located, a 2500m^2 area of occupation has been examined in detail,
and trial cuttings show that similar deposits continue for at least 30m to
both north and south. Post-built structures, a number of stake alignments
and numerous pits have been defined, apparently laid out in regular
zones, which perhaps relate to individual properties. These features are
dated broadly to the Anglian period by a suite of artifacts including metalwork and pottery of the type first recognized at 16–22 Coppergate. It is
hoped that greater precision will be supplied by coin finds, which include
a hoard of four *sceattas,* at least some of which are of the "London" type
series L dated to around the second quarter of the eighth century. Evidence for crafts or industry includes loom weights. comb-making debris
and metalworking crucibles; a fragment of lava quern may represent
contemporary contact with the Rhineland, and imported pottery has also
been recognized.

Anglian York was the first target of the *micel here* of Viking warriors who captured it in 866. Documentary sources, among which the silver penny coinage minted in York for the first time at the very end of the ninth century may be included, show that Viking Age York was a prize hotly contested by rival Scandinavian kings and the English until, with the final expulsion of Erik Bloodaxe in 954, York and Northumbria were incorporated into the new pan-English state. Through all these political uncertainties the city continued to flourish, and in *Domesday Book* it is the largest urban site, surpassed only, it is supposed, by London. Yet Anglo-Scandinavian *Jorvik,* as it became known, remains almost as mysterious in many of its aspects as does Anglian *Eoforwic.*

Various pre- and post-Conquest sources include comments on the city's defenses[46] to which may be added the *Anonymous Life of St. Oswald* and the *Historia de Sancto Cuthberto.*[47] However in each case their reliability may be questioned, and archaeology alone will provide information on the extent of the defended area. Within the Roman fortress area Davison's defensive sequence adjacent to the Anglian Tower (1) extends into the Viking Age,[48] and additions to the rampart have been noted adjacent to 1–5 Aldwark (18).[49] Furthermore, Radley reinterpreted three sections dug across the north-west and north-east sides of the Roman fortress defenses by Miller in 1925–7 as also containing pre-Norman defensive elements (19–21).[50] By contrast it seems that the fortress's southeast and south-west defenses became increasingly less formidable as occupation material and other debris accumulated around them. This is the picture gained from a series of observations and excavations by Radley,[51] Ramm,[52] Stead,[53] and Wenham.[54] The evidence of street lines and property and parish boundaries equally emphasizes the continued role of the Roman defensive lines as topographical determinants, if not defensive barriers, into the eleventh and twelfth centuries at least. Definitive pronouncements on the degree of the wall's above-ground survival at any time are often impossible to make, either due to its obvious removal at a more recent date, as encountered at 7–9 Aldwark (22),[55] or because of the possibility of its earlier truncation above an already buried and thus surviving portion.

The development of the Roman fortress area in the Anglo-Scandinavian period remains a major historical *lacuna* The archbishopric was not extinguished by the Vikings and continued throughout the political turmoil, but no traces of a Viking Age cathedral were uncovered in Phillips's excavation, although a graveyard with Anglo-Scandinavian marker stones suggests that the church is close by. Extremely restricted excavation behind the Nuffield Purey Cust Hospital some 75m north-west of the Minster (23), just within the defenses and to the north of the Roman *porta principalis dextra,* has yielded a coin of the Viking king of York, Cnut (ca. 900), perhaps suggesting activity hereabouts at that time, although the nature of this activity could not be recognized.[56] This apart, there is nothing to add to the meager data presented in the last published survey.[57]

Across the River Ouse in the *colonia* area there is as yet no evidence for Viking Age defenses, but no recent excavation has penetrated the later medieval rampart layers. Palliser has suggested that the area was planned in an essentially grided layout, perhaps under the inspiration of the pre-Conquest archbishops who held land here, but that this grid has been camouflaged by later ecclesiastical changes and Norman military works.[58]

Architecture, sculpture and *Domesday Book* point to Anglo-Scandinavian churches on the sites of St. Mary Bishophill Senior (24) and Junior (7), St. Martin (9), and Holy Trinity (6) churches. At Clementhorpe (10) (see above) the possible Anglian church structure seems to have continued in use at this period, with the eponymous dedication to St. Clement perhaps originating under Scandinavian influence in the tenth or eleventh century.[59] Holy Trinity (alias Christchurch), perhaps the eighth century *monastarium,* was a particularly important church in the Anglo-Scandinavian period, enjoying rights and privileges extended elsewhere in Northumbria only to the minsters at York, Ripon, Beverley, and the church at Durham. All these south-bank churches indicate the presence of communities of some sort,[60] most clearly identified in Wenham's discovery of Scandinavian settlers buried around St. Mary Bishophill Junior in the 920s.[61]

Moulden and Tweddle's survey of archaeological and chance finds in this area shows a distribution of Anglo-Scandinavian material right across the *colonia.*[62] Apparent concentrations north of Micklegate, "the great street" (where nothing has been found because virtually no rebuilding has occurred since the eighteenth century), and to the east at Skeldergate Bridge/Baile Hall, probably reflect no more than the incidence of principal nineteenth century building works, and comparison of these two "concentrations" with the distribution of contemporary churches highlights the imbalance of the evidence. Certainly the density of Anglo-Scandinavian settlement is not known, for only five sites have produced archaeologically excavated evidence for secular occupation or activity. Buildings have been recovered only at 58–9 Skeldergate (13), where they were laid out in the late ninth or early tenth century.[63] A few pits were located at 37 Bishophill Senior (25),[64] occupation deposits were uncovered at Baile Hill,[65] as well as apparently unassociated finds at 5 Rougier Street (5) and 24–30 Tanner Row (26).[66] In all, the finds are overwhelmingly domestic in nature—there is little evidence for manufacturing or commerce.

This contrasts with the evidence from the area east of the fortress on the spit or *ness* between the two rivers. This area had been extramural in the Roman period, but the defensive enclosure which encompassed it in the later medieval period probably originated before the conquest. A similar Anglo-Scandinavian extension of the Roman defenses has been suggested at Chester.[67] Indeed a more positive method of determining when the south-west and south-east sides of the fortress became obsolete (see above) requires the examination of additions to the fortress walls running to the Ouse from near the west corner and towards the Foss from off the east corner; opportunities here have not yet arisen. An enlargement of the defended circuit has long been recognized, and was illustrated by Radley,[68] but the precise course depicted there is certainly based on some misapprehensions. Elements in it, such as the "stockade" at 27 High Ousegate, or the "rampart" at Hungate (12), can be reinterpreted[69] and attention should be focused not on Radley's illustration but on his accompanying text.[70]

Within this area, from partial excavation of just five tenements and from observations in a few others, there is now evidence for the practice of a range of crafts, including leatherworking, in particular cobbling/cordwaining,[71] the working of jet, amber, iron, lead, copper alloy, silver and gold,[72] glassworking[73] and the lathe-turning of wooden bowls and cups.[74] In addition bone/antler working[75] and textile manufacture and dyeing[76] may have been carried out on either a commercial or a domestic scale of production. This area has also produced evidence for the contacts Jorvik enjoyed—a wide-ranging orbit centered on Scandinavia, the Scandinavian colonies in Scotland and Ireland, and north-western Europe, but extending to the east end of the Mediterranean, the Near East and as far as Samarkand. The objects that emanated from these areas did not, of course, all reach York as the result of trading activities, but some, such as the quantity of Byzantine silks found at 16–22 Coppergate, almost certainly did.

The chronology of this movement back to an area largely barren of indications of Anglian occupation has been established at 16–22 Coppergate (11). After desertion throughout the fifth to mid ninth centuries, activity began again just at or slightly before the Viking takeover. By ca. 900 elements of what was to be an enduring layout were in being, and by ca. 930/5 tenements were well established. The motives and personnel behind these developments remain speculative, however. Was a royal prerogative behind the planning of the regular tenements, or the initiative of aristocrats or entrepreneurs? How much of Coppergate and the surrounding locale was treated in this way? There are indications of broadly similar developments between 25–7 High Ousegate and 5–7 Coppergate (27),[77] but their chronology is unknown.

Further developments at 16–22 Coppergate took place ca. 975 when two ranks of buildings at the head of most tenements replaced the earlier single structures there, perhaps reflecting a specialized use of one rank for craft purposes rather than a growing population. Subsequently the erection of what may have been a warehouse nearer the Foss river front on one tenement took place in the 1030s.

Another indication of the rebirth of this area comes from excavation at 21–33 Aldwark (28), a site immediately south-east of the fortress, where the church of St. Helen-on-the-Walls was shown to have had its origin in the tenth century.[78] This indication of a community contrasts with the general absence of earlier pre-Conquest material in the vicinity, and particularly with the absence of any signs of pre-church occupation above the remains of an underlying Roman townhouse.

It should be appreciated that the picture of a densely occupied manufacturing/artisan quarter now well established in the Coppergate-Ousegate-Pavement area may also be applicable to much of the fortress area. The archaeological difficulties here include the lack of opportunity for excavation and the later medieval removal of relevant levels; to these may be coupled the general absence of waterlogged deposits.

Occupation and activity also extended eastward across the River Foss into the Walmgate area. The church of St. Denys (29) was a pre-Conquest foundation, attested by sculpture. Occupation deposits have been examined at 118–26 Walmgate (15), some 400m from the present bridging-point of the Foss,[79] and the tenth–twelfth century comb-making debris has been retrieved at Leadmill Lane (30).[80] The sections through the ramparts adjacent toWalmgate Bar (16) that proved that there was no pre-Conquest defensive line here did reveal traces of Anglo-Scandinavian activity.[81] This, however, leaves the question of whether there was a defended bridgehead east of the Foss crossing, and if so, where it lay. The Anglo-Scandinavian Walmgate area merged with Fishergate, where the late-eleventh century archbishops enjoyed rights, as they did directly across the River Ouse in Clementhorpe.

The final component of Jorvik was an area between the Roman fortress and Marygate, where there had been a defended Roman enclosure. This area was known to the eighteenth century historian Drake as *Earlsburgh,* and here, according to the *Anglo-Saxon Chronicle,* Earl Siward (ca. 1030–55) had built (or perhaps rebuilt) a church which he dedicated to St. Olaf. This, taken in conjunction with the place-name, leaves little room to doubt that the palace of the Anglo-Scandinavian earls was nearby.

The care with which these earls, and the archbishops of York were chosen by the English kings indicates their desire to control Jorvik, not only to negate a political welcome for Scandinavian invaders, but also to ensure that the city's wealth was available to the English economy and to the kings themselves. In 1066 King Harold Godwinson had two reeves in the city, presumably to look after royal commercial interests, and if political necessity had not focused William I's attention on York, economic desirability would undoubtedly have done so.

ACKNOWLEDGMENTS

I am most grateful to all my colleagues at York Archaeological Trust who have discussed aspects of this paper with me. The illustrations were prepared by Erich Kadow, and the text was typed by Stephanie Crosby.

NOTES

[1] P. J. Ottaway, "Colonia Eburacensis: A Review of Recent Work," in P. V. Addyman and V. E. Black, eds., *Archaeological Papers from York Presented to M. W. Barley* (York, 1984), 28–33, at pp. 32–33.

[2] J. N. L. Myres, *The English Settlements* (Oxford, 1986; corrected ed. 1989), 196.

[3] B. N. Eagles, *The Anglo-Saxon Settlement of Humberside,* B.A.R. Brit. ser. 68 (Oxford, 1979), 240–41.

[4] M. L. Faull, "Roman and Anglian Settlement Patterns in Yorkshire," *Northern Hist.* 9 (1974), 1–25, at p. 23; M. L. Faull, "British Survival in Anglo-Saxon Northumbria," in L. Laing, ed., *Studies in Celtic Survival,* B.A.R. Int. ser. 37 (Oxford, 1977), 1–55, at pp 2–3.

[5] H. G. Ramm, "The End of Roman York," in R. M. Butler, ed., *Soldier and Civilian in Roman Yorkshire* (Leicester, 1971), 179–99, at pp. 181–83; J. Radley and C. Simms, *Yorkshire Flooding—Some Effects on Man and Nature* (York, 1971), 9.

[6] D. Phillips, "Excavations at York Minster 1967–73," *Friends of York Minster 46th Annual Report, 1975,* 19–27, at p. 24. For the sculpture from York Min-

ster see, J. Lang, *Corpus of Anglo-Saxon Stone Sculpture 3. York and Eastern Yorkshire* (Oxford, 1991), 53–78.

[7] D. Phillips, *Excavations at York Minster II: The Cathedral of Archbishop Thomas of Bayeux* (London, 1985), 50ff.

[8] M. Biddle and D. Hudson, *The Future of London's Past* (Worcester, 1973), 20.

[9] J. Radley, "Excavations in the Defenses of the City of York: An Early Medieval Stone Tower and the Successive Earth Ramparts," *Yorkshire Archaeol. J.* 44 (1972), 38–64.

[10] L. Webster and J. Cherry, "Medieval Britain in 1971," *M.A.* 16 (1972), 147–212, at pp.165–67; R. Hall and B. K. Davison, "Investigations Adjacent to the Anglian Tower, 1970," in P. V. Addyman, ed., The Archaeol. of York 11 (forthcoming). Some useful background is provided in R. A. Hall, P. Ottaway and B. K. Davison, "B. K. Davison's Investigations of York's Defences between the Multangular and Anglian Towers, 1970," in P. J. Ottaway, *Excavations and Observations on the Defences and Adjacent Sites 1971–90,* P. V. Addyman, ed., The Archaeol. of York 3.3 (1996), 256–72.

[11] D. R. Wilson, "Roman Britain in 1971. Sites Explored," *Britannia* 3 (1972), 299–351, at p. 309.

[12] P. C. Buckland, "The 'Anglian Tower' and the use of Jurrasic Limestone in York," in Addyman and Black, *Archaeological Papers from York,* 51–57.

[13] J. Radley, "Excavations in the Defences of the City of York," 46.

[14] R.C.A.H.M., *An Inventory of Monuments in the City of York, 5, The Central Area,* (London, 1981), 94.

[15] P. V. Addyman, "York Archaeological Trust Work in 1975," *Ann. Rep. Yorkshire Philosoph. Soc., 1975,* 30–37, at p. 34.

[16] G. Andrews, "Archaeology in York: An Assessment," in Addyman and Black, *Archaeological Papers from York,* 173–208, at p. 199.

[17] Cf. D. Tweddle, "A Fragment of Anglian Metalwork from Blake Street," in ibid., 58–62.

[18] R. Cramp, *Anglian and Viking York,* Borthwick Papers 33 (1967), pl. IV.

[19] L. P. Wenham, "Excavations and Discoveries within the Legionary Fortress in Davygate, York, 1955–8," *Yorkshire Archaeol. J.* 40 (1962), 507–87, at p. 547, fig. 18, no. 120.

[20] J. Moulden and D. Tweddle, *Anglo-Scandinavian Settlement South-west of the Ouse,* in P. V. Addyman, ed., The Archaeol. of York 8.1 (1986), 7, 16.

[21] D. M. Wilson, "Two 9th-century Strap-ends from York," *M.A.* 8 (1964), 214–16.

[22] P. V. Addyman, "York Archaeological Trust Work in 1981," *Ann. Rep. Yorkshire Philosoph. Soc. 1981,* 34–53, at p. 45 and pl. 16.

[23] D. M. Palliser, "York's West Bank: Medieval Suburb or Urban Nucleus," in Addyman and Black, *Archaeological Papers from York,* 101–08, at pp. 104–05.

[24] R. Morris, "Alcuin, York and the Alma Sophia," in L. A. S. Butler and R. K. Morris, eds., *The Anglo-Saxon Church: Papers on History, Architecture and Archaeology in Honour of Dr. H. M. Taylor,* C.B.A. Research Rep. 60 (London, 1986), 80–89.

[25] R. B. Dobson and S. Donaghey, *The History of Clementhorpe Nunnery,* in P. V. Addyman, ed., The Archaeol. of York 2.1 (London, 1984), 7; D. Brinklow, "A pre-Conquest Structure at Clementhorpe," in Moulden and Tweddle, *Anglo-Scandinavian Settlement,* 57–61.

[26] D. M. Waterman, "Late Saxon, Viking and Early Medieval Finds from York," *Archaeologia* 97 (1959), 59–106, at p. 80 and fig. 10.6.

[27] D. Tweddle, *The Coppergate Helmet* (York, 1984); see also D. Tweddle, *The Anglian Helmet from 16–22 Coppergate,* in P. V. Addyman, ed., *The Archaeol.* of York 17.8 (London, 1992).

[28] A. J. Mainman, *Anglo-Scandinavian Pottery from 16–22 Coppergate,* in P. V. Addyman, ed., The Archaeol. of York 16.5 (London, 1990).

[29] P. V. Addyman, "Archaeology in York 1831–1981," in C. H. Feinstein, ed., *York 1831–1981* (York, 1981), 53–87, at p. 69.

[30] K. M. Richardson, "Excavations in Hungate, York," *Archaeol. J.* 116 (1959), 51–114, *passim.*

[31] S. Donaghey and R. A. Hall, "Anglo-Scandinavian Structures and Features at Skeldergate and Bishophill: 58–59 Skeldergate," in Moulden and Tweddle, *Anglo-Scandinavian Settlement,* 37–52, at p. 48.

[32] D. Whitelock, *English Historic Documents I c. 500–1042* (London, 1955), 725.

[33] J. G. Hurst, "The Wharram Research Project: Results to 1983," *M.A.* 28 (1984), 77–111, at p. 82.

[34] E. J. E. Pirie, *Post-Roman Coins from York Excavations 1971–81,* in P. V. Addyman, ed., The Archaeol. of York 18.1 (London, 1986), 51.

[35] D. M. Metcalf, "Monetary Circulation in Southern England in the First Half of the Eighth Century," in D. H. Hill and D. M. Metcalf, eds., *Sceattas in England and on the Continent,* B.A.R. Brit. ser. 128 (Oxford, 1984), 27–69, at pp. 68–69.

[36] E. J. E. Pirie, "Some Northumbrian Finds of Sceattas," in Hill and Metcalf, *Sceattas in England and on the Continent,* 207–16, at pp. 208–09.

[37] I. Stewart, "Anglo-Saxon Gold Coins," in R. A. G. Carson and C. M. Kraay, eds., *Scripta nummaria Romana: Essays Presented to Humphrey Sutherland* (London, 1978), 143–72, at p. 149; P. Grierson and M. Blackburn, *Medieval*

European Coinage 1: The Early Middle Ages (5th–10th Centuries) (Cambridge, 1986), 643.

[38] Pirie, "Some Northumbrian Finds of Sceattas," 209–11.

[39] J. Booth, "Sceattas in Northumbria," in Hill and Metcalf, *Sceattas in England and on the Continent,* 32–95, at p. 88.

[40] S. Reynolds, *An Introduction to the History of English Medieval Towns* (Oxford, 1977), 24–27; A. R. Rumble, "HAMTVN alias HAMWIC (Saxon Southampton): The Place-name Traditions and their Significance," in P. Holdsworth, *Excavations at Melbourne Street, Southampton, 1971–76,* C.B.A. Research Rep. 33 (London, 1980), 7–19, at p. 11.

[41] Palliser, "York's West Bank," 103, 107–08.

[42] M. Redmond, "Swimming Pool Site, Paragon Street: Anglian Finds," in P. V. Addyman, *Excavations in York 1973–1974, Second Interim Report* (York, 1976), 12.

[43] P. V. Addyman, "York Archaeological Trust Work in 1979," *Ann. Rep. Yorkshire Philosophical Soc., 1979,* 28–50, at p. 33.

[44] B. Barber, "Excavations Through the City Defences near Walmgate Bar," in P. V. Addyman, ed., The Archaeol. of York 11, forthcoming.

[45] Cramp, *Anglian and Viking York,* 18 and pl. viib.

[46] Waterman, "Late Saxon, Viking and Early Medieval Finds," 67.

[47] J. Raine, ed., *The Historians of the Church of York and its Archbishops,* Rolls Series 71, 3 vols. (London, 1879) vol. 1, 454; J. Hinde, ed., *Symeonis Dunelmensis Opera et Collectanea,* Surtees Society LI (Durham, 1868), 144.

[48] Hall and Davison, "Investigations Adjacent to the Anglian Tower."

[49] H. MacGregor and R. A. Hall, "Structures on the North-East Side of Aldwark Adjacent to 1–5 Aldwark," in R. A. Hall, H. MacGregor, M. Stockwell, *Medieval Tenements in Aldwark and Other Sites,* in P. V. Addyman, ed., The Archaeol. of York 10.2 (London, 1988), 63–88.

[50] Radley, "Excavations in the Defences of the City of York," 57–58.

[51] J. Radley, "Two Interval Towers and New Sections of the Roman Fortress Wall, York," *Yorkshire Archaeol. J.* 42 (1970), 399–402.

[52] H. G. Ramm, "Roman York: Excavations in 1955," *J. Roman Stud.* 46 (1956), 76–90.

[53] I. M. Stead, "Excavations at the South Corner Tower of the Roman Fortress at York 1956," *Yorkshire Archaeol. J.* 39 (1958), 515–37; I. M. Stead, "An Excavation at King's Square, York, 1957," *Yorkshire Archaeol. J.* 42 (1968), 151–64.

[54] J. Dyer and L. P. Wenham, "Excavations and Discoveries in a Cellar in Messrs. Chas Hart's Premises, Feasgate, York, 1956," *Yorkshire Archaeol. J.* 39 (1958), 419–25; L. P. Wenham, "Excavations and Discoveries Adjoining the South-West Wall of the Roman Legionary Fortress in Feasgate, York, 1955–

1957," *Yorkshire Archaeol. J.* 40 (1961), 329–50; Wenham, "Excavations and Discoveries within the Legionary Fortress in Davygate"; L. P. Wenham, "Discoveries in King's Square, York, 1963," *Yorkshire Archaeol J.* 42 (1968), 165–68.

[55] M. Stockwell and P. J. Ottaway, "Medieval Levels at 7–9 Aldwark," in Hall, MacGregor and Stockwell, *Medieval Tenements in Aldwark,* 112–16.

[56] N. F. Pearson, "Excavations at the Nuffield Purey Cust Hospital," in P. V. Addyman, ed., The Archaeol. of York (forthcoming).

[57] R. A. Hall, "The Topography of Anglo-Scandinavian York," in R. A. Hall, ed., *Viking Age York and the North,* C.B.A. Research Rep. 27 (London, 1978), 31–36, at p. 34.

[58] Palliser, "York's West Bank," 105.

[59] Dobson and Donaghey, *The History of Clementhorpe,* 7.

[60] Cf. C. Briden and D. Stocker, "The Tower of the Church of St. Mary Bishophill Junior," in L. P. Wenham, R. A. Hall, C. Briden and D. Stocker, *St. Mary Bishophill Junior and St. Mary Castlegate,* in P.V. Addyman, ed., The Archaeol. of York 8.2 (London, 1987), 84–146.

[61] L. P. Wenham and R. A. Hall, "St. Mary Bishophill Junior Excavation to the North of the Church," in ibid., 74–83.

[62] Moulden and Tweddle, *Anglo-Scandinavian Settlement.*

[63] Donaghey and Hall, "Anglo-Scandinavian Structures."

[64] M. Carver, "Anglo-Scandinavian Structures and Features at Skeldergate and Bishophill: 37 Bishophill Senior," in Moulden and Tweddle, *Anglo-Scandinavian Settlement,* 53–56.

[65] P. V. Addyman and J. Priestley, "Baile Hill, York." *Archaeol. J.* 134 (1977), 115–56, at pp. 122–24.

[66] Moulden and Tweddle, *Anglo-Scandinavian Settlement,* 12.

[67] D. J. P. Mason, *Excavations at Chester, 26–42 Lower Bridge Street 1974–6. The Dark Age and Saxon Periods,* Grosvenor Mus. Archaeol. Excavation and Survey Rep. 3, (Chester, 1985), 38.

[68] J. Radley, "Economic Aspects of Anglo-Danish York," *M.A.* 15 (1971), 37–57, at fig. 5.

[69] R. A. Hall, "Observations at 5–7 Coppergate," in P. V. Addyman and R. A. Hall, *Urban Structures and Defences, Including the Lloyds Bank Excavations,* in P. V. Addyman, ed., The Archaeol. of York 8.3 (London, 1991), 238–50. See also, R. A. Hall, "Anglo-Scandinavian Defences North-East of the Ouse," in ibid., 264–77.

[70] Radley, "Economic Aspects of Anglo-Danish York," 39.

[71] A. MacGregor, *Anglo-Scandinavian Finds from Lloyds Bank, Pavement and other Sites,* in P.V. Addyman, ed., The Archaeol. of York 17.3 (London, 1982), 136ff.

[72] E. Roesdahl, et al., *The Vikings in England* (London, 1981), *passim.*

[73] J. Bayley, "Non-ferrous Metal and Glass-working in Anglo-Scandinavian England: An Interim Statement," *Pact 7* (1982), 487–96, at pp. 493–95; J. Bayley, "Viking Glassworking: The Evidence from York," *Annales du 10e congrès de l'Association Internationale pour l'Histoire du Verre* (Madrid & Segovia, 1987), 245–54.

[74] C. Morris, "Aspects of Anglo-Saxon and Anglo-Scandinavian Lathe-turning," in S. McGrail, ed., *Woodworking Techniques before A.D. 1500,* B.A.R. Int. ser. 129 (Oxford, 1982), 245–61.

[75] Roesdahl, et al., *The Vikings in England,* 112–16.

[76] MacGregor, *Anglo-Scandinavian Finds from Lloyds Bank,* 100–36; R. A. Hall, et al., "Dyeplants from Viking York," *Antiquity* 58 (1984), 58–60.

[77] G. Benson, "Notes on Excavations at 25, 26 and 27 High Ousegate, York" *Ann. Rep. of the Yorkshire Philosoph. Soc. For 1902,* 64–67; Hall, "Observations at 5–7 Coppergate."

[78] J. R. Magilton, *The Church of St. Helen-on-the-Walls, Aldgate,* in P. V. Addyman, ed., The Archaeol. of York 10.1 (London, 1980), 37.

[79] Andrews, "Archaeology in York," 202.

[80] MacGregor, *Anglo-Scandinavian Finds from Lloyds Bank,* 94–95.

[81] Barber, "Excavations Through the City Defences."

CHAPTER 6

Monkwearmouth and Jarrow in their Continental Context

ROSEMARY CRAMP

When the twin foundations of St. Peter's Wearmouth and St. Paul's Jarrow were founded in 674 and 682 respectively,[1] the monastic movement was already long established in Europe, the British Isles and Ireland, and many monastic houses, such as the influential center of St. Honorat Lérins had already accepted and modified, or exchanged, different Rules for the conduct of their lives. To say before the ninth century that a monk "followed a Rule" simply implied that he lived in accordance with an ideal of asceticism and prayerful relationship to God, established long before by the Desert Fathers of the movement, and which the founder of his institution had transmitted as a personal adaptation.

In his dying address to his community, Benedict Biscop, the founder of Wearmouth/Jarrow, declared, according to Bede's well known account, that he had derived his "Rule" from the best employed in seventeen monasteries in England and the Continent[2]; but it is hard today to establish what manner of choice he had. We only know for certain two or three establishments, such as Lérins and Canterbury, which would have been included in the seventeen; but even if we knew the names of the others, we have neither enough textual nor archaeological evidence to determine the appearance, life style, or economic base of any of them. It may be thought, therefore, that this is a topic in which one can reach very few firm conclusions. Nevertheless, despite the fact that there are for the seventh to eighth centuries no completely excavated monastic sites from Britain and Europe, and from Ireland only two small hermitages, excavations are in progress on several sites, and there is today a welcome tendency to look to the outer periphery of these often very large settlements and not just at the churches and cult centers. It seems then a convenient moment to take stock of what we know currently concerning early medieval monasteries, whose communities filled such a gap in the education of the post-Roman and pre-Carolingian era and produced from their scriptoria and other workshops books, metalwork and sculpture, which survive to be admired today.

In this short space I can only be selective; but I shall attempt to consider the plans and physical appearance of these sites and then some of the evidence for the supporting economy of the two specific sites of my title. The appearance of Wearmouth and Jarrow is of interest because their founder clearly made a conscious choice to create in them something new and carefully contrived. The buildings of the first generation of western monasteries were not distinctive in their forms and layout. The founders sometimes converted one of their houses for communal monastic use or constructed a simple building in the local style. Sometimes they followed the example of the desert ascetics by living in wooden cabins and caves in the rocks as St. Martin did at Marmoutier or St. Benedict at Subiaco.[3]

PLANS AND PHYSICAL APPEARANCE:
EARLIER MODELS

Edward James who has discussed fully the evidence for Gaulish monasticism, in reminding us that in the sixth century many of the Gaulish monastic buildings may have been in wood, noted the description of Condat with its wooden buildings comprising "individual cells attached to each other by beams," and also that it had been "doubled by finely built upper storeys."[4] This form may have existed also in Britain, since the account of the ancient monastery of Abingdon describes individual cells attached to the surrounding wall, although nothing has been found to support this.[5] Likewise, the crop-mark revealed by aerial photography near the church at Ninekirks, Cumbria, occurs on a site which has been traditionally associated with the sixth-century bishop Ninian. The site consists of a wooden enclosure and wooden buildings attached to it,[6] and there are caves on the opposite side of the river, which were used as late as the eighteenth century, and so this could have been a British monastery with associated eremetical buildings. Of course the site could equally have been secular rather than monastic, and this exemplifies the continuing problem of how to identify early monastic sites and to distinguish them from early medieval secular sites, which was voiced as long

ago as a monastic conference held at Edinburgh in 1973.[7] The functions
of recently excavated sites, such as Brandon and Flixborough, are similarly ambiguous, although it may be reasonable to see them as exempla
of the variety in form such sites could take.[8] It is unfortunate that so little
is known concerning the early appearance of the important site of Glastonbury, and indeed that the sixth-century monastic sites in Wales[9] and
Cornwall[10] are also hardly capable of reconstruction outside the texts. It
is particularly unfortunate also that we know so little about the appearance of anything save the churches of the monasteries founded by the
Augustinian mission in Kent, since Benedict Biscop must have known at
least the monastery of St. Peter and St. Paul well when he was acting
abbot there, before he founded Wearmouth and Jarrow.

However, before Benedict Biscop set off about 653 on his first trav-
els abroad, he could have seen at first hand in his native Northumbria
several of the monasteries built in the first fifteen years of the Ionan mission, and he would not necessarily have excluded their customs when he
later assembled the Rule of his House. The appearance of these "Ionan"
monasteries would certainly have included such features as prominent
enclosures, as well as timber buildings in the Irish manner such as have
been excavated at Iona.[11] The Saxon buildings of the mother house of the
Ionan mission at Lindisfarne have not been excavated; but some parts of
Hartlepool and Whitby, two of its colonies, have been. Both of these had
links, through St. Hilda, with Gaulish double monasteries in northern
France, to which it had been customary to send high-born Anglo-Saxon
female postulants. I have discussed these sites elsewhere,[12] and here I
wish only to stress three points, two of which will recur again. First, the
scale of the distribution of the remains at Hartlepool, which probably
filled the whole headland up to the medieval boundary, reminds one of
how widespread were the activities on these early sites. Second, the
buildings are identical in form and in their constructional development—
from spaced posts to post-in-trench—with Middle Saxon secular buildings. Third, the more unusual development from earth-fast timbers to
timbers set on a groundsill of stone is well dated at Hartlepool.[13] This
construction may be the same as that which has recently been discovered
at Whithorn in Galloway, where an ancient timber church was reset on
stone foundations and a funerary chapel of painted daub was constructed
on such foundations.[14] Such a construction seems to have been described
also in the Life of Saint Philibert at Jumièges, when his cell is stated to be
"petreo margine florescente"—"adorned with a stone border." The problems of interpreting this phrase are discussed by James;[15] but the idea

that one is "improving" a wooden building by adding a stone base is borne out by Whithorn and the rebuilding of Whitby.

After Benedict Biscop's visits to Rome and his sojourn and ton-suring at Lérins, his intention was, as mentioned above, to build a monastery which was different from the buildings of the Celtic mission and the native Anglo-Saxon buildings, since it was to be "in the Roman manner." There is not much at Lérins today which indicates whether any buildings there served as a model. The surviving churches are, as on so many Merovingian sites, the only excavated features to compare with Wearmouth/Jarrow.[16] It seems probable that the unknown monastery in Gaul, from which Benedict acquired his builders, could have been in the northern half of France, since such sites as Evrecy have yielded compa-rable architectural sculpture.[17] The fact that he sent to Gaul rather than to Italy for masons to accomplish his ideal may mean that he had to be pragmatic when looking for easily available talent—the Roman tradition was a complex one at that time and recoverable in many places. As we shall see, by the time he constructed Jarrow, he seems to have derived some inspiration as well as raw material from the surviving Roman buildings in his own country.

PLANS AND PHYSICAL APPEARANCE: WEARMOUTH/JARROW

The site which the king gave him at the mouth of the River Wear for his first monastic establishment may have already been a lay burial ground.[18] There are also some buildings, such as D (which may be a structure with stone footings and wooden superstructure, like the Hartlepool and Whitby buildings), which were built before the Gaulish masons arrived (fig. 6.1).

The first and most important building certainly to be constructed by the Gaulish craftsmen was the church. The church of St. Peter, built within a year between 674 and 675, was not a large building, although its nave proportions of 5.64 by 19.5m (18 ft. 6 in. by 64 ft.) are not dissimi-lar to those of many Merovingian churches. The church may originally have had, like Jarrow, narrow aisles both to north and south or only on one side. Narrow naves with a single narrow aisle on the north side may have originated in Syria, and the Merovingian church of St. Martin's at Angers also possessed a single narrow aisle on the south,[19] while the fu-nerary church of St. Peter at Moutier Grandval possessed a very narrow southern aisle of the proportions of Wearmouth/Jarrow,[20] and it is prob-

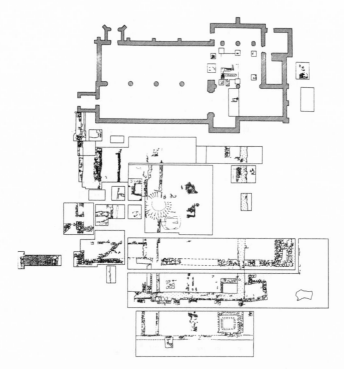

Fig. 6.1. Wearmouth. General Plan of Excavated Stone Structures.

able that the church of St. Mary's, Lyminge, Kent, also had narrow side aisles.[21]

There was some sort of western adjunct at Monkwearmouth which preceded the porch; but its form is uncertain, since only a small area of walling was noted by the author in an electricity cable trench. There also seems to have been a narthex, which preceded the porch, and it seems likely that there were two chambers at the east end, not only because of the vestiges of walls excavated on the north, but because of the description of the icons which Benedict hung across the east wall.[22] The precise form of the chancel is unknown; but the east end of the church was used as a funerary *"porticus,"* where the abbots were buried.[23] This may have been considered either as a chancel or as a separate adjunct.

Benedict, one year after his building work had begun, sent again to Gaul for glaziers to glaze the windows of the church, upper chambers or refectories, and the *porticus*. This raises two issues, the glass and the nature of the porticus. Colored window glass from both Monkwear-mouth and Jarrow has been recovered in some quantity,[24] and recent re-search suggests that in appearance and chemical type it is very similar to the glass from the ongoing excavations at San Vincenzo al Volturno.[25] The word *"porticus,"* it is clear from the usage of other early Christian writers, could have referred to a long narrow adjunct like an aisle or gallery, or a smaller chamber such as a sacristy. The long corridor at Monkwearmouth (fig. 6.2), which is joined to wall K at foundation level and peters out by modern drains 35.5m (110 ft.) to the north, is a distinc-tive feature south of the church. It may have joined an aisle or range of porticus of the church. James compares this feature with the account of the restoration work undertaken in the early ninth century by Ansegis, abbot of Luxeuil, in which "he renewed the *porticus* that went from the church of St. Peter to the church of St. Martin, and he covered it, fixing wooden shingles to it with iron nails."[26] It is not certain what the corridor at Monkwearmouth led to; but in the fashion of other English sites like Canterbury or Hexham, or of continental sites such as Nivelles, at least

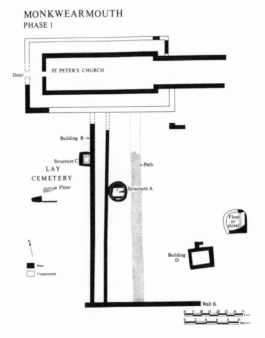

Fig. 6.2. Wearmouth. Saxon Phase 1.

two other churches or chapels are recorded at Wearmouth, and so perhaps the Monkwearmouth corridor led, as at Luxeuil or the later church of St. Riquier, to another church. This might have been the chapel of St. Lawrence, which Bede tells us was in or against the dormitory of the brethren, and which Abbot Ceolfrith visited on his way down to the river when he left on his last journey in 716.[27] The corridor, as well as being a covered way between buildings, may also have served to divide off the lay burial ground, with its densely packed graves of men, women and children to the west, from the monastic burial ground to its east.

The early structures (fig. 6.3), including the church, corridor and substantial enclosure wall of period 2, are all constructed in a poured-concrete technique. One certain and another possible mortar mixer have been found, and the constructional technique of making the walls was well illustrated by the southern termination of the corridor, in which it could be seen that the walls were built against the face of undisturbed sand, perhaps in shuttering.

Despite the fact that Wearmouth was, as Bede records, the larger of

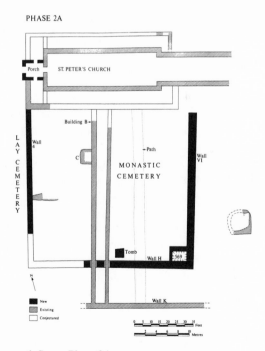

Fig. 6.3. Wearmouth Saxon Phase 2A.

PHASE 2B

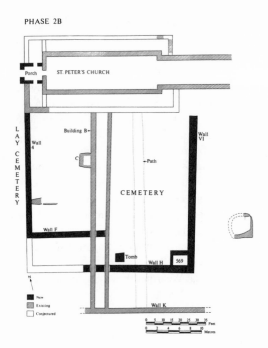

Fig. 6.4. Wearmouth. Saxon Phase 2B.

the two parts of the twin monastery, we do not know how large, since no termination has been found on any side. There was obviously pressure on space, though, within the area enclosed, since large buildings, perhaps of two stories, were inserted into the space enclosed in phases 2 and 3 (figs. 6.3 and 6.4), some parts of them covering areas of the lay cemetery. The corridor was not cut; but the new buildings were built up to and perhaps over it. Unfortunately I do not know the function of any of the buildings at Wearmouth; but the potentially two-storied buildings at the south could have contained dormitories, and if two-storied they could have been used for other functions at ground level. They are not of the scale of the much discussed dormitory at Jumièges described in St. Filibert's *Vita*. This lay to the south of the church, was two-storied, 290 "feet" long and fifty "feet" wide, with a glass window lighting every bed.[28] Its ground floor was divided for two purposes, the storage of wine and the preparation of food.

    The latest Saxon plan of Wearmouth (fig. 6.5), with the buildings, of its cult center at least, joined by a corridor and enclosed within a wall in

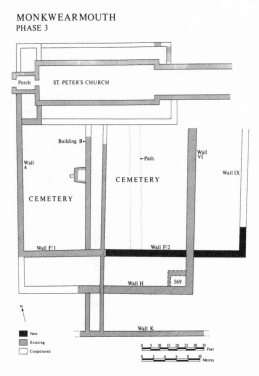

MONKWEARMOUTH
PHASE 3

Porch   ST. PETER'S CHURCH

Building B

Wall
4

←Path

Wall
VI

C   CEMETERY   Wall IX

CEMETERY

Wall F/1   Wall F/2

Wall H   569

Wall K

■ New
▨ Existing
□ Conjectured

Fig. 6.5. Wearmouth. Saxon Phase 3.

an orderly layout, is very Roman in appearance, an appearance which must have been accentuated by the painted striped plaster on some of the walls, the painted balusters, and the red-brick floors, not to mention the colored glass windows. However, the fragments of decorated pilasters and panels which have been excavated, together with the elaborate little open portal and façade of the church porch, present a non-Roman appearance and one which combines both insular and continental ornamental details.[29]

I have no firm evidence to date the various phases of the Monkwearmouth building development, save that the porch seems to have been added to the church before the burial of Eosterwine there ca. 685/6,[30] and that the enclosure wall is bonded into and is of the same constructional type as the church and porch, whilst wall H, although rebuilt almost from foundation level, is of the same type. Only wall F/2 has clay-bonded cobble foundations, and is more like the Jarrow constructions.

It seems probable that, like the other visiting experts such as John the arch-cantor, the Gaulish masons went back to their homeland after some time, having trained English successors, and it is not implied from contemporary accounts that they took part in the building of Jarrow.[31] What is certain is that the building program, from ca. 681/2, when the Wearmouth brethren went to the site, to the dedication, although not necessarily the completion, of the "basilica" of St. Paul in 685, was not as speedy as the building of St. Peter's. Nor was the Roman manner the same. It seems to be the manner of local Roman buildings, such as would have been found at the nearby fort of South Shields or on the Roman Wall across the Tyne to the north. The small neat sandstone blocks form the superstructure of trench-built walls with clay-and-cobble foundations, and this is the method of construction of the larger western church—the basilica, and also of Building A, which may be a refectory with a dormitory above. On the other hand, Building B and the eastern church, which survives as the present chancel, have simpler foundations (fig.6.6).

I have written elsewhere about the similarities of the churches at Wearmouth and Jarrow in their proportions and style.[32] Both had naves about 5.6m wide and 19.8m long internally, and both originally had a

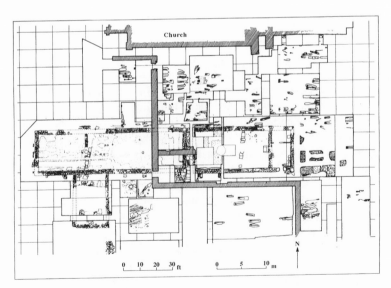

Fig. 6.6. Jarrow. Saxon Cemetery and Buildings A and B.

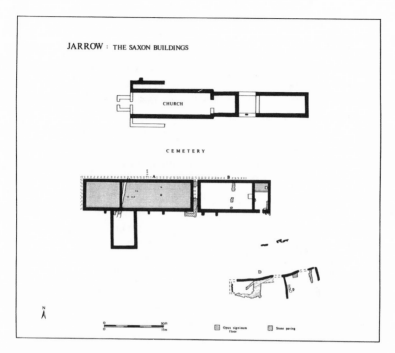

Fig. 6.7. Jarrow. Excavated Saxon Stone Buildings.

narrow aisle. It is possible that from the beginning St. Paul's Jarrow had a porch of entry, and it is certain that it had a square-ended chancel. At Jarrow (fig. 6.6, 6.7) the originally independent eastern church is plausibly interpreted as a funerary chapel, like the eastern porticus at Wearmouth. It is sited in the middle of an early cemetery, with doors opening north and south into the cemetery, and, if the two upright stones at the base of the east wall were some form of oculus, then it might have housed a prestigious tomb or tombs. This position of the funerary chapel to the east of the main church is also paralleled at Whithorn, as described below. We do not know any more of the relative building dates of the east and west churches than of the relative building dates of Buildings A and B, which lie to the south of the cemetery, about 15.24m from the church, because by great misfortune the stratigraphy between them is cut by modern buildings.

Building B sits very neatly in the center of the church complex, if one assumes that both the churches co-existed from the beginning, and, if its position was determined by a pre-existing cemetery, it may have been built first. On the other hand the division wall of Building A, which creates to the east of it a building of the same dimensions as B, lines up neatly with the west wall of the nave, and the decorative wall plaques, as well as the column with vine-scroll ornament discovered within its ruins, compare very well in style and quality with the decorative friezes which by tradition derive from the church.[33]

Both buildings are constructed on the same modules, and both must, I think, belong to the first building phase, although there are modifications to Building A in later phases. Building A has been interpreted as a refectory, and Building B as a meeting or communal work room.[34] The original appearance of A, if the larger eastern section were for eating and the small western section for storage, reminds one of the description of the divided refectory at Fontenelle,[35] while both on that site and on early monastic sites in Ireland there are, as well as the refectory, a few other large multi-purpose buildings.[36] Whether these interpretations are correct or not, buildings A and B may in any case be seen as a development of the two buildings within the same range at Wearmouth; but they are not joined to the church by a corridor, nor are they enclosed within a surrounding wall. In fact it is difficult to relate them to known openings, in or between the churches, to form a coherent plan.

The layout of these large public buildings, end to end and with narrow gaps or junction structures between them, is very like the layout of secular buildings at, for example, Chalton or Yeavering, with which I have compared them in the past.[37] There are also similarities in plan between Building B, with its large public room and smaller subdivided section at the east end, and some of the structures from Yeavering or Cowdery's Down. The Anglo-Saxon building tradition, and indeed its affiliations with the Roman stone building traditions which preceded it, have been discussed recently by James, Marshall and Millett.[38] The authors note the existence of a cross passage as a characteristic of Saxon buildings, but not of Roman, and in this the Jarrow buildings are more typical of the Roman than the Saxon, since a careful analysis has revealed that they could never have had opposed doors in their long walls. The supposition then that the Jarrow buildings actually copied nearby Roman stone structures is very plausible. There is not space here to discuss the tradition behind the construction of the scooped structure, Building D, interpreted as a guest-house later turned into workshops, but that tradition is most plausibly insular.

It would seem then that, although the founders of Wearmouth and Jarrow maintained some elements of a common model in the cult centers of the larger and the smaller sites, they adapted their ideas of "Romanitas" to available models and to the topography of the sites. Possibly also there was a response to new models, such as for example Wilfrid's continental work at Hexham, with which Jarrow at least has similarities, not only in its sculpture[39] but also in its plan.[40]

The founders may also have established practices in building which could be transmitted as "the Roman tradition" to other sites in the British Isles. Nechtan of the Picts' request of ca. 710 to Wearmouth/Jarrow for masons to build him a church of stone in the Roman manner, although often quoted, has not so far produced convincing examples of what that could mean. At Whithorn, however, a center which is recorded as coming under Northumbrian influence in the mid-eighth century, recent excavations have revealed ranges of timber buildings, followed by timber-on-stone foundations, which are plausibly interpreted as a church with a mausoleum to the east, later joined together. Other ranges of buildings in parallel terraces down the slope are also very reminiscent of the Jarrow layout, although constructional details and the nature of the platform on which they are built could well derive from insular prototypes.

It is clear from the archaeological evidence that the Wearmouth/Jarrow communities continued in existence into the second half of the ninth century, and the modifications which joined the churches at Jarrow by a tower could well date to that period. It is unfortunate, however, that organized life on the two sites ended soon after the mid-ninth century, the period in which monastic houses on the Continent increased in scale and organization. San Vincenzo al Volturno, the site which has produced examples of colored glass closest in type to Wearmouth/Jarrow, increased in scale tenfold in the tenth century.[41] The important Breton monastery of Landevennec, which is currently being excavated, has produced little evidence for the period of the early "Celtic" church, save perhaps a large wall; but by the ninth century not only is there a complex church, but also a range of buildings and a cloister walk.[42]

The churches from the two sites compare in scale with the contemporary churches in northern and eastern Francia, and they are considerably larger than, for example, the church of the eighth-century monastery at Pfalzel, which has a nave only about 12m. long;[43] but there is a vast increase in scale, for example in the churches at Hersfeld, between the seventh/eighth and tenth centuries.[44] The complex which is nearest in type to Wearmouth/Jarrow is Lorsch; but there are ambiguities in the form and chronology of the plan.[45] Large rectangular buildings are grouped round a central space, as in the latest plan of Wearmouth; but it is important to remember that before 800 the walls at Lorsch enclosed more than

25,000 square meters. Neither at Wearmouth nor at Jarrow do we know the extent of the area enclosed; but it is not likely to have been so large.

SUPPORTING ECONOMY

The large scale of some of the Irish monasteries has been demonstrated clearly from air photographs and from the current excavations at Armagh, where the craft workshops of that famous monastery are at a considerable distance from the cathedral.[46] Recently, in Scotland, the ditch which surrounded the site of Hoddom in Dumfriesshire has been traced, and the excavator, Mr. Christopher Lowe, has kindly informed me in advance of publication that this encloses 20 hectares. On the outer edge of the enclosure were large domestic buildings, and these are almost out of sight of the church and cemetery, which not only has produced in the past a well known series of eighth/ninth-century crosses, but also a new series of grave slabs in the 1991 excavations.

At Jarrow the craft workshops by the river are only about 30.48m (100 ft.) south of the church. They have produced evidence of intermittent use for metalwork and glass melting before the ninth century, but no evidence, as at Whitby, for textile manufacture or working, which leads one to speculate as to whether male and female monasteries maintained specialized workshops and operated an exchange system. There was a burst of more intense craft activity at Jarrow in the ninth century, associated with metal-and glassworking. In that phase there is a hint that the occupation is of a more "lay" type, in that the contents of layers include silver and bronze dress fastenings, coinage and some animal bones. Similar craft activities have been found on other monastic sites such as Barking, or on sites such as Brandon and Flixborough, which could be the industrial *vici* of monasteries, for which we have not yet discovered the cult centers.[47] The areas of craft activity at, for example, Flixborough, are more intensively used, leaving much more industrial residue, pottery and animal bones, than in any of the layers at Jarrow; but of course we have not found the craft area of the larger of the pair at Wearmouth, and that could have sustained a more intense activity.

The mechanisms whereby a monastic community was supported, and how it paid for that support at this period, are still imperfectly understood. The original endowments of Wearmouth/Jarrow, together with what was added afterwards, gave a total support of about 150 households by the time that Abbot Ceolfrith departed for Rome in 716. These households would no doubt contribute produce and work service as their rent, later perhaps even cash. At the same time Ceolfrith left behind a *cohors militum Christi,* 600 strong, some of whom must have taken part in the manual work of the monastic farms and craft shops, and all of whom would need a minimum of food, together with clothing, shoes, a belt, a knife and a drinking vessel. The churches and other buildings would need constant repair and improvement. How, therefore, can one assess from the archaeological evidence the activities which such needs and such support would engender? I think that it is very difficult to assess from the productive areas of these sites whether one is seeing the evidence of a subsistence economy or of a specialized economy which is producing a surplus.

The relationship between the monastic and lay economic networks is still very obscure. These early monasteries had an obvious social value. They provided the lay community with hospitality for visitors of all sorts and royal servants in particular. They also maintained specialist craftsmen, such as architects or stone carvers, who could produce prestige monuments. Kings and important laymen may have expected to draw on other specialist skills, such as literacy or medical knowledge, and all may have hoped for the support of prayer in life and death. But these are intangible benefits, as Bede saw, when one considers how much land was in monastic hands by the ninth century. The predatory wish of kings and nobles to acquire some of these land holdings is already evident in the documents dating from before the Viking Age invasions and settlements brought about the opportunity for the reallocation of monastic land blocks.[48] The process whereby this change took place is still uncertain; but it is unfortunately in the ninth century, when on the Continent the monasteries began their great reforms and redevelopments, that the monasteries in northern England vanished into an obscurity from which they did not emerge until the eleventh century.

NOTES

[1]C. Plummer, ed., *Venerabilis Baedae Historium ecclesiasticam gentis Anglorum, Historia Abbatum,* 2 vols. in 1 (Oxford, 1896), ii, 328–29, 352–53, 373. Hereafter *H.A.B.*

[2] *H.A.B.,* ii, 11; *H.A.B.* i, 374–75.

[3] W. Braunfels, *Monasteries of Western Europe* (London, 1972), 19–22.

[4] E. James, "Archaeology and Merovingian Monasticism," in H. B. Clarke and M. Brennan, eds., *Columbanus and Merovingian Monasticism,* B.A.R. Int. ser. 113 (Oxford, 1981), 33–58, at p. 36.

[5] R. Cramp, "Monastic Sites," in D. Wilson, ed., *The Archaeology of Anglo-Saxon England* (London, 1976), 201–52, at pp. 216–17.

[6] N. J. Higham, The Northern Counties to A.D. *1000* (London, 1986), 276–77.

[7] P. Rahtz, "Monasteries as Settlements," *Scottish Archaeol. Forum* 5 (1974 for 1973), 125–35; I. C. G. Burrow, "Tintagel—Some Problems," ibid., 99–103; see also, C. A. R. Radford, "Summary and Discussion," ibid., 136–40.

[8] L. Webster and J. Backhouse, eds., *The Making of England, Anglo-Saxon Art and Culture* A.D. 600–900 (London, 1991), 79–100.

[9] W. Davies, *Wales in the Early Middle Ages* (Leicester, 1982), 146–57.

[10] L. Olsen, *Early Monasteries in Cornwall* (Woodbridge & Wolfeboro, 1989), 34–50.

[11] R.C.A.H.M.S., *Argyll, An Inventory of the Monuments, 4, Iona* (Edinburgh, 1982), 31–49, fig. p. 32.

[12] R. Cramp, "A Reconsideration of the Monastic Site of Whitby," in R. M. Spearman and J. Higgitt, eds., *The Age of Migrating Ideas: Early Medieval Art in Northern Britain and Ireland* (Edinburgh, 1993), 64–73.

[13] R. Daniels, "The Anglo-Saxon Monastery at Church Close, Hartlepool," *Cleveland Archaeol. J.* 145 (1988), 158–210.

[14] P. Hill and D. Pollack, *The Whithorn Dig,* 2nd ed. (Whithorn, 1992); P. Hill, *Whithorn 4: Excavations of Whithorn Priory 1990–91* (Whithorn, 1992). See now also P. Hill, *Whithorn and St. Ninian: The Excavation of a Monastic Town 1984–91* (Stroud, 1997).

[15] James, "Archaeology and Merovingian Monasticism," 38–40, note 4.

[16] E. Fletcher, "The Monastery of Lérins," *J.B.A.A.* 133 (1980), 17–29; I. Smith, "The Survey of Lérins," *Archaeol. Reports for the Univ. of Durham and Univ. of Newcastle for 1983* (Durham, 1984), figs. 1, 2.

[17] L. Musset, "L'église d'Evrecy (Calvados) et ses sculptures préromanes," *Bul. Soc. Antiq. de Normandie* 53 (1957 for 1955–56), 1–81, figs. 2, 7.

[18] R. Cramp, "Excavations at the Saxon Monastic Sites of Wearmouth and Jarrow, Co. Durham: An Interim Report," *M.A.* 13 (1969), 21–66, at pp. 31–34.

[19] N. Duval, "L'architecture culturelle," in N. Duval, J. Fontaine, P.-A. Février, J.-C. Picard, and G. Barruol, eds., *Naissance des arts chrétiens. Atlas des Monuments paléochrétiens de la France* (Paris, 1991), 212–13.

[20] G. A. de Maillé, *Les cryptes de Jouarre. Plans et relevés de P. Rousseau* (Paris, 1971), 190, fig. 20.

[21] B. Cherry, "Ecclesiastical Architecture," in Wilson, *Archaeology of Anglo-Saxon England,* 151–200, at p. 162, fig. 4.4.

[22] *H.A.B.,* i, 368–70; R. Cramp, report on the excavations, forthcoming.

[23] *H.A.B.,* i, 384–85.

[24] R. Cramp, "Decorated Window-glass and Millefiori from Monkwearmouth," *Antiquaries J.* 50 (1970), 327–35; R. Cramp, "Window-glass from the Monastic Site of Jarrow, " *J. Glass Studies* 17 (1975), 88–96.

[25] R. Brill, pers. comm.

[26] James, "Archaeology and Merovingian Monasticism," 46.

[27] *H.A.B.,* i, 383.

[28] Braunfels, *Monasteries of Western Europe,* 234.

[29] R. Cramp, *Corpus of Anglo-Saxon Stone Sculpture,* vol.1. *County Durham and Northumberland* (Oxford, 1984), 124–34. Hereafter *Corpus* 1.

[30] *H.A.B.,* i, 371–73; ii, 362, 369.

[31] *H.A.B.,* i, 374–76, 391–92.

[32] R. Cramp, "Jarrow Church," *Archaeol. J.* 133 (1976), 220–28; R. Cramp, "Monkwearmouth," ibid., 230–37.

[33] *Corpus* 1, 114–22.

[34] R. Cramp, "Monkwearmouth and Jarrow," in G. Bonner, ed., *Famulus Christi* (London, 1976), 12–14.

[35] Braunfels, *Monasteries of Western Europe,* 236.

[36] K. Hughes and A. Hamlin, *The Modern Traveller to the Early Irish Church* (London, 1977), 54–79.

[37] Cramp, "Monkwearmouth and Jarrow," 14.

[38] S. James, A. Marshall and M. Millett, " An Early Medieval Building Tradition," *Archaeol. J.* 141 (1984), 182–215 and Chap. 5 above.

[39] *Corpus* 1, 26, 128.

[40] R. Bailey, "St. Wilfrid. Ripon and Hexham," in C. Karkov and R. Farrell, eds., *Studies in Insular Art and Archaeology,* American Early Medieval Studies 1 (Oxford, OH, 1991), 3–23.

[41] R. Hodges and J. Mitchell, eds., *San Vincenzo al Volturno, the Archaeology Art and Territory of an Early Medieval Monastery,* B.A.R. Int. ser. 252 (Oxford, 1985).

[42] A. Bardel, "L'Abbaye Saint-Gwenole de Landevennec," *Archéologie Médieval* 21 (1991), 51–101, esp. Fig. 3.

[43] N. Gauthier, *L'évangélisation des pays de la Moselle: la province romaine de Première Belgique entre Antiquité et Moyen Âge* (Paris, 1980), 333.

[44] Braunfels, *Monasteries of Western Europe,* 30, fig. 19.

[45] F. Behn, *Die karolingische Klosterkirche von Lorsch* (Berlin & Leipzig, 1934).

[46] M. Ryan, "Fine Metalworking and Early Irish Monasteries," in J. Bradley, ed., *Settlement and Society in Medieval Ireland* (Kilkenny, 1988), 33–48.

[47] Webster and Backhouse, *The Making of England,* 79–100.

[48] D. Whitelock, *English Historical Documents, c. 500–1042* (London, 1955; 2nd ed. 1996), 674–75.

CHAPTER 7

The Anglo-Saxon Cathedral Church at Canterbury

H. M. TAYLOR

1. INTRODUCTION

The Anglo-Saxon cathedral church at Canterbury was destroyed by fire in 1067 and was demolished three years later by Archbishop Lanfranc to make way for his great Norman building. By great good fortune we have a fairly full description of the vanished Anglo-Saxon church in the words of a Canterbury monk Eadmer, who was a child at the time of the fire and was shortly thereafter a pupil at the cathedral school.[1] Eadmer also gave a short description of the steps taken by Lanfranc to rebuild the cathedral.

The object of this paper is to make a reappraisal of the nature of the Anglo-Saxon cathedral and of its architectural history. The primary evidence is, of course, Eadmer's contemporary description of the building; but important help can be given by recent discoveries about similar buildings elsewhere, particularly by the excavations in the crypt of Old St. Peter's at Rome, a building which Eadmer compared directly with the cathedral at Canterbury.

A brief summary is given in Appendix I of the principal previous essays on this subject, namely those of Robert Willis (1845), G. G. Scott the Younger (1881), G. Baldwin Brown (1903), William St. J. Hope (1918) and A. W. Clapham (1930). None of these writers had accurate knowledge of the crypt of Old St. Peter's, but each of them made distinctive contributions to our knowledge of the cathedral at Canterbury. In particular, Robert Willis had an almost uncanny ability to translate Eadmer's brief description into a living architectural outline, while resisting the temptation to insert detail for which evidence was not available. I

155

have therefore drawn heavily on Willis, more particularly because he provided a very full account of the primary historical material both in the original Latin and also in translation. It will be seen that where my reconstruction and conjectural architectural history differ from those of Willis the differences are usually due to fresh discoveries in the intervening years rather than to shortcomings in the work of Willis himself.

In the light of modern knowledge of similar buildings I have dared to go a little further than did Willis or any of his successors in the matter of conjectural reconstruction of features for which Eadmer's description does not give evidence. I must, however, underline Willis's warning that any such reconstruction is to be regarded only as a model, without authority; and I hope it will not be felt that my reconstruction has proceeded beyond the bounds of reasonable probability.

In the intervening years since Willis wrote, there has been a considerable increase in the ease of accessibility of the original records, for many of Eadmer's writings have been republished in modern historical works and one that was previously available only in the original manuscript has now been published. In Appendix II I have given the Latin text corresponding to all the historical and architectural passages that are given in translation in Sections 2 and 3, and in addition I have given references both to Willis's version of the Latin text and also to the general works in which the original material is published. I have read the material in both places and it does not appear that modern scrutiny of the sources has produced any change that affects the architectural study.

2. THE HISTORY OF THE CHURCH

Eadmer's description of the cathedral as given in Section 3 relates to the church that was burnt in 1067 and does not of itself give any indication when the several parts were built. It will probably never be possible to reach any certainty about such historical details; but it is, nevertheless, possible to make some progress in that direction by closer study of the evidence. This evidence was set out in full by Willis, both in translation and in the original Latin.[2] The summarized account given below omits all passages that do not relate to the architectural history, but otherwise retains the words and numbered paragraphs used by Willis except where changes are indicated by footnotes. The Latin text is given in Appendix II, using the same numbered paragraphs, and with full reference to the published sources; there is therefore no need for footnotes in this Section except to indicate where I have diverged from the translation or the dates given by Willis.

1. When Augustine had received the episcopal see in the royal city, he restored in it with the king's support a church which he had learnt had been built there of old by the work of Roman believers, and consecrated it in the name of the holy Savior our Lord and God Jesus Christ, and established there a residence for himself and his successors.[3]

2. Cuthbert (the eleventh archbishop, 740–60)[4] amongst his other good works constructed a church to the east of the great church, and almost touching it, which he solemnly dedicated in honor of St. John the Baptist. He fabricated this church for the following purposes; that baptisms might be celebrated therein; that certain judicial trials which are wont to be held in the church might be carried on there; and lastly that the bodies of the archbishops might therein be buried, thus departing from the ordinary ancient custom of burial beyond the walls of the city. And he was accordingly buried in the aforesaid church of St. John.

4. Archbishop Bregwin (the twelfth, 761–64) was buried in the aforesaid church of St. John, near the body of the reverend Cuthbert.

6. In the days of Archbishop Odo (the twenty-second, 942–58) the roof of Christ Church had become rotten from excessive age and rested throughout on half-shattered pieces: wherefore he set about to reconstruct it; and, being also desirous of giving the walls a more aspiring altitude, he directed his assembled workmen to remove altogether the disjointed structure above and commanded them to supply the deficient height of the walls by raising them. . . . During three years in which the walls of the church were being carried upwards, the whole building remained open to the sky: yet did no rain fall either within the walls of the church or even within the walls of the city.

10. Now on the day of the coming of Dunstan to Canterbury, he was celebrating mass at the altar of the Savior, when suddenly the house was covered with a cloud, and that dove which erst was seen of John in Jordan again appeared and hovered over him. And when the sacrifice was completed, it rested upon the memorial[5] of the blessed Odo which was constructed in the fashion of a pyramid to the south of the altar.

11. Archbishop Dunstan (the twenty-fifth, 960–88) was buried in the spot which he himself had chosen, the place to wit where the divine office was daily celebrated by the brethren and which was before the steps that led up to the altar of the Lord Christ. Here in

the midst of the choir his body was deposited in a leaden coffin deep in the ground according to the ancient custom of the English, and the depth of his grave was made equal to the stature of an ordinary man. A memorial[6] was afterwards constructed over him, in the form of a large and lofty pyramid and having at the head of the saint the matutinal altar.

12. In the primacy of Archbishop Elphege (the twenty-eighth, 1005–12), the sack of Canterbury by the Danes took place; . . . the people were slain, the city burnt, and the church profaned, searched, and despoiled; the archbishop was led away bound, and after enduring imprisonment and torture for seven months was finally slain.

13. It must be remarked, however, that the church itself at the time of the suffering of the blessed martyr Elphege was neither consumed by fire nor were its walls or roof destroyed.

14. (A.D. 1067) After these things, and while misfortunes fell thick upon all parts of England, it happened that the city of Canterbury was set on fire by the carelessness of some individuals and that the rising flames caught the mother church thereof. How can I tell it? The whole was consumed, and nearly all the monastic offices that appertained to it, as well as the church of the blessed John the Baptist where as aforesaid the remains of the archbishops were buried.

16(a). In the conflagration, however, by the Divine mercy and the intercession of the pious Dunstan it happened that two houses indispensably necessary to the existence of the brethren remained unhurt: the refectory, namely, and the dormitory as well as the cloisters which were attached to them.

16(b). After this, there was erected over the resting place of the blessed man a house of small magnitude, and in this were performed daily over his holy body masses together with other services.

17(a). Now after this lamentable fire the bodies of the pontiffs (namely Cuthbert, Bregwin, and their successors) rested undisturbed in their coffins for three years until that most energetic and honorable man Lanfranc, abbot of Caen, was made Archbishop of Canterbury. . . . He pulled down all that he found of the burnt monastery, whether of buildings or the wasted remains of buildings, and, having dug out their foundations from under the earth he constructed others in their stead.

17(b). He ordered the said archbishops to be raised and placed in safety until the new church had been completed, in which they could be honorably placed. And this was done.[7]

17(c). As for the church which the aforesaid fire combined with its age had rendered completely unserviceable, he set about to destroy it utterly and erect a more noble one.

17(d). And in the space of seven years he raised this new church from the very foundations and rendered it nearly perfect.

17(e). But before the work began he commanded that the bodies of the saints which were buried in the eastern end of the church should be moved to the western part where the oratory of the blessed Virgin Mary stood. Wherefore after a three days fast the bodies of those most precious priests of the Lord, Dunstan and Elphege,[8] were raised and in presence of an innumerable multitude conveyed to the destined place of interment and there decently buried. To which I Eadmer can bear witness for I was a boy at the school.

18. But in process of time as the new work begun on the church proceeded it became necessary to take down the old work where the bodies of the saints just mentioned were deposited. Having prepared therefore the refectory of the brethren for the celebration of Divine Service we all proceeded thither from the old church in festal procession bearing with honor and reverence our glorious and sweet fathers Dunstan and Elphege.

19. When the high altar of the old church was taken down the relics of the blessed Wilfrid were found and placed in a reliquary. But after some years the brethren were of the opinion that they ought to have a more permanent resting place and accordingly a sepulcher was prepared for them on the north side of an altar in which they were reverently enclosed.

20. After a few years the bodies of the pontiffs Cuthbert, Bregwin, and their successors, were brought into the newly founded church and placed in the north part upon a vault, each in a separate wooden coffin, and there daily the mystery of the Sacrifice of Salvation was celebrated.

3. EADMER'S DESCRIPTION OF THE CHURCH

The whole of Eadmer's important description of the Anglo-Saxon cathedral church was translated by Willis into a single paragraph which he numbered 15. For ease of subsequent reference it is convenient to have this long passage split into a number of separate paragraphs; but in order to avoid confusion I have retained the number 15 and have used sub-paragraphs 15(a) to 15(k). Throughout the text I have followed the translation given by Willis except were I have drawn attention to any difference in a footnote. The original Latin is given in Appendix II, divided into the same sub-paragraphs.

15(a). This was that very church (asking patience for a digression) which had been built by Romans, as Bede bears witness in his history; and which was duly arranged in some parts in imitation of the church of the blessed Prince of the Apostles, Peter, in which his relics are exalted by the veneration of the whole world.[9]

15(b). The venerable Odo had translated the body of the blessed Wilfrid Archbishop of York from Ripon to Canterbury and had worthily placed it in a more lofty receptacle, to use his own words, that is to say in the great altar which was constructed of rough stones and mortar close to the wall at the eastern part of the presbytery.

15(c). Afterwards another altar was placed at a convenient distance before the aforesaid altar and dedicated in honor of our Lord Jesus Christ, at which the divine mysteries were daily celebrated. In this altar the blessed Elphege had solemnly deposited the head of St. Swithin which he had brought with him when he was translated from Winchester to Canterbury, and also many relics of other saints.

15(d). To reach these altars there was an ascent of several steps from the choir of the singers, because there was beneath them a crypt which the Romans call a confessionary.[10] This crypt was fabricated in the likeness of the confessionary of St. Peter, the vault of which was raised so high that the part above could only be reached by many steps.

15(e). Within, the crypt had at the east end an altar in which was enclosed the head of the blessed Furseus, as of old it was asserted. Moreover the single passage which ran westward from the curved part of the crypt reached from thence up to the resting place of the blessed Dunstan, which was separated from the crypt itself by a strong wall.[11] For that holy father was interred before the aforesaid steps at a great depth in the ground, and at the head of the saint stood the matutinal altar.

15(f). Thence the choir of the singers was extended westward into the body of the church, and shut out from the multitude by a proper enclosure.

15(g). In the next place, beyond the middle of the length of the body, there were two towers which projected above the aisles of the church.[12] The south tower had an altar in the midst of it, dedicated in honor of the blessed pope Gregory. At the side was the principal door of the church which as of old by the English so even now is called SUTHDURE and is often mentioned by this name in the law books of the ancient kings. For all disputes from the whole kingdom which cannot legally be resolved within the hundreds or the counties, or even in the king's court, must be settled here as if in the high king's court.

15(h). Opposite to this tower, and on the north, the other tower was built in honor of the blessed Martin and had cloisters about it for the use of the monks. And as the first tower was devoted to legal contentions and judgments of this world, so in the second the younger brethren were instructed in the knowledge of the offices of the church, for the different seasons and hours of the day and night.

15(i). The extremity of the church was adorned by the oratory of Mary, the blessed Mother of God; which oratory was so constructed that access could only be had to it by steps. At its eastern part there was an altar consecrated to the worship of that Lady, which had within it the head of the blessed virgin Austroberta.

15(j). When the priest performed the divine mysteries at this altar he had his face turned towards the east, towards the people who stood below. Behind him to the west was the pontifical chair constructed with handsome workmanship and of large stones and cement, and far removed from the Lord's table, being contiguous to the wall of the church which embraced the entire area of the building.

15(k). And this was the plan of the church at Canterbury. These things we have shortly described in order that the men of the present and future generations when they find them mentioned in writings of old perceive that the existing things do not coincide with their narratives may know that all these old things have passed away and that new ones have taken their place. For after the innumerable vicissitudes which this church underwent the whole was finally consumed in our own days by fire as we have above related.

4. OLD ST. PETER'S AT ROME

Since Eadmer says that the crypt at Canterbury was fashioned in the like-ness of the confessionary of St. Peter and that the church was arranged in some parts in imitation of St. Peter's, it is clear that an accurate interpre- tation of Eadmer's description will be helped by an accurate knowledge of the arrangements at St. Peter's in Rome.

The importance of this comparative study was fully appreciated by Willis, who devoted the first five pages of his Chapter II to a study of St. Peter's, and who also drew attention to the fact that Eadmer was well qualified to judge the resemblance between the two churches since he had accompanied Anselm to Rome.

Now in the knowledge of Old St. Peter's there have been important advances since Willis wrote, particularly as a result of the excavations undertaken there during and after the Second World War. Moreover these excavations have not only greatly increased our knowledge of the de-tailed arrangements of the ring crypt but they have also established be-yond reasonable doubt that it was built by Pope Gregory the Great (590–604) in order to provide that mass could be celebrated directly above the spot that was believed to be the burial place of St. Peter.[13]

In figure 7.1 there are shown two reconstructions in very diagram-matic form of the sanctuary area of Old St. Peter's as it is shown by the excavations to have been at two decisive times in the history of that church. At A the isometric drawing shows the apse and the adjoining part of the transept as they were laid out to the orders of Constantine the Great early in the fourth century; the whole floor of the church was at a uniform level, and the previously-existing memorial over the Apostle's tomb was enclosed in a shrine which is represented diagrammatically at M while the six simple cubical bases represent the supports for six twisted columns that supported a screen and a canopy over the shrine. The second drawing B shows the same area of the apse and transept after the modifications that were made between 590 and 604 by Pope Gregory the Great in order to provide for the high altar, N, to be placed directly over the tomb. It will be seen how this was achieved by raising the whole area of the sanctuary, which was now approached up the flights of steps W. In order to provide direct access to the tomb, entries were made on ei-ther side of the raised area at X and X, down a few steps in each case, to a corridor which followed a curved path beside the wall of the apse and which was covered by flat paving slabs. In the third diagram C there is shown a plan of this curved underground passage or ring crypt.

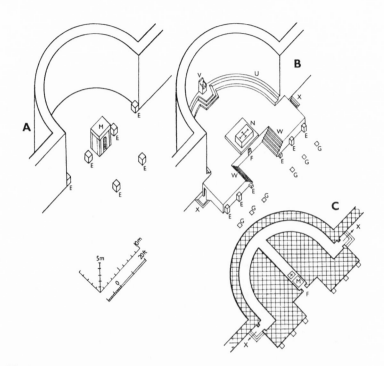

Fig. 7.1. Old St. Peter's, Rome. In Fig. 7.1A the transept and apse are shown as built by Constantine the Great about A.D. 330, while Fig. 7.1B shows the same area as reconstructed about 600 by Pope Gregory the Great. Fig. 7.1C shows a plan of the crypt beneath Gregory's raised sanctuary; E, bases for the twisted marble columns that shut off the apse and screened the shrine; F, the *fenestella;* G, the bases for six further columns added in the eighth century; M, the shrine which Constantine built to enclose the original memorial of St. Peter; N, Gregory's high altar, replacing Constantine's shrine without displacing the original memorial; U, stone seats for clergy; V, throne for the Pope; W, flights of steps up to the sanctuary; X, flights of steps down to the crypt.

It will at once be noted how close a resemblance these arrangements bear to the description given by Eadmer of the main sanctuary area at Canterbury where "to reach the altars there was an ascent of several steps from the choir of the singers because there was beneath them a crypt which the Romans call a confessionary," and where a "single passage ran westward from the curved part of the crypt."

This arrangement of a curved ring crypt with a central straight passage leading to the *confessio* was adopted in many continental churches, no doubt inspired by Old St. Peter's at Rome.[14] The altar standing above, in the sanctuary, at the center of the chord of the apse, was normally placed directly above an important relic that was housed in or beneath the *confessio* chamber, at the end of the straight passage of the crypt. The importance of Old St. Peter's in the understanding of the development of this type of crypt is that the arrangement developed organically at Old St. Peter's because the tomb that had long been believed to be that of St. Peter, and the memorial standing above it, were incorporated by Constantine the Great into his imposing fourth-century church, as shown at M in diagram A; in the more developed liturgy of the sixth century the memorial M represented a hindrance to the service of the mass directly above the tomb, and therefore Gregory the Great changed the layout of the sanctuary area as shown in diagram B. The close contacts between Canterbury and Rome from the time when Augustine was first sent there by Gregory the Great would provide good reason for the provision of a similar arrangement in the sanctuary of the principal church in Canterbury. The associated question of the probable date of the crypt at Canterbury is considered more fully in Section 6, below.

5. TENTATIVE RECONSTRUCTION OF THE ANGLO-SAXON CATHEDRAL

In building up a reconstruction of the Anglo-Saxon cathedral at Canterbury it is convenient to proceed as did Willis from Old St. Peter's at Rome, testing the propriety of including or rejecting individual features by reference to the description of the Canterbury church as given by Eadmer. For this purpose let us therefore summarize very briefly Eadmer's description as given in Section 3, using the same letters (*a*) to (*k*) for the much shorter wording that is given below but is based on paragraphs 15(*a*) to 15(*k*); and let us add three further items (*l*), (*m*) and (*n*) taken from Section 2, paragraphs 2, 10, and 11:

(*a*) Some parts of the church imitated St. Peter's at Rome.

(*b*) There was a stone altar close to the wall at the east of the presbytery.

(*c*) There was a second altar dedicated to our Savior some distance in front of the first altar.

(*d*) A flight of several steps led up from the choir to these altars, and there was a crypt beneath, like that at St. Peter's.

(e) The crypt had a curved passage, with an altar at the east, and a single passage running westward to Dunstan's burial place before the steps, with the matutinal altar at his head.

(f) The choir extended westward from this altar and was enclosed.

(g) Beyond the middle of the church there were towers above (or beyond) the aisles. The south tower had an altar in it dedicated in honor of St. Gregory, and it also served as the principal entry to the church. It was used for legal proceedings.

(h) The north tower, opposite, was built in honor of St. Martin. It had the cloisters about it and was used for instruction of the younger brethren.

(i) The west end of the church was a chapel of the Virgin Mary, approached up a flight of steps, and with its altar at the east.

(j) The priest celebrating mass here stood facing east with the people standing below. Far behind him to the west the archbishop's stone chair stood against the west wall.

(k) This was the plan of the church.

(l) To the east of the great church and almost touching it was the church of St. John the Baptist, built by Archbishop Cuthbert (740–60) as a baptistery, as a burial place for the archbishops and for certain legal trials.

(m) South of the altar of our Savior was the memorial of Archbishop Odo.

(n) A large and lofty memorial was built over the place of St. Dunstan's burial.

The model which I very tentatively offer on the evidence given above is shown in figure 7.2; which should be compared and contrasted with earlier reconstructions shown in Appendix I, figures 7.3 and 7.4.

Eadmer's description makes no reference to a transept, and therefore none has been shown in figure 7.2, particularly because there is as yet no evidence for early transepts in England. The crypt has a curved passage and therefore it seems legitimate to assume an apsidal east end, for which there is supporting evidence from other early churches in Kent. The apse is shown curved both internally and externally; but it could well have been curved internally and polygonal externally, as at Reculver and Brixworth.

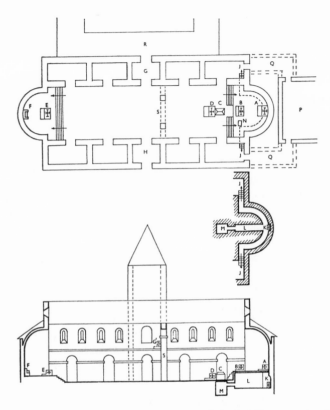

Fig. 7.2. Tentative Reconstruction of Canterbury Cathedral. The reconstruction shows a plan of the church as a whole, a plan of the crypt, and a longitudinal section of the church. This latter is even more tentative than the plans; A, eastern altar with relics of St. Wilfrid; B, altar of our Lord; C, memorial of St. Dunstan; D, matutinal altar; E, altar of the Virgin Mary; F, archbishop's throne; G, porch and tower of St. Martin; G[1,] altar of St. Martin in upper chamber of the tower (shown by broken lines through the north wall of the nave); H, porch and tower of St. Gregory, with principal entry to the church; J, stairs up from the ring crypt; K, altar at east end of ring crypt, with relics of St. Furseus; L, *confessio* passage; M, burial place of St. Dunstan; N, memorial of Archbishop Odo; P, site of church of St. John the Baptist; Q, tentative arrangement of corridors connecting the two churches; R, position of south walk of cloister; S, triple arch and screen separating the nave from the choir of the singers.

Much of the reconstruction is necessarily speculative; in particular there is no evidence for the number or nature of the windows, or for the number or shape of the openings from the nave to the side-chapels.

Willis and others following him have shown square piers between the nave and the aisles rather than the round columns which were used at St. Peter's although Eadmer gives no evidence either way. I have dared to diverge even further from St. Peter's by following the example of the surviving early churches at Brixworth and Wing, which both have apsidal chancels above crypts, and in both of which the nave is divided from the aisles or side-chapels by broad rectangular piers which at Brixworth are wider than the openings between them. In Kent itself there are also examples of a central nave divided from side-chapels by almost continuous walls; notably at Reculver, and at St. Augustine's abbey in Canterbury.

On the enclosure of the choir Willis and others following him used a Roman model of a screened off area narrower than the nave. Here again I have followed an English pattern rather than a Roman one and have assumed that the choir of the singers occupied the whole width of the central space and was divided from the nave (also of the same width) by a triple arch such as we know to have served just this purpose at Brixworth.

It is convenient to list next a number of arrangements that seem to follow quite straightforwardly from Eadmer's description. A and B are the two altars in the raised presbytery, which is reached by the wide flight of steps from the choir. C is the lofty memorial over the place of St. Dunstan's burial, and D is the matutinal altar. Beneath the raised presbytery the curved passage of the ring crypt is reached down flights of steps J, J; and at the east end of this curved passage (shown both in the section and in the plan of the crypt) there is the altar K. From this altar a straight passage, L, leads back westward towards M, the burial place of St. Dunstan which is at a great depth below his memorial C and is separated by a thick wall from the *confessio* passage L.[15] I have shown a small opening or *fenestella* allowing a view of the burial place, M, although Eadmer mentions nothing of the sort. In other places such a *fenestella* was a common arrangement to allow veneration of relics, and its presence here would explain Eadmer's perhaps otherwise unexpected certainty about the thickness of the wall and depth of the burial. Finally, E is the altar of the Virgin Mary, reached up steps from the nave, and F is the archbishop's throne at the west end of the church.

By contrast with these straightforward matters, the following arrangements in the reconstruction seem to call for some detailed further consideration:

(i) *The west end.* This has been shown curved like the east end although Eadmer does not explicitly say so. The presence of the archbishop's stone chair suggests an analogy with the pope's chair in the apse at Rome, but again this does not necessarily prove that the west end was enclosed by a curved wall. But although the apsidal shape at the west end is not a certainty, there can be no doubt that the general arrangement of the church comprised an apsidal sanctuary at the east and a second sanctuary at the west, probably but not certainly apsidal.

(ii) The towers. I have shown the towers above the aisles or side-chapels rather than outside them as shown by Willis. I believe that *duae turres erant, prominentes ultra alas ecclesiae* is capable of this interpretation, and there is good evidence at Deerhurst for just such a building of upper stories on side-chapels quite early in the Anglo-Saxon era. This interpretation is not new, having been given first by William St. John Hope and later by Alfred Clapham.[16]

(iii) The altars of St. Gregory and St. Martin. I believe that the north tower should be assumed to have an altar of St. Martin although Eadmer explicitly names an altar only in the south tower and uses the expression "built in honor of the blessed Martin" for the north tower. For both altars I believe that the most probable position would be on the first floor where the altar of St. Martin is shown in my longitudinal section.[17] This would leave the ground floor chambers free for the other uses described by Eadmer, namely law-suits in the south porch and instruction of younger brethren in the north one; moreover it would leave the porches free for passage, a need which seems to be specially underlined by Eadmer's note that the south door was the principal entry to the church.

(iv) The church of St. John. I have shown this baptistery-mortuary chapel in purely diagrammatic form in the same alignment as the principal church and just to its east. We have no evidence for the shape of this church, but I suggest that the analogue of the alignment of churches so strikingly provided at St. Augustine's abbey within a few hundred yards of the cathedral gives good support for some such arrangement. Following continental examples, the two churches might have been connected by a passage such as is shown by Willis, or might even more probably have had a covered way laid out like an atrium as is shown by the dotted passages Q, Q. This whole layout must be regarded as very tentative.

Finally, the longitudinal section shown in figure 7.2, must be regarded simply as an attempt to indicate how the church might look.[18]

6. AN ATTEMPT TO DATE THE CHURCH DESCRIBED BY EADMER

We have seen in Section 5 the considerable uncertainties that remain in any reconstruction of the church notwithstanding the fairly detailed description which Eadmer gives of it; therefore it will be apparent that much greater difficulties confront us in attempting to decide when its several parts were built, for Eadmer gives us very little information on this matter. The most prudent course would be to follow Willis and say:

> As to the history of these arrangements of the church, we can offer little beyond conjecture; Eadmer describes it as he knew it and had seen it during its demolition; and we know that Odo raised the walls when he made a new roof, and that this operation took three years. . . . But whether the said church was the ancient Roman Christian building or whether Augustine or one of his successors might not have rebuilt it, who can tell?[19]

Nevertheless I believe that there is a duty imposed upon those who make a serious study of these monuments that they should examine all the evidence and should then state their considered opinion about the most probable history of the buildings.

Let us therefore look afresh at such evidence as is given in Eadmer's words, in Section 2, above:

> The first reference to building is in para. 2 which records that Cuthbert added a new church of St. John the Baptist almost touching the east end of the cathedral.
>
> The second reference is in para. 6 which records Odo's extensive three-year program of reconstruction. It should, however, be noted that Eadmer very specifically describes this work as a reconstruction of the roofs that had become rotten through age, and a raising of the walls to give a more aspiring altitude.
>
> The third reference is of a negative character, in para. 13, where Eadmer asserts most explicitly that the Danish sack of Canterbury in 1012 did not result in destruction of the walls or roof of the cathedral.
>
> It could also be claimed that a fourth reference is contained in para. 15(a) of section 3 where Eadmer asserts that "this was that very church . . . which had been built by the Romans." But this must be regarded as a very indirect piece of evidence.

In assessing the evidence it is important to remember that it is assembled from a variety of sources even though most are writings by the same author. Eadmer did not compose a single work on the architectural history of the cathedral; therefore the absence of a reference to a complete rebuilding cannot be taken as absolute evidence that no such rebuilding took place. Moreover on the record of Odo's reconstruction of the roofs it could be objected that this was already shrouded in the obscurity of over a hundred years of tradition when Eadmer wrote about it, and that therefore Odo might have done more than Eadmer believed, and might perhaps have extended a smaller church eastward by building the whole of the eastern apse with its crypt beneath it.

In order to resolve these uncertainties I think it is necessary to look at all the evidence and also to review the probabilities in the light of our knowledge of building practices throughout western Europe at all the relevant times. In this respect we are now very much better informed than was Willis when he first attacked this problem over a hundred years ago.

In the first place, then, Archbishop Cuthbert's church of St. John gives us some help, since we know that one of its purposes was to provide a burial place for the archbishops. Now there are many examples from all over the Continent to show that a favored place for such burial chapels was immediately beside the sanctuary of the main church, so that the bodies of the faithful would rest as close as possible to the place where the sacrament of Holy Communion was celebrated. This therefore supports the reliability of Eadmer's assertion that the church of St. John almost touched the east end of the cathedral. Moreover it supports the probability that this contiguity of the two churches dated from the time when Cuthbert built the church of St. John (740–60) and that it was not a result of later eastward extension of the cathedral.

The next architectural consideration is the ring crypt itself. These ring crypts were a very sophisticated arrangement based, as we have noted above, upon the very special requirement of placing the high altar above an important relic which was housed in or below the *confessio* at the end of the straight central passage of the crypt. Now the remarkable thing about Eadmer's description is that, while there are detailed accounts of the deposition of relics by a number of archbishops in a variety of places, there is no mention at all of any relic in the *confessio* passage beneath the high altar. This seems to me important evidence that the whole crypt dated from an early period and that the basic reason for its existence had become forgotten by Eadmer's time. Since Eadmer's works are very specially devoted to the relics preserved in Canterbury Cathedral it seems to me inconceivable that he would have omitted to mention a relic at this important place in the *confessio* passage if there had been any memory of one available to him. Moreover it seems equally unlikely that if, as some writers have thought Odo (942–58) was the builder of the eastern apse he would have built a ring crypt at all unless its *confessio* was to house an important relic of our Lord beneath the high altar dedicated to Him.[20] Equally, it seems impossible to believe that the presence of such a relic would be forgotten between the times of Odo and Eadmer.

Discussion of the Comparative Architectural Evidence, and Conclusions From It

I have discussed elsewhere the important changes that have been produced in the dating of ring crypts by the post-war evidence that the ring crypt at Old St. Peter's in Rome is the work of Gregory the Great (590–604).[21] In particular I have there underlined how these changes enable us to accept at its face value the evidence at Brixworth of identity of fabric in the walls of the ring crypt and of the nave, with the consequence that the ring crypt should now be accepted as being contemporary with the nave, late in the seventh century or early in the eighth. Augustine must be assumed to have been familiar with Gregory's work at Old St. Peter's, and so also were the great Anglo-Saxon church builders of the seventh century such as Wilfrid and Benedict Biscop, both of whom had made several visits to Rome. Therefore any one of these could have provided the inspiration for the ring crypts at Brixworth and at Canterbury Cathedral. So indeed could have Archbishop Theodore, or Abbot Hadrian of St. Augustine's, both of whom came from Rome and had important links respectively with centers of architectural activity in Asia Minor and North Africa. On the whole I believe it is highly probable that so distinctive a feature as a ring crypt, with its very special implications of close association with Rome, would be introduced into the cathedral church at Canterbury before it would appear elsewhere in England. The late-seventh or early-eighth century date for its appearance at Brixworth would therefore suggest that its appearance at Canterbury should not be later than the archbishopric of Cuthbert (740–60). The records of building in this period name only Augustine, who restored the church that had been built by Roman believers, and Cuthbert, who built the church of St. John close to the east end of the cathedral.

Conclusion

The straightforward conclusion from all these considerations is that we should accept Eadmer's record at its face value and assign to Augustine himself the building of the essential parts of the church described by Eadmer, at any rate in ground plan; this would also imply that we accept Eadmer's evidence that Odo's work in the tenth century was limited in the main to a repairing of the decayed roof, but that it included a substantial raising of the height of the church, and no doubt also the erection of the towers above the north and south *porticus.*

Alternative Elaborated Conclusion

Nevertheless, we cannot rule out the possibility that the traditions of Eadmer's day had lost account of a major enlargement of Augustine's original church at some intermediate time. Moreover the presence of the archbishop's throne in the western sanctuary is difficult to reconcile with the clear priority of the eastern sanctuary dedicated to our Savior, unless we assume that the first state of the building had only the western sanctuary. This process of thought would then lead to a tentative architectural history along the following lines: Augustine took over, restored, and dedicated to our Savior, a small church which had only a western apse (like the known Romano-British survival at Silchester); at the head of this western apse he placed his throne, and at the center of the apse he placed the altar, just as at St. Peter's in Rome save that as yet there seems to have been no crypt at Canterbury; no doubt also he provided the nave with side chapels or *porticus* such as we know he designed at the church of St. Peter and St. Paul in St. Augustine's abbey. Thereafter it would be necessary to assume a fresh phase of building in which the eastern apse was provided, along with its ring crypt. The provision of such a crypt would have been a very natural consequence of the acquisition, say by gift from Rome, of some relic associated with our Lord or his Passion; and, if at the same time there was felt to be a need for enlargement of the church, it could well have seemed desirable to provide for the housing of the relic in a newly built addition at the other end of the church rather than to modify the existing sanctuary.[22] It is difficult to suggest what would have been the most likely time for such an addition to the original cathedral, but there are good reasons for thinking that the time of Archbishop Theodore (668–90) is a possibility: in the first place we know that under him there was an upsurge of activity in the arts as well as in religion, and secondly his friend Abbot Hadrian of St. Augustine's abbey was a native of North Africa and would have been familiar with the use in that country of apses at both ends of a church. Moreover we have already given reason for believing that the eastern apse was completed before Cuthbert added the chapel of St. John.

Relative Probability of the Two Conclusions

It is difficult to decide between these alternative conclusions: the first and simpler one is closer to the record provided by Eadmer, while the second seems more closely to fit all the architectural evidence. In any event I should again point out that here, as in the reconstruction of the church, we cannot achieve certainty but only a most probable solution. On the whole it seems to me that the most probable solution, based on the evidence which is at present available, is along the lines of the second of the conclusions described above.

I have not been able to find from the historical evidence any straightforward clue to the development of the ring crypt. Bede does indeed record (*H.E.* i, 29) that about 601 Pope Gregory sent to Augustine "relics of the holy apostles and martyrs," but such relics do not seem appropriate for use in this particular *confessio* beneath the altar dedicated to our Lord. On the other hand, Bede's record of Augustine's coming to Britain (*H.E.* i, 25) tells that the band of missionaries, when they first met King Ethelbert, came "bearing a silver cross for their banner and the image of our Lord and Savior painted on a board"; and the same chapter tells that the same emblems were carried at the head of the column as they later entered Canterbury after the King had given them permission to do so. I believe it would be well within the bounds of the medieval concept of relics that these emblems, which had in some measure served to win the King's acceptance of Christ, could be regarded as the appropriate relics to be deposited beneath the altar of our Savior in the cathedral church shortly after the campaign for the conversion of England had been ended. From Eadmer's record it is abundantly clear that by the tenth and eleventh centuries the interest in relics had moved strongly towards the accumulating of the bodies of local and national saints; and this could perhaps account for the otherwise remarkable absence of any record of the relic in the *confessio* beneath the high altar.

7. SOME FURTHER ARCHITECTURAL AND HISTORICAL DEDUCTIONS

The Site of the Early Cathedral

The evidence for the site of the early cathedral can be summarized as follows in terms of extracts from the history recorded in Section 2:

(*a*) After the fire a small chapel (*domus*) was erected over the site of St. Dunstan's burial-place for the daily services (para. 16*b*).

(b) The bodies of the archbishops (Cuthbert, Bregwin and their succes-
        sors) rested undisturbed in the burnt church of St. John for three
        years until Lanfranc began his rebuilding (para. 17a).
(c) At a time not specified, but by implication before the rebuilding of
        the church, the bodies of these archbishops were raised and put in
        safety in an unspecified place (para. 17b).[23]
(d) Lanfranc destroyed the cathedral church completely and built a new
        one from the foundations (paras. 17c and d).
(e) Before the work began he moved the bodies of the archbishops who
        had been buried in the eastern part of the cathedral; Dunstan and
        Elphege were therefore moved and reburied in the western sanctu-
        ary, the oratory of the Virgin Mary (para. 17e).[24]
(f) As time went on, this oratory had to be pulled down; and the bodies
        of the saints were again translated (para. 18).
(g) After a few years the bodies of the archbishops Cuthbert and Breg-
        win and their successors were translated to a chapel in an upper
        story of the new cathedral (para. 20).

As Willis pointed out, these records show clearly that the work of rebuilding was carried out in the usual way, beginning at the east so that the
new sanctuary was the first part to be completed; then in due course work
began on the rebuilding of the nave.

Since the archbishops buried in the church of St. John were moved
in the early stages of the work it follows that Lanfranc's building went at
least as far east as that church; and since it later became necessary to
move the bodies of St. Dunstan and St. Elphege from their temporary
resting place in the oratory of the Virgin Mary it is clear that the nave of
Lanfranc's new church went up to or beyond the extreme west end of the
old church. It therefore seems clear that Lanfranc's church covered the
whole site of the earlier cathedral, including the separate church of St.
John, but that we cannot be certain how much further eastward or westward it went than its predecessor.

Arrangement of Altars

The plan of the church shown in figure 7.2 as a reconstruction of the
building described by Eadmer represents a remarkably simple layout for
the metropolitan church of the province of Canterbury in the year 1067,
even if we admit that there may have been additional features which Eadmer did not think it necessary to mention. If we compare it with the
church described by Alcuin as having been built by Archbishop Albert

(767–80) at York, we cannot fail to be struck by the apparent inadequacy of the church at Canterbury in which, for example, Eadmer described only six altars,[25] by comparison with the thirty described by Alcuin at York. This seems to me yet another reason for thinking that the church which was burnt in 1067 was not a ninth- or tenth-century construction but was a survival from very early days and was so deeply revered that it had not been modified to keep it in fashion.

Bi-Polar Planning with Sanctuaries at the East and West

The presence of sanctuaries at the two ends of the old cathedral at Canterbury is of sufficient importance to warrant further study. It should again be emphasized that, although there is some element of doubt about the precise shape of the western sanctuary, Eadmer's record leaves no doubt whatever that there were two sanctuaries, of which that at the east had an altar in honor of our Savior and that at the west had an altar in honor of the Virgin Mary.

While there can be little doubt that St. Peter's at Rome was the source of inspiration for the principal sanctuary with its ring crypt below, this of itself gives no help towards explaining the second sanctuary at the other end of the church, because at St. Peter's this was the place of the great entrance doorways. The most probable explanation of the double-ended arrangement at Canterbury seems to me to be the purely functional development which has been sketched in Section 6, above, on the assumption that the Romano-British church which Augustine took over and repaired had only one sanctuary, at the west; and that the duplication of sanctuaries arose from a need to enlarge the church and provide a ring crypt so that mass could be celebrated directly above a newly acquired relic of our Savior.

This functional solution fits Eadmer's record, and seems to me more probable than Baldwin Brown's suggestion that the double sanctuary may have been copied from an Austrasian example in the time of Archbishop Odo.[26] In particular among the considerable number of German churches with double sanctuaries, I know of no instance that shows the arrangement peculiar to Canterbury of placing the archbishop's throne at the head of one apsidal sanctuary and the ring crypt beneath the opposite sanctuary. By contrast, as will appear below, I believe that the German and English examples of bi-polar churches are a parallel and independent development; of which the English one seems to be earlier. The priority of the development in England would follow straightforwardly if my dating in Section 6 should be proved correct, since this would place the double sanctuary at Canterbury before Archbishop Cuthbert (740–60) and probably not later than Theodore (668–90), whereas the first German example seems to be Fulda which was given its double-ended form in the reconstructions which were carried through by Abbot Ratger (802–17).

Since Fulda is particularly associated with the Anglo-Saxon missionary Boniface, and since the incidence of the double-ended churches in Germany agrees roughly with the area of his missions it might be tempting to infer that the idea of the double sanctuary was transmitted by them to Germany. Nevertheless it seems to me more likely that the development was an independent and functional one in Germany because the church at Fulda originally had a single eastern apse and Ratger's reconstruction seems to have had as its special object the provision of a resting place for Boniface's remains at the junction of a western transept and western sanctuary in very direct imitation of those of St. Peter's at Rome.

Finally, mention should also be made of the other site in England where there is record of an early church with apses at both east and west, namely Abingdon. The church said to have been built there during the reign of Ine, King of Wessex (688–726), is described by the chronicler as having been 120 ft. long and round both at the east and the west. Moreover the successor built during the abbacy of Ethelwold (ca. 954–63) is described as having a round sanctuary, a round nave twice as long, and a tower which was also round.[27] Unfortunately the evidence for the early church at Abingdon is less authoritative than that for Canterbury since it was based on tradition rather than eye-witness.[28] Excavations made at Abingdon in 1921–2 seem to have yielded little result.[29] Nevertheless, the tradition is of considerable interest when taken in conjunction with Eadmer's clear evidence for the two sanctuaries at Canterbury.

APPENDIX I: EARLIER STUDIES OF THE CATHEDRAL

In order to understand fully the new reconstruction and architectural history set out above for the Anglo-Saxon cathedral church at Canterbury and in order also to appreciate to the full the arguments for and against its several innovations it is important to have a clear grasp of the earlier attempts that have been made to solve these problems.

These earlier studies are set out in three major articles, namely, Willis (1845), Scott (1881), and Hope (1918); and in two incidental treatments in general textbooks, namely, Brown (1903); 260–63 and 267; and Clapham (1930), 85–87, 98 and 122.[30] The first four of these studies are accompanied by ground plans which illustrate the reconstruction proposed by their authors. As originally published, these plans where of different sizes, but to facilitate comparison between them I have reproduced all four in figures 7.3 and 7.4 as nearly as possible at a uniform size. I have also introduced a uniform system of lettering to denote the principal features on each of the plans, namely:

Z: Entry or entries to the crypt   U: Cloister (Willis only)
Y: Ring corridor of the crypt   T: Towers
X: Central passage or chamber   S: Choir of the singers
W: Cross passage (Brown only)   R: Western *porticus* (Brown only)
V: Western sanctuary   Q: Church of St. John
P: Straight joint between earlier
   western church and later eastern
   addition (Hope and Scott)

For greater clarity I have also shown beside each ground plan a separate plan of the crypt. In the case of Willis this plan of the crypt is open to some uncertainty because his ground plan does not show the crypt and his description in words is not without ambiguity.[31] The other three crypts were specified fairly precisely on the ground plans proposed by their authors, though Scott's is open to ambiguity about the length of the central passage, and Hope does not explicitly specify that he intended entry to the Church of St. John to be by way of the ring corridor as I have shown in my plan of his crypt.

The General Arrangements of the Church

It will be seen that in the general arrangement of the cathedral itself there is little difference between the plans of Willis, Scott, and Brown; but that

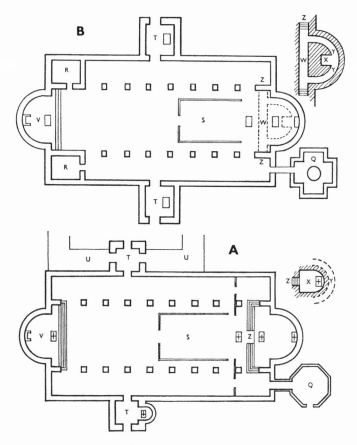

Fig. 7.3. Reconstructions of Willis (plan A) and Brown (plan B). The lettering is explained on p. 177 of Appendix I.

Hope introduces two major changes; first by introducing a transept (for which Eadmer gives no authority) and secondly by placing the towers over the aisles instead of outside them.

Brown makes no reference in his text to the two *porticus* R which he introduces at the west of his aisles. I imagine they must have been inspired by the arrangement of lateral western chambers at Silchester, although the plan of Silchester gives no authority for his placing of the doorways. He also showed the eastern sanctuary without its flight or flights of steps, no doubt in order to allow greater elaboration of the broken lines that serve to indicate his crypt.

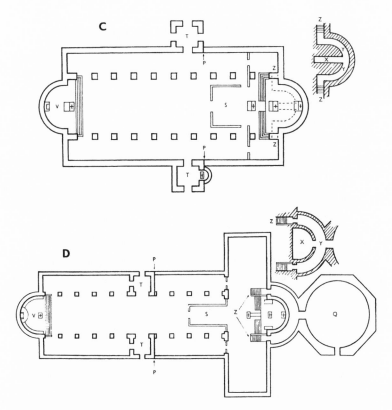

Fig. 7.4. Reconstructions of Scott (plan C) and Hope (plan D). The lettering is explained on p. 177 of Appendix I.

All four plans agree in showing the church with aisles separated from the central space by rows of square piers, although Eadmer's text gives no authority for this. I have therefore preferred to follow the example of the surviving major churches at Brixworth and Wing where the openings are in the form of widely spaced arches pierced through a solid wall. This also fits the pattern of the smaller Kentish churches, which we know to have had naves that opened through doorways to lateral *porticus*.

All four plans show the choir of the singers enclosed within screens in a space appreciably narrower than the nave. So far as I know there is no analogue for this in England, and I have therefore preferred to follow the pattern for which there is surviving structural evidence at Brixworth, and to which Eadmer's words seem to me equally applicable.

The Crypt

On the important matter of the crypt both Willis and Hope seem to me to have been led astray by a preconceived idea that there must have been an open central space of some considerable area. It was (I believe) this preconceived idea that led Willis to insert the words "of entrance" into his translation of para. 15(*e*) of Eadmer's account of the crypt, where no such words occur in the Latin. His description of his reconstruction of the crypt reads as follows:

> This crypt has an altar within, and a single entrance in the middle of its western face. . . . No mention is made of any outer crypt behind the principal one, and similar to the polyandrum of St. Peter's. But such a circumscribing crypt has been discovered in the ancient church of Brixworth running, however, outside the apse.[32]

My representation of Willis's crypt is, therefore, rather conjectural, showing the apsidal chamber x with its eastern altar and western entrance stairway, together with a possible but doubtful outer ring passage. Willis was cramped in his interpretation of Eadmer's text by an incomplete knowledge of the arrangements at St. Peter's to which Eadmer was comparing the crypt at Canterbury.

By contrast it is strange that Hope should have been so firmly attached to the idea of a large open central area within the crypt, for he was well aware of Scott's reconstruction with its straight central *confessio* passage which we now know to be a very accurate representation of the state of affairs at St. Peter's. The passage describing the crypt in Eadmer's manuscript (our paragraph 15 (*e*)) is not an easy one to translate, but in spite of the impressive list of authorities advanced by Hope in favor of his alternative translation I find Willis's translation given in Section 4 para.15 (*e*) preferable to Hope's alternative:

> Moreover a passage, that upon its western edge the curvature of the same crypt bounded, extended as far as the resting place of the blessed Dunstan.[33]

Two further objections can be advanced on architectural grounds against Hope's reconstruction of the crypt: first that there is no convenient place either in the crypt x or the ring passage y for the eastern altar that contained the head of St. Furseus, and secondly (as Hope himself seems to have appreciated) that it is a very forced interpretation of Eadmer's words to regard the passages, z, z, as "extending as far as the resting place of the blessed Dunstan."

Scott's reconstruction of 1881 seems to me to have provided the correct interpretation of the crypt; and in the main it was followed by Brown in 1903 except for the cross passage (w in my fig. 7.3) which Brown introduced with the words "At Canterbury to judge by the description the two ends were joined by a straight passage forming the chord of the arc."[34] I do not myself believe that there is any justification for this passage, either in Eadmer's text or in the remains at St. Peter's.

The Church of St. John (Baptistery, Mausoleum, and Law Court)

At first sight it is tempting to accept as plausible the chapels suggested in octagonal form by Willis or cruciform plan by Brown, having in mind early Mediterranean baptisteries which were based on the square, the octagon, or variants obtained by incorporating recesses into these shapes. But there is almost certainly an anachronism inherent in this suggestion, because the Italian examples of such baptisteries belong to the fifth century or thereabouts, and even in southern France where there is a cluster of octagonal baptisteries at Aix-en-Provence, Fréjus, Riez, and Marseille, these are also to be dated in the fifth and sixth centuries, so that their use as a model for Cuthbert's mid-eighth-century work at Canterbury is very improbable. Hope's large axial circular and octagonal building was admittedly based on Wulfric's eleventh-century work at St. Augustine's abbey; moreover it seems directly at variance to Eadmer's text which describes the two churches as "almost touching" and not as being joined together.

Since Cuthbert had before him the time-honored example of the church of St. Peter and St. Paul in St. Augustine's abbey I believe it is much more probable that he would have planned his church of St. John on somewhat similar lines, so that its nave could be used for baptisms and law-suits, while its *porticus* would provide convenient places for the burial of the archbishops, some dozen of whom we know to have been buried there before Dunstan set a new fashion for burial within the cathedral itself.

The Altar of St. Gregory

The inconvenience of an altar in the main entrance porch was appreciated by Willis who therefore provided space for it by throwing out an eastern apse. Scott followed this plan; but Brown correctly pointed out that Eadmer described no such apse. Brown therefore proposed an alternative solution based upon known examples of lateral displacement of doorways into *porticus* to allow space for altars, as at Bishopstone and Bradford-on-Avon.

Privacy for the chapel of St. Gregory would, however, be much more completely achieved by placing it on an upper floor, above the entrance porch, a position which is in no way precluded by Eadmer's text and for which we have a clear-cut example in the (western) entrance porch at Deerhurst.

The Cloister

Willis alone of the four shows a tentative cloister, which, as Eadmer describes, lies on either side of the tower of St. Martin (*hinc inde*). This description of the cloister seems to me the one serious objection to the supposition that the towers stood above the aisles (or *porticus*) rather than at their sides, for a cloister running along the north wall of the church can less easily be described as *hinc et inde* to a tower like that of Hope than to those of Willis, Scott, and Brown.

Architectural History

Scott proposed in some detail an architectural history which assumed that Augustine took over and brought into use a surviving church with a single western apse, and that later the church was roughly doubled in size by adding the choir of the singers and the eastern apse. Hope adopted this same pattern and in the plans by both writers the region of junction of the two churches is shown by straight joints P, P. Brown followed much the same pattern in his description but did not differentiate the building dates in his plan. Moreover he emphasized that the towers were most probably raised later upon what were at first lateral *porticus,* and that even these *porticus* were more likely to have been additions made in the seventh century than original parts of the Romano-British building.[35]

In the same place Brown argues that the baptistery is most logically placed near the entry of the church and that therefore: (*a*) the entry was probably originally at the east and only later changed to the south; and (*b*) that these changes probably took place when the eastern apse and crypt were built; and (*c*) that therefore the eastern apse and crypt are later than Cuthbert's baptistery, and are probably Odo's work, carried out during his great three-year repair of the roofs.

While it is indeed logical to argue for a baptistery at an entry to the church (and while there are good surviving examples of this on the Continent as widely spaced as Fréjus in the south of France and Essen in northern Germany) it does not at all follow that the building of the eastern apse and crypt before Cuthbert's baptistery would have hindered the logical use of the baptistery as an entrance to church during baptismal services. My figure 7.2 shows the baptistery linked to the cathedral church by atrium-like passages, Q, Q such as survive at Essen between the baptistery-church of St. John and the Cathedral, where to this day these passages have lateral access doorways. Such an arrangement would give a good circulation even for crowded baptismal services, and it would in no way preclude the use of the doorway below the south tower as the main entrance to the church.

Clapham's Summary

Clapham[36] gave no plan of the cathedral but in a brief summary he set out his view which may be even further summarized to say:

(*a*) The building as it stood in 1066 must have been in form and arrangement rather a work of Odo than of any earlier age.

(*b*) Any use of towers would have been unusual (even impossible) either in the Romano-British church or by Augustine.

(*c*) Twin flanking chapels or *porticus* are a distinctive feature of the early Kentish churches; and the dedications to St. Martin and St. Gregory strengthen the assumption that St. Augustine built these projecting chapels.

(*d*) The towers were later additions to these chapels, probably in the tenth century, when we know that similar additions were made elsewhere.

(*e*) It seems probable that the church had apses at both ends but as to the date of either it would be idle to speculate.

A Recent Reconstruction by Gilbert

In conclusion, reference should be made to a recent reconstruction proposed by Edward Gilbert in an article mainly devoted to a general study of the English basilica and to Brixworth in particular.[37] His reconstruction shows the crypt in the form indicated by Willis, as a large chamber entered by a single passage from the west. This reconstruction seems to be contrary both to Eadmer's description in words and also to his clear assertion that the crypt was "fabricated in the likeness of the confessionary of St. Peter."

It is necessary also to refer briefly to Gilbert's claims that "it can be taken as proved that the building dates from Wulfred's rule here, and is about A.D. 813." In my opinion this claim for a proved date for the building of the Anglo-Saxon cathedral church is based upon a misinterpretation of a privilege of Archbishop Wulfred (fifteenth archbishop, 805–32).[38] The relevant text reads as follows:

> Anno ab incarnatione ejusdem Dei et redemptionis mundi DCCCXIII Indict VI praesidente Christi gratia Archpontifice Ulfredo metropolitano sedem Ecclesiae Christi, quae sita est in Durovernia civitate, anno vii episcopatus ejusdem Archiepiscopi, Divina ac fraterna pietate ductus, amore Deo auxiliante, renovando et restaurando pro honore et amore Dei sanctum monasterium Durovernensis ecclesiae reaedificando refici, auxiliantibus ejusdem Ecclesiae presbiteris et diaconibus cunctoque clero Domino Deo serventium simul.

The passage as a whole should, I believe, be translated thus:

> In the year of the Incarnation of the same God and Redeemer of the world 813, Indiction 6, the metropolitan archpontif Wulfred, being by the grace of God in charge of the see of the church of Christ which is situated in the city of Canterbury, in year 7 of the episcopate of the said archbishop, I, moved by divine and fraternal piety, the love of God assisting, have repaired by renewing restoring and rebuilding for the honor of God the holy monastery of the church of Canterbury, with the help of the priests and deacons of the same church and likewise of all the clergy serving the Lord God.

From the point of view of the architectural historian the important words are *monasterium Durovernensis ecclesiae refici,* and these seem to me to involve the translation, "I have repaired the monastery of the church of Canterbury." The whole content of the privilege relates to a renewal of monastic life and therefore also strengthens the belief that this natural translation of the Latin gives a correct interpretation of Wulfred's contribution to Canterbury cathedral, namely a reconstruction of derelict monastic buildings and a re-introduction of stricter monastic life. I do not for a moment suggest that the text can be taken as proving that Wulfred did not carry out work on the church itself; but I think it is wrong to use this text as proof that the church described by Eadmer was substantially Wulfred's work. From the translation given above it will be seen that I also disagree with Gilbert's belief that *sedem* should be translated "temple."

APPENDIX II: THE ORIGINAL SOURCES

General Notes

The consecutive account of the history of Canterbury Cathedral set out in Willis's Chapter 1 and abbreviated in my Section 2 was compiled by Willis from a number of separate writings, mostly by Eadmer, but including also three that have generally been attributed to Osbern who wrote about the end of the eleventh century. This variety of sources means that arguments from silence are reduced in value, and that there is great danger of misinterpretation unless the utmost care is taken to ensure that passages which are associated in the composite history do indeed relate to one and the same event. My independent checking of Willis's work in these respects has greatly impressed me with his accuracy.

In order to direct attention to the variety of sources and at the same time to provide abbreviated references to them, there are listed in Table A the nine separate works from which quotation is made, together with an abbreviation for each work, and a list of the paragraphs of Sections 2 and 3 that are taken from it. It will be noted that while the history of the cathedral contained in Section 2 is derived from all nine works, the de-

Table A

	Work	Abbreviated Title	Paragraphs Taken From Each Work
Eadmer	*Vita Sancti Bregwini*	EB	2, 4, 14, 17(*a*), 20
Osbern (Eadmer?)	*Vita Odonis*	OO	6
Osbern	*Vita Sancti Dunstani*	OD	10, 11(*a*)
Eadmer	*Liber miraculorum Sancti Dunstani*	EMD	16(*a*), 16(*b*), 17(*c*), 17(*e*), 1, 18
Eadmer	*Epistola ad Glastonienses de corpore S. Dunstani*	EGD	11(*b*), 13, 17(*e*)[2]
Eadmer	*De reliquiis Sancti Audoeni . . .*	ERA	11(*c*), All of 15
Osbern	*Vita sancti Elphegi*	OE	12
Eadmer	*Historia Novorum in Anglia*	EH	17(*d*)
Eadmer	*Vita sancti Wilfridi*	EW	19

scription of the building in Section 3, para. 15, is wholly taken from one work, thus greatly increasing its reliability.

Sources for Section 2

The following paragraphs of Latin text are numbered to correspond to the paragraphs of the English translation in Section 2. After each paragraph or sub-paragraph the reference in square brackets gives the following items of information:

> Where the Latin text is referred to or quoted in Willis, *Architectural History of Canterbury Cathedral* (London, 1845).
> The original work from which it is taken, using the abbreviations in Table A, above.
> Abbreviations are footnoted.

Thus for para. 2, the note indicates that Willis cites the text on his page 2, note b; that it comes from Eadmer's *Vita sancti Bregwini;* and that it is published in H. Wharton's *Anglia Sacra* (1691), vol. 2, p. 186. In each case my text follows that of the last-named authority rather than that of Willis when there is any discrepancy.

>2. Is inter alia bona . . . fecit Ecclesiam in Orientali parte majoris Ecclesiae eidem pene contiguam; eamque in honorem beati Johannis Baptistae solenniter dedicavit. Hanc Ecclesiam eo respectu fabricavit; ut baptisteria & examinationes judiciorum pro diversis causis constituorum, quae ad correctionem sceleratorum in Ecclesia Dei fieri solent, inibi celebrarentur, & Archiepiscoporum corpora in ea sepelirentur: sublata de medio antiqua consuetudine, qua eatenus tumulari solebant extra civitatem in Ecclesia Beatorum Apostolorum Petri & Pauli, ubi posita sunt corpora omnium antecessorum suorum. Hic . . . in praefata Ecclesia Beati Johannis decenter sepultus. [W2, note *b*; EB; *Anglia Sacra,* vol. 2, 186]
>4. Sepultus sane est in praefata Ecclesia Beati Baptistae Johannis prope corpus Reverendi Pontificis Cuthberti. [W2, note *e*; EB; *Anglia Sacra,* vol. 2, 187]
>6. Tectum ejusdem Ecclesiae Christi nimia vetustate corruptum, semirutis per totum partibus pendebat. Quod ille renovare cupiens, murum quoque in porrectiorem celsitudinem exaltari desiderans, congregatis artificibus praecepit & quod dissolutum

desuper eminebat penitus tolli, & quod minus in altitudine murus habebat jussit extolli . . . .Factum est, ut in tribus annis, quibus Ecclesiae muri in altum porrigebantur, tota fabrica desuper pateret, nec tamen non dico infra ambitum solius Ecclesiae, sed nec intra muros totius civitatis imber aliquando descenderet. [W3, note *g*; OO; *Anglia Sacra,* vol. 2, 83]

10. Nam cum die adventus sui primo sacris altaribus assisteret [ad altare Domini Salvatoris Cantuariae] repente contecta nube domo columba in Jordane a Johanne olim visa iterum apparuit; quae quousque sacrificium fuisset consumptum super illum mansit. Cumque consumptum fuisset sacrificium; requievit supra memoriam Beati Odonis, quae ad australem partem altaris in modum pyramidis exstructa fuit. [W6, note *m*; OD; *Anglia Sacra,* vol. 2, 110 (except for words in squaɪe brackets which come from OO; *Anglia Sacra,* vol. 2, 86)]

11(a). Sepultus sane est in loco quo ipse disposuerat, loco scilicet ubi quotidie divinum officium a fratribus celebrabatur, quod fuit ante gradus quibus ad altare Domini Christi ascendebatur. [W6, note *n;* OD; RS 63,[39] 221]

11(*b*). In medio chori ante gradus, quibus ad majus altare ascendebatur, corpus Beati Dunstani humatum fuit, in plumbeo loculo, et illo in magna profunditate terrae locato, uti Anglis olim moris erat suorum cadavera tumulare. . . . Infra terram ad staturam virilis corporis foveae profunditas penetraverit. [W6, note *n;* EGD; RS 63, 419 and 418]

11(c). Tumba super eum in modum pyramidis grandi sublimique constructa habente ad caput sancti altare matutinale. [W6, note *n;* ERA; Willmart, 1935, 365][40]

12. Jam populo caeso, jam urbe flammata, jam denique Christi templo violato, perscrutato, spoliato, extrahitur Sanctus toto corpore vinctus, furientis populi manibus occidentus . . . .Ibi menses septem duodeno milite septum servavere . . . .Deinde alii atque alii eum lapidibus obruunt. [W7, note *p;* OE; *Anglia Sacra,* vol. 2, 136, 137, 140]

13. Ecclesia ipsa in passioni beatissimi martyris [Elphegi] nec igne consumpta, nec tecto aut parietibus diruta fuit. [W8, note *u;* EGD; RS 63, 418]

14. Post haec multis malis quaque per Angliam crebrescentibus, contigit civitatem Cantuariam ex incuria flammis in matrem Ecclesiam inibi consistentem incendium ferri. Quid dicam?

Combusta est tota cum officinis Monachorum ibi degentium pene omnibus, simul & Ecclesia Beati Johannis Baptistae, ubi ut praedictum est Archiepiscoporum reliquiae jacebant humatae. [W9, note *x;* EB; *Anglia Sacra,* vol. 2, 187–8]

16. In qua tamen conflagratione magna miseracordia [Dei] et inter-cessione pii Dunstani actum est ut duae domus, sine quibus fratres esse non poterant, illaesae ab incendio remanerent; refec-torium, videlicet, et dormitorium cum claustris quae appenda-bant. Dehinc aedificata est domus non adeo grandis super locum quietis beati viri, et in ea circa sacrum corpus ejus missae cum reliquo sevitio Dei quotidie fiebant. [W13, note *c;* EMD; RS 63, 231]

17(*a*). Post istud gemendum incendium corpora Pontificum supra memoratorum suis loculis immota quiescebant; donec ille viro-rum strenuissimus & cum omni honore nominandus Lanfrancus videlicet Cadomensis coenobii abbas Archiepiscopatu Cantuari-ensi functus est. Is quippe omnia quae combusti monasterii rep-perit vel aedificia vel aedificiorum detrita monumenta terrae coaequans, & quae sub terra erant fundamenta effodiens, cuncta nova extruxit. [W13, first quotation in note *d;* EB; *Anglia Sacra,* vol. 2, 188]

17(*b*). Et praefatos antistites levari ac in tuto locari constituit; donec ea quam coeperat Ecclesia facta esset, in qua decenter poni valerent. Et ita factum est. [W13, first quotation in note *d;* EB, *Anglia Sacra,* vol. 2, 188]

17(*c*). Lanfrancus . . . ecclesiam Salvatoris, quam cum praefatum incendium tum vetustas inutilem fecerat funditus destruere et augustiorem construere cupiens, . . . [W13, fourth quotation in note *d;* EMD; RS 63, 232]

17(*d*). Ecclesiam praeterea quam spatio septem annorum a funda-mentis ferme totam perfectam reddidit. [W13, second quotation in note *d;* EH; RS 81, 13[41]]

17(e). 1. Jussit corpora sanctorum, quae in orientali parte ipsius ec-clesiae humata erant, in occidentalem partem, ubi memoria beatae Dei genetricis et perpetuae Virginis Mariae celebris habebatur, demutari. Quamobrem celebrato triduano jejunio, sub innumera hominum multitudine levata sunt corpora pretio-sissimorum pontificum Christi Dunstani atque Elfegi; jam trans-ferebantur ad destinatum locum sepulturae. [W14, fourth quotation in note *d;* EMD; RS 63, 232]

2. Testis enim est mihi omnia sciens & disponens veritas Deus; quia cum adhuc in scholis puerulus essem. [W14, sixth quotation in note *d;* EGD; *Anglia Sacra,* vol. 2, 222]

18. Inter haec proficiente novo opere coeptae ecclesiae, res exegit residuum vetusti operis, ubi memorata sanctorum corpora erant locata, subverti; parato igitur refectorio fratrum ad divinum officium inibi celebrandum, omnes cum festiva processione illuc a veteri ecclesia perreximus, praeferentes cum honore et reverentia gloriosos ac dulcissimos patres nostros Dunstanum atque Elfegum. [W15, note *g;* EMD; RS 63, 236]

19. Cum ergo praedictum altare subverteretur, reliquiae beati Wilfridi repertae ac levatae sunt, atque in scrinio collocatae. Verum cum post aliquot annos fratrum voluntas in eo consentiret, ut magis fixo loco clauderentur; sepulcrum eis in aquilonari parte altaris factum est, et in eo sunt quarto idus Octobris reverenter inclusae. [W15, note *i;* EW; RS 71, vol. 1, 226][42]

20. Post aliquot annos in Ecclesiam jam fundatam illati sunt, & in aquilonali parte super voltum singuli sub singulis ligneis locellis, ubi quotidie mysterium Sacrificii salutaris celebratur, positi sunt. [W16, note *k;* EB; *Anglia Sacra,* vol. 2, 188]

Sources for Section 3

As for Section 2, the paragraphs of the Latin text are numbered to agree with the English translation. By contrast with Section 2 the whole Latin text of Section 3 comes from a continuous passage in Eadmer's *De reliquiis sancti Audoeni et quorundam aliorum sanctorum quae Cantuariae in aecclesia Domini Salvatoris habentur.* Most of the Latin Text is quoted in W10 note *y* and W12 note *a;* the full text is given in Willmart;[43] and also in RS 73, vol. 1, 8,[44] in the form in which it was quoted by Gervase of Canterbury writing later in the twelfth century. Therefore no references are given here for individual paragraphs as is done above for Section 2. The text quoted below is taken from Willmart.

15(*a*). Erat enim ipsa aecclesia—quod per excessum dici patienter, quaeso, accipiatur—sicut in historiis Beda testatur, Romanorum opere facta, et ex quadam parte ad imitationem aecclesiae beati aposto[lo]rum principis Petri, in qua sacratissimae reliquiae illius totius orbis ueneratione celebrantur, decenter composita.

15(*b*). Ipsis pene diebus idem uenerabilis Odo corpus beati Wilfridi pontificis Eboracensium de Rhipis sublatum, Cantuarium trans-tulerat, et illud in editiore entheca, ut ipsimet scribit, hoc est in maiori altari, quod in orientali presbiterii parte, parieti contiguum, de impolitis lapidibus et cemento extructum erat, digniter collocauerat.

15(*c*). Porro aliud altare, congruo spatio antepositum praedicto altari, erat dedicatum in honorem domini nostri Jesu Christi, ubi cotidie diuina misteria celebrabantur. In quo altari beatus Aelfegus caput sancti Suuithuni, quod ipse, a pontificatu Wintoniensi in archiepiscopatum Cantuariensem translatus, secum tulerat, cum multis aliorum sanctorum reliquiis solenniter reposuerat.

15(*d*). Ad haec altaria nonnullis gradibus ascendebatur a choro cantorum, quoniam cripta, quam confessionem Romani uocant, subtus erat, adinstar confessionis sancti Petri fabricata, cuius fornix eo in altum tendebatur, ut superiora eius non nisi per plures gradus possent adiri.

15(*e*). Haec intus ad orientem altare habebat, quod caput beati Fursei, ut antiquitas fatebatur, in se habebat. Sane uia una, quam curuatura criptae ipsius ad occidentem uergentem concipiebat, usque ad locum quietis beati Dunstani tendebatur, qui maceria forti ab ipsa cripta dirimebatur. Ipse nanque sanctissimus pater ante ipsos gradus in magna profunditate terrae iacebat humatus, tumba super eum in modum piramidis grandi sullimique constructa, habente ad caput sancti altare matutinale.

15(*f*). Inde ad occidentem chorus psallentium in aulam aecclesiae porrigebatur, decenti fabrica a frequentia turbae seclusus.

15(*g*). Dein sub medio longitudinis aulae ipsius duae turres erant, prominentes ultra aecclesiae alas. Quarum una, quae in austro erat, sub honore beati Gregorii papae altare in medio sui dedicatum habebat, et in latere principale ostium aecclesiae, quod antiquitus ab Anglis et nunc usque SUTHDURE dicitur. Quod ostium in antiquorum legibus regum suo nomine sepe exprimitur, in quibus etiam omnes querelas totius regni quae in hundredis uel comitatibus uno uel pluribus uel certe in curia regis non possent legaliter definiri, finem inibi, sicut in curia regis summi, sortiri debere decernitur.

15(*h*). Alia uero turris in plaga aquilonali e regione illius condita fuit in honorem beati Martini, claustra in quibus monachi conuersabantur hinc inde habens. Et sicut ante aliam forenses lites et saecularia placita exercebantur, ita in ista adolescentiores fratres in discendo aecclesiastica officia die ac nocte pro temporum uicibus instituabantur.

15(*i*). Finis aecclesiae ornabatur oratorio beatae matris dei Mariae. Ad quod, quia structura eius talis erat, non nisi per gradus cuius patebat accessus. In cuius parte orientali erat altare in ueneratione ipsius dominae consecratum, et in eo caput beatae uirginis Astrobertae honorabatur inclusum.

15(*j*). Ad hoc altare cum sacerdos ageret diuina misteria, faciem ad populum qui deorsum stabat ad orientem uersam habebat, post se uero ad occidentem cathedram pontificalem, decenti opere ex magnis lapidibus et cemento constructam, et hanc longe a dominica mensa remotam, utpote parieti aecclesiae qui totius templi complexio erat omnino contiguam.

15(*k*). Hic situs fuerat aecclesiae Cantuariensis. Quem ea re hic ita paucis descripsimus, ut, cum praesentis aetatis homines et futurae antiquorum de hoc scripta audierint, nec iuxta relationem illorum quicquam inuenerint, sciant illa uetera transisse et omnia noua facta esse. Siquidem post innumeras persecutiones, quas sepissime passa est intus et foris, occulto nostris diebus, sed iusto iudicio dei, incendio consumpta est, et cum omnibis ornamentis et utensilibus suis in nichilum pene redacta.

NOTES

[1] The dates of Eadmer's birth and death are not known with certainty; the former must have been about 1060 and the latter probably 1130, although claims have been made for a date as late as 1144. See R. W. Southern, *Saint Anselm and his Biographer* (Cambridge, 1963), 231, 239 for the arguments supporting 1060 and 1130.

[2] R. Willis, *Architectural History of Canterbury Cathedral* (London, 1845).

[3] D. Whitelock, ed., *English Historical Documents,* vol. 1 (London, 1955; 2nd ed., 1996), 604; translating from Bede's *Historia Ecclesiastica.*

[4] My serial numbers and dates for the archbishops differ slightly from those cited in Willis: mine are taken from F. M. Powicke and E. B. Fryde, eds., *Handbook of British Chronology,* 2nd ed. (London, 1961), 209–10, omitting Wigheard who did not live to take up office.

[5] Here and in para. 11, I have used "memorial" for the monument placed above the place of burial. The Latin word used here is "memoria," while in para. 11 it is "tumba." That Odo was in fact buried beneath the memorial is made clear by Osbern, who relates the same episode in his *Vita sancti Odonis* and there

includes the words "ubi Venerabilis Odo tumulatus jacebat" (H. Wharton, *Anglia Sacra,* vol. 2 [London, 1691], 86).

6 See footnote 5. The coffin has been specified as having been placed deep underground; the large and lofty pyramid was therefore clearly a memorial rather than a tomb.

7 Although Willis included this passage in the original Latin in his footnote d (Willis, *Canterbury Cathedral,* 13), he did not give it any place in the composite English translation of his para. 17 which is built up from a number of separate original sources. I am much indebted to Martin Biddle for having pointed out to me the relevance of this passage to the consideration of the details of the extent of Lanfranc's rebuilding in relation to the Anglo-Saxon cathedral.

8 The "D" version of the *Anglo-Saxon Chronicle* records under 1023 that in that year the body of Elphege was translated from London to Canterbury and buried on the north side of the altar of Christ.

9 That is to say the church known as Old St. Peter's at Rome.

10 Here Willis says: "To reach these altars, a certain crypt which the Romans call a confessionary had to be ascended by means of several steps from the choir of the singers. This crypt was fabricated beneath in the likeness . . ."

11 In his translation Willis has inserted the words "of entrance" near the beginning of this sentence so that it reads, "Moreover the single passage (of entrance) which ran westward . . ." No such words occur in the Latin, and I believe that their insertion obscures, and indeed incorrectly changes, Eadmer's meaning.

12 In this sentence Willis says: "which projected beyond the aisles of the church." The Latin is "ultra," which I think is capable of either meaning. See Section 5 for arguments supporting my belief that Eadmer intended to convey the meaning that the towers projected above the aisles. In the final sentence of this paragraph my translation also differs from that of Willis, but the change has no architectural significance.

13 For a full account of the considerations that are set out very briefly in this section, see J. Toynbee and J. Ward Perkins, *The Shrine of St. Peter* (London, 1956), or E. Kirschbaum, *The Tombs of St. Peter and St. Paul* (London, 1959), or the original reports of the excavators to which full references are given in the two books named.

14 For a detailed account of the development of ring crypts and their distribution both on the Continent and in England, see H. M. Taylor, "Corridor Crypts on the Continent and in England," *North Staffordshire J. of Field Stud.* 9 (1969), 17–52

15 In the normal arrangement of a ring crypt there would be a major relic in or below the *confessio* chamber, and therefore directly below the high altar B. Eadmer makes no mention of any such relic; I return to this point in Section 6.

[16] W. St. John Hope, "The First Cathedral Church of Canterbury," *Proc. of the Soc. of Antiquaries of London,* 2nd ser. 30 (1918), 136–58; A. W. Clapham, *English Romanesque Architecture Before the Conquest* (Oxford, 1930).

[17] The idea that these chapels were placed on the upper floors of the towers does not seem to have been suggested previously in any English text. It was put forward some time ago on the Continent at the second International Congress for the Study of the Art of the Early Middle Ages, see. P. Verdier, "Transepts de nef." *Arte del primo millenio* (Pavia, 1954), 354–61, at p. 357. Evidence for two such chapels in the upper stories of an entrance porch or tower has survived at Deerhurst, see H. M. Taylor and Joan Taylor, *Anglo-Saxon Architecture* (Cambridge, 1965), 197, 205.

[18] For an alternative reconstruction that shows square piers and wide arches instead of a continuous wall and narrow doorways, see Taylor, "Corridor Crypts," fig. 11.

[19] Willis, *Canterbury Cathedral,* 30.

[20] Tentative assignments to Odo are made by G. B. Brown, *The Arts in Early England,* vol. 2, *Anglo-Saxon Architecture,* 2nd ed. (London, 1925), 232–33 and by Clapham, *English Romanesque Architecture,* 87. An assignment to about this time is also implicit in Conant's statement referring to works of the time of King Edgar and saying that "we know from texts that there was a considerable amount of cathedral building including Canterbury which was rebuilt as a 'double-ender' with two lateral porticus" (K. Conant, *Carolingian and Romanesque Architecture, 800–1200* [London, 1959], 32). This statement, particularly in its implied certainty in the dating of the double eastern and western sanctuaries at Canterbury, seems to me a very dangerous misrepresentation of the facts.

[21] Taylor, "Corridor Crypts."

[22] The cathedral at Fulda provides a good example of such an operation, although at Fulda the early sanctuary was at the east and the new sanctuary added during the enlargement was at the west.

[23] Willis omitted this passage from his para. 17; see footnote 7.

[24] It seems clear beyond doubt from para. 10 and note 5 that Odo was buried at the south of the altar of our Savior. It is therefore strange that in his accounts of the translations of the saints who had been buried within the cathedral Eadmer should so clearly refer in paras. 17 and 18 only to Dunstan and Elphege, and should omit Odo. This indicates very clearly the dangers of arguments based on silence, particularly when the original sources are so diverse (see also Appendix II).

[25] Or seven, if we accept my suggestion that there was an altar dedicated to St. Martin in the north tower.

[26] G. B. Brown, *The Arts in Early England,* vol. 2, *Anglo-Saxon Architecture* (London, 1903), 263; and Brown, *Anglo-Saxon Architecture,* 2nd ed., 232–33.

[27] *Chronicon Monasterii de Abingdon,* ed. J. Stevenson, Rolls Series 2 (London, 1858), vol. 2, 272 and 277.

[28] See F. M. Stenton, *Early History of the Abbey of Abingdon* (Oxford, 1913), 1–2. The three manuscripts of this chronicle are all of the thirteenth century although one contains evidence that establishes it as a copy of a work written by a monk who was an inmate of the abbey in 1117. Unfortunately the details of the buildings are contained only in the manuscript which Stenton regarded as the least reliable of the three.

[29] Clapham, *English Romanesque Architecture,* 156.

[30] Willis, *Canterbury Cathedral*; G. G. Scott (the Younger) *History of English Church Architecture* (London, 1881); Hope, "First Cathedral Church of Canterbury"; Brown, *Anglo-Saxon Architecture*; Clapham, *English Romanesque Architecture.*

[31] Willis, *Canterbury Cathedral,* 25–26.

[32] Ibid.

[33] Hope, "First Cathedral Church of Canterbury," 152.

[34] Brown, *Anglo-Saxon Architecture,* 262.

[35] Ibid.

[36] Clapham, *English Romanesque Architecture.*

[37] E. Gilbert, "Brixworth and the English Basilica," *Art Bulletin* 47 (1965), 1–20, at pp. 9–10, and fig. 10.

[38] A. W. Hadden and W. Stubbs, *Councils and Ecclesiastical Documents Relating to Great Britain and Ireland,* vol. 3 (Oxford, 1871), 575; A. W. Birch, *Cartularium Saxonicum* (London, 1883–93), no. 342.

[39] W. Stubbs, ed., *Memorials of St. Dunstan,* Rolls Series 63 (London, 1874).

[40] A. Willmart, "Opuscula: Edmeri Cantuarensis cantoris nova opuscula de sanctorum veneratione et obsecratione," *Revue des Sciences Religieuses* 15 (1935), 184–219 and 354–79.

[41] M. Rule, ed., *Eadmer's Historia Novorum in Anglia,* Rolls Series 81 (London, 1884).

[42] J. Raine, ed., *Historians of the Church of York,* Rolls Series 71 (London, 1879), vol. 1.

[43] Willmart, "Opuscula," 365–66.

[44] W. Stubbs, ed., *The Historical Works of Gervase of Canterbury,* Rolls Series 73 (London, 1878), vol. 1, 8.

CHAPTER 8

Anglo-Saxon Church Building
Aspects of Design and Construction

WARWICK RODWELL

BACKGROUND

Although my interest in the archaeology of buildings was first aroused more than twenty years ago, it was not until 1971 that the opportunity arose to undertake a large-scale investigation on a completely intact parish church, when a three-year project was initiated at Rivenhall, Essex. The project involved not only extensive excavations around the parish church, but also detailed recording of the entire upstanding fabric. Rivenhall church had generally been dismissed as a building of minimal architectural interest, on the presumption that it was a largely Victorian rebuild. However, investigation demonstrated that the hitherto unknown shell of an Anglo-Saxon nave and chancel still stood to a height of 6.25m behind a mantle of recent stucco.[1]

Although the church lacked sumptuous sculpture and most of the diagnostic architectural detailing normally associated with Anglo-Saxon buildings, it had much to offer by way of constructional evidence. The Rivenhall discovery came at an opportune moment, when Harold Taylor was searching for fresh means to advance our knowledge of the constructional history and chronology of Anglo-Saxon church architecture. In pursuit of this aim he was jointly responsible for the initiation of research projects at Deerhurst in 1973 and at Repton in 1974; and he was instrumental in the promotion of a program of excavation and structural study at Hadstock, also begun in 1974. From the outset all three sites returned impressive yields of fresh information, demanding significant changes to the generally accepted architectural histories of those buildings. But more than this, the techniques and equipment of the Anglo-Saxon builders began to be unveiled: at last it became possible to comprehend these churches not just as specimens of art history, but also as works of constructional engineering.

Rivenhall, Deerhurst, Repton, and Hadstock all have living churches, and the extent to which their sites and fabrics can be disturbed in pursuit of academic knowledge must, perforce, be limited. What was really needed—to obtain the maximum yield of evidence—was a substantial Anglo-Saxon church where there was no obstacle to mounting a program of intensive archaeological and architectural study on the building and its site, both internally and externally. The redundant church of St. Peter, Barton-upon-Humber, met all the required conditions, and it must be acknowledged that one of Harold Taylor's major achievements was to persuade the Department of the Environment in 1977 to facilitate and fund at Barton the fullest program of investigation so far to take place on a parish church in Britain. For the first time it has been possible to study an Anglo-Saxon (and medieval) stone building, and the processes involved in its construction, from the foundations to the roofs.

Barton-upon-Humber was a particularly apt choice for investigation, since it is a church about which a great deal has been written, and it is instructive to compare previous attempts to expound its architectural history with the evidence now fully revealed.[2] St. Peter's Church made its debut in architectural history in 1819 with Thomas Rickman, and has subsequently been discussed by numerous scholars. By 1974 the possibilities for further superficial study of the church had reached the point of exhaustion; with typical Taylorian succinctness, the situation was summed up thus: "It will be clear from what has been said that much of the history of this important church remains uncertain. . . . It is very much hoped that full opportunity will be taken of the present period of redundancy to enable a thorough investigation to be made, both inside and around it, using all the specialized techniques of modern archaeology . . ."[3]

It is not appropriate in this paper to expound the results of archaeological investigations at either Barton-upon-Humber or any other particular site; instead an attempt will be made to outline some of the classes of constructional evidence which have been studied in recent years, in varying depths, on a score of Anglo-Saxon buildings.

STRUCTURAL CRITICISM
AND STRUCTURAL DISSECTION

The need to examine carefully and appraise critically all the component parts of an Anglo-Saxon church has been discussed by Taylor,[4] particularly in relation to vertical joints in walls, quoin types, fabric changes, and inserted features. The processes he describes, and has himself used extensively, Taylor calls "structural criticism." They are non-destructive and therefore essentially superficial, and can thus be applied to any building without detriment to fabric or decoration. It is, however, readily apparent when undertaking structural criticism that, if circumstances allow, a much deeper probing into the stone and timber fabric of a church will yield greater returns of information, and will permit enigmatic features to be explored and ambiguous relationships to be correctly determined. This process, which we might term "structural dissection," is essentially an extension above ground of the principles and techniques of archaeological excavation.

The purpose of structural dissection is similar to that of biological dissection: to open up the specimen, to discover and examine its constituent parts, and to ascertain their composition, interrelationships, and mode of functioning. While structural dissection, like structural criticism, can be used to examine a particular feature, or features, within a building, it can be as dangerous and misinformative as keyhole excavation. Its real value lies in its ability to demonstrate, stage by stage, the processes involved in the erection of a building. Anomalies such as inserted features, raised walls, patched or refaced masonry, and even recycled materials will almost automatically proclaim themselves if the principles of building and the techniques of dissection are correctly understood and applied. In essence, the investigator has temporarily to assume the role of the Anglo-Saxon builder, and follow the construction of the church, stone by stone and timber by timber.

It would be premature to attempt a treatise on Anglo-Saxon building, since few standing structures have been intensively investigated, and since building practice clearly varied from one geographical region to another. What follows here is essentially an introduction to some of the classes of evidence for Anglo-Saxon building technique, as revealed by recent investigations on a small number of churches, augmented by some more generalized observations.

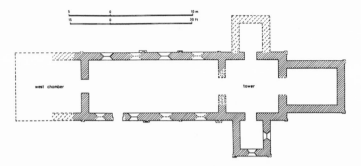

Fig. 8.1. Breamore: reconstructed plan of the Anglo-Saxon church, which is based on the Northern rod (15 N feet). The tower is externally 25 N ft. square (1⅔ N rods), and the nave is a double square of the same dimension (25 by 50 N ft.), with the pilasters approximately marking bays. The *porticus* were added as squares, half the size of the tower, and the chancel is 20 N ft. (1⅓ N rods) in length.

ELEMENTS OF CHURCH CONSTRUCTION

1. Ground Plans and Foundations

It has often been assumed that because a significant number of Anglo-Saxon churches display irregularities in their ground plans no precise unit of measurement or procedure for laying out the foundations could have been employed (e.g. Bosham, Sussex). Serious doubts are now being cast upon this premise, for two reasons. First, careful recording has recently demonstrated that many secular and ecclesiastical buildings, both in timber and in stone, exhibit ratios between the lengths of their walls which presuppose the use of a standardized measuring rod of fifteen "northern" or long Roman feet, equivalent to 16½ statute feet, or 5.03m.[5] Secondly, churches which may be geographically distant from one another, or locally grouped, can display such similarities of proportion or absolute measurement as to leave little room for doubt that master-plans existed in pre-Conquest England.

Birthe Kjølbye-Biddle has convincingly demonstrated that a large, multi-cellular church such as the Old Minster at Winchester was designed and laid out with the Drusian foot as the unit of measurement.[6] The smaller minster church at Breamore, Hants., exhibits an impressively regular plan, based on the Roman foot (fig. 8.1),[7] as does the much simpler two-celled Rivenhall church.[8] Some notable irregularities in church plans, such as the skewed west end at Hadstock, have turned out upon investigation to be later interferences with the Anglo-Saxon plan;[9] but in other instances the anomalous ground plan is demonstrably original. This applies at Barton-upon-Humber, where the western baptistery is set askew to the turriform nave (see fig. 8.13): it is plainly obvious that the baptistery was intended to be a mirror-image of the chancel, but that a simple error occurred during setting out.[10] Builders' errors in setting out have always been, and still are, commonplace; scrutiny of an accurate plan can frequently explain the nature and magnitude of the error, even if the reason for its occurrence is not always apparent. Foundation plans often differ from wall plans, and it is not uncommon to find that an accurately planned church could rest upon seemingly irregular foundations (cf. the Old Minster, Winchester). The converse can also be true; and one wonders, for example, what the foundation plan of Chickney, Essex, might look like. There, the nave and chancel appear to be parallelograms, a circumstance repeated in the plan of the twelfth-century Fishermen's Chapel at St. Brelade, Jersey; but recent excavation of the chapel has shown that it rests upon a broad foundation of contemporary date and rectangular plan.

Most of the excavations at churches on clay and sandy subsoils in lowland England have revealed foundations of layered form, extending to a depth of up to one meter. These foundations usually comprise two distinct materials, deposited and compacted in alternating layers: one material is coarse and granular (gravel, chalk, or stone rubble), while the other is finer and more cohesive (clay, sand, or crushed mortar from demolished structures). Foundations of this nature have a remarkable stability in ground which is liable to slight seasonal movement.

On waterlogged and unstable ground timber or timber-laced foundations were constructed, and a splendid example of the latter was recorded in one of the lateral apses of the Old Minster at Winchester.[11] Here, a chalk raft-foundation was spinally laced with jointed timbers (fig. 8.2). The Anglo-Saxon church at Headbourne Worthy, Hants., rests on a mud-bank and is almost entirely surrounded by water, a tributary of the river Itchen. When its walls were underpinned some years ago the church was described as having no foundations, and it seems probable that the building was erected on a timber or brushwood raft which had decayed, leaving the superstructure virtually unsupported.

2. Wall Construction

Three basic forms of construction were used in Anglo-Saxon walling: coursed ashlar, roughly coursed stone, and small rubble. The stone-

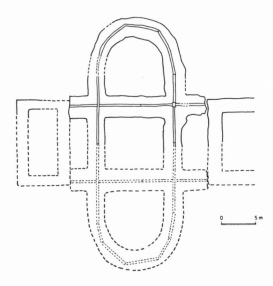

Fig. 8.2. Winchester Old Minster: foundation plan of the late Saxon west end, showing the timber-laced chalk raft which supported an axial tower and lateral apses; the southern half is a reconstruction.

masonry techniques involved differed for each form of construction. Coursed ashlar is the most straightforward and in some ways is the least informative archaeologically, although much can be learnt about the reuse of earlier, generally Roman, masonry by examining tooling patterns and secondary cutting marks on faces which now run into a wall and are normally concealed by pointing.

The commonest form of Anglo-Saxon walling in central and southern England is undressed stone rubble laid only in very approximate courses, as seen at Brixworth or Barton-upon-Humber. There, and elsewhere, one can see with remarkable clarity the vertical stages in which the walling was raised, and within the stages it is sometimes possible to detect the laying of several masons working alongside one another. Each man would have between 1.5m and 3m of wall length to work on, and it is commonly observable that a relatively well coursed section of walling will abut and intermesh with a section of very haphazard build, where the individual stones are neither coursed nor always horizontally bedded. The most apt description for this technique is "heap building" (fig. 8.3). Surely we see in this widespread phenomenon the presence of masons and their apprentices working side by side on the scaffold? By the time a

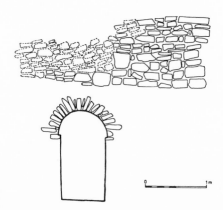

Fig. 8.3. Barton-upon-Humber: detail from interior of north wall of baptistery, showing rear arch of double-splayed window with slight ledges to support centering; above is a sample of rubble walling showing roughly coursed masonry on the right, interleaved with "heap" building (dotted outline) on the left.

wall had been raised 0.5m or 0.75m its upper edge had to be leveled to remove the ever-increasing switchback effect caused by irregular building. Thus one or two leveling courses, laid by a competent mason, would be introduced; these were generally coursed in with the ashlars that formed quoins and lined openings. Thus stone walls of this kind tend to exhibit a series of readily definable "lifts," each of which seems to represent a single working session, perhaps a day.

The pause between working sessions may be punctuated in two ways. At the close of a day's work the upper surface of the wall would be roughly flattened with the trowel, compressing the wet mortar and smearing some over the laid stones. Then, when work resumed, a bed of fresh mortar was laid to take the next course of rubble. Thus a slightly thicker joint than usual could be created. In addition, if there was a time gap of a day or more between lifts the exposed mortar surface would dry out sufficiently for there to be an imperfect union between the old and the new courses, resulting in a permanent hairline crack at the interface. To the trained eye this is readily detectable. Observation is made easier when there is a ferruginous component in the sand, and iron salts consequently migrate to the drying surface of the mortar, staining the interface brown.

When large stones were used to form quoins and to dress openings these were invariably set in position first, and then the stonework infilled

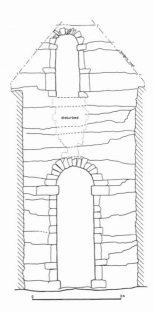

Fig. 8.4. Barton-upon-Humber: west face of tower, seen inside the baptistery. Interpretation diagram of the building lifts, showing typical features of rubble-wall construction: coincidence of some lifts with joints in the ashlar dressings; "humping" of the lift which incorporates the major arch; and stepping of courses towards the outer walls, owing to the corners having been built up first.

between, frequently accompanied by a slight sagging of the courses towards the center of the wall length. The reverse phenomenon is seen as walling on either side of an arched opening approached the crown, and the stones may tilt within their courses, and the entire lift may exhibit "humping" over the voussoirs (fig. 8.4). This provides a reliable indication of the originality of an arch to its adjacent walling. These features are well demonstrated in the east and west arches of the turriform nave at Barton-upon-Humber, in the lateral nave arches at Brixworth, and at Heysham, Lancs.

Building with irregular rubble inherently involved the use of prodigious quantities of mortar, with the consequence that drying and setting were not rapid processes, particularly in cool or damp weather. There was thus a limit to the number of courses that could safely be laid in a single session, without the risk of slumping: on average, some 0.5 to

0.6m of walling constitutes a single lift. When small flint nodules comprised the basic building material (as in East Anglia and much of southern England), the problem of slumping was greatly exacerbated. On average, a rubble wall built with small flints has 30% mortar in its volume, and the impervious nature of flint means that it does not exert any significant suction on the wet mortar, resulting in a considerable increase in the required drying time. It is thus extremely difficult and laborious to construct thick and tall walls in flint, but the Anglo-Saxon builders—like the Romans before them—overcame this problem with the use of timber shuttering. Flint and other walls of small rubble were built in coursed lifts between tiers of horizontal planks laid on edge and supported by lines of vertical posts and raking shores (fig. 8.5). The planks were mostly cut to a standard width of about one foot (0.3m), which determined the height of the lifts. Series of postholes set hard against the wall faces at Hadstock and Winchester Old Minster provide clear evidence for the shuttering supports needed to build those flint churches (fig. 8.6).

Where there was a ready supply of Roman brick or stone which could be employed to dress openings and quoins—and at the same time to give them added strength—advantage was taken of this. Thus numerous churches of the Rivenhall type exhibit an admixture of flint and brick, but others are wholly of flint. There is no better example than the late Saxon tower at Little Bardfield, Essex, the angles of which are entirely devoid of dressings (pl. 8.1). Since a complete carcase of timber

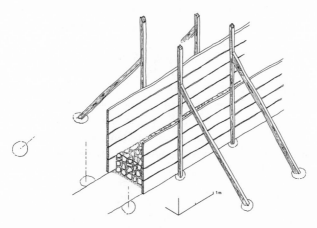

Fig. 8.5. Reconstruction of the timber shuttering required to build walls of small flint rubble in vertical lifts of 0.3m.

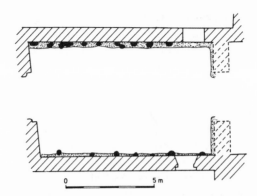

Fig. 8.6. Hadstock: plan of the nave, showing postholes used for supporting temporary wall shuttering; note that these holes pierce the top of the hoggin foundation (stippled).

shuttering had to be constructed for the erection of this tower there was no compelling need to form separate quoins. Circular flint towers were somewhat more difficult to build, in that the shuttering had to be erected in short vertical lengths and strapped around the entire circumference, in barrel-fashion.

Rubble walls were often provided with some kind of stiffening at approximately regular intervals through their height. This commonly took the form of two or three bonding courses of Roman brick or thin stone slabs; alternatively, courses of pitched or "herringbone" masonry could be introduced at intervals. The strength of the bond in herringbone work is several times greater than that of horizontally coursed masonry. In most if not all cases herringboning was not a decorative technique, since it is clear that Anglo-Saxon rubble masonry was generally plastered both internally and externally. As a third alternative walls, like foundations, could be timber laced for strength.[12] This technique, derived from the Romans and much used by the Normans, has only recently been recognized in pre-Conquest churches. When the tower of Sompting church in Sussex was repointed in 1962 the voids of horizontal mid-wall lacing beams were discovered both above and below the belfry openings.

At Barton-upon-Humber oak beans which are flush with the inner faces of the walls of the turriform nave still survive at two levels on the north and south sides. These timbers not only laced the walls but also formed seatings for the ends of the joists of the first and second floor lev-

Pl.8.1. Little Bardfield: tower built wholly of small flint rubble, erected in five stages (photo: W. Rodwell).

els within the tower. The exceptionally tall tower at Clapham, Beds., was laced by its own floor joists on three levels. The joists ran alternatively north–south and east–west, tying the walls of the tower together; their lacing properties derived from the rigidity provided by nailed floor boards.

3. Scaffolding

Two types of scaffolding have been observed in Anglo-Saxon churches: groundfast and cantilevered. For the most part the former was reusable and the latter non-reusable. There were three elements to the framework of the groundfast scaffold, namely standards, ledgers, and putlogs. The standards were set vertically in rows on either side of the wall to be constructed, at a distance of 1.0 to 1.25m from its face; the spacing between individual poles varied according to the nature of the work under construction, but was usually between 1.5 and 2.0m. The postholes used to support scaffold poles are frequently encountered in church excavations, and a virtually complete pattern has been obtained from the internal excavations at Barton-upon-Humber. A less complete pattern has been recovered at Hadstock. Owing to the disturbances caused by grave-digging it is very rare to discover early scaffold settings outside churches. Postholes inside churches have caused much confusion in the archaeological record: Professor Olaf Olsen has pointed out that the so-called pagan timber temple at Gamla Uppsala in Sweden is a misinterpretation; it could be scaffolding for the construction of the first stone church on the site.[13] At Wharram Percy, Yorks., some but not all of the internal postholes clearly belong to the scaffolding of the first stone church; other holes may be assignable to a previous timber structure.[14] It is worth noting that postholes found very close to walls cannot normally be interpreted as scaffolding for their construction: they are usually associated with shuttering (see above) or other fixtures such as benches or doorcases.

At each scaffold stage the standards were tied together with a horizontal ledger, which supported the outer ends of the putlogs; their inner ends were embedded in the masonry of the wall. The depth of penetration may be as little as 0.1m, but it is usually twice this. When the end of the putlog had been laid on the fresh wall top it was often flanked by a pair of squarish stones (or sometimes several pieces of Roman brick), and then capped with a large flat stone (fig. 8.7, nos. 5, 6). The embedded putlog was thus framed with stone, preventing the timber from becoming

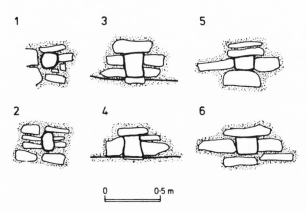

Fig. 8.7. Barton-upon-Humber: examples of putlog holes in the tower: 1, 2, built-in putlogs of branchwood; 3, 4, built-in squared timbers serving both for scaffolding and internal framing (note these features rest on building lifts); 5, 6, removable putlogs of squared timber.

too firmly embedded in the wet mortar, and facilitating its withdrawal when the scaffolding was struck (i.e. dismantled). These reusable put-logs were often of squared timber having sides of 100 to 120mm. The vertical stages in an Anglo-Saxon scaffold could vary between ca. 1.3m (Rivenhall) and ca. 2m (Barton-upon-Humber), and the ground stage was often taller than all subsequent stages. This is seen particularly well at St. Peter's, Bradwell-on-Sea, Essex, where the complete scaffolding scheme for the outer face of the south wall can be read in the fabric (fig. 8.8). The first scaffold stage, which appears only on the west end of the chapel, is at 1.5m above ground; this is omitted from the south side, where stage two alone appears at 2.5m above the ground. Stage 3 is at a further 1.7m, where it was designed to clear the tops of the pilaster-but-tresses and permit some putlogs to pass through window openings, rest-ing on the cills. The fourth stage was placed only 1.3m above the third, being determined by the height of the apse wall at the east end of the chapel. Stage 4, at the east end, would not have continued around the apse, but would have run across the tops of its walls against the east face of the chancel arch. A further 1.5m above the fourth stage was wall-plate level along the sides of the nave; this equated with stage 5 of the scaffold, which was only required at the east and west ends, for the construction of the gables. Thus, what looks at fist sight a somewhat irregular pattern of

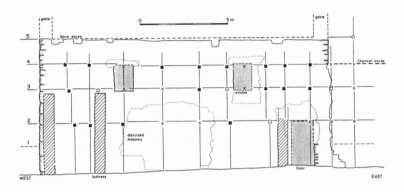

Fig. 8.8. St. Peter's Chapel, Bradwell-on-Sea: south elevation, with putlog positions indicative of five scaffold stages; blocked putlog holes are shown as black squares (certain examples), and open squares (probable); crosses indicate presumed putlogs for which no evidence has survived.

scaffolding at Bradwell is in fact an entirely logical and economical scheme.

Where a tower or other high structure, such as a clerestory (e.g. at Brixworth), was to be erected above the general eaves level of the nave, another type of scaffolding was often employed which did not involve the use of groundfast poles. Instead, long putlogs (ca. 3m in length) were laid across the tops of the walls, with equal projections inside and outside the building; unsquared branchwood tended to be used, sometimes with a diameter of less than 80mm. A few courses of masonry were laid over the putlogs, firmly embedding them in the fabric of the wall. There was no necessity to support the outer ends of the putlogs: Anglo-Saxon builders clearly did not have any qualms about working on a rather springy, cantilevered scaffold. In order to carry the scaffold platform around the outer angles of a tower putlogs were set diagonally through the corner of the walls; this is clearly seen in the second stage of the tower at Barton-upon-Humber (fig. 8.9).

The building of towers and other upper stories usually involved the simultaneous construction of timber floors, the joists of which were bedded directly into the wall fabric. These floors naturally provided ready-made internal working platforms upon which supplies of stone and mortar could be stacked, and from there passed out to the masons working from the flimsy cantilevered scaffolds. There was thus not always a

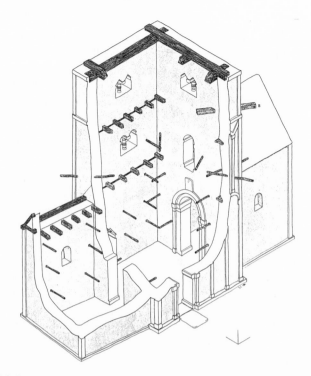

Fig. 8.9. Barton-upon-Humber: cutaway isometric drawing of the Anglo-Saxon church, showing positions of recorded putlogs, floor and roof timbers, and crane beam (B) (drawn by Steve Coll).

need for high-level scaffolds to support great weights. Materials, particularly heavy stones which were required for quoins, arches, and string-courses, were hauled up from the ground with the aid of temporary jibs and other crane-like contrivances. The socket for a cantilevered beam ca. 0.45m square was found running diagonally through the south-east corner of the tower at Barton-upon-Humber, just above second floor level (fig. 8.9). A rope and pulleys attached to the outer end of this jib would have allowed large blocks of stone to be raised from the ground immediately beside the chancel, and then swung onto a platform resting on the tops of the chancel walls (there was in any case an Anglo-Saxon floor at this level). In a second operation the stone could be hoisted to the required position on the tower. The same beam could also be used for internal hoisting.

Putlogs of branchwood which were deeply embedded in wall cores, or which passed right through walls, could not be recovered for reuse (see fig. 8.7, nos. 1, 2). They were simply cut off flush with the wall-face. The decayed remains of several have been discovered during recent archaeological investigations: one at Barton-upon-Humber is of silver birch, and one at Deerhurst is of ash;[15] hawthorn was used at Clapham.[16] Brixworth has yielded fragments of several putlogs, and a discussion of scaffolding arrangements in relation to that church has been offered by David Parsons.[17]

Anglo-Saxon towers built of flint rubble required a more substantial scaffolding arrangement for the upper stages because this had not only to support working platforms but also the shuttering needed to contain the flint walls. Thus at Little Bardfield squared putlogs passed right through the walls of the tower.[18] This flint tower was erected in five separate stages, each inset slightly from the last in order to establish a firm new bed to take the weight of shuttering. The first shuttering stage (from ground level) rises to the same height as the side walls of the nave, but the subsequent stages are considerably shorter. In a few instances even the walls of a flint-built nave of moderate height were shuttered in two distinct stages, with a horizontal offset halfway up, usually at window cill level (e.g. Little Easton and Elsenham, Essex).

4. Arches, Vaults and Centering

Wherever possible, internal and external scaffolds were tied together by passing putlogs through window and door openings, and scaffold stages are frequently seen to correspond to cill and impost levels. This was partly for convenience of working on the construction of these features, and partly to enable window templates and arch centering to be given temporary support by props from the scaffold. Numerous churches containing Anglo-Saxon and Norman round-arched windows retain impressions of timber centering in the mortar of their splays and archivolts, showing the several methods of construction employed. Single-splayed windows built of rubble or small ashlar normally had both their inner and outer apertures built around prefabricated wooden templates, which could be used over and over again. The conical archivolt between the two apertures was formed by building a barrel-like construction of tapered staves between the two templates; and in each reveal, at the point where the vertical face meets the archivolt, a narrow ledge is often seen. The function of this was to provide support for the centering staves through the full thickness of the wall. This arrangement is very clearly seen inside the towers at Clapham and Sompting; see also fig. 8.3.

A different construction was required for double-splayed windows, where the narrowest aperture was at or near the center of the wall. Here, a carpentered frame or pierced board was built into the wall, and conical archivolt shuttering had to be constructed on both sides. Pre-formed templates were once again provided at the inner and outer apertures, but instead of using staves for centering under the archivolt a hood of woven basketwork was formed in situ. The mid-wall frame was drilled, from both sides, with a semicircle of small holes around the head of the aperture, so that the basket hood could be firmly plugged in position (pl. 8.2). This was essential to ensure that the basketwork did not distort under the weight of rubble and wet mortar piled upon it to form the window arch. When the mortar had set and the masonry arch was firm the timber formwork could be removed from the apertures, but the basketwork was of course irretrievably embedded; it was simply plastered over and left in position. Traces of basket hoods survive in the mortar at Hadstock (outer splay) and at Hales, Norfolk (inner splay).[19] In some instances the mid-wall frame was of stone and not timber, but the principle of construction

Pl. 8.2. Hadstock: semicircular head of a jointed window frame, showing arc of small holes used to anchor the basketwork hood which served as a former for the arch of flint rubble (photo: W. Rodwell).

was exactly the same and the stone had to be drilled to receive the basket-work (cf. Avebury).[20]

The seven double-splayed windows at Clapham are interesting hybrids: the wooden frames are set one-third of the way in from the outer face of the wall (as at Witley, Surrey, where window boards have also been found). Basketwork hoods were formed in the external splays, while the inner ones were arched with wooden staves (see above).

The construction of an arch which passed straight through a wall could be achieved on two or three semicircular templates resting directly upon the projections of the imposts, if long voussoirs were available. When smaller stones were used a complete half-cylinder of timber formwork had to be erected on the imposts. Some windows, belfry openings, and small doorways were formed with monolithic stone heads at the wall faces and infilled between with a rubble core carried on timber formwork (e.g. Barton-upon-Humber, fig. 8.10).

The great arches in the north and south walls of the nave at Brixworth are formed with double rings of recycled Roman bricks, built on staved formwork. But it is apparent from the arrangement of bricks and adjoining masonry in the wall faces that a more sophisticated type of centering was used than a mere half-cylinder of staves: there were also semicircular flanges on the ends of the formwork, giving the appearance of giant cotton-reels or cable-drums. The method of building the Brixworth arcades can be read from the fabric (fig. 8.11). First, the rectangular piers and responds to east and west were raised to springer level. Secondly, diminutive imposts were formed by corbelling out two or three

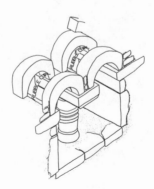

Fig. 8.10. Barton-upon-Humber: isometric drawing of one of the gallery windows in the tower, showing semicircular stone facings to a rubble vault erected on timber centering (drawn by Steve Coll).

courses of Roman brick; these imposts not only ran through the thickness of the wall, but were also returned along the inner and outer faces for a distance of ca. 0.3m. Thirdly, the cable-drum-shaped wooden formers were erected upon the imposts, with their flanged ends resting on the returns of the imposts. Fourthly, the formers were anchored firmly in position by laying a few courses of masonry and some bricks on top of the imposts, between the wooden flanges. Fifthly, the inner orders of the arches were constructed, using the rims of the wooden flanges to guide the arcature of the extrados. The masonry which anchored the formwork served the equally vital function of preventing the brickwork of the inner arches from spreading laterally under its own weight while the mortar was setting. In some of the arches it is also evident that the lowest parts of the outer ring of bricks (or stones) were laid while the inner ring was being built, in order to give additional lateral support. The sixth stage was the forming of the outer ring, and the seventh was the infilling of the masonry spandrels between the arches.

Some Anglo-Saxon arches exhibit a deformity which clearly occurred during construction as a result of partial failure of the centering. If not properly secured, the formwork could move on the imposts or could become distorted through too much weight of masonry being applied on one side, without being counteracted on the other side. This effect is seen

Fig. 8.11. Brixworth: diagram to illustrate the constructional processes in the nave arcades, based on evidence from the easternmost arch on the south side; the timber framework is omitted from stages 4 to 6 for clarity.

Fig. 8.12. Stow: arch in west wall of north *porticus,* showing distortion caused by the thrust of masonry on the left-hand side; additional weight at the center was provided by an outer ring of rough voussoirs (stippled), and rubble was piled to the right (dotted outline).

in the small archway in the west side of the north *porticus* at Stow (fig. 8.12).

Viewed from inside the *porticus,* the intrados has a tighter arcature on the right than on the left. The reason for this is that the voussoirs on the left are much more massive than those in the middle and on the right, resulting in the exertion of unequal thrust on the centering. The mason building the arch perceived what was happening and quickly added an outer ring on top to equalize the pressure; the adjacent walling was then built up, the courses dipping slightly towards that ring. This is, incidentally, a clear case where, on constructional evidence, the archway and the wall containing it must be contemporaneous.

Finally, Anglo-Saxon and Norman rubble-built vaults—surmounting crypts, passages, spiral stairs, and features such as the semi-domed recesses incorporated in the primary west front of Lincoln Cathedral—were all built on timber formwork related to that described above in connection with window splays. The subject has been discussed by David Parsons in relation to barrel-vaulted staircases,[21] and all the evidence for the nature of the formwork can be seen in the Anglo-Saxon stair-turret at Broughton, Humbs. There is, however, one detail in Parsons's reconstruction of the centering used in helical barrel-vaults which requires re-examination, and that is the use of nails. These seem to have been a precious commodity in Anglo-Saxon England and were not used liberally. If all the staves forming the staircase vault at Broughton were nailed to the cross battens a minimum of 500 nails would have been required. Pegs would probably have been used if any fixings were required; but since there are no marks of nail-heads or peg-ends in the preserved mortar imprints of the timber formwork, it seems likely that neither was used. If the formwork and masonry of a staircase were raised together the staves should hold themselves in position under the weight of rubble.

5. Window-Frames and Doorcases

Until recently it was not generally accepted that wooden window-frames, exposed to the natural elements for a millennium could have survived down to the present day. Taylor and Taylor argued for the acceptance of the mid-wall frames at Hadstock as being original to the fabric of the nave,[22] and in 1981 it was discovered that two of the windows in the tower at Clapham also retained similar frames. At Odda's Chapel (Deerhurst) and Thursley, Surrey, mid-wall slabs of oak survive in round-headed windows, while at Barton-upon-Humber perforated oak boards remain in two small circular windows in the west wall of the baptistery. These latter also exhibit small holes around the edge of the aperture to which conical basket formwork was affixed. Similar evidence has been recorded at South Lopham and Framingham Earl, Norfolk.

In 1979 the opportunity arose to study in detail the four surviving carpentered frames at Hadstock and to correct previous reconstructions published by Cecil Hewett.[23] While it seems probable that all double-splayed windows had a mid-wall frame or slab of timber or stone, there is little evidence at present for frames in single-splayed windows. Examination of the Anglo-Saxon windows at Rivenhall, during unblocking indicated fairly conclusively that there had been no original frames; in the north chancel window, however, an oak cill board was discovered and shown to be a secondary insertion. It yielded a radiocarbon date of A.D. 1000 ± 60 (HAR 2427). The cill was associated with a mortar fillet which had secured some form of secondary glazing close to the outer aperture.[24] Although the wooden frames at Bradwell-on-Sea are all modern, it seems possible that these replace original work of generally similar form, at least in the four side windows of the nave. Here the openings are rectangular and single-splayed, and the survival of Anglo-Saxon masonry above them indicates that the windows were always square-headed (see fig. 8.8). The openings were bridged with a series of heavy timber lintels set side by side.

A similar form of construction was used in the small square-headed doorway at Clapham which led from first floor level in the tower to the roof-space over the nave. The jambs of this doorway are formed in stone, but the head comprises six oak lintels set side by side, through the thickness of the wall. This feature, which seems not to have been previously noticed, is entirely original and undisturbed.

It has long been appreciated that Anglo-Saxon doorways, especially those constructed of very large stones, are seldom internally rebated for hanging a door, and in some cases it may be argued that all iron crooks and staples in a given doorway are post-conquest additions. Furthermore, it is noticeable that the stonework used to line Anglo-Saxon doorways usually presents an unadorned and relatively rough face to the interior of the church. There is thus good reason to postulate that the doors themselves originally hung in timber surrounds, or doorcases. The dilemma was resolved in 1974, when excavations inside Hadstock church revealed a pair of deep and substantial postholes flanking the doorway into the north *porticus*. It was suggested that these represented the groundfast posts of a timber doorcase,[25] an interpretation which received striking confirmation by excavation at Barton-upon-Humber in 1979 (fig. 8.13). Here, deep postholes were discovered against the inner faces of both north and south doorways, complete with the "ghosts" of squared timbers.[26] Similarly, paired postholes have been found to flank internal archways at Barton and Hadstock; these were shallower features which may

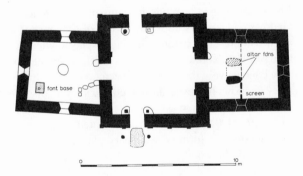

Fig. 8.13. Barton-upon-Humber: excavated plan of the Anglo-Saxon church, showing evidence for furnishings and structural fixtures such as timber doorcases.

not have supported doorcases, but ornate timber architraves surrounding the openings. It is probably legitimate to turn to the Norwegian stave churches for illumination of this subject, where timber doorcases and architraves abound.

There are hints also that shallow porch-like timber structures may have been built outside the doorways of Anglo-Saxon churches, and Barton again provides evidence in the form of a pair of postholes flanking the stone threshold and set 0.6m in front of the pilaster strips which frame the south doorway. The south doorway to the tower at Barnack, Cambs., embodies three large, square stones having the appearance of plain corbels; two rest upon the imposts, and the third on the crown of the arch, where it serves as a base for a pilaster-strip. The size and projection of these blocks might indicate that they were designed to support timbers. Could they therefore be associated with a former porch?

6. Timber Floors and Roofs

Cecil Hewett's assertion that certain floor and roof timbers in Anglo-Saxon churches are of similar age to the buildings themselves added a new dimension to the study of pre-conquest architecture.[27] The spire at Sompting he claims to be Anglo-Saxon, but archaeological examination of the top of the tower suggests that the principal timbers here are not coeval with the masonry. The same may be said about the roofs of St. Martin's, Canterbury, or the Harlowbury Chapel,[28] both of which appear to be of fourteenth century date with, at present, little plausible evidence for earlier roof forms. Hewett also maintains that upper floors in the towers at Sompting and Holy Trinity, Colchester, are original; and some timbers in Earls Barton and other Anglo-Saxon towers may be primary, if not actually in situ. Indeed, there is every likelihood that some Anglo-Saxon and early Norman timbers survive, unrecognized, amongst later work in floors and roofs since it is commonplace to find reused timbers in fourteenth and fifteenth century refurbishments of tower interiors. Only detailed archaeological scrutiny and the selected application of dating methods will reveal the extent to which early timbers have survived.

While at present the spire at Sompting stands alone, several other church roofs may potentially incorporate Anglo-Saxon elements, most notable of which are the nave at Hadstock (tie-beams, a wall-strut, and other timbers) and the stepped pyramidal roof of the central tower at Breamore.

When a roof has entirely disappeared it is not usually possible even to reconstruct its basic form (although Barton-upon-Humber provides an exception, see below), but the situation is different in respect of timber floors within towers and upper parts of churches. A good deal of evidence for the positions, and the construction, of upper floors and galleries remains in Anglo-Saxon churches. High-level doorways and windows have been recorded by Taylor, and their structural implications assessed, for example at St. Mary, Deerhurst, and Tredington.[29] In other churches, such as Clapham, there is a good deal of evidence—only recently noticed and recorded—for the original timber floors within the tower. None now survives, but the sockets which formerly housed the ends of the joists can be discerned, albeit that they are blocked. Thus, one can recover the levels of the three original floors, the directions of the joists (two sets north–south, the other east–west), the number of joists (five) per floor, and the precise dimensions of every timber.

It will be useful to discuss here, in brief, the case of Barton-upon-Humber as an illustration of the extent to which evidence for Anglo-Saxon roofs and floors remains latent in the fabric and can be revealed by structural dissection. Once fully revealed and recorded, the evidence can be used to make considerable progress with the reconstruction of the timber components in a church. When structural dissection began in 1978 no evidence of any kind for Anglo-Saxon timberwork in St. Peter's Church had been adduced, save the two fragmentary mid-wall slabs in the small circular windows at the west end. The three upper floors in the tower were demonstrably Victorian, with some old joists apparently reused in the second floor. The treatment of the internal wall faces varied: ancient crumbling plaster, Victorian plaster, and plaster of 1920 covered some surfaces, while others had been stripped and the rubble walling pointed in 1897. In the process of dissection everything, down to the most modern, has been recorded. The nineteenth and twentieth century plasters and cement pointing have all been removed, disclosing not just the Anglo-Saxon fabric but also sizeable patches of original wallplaster. Some 300 archaeological "features" were detected in the Anglo-Saxon fabric, including putlog holes; sockets for floor joists, roof fixings, and bell hanging; disturbances resulting from the construction and their later removal of staircases, galleries, and other fixtures; and patches and repairs of all ages. As far as possible these features have all been excavated and recorded in the normal stratigraphic manner: plans, sections, and elevations were prepared both of individual features and complete walls. From these overall records phase-plans and phase-elevations have been extrapolated, and these in turn have been used to prepare three-dimensional reconstructions, period by period.

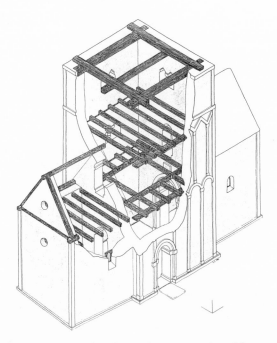

Fig. 8.14. Barton-upon-Humber: isometric reconstruction of floor and roof timbers in the Anglo-Saxon church, based on evidence encapsulated in the walls (drawn by Steve Coll).

Three levels of primary timbering could be reconstructed within the tower at Barton: a first-floor gallery, a belfry floor, and a base-frame for the roof structure (fig. 8.14). The turriform nave was without windows at ground level, and derived its illumination from double windows in the north and south walls of the chamber above. For this and other reasons, the first floor cannot have been a solid construction, but must have been galleried, and the arrangement of joists supports this notion. There were six north–south joists, the central pair of which would have been trimmer-joists rather than continuous timbers spanning the full width of the tower. A four-sided gallery was thus created around a void 3.4m square; the walkway was 1.6m wide. The gallery floor lay at the threshold of the two high-level doorways opening to east and west; access from the ground was by ladder, probably in the north-west corner. The belfry floor above was carried on seven continuous north–south joists, presumably with ladder access from the gallery.

A massive frame was embedded in the tower at wall-top level. Two east–west beams were set flush with the top of the masonry; partially trenched into these were two north–south beams, which projected above the wall-top; and these were given additional support from below by a fifth (east–west) beam. The arrangement was plainly designed to support and anchor a roof structure of substance; further large timber sockets at a lower level (not illustrated here) are less certainly associated with this primary roof. Neither a flat roof nor a very low pyramidal one would have called for such an arrangement of timbering, and two alternative reconstructions would fit the evidence, although these cannot be argued in detail here. First, a stepped pyramidal roof, related to the Breamore type, and secondly a modest spire may be proposed. The latter, in particular, has much to commend it. While the Sompting spire is supported on masonry gables, the arrangement envisaged at Barton would only have had timber-framed gables, mounted on the wall-top frame. A spire of this kind, with four shingle-covered gables, is depicted on the tenth-century bronze censor-cover from Pershore.[30] The form of the roofs which covered the east and west chambers at Barton can be ascertained with precision. Each chamber was floored at wall-top level with six north–south joists; one of these joists over the baptistery remains in situ to this day, and the sawn-off stubs of others survive in the side walls. The chancel and baptistery thus had flat ceilings with attics above, lit by small circular windows in the end-gables. Floor level was continuous with that of the nave gallery. The roof rafters were carried between wall-plates, set against the outer faces of the north and south walls, and a ridge-piece. All three timbers were deeply socketed into the tower walls at their inner ends, while the outer ends of the wall-plates appear to have been secured by a tie-beam housed within the masonry of the gable. The pitch of these lower roofs was sixty degrees. A sample from the complete floor joist in the baptistery was submitted for radiocarbon dating and returned the result of A.D. 900± 70 (HAR 3106).

In the mid to late eleventh century the tower roof at Barton-upon-Humber was removed and a new belfry stage was constructed on top of the old walls. The base-frame of the previous roof was allowed to remain in situ, providing support for internal scaffolding and a working floor. The new belfry was built from cantilevered scaffolding which, unlike that used in the earlier Saxon construction, was of substantial squared timber, not branchwood (pp. 209–210). There were three levels of timbering, for which nearly all the wall-sockets have been found and recorded (fig. 8.15). The very precise siting of these timbers, including

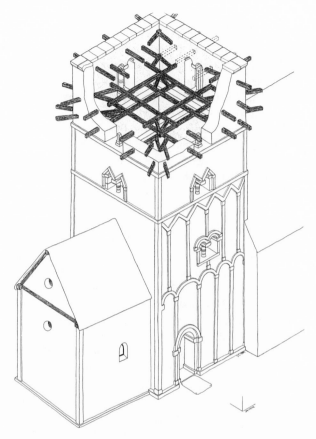

Fig. 8.15. Barton-upon-Humber: cutaway isometric drawing showing reconstruction of the timber framing erected as part of the Saxo-Norman belfry on top of the earlier tower; this framing probably served to anchor a roof spire, and also projected through the walls as cantilevered scaffolding (drawn by Steve Coll).

those obliquely positioned at the corners, revealed a dual function. They served not just a temporary purpose for scaffolding, but were conceived as fully-jointed internal frames in which the bells were hung. Moreover, the timber-framing could have been, and probably was, used to anchor a spire-like roof onto the tower. The ends of the frame timbers which projected through the walls to support cantilevered scaffolding were, of course, cut off flush with outer faces upon completion of the new belfry; for the putlog holes see fig. 8.7, nos. 3, 4.

MASONS OR CARPENTERS?

Although it is the work of the mason which has principally survived in
the extant Anglo-Saxon churches, it must be apparent from the foregoing
that the role of the carpenter and joiner was in no way less significant.
Recent research has demonstrated that there was considerably more
structural and other functional timberwork in the early churches than has
perhaps hitherto been appreciated. Add to this the requirement of scaffolding, formwork, centering, and wall shuttering, and it is self-evident
that the number of carpenters employed in church construction can
hardly have been smaller than the number of masons. Moreover, when it
is recalled that the vast majority of other buildings associated with religious life, and almost all secular buildings, were also of wooden construction, the pre-eminence of a timber technology in Anglo-Saxon
England needs no justification. Nor does the fact that the verb *timbrian*
simply meant "to build". Stonemasonry was by far the lesser craft in the
construction industry down to the end of the eleventh century.

While to a large extent our knowledge of pre-conquest timber
churches lies in the realms of speculation—there being but one extant
example (Greenstead-juxta-Ongar), a few written descriptions, and less
than a score of excavated plans—there are powerful arguments to be advanced for the former existence of a very great number of these between
the beginning of the seventh and the close of the eleventh centuries. Archaeological investigations have so far failed to increase, to any significant degree, the total of Anglo-Saxon stone-built churches antedating the
late tenth century, beyond the generally accepted legacy of such buildings. In particular, very little stonemasonry can be attributed to the period between the later eighth and the mid tenth century.

Thus when a church such as St. Peter's, Barton-upon-Humber, or the
tower at Earls Barton was erected it was at the end of a long era of timber
technology. Consequently, the question to which we must address our-
selves is, whence came the stonemasons responsible for such constructions. Some men were doubtless imported from the Continent, but it is
scarcely plausible to imagine that masons and their apprentices arrived in
England in scores, let alone in hundreds. It is inherently far more likely
that much pre-Conquest church-building, especially in the Lowland
zone, was undertaken by men who were turning their hands from the
skills of the carpenter to those of the mason. While this proposition may
initially be difficult to embrace, a carefully objective and dispassionate
examination of the extant structural evidence lends no small measure of

support. To do this one must examine churches through the eyes of the practical builder, rather than those of the architectural historian. There are several strands of evidence to consider.

First, those buildings constructed of flint or other small rubble, with little or no dressed stone, even for quoins and arched openings (pp. 199–206), testify to the skill of the carpenter rather than that of the mason. A tower like that at Little Bardfield (p. 205) took its form from the enormous timber carcase which had to be constructed, albeit in stages, as a mould into which mortar and flints were poured. The art of the stonemason proper is absent in such a building. Secondly, a mistrust of the cohesive strength of rubble masonry is suggested by the use of lacing and other large timbers in walls; mention might also be made of the unnecessarily deep seatings provided for joists and beams. Thirdly, a number of architectural features in stone which have load-bearing functions can be seen as direct copies of timber prototypes. No better example than double-belfry openings can be cited, where the through-stone and mid-wall shaft represent a highly unsatisfactory use of masonry in place of timber. The concept is that of a counterbalanced beam pivotally supported on an upright post, and is precisely the kind of everyday propping arrangement which would have been used by Anglo-Saxon carpenters in the construction of centering and formwork. But in belfry windows it has been translated into the permanence of stone. The weight of the inner and outer arched openings, and the walling above them, apply shearing forces to the through-stone which must have resulted in many failures and consequent collapses (one of the through-stones at Barton-upon-Humber sheared under its load in 1979). No-one properly schooled in masoncraft could have invented such a concoction, or would willingly have permitted its use in a stone building. The mason's method of constructing a double (or multiple) opening of the kind in question would be either to build a thin spine wall between the arches, or to carry them not on a through-stone, but on a through-lintel. There, the stone passing through the thickness of the wall would have been supported at both extremities by columns, placing it under more uniform compression.

The mid-wall shaft employed in double openings and multiple openings, as at Earl's Barton, is also a transmutation into stone of a lathe-turned wooden baluster. The bulbous shapes, with ribs, grooves, and neckings, are quickly and easily turned on the wood lathe: they are an unmistakable hallmark of the turner. But to imitate concentric work of this nature without the use of a lathe—and most, if not all, Anglo-Saxon stone balusters were demonstrably not lathe-turned—is an incredibly

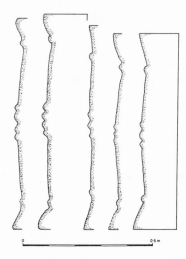

Fig. 8.16. Barton-upon-Humber: profiles of stone mid-wall shafts, hand-cut in imitation of lathe-turned wooden balusters; there is no structural reason for the varying lengths of the shafts: they probably reflect the dimensions of the Roman stones from which they were cut.

laborious and pointless activity (fig. 8.16). There is a difference between producing circular drums for a Roman or Norman columnar structure, and the fashioning of one-piece balusters.

Although larger in scale, columns such as those in the crypt at Repton were made basically in the same manner as balusters, and once again are copies of wooden prototypes. The coarse, barley-sugar twist with a raised rib seen on the Repton column shafts has been laboriously cut in emulation of spiral wood turning (an advanced technique involving considerably more skill than plain turning). This is not quite the same thing as spiral fluting, and Fernie's comparison of Repton with Utrecht is invalid.[31]

The fourth category of evidence to consider includes all those features that are non-load-bearing, and not of major structural importance, found in certain stone buildings and for which no entirely satisfactory explanation has yet been forthcoming. Translated into timber, some of these features—such as pilaster strips—can immediately be appreciated as integral components of a framed structure. There has been much discussion of the origin and purpose of pilaster strips in Anglo-Saxon buildings, and the arguments have been admirably summarized by Taylor.[32] One early suggestion, that the strips are purely decorative and merely imitate wooden framed construction, has fallen out of academic favor, but is urgently in need of resurrection. Examination of the pilaster strips on the tower at Barton-upon-Humber has shown that they are cut from reused Roman ashlars of varying dimensions, and they do not seem to be set into the rubble walling to a consistent depth. Indeed, some are very shallowly bedded, and it is difficult to envisage any structural function that they could perform. Long vertical joints introduce weakness into a wall, especially when poorly bedded with sizable voids in the mortar. I therefore incline to the view that the principal function of pilaster strips and the blind arcading frequently associated with them was ornamental. Indeed, a glance at the hopeless jumble of arcading on the tower at Earls Barton is sufficient to make the point.

Previous discussions of the origins of pilaster strips have tended to concentrate on geographical and art historical considerations, with little attention directed to constructional details. It is to those that we must now turn, since they beyond all else betoken the influence of the carpenter. The form of jointing used in gable-headed openings and arcading was in the great majority of cases lifted directly from the carpenter's repertoire: gable stones were angled at their bases in order to rest on the imposts and, more particularly, they were mitered at the apex joint. This is clearly demonstrated by the double window in the east face of the tower at Deerhurst (fig. 8.17C). Roman gritstone blocks were being recut for use as dressings at Barton-upon-Humber and consequently some compromises were permitted in order to accommodate stones of predetermined dimension; thus in the belfry openings there was a tendency to butt and lap stones in a variety of ways. In only one gable head was a proper mason's miter used with an apex block and right-angled joints (fig. 8.17A, right). In contrast to this is the remarkable expedient found in two of the four belfry openings, where wooden boards were used in place of gable stones on the inner face of the tower (fig. 8.18). In both the openings where this original feature is found boards of much slighter dimensions than the adjoining gable stones have been employed to form the V-shape resting on the through-stone. Gritstone slabs were evidently scarce in supply by the time the builders reached the uppermost levels of the tower, and the substitution of timber in places where it would not be noticed was a natural solution. Such a compromise would be unthinkable to a true mason, emphasizing that the builders of the Barton tower were carpenters at heart.

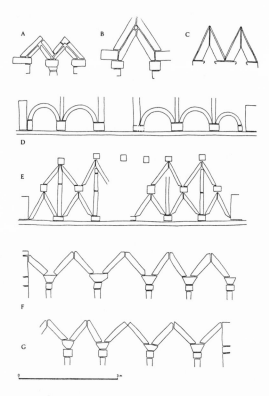

Fig. 8.17. Pilaster-strips and gable-headed features: A, Barton-upon-Humber: belfry opening, north side; B, Barton-upon-Humber: north doorway; C, Deerhurst: tower windows, east side; D, Earls Barton: arcading, south side; E, Earls Barton: gable-headed features, south side; F, Barton-upon-Humber: arcading, south side; G, Barton-upon-Humber: arcading, north side.

The treatment of the north doorway at Barton is interesting, with carpenters' joints between the gable stones and the imposts; the apex joints are also carpenters' miters, but with the ad hoc addition of two filler pieces (fig. 8.17B). These were necessitated by the fact that the Roman stones were slightly too short to receive full-length miters, like those at Deerhurst. The same problem is encountered in the gable stones of the blind arcading at Barton (fig. 8.17F, G): all the mitered joints on that work are of carpenters' type, not masons'.

A similar situation is found at Earls Barton, on the gable-headed arcading of the tower (fig. 8.17E). Here, additional evidence for Anglo-

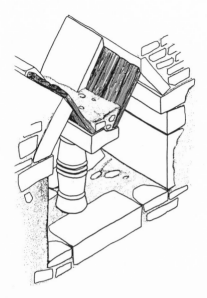

Fig. 8.18. Barton-upon-Humber: isometric view (internal) of a belfry opening showing wooden boards used instead of stone slabs to form parts of the gable heads (drawn by Steve Coll).

Saxon building practice is seen, in the form of prefabricated components. The gable stones all have carpenters' miters at the apex and at the feet, and while the former joints are correctly fitted together, the latter are for the most part obvious misfits. In particular, it is evident that the feet of the gable stones are too acutely angled for the bases which carry them. In effect the gable stones stand on tip-toe. The explanation for this is found in one gable head on the south side (fig. 8.17E, left); this is illustrated diagramatically in figure 8.19A. What we see here is an imitation of a form of lap joint used by carpenters for bracing a vertical post (cf. the braced post in fig. 8.19D, and the bracing of the spire mast at Sompting, fig. 8.19C). The design for the jointing at Earls Barton was not, however, followed rigorously, and most of the pilasters were not clasped by the gable stones; instead, the more expedient arrangement shown diagramatically in figure 8.19B was adopted. This copied the carpenter's mitered lap joint (cf. fig 8.19E), and would have made little visual difference to the finished work were it not for the fact that the gable stones had already been cut to length and angled at both ends for the joint-types previously described. The effect was to steepen the pitch of the gabling and narrow the span (fig. 8.19B).

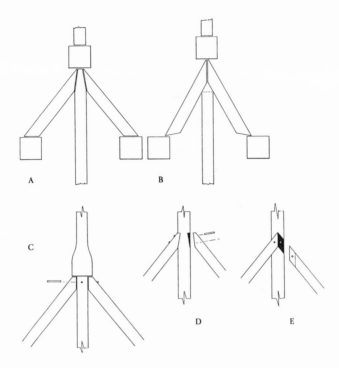

Fig. 8.19. Earls Barton: diagrams to illustrate the use of carpentry joints in the pilaster-stripwork of the tower (not to scale): A, pilaster with braced lap joint; B, pilaster with mitered lap joint; C, spire mast at Sompting with wooden braces; D, wooden post with lap-jointed braces; E, wooden post with mitered and lap-jointed braces.

There are many curiosities about the tower at Earls Barton which lead one to believe that the design of its prototype was wholly for timber, where prefabricated framing would be brought onto site ready for erection. The concept was translated into stone, even down to prefabrication, but something went drastically wrong with the erection process and one cannot help but feel that the design drawings were mislaid. As a result the "kit of parts" was incorrectly assembled, to such an extent that I believe major elements to have become transposed. For example, the thin, semicircular hoops which stand on a string-course were surely intended to be heads for arcading, as at Barton-upon-Humber (fig. 8.17D). The hoops have, incidentally, been cut as one-piece stones with a greater labor input than would have been required for the production of their timber prototypes (simple rings turned on the wood lathe, and then cut in half).

The fifth, and final, category of evidence which will be mentioned here in connection with the transmutation of wooden architecture into stone concerns decorative elements. There are many cases where a piece of stone has been handled and decorated as though it were a balk of timber. Two examples will suffice to make the point. The shallow, concentric grooves on the face of a semicircular arch stone, as at St. Patrick's Chapel, Heysham, are in imitation of faceplate-turning done on the wood lathe. Mid-wall slabs used in belfry and window openings were easily made from timber (pp. 215-217), but could also, with commendable skill, be cut in stone, and slotted into the fabric in exactly the same way; these are best seen at Barnack and Earls Barton. The former has examples of both pierced scroll decoration and slotted openings exactly like those still to be found in medieval boards in belfry openings.

CONCLUSION

Many aspects of Anglo-Saxon buildings have been discussed by Taylor in recent years in varying detail, according to the evidence currently available.

However, in a very short space of time a mass of fresh data has become available through excavation and structural dissection, and it has been a very great pleasure to work with Harold Taylor in the collection and analysis of this material. I offer this essay as a series of footnotes to his publications. The definitive account of the Anglo-Saxon builder has yet to be written.

NOTES

[1] W. Rodwell and K. Rodwell, "Excavations at Rivenhall Church, Essex: An Interim Report," *Antiquaries J.* 53 (1973), 219–31.

[2] W. Rodwell and K. Rodwell, "St Peter's Church, Barton-upon-Humber: Excavation and Structural Study, 1978–81," *Antiquaries J.* 62 (1982), 283–315, at pp. 283–88.

[3] H. M. Taylor, "Old St Peter's Church, Barton-on-Humber," *Archaeol. J.* 131 (1974), 369–73, at p. 373.

[4] H. M. Taylor, "Structural Criticism: A Plea for More Systematic Study of Anglo-Saxon Buildings," *A.S.E.* 1 (1972), 259–72.

[5] P. J. Huggins, K. Rodwell, and W. Rodwell, "Anglo-Saxon and Scandinavian Building Measurements," in P. J. Drury, ed., *Structural Reconstruction: Ap-*

proaches to the Interpretation of the Excavated Remains of Buildings, B.A.R. Brit. ser. 110 (Oxford, 1982), 21–65.

⁶ B. Kjølbye-Biddle, "The 7th-Century Minster at Winchester Interpreted," in L. A. S. Butler and R. K. Morris, eds., *The Anglo-Saxon Church: Papers on History, Architecture, and Archaeology in Honour of Dr. H. M. Taylor,* C.B.A. Research Rep. 60 (London, 1986), 196–209.

⁷ W. Rodwell and E. C. Rouse, "The Anglo-Saxon Rood and other Features in the South Porch of St. Mary's Church, Breamore, Hampshire," *Antiquaries J.* 64 (1984), 298–325.

⁸ Huggins, Rodwell and Rodwell, "Anglo-Saxon and Scandinavian Building Measurements," fig. 2.14; W. Rodwell and K. Rodwell, *Rivenhall: Investigations on the Roman Villa, Church and Village, 1950–75,* C.B.A. Research Rep. 55 (Chelmsford, 1993).

⁹ W. Rodwell, "The Archaeological Investigation of Hadstock Church, Essex: An Interim Report," *Antiquaries J.* 56 (1976), 55–71, at pp. 60–61.

¹⁰ Rodwell and Rodwell, "St Peter's Church, Barton-upon-Humber," 296.

¹¹ M. Biddle, "Excavations at Winchester, 1968: Seventh Interim Report," *Antiquaries J.* 49 (1969), 295–329, at fig. 6 and pls. LXIV–LXVI.

¹² R. P. Wilcox, *Timber and Iron Reinforcement in Early Buildings* (London, 1981).

¹³ O. Olsen, "Is there a Relationship between Pagan and Christian Places of Worship in Scandinavia?" in Butler and Morris, *The Anglo-Saxon Church,* 126–30, at p. 126.

¹⁴ J. G. Hurst, "Wharram Percy: St Martin's Church," in P. V. Addyman and R. K. Morris, eds., *The Archaeological Study of Churches,* C.B.A. Research Rep. 13 (London, 1976), 36–39, at fig. 13.

¹⁵ H. M. Taylor, *Deerhurst Studies* 1 (1977), privately printed, 14.

¹⁶ Information from M. Hare.

¹⁷ D. Parsons, "A Dated Timber Fragment from Brixworth Church, Northamptonshire," *J.B.A.A.* 133 (1980), 30–6.

¹⁸ C. A. Hewitt, "Anglo-Saxon Carpentry," *A.S.E.* 7 (1978), 305–30, at p. 327.

¹⁹ H. M. Taylor and J. Taylor, *Anglo-Saxon Architecture,* 2 vols. (London, 1965), fig. 483.

²⁰ H. M. Taylor, *Anglo-Saxon Architecture,* vol. 3 (London, 1978), 1062–63.

²¹ D. Parsons, "Barrel-vaulted Staircases in England and on the Continent." *Zeitschrift für Archaeölogie des Mittelalters* 6 (1978), 129–47.

²² Taylor and Taylor, *Anglo-Saxon Architecture,* 275.

²³ Hewett, "Anglo-Saxon Carpentry," fig. 13; C. A. Hewett, *English Historic Carpentry* (London, 1980), fig. 21.

²⁴ Rodwell and Rodwell, *Rivenhall.*

[25] W. Rodwell, "The Archaeological Investigation of Hadstock Church"; W. Rodwell, *The Archaeology of the English Church* (London, 1981), fig. 52.

[26] Rodwell and Rodwell, "St Peter's Church, Barton-upon-Humber," 298 and fig. 6.

[27] Hewett, "Anglo-Saxon Carpentry"; Hewett, *English Historic Carpentry*, chap. 1.

[28] C. A. Hewett and H. M. Taylor, "The Chapel at Harlowbury, Harlow, Essex," *M.A.* 23 (1979), 223–25.

[29] For summary, see Taylor, *Anglo-Saxon Architecture* 3, 1017–19.

[30] D. M. Wilson, *Anglo-Saxon Ornamental Metalwork, 700–1100, in the British Museum* (London, 1964), no. 56.

[31] E. C. Fernie, *The Architecture of the Anglo-Saxons* (London, 1983), 120.

[32] H. M. Taylor, "The Origin, Purpose and Date of Pilaster-strips in Anglo-Saxon Architecture," *North Staffordshire J. Field Stud.* 10 (1970), 21–47.

CHAPTER 9

Archaeology and the Cult of St. Oswald in Pre-Conquest Northumbria

ERIC CAMBRIDGE

INTRODUCTION

The evidence for those of the numerous dedications to St. Oswald in the north of England which can be traced back to before the Reformation has been collected by Alison Binns;[1] the purpose of the present paper is to venture into all but uncharted waters by attempting to consider how many of those dedications (whether or not their medieval ancestry is demonstrable) may date to before the Norman Conquest. Where possible, it will attempt to place them within the four centuries or so which separate Oswald's death from the Norman invasion, and to consider why Oswald came to be chosen as the dedicatee. Given that there are few Oswald dedications indeed which can be demonstrated to be early by documentary evidence, it must be stressed at the outset that this paper cannot pretend to supply conclusive answers to questions of this kind; rather, it attempts to outline a general historical and archaeological framework within which they may be appropriately considered. Of course, future detailed studies of particular sites, which are so urgently needed, may often require the interpretations tentatively advanced here to be revised; but at least enough may have been said to establish that there is an archaeological dimension which deserves to be considered in such analyses. Only the fifty-nine dedications recorded in the north of the country, that is, those anciently in northern Mercia and Northumbria, will be examined; for it is surely here, in the territory of Oswald's native land and where all of the most ancient centers of his cult lie, that the earliest dedications are most likely to be encountered.

Fig. 9.1 Oswald's World.

The only explicit documentation of a dedication to Oswald in pre-Viking Northumbria concerns the site of *Scythlescester,* where a church commemorating the site of the murder of King Ælfwald of Northumbria in 788 was dedicated to Saints Oswald and Cuthbert.[2] The importance of this chance reference lies in its implication that the practice of dedicating churches to indigenous saints was established by the late eighth century in Northumbria.[3]

The evidence of place-names in the form Oswaldkirk and Kirkoswald, which incorporate the element *Oswald* as a specific, provides another potential means of dating the church dedications which they presuppose, albeit an indirect and considerably less precise one. Four such names are recorded: Oswaldkirk in the North Riding of Yorkshire; Kirkoswald in

Cumberland; and the two Kirkoswalds in Ayrshire. The form of the generic element indicates a derivation from Old Norse *kirkja,* a church. The two English examples must therefore have been coined between the arrival of Viking settlers in the regions in which they are situated and their first mention in documentary records. This gives *termini* of between ca. 900 and 1162 for the Cumberland Kirkoswald and ca. 876 and 1086 for Oswaldkirk;[4] a pre-Conquest date for the formulation of the latter at least is thus highly probable. What is more, the distinction between the period in which such names came into existence in their current form, and the time of the dedication to Oswald of the churches to which they bear witness, must be kept clearly in mind. Both these names leave open the possibility that the Oswald dedication, if not also the practice of distinguishing those places as "Oswald's church," might have been older (perhaps considerably so) and, as will be explained below, there are other grounds for suspecting this to be so.[5] The date of formulation of the place-name and the date of the original dedication of the church are likely to have diverged even more markedly in the case of the two Scottish Kirkoswalds, both of them in Ayrshire. The class of *kirk*-compound names to which these belong continued to be coined in this area of southwest Scotland until late in the Middle Ages.[6] The possibility that the Oswald dedications implied by these names merely reflect the individual devotional preferences of, say, twelfth-century settlers, cannot therefore be ruled out on purely onomastic grounds (and indeed, the presence of a dedication to this saint as far north as Cathcart, just south of Glasgow, is perhaps best explained as belonging to such a chronological stratum). Nevertheless, from an historical perspective, the likeliest context in this part of Britain for the dedication of churches to such a quintessentially Northumbrian saint arguably lies much further back, during the period of Northumbrian occupation. In the southern parts of the area this had begun well before the establishment of a Northumbrian bishopric at Whithorn ca. 730, while the most plausible explanation for the presence of the two churches dedicated to Oswald further north in Carrick is that their dedications originated in a period beginning some time before the Northumbrian conquest of Kyle (the area immediately to the north) in 750, and ending with the eventual loss of both regions to the kingdom of Strathclyde, perhaps during the later ninth century.[7]

Meager though the harvest of the documentary, onomastic, and historical sources may seem, even a skeptic will be forced to concede that some churches had been dedicated to Oswald well before the Norman Conquest, and at least one in the pre-Viking period. And given that the Northumbrians had a more obvious motive for promoting Oswald's commemoration in this way than their Viking successors, it seems not unlikely that there were other dedications to the saint of comparable antiquity. It is therefore at least possible that some of the dedications to Oswald recorded only at a much later period might have originated centuries earlier. The most immediate obstacle when it comes to trying to determine which are early, and which not, is that Oswald's cult remained popular throughout the Middle Ages, so that other Oswald dedications might equally well reflect later medieval rather than Anglo-Saxon piety. One possible way round this problem is to consider whether there are any distinctive archaeological characteristics associated with the sites of Oswald dedications and their immediate environs which might point to a possible period of origin for the dedication, and whether such characteristics might change over time, thus enabling the dedications to be placed in an appropriate chronological sequence.

Inference from such inherently ambiguous evidence is obviously a procedure fraught with difficulties. For example, some ecclesiastical sites with early archaeological features may nevertheless contain churches which only came to be dedicated to Oswald centuries later, and there can be no knowing how often this might have occurred. Other churches dedicated to Oswald may have shed their original archaeological context by moving their site, while others again may subsequently have been rededicated to another saint, so rendering their previous Oswald associations undetectable. Later loss and destruction of archaeological evidence (and perhaps also the failure to recognize the potential significance of what does survive) presumably also means that fewer sites retain identifiable evidence of an early context today than was once the case. The presence of archaeological indications at a site suggestive of a pre-Conquest context thus need not imply that the dedication to Oswald of a church there is early, nor their absence that it might not be.

Bearing all these caveats in mind, four criteria have been selected to provide as comprehensive a basis for comparison as possible: the presence or absence of Anglian (that is, pre-Viking) sculpture; the presence or absence of Viking-age sculpture; the degree of proximity to sites which have produced Anglian sculpture; and the degree of proximity to roads of Roman origin. The results have been summarized in the Appendix (pp. 265–267). Before considering the possible implications, two of these criteria, and the hazards of interpreting them, need further explanation.

First, the evidence of stone sculpture has been included, as this is the most widely distributed type of artifact surviving from the early Middle Ages. Its possible implications for the function of the sites at which it occurs is controversial; but it is almost always found in ecclesiastical contexts, which at least raises the possibility that churches at sites where it is present might have been in existence comparatively early. Carvings of the pre-Viking period are more common in the north of England and the adjacent parts of southern Scotland and the north midlands than in any of the regions further south; yet it remains a comparatively unusual phenomenon even in these areas. Though it is not always possible to distinguish carvings of this period from those of the Viking age (dubious examples being indicated with question marks and linked by a horizontal line in the Appendix), this can be done with confidence in the majority of cases. The point is of importance because the distribution of sculpture datable to the Viking age differs significantly from that of the earlier material; while most of the sites which have produced pre-Viking carvings have also produced Viking-age stones (though there are significant exceptions), there are perhaps as many sites again which have *only* produced Viking-age carvings.

Second, though it is generally recognized that there are significant relationships between early ecclesiastical sites and Roman roads,[8] the evidence for the latter raises problems of its own. By no means all roads which have been claimed as Roman are accepted as such by more cautious scholarship; and even if they are, some parts of their courses remain more or less inferential. Sometimes the equivalent medieval routes deviated partly or wholly from their Roman predecessors, as, for example, Morris's detailed survey of Ermine Street north of Lincoln clearly shows.[9] While many Roman roads clearly continued in use into the early Middle Ages, not all did, so some instances of juxtaposition with church sites may be fortuitous; on the other hand, those which continued in use throughout the medieval period and into modern times might give rise to juxtapositions which, even if not accidental, derive only from the circumstances of a much later period. What is more, even if proximity is defined fairly strictly, as here (within three miles), the likelihood of fortuitousness increases appreciably in circumstances such as proximity to major route centers approached by several roads (such as York or Chester), or where roads run through pronounced valleys; in either case, churches erected at any date could hardly have avoided being near the line of a Roman road. Indeed, it is abundantly clear from existing case studies that many instances of proximity need carry no implication of an early medieval origin.[10] Clearly, then, this criterion is a crude and potentially misleading instrument, and much detailed fieldwork both on the routes themselves and on their relationship to settlement morphology would be required before the possible significance of juxtapositions between churches and roads of Roman origin can even begin to be properly evaluated; nevertheless, such evidence has been included as it may be potentially significant in combination with other factors. Instances which appear *prima facie* to be dubious are indicated by brackets in the Appendix.

Do any significant correlations at all emerge from the data presented in the Appendix?[11] First, it is doubtful whether any *general* importance should be attached to the number of sites with Oswald dedications at which pre-Conquest sculpture has been found.[12] A skeptic might justifiably argue that, in a random sample of this size taken in the north of England, a few examples of church sites with Anglian material, and rather more with only Viking-age sculpture, would be precisely what one would expect. And even if the number of sites within three miles of a road of Roman origin, that is, somewhere between one-third and perhaps as many as half of the total, seems unexpectedly high given that there is no obvious *prima facie* reason to expect any significant correlation between the two, the problems of interpretation outlined above make it hazardous to assess whether or in what way this phenomenon is significant.[13]

By far the most striking correlation is the number of Oswald dedications—somewhere between one quarter and one third—which are *adjacent* to a site which has produced Anglian sculpture.[14] Again, the juxtapositions may well be fortuitous in a number of cases: for example, by casual migration of early carvings to adjacent sites, or by the dedication of later churches near early sites (or the rededication of ancient ones) to Oswald. But it has already been noted that sites at which this material occurs are comparatively uncommon, and as there is again no obvious *prima facie* reason why Oswald dedications should be juxtaposed with them in this way, the degree of correlation does appear to be significantly high. What is more, at least half of the Oswald sites at which Viking-age sculpture has been found are also close to sites which have produced Anglian material; and most of them are also near to roads of Roman origin.

It seems, then, that some potentially significant combinations of characteristics do begin to emerge when the archaeological contexts of Oswald dedications are examined. The likelihood that this is not wholly fortuitous is appreciably strengthened when the evidence of regional variation is taken into account. Thus the degree of correlation between Oswald dedications and sites with any of the above material characteristics is markedly low in Lincolnshire, particularly when the sole example of a site with Viking-age sculpture (Crowle) should probably be placed in the early Anglo-Saxon *regio* of *Hæthfeld* (Hatfield), a distinct territory lying on the borders of Northumbria, Mercia, and Lindsey, rather than in the kingdom of Lindsey proper.[15] Though Anglian-period sculpture is markedly less frequent here than further north, this is not true of Viking-age material nor of Roman roads, so the lack of correlation may be significant, perhaps lending some support to the suggestion that most of the Lincolnshire dedications are not early but rather reflect the refoundation of Bardney Abbey in the late eleventh century.[16] Conversely, this variation gives one some confidence in supposing that the notably high degree of correlation in some regions (Yorkshire, Cumberland and Westmorland, and perhaps also Cheshire) may indicate that appreciable numbers of early Oswald dedications with distinctive archaeological profiles may survive there.

If it is accepted that there may be significant trends in the material evidence associated with the sites of churches dedicated to Oswald, the next problem is to explain what these apparent patterns might mean. This question is probably best tackled only after reviewing in detail a number of particular sites where there is evidence (not invariably confined to the archaeological evidence) to indicate the date and context in which the Oswald dedication, if early, might have arisen.

CULT CENTERS

It will be as well to begin with Bamburgh (fig. 9.5, no.7), for its association with Oswald is demonstrably early; according to Bede, this was the place at which major relics of St. Oswald, his arms and hands, were enshrined within a generation of his death, having been retrieved by Oswald's brother and successor, Oswiu, and placed in a church dedicated to St. Peter.[17] This church must therefore have been in existence before Oswiu's death in 670. Yet there is another (considerably later) tradition that there were two churches in Bamburgh, dedicated respectively to St. Oswald and St. Aidan, but with no mention by this time of a church of St. Peter. The evidence is principally contained in a group of twelfth-century and later charters granted in favor of the priory of Nostell in Yorkshire, which in consequence became the proprietor of the parish church of Bamburgh and established a small dependent monastery or cell there. How are these apparent discrepancies between the number of churches in early medieval Bamburgh, and the saints to whom they were dedicated to be explained?

One major difficulty in understanding the charter evidence must be faced at the outset, for it seems that there are two distinct versions, the first recording the grant of only one church without specifying its dedication,[18] while the second (attested only in charters of confirmation) records the grant of the two churches of St. Oswald and St. Aidan as noted above.[19] One commentator has sought to account for the second version as merely an attempt to amplify the terms of the original grant,[20] but while this may be on the right lines, the discrepancies seem too substantial as they stand to be wholly explained in this way. Alternatively, the traditions might be reconciled by supposing that there were originally two separate grants of two different churches, though evidence for only one now survives (in the first version), and that their dedications came to be specified in subsequent confirmations in order to distinguish the two. But if that were the case, it would be difficult to explain why that first version, mentioning only one church without giving its dedication, persisted alongside the other for so long. One may even wonder whether there was in fact only one church involved all the way through (though there may have been two grants of it in different terms), and the references to two churches only arose later, as a result of confusion.[21]

The evidence of the Nostell charters alone thus provides an insecure basis from which to infer the presence of two churches dedicated to St. Oswald and St. Aidan in twelfth-century Bamburgh. That there was a church dedicated to St. Aidan there at least seems reasonably probable on other grounds, however. The present-day parish church is situated about one-third of a mile west of the castle rock, at the opposite end of the modern village (fig. 9.2a). Though largely of thirteenth-century and later date, its earliest extant fabric is Romanesque, and enough of this survives to indicate that already in the twelfth century the church was an elaborate cruciform structure.[22] As the church is dedicated to St. Aidan, it seems reasonable *prima facie* to identify it with the one mentioned in the twelfth-century charters, and this presumption must be considerably strengthened by the consideration that this dedication—perhaps surprisingly—was apparently unique in England until modern times.[23] What is more, its rarity strongly suggests that the church was dedicated to that saint for a particular reason. The probable explanation is provided by Bede's account of Aidan's death as he was leaning against the buttress of a church in a royal estate center (*uilla regia*), in which he also had a residence, not far from the fortress (*urbs*) of Bamburgh[24] The buttress miraculously survived two fires and was preserved as a relic in the rebuilt church.[25] It is difficult not to believe that the existence of this early cult site accounts for the unusual later medieval dedication. While it is always possible that the latter reflects no more than the piety of later generations familiar with Bede's account, the apparent general unpopularity of Aidan's cult in the later Middle Ages, and the incentive to favor a dedication to

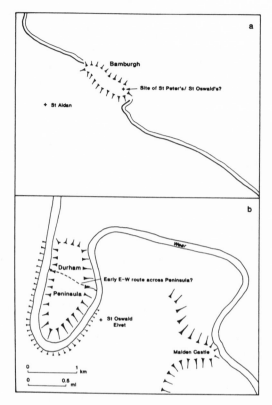

Fig. 9.2. Early Churches and Settlements.

Oswald rather than Aidan once the church had passed to the priory of Nostell, combine to make this explanation unlikely.[26]

Despite the considerable difficulties of interpreting the charter evidence, it may be that the former existence of a church of St. Oswald at Bamburgh cannot be entirely rejected, since one containing relics of Oswald is mentioned in Reginald of Durham's Life of the saint and, as will be explained elsewhere, this text does seem to incorporate genuine traditions about Bamburgh in the late pre-Conquest period.[27] If so, then it seems likely that, as Bateson long ago surmised, the church which had become identified with St. Oswald by that time was identical to (or at any rate a successor of) the seventh-century church of St. Peter.[28] The assimilation of the dedicatee of a church to the saint whose relic it had long housed is a phenomenon which can be paralleled elsewhere, at Repton in Derbyshire, for example; if such an explanation holds good at Bamburgh, assimilation had evidently still not taken place at the end of the eighth century.[29] Assuming that St. Peter's is indeed to be identified with the later St. Oswald's, where was it located? According to Bede and to the annals in the *Historia Regum* St. Peter's lay within the *urbs* of Bamburgh, that is, presumably, the defensible area on the rocky outcrop now occupied by the twelfth-century and later royal castle,[30] and Bateson may well also be right in supposing that the twelfth-century castle chapel on the south-eastern extremity of the rock perpetuates its site.[31] In turn, this evidence suggests that the interpretation of the Nostell charters as indicating grants of two different churches cannot be dismissed out of hand either. Indeed, given the long struggle of the Nostell monks to gain effective control of the revenues of St. Aidan's, is it possible that their earliest foothold in Bamburgh was in fact within the castle?[32]

What does seem reasonably clear from the foregoing discussion is that there are grounds for assuming continuity of site as regards the present-day parish church and Aidan's church and residence on the one hand, and (though its precise location on the rock remains in some doubt) the Romanesque castle chapel and the church of St. Peter's/St. Oswald's on the other. The nature of the topographical relationship between these two sites (fig. 9.2a) has been obscured to some extent by a misunderstanding of what Bede has to say about Aidan's church and residence. In particular, the *uilla regia* at which Aidan died seems sometimes to have been interpreted as distinct from Bamburgh itself,[33] whereas the topographical evidence presented above suggests rather that the two formed part of the same estate, and therefore that Bede thought of the *uilla regia* as a polyfocal settlement comprising both the *urbs* and Aidan's church and residence (and conceivably other components not mentioned).[34] Bede's account makes it clear that one of the functions of Aidan's residence was to serve as a base from which to carry out preaching tours in the surrounding area. If the contention that the later parish church perpetuated its site is correct, these two facts together suggest that the pastoral needs of the surrounding area have always been served from this church. In contrast, there are no grounds for supposing that they were ever exercised from the church of St. Peter/St. Oswald; from its location and its early function as the place in which a major dynastic relic was housed, this must presumably be envisaged as the palace chapel of the Bernician royal fortress, later perpetuated as a shrine church after the political importance of the site declined. It appears, then, that we may have here an early and comparatively well documented example of a church at an episcopal residence, near to yet distinct from the secular focus of a great royal estate, and remaining (as had been intended from the start) the center of pastoral care for the area. Initially occupied periodically by the bishop of Lindisfarne in person (or perhaps by one of his priests in his absence), it may in time have come to have a permanently resident staff, and to have been provided with endowments of its own.[35]

Evidence for the date at which other early cult sites associated with Oswald came to possess churches dedicated to him is uncertain. It can be assumed that Bardney in Lincolnshire (fig. 9.5, no. 68), like Bamburgh, must have had another dedication at the outset, because it was obviously already in existence when Oswald's relics were installed there. There is no evidence on the point, but it is conceivable that the twelfth-century and later dedication of the refounded abbey to saints Peter, Paul, and Oswald perpetuates a memory of the primary dedication combined with a commemoration of Oswald, whose relics had been housed in the church between the late seventh and early tenth centuries.[36] The evidence regarding Oswald's death-site at *Maserfelth* is even more tenuous given the controversy as to its location, though Stancliffe has made a plausible case for identifying it with Oswestry in Shropshire (fig. 9.6, no. 53). The church there was known by the early twelfth century simply as "the church of St. Oswald" in a way which implies that its dedication to the saint was already well established, and therefore it can probably be assigned to at least the late pre-Conquest period.[37] Finally, the church at Heavenfield in Northumberland (fig. 9.5, no. 8) might have been dedicated to Oswald from the period of its construction in the early eighth century since it was specially built to honor a site associated with the saint. The only direct documentation of the dedication is much later, however, so such an interpretation must remain hypothetical.[38] There is thus at least no evidence from the other early cult sites to contradict the sequence suggested by the evidence relating to Bamburgh (that is, that the dedication to Oswald only came about comparatively late in the pre-Conquest period), though a dedication to Oswald may be more likely to be early in cases where the church was purpose built to honor his cult than where one was already in existence before the Oswald association arose.

MONASTIC SITES

Though the church at Lythe,[39] in the North Riding of Yorkshire (fig. 9.5, no. 26), boasts a large collection of Viking-age sculpture, the only earlier carving from the site is probably architectural in character. This has been identified and interpreted by James Lang as a gable-finial from a stone church; its nearest analogues, at Lastingham, Yorkshire, and Heysham,

Lancashire, lie firmly in pre-Viking contexts, and the former is also doc-umented as a monastic site.[40] What is more, given the tendency for early stone churches in Northumbria to be associated with monastic sites,[41] the presence of such a carving at the site would strengthen the case for a monastic association. The proximity of Lythe to Whitby, which lies only four miles south-east, and has itself produced pre-Viking sculpture in quantity, suggests an association with the latter (fig. 9.3a); if this spec-ulation is right, Lythe may be seen as falling within a context of royal patronage, for Whitby is probably to be identified with *Streanaeshalch,* the monastery which contained the dynastic mausoleum of the Deiran ruling family.[42] It therefore raises the possibility that the community

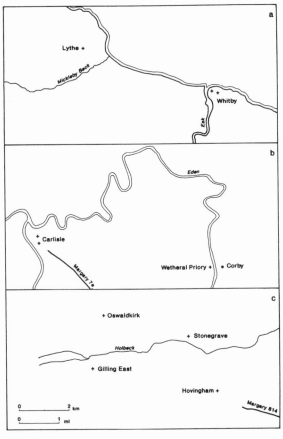

Fig. 9.3. Oswald Dedications and Early Settlements, I.

whose principal church housed the relics of Edwin and the tombs of several prominent royal descendants also had associated with it a church dedicated to the other great Northumbrian royal saint, Edwin's nephew, Oswald.[43]

The place-name Lythe is Norse in origin and so (like Whitby itself) the earlier name of the site may have been completely different.[44] If the association with Whitby suggested above is correct, however, the site should perhaps be considered as a candidate for the location of *Osingadun,* the place at which St. Cuthbert had a premonition of the death of one of the Whitby brethren while feasting the day before dedicating a church there for Abbess Ælfflæd.[45] This site has not been convincingly identified hitherto. As I have pointed out elsewhere, the internal evidence of the story, in which the messenger sent by the abbess to Whitby to verify Cuthbert's vision made the return journey before the dedication ceremony on the day following the feast, implies that *Osingadun* was located fairly close to Whitby;[46] this makes Colgrave's suggestion of Kirkdale (thirty miles south-west over difficult terrain) unlikely.[47] I have also argued that the vocabulary used to describe the church suggests that it was intended to house monks (and thus perhaps was meant to form the principal male focus of the double monastery). This would be consistent with the implication of the presence of an early stone church suggested by the carved fragment. What is more, the potential significance of the Lythe carving increases in the light of the fact that it is the only site at all close to Whitby which has produced pre-Viking sculpture of any kind. The above interpretation is, it must be frankly admitted, highly speculative. Nevertheless, it involves one intriguing implication, and that is that the surviving carved fragment is actually from the church dedicated by Cuthbert. What remains, alas, unknowable, is the identity of the saint to whom he dedicated it; but the possibility that the Oswald dedication might go back as far as ca. 686 cannot be ruled out.[48]

In addition to Lythe, Filey in the East Riding of Yorkshire (fig. 9.5, no. 31) and Wetheral in Cumberland (fig. 9.5, no. 10) are further examples of the small group of sites at which dedications to Oswald and finds of indisputably pre-Viking sculpture occur together. Wetheral lies four and a half miles east of Carlisle, which is well documented as an important monastic center (fig. 9.3b). Though the precise location of the chapel dedicated to Oswald, which is mentioned in a thirteenth-century source, is not known, it seems to have been near the site of the later medieval priory. What is more, as Carlisle seems to have been a double monastery in origin,[49] it is tempting to compare the possible relationship between it and Wetheral with that proposed above for Whitby and Lythe.

The church of Filey lies three miles north-east of that at Hunmanby, which has produced sculpture of Viking-age date and perhaps also a pre-Viking piece;[50] though no early documentation survives for either site, indirect evidence of the pre-Conquest importance of Hunmanby is provided by the extensive parish which was formerly dependent on it. What is more, before that parish became fragmented later in the Middle Ages, the parish of Filey directly adjoined that of Hunmanby, and it may be that the two sites had once been associated.[51] By analogy with the sites already mentioned it is tempting to suppose that the Oswald dedication might be early, perhaps originally associated with the adjacent early ecclesiastical center at Hunmanby. As with Lythe and Whitby, the comparative rarity in eastern Yorkshire both of pre-Viking sculpture and of churches dedicated to Oswald must be particularly emphasized; this suggests that the juxtaposition of these two categories of evidence here is unlikely to be coincidental.[52]

Unlike the sites considered so far, there is no pre-Viking sculpture at Oswaldkirk in the North Riding of Yorkshire (fig. 9.5, no. 30), where the surviving stone carving dates only from the Viking period.[53] Nevertheless, there are some grounds for supposing that it may belong in a similar context, for its parish lies immediately adjacent to that of Stonegrave, the church of which lies just over two miles south-east. Stonegrave is documented as a *monasterium* by a chance reference in a papal adjudication of an ownership dispute in the mid eighth century;[54] pre-Viking sculpture has also been found there. Admittedly, this may be of less significance than the case of Filey/Hunmanby considered above, for carving of pre-Viking date is comparatively common in this area of Yorkshire, and is also present at Gilling, the parish immediately adjacent to the south, though the major center in the area is presumably Hovingham (fig. 9.3c).[55] Nevertheless, the archaeological context may well suggest that a church dedicated to Oswald and associated with a documented adjacent Anglian ecclesiastical center was in existence in the pre-Viking period, that is, before its existence was registered either archaeologically or onomastically.[56]

EPISCOPAL RESIDENCES

Tempting though it may be to attempt to interpret the remaining evidence for sites with potentially early dedications to Oswald as monastic dependencies along the lines argued above, this would certainly be unwise, for in at least one case there are grounds for supposing that another kind of ecclesiastical function may be involved. The evidence relates to the church of Guiseley in the West Riding of Yorkshire (fig. 9.5, no. 35).

For an unknown period anterior to the late tenth century Guiseley had formed a component of a large estate centered on Otley, the archaeological evidence from which marks it out as the most important pre-Viking ecclesiastical center in Wharfedale.[57] By the 970s the Otley estate had come under the control of the archbishops of York, for a memorandum of that time records that during the episcopate of Archbishop Oswald (972–92) several of its components, including Guiseley, were alienated from the see. Guiseley itself was recovered by the archbishops between ca. 1020 and 1086.[58] The surviving sculpture from the site may be dated stylistically to the late ninth or earlier tenth century,[59] though whether or not it was produced under archiepiscopal patronage remains uncertain. At any rate, the available evidence does not enable one to determine whether there was an ecclesiastical site of any kind at Guiseley as early as the pre-Viking period, nor whether archiepiscopal ownership of the settlement stretched back that far.

Nevertheless, the possibility that the ecclesiastical site at Guiseley might have originated in a pre-Viking context should not be ruled out. Addingham, some ten miles further north-west up Wharfedale, and on the same Roman road which passes just over a mile north of Guiseley, was probably an archiepiscopal residence in the late ninth century; at any rate, this appears to be the likeliest explanation of why it was chosen as a refuge by Archbishop Wulfhere following his flight from York after the Viking assault in 867.[60] Addingham itself is not dedicated to Oswald, but twelve miles down the valley from Guiseley, approximately equidistant between it and York, lies Collingham, another Oswald dedication which may be of early date, and a site which has produced Viking-age and also pre-Viking sculpture.[61] Richard Bailey has drawn attention to the possible role of the Roman roads as a determinant of the stylistic relationships of Viking-age monuments in the Warfe valley and adjacent areas;[62] the above evidence may provide a possible pre-Viking context for the importance of such routes, and the ecclesiastical settlements connected by them. Even if the possibility that Guiseley might have originated in this way is accepted, however, this is very far from proving that its dedication to Oswald is of comparable antiquity. But it may be worth advancing the speculation that the Oswald dedications at Guiseley and Collingham should be seen as components in a sequence of archiepiscopal possessions stretching westwards along one of the main routes from York across the Pennines, and one which must have been of fundamental importance to the episcopal administration of southern Cumbria and northern Lancashire which, it may be assumed, were already in the pre-Viking period (as certainly later) within the see of York.[63]

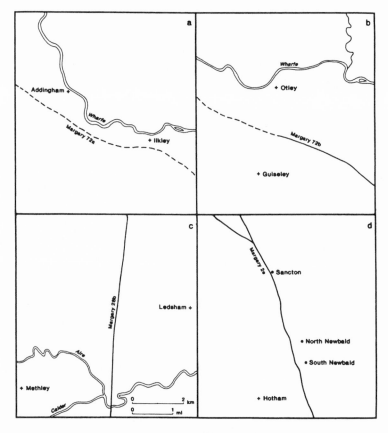

Fig. 9.4. Oswald Dedications and Early Settlements, II.

One further aspect of the siting of Guiseley calls for comment. This is its situation adjacent to, yet distinct from, the major early ecclesiastical center of Otley, which lies two and a half miles to the north, on the other side of the Roman road (fig. 9.4b). It has been noted above that, by the later pre-Conquest period, Guiseley had come to form a component of the Otley estate, though the antiquity of the territorial association between the two remains uncertain. Their juxtaposition is, nevertheless, comparable to that of Addingham and Ilkley (fig. 9.4a). As has been seen, there is some evidence to suggest that the former may have been a pre-Viking episcopal residence; as at Guiseley, Viking-age sculpture has been recovered from the site.[64] In contrast, Ilkley, like Otley, preserves a large collection of Anglian sculpture,[65] suggesting that it was second only to the latter as an early ecclesiastical center in Wharfedale.

OTHER EARLY ECCLESIASTICAL CENTERS

Although there is evidence to suggest that other churches dedicated to Oswald may well belong in a pre-Viking ecclesiastical context of some kind, there seems to be no possibility of determining their function more precisely. In view of its place-name, the most important of these is probably Kirkoswald in Cumberland (fig. 9.5, no. 11). A mile to the southeast lies the site of Addingham (now submerged beneath the river Eden).[66] To judge by its sculptural remains, that site must have been the major Anglian ecclesiastical center of the middle Eden valley.[67] At Kirkoswald itself there is sculpture which may also be pre-Viking in date, though a later date cannot be ruled out.[68] As with its Yorkshire counterpart at Oswaldkirk, the possibility therefore arises that the dedication of the church may be appreciably older than the date of formation of the place-name in the tenth century or later.

In other instances the absence of any early material context at the site of an Oswald dedication perhaps makes the possibility of a pre-Viking context weaker; nevertheless, the proximity of the church of Dean in Cumberland (fig. 9.5, no. 12) to the major pre-Viking center of Brigham may be significant,[69] as might the possible relationship between Methley (fig. 9.5, no. 40) and the important pre-Viking church of Ledsham in the West Riding of Yorkshire (fig. 9.4c).[70] Finally, it is conceivable that the phenomenon extends beyond Northumbria into parts of northern Mercia, where the scarcity of pre-Viking sculpture makes the juxtapositions all the more striking. For example, in Cheshire, the church at Brereton (fig. 9.5, no. 51) may stand in a comparable situation with respect to Sandbach, which has produced major pre-Viking sculpture; so might Bidston (fig. 9.5, no. 46), which lies one and a quarter miles northeast of Overchurch where such carving has also been found.[71] In some cases there may also be significant relationships to the Roman road network (see Appendix).

ROYAL CENTERS

The final category of potentially early dedications to Oswald which remains to be considered consists of those whose most significant relationship appears to be not with an ecclesiastical center, but rather with an adjacent secular settlement.

The dedication of the church of Elvet in Durham City (fig. 9.5, no. 9) to St. Oswald was first recorded in the late twelfth century, and the earliest extant fabric dates from that same period;[72] but if one can assume that the pre-Conquest carving found reused in the church tower anciently belonged here, it points to a significantly earlier stratum in the site's ecclesiastical use. This cross-shaft has been variously dated to between the late ninth and early eleventh centuries. Advocates of the later date stress the similarity of some of its motifs to those on carvings found at the cathedral site itself, which are usually assumed to date from after the Cuthbert Community's arrival there in 995.[73] These motifs are, however, also found on carvings elsewhere in the region which are usually dated to the late ninth or early tenth centuries, at Tynemouth and Aycliffe for example.[74] The date of the St. Oswald's cross thus depends on the possibility of making a fine distinction between the first currency of the motifs ca. 900 and their apparent revival at Durham in the early eleventh century. For present purposes, only two features of this controversy are significant. One is that the earlier possibility is one factor among others pointing to the existence of an ecclesiastical presence at Elvet before the arrival of the Community of St. Cuthbert on the Durham peninsula in 995; the second is that, whatever its date, this carving clearly belongs in a Viking-age rather than pre-Viking context.

More specific in its chronological implications than the uncertain evidence of the sculptural finds is the place-name Elvet, for it is generally accepted that this is to be identified with the *Aelfet ee* at which, according to one of the versions of the *Anglo-Saxon Chronicle,* Pehtwine was consecrated bishop of Whithorn in 762.[75] If this identification is correct it implies that a settlement of some importance was present in or near Elvet long before the surviving sculpture (whatever date is preferred for it) was carved. The possible topographical reference of the place-name is ambivalent, however. The meaning of the specific element *Aelfet* ("swan") is clear enough; but the generic element *ee* is more ambiguous, for it may represent either Old English *ea* ("stream") or *eg* ("island").[76] The present location of Elvet on the eastern bank of the loop of the river Wear may seem to make the former the more likely interpretation, as its topography is not very obviously insular (fig. 9.2b). Other considerations, however, suggest that we should be wary of accepting that the *prima facie* interpretation is necessarily the correct one; and that it may be misleading to assume that the ancient reference of the name was so restricted, for besides meaning island in the modern sense *eg* was also used to refer to peninsulas, whether defined by water or simply a hill projecting from flatter land.[77]

Two recent discussions of place-names incorporating the generic *eg* are particularly relevant to our understanding both of the possible original reference of the name *Aelfet ee* and of its significance as a settlement. The first is the suggestion that the original topographical reference of the name Lindsey (Old English *Lindes-eg*), which came to be applied to an entire Anglo-Saxon kingdom (fig. 9.1), was to the prominently elevated upper parts of the city of Lincoln rather than to a low-lying island near the river below.[78] The second is provided by an early form of the place-name now familiar to us as Hexham, which occurs in early sources as *(H)agustaldesei*. Of particular significance as regards the original meaning of *Aelfet ee* is the fact that, in this case, there are enough early attestations to enable it to be determined that the element represented by *ei* (alternatively *ae, iae*) in the early forms is more likely to be the generic *eg* than *ea*.[79] The Anglo-Saxon monastery at Hexham (the site of which is certainly perpetuated by the existing abbey church) was situated on a pronounced bluff clearly visible from across the Tyre valley. What is more, it has been suggested that the first element of this name implies that the settlement was held by a person of high status before the monastery was founded there.[80] These examples thus not only provide parallels for the application of the generic element *eg* to prominent peninsular sites, but also raise the intriguing possibility that such sites were favored locations for early centers of secular power.

In the light of this comparative evidence, the possibility that *Aelfet ee* might originally have referred to the Durham peninsula itself needs to be considered. The name Durham is late Old English in origin (*dun holm*, "hill island"), the element *holmr* being of Old Norse derivation.[81] The fact that this later name describes the peninsula as an island may be significant here, for it raises the possibility that it perpetuated the topographical reference of the generic element of a more ancient name which it in part supplanted. In other words, it implies, like the comparative evidence adduced above, that the peninsula could appropriately have been described by the generic *eg,* and hence that *Aelfet ee* might originally have been coined with reference to it.[82] Of course, the peninsula is not the only available candidate which might be described as an *eg* in this sense—the hill east of present-day Elvet known as Maiden Castle should not be ruled out, for example—but it does appear to be the most obvious one in the area.

The physical separation of the peninsula from the ecclesiastical site at Elvet (fig. 9.2b) may seem to raise a difficulty with the above interpretation, for it is not immediately apparent how a name which originally referred to the peninsula should have come to refer to an area on the opposite side of the river, nor why the latter should have perpetuated the early name after it had been abandoned with respect to its original point of reference. In practice it is not difficult to envisage how this might have come about, as the phenomenon of extending the original terms of reference of a place-name to the surrounding territory can be paralleled in other Anglo-Saxon contexts. Again Bamburgh supplies a local parallel: the name which had in origin applied to the fortress on the rock was used for the parish church one third of a mile distant by the twelfth century, and probably long before (fig. 9.2a). Similarly, a recent analysis of Selsey in Sussex (Old English *Sealæs-eg* "seal island") has demonstrated that the name referred to an extensive adjacent territory from an early period and was not restricted to the coastal peninsular site itself.[83]

If the above suggestion is right, how, then, did the name Elvet later come to be restricted to the suburbs east of the peninsula? This usage may be explicable as a relict use of the old name. The obvious context for this would have been a time when settlement was disrupted on the peninsula itself but continued on the eastern bank of the river thanks to the persistence of an ecclesiastical center in the area. This would also explain why the *eg* element of the name subsequently dropped out of use. The likeliest period for the renaming of the peninsula in the late Saxon period must surely be the arrival of the Cuthbert Community there ca. 995. If this interpretation is right, the fact that a renaming took place at all would suggest that (in contrast to sites such as Bamburgh) there had been major discontinuity in the occupation of the peninsula itself, a circumstance which might be explained by supposing that the site became much more marginal in the Viking period, when it lay near the border with the Viking kingdom of York, than it had been previously, when it lay mid-way between the Bernician and Deiran centers of power.

The above hypothesis also implies that the ecclesiastical site at Elvet is likely to have originated appreciably earlier than its archaeological context alone would indicate. Again, comparative evidence suggests that there is nothing unlikely about this. A site where there are grounds for supposing that the associated archaeological evidence appears significantly later than the likely period of origin has already been encountered at Oswaldkirk; another, more local example, at Coniscliffe, is discussed below. A further point is that recent work on the relationship between early ecclesiastical sites and their secular counterparts suggests that a degree of separation is precisely what one would expect.[84] If the recent proposal to identify the *urbs regis* called *Inbroninis* mentioned in Stephen's *Life of Wilfrid* with the rock of Beblowe (now the site of the castle) on Lindisfarne is correct, a comparable disjunction of secular and ecclesiastical centers would have applied to Lindisfarne itself, at least in the seventh century; and as we have already seen, Bamburgh is another local example of similar date.[85] It seems likely therefore that the early ecclesiastical settlement at *Aelfet ee* would have been adjacent to the secular focus but would not have been sited actually within it. None of this, of course, proves that the present-day church of Elvet perpetuates the site of an eighth-century predecessor, but it does mean that this location should not be considered at all anomalous in terms of what is known about how such early settlements were laid out. It may therefore be misleading to treat the site at Elvet in isolation and as antecedent to the establishment of any settlement on the peninsula, as previous discussions have tended to do;[86] recent research suggests rather that the two locations would more likely have been complementary in function and chronologically contemporaneous rather than successive.

If the above interpretation of the place-name *Aelfet ee* is accepted, the implications for the status of the proposed early settlement on the peninsula which it originally designated remain to be considered. It has already been noted that the consecration of a bishop at this place suggests a settlement of high status; the comparative evidence of the kinds of site designated by the element *eg* appears to point in the same direction. Other considerations may hint at the former presence of a royal center on the Durham peninsula. The active support of the earl of Northumbria in establishing the Cuthbert Community on the peninsula may itself hint that it had been inherited (like Bamburgh itself) by the earls as successors of the Northumbrian kings. What is more, its proximity to the likely course of the eastern of the two Roman roads running through the Tyne-Tees area perhaps suggests that its location may have been important in the pre-Viking period, when north-south communications must have been essential to the viability of the Northumbrian kingdom.[87]

Neither of the preceding considerations is at all conclusive when taken in isolation; when seen in the light of an important piece of comparative evidence, however, they may lend support to the contention that the church of Elvet was associated with a pre-Viking royal center. This relates to High Coniscliffe, on the north bank of the Tees, the traditional dedicatee of which is another Northumbrian sainted king, Edwin. It must be admitted that there seems to be no direct medieval documentation of this dedication; but its rarity perhaps argues in favor of its authenticity.[88] As the place-name itself suggests, the church was probably situated on a royal estate,[89] and this may receive further indirect support from a record of the murder there in 778 of a Northumbrian *ealdorman* on the orders of King Æthelred of Northumbria.[90] Further, the site is only a mile east of Dere Street, and proximity to Roman roads has already been noted as a characteristic of (among others) early royal centers. What makes this evidence particularly significant for present purposes is that the early royal associations of the site are independently documented. Furthermore, the unusual choice of dedicatee presumably reflects the site's royal status; it also seems most likely to have arisen in a pre-Viking context, for it is possible to envisage that a later Anglo-Saxon king of Northumbria might have wished to dedicate a church on one of his estates to a sainted royal predecessor, but difficult to see why any later lord would have been motivated to commemorate an increasingly obscure saint.[91] The archaeological implications of the comparison with Coniscliffe are also important; for, despite the circumstantial evidence that its church dates from the pre-Viking period, the existing fabric contains no features datable to the pre-Conquest period, while none of the stone sculptures from the site is earlier than the Viking period.[92] This suggests that the similar archaeological profile of Elvet by no means argues against its having been an important place in the pre-Viking period; on the contrary, the lack of pre-Viking material remains of this kind may be precisely what one should expect from churches serving such royal estate centers.[93]

The preceding evidence thus offers some support for the hypothesis outlined above: that is, the existence of a pre-Viking royal center, probably on the Durham peninsula, served by its associated ecclesiastical settlement nearby at Elvet, and both originally known as *Aelfet ee*. The significance of the dedication of Elvet church to St. Oswald, particularly in view of its rarity north of the Tees at any period of the Middle Ages, therefore needs to be assessed in the light of it. If the possibility that the dedication is early can be accepted, there are two ways in which it might have come about. The first is that, as at Coniscliffe, the dedication is a direct consequence of the presence nearby of a royal center, reflecting an interest on the part of the Northumbrian kings in promoting the cult of their sainted ancestor. The second (which does not necessarily exclude the first) depends upon the topographical analogy between Durham/Elvet and sites such as Bamburgh, as analyzed above (fig. 9.2); this may imply that the church of Elvet originated in an episcopal residence adjacent to the royal center.[94] If so, this need not have been for the benefit of the bishops of Lindisfarne, particularly if, as I have argued elsewhere, the latter may already have had a residence nearby at Chester-le-Street long before that site became the resting place of Cuthbert's relics in 883;[95] what is more, the church of Elvet is conspicuous by its absence from the extensive and comparatively well documented pre-Conquest possessions of the Cuthbert Community. The bishops of Hexham would also have needed similar provision at the principal royal centers within their diocese, of which, if the above speculation is right, *Aelfet ee*/Durham would have been one. Moreover, Durham lies at the first point at which the eastern of the two principal north–south Roman roads traversing the county is easily accessible from Dere Street, the obvious route south from Hexham.[96] If the suggestion of a Hexham rather than a Lindisfarne link is right, the Oswald dedication would become more easily comprehensible given the active promotion of Oswald's cult on the part of the Hexham community.[97]

Another Oswald dedication which may be explicable in terms of an association with a possible pre-Viking royal center is the church of Hotham (fig. 9.5, no. 39) in the East Riding of Yorkshire. It must at once be admitted that nothing in the fabric of the church itself gives any indication of a pre-Conquest origin; the argument depends rather on its archaeological context. Three miles north-east of Hotham, on the other side of the Roman road from Lincoln to York, lies Sancton, the most extensive of the Deiran cremation cemeteries (fig. 9.4d), and five miles north lies Goodmanham, site of the pagan sanctuary mentioned in a famous episode in Bede's *Ecclesiastical History.*[98] In the light of these associations, Higham has recently postulated an early palace site within Sancton parish, pointing to a field-name which incorporates the element *cyning* in support of its early royal associations, and suggesting that it may have been succeeded by a later royal residence nearby at Newbald (Old English *niwe bold,* "new building" or "new palace"), one and a half miles east of Hotham on the other side of the Roman road.[99] The rarity of dedications to Oswald in this area of Yorkshire in contrast to their apparent frequency in others (fig. 9.5) may lend some support to the hypothesis that the one at Hotham originated in association with an adjacent pre-Viking royal center. A second site in the same county for which an early royal context may be tentatively suggested is Flamborough (fig. 9.5 no. 32). Here the coastal peninsular site is not unlike Bamburgh's, and the possibility that the Danes' Dyke (the great linear earthwork which defends the peninsula on its landward side) is early Anglian in date suggests that its occupation sequence might also have been similar, originating as a pre-Christian stronghold and continuing as an important center into the post-conversion period.[100] Finally, as regards Wittingehame in East Lothian (fig. 9.5, no. 6), two preliminary observations may be made, though more work is urgently needed to establish the antiquity both of its dedication and of the present-day location of the church. First, the place-name in -*ingaham* may indicate an early phase in the Anglian settlement of the region.[101] Second, the site's location, a mile and a half south-east of the major late Iron-age and sub-Roman fortress of Traprain Law, may be significant: their relative location is reminiscent of that of Yeavering Bell on the one hand, and the potentially early ecclesiastical site of Kirknewton on the other. Close to these two lies the early Anglo-Saxon palace site at Yeavering itself;[102] so, if this comparison has any validity it implies the existence of another, possibly royal, site in the immediate vicinity of Wittingehame and Traprain; at least one other neighboring and independently documented royal site, at Dunbar, would presumably also have been in existence contemporaneously, suggesting a major focus of Northumbrian royal power in this area of Lothian.

The above group of sites, together with analogous settlements like Coniscliffe and Bamburgh, suggests that there is a significant correlation between dedications to Oswald and early royal centers. The Oswald sites themselves may be explained either as royal chapels or (perhaps more likely in view of the evidence for their subsidiary locations) in terms of nearby episcopal residences. They may therefore not differ as much as might at first appear from episcopal residences adjacent to ecclesiastical centers, as already postulated for such sites as Guiseley.

CONCLUSIONS

It must be stressed that the preceding survey of the variety of contexts in which dedications to Oswald might have originated in pre-Viking Northumbria has of necessity been put forward only tentatively; clearly much more detailed work on both the history (including the later medieval history) and the archaeology of individual sites is required before the degree of probability that any dedication to Oswald really does belong in so early a context, and if so, in what sort of context, can be properly assessed. Nevertheless, there seems to be at least enough *prima facie* evidence to suggest that a number may well have arisen in that period. Though it is undoubtedly hazardous to go further at present, several more general observations may be made.

The range of possible functional contexts suggested for sites at which potentially early Oswald dedications occur should not be allowed to obscure the one feature they appear to have in common to a striking degree, and that is their tendency to be dependent in some way on other adjacent places of higher status; only rarely can a case be made for an early dedication to Oswald being at a high-status site itself. In ecclesiastical complexes at least this may in part reflect a preference for dedicating the principal church to a universal saint, restricting indigenous dedicatees to subsidiary contexts. More fundamentally, however, it presumably reflects one of the basic characteristics of the structure of early medieval settlement, in which the principal focus is surrounded by a series of dependent settlements, one of which happens to have become fossilized as a result of its ecclesiastical associations. In favor of this interpretation is the way in which the feature seems to be common to dedications associated with high-status secular centers as well as ecclesiastical ones. On the other hand, one should perhaps be wary of too readily assuming that all examples of dependent and focal settlements are instances of the *same* phenomenon; there may also be significant differences. For example, possible instances of episcopal residences near to royal centers, as suggested at Bamburgh and Durham (fig. 9.2), appear to be significantly closer to each other than those associated with major ecclesiastical centers, as postulated at Guiseley (fig. 9.4b); other sites, such as Whitby and Lythe, or Carlisle and Wetheral, for which a monastic context has been suggested, seem to be significantly further apart again (fig. 9.3a). Whether such differences are to be explained in functional or chronological terms (or both) raises questions about the morphology of early medieval settlement which cannot be entered into here; but the potential significance of this evidence for addressing such questions should at least be apparent.[103]

One general feature of the dedications identified above as possibly pre-Viking remains to be considered, and that is the significance of their overall distribution, which appears not to be confined to Northumbria, but extends into northern Mercia. Of course, from the beginning Oswald's had not been an exclusively Northumbrian cult, receiving Mercian royal patronage from as early as ca. 700.[104] Given that at least one (Bardney) if not two (*Maserfelth*/Oswestry) major centers of the saint's cult lay within Mercian territory, it should not be surprising if this were reflected in early dedications to the saint to some extent. It is notable, however, that Bardney, though the best attested early site outside of Northumbria, seems to have generated no identifiably early dedications in its region; perhaps the anti-Northumbrian sentiments which led to the initial rejection of Oswald's relics by the monks of Bardney died hard in Lindsey. In contrast, a case can be made for some of those in north-western Mercia being early, such as Brereton and Bidston in Cheshire (fig.

9.5, nos. 51, 46), and Winwick in south Lancashire (fig. 9.5, no. 45).[105] This perhaps lends support to Stancliffe's suggestion that Oswald's death-site lay in that same region, and may have had a continuous existence as a cult-center in the early Middle Ages.[106]

Within Northumbria itself there are marked contrasts in the distribution of Oswald dedications. They are rare north of the Tees at any period (fig. 9.5, nos. 6–9), the few examples being certainly or probably early in date; whereas they appear to be significantly more common south of the Tees and west of the Pennines, not only in the later Middle Ages but also, if the preceding analysis is correct, in the pre-Viking period (fig. 9.5). Despite the considerable uncertainty which accompanies any attempt to define the geographical extent of the pre-Viking Northumbrian dioceses, it may be worth speculating that these contrasts are in some way to be associated with differing attitudes on the part of the various sees at any rate so far as their core territories are concerned. To judge by the promotion of the battle site of Heavenfield, Hexham was an active supporter of Oswald's cult, at any rate from the early eighth century, while the dedications at *Scythlescester* and (if the arguments set out above are accepted) that of Elvet are almost certainly also to be associated with that diocese.[107] The number of potentially early dedications south of the Tees suggests that the cult was also vigorously promoted within the diocese of York, both in its core territory east of the Pennines in Deira, and in areas west of the Pennines which probably also came under its control.[108] From this perspective, the almost total absence of Oswald dedications in the diocese of Lindisfarne becomes all the more striking. It is tempting to conclude that there was a positive antipathy to Oswald dedications at Lindisfarne, despite the presence of major corporeal relics at both Bamburgh and Lindisfarne itself. The attitude of the Lindisfarne community towards its relic seems to have been remarkably ambivalent.[109] How might this state of affairs be explained? Possibly the espousal of Oswald's cult by Hexham presented an unwelcome (and perhaps all too successful) challenge to Lindisfarne as a center of his cult. From this point of view, the alternative promotion of Cuthbert's cult after the elevation of his relics in 698 had the distinct advantage of being exclusively under Lindisfarne's control. It may not be coincidental that the distribution of potentially early Cuthbert dedications is to some extent complementary to that of the Oswald ones, for, though by no means confined to the area north of the Tees, they are notably more common there.

There may also have been political overtones in the promotion of Oswald's cult in parts of pre-Viking Northumbria. If Alcuin's poem on the bishops, kings and saints of York is any guide to the way in which Oswald was perceived at York by the later eighth century, the saint had clearly acquired something of the status of a Christian founding father of the Northumbrian nation. In the light of Godman's observations on the increasing political status of the archbishops of York in the later eighth century, as royal power was eroded by dynastic conflict,[110] their patronage may well have been an important factor behind the number of probable pre-Viking Oswald dedications in southern and western Northumbria. Circumstantial evidence has been adduced in support of archiepiscopal involvement in the case of Guiseley; others may have arisen in similar circumstances.[111]

The distribution of sites with potentially early dedications to Oswald within Deira may itself be significant, for these are confined to two areas: the Deiran heartland east of Dere Street, in which lie Lythe, Oswaldkirk, Filey, Flamborough and Hotham (fig. 9.5, nos. 26, 30–32 and 39); and Elmet, containing Guiseley, Collingham and Methley (fig. 9.5, nos. 35, 37 and 40). Whether a further contrast should be drawn, on the basis of the foregoing analysis, between the apparently royal and monastic associations of the eastern sites and the possible archiepiscopal ones of those in Elmet, it is difficult to decide, though in view of the landed interests of later archbishops in the latter area it may not be wholly inappropriate to do so. What does seem clear is the contrast between the southern and eastern distribution of all the potentially early sites on the one hand and the more northerly and westerly distribution of pre-Reformation dedications to Oswald in Yorkshire as a whole on the other (fig. 9.5). However this apparent shift is to be explained, it seems unlikely to be fortuitous, which suggests that the identification of the early sites may not be altogether wide of the mark.

Besides going some way towards explaining the disparity between the small number of dedications to Oswald within the diocese of Lindisfarne and those elsewhere, the increasing popularity of the saint in episcopal circles other than Lindisfarne may also supply a clue to their chronological sequence. If the apparent indifference to Oswald on the part of the Lindisfarne community and its bishops was indeed a consequence of the desire to promote Cuthbert's cult from 698 onwards, their attitude before that momentous event, in the half-century or so after Oswald's death, need not have been so negative. Indeed, the possibility that Cuthbert might himself have dedicated a church to Oswald has been raised in connection with Lythe, and if the possible dedication at Wetheral is rightly interpreted as dependent on the important monastery at Carlisle, which appears to have been under Lindisfarne's control (at least during Cuthbert's lifetime), it may also be best explained as originating in a later seventh-century context. Slight though the evidence is, it suggests that the earliest Oswald dedications tended to be associated either with royal centers (such as Hotham or Elvet) or with major monasteries (such as Whitby or Carlisle). Their rarity in the diocese of Lindisfarne, may, however, suggest that they only became more common in Northumbria as a whole from the eighth century onwards, and that this fashion failed to take root (or was actively discouraged) in that diocese, due to the vigorous promotion of Cuthbert's cult there after 698. The more general spread of Oswald dedications elsewhere in Northumbria might then be seen as a later, eighth- to ninth-century, phenomenon, the consequence of the more universalized view of the saint's status as reflected in the verses of Alcuin. It must be stressed that Cuthbert also figures prominently in Alcuin's poem, so there is no attempt to present the cults as rivals, at least in York circles. The dedication to Oswald and Cuthbert jointly at *Scythlescester* at much the same time Alcuin was writing may reflect a comparable outlook. So may the way in which churches dedicated to Oswald in south-west Scotland tend to occur beside others dedicated to Cuthbert.[112] It has already been noted that the most plausible historical context for the establishment of the Oswald dedications in this region is an early one.[113] Of course, even it this is correct, there can be no certainty that the Cuthbert dedications are contemporaneous with those to Oswald. Nevertheless, in a region in which dedications to native Northumbrian saints were probably always uncommon, such strikingly similar distribution patterns seem unlikely to be coincidental, and might belong in a similar conceptual and chronological context.[114] And here, in the farthest outposts of Northumbrian rule, the political (indeed, propagandist) overtones are surely unmistakable; nor should the possibility that such a message was also intended by similar juxtaposition elsewhere in Northumbria be ruled out.[115] It seems that, by the late eighth century, Oswald (whether in conjunction with Cuthbert or alone) was being widely promoted by the Northumbrian establishment, both ecclesiastical and secular, the patriotic overtones of his cult being succinctly captured in Alcuin's characterization: "vir virtute potens, patriae tutator, amator."[116]

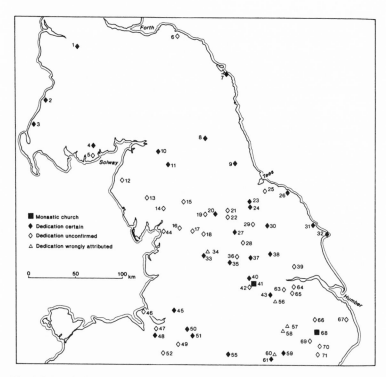

Fig. 9.5. Pre-Reformation Dedications to St. Oswald, I: North and Midlands.

Key to Figure 9.5

1 Cathcart, Renfrewshire

2 Kirkoswaald (of Turnberry), Ayrshire

3 Kirkoswald (alias Balmaknele), Ayrshire

4 Kelton, Kirkcudbrightshire

5 Kirkcarswell, Kirkcudbrightshire

6 Whittingehame, East Lothian

7 Bamburgh, Northumberland

8 St. Oswald in Lee (Heavenfield), Northumberland

9 Elvet (Durham City), County Durham

10 Wetheral, Cumberland

11 Kirkoswald, Cumberland

12 Dean, Cumberland

13 Grasmere, Westmorland

14 Burneside, Westmorland

15 Ravenstonedale, Westmorland

16 Thornton in Lonsdale, Yorkshire

17 Horton in Ribblesdale, Yorkshire

18 Arncliffe, Yorkshire

19 Askrigg, Yorkshire

20 Castle Bolton, Yorkshire

21 Hauxwell, Yorkshire

22 Thornton Steward, Yorkshire

23 West Rounton, Yorkshire

24 East Harlsey, Yorkshire

25 Newton in Cleveland, Yorkshire

26 Lythe, Yorkshire

27 Winksley (cum Grantley), Yorkshire

28 Farnham, Yorkshire

29 Sowerby, Yorkshire

30 Oswaldkirk, Yorkshire

31 Filey, Yorkshire

32 Flamborough, Yorkshire

33 Thornton in Craven, Yorkshire

Fig. 9.5. (*cont.*)

34 Broughton in Craven, Yorkshire
35 Guisely, Yorkshire
36 Leathley, Yorkshire
37 Collingham, Yorkshire
38 Fulford, Yorkshire
39 Hotham, Yorkshire
40 Methley, Yorkshire
41 Nostell Priory, Yorkshire
42 Wragby, Yorkshire
43 Kirk Sandall, Yorkshire
44 Warton, Lancashire
45 Winwick, Lancashire
46 Bidston, Chesire
47 Backford, Cheshire
48 Chester, Cheshire
49 Worleston, Cheshire
50 Lower Peover, Cheshire
51 Brereton (with Smethwick), Cheshire
52 Malpas, Cheshire

53 Oswestry, Shropshire
54 Hinstock, Shropshire
55 Ashbourne, Derbyshire
56 Finningley, Nottinghamshire
57 Dunham, Nottinghamshire
58 Ragnall, Nottinghamshire
59 East Stoke, Nottinghamshire
60 Bulcote, Nottinghamshire
61 Burton Joyce, Nottinghamshire
62 Broughton Sulney, Nottinghamshire
63 Crowle, Lincolnshire
64 Luddington, Lincolnshire
65 Althorpe, Lincolnshire
66 Rand, Lincolnshire
67 Strubby, Lincolnshire
68 Bardney Abbey, Lincolnshire
69 Blankney, Lincolnshire
70 Walcot, Lincolnshire
71 Howell, Lincolnshire

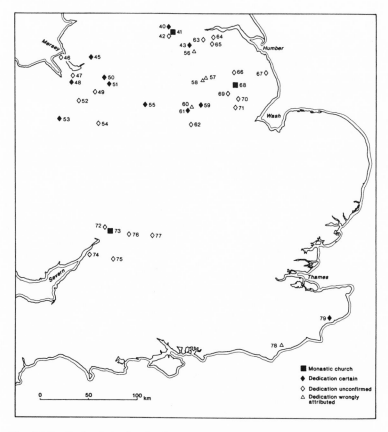

Fig. 9.6 Pre-Reformation Dedications to St. Oswald, II: Midlands and South.

Key to Figure 9.6

40 Methley, Yorkshire	52 Malpas, Cheshire
41 Nostell Priory, Yorkshire	53 Oswestry, Shropshire
42 Wragby, Yorkshire	54 Hinstock, Shropshire
43 Kirk Sandall, Yorkshire	55 Ashbourne, Derbyshire
44 Warton, Lancashire	56 Finningley, Nottinghamshire
45 Winwick, Lancashire	57 Dunham, Nottinghamshire
46 Bidston, Cheshire	58 Ragnall, Nottinghamshire
47 Backford, Cheshire	59 East Stoke, Nottinghamshire
48 Chester, Cheshire	60 Bulcote, Nottinghamshire
49 Worleston, Cheshire	61 Burton Joyce, Nottinghamshire
50 Lower Peover, Cheshire	62 Broughton Sulney, Nottinghamshire
51 Brereton (with Smethwick), Cheshire	63 Crowle, Lincolnshire

Fig. 9.6. (*cont.*)

64 Luddington, Lincolnshire	72 Lassington, Gloucestershire
65 Althorpe, Lincolnshire	73 Gloucester Priory, Gloucestershire
66 Rand, Lincolnshire	74 Rockhampton, Gloucestershire
67 Strubby, Lincolnshire	75 Shipton Oliffe, Gloucestershire
68 Bardney Abbey, Lincolnshire	76 Compton Abdale, Gloucestershire
69 Blankney, Lincolnshire	77 Widford, Oxfordshire
70 Walcot, Lincolnshire	78 Hooe, Sussex
71 Howell, Lincolnshire	79 Paddlesworth, Kent

ACKNOWLEDGEMENTS

I am particularly indebted to Richard Bailey for reading and commenting on several drafts of this paper, and to the following for their help and advice on particular points: Daphne Brooke; Tom Corfe; Derek Craig; Rosemary Cramp; Jane Cunningham; Margaret Gelling; Martin Snape; Clare Stancliffe; and Victor Watts.

ADDENDA

pp. 245–246, Oswaldkirk (Yorks.). On Oswaldkirk, cf. also G. [R. J.] Jones, "The Multiple Estates of (Holy) Islandshire, Hovingham and Kirby Moorside," *Medieval Europe 1992: Rural Settlement, Pre-printed Papers* 8 (York, 1992), 79–84, at pp. 81–83 and Fig. 2.

pp. 246–248, Guisley. On Guisley, see now G. R. J. Jones, "Some Donations to Bishop Wilfrid in Northern England," *Northern Hist.* 31 (1995), 22–38, at pp. 31–36.

EXPLANATORY NOTE FOR THE FOLLOWING APPENDIX

Oswald dedication numbers are as for Figs. 9.5–9.6. Roman road numbers after I. D. Margary, *Roman Roads in Britain,* 2nd edition (London, 1967), except for the one near to Burneside, Westmorland, for which see J. S. and J. A. Andrews, "A Roman Road from Kendal to Ambleside. A Field Survey. Part I: Kendal to Broadgate," *Trans. of the Cumberland and Westmorland Antiq. and Archaeol. Soc.* 91 (1991), 49–57. Brackets indicate significant uncertainty about the date of road or line of route.

ABBREVIATIONS AND SYMBOLS USED

ANG, Anglian; VA, Viking-age; *, presence; *?, evidence uncertain; *?——*?, date uncertain as between Anglian and Viking-age.

APPENDIX

Oswald Dedications and Archaeological Features

Oswald Dedication	Sculpture ANG VA	Anglian Sculpture within 5 miles	Roman Road within 3 miles
CHESHIRE			
47. Backford		Chester	(670/701)
46. Bidston		Overchurch	
51. Brereton		Sandbach	
48. Chester	*?		(6a/7a)
50. Lower Peover			(700)
52. Malpas			6a
49. Worleston			(700)
CUMBERLAND/WESTMORLAND			
12.Dean (Cu)		Brigham	(75)
11. Kirkoswald (Cu)	*?——*?	Addingham	
10. Wetheral (Cu)	*	Carlisle	7e/85b
14. Burneside (We)		Kendal	()
13. Grasmere (We)			
15. Ravenstonedale (We)		Kirkby Stephen	
DERBYSHIRE			
55. Ashbourne			
DURHAM			
9. Elvet	*		(80a)
LANCASHIRE			
44. Warton		Halton	
45. Winwick	*		70a

Oswald Dedication	Sculpture ANG	VA	Anglian Sculpture within 5 miles	Roman Road within 3 miles
LINCOLNSHIRE				
65. Althorpe				
68. Bardney Abbey				
69. Blankney				
63. Crowle		*		
71. Howell				
64. Luddington				
66. Rand				(27/272)
67. Strubby				
70. Walcot				
NORTHUMBERLAND				
7. Bamburgh	*? ——	*?		
8. St. Oswald in Lee	*?			8c/86
NOTTINGHAMSHIRE				
62. Broughton Sulney				5f/58a
61. Burton Joyce				
59. East Stoke				5f
SHROPSHIRE				
54. Hinstock				19
53. Oswestry				
YORKSHIRE				
18. Arncliffe				(731)
19. Askrigg				73/730
20. Castle Bolton			West Witton	
37. Collingham	*	*		72b
24. East Harlsey				80

Oswald Dedication	Sculpture ANG VA	Anglian Sculpture within 5 miles	Roman Road within 3 miles
YORKSHIRE (*cont.*)			
28. Farnham			(720b)
31. Filey	*	Hunmanby	(816)
32. Flamborough			810/811
38. Fulford	*	York	(28c)
35. Guiseley	*	Otley	72b
21. Hauxwell	*		
17. Horton in Ribblesdale			
39. Hotham			2e
43. Kirk Sandall			
36. Leathley		Otley	72b
26. Lythe	* *	Whitby	
40. Methley	*?	Ledsham	28b
25. Newton in Cleveland			
30. Oswaldkirk	*	Gilling East, Stonegrave	
29. Sowerby			80
33. Thornton in Craven			72a
16. Thornton in Lonsdale			
22. Thornton Steward	*		
23. West Rounton			80
27. Winksley cum Grantley		Ripon	
42. Wragby		Crofton	

NOTES

[1] A. Binns, "Pre-Reformation Dedications to St. Oswald in England and Scotland: A Gazetteer," in C. Stancliffe and E. Cambridge, eds., *Oswald Northumbrian King to European Saint* (Stamford, 1995), 241–71.

[2] *Historia Regum Symeonis Monachi Opera Omnia* (hereafter *H.R.*), ed. T. Arnold, Rolls Series 75, 2 vols. (London, 1882–85) *sub anno* 788. On the pre-Conquest annalistic material incorporated into the *Historia Regum,* see P. Hunter

Blair, "Some Observations on the *Historia Regum* attributed to Symeon of Durham," in N. K. Chadwick, ed., *Celt and Saxon: Studies in the Early British Border* (Cambridge, 1963), 63–118, at pp. 86–99, 117. On *Scythlescester,* see further Binns, "Pre-Reformation Dedications," 255.

[3] At first sight the joint dedication looks like an early example of that pairing of Cuthbert and Oswald which became popular in Durham iconography from the late twelfth century (R. N. Bailey, "St. Oswald's Heads," in Stancliffe and Cambridge, *Oswald,* 195–209); such an interpretation would, however, probably be anachronistic given the Lindisfarne community's apparent indifference (or even antipathy) to Oswald's cult at this period (see above, and A. Thacker, *"Membra Disjecta:* The Division of the Body and Diffusion of the Cult," ibid., 97–127, at pp. 101–02). The intention here may rather have been to promote the cult of a new royal martyr by associating him with the two most important indigenous Northumbrian cults.

[4] G. Fellows-Jensen, *Scandinavian Settlement Names in Yorkshire* (Copenhagen, 1972), 134, 246; Kirkoswald is first recorded in 1167: G. Fellows-Jensen, *Scandinavian Settlement Names in the North-West* (Copenhagen, 1985), 200.

[5] For Kirkoswald in Cumberland, see above, p. 249, and for Oswaldkirk, p. 246.

[6] D. Brooke, "Kirk-compound Place-names of Galloway and Carrick," *Trans. of the Dumfries. and Galloway Nat. Hist. and Antiq. Soc.,* 3rd series 58 (1983), 56–71.

[7] For the north shores of the Solway, see D. Brooke, "The Northumbrian Settlements in Galloway and Carrick: An Historical Assessment," *Proc. Soc. Antiq. of Scotland* 121 (1991), 295–327, at pp. 300–1. Eadberht's conquest of Kyle is recorded in the annals added to Bede's *Ecclesiastical History* (*H.E.,* 574–75) (see, B. Colgrave and R. A. B. Mynors, eds., *Bede's Ecclesiastical History of the English People* [Oxford, 1969; repr. 1991]). Strathclyde had probably advanced as far south as the northern parts of English Cumbria by the early tenth century (R. N. Bailey and R. J. Cramp, *Corpus of Anglo-Saxon Stone Sculpture in England,* vol. 2, *Cumberland, Westmorland and Lancashire North-of-the-Sands* [Oxford, 1988] [hereafter cited as *Corpus* 2], p. 6); this suggests that the loss of Anglian control in parts of south-west Scotland would have been earlier.

[8] R. Morris, *Churches in the Landscape* (London, 1989), 113, fig. 25.

[9] Ibid., fig. 64.

[10] Ibid., figs. 26, 64.

[11] In the following notes, the minimum figure is given first, followed by the maximum possible (in brackets). All instances where there is reason to doubt either the quality or relevance of the evidence are included in the bracketed figures.

[12] Anglian sculpture occurs at four (eight) sites, Viking-age sculpture at ten (thirteen) sites with Oswald dedications in the north.

[13] Roman roads run within three mile of seventeen (thirty) sites with Oswald dedications in the north.

[14] Sites with Anglian sculpture lie within five miles of seventeen (nineteen) sites with Oswald dedications in the north.

[15] M. S. Parker, "The Province of Hatfield," *Northern Hist.* 28 (1992), 42–69, at pp. 48–49, 60, map. 6 on p. 61.

[16] L. A. S. Butler, "Church Dedications and the Cults of the Anglo-Saxon Saints in England," in L. A. S. Butler and R. K. Morris, eds., *The Anglo-Saxon Church: Papers on History, Architecture and Archaeology in Honour of Dr. H. M. Taylor,* C.B.A. Research Rep. 60 (London, 1986), 44–50, at p. 45.

[17] *H.E.* iii, 6, 12.

[18] The formula "ecclesiam de Baenburch" (alternatively "ecclesiam suam de Bamburgh") first occurs in a grant of Henry I dated ca. 1119 (London, B. L., Vespasian Exix, f.8) (E. Bateson, *A History of Northumberland,* vol. 1, *The Parish of Bamburgh with the Chapelry of Belford* [Newcastle upon Tyne & London, 1893], 74, note 1; *Regesta Regum Anglo-Normannorum, 1066–1154,* vol. 2, *1100–35* [ed. C. Johnson and H. A. Cronne; Oxford, 1956], no. 1217; W. Farrer, ed., *Early Yorkshire Charters,* 12 vols. [Edinburgh, 1914–16], vol. 2, no. 1424). It is followed by a mandate of Henry II to Bishop Hugh Le Puiset of Durham (Vespasian Exix, f.6 [ibid, no. 1456]); and a notification by the former to the latter concerning the royal clerk Hugh Murdac (Vespasian Exix, f.7 [ibid, no. 1457]), which is in turn confirmed by Le Puiset (Vespasian Exix, f.7); three further royal documents of the reign of King John (Vespasian Exix, f.8) also refer to the church in these terms.

[19] The formula "ecclesias sancti Osualdi ed [sancti] Aidani de Bamburg sicut Algarus presbiter unquam eas melius tenuit" first occurs in a general confirmation of Henry I dated to between 1121 and 1127 (Vespasian Exix, f.150 [Farrer, *Early Yorkshire Charters,* vol. 2, no. 1428]). It is followed by: a general confirmation of Henry II (adding "cum capellis" [ibid, vol. 3, p. 135]); a Le Puiset confirmation of ca. 1160 (also mentioning Hugh Murdac) (Vespasian Exix, f.118); and by later royal confirmations of Richard I, John, and Henry III (respectively Vespasian Exix, ff.4, 5, 8).

[20] Bateson, *Bamburgh,* 74

[21] Confusion could have arisen if that church had (or had acquired) a double dedication, which could then easily have been misinterpreted as referring to two different buildings. As none of the documents is known to survive in the original, it is unclear whether confusion might have arisen at the hands of a twelfth-century forger or of the later medieval copyist of the Nostell cartulary, which is our only surviving source for their texts. A dedication to Oswald might even have been added by the monks of Nostell, given their obvious interest in the saint (see D. Rollason, "St. Oswald in Post-Conquest England," in Stancliffe and Cambridge,

Oswald, 164–77, at pp. 173–74); for the likelihood that the dedication to Aidan is early, see above.

[22] Bateson, *Bamburgh,* 104.

[23] F. Arnold-Foster, *Studies in Church Dedications: Or, England's Patron Saints,* 3 vols., (London, 1879), vol. 2, 235. The rarity of the dedication may be an indication of how successfully the Cuthbert Community eclipsed the cult of Aidan by promoting that of Cuthbert.

[24] "Erat in uilla regia non longe ab urbe . . . In hac enim habens ecclesiam et cubiculum . . ." (*H.E.* iii, 17).

[25] Ibid.

[26] See above, note 21. Bullough seems to have considered the above possibility, though later he doubts the antiquity of the dedication to Aidan. His grounds for considering this site to have been monastic in the seventh century are not clear, however: see D. Bullough, "The Missions to the English and Picts and their Heritage," in H Löwe, ed., *Die Iren und Europa,* 2 vols. (Stuttgart, 1982), vol. 1, 80–98, at pp. 86–87, note 20.

[27] The evidence is discussed by R. N. Bailey, "St. Oswald's Heads," 198–99; V. Tudor, "Reginald's *Life of St. Oswald,*" in Stancliffe and Cambridge, *Oswald,* 178–94, at p. 189.

[28] Bateson, *Bamburgh,* 74.

[29] For the phenomenon in general, see W. Levison, "Medieval Church Dedications in England: Some Problems," *Trans. Archit. and Archaeol. Societies of Durham and Northumberland* 10 (1946), 55–79, at p. 78. The existence at Repton of structures presumably associated with the monastery documented from the late seventh century (for which see *Felix's Life of St. Guthlac,* ed. and trans. B. Colgrave [Cambridge, 1956], 178–79), but in any case dating from well before the interment of the remains of the present dedicatee there in 849, has been demonstrated by archaeological and structural analysis: see H. M. Taylor, "St. Wystan's Church, Repton, Derbyshire. A Reconstruction Essay," *Archaeol. J.* 144 (1987), 205–45, at pp. 211, 243–44. The church of St. Peter at Bamburgh is referred to by Alcuin, *The Bishops, Kings, and Saints of York,* ed. P. Goodman (Oxford, 1982), lines 304–07.

[30] *H.E.* iii, 6, 12. (It is clear from the circumstantial details of Bede's account of Penda's attempt to raze the *urbs* by fire in *H.E.* iii, 16 that he thought of it as confined to the rock.) *H.R. sub anno* 774; J. Campbell, "Bede's Words for Places," in P. H. Sawyer, ed., *Names, Words and Graves* (Leeds, 1979), 34–51, at pp. 35, 39.

[31] Bateson, *Bamburgh,* 57, 74. A fragment of pre-Viking sculpture from the castle site, convincingly interpreted by Cramp as the arm of a chair, may have been associated with St. Peter's, though its context is not certainly ecclesiastical

(R. Cramp, *Corpus of Anglo-Saxon Stone Sculpture in England,* vol. 1, *County Durham and Northumberland* [Oxford, 1984] [hereafter cited as *Corpus* 1], 162–63, fig. 18, ills. 812–17).

[32] Bateson, *Bamburgh,* 75–83.

[33] Colgrave (*H.E.,* 263) seems to take the passage in this sense, as do Campbell, ("Bede's Words for Places," 46, and L. Alcock, *Bede, Eddius, and the Forts of the North Britons,* Jarrow Lecture 1988 (Jarrow, 1989), 11.

[34] These might have included the "uiculis in uicinia urbis" demolished by Penda to provide fuel for his attempt to set fire to the *urbs* (*H.E.* iii, 16). Aidan's buildings might have counted as a *uiculus* for these purposes, since the church at which he died, together with its *uicus,* were burnt by Penda in the course of a later attack on Bamburgh during the episcopate of Aidan's successor (*H.E.* iii, 17), and since there are contexts in Bede's writings in which it is certain that *uicus* and *uiculus* are being used interchangeably (Campbell, "Bede's Words for Places," 43). Alternatively Bede may mean that this satellite settlement near the *urbs* was itself capable of being described as a *uilla regia,* though this seems unlikely as recorded occurrences of the term *uilla regia* generally refer to the principal settlement of an estate (ibid., 46–48.)

[35] If Bede's statement in *H.E.* iii, 17 that Aidan ". . . owned nothing except his own church and small adjacent fields" (". . . nil propriae possessionis excepta ecclesia sua et adiacentibus agellis habens") is correctly interpreted as referring not to his church at Bamburgh but rather to his monastery on Lindisfarne (see C. Stancliffe, "Oswald, Most Holy and Most Victorious King of the Northumbrians," in Stancliffe and Cambridge, *Oswald,* 33–83, at p. 65), the implication is that, in the beginning at least, not even the church and accommodation at Bamburgh and at other royal vills were owned by the bishop, but rather were provided by the king for his use. The possible modes of development of such episcopal churches in royal centers are briefly considered by P. H. Sawyer, "The Royal Tun in pre-Conquest England," in P. Wormald, ed., with D. Bullough and R. Collins, *Ideal and Reality in Frankish and Anglo-Saxon Society: Studies Presented to J. M. Wallace-Hadrill* (Oxford, 1983), 273–99, at pp. 277–78.

[36] See Thacker, *"Membra Disjecta"* 104–05; and Binns, "Pre-Reformation Dedications," 253. St. Oswald's Gloucester had apparently originally been dedicated to St. Peter at its foundation ca. 900 (see M. Hare, *The Two Anglo-Saxon Minsters at Gloucester,* Deerhurst Lecture 1992 [Deerhurst, 1993], 6). The dedication must have changed to St. Oswald after the translation there of his relics in 909 and before the later eleventh century, by which time Oswald seems to have been well established as the patron saint: see Binns, "Pre-Reformation Dedications," 250.

[37] See C. Stancliffe, "Where was Oswald Killed?" in Stancliffe and Cambridge, *Oswald,* 84–96. Her interpretation of the Welsh name for Oswestry, *Croesoswald,* implies that a cross commemorating the saint predated the church (ibid, 88–91). See also Binns, "Pre-Reformation Dedications," 258.

[38] Ibid., 255.

[39] The grant of this church to Nostell Priory in the twelfth century may suggest that its dedication to Oswald is ancient: see Rollason, "St. Oswald in Post-Conquest England," 173, n.44, and Binns, "Pre-Reformation Dedications," 263.

[40] I am most grateful to James Lang for supplying information about this carving, and for drawing to my attention a second stone at Lythe which (to judge from the lack of taper and the fact that carving occurs only on one face) may also have been architectural in function (presumably an impost): see W. G. Collingwood, "Anglian and Anglo-Danish Sculpture in the East Riding, with addenda to the North Riding," *Yorkshire Archaeol. J.* 21 (1911), 254–302, at p. 288, fig. k on p. 289. The form of the interlace suggests that this piece must be considerably later than the late seventh century, however. For the Lastingham finial, see J. T. Lang, *Corpus of Anglo-Saxon Stone Sculpture in England,* vol. 3, *York and Eastern Yorkshire* (Oxford, 1991) (hereafter cited as *Corpus* 3), 171–72, ills. 610–13; and for that at Heysham, R. D. Andrews, "St. Patrick's Chapel, Heysham, Lancashire," *Bul. of the C.B.A. Churches Com.* 8 (1978), 2.

[41] E. Cambridge, "The Early Church in County Durham: A Reassessment," *J.B.A.A.* 137 (1984), 65–85, at pp. 66–71.

[42] For the difficulties see Butler, "Dedications," n. 11, pp. 49–50. While Hunter Blair perhaps too easily dismissed the possibility of an identification with Strensall, his discussion of Bede's interpretation of the name (as *sinus fari,* "bay of light") still points to a coastal location (P. Hunter Blair, "Whitby as a Centre of Learning in the Seventh Century," in M. Lapidge and H. Gneuss, eds., *Learning and Literature in Anglo-Saxon England. Studies Presented to Peter Clemoes* [Cambridge, 1985], 3–32, at pp. 9–12). For the archaeology see R. Cramp, "A Reconsideration of the Monastic Site of Whitby," in R. N. Spearman and J. Higgitt, eds., *The Age of Migrating Ideas. Early Medieval Art in Northern Britain and Ireland* (Edinburgh & Stroud, 1993), 64–73.

[43] Oswald's Deiran blood may have been one factor underlying his choice as dedicatee (*H.E.* iii, 6); but surely more pertinent is the fact that Oswiu, his brother and successor, who was clearly instrumental in establishing his cult at Bamburgh (see above, p. 239), was himself buried at Whitby (*H.E.* iii, 24).

[44] Fellows-Jensen, *Scandinavian Settlement Names in Yorkshire,* 100.

[45] *Vita Sancti Cuthberti Auctore Anonymo,* the anonymous *Life of St. Cuthbert,* ed. and trans. B. Colgrave, *Two Lives of St. Cuthbert* (Cambridge, 1940; reprinted 1985), IV, 10 (pp. 126–29); *Vita Sancti Cuthberti Auctore Beda,* Bede's Prose *Life of St. Cuthbert,* in ibid., ch. 34 (pp. 260–65).

[46] Cambridge, "Early Church," 74.

[47] B. Colgrave, ed. and trans., *The Earliest Life of Gregory the Great* (Cambridge, 1968), 41.

[48] A recent suggestion that the whole *Osingadun* episode was originally set near Carlisle (S. Hollis, *Anglo-Saxon Women and the Church: Sharing a Common Fate* [Woodbridge, 1992], 202, n. 112, cf. 203, n. 116) ignores the other possible interpretations of the phrase "in parrochia eius" in the anonymous *Life of St. Cuthbert IV,* 10 (discussed in Cambridge, "Early Church," 84, n. 62).

[49] *Corpus* 2, 84, n. 1.

[50] For Hunmanby, see *Corpus* 3, 148–49, ills. 500, 502; for Filey, ibid., 130, ill. 450.

[51] Morris, *Churches,* figs. 32, 27, 29.

[52] *Corpus* 3, fig. 3; fig. 8.

[53] *Corpus* 3, 197–98, ills. 741–44.

[54] Printed in A. W. Haddon and W. Stubbs, *Councils and Ecclesiastical Documents Relating to Great Britain and Ireland,* 3 vols. (Oxford, 1869–78), vol. 3, 394–96.

[55] For Stonegrave, see *Corpus* 3, 216–17, ills. 824–25, 827–28; for Gilling, ibid., 133, ill. 440; for Hovingham, ibid., 145–48, ills. 484, 490–99.

[56] Conceivably Collingham, the only other Yorkshire Oswald dedication which has produced pre-Viking (as well as Viking-age) sculpture (W. G. Collingwood, "Anglian and Anglo-Danish Sculpture in the West Riding, with Addenda to the North and East Ridings and York, and a General Review of the Early Christian Monuments of Yorkshire," *Yorkshire Archaeol. J.* 23 [1915], 129–299, at pp. 155–61), should also be thought of in a monastic context. But it differs from the others in showing no discernible sign of being associated with any other adjacent sites.

[57] Collingwood, "West Riding," 224–31. Some possible implications of the sculpture for the function of the site are discussed in I. N. Wood, "Anglo-Saxon Otley: An Archiepiscopal Estate and its Crosses in a Northumbrian Context," *Northern Hist.* 23 (1987), 20–37, at pp. 30–36.

[58] For a summary of the documentary evidence relating to Guiseley, see Wood, ibid., 20–23.

[59] Collingwood, "West Riding," 179–81.

[60] Wood, "Anglo-Saxon Otley," 23.

[61] See above, n. 56.

[62] R. N. Bailey, *Viking Age Sculpture in Northern England* (London, 1980), 189–90, fig. 52.

[63] I have drawn attention elsewhere to a comparable north–south sequence of sites associated with the bishops of Lindisfarne (E. Cambridge, "Why did the Community of St. Cuthbert Settle at Chester-le-Street," in G. Bonner, D.

Rollason and C. Stancliffe, eds., *St. Cuthbert, His Cult and His Community to A.D. 1200* [Woodbridge, 1989], 367–86, at pp. 380–85); it is possible that such a context may also help to explain some of the Oswald dedications in the High Pennines (notably Thornton in Craven, which lies on the line of a Roman road), and perhaps also some of those in Cumberland and Westmorland.

[64] Bailey, *Viking Age Sculpture,* 170, 189, fig. 40 on p. 162.

[65] Collingwood, "West Riding," 185–97.

[66] C. J. Gordon, "A Submerged Church in the River Eden," *Trans. of the Cumberland and Westmorland Antiq. and Archaeol. Soc.,* 2nd ser. 14 (1914), 328–36, fig. facing p. 328.

[67] *Corpus* 2, 46–48; not to be confused with Addingham, Yorkshire (see p. 247, above).

[68] *Corpus* 2, 125.

[69] *Corpus* 2, 74–75; for the extent of the large medieval parish, see A. Winchester, "Medieval Cockermouth," *Trans. of the Cumberland and Westmorland Antiq. and Archaeol. Soc.,* 2nd ser. 86 (1986), 109–28, at pp. 122–25, fig. 4.

[70] H. M. and J. Taylor, *Anglo-Saxon Architecture,* 2 vols. (Cambridge, 1965), vol. 1, 378–84.

[71] On the other hand, Brereton seems to have been dependent on Astbury in the later pre-Conquest period at least (see Binns, "Pre-Reformation Dedications," 246); on Sandbach see J. D. Bu'lock, *Pre-Conquest Cheshire 383–1066* (Chester, 1972), 45–48. On Overchurch, see ibid., 48–49; a possible pre-Conquest association between Overchurch and Bidston has been postulated by Bu'lock on other grounds (ibid., 80).

[72] N. Pevsner, et al., *The Buildings of England, County Durham,* 2nd ed. (Harmondsworth, 1983), 223.

[73] Summarized in *Corpus* 1, 32; see also 66–67, ills. 189–92. For a cautionary note on the latter assumption see R. N. Bailey, "The Chronology of Viking-Age Sculpture in Northumbria," in J. Lang, ed., *Anglo-Saxon and Viking Age Sculpture,* B.A.R., Brit. ser. 49 (Oxford, 1978), 173–203, at pp. 173–74.

[74] *Corpus* 1, ill. 1266 (Tynemouth 4A), ill. 28 (Aycliffe 1D) (cf. ill. 189); Bailey, *Viking Age Sculpture,* 194–95.

[75] C. Plummer and J. Earle, *Two of the Saxon Chronicles Parallel,* 2 vols. (Oxford, 1892), "E", *sub anno* 762. Hereafter *A.S.C.*

[76] These two elements are ultimately connected and sometimes confused: see A. H. Smith, *English Place-Name Elements,* vol. 1, English Place-Name Society 25 (Cambridge, 1958), 147; for Elvet see E. Ekwell, *The Concise Oxford Dictionary of English Place-Names,* 4th ed. (Oxford, 1960), 166 (*sub* "Elvet Hall"). I am grateful to Victor Watts for pointing out to me that the recorded forms of the name do not enable the form of the generic to be determined on linguistic grounds.

[77] M. Gelling, *Place-Names in the Landscape* (London, 1984), 36.

[78] B. Yorke, "Lindsey: the Lost Kingdom Found?" in A. Vince, ed., *Pre-Viking Lindsey* (Lincoln, 1993), 141–50, at p. 143, quoting a suggestion by M. Gelling.

[79] For the early forms, see B. Colgrave, ed., *The Life of Bishop Wilfrid by Eddius Stephanus* (Cambridge, 1927; reprinted 1985), 22, 44, 51, 60, 62, 65 (pp. 44, 90, 106, 132, 134, 140). I am grateful to Victor Watts for the information on the generic.

[80] See, for example, Ekwall, *Place-Names,* 237 (*sub* "Hestercombe"). I am most grateful to Tom Corfe for allowing me to see his unpublished work on this topic.

[81] Ekwell, *Place-Names,* 154.

[82] Smith (*English Place-Name Elements,* 147) points out that *holmr* is used as the equivalent of *eg* in the areas of Scandinavian settlement.

[83] For the phenomenon in general, see Campbell, "Bede's Words for Places," 45–46; for Bamburgh, see above, 240–243; for Selsey (a former royal vill given to found a monastery), see G. R. J. Jones, "Broninis," *Bul. of the Board of Celtic Studies* 37 (1990), 125–32, at pp. 127–28. If his identification of *In-broninis* with Lindisfarne is correct, its generic element *ynys* ("island") may provide a British parallel to the use of Old English *eg* proposed above, for he argues that the name referred to the extensive mainland territory dependent on Lindisfarne and not just to the island itself (ibid., 131).

[84] For the phenomenon in general see J. Blair, "Minster Churches in the Landscape," in D. Hooke, ed., *Anglo-Saxon Settlements* (Oxford, 1988), 35–58, at pp. 40–48.

[85] Jones, "Broninis," 129–30; see above, 240–243.

[86] For example, H. Gee, "City of Durham: General History of the City," *Durham,* vol. 3, Victoria County History of the Counties of England (London, 1900), 1–52, at pp. 6–7.

[87] Compare the relationship of Coniscliffe to Dere Street (discussed above, p. 253–254).

[88] F. Arnold-Forster, *Studies in Church Dedications,* vol. 3, 360. For the possibility that the place-name Edwinstowe (Nottinghamshire) reflects a (perhaps early) dedication to Edwin, see Butler, "Dedications," 47–48. The subsequent unpopularity of Edwin's cult may have resulted in other early dedications being supplanted elsewhere, so that the contrast with the number of Oswald dedications may have been somewhat less pronounced in the pre-Viking period.

[89] It is a Scandinavianized version of Old English *Ciningesclif,* "the king's cliff" (Ekwell, *Place-Names,* 120). For the likelihood that it is to be identified with *Ædwinesclif,* the setting of a royal murder in 761 (*A.S.C.*, "E", *sub anno* 761), see W. Pearson, "Edwin, Coniscliffe and the Quest for Hela and 'Thorns'," *Durham Archaeol. J.* 7 (1991), 113–21, at pp. 113–14.

[90] *A.S.C.*, "E", *sub anno* 778. For other examples of murder carried out at royal vills see Sawyer, "Royal Tun," 276.

[91] Particularly if Coniscliffe, on the north bank of the Tees, was regarded as part of Deira, to whose ruling dynasty Edwin belonged and where (at Whitby) his relics were enshrined (see above, pp. 244-245, and Thacker, *"Membra Disjecta,"* 105).

[92] For the church, see P. F. Ryder, "St. Edwin's Church, High Coniscliffe," *Durham Archaeol. J.* 5 (1989), 55–65. Might the extraordinarily long and narrow proportions of the nave (ibid., fig. 1, p. 56) conceivably have been to some extent determined by a timber predecessor? For the sculpture, see *Corpus* 1, 59–61, ills. 152–55, 157–59 (with Ryder's correction, "St. Edwin's Church,". 64, n. 11).

[93] I have suggested elsewhere that these features typify non-monastic churches serving estate centers (Cambridge, "Early Church," 81). St. Aidan's at Bamburgh also appears to conform to this pattern.

[94] The street leading from the Durham peninsula to the ford giving access to the east bank of the river and St. Oswald's church may thus be a significant early surviving feature of the settlement plan. Might its later medieval name, Kingsgate, preserve a memory of its early function in linking the royal and ecclesiastical settlements? It seems to have formed the principal east–west route across the peninsula (fig. 9.2b) before its displacement northwards by the construction of the two bridges in the twelfth century.

[95] Cambridge, "Chester-le-Street," 379–86.

[96] Ibid., fig. 33, p. 381.

[97] Thacker, *"Membra Disjecta,"* 107–11.

[98] *H.E.* ii, 13.

[99] N. J. Higham, *The Kingdom of Northumbria A.D. 350–1100* (Stroud, 1993), 81. (For the name, see Ekwall, *Place-Names,* 339.) The complex intermingling of adjacent parts of the parishes of Hotham and North and South Newbald, an arrangement which was apparently established as early as 963, not only attests the antiquity of their relationship, but may also suggest that they had anciently been part of a single territory: see M. H. Long and M. F. Pickles, "Newbald," in H. E. J. Le Patourel, M. H. Long, and M. F. Pickles, eds., *Yorkshire Boundaries* (Leeds, 1993), 135–41, at p. 136, and fig. 49 on p. 138.

[100] The first element in the place-name is a personal name of Scandinavian origin (Ekwell, *Place-Names,* 181); conceivably, however, the generic might have been formulated earlier, like that of Bamburgh. For the possible date of the Danes' Dyke, see J. R. Watkin, "The Archaeology of Anglian East Yorkshire—A Review of Some Published Evidence and Proposals for Future Research," *East Riding Archaeol.* 7 (1983), 25–39, at p. 33, and for early Anglian settlement within it, p. 31.

[101] W. F. H. Nicolaisen, *Scottish Place-Names, Their Study and Significance* (London, 1976), 20, 72.

[102] B. Hope-Taylor, *Yeavering: An Anglo-British Centre of Early Northumbria* (London, 1977), fig. 2.

[103] The way in which several complexes appear to straddle the Roman roads to which they are adjacent, the subsidiary element lying on the opposite side to the principal one, may also be a diagnostic early feature (for example, Guiseley and Otley [fig. 9.4b], Hotham and Sancton/Newbald [fig. 9.4d], and perhaps also Methley and Ledsham [fig. 9.4c]); it is not, of course, restricted to sites containing Oswald dedications.

[104] Æthelred of Mercia retired to the monastery of Bardney in 704 (*H.E.* v, 24); his queen, Osthryth, had earlier translated relics of Oswald there (see Thacker, "*Membra Disjecta,*" 104–05). For Offa's bequests to Bardney in the later eighth century, see Alcuin, *Bishops, Kings and Saints,* lines 388ff.

[105] See above, p. 249, and Appendix, p. 265.

[106] See Stancliffe, "Where was Oswald Killed."

[107] See Thacker, "*Membra Disjecta,*" 107–08, 113, and Binns, "Pre-Reformation Dedications," 255, 249.

[108] See above, p. 247 and n. 63. Oswald's popularity in these regions may in part reflect the failure of widely popular saints' cults to establish themselves either at York itself or within its diocese.

[109] See Thacker, "*Membra Disjecta,*" 101–02, 104, and Bailey, "St. Oswald's Heads," 198.

[110] Alcuin, *Bishops, Kings and Saints,* lix–lx.

[111] The correlation between episcopal estates and early dedications to St. Chad in the north-west midlands to which Alan Thacker has recently drawn attention forms an instructive parallel, particularly as in at least one instance (Tushingham) the dedication to Chad apparently occurs in a subsidiary context: see The Victoria History of the Counties of England, *Chesire* (London, 1979), vol. 1, 266, 271.

[112] Daphne Brooke has drawn attention to the juxtaposition of the Oswald dedication implied by the name Kirkoswald of Turnberry (fig. 9.5, no. 2) with the Cuthbert dedication in the adjacent parish of Maybole (Brooke, "Northumbrian Settlements," 310–11). A similar situation arises with Kirkoswald, alias Balmaknele (fig. 9.5, no. 3), and Ballantrae; the first element of the ancient name of the latter, *Kirkcudbright-Innertig,* fossilizes its Cuthbert dedication, and though the site of the former is uncertain, it was clearly within Ballantrae parish. A further example may occur in the southern part of this region, where the Oswald dedication at Kelton (and, if the place-name is correctly interpreted, that at Kirkcarswell: fig. 9.5, nos. 4–5) is near to Kirkcudbright, the specific of which again fossilizes a dedication to Cuthbert.

[113] See above, p. 235.

[114] This also suggests that the attitude of the bishops of Whithorn resembled that of York and Hexham, and not that of Lindisfarne.

[115] The occurrence of Oswald and Cuthbert dedications near to one another in areas where neither is common, such as Warton (fig. 9.5, no. 44) and St. Cuthbert at Over Kellet in north Lancashire, or Filey (fig. 9.5, no. 31) and St. Cuthbert at Burton Fleming (both perhaps to be associated with a major center at Hunmanby, see above p. 246) in eastern Yorkshire, are reminiscent of the south-west Scottish examples.

[116] "A man of mighty virtue, guardian and lover of the fatherland," Alcuin, *Bishops, Kings, and Saints,* line 267.

CHAPTER 10

The Anglo-Saxon Cemetery at Sutton Hoo
An Interim Report

MARTIN O. H. CARVER

Field-work at Sutton Hoo finished in April 1992. As the final interim report went to press the excavations were being back-filled, and, in realization of a cherished dream, Mound 2 was being rebuilt to its original seventh-century height—a great yellow-streaked hill similar in size and presence to Ottarshögen or one of the mounds at Gamla Uppsala. With the soil so freshly returned, and the compendious records so recently sorted and filed, readers will not be expecting a definitive account either of the curious burial practices of the Anglo-Saxons at this place, or of its role in history. Nevertheless, this is a special moment, that which immediately follows the closure of an archaeological site,—when the imagination is still feverish with discovery, and not yet sobered by analysis, mocked by lost records or dulled by delay. It is a time of excitement, optimism and speculation, when a *loi de carnaval* applies and we may still proffer the unprovable and think the unthinkable.

In this spirit, an interim report is given here, as a foretaste of the monograph on the Anglo-Saxon cemetery to be published, after analysis of the finds, by the Society of Antiquaries and the British Museum. This interim report is dedicated to three matters only: briefly, a description of the recorded investigations at Sutton Hoo; secondly and more generously an account of what has been discovered there relating to the early Middle Ages, and thirdly and most sketchily, what these discoveries may be currently contrived to mean. The report is thus both a record and an agenda for research on Anglo-Saxon Sutton Hoo. Not discussed or hardly referred to are the two other research areas which comprised a major part of our efforts: the prehistoric (mainly late Neolithic and early Bronze

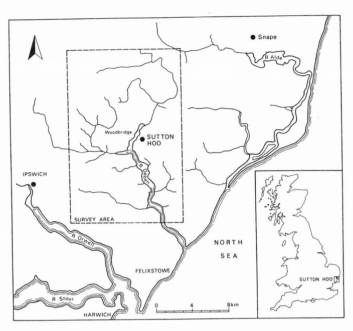

Fig. 10.1. Sutton Hoo: Location.

Age) settlement and the methodological developments, both of which are the subject of quite separate studies.

THE INVESTIGATIONS AND WHAT
THEY ENCOUNTERED, BEFORE 1983

The earliest investigation of which we have any record occurs in the Ipswich Journal for 1860, and it is worth quoting in full if only because the excavations that are intimated were to become so closely entangled with our own:

> ROMAN MOUNDS or BARROWS.—It is not known by many that not less than five Roman Barrows, lying close to each other, may be seen on a farm occupied by Mr Barritt, at Sutton, about 500 yards from the banks of the Deben, immediately opposite Woodbridge. One of these mounds was recently opened, when a considerable number (nearly two bushels) of iron screw bolts were found, all of which were sent to the blacksmith to be converted into horse shoes! It is hoped,

when leave is granted to open the others, some more important antiquities may be discovered. These barrows were laid down in the Admiralty surveys by Captain Stanley during the stay of the *Blazer*, when taking the soundings of the above-named river some years since.[1]

The mounds shown in the Admiralty survey are 1–4 and 6–8, so the victim should have been one of these,[2] and from what we have since learnt the candidates can only be Mounds 2 or 8. Of these Mound 2 certainly contained ship-rivets, no doubt the "iron screw bolts" of the journalist, and provided (on re-examination in 1986) a compatible setting for the barrow-opening of 1860. Leave, it seems, was subsequently granted to open at least some of the others, for the innocent-sounding announcement

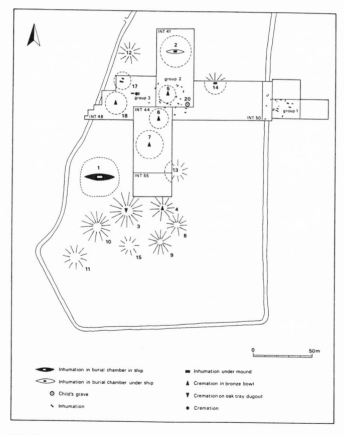

Fig. 10.2. Sutton Hoo: Known and Possible Anglo-Saxon Burials and Extent of the Anglo-Saxon Site.

either heralds, or perhaps conceals, what was discovered on the ground to be a major nineteenth-century excavation campaign, involving the opening of Mound 2 and at least six others. No records have been located and what became of the finds is quite unknown, although it may of course yet be discovered. The 1860 adventure at Sutton Hoo, unlike its sister excavation at Snape two years later,[3] had at any rate been completely forgotten by 1938 when Mrs. Pretty, the new landowner and Justice of the Peace, conceived (as landowners sometimes do) a curiosity about the humps and bumps of her barrow cemetery, by this time nearly flattened and covered in bracken. Assisted by Ipswich Museum and by the services of the freelance self-taught Suffolk excavator Basil Brown, Mrs. Pretty caused to be opened, by the traditional method of trenching, Mounds 2, 3 and 4. In each case the finds (Table 10.1) showed the burial to have been Anglo-Saxon, and in each case to have been previously disturbed. Mounds 3 and 4 had contained cremations, while Mound 2 had included iron rivets of a type used to fasten the planking of early medieval clinker-built ships.

Encouraged, or at least not discouraged, by these encounters, Mrs. Pretty's team returned in 1939 to confront the then largest mound, Mound 1. Here the green fingers of Basil Brown, alerted by the early discovery of rivets, were able to trace the 27m long outline of a clinker-built rowing-boat buried in a trench below ground level (fig. 10.3; pl. 10.3). In the center of this ship, still the largest known from the early Middle Ages, was a dark rectangle ". . . the place where I expect the chief lies" as Basil Brown remarked in his diary for 3 July,[4] which proved indeed to be the remains of a collapsed but otherwise undisturbed burial-chamber. In the sordid and profane history of British heritage management, such preservation from the hands of looters, treasure-hunters, and acquisitive royal agents must be counted a miraculous deliverance, the true benefits of which were soon to be revealed.

Following the intervention of the British Museum (spurred by Christopher Hawkes) and the Ministry of Public Buildings and Works, a scratch team led by Charles Phillips and including in its illustrious contingent W. F. Grimes, Graham Clark, Peggy Guido and Stuart Piggott, dismantled the burial-deposit with its 263 finds in an astonishing ten days. This was one of the heroic episodes of British archaeology, the expeditious but measured, courageous but not cavalier retrieval of the richest burial-assemblage so far discovered in Britain, under pressure from heat, wind, unfamiliarity, negligible resources, an inquisitive public and the approach of war. Given the circumstances of discovery, together with the immediate production of a report[5] and the selfless gift of the entire treasure to the nation by Mrs. Pretty, it is scarcely surprising that this

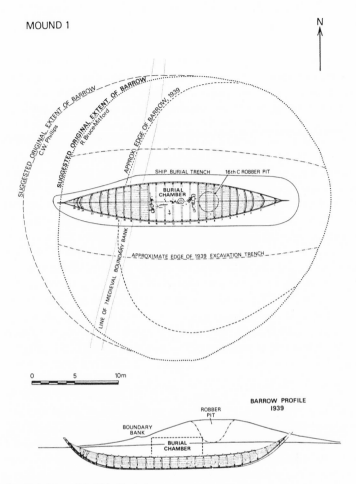

Fig. 10.3. Mound 1: Ship Burial.

grave-group made the name of Sutton Hoo famous; it became and has remained an inspiration for the researches and speculations of archaeologists, art historians, historians, anthropologists, teachers and members of
the general public alike.

Equally heroic, in its persistence and meticulous attention to detail,
was the work of the British Museum team under Rupert Bruce-Mitford
which conserved, reconstructed and studied the assemblage over the
forty years which followed. The program included a return to the field of
battle from 1966 to 1971, in order to re-excavate the ship-burial, abandoned since 1939, test for the presence of "Mound 5" and investigate the
character of the prehistoric site first reported by Basil Brown. This successful campaign enabled the inventory of the Mound 1 assemblage, and

the account of the burial rite employed to be completed,[6] Mound 5 to be identified[7] and the prehistoric site to be broadly defined: a settlement area exploited from the middle Neolithic period to the Iron Age.[8] Two new types of burial were also encountered: flat graves containing sand-bodies and (less certainly Anglo-Saxon) two cremations (Table 10.1 nos. 13, 14, 45, 50, 51, 56).[9] Bruce-Mitford's publication, a monument in its own right, provides not only a means for the world to share the treasure, but a point of departure for new interpretation, as understanding of the significance of the find and its context is altered by new discoveries, new students and above all by new archaeological theory.

THEORY AND HYPOTHESIS

The Mound 1 burial will be reviewed in the context of the present campaign, the object of which is of course to publish the cemetery as a whole. In the final report, the Mound 1 burial will therefore reappear before the public, dressed as before but playing a new role. While hastening to relieve the reader of any anxiety that I might attempt such a reinterpretation here, it will be worth recounting how fundamentally perceptions of Mound 1 have changed since its discovery, so providing both the theoretical background and a prelude to the work of the recent campaign which is about to be reported. In 1939, and in spite of incompatible (and imprecise) archaeological dating, Chadwick identified Mound 1 as the burial of Raedwald, a documented king of East Anglia who died ca. 625 A.D.[10] The arguments were simple and have been improved in presentation rather than substance in the hands of Bruce-Mitford: the wealth of the burial implies a king; that it now lies in East Anglia implies a king of East Anglia, and the date (early seventh century) implies an East Anglian king who died at about that time. The prime candidates are therefore Raedwald (died ca. 624), Eorpwald (died ca. 628), Sigeberht (died ca. 637), and Ecgric (died ca. 637). Each has had his champions, but Raedwald has carried the day with his successful capture of Chapter 10 in the definitive report.[11]

Behind such an attribution there are of course a number of assumptions, none of which need be wrong but none of which will enjoy many points of contact with a strictly archaeological inquiry. Archaeologists deal in material culture which is rarely specific or individual and has very little to say about who ruled which polity or where they were buried. Even if a personal attribution were plausible, it is hard to see that much has been thereby added to our knowledge of the ideas and practices of the Anglo-Saxons. Raedwald may indeed have been buried in Mound 1 (or indeed, as we shall see, in Mound 2), and Wuffa may be the bloodthirsty occupant of Mound 5. But attractive as they certainly are to public sentiment, these unprovable ascriptions have only passing relevance to the real business of archaeology: constructing the image of a people and their community in transition.

The change in archaeological interests from rather specific questions of cultural history to more general hypotheses about social process reached Anglo-Saxon archaeology during the 1970s, and was an influential force at about the time that the new campaign began in 1983. The questions to be asked became not "who was buried in these mounds?" or even "was this a royal burial ground?" but "what was the structure of Anglo-Saxon society in the seventh century and how did it change?"; "what was a king?" and "did the Anglo-Saxons have them?" And "if so, when?" and "why then, why there?" As late as 1983 *Rescue News,* objecting to the new campaign, asserted that "we know how the Anglo-Saxons buried their kings in the seventh century," a statement which illustrates in concentrated form the number of assumptions that Sutton Hoo had trailed after it into the 1980s. The new approach did not deny the likelihood of Sutton Hoo being a royal burial ground or one containing the mortal remains of Raedwald, it only suggested that there were more important questions to be asked, questions concerning the very fabric of early English society, and that Sutton Hoo was a site that could help answer them: how was that society structured? How did its members think? How did ideas, ideology and allegiance change during the seventh century? The questions were ambitious ones, and they were meant to be; the campaign was to generate a new page one for English history, otherwise there could be no justification for destroying the monument, however partially or systematically this might be done.[12]

The research plans which were laid in 1983, therefore took it for granted that the bigger picture would require a bigger canvas. It would be assumed that the "Anglo-Saxons" were a compound of indigenous with immigrant peoples from the coastal areas of north Germany and Denmark (following Bede) and from south-west Norway,[13] and most probably from other areas also of the North Sea litoral in which early states or "kingdoms" were already forming.[14] The immigrant folk first took root in fifth-century East Anglia[15] and their subsequent social evolution can be followed through material culture.[16] The early *settlements* were small and dispersed (West Stow providing the paradigm), but by the late sixth century were augmented or replaced by nucleated proto-manors (such as Brandon or Wicken Bonhunt) or emporia (Ipswich). The early *cemeteries* were large and already hierarchical (Spong Hill) but by the late sixth century had become more demonstratively extravagant for an aristocratic minority. This extravagance included wealthy barrow-burial, which, to-gether with the new types of settlement can be read as indicating the onset of that particular social strategy known as kingship.[17]

It was with the testing of this model that the Sutton Hoo project was to be mainly concerned. Accordingly, there were to be three concentric research zones: a North Sea zone where comparative studies would be made of the formation processes of contemporary and near contempo-rary states, a regional zone where the settlement pattern and burial reper-toire would be surveyed and sampled in the search for social and economic change, and a little patch of hectares around the Sutton Hoo burial ground itself. Of these, the *comparative studies* were to flourish through seminars organized at Ipswich, Cambridge, Oxford and York. The *regional studies* developed in the systematic hands of East Anglia's archaeological units and Suffolk's John Newman in particular.[18] The *site* itself was the nodal point of the campaign: not only would it be asked the hardest questions, but would be obliged to bear the publicity and the irre-versible loss of destruction by excavation (pls. 10.1, 10.2).[19]

Even when the die was cast and the long itinerary from data acquisi-tion to analysis had begun, theory would not lie down, and hypothesis would not sleep. During our eight years cultivating data in the field, the kitchen of British archaeology changed its cuisine, from processual to structuralist flavors, just as it had changed from a cultural-history to processual viewpoint ten years earlier. And just as before, the adrenalin provided by the theoretical debate was entirely beneficial to the Anglo-Saxon archaeology of Sutton Hoo. Without invalidating our quest for ev-idence for the formation of an early English kingdom, we were able to add to our agenda the subtle levels of interpretation allowable by the new post-processual thinking and so appropriate to burials. Mound 1 was not to be construed as some mindless custom, the helpless betrayal of a fos-silized social system, but the artificial contrivance of a creative mind; not so much an assemblage of finds, as a statement or text, composed of carefully selected symbols. Far from being hard evidence for the reality of the heroic world of *Beowulf,* the Mound 1 ship-burial was itself a poem, a heroic dirge declaimed in a theater of death, which (assuming we can read it) carries all the aspirations and agonies of the Anglo-Saxon political soul in transition. In short, the *historicity* of each burial mound came back into fashion, at the time we were finding on the ground that the Anglo-Saxons had indeed concentrated their ideological investment upon them. Henceforward, our interpretative statements could claim each mound as a signal of political dogma and allegiance; our excavations were not chronicling changes in social and economic strategy but changes in Anglo-Saxon attitudes.[20] Therefore, just as the beginning of the Sutton Hoo campaign coincided with the optimism of processual archaeology and its assumed ability to sample social systems in the field, so its conclusion coincides with the optimism of structural and contextual archaeology, with its assumed ability to see deep into the minds of long dead Anglo-Saxon aristocrats. Finding myself thus a member of an anti-empirical community, hungry for meaning and stories, is a piece of good fortune I have no intention of ignoring.

EVALUATION AND STRATEGY

Fieldwork began in 1983, but it was to be three years before any burial mound was newly broached. It was not enough to have a rigorous research program; there had to be some confidence that the Sutton Hoo site could actually still answer the questions to be posed. There was also an ethical principle to include in the reckoning: I did not and do not feel that any of us is justified in excavating the *whole* of any site, however defined. The 1980s passion for so-called total excavation struck me then, as it strikes me now, not only as immoral but unscientific. If we had no questions to ask, then no digging at all was justified. If we had questions, but the destruction of the whole site was required to answer them, then they were the wrong questions and we should think again. Accordingly an intensive period of nondestructive investigation was required to establish the extent and quality of the archaeological deposits still present at Sutton Hoo. This was the three year "evaluation," requested from and granted by the imaginative, intelligent and patient Sutton Hoo Research Trust which governed the project.[21]

The predictions of the evaluation were reasonably straightforward, and as we can now see with hindsight, not too wide of the mark. A prehistoric settlement of about 12 ha. in extent comprised boundary-ditches and buildings as well as a few cremations, and flourished between the middle Neolithic and the Iron Age, peaking in the Beaker period (ca. 2000 B.C.). Whether the prehistoric settlement remained recognizable by the Anglo-Saxons—at least as an element of the vocabulary of the landscape—has yet to be determined. But it was after two millennia of no great activity on the same modest promontory overlooking the River Deben that the Anglo-Saxons initiated their prestigious cemetery, extending to 4.5 ha. and expected to contain cremations and flat-graves in large numbers as well as barrow-burials. Fairly intensive looting of most but not all the mounds was surmised, and it was plain that there had been many holes dug between and around the mounds as well as in them, for reasons that were not likely to have been scientific. It was supposed (and afterwards demonstrated) that the barrow cemetery had been rubbed nearly flat through cultivation; so that, ploughed by farmers, looted by treasure-seekers, tunneled by rabbits, scrambled by bracken and shot at by the army (which trained there in the war), the site had been sadly impoverished by time and neglect. The terrain—an acid porous sand and light gravel—had also played its part in the reduction of the archaeological assets. The bodies of the Anglo-Saxons left very little skeletal material, but were recognizable as sandy lumps carrying the shape of the flesh—the anthropomorphs or "sandmen" so beloved of the media. Ageing, sexing and dating our population would therefore be a problem.

In spite of these obvious deficiencies, burial rite was still generally readable, even in previously excavated chambers, as Basil Brown had already demonstrated in 1938, and a strategy for excavation could be proposed within a more general data-acquisition package,[22] which was feasible and important enough to justify the destruction of part of the site. Our objectives were clear: to explore a changing early English community and its ideology by chronicling its changing burial rites. A sample of these burial rites would be obtained by excavating a transect 32m wide form the western edge to the eastern edge of the burial ground. If I believed that I knew where the western edge was, (on the undulating crest of the promontory where the ground fell rapidly away to the flood plain of the river Deben), the eastern (inland) edge was unlocated and we would have to dig for it. The 150m long transect was therefore extended eastwards for some 50m beyond the most easterly burial, an operation tedious but conclusive. The width of the transect was suggested by the geography of the seventh-century palace site at Yeavering;[23] if there were buildings they should not be able to escape us.

The rationale behind this transect was that the Sutton Hoo community would begin burying on the crest and continue eastwards, that is inland, until overtaken by history. This assumption bore heavily on an (unproven) Anglo-Saxon sense of logic. No such "axis of growth" may have been intended or adopted by them. The buried population might grow organically from several nodes, or wander northwards or southwards along the crest or enter their final resting places in a manner which for us was entirely random. Accordingly a north–south transect, 138m long, was planned at right-angles to the first, so that any geographical of chronological trends might be captured. The cruciform transect so formed offered a sample almost exactly 1 ha. in extent: an expenditure of the resource of slightly over 20% (fig. 10.2; pl. 10.4).[24] This area was declared the largest that we could be justified in taking and the smallest that would make sense. It was sited at the northern end where the majority of the recorded excavations had taken place, and the mounds were among the most damaged. The sectors reserved for the future should be both the biggest and the best. And in 1986, with the agreement of the authorities, the grudging concord of the professional fraternity and the tireless support of the Sutton Hoo Research Trust, excavation began.

WHAT HAS BEEN FOUND

The areas examined were dug in large pieces as "interventions," beginning in the extreme east "INT 32, 39" then north "INT 41," then south "INT 44, 55" then east again "INT 50, 52" and then west "INT 48" (fig. 10.2). I now propose to take readers on a site-tour showing them, and briefly describing to them, the Anglo-Saxon burials discovered in approximately the order of their discovery. The inventory of all burials so far known at Sutton Hoo and identified as Anglo-Saxon is contained in Table 10.1.

Eastern Cementery

Accordingly we must begin, as we did in 1986, out in the fields, in our extreme eastern sector. Here the original purpose was to determine the limits of the cemetery (see above), but the peripheral group of burials that was defined there did little to establish a "norm" against which to set the extravagance of the barrows. These twenty-three graves (fig. 10.4)

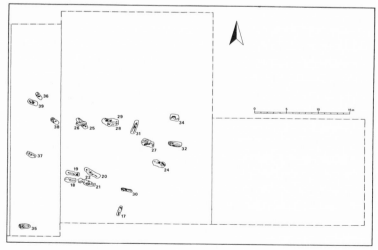

Fig. 10.4. Eastern Sacrificial Group.

were in general without grave goods or constructional features, although there were two well-defined coffins, a box or chest, signs of a cairn, a joint of meat and an ard (Table 10.1; burials 20, 27, 34). The principal attributes of each grave were therefore the orientation and posture of the body, and here there was great variety: some were supine, some were prone, some were kneeling, some were flexed and some were extended. What characterized the group, other than their variety, was the recurrent stress implicit in the body position. In four cases, the juxtaposition of limbs implied that wrists or ankles had been tied. In three others the head had been removed or the neck broken (pl. 10.5). Early attempts to rationalize these burials as the work of a "shoddy undertaker," who dumped corpses in graves that were too small, were soon confounded: one grave had been dug much longer and another much broader than was necessary (Burials 29, 27). The additional investment, the trauma or post-mortem abuse, and the curious if exiguous furnishing were most easily explained as having ritual meaning. The dating so far is seventh to eighth century, broadly contemporary with the mound-burials further west (Table 10.1). Were these people the victims of battle, execution or sacrifice? There are no military honors here, and the trauma for which we have evidence (hanging and beheading) hardly implies them. Execution and sacrifice are hard to distinguish archaeologically—and no easier, it might be argued for an eye-witness. How should a spectator at a public hanging in the nineteenth century distinguish the moral from the ritual in the ideology of the state? Further support for a ritual interpretation comes from the plan. Far from heralding contact with a densely packed burial ground extending to the west, the group appeared to be arranged in an isolated circle, continuing neither to north, east, south or west (figs. 10.2, 10.4). In the center of this circle was an unexceptional pit containing nothing that would suggest it was itself a burial or a structure, merely the undated natural deposits attributed elsewhere to a rotted root-mantle: it was a tree. At this moment therefore and in anticipation of the analytical and dating exercises that are still to be carried out, I feel obliged to suggest that the eastern group of graves is destined to be interpreted as a ritual area, contemporary with the mounds and involving human sacrifices around a tree.

North Sector

With some relief, we may now travel to the sector which represents the northern arm of the excavation sample and contains Mounds 2 and 5 (pl. 10.7). Mound 2 was one of those explored by Basil Brown in 1938, and his excavation trench was re-used during the evaluation phase of the pre-

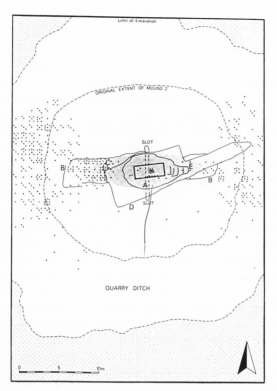

Ship Rivet / Rivet Fragment   plotted to the nearest metre

A Burial Chamber Pit—7th cent. AD
B Robbers' Trench—?
C Robbers' Steps
D Basil Brown's Trench—1938
E Basil Brown's Steps

☐ Burial Chamber

⬬ Supposed Ship Position

Fig. 10.5. Mound 2: Ship Burial.

sent campaign in order to study the problems of mound excavation. Mound 2 and the quarry ditch that appeared around it were subsequently completely dissected, and provided our most credible evidence for the way that mounds were built. Inside the mound was a veritable Chinese puzzle of earlier cuts and intrusions, which resolved into three principal episodes: a chamber-grave, a robbing operation probably of the nineteenth century, and the east–west trench cut by Basil Brown, who unwittingly spent the greater part of his excavation inside the trench cut by his predecessor (pl. 10.6). To the finds collected by Basil Brown,[25] were added a further 140 scraps of gold, silver, bronze and other materials, as well as nearly 500 ship-rivets, from the robber-trench or its spoil-heaps. On the floor of the chamber itself, traces of rusty soil and other anomalies enhanced by chemical mapping indicated the original positions of large objects of iron and copper-alloy, and indeed that of the body itself.[26]

In spite of the trail of confusion left in the center of this much-visited monument, the original ritual could be plausibly modeled. A chamber 3.8 by 1.5m had first been dug more than 2m deep, through topsoil and sand and gravel subsoil, to provide a rectangular room revetted with vertical timber planking. The body of a man laid at the west end (and therefore feet most probably to the east) had been accompanied by a sword, shield, drinking horns, silver-mounted cup, five knives in their sheaths, a blue glass jar, an iron-bound bucket and a cauldron, to list only those items whose original presence is reasonably certain. Basil Brown had not been wrong in supposing that Mound 2 contained a ship, only in that the ship had been underground. The distribution of the ship-rivets makes it plain that early excavators had encountered a ship all along the length of their trench, which had followed the yet intact old ground surface (fig. 10.5). The types of rivets present indicate that while there is a full complement (155) of rivets with angled roves—from the two ends—the majority from the center are missing. These indications suggest that the ship originally lay at ground level on top of the chamber, as in the much later example found at Haithabu.[27] Such a vessel would have eventually collapsed amidships under the weight of the mound, depositing within the chamber a mass of rivets—some still attached to the planking. This eventuality offers a context for the disingenuous announcement in the Ipswich Journal already cited, and an explanation for the rivet patterns which understandably misled Brown. The ship buried in Mound 2 would have been in the order of 20m (60 ft.) long, and the burial which lay beneath must have scored highly on the scale of contemporary wealth. Mound 1 and Mound 2, both rich ship-burials, show no great differences from each other in either rank or date, and only a thematic variation, if an intriguing one, in the burial rite employed.

The curious ritual composition was covered by a mound, which, from the geometry of the quarry ditch can be shown to have risen over 4m from its contemporary ground surface—a giant of a barrow and one unlikely to have been easily robbed before its reduction by those hungry for topsoil. Such a reduction had already rendered Mound 5 almost invisible, but it was in its day a monument no less significant than Mounds 1 or 2—although for a very different reason. The original burial here, subsequently robbed at least twice, had been a cremation wrapped in cloth and placed in a bronze bowl accompanied by a comb, shears, and gaming pieces among other less identifiable objects. The head of the cremated person had been cloven, probably by a sword. Over this burial, Mound 5 was erected, but the spoil here was gained not from a quarry ditch but a series of pits, originally linked at ground level. The altitude of the ground surface under Mound 5, and the rather hesitant technique of construction suggest it to have been among the earliest. But it was not in that that the primary interest lay. The three bodies discovered and excavated by the British Museum team in the 1960s proved to belong to a set of sixteen disposed in a gentle arc around the putative periphery of the original Mound 5 (fig. 10.6). They shared some of the gruesome attributes of the eastern group: evidence for binding, hanging and beheading (Table 10.1; pl. 10.5). They should certainly be closely associated with Mound 5— not only thanks to their position in plan, but because in six cases graves had been cut into the base of quarry pits which had partially silted up. These burials ("Group 2") were named by us "satellite burials" after their relationship in space to the mound. Like the examples in the eastern field ("Group 1") they may be seen as sacrifices—in this case added to the Mound 5 obsequies immediately after its construction and thereafter at intervals for an indefinite but not extended period; the observation of silting patterns in open ditches during our own fieldwork suggests a total span of years rather than decades.

The fashion of cremation was found to continue in the *southern* sec-

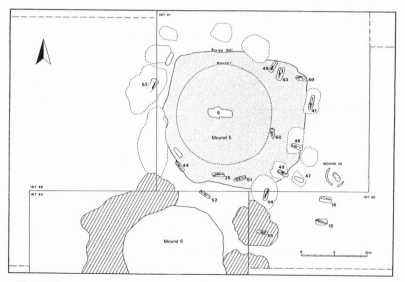

Fig. 10.6. Mound 5 and Satellite Burials.

tor: Mounds 6 and 7 were both cremations in origin, although both had been hideously transformed by earlier excavators. The methodology of the early diggers here resembled those who had entered Mound 2 and the morphology of their work-pattern was still clearer (fig. 10.8). The excavators' trench of the time was characteristically "bull-nosed" and "fish-tailed" and ran west to east. The trench was driven in to the mound at one side, following the brown soil of the old ground surface until it was interrupted by the bright sand of a back-filled burial pit. At the bull-nosed end steps were cut down into the burial chamber—and it was here on a ledge that the gentlemen antiquary could stand, in tail coat and top-hat no doubt, stooping only to receive the good things which the earth had to offer. At the other end, splayed towards the spoil heaps, were the barrow-runs of the honest rustics, earning a supplementary shilling by removing, and in the case of Mounds 6 and 7, sieving, four or five hundred tons of sandy soil. What little survived from these exceptionally diligent exertions, allows Mound 6 to be stated as containing a cremation wrapped in cloth and placed in a bronze bowl accompanied by a bronze sword-pyramid and bone comb; and Mound 7 to have been a cremation, also most probably in a bronze bowl, and accompanied (at the least) by a playing piece and a reticella bead. The southern sector was eventually extended

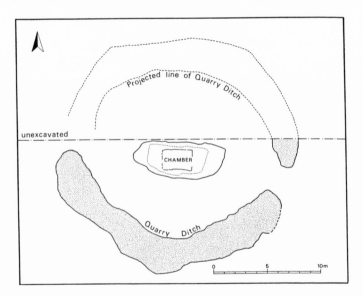

Fig. 10.7. Mound 14.

to join hands with Mounds 3 and 4, which like Mound 13 (sectioned in 1991), had been involved in the nineteenth century campaign. The excavators may have continued on to Mound 10, which is scarred by the dent characteristic of all mounds found to have been robbed. Our jolly diggers therefore denied themselves a rather particular treat: Mound 1. Why did they stop? It would have been more human to lay their trench across it, as across all the others—but perhaps they tried. It was after all very much deeper and the burial rite meant that the usual tell-tale guide to the location of the burial chamber (an interruption to the buried soil) was lacking. At any rate they turned away—and the early history of England was richer as a result.

Eastern Arm

The eastern arm (INT 50) was the large open area, crossed by a medieval hollow way, which connects the group of peripheral burials named as group 1 (above) with the world of the burial mounds, 5, 6 and 7. Any expectations that this sector would be densely packed with flat graves on the one hand or reserved for hall buildings or a church on the other were speedily disappointed. The sector was nearly, but not quite, empty of Anglo-Saxon features. Near the barrows lay a row of three graves, each of them furnished. The more northerly ("Mound 20") was the burial of a child of less than four years old in a coffin, accompanied by a tiny spear and tiny buckle. Equally diminutive was the mound that had once covered it, betrayed by a circular truncated ditch; the mound could hardly have been 2m in diameter. The companions of this grave, which were parallel to it to the south, were probably also young, adolescents or young adults. They too were in coffins and modestly furnished with bronze and ironwork (Table 10.1), but with no evidence for mounds. Some meters to the east lay the unobtrusive profile of Mound 14, which the sector was designed to cut in half, exposing the residual mound and its buried soil in section and any central burial in plan (fig. 10.7; pl. 10.8). The quarry ditch was of the "Mound 2" type, ragged but continuous except for interruptions at the east and west, and in the middle lay the lozenge-shaped depression of a robbed chamber-grave. The chamber was a delicate affair, built with thin planks set vertically in a technique which also echoed that of Mound 2. By good fortune the pillaging of Mound 14 had been interrupted by an East Anglian squall:—fans of rain-washed silt were defined above the natural subsoil to the east, while the west had turned into an extensive mush. At a given moment the looters of

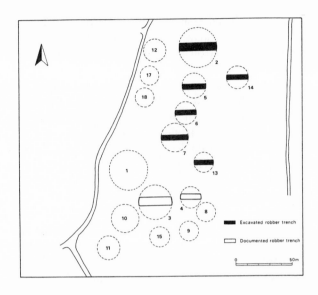

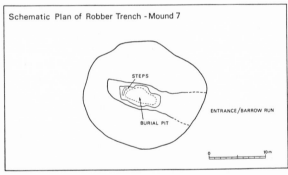

Fig. 10.8. The Nineteenth-Century Excavation Campaign, with (below) Diagram of the Excavators' Methodology at Mound 7.

Mound 14 must have decided to call it a day, since they departed, abandoning within the "mush" of their sodden tread more than one hundred finds. Enticing things have since been glimpsed in this assemblage, as it lies in the intensive care of the British Museum: a small silver buckle, a silver chain, a chatelaine—enough to promise an important statement from a grave which is set fair to be the first burial at Sutton Hoo which is incontravertibly the inhumation of a female.

The West

The last sector to be explored, reaching over the crest into Top Hat Wood with the river beyond, should have been the first to be exploited—and this may well prove to be the case. The British Museum excavations of the 1960s had located here two putative cremations (neither wholly convincing as Anglo-Saxon) and a grave containing only a skull (Table 10.1, no. 56[28]). To these we would add two burial mounds (nos. 17 and 18). The damage suffered by the western end of the site, owed most likely to ploughing and erosion, had reduced the earthworks to shadows. Mound 18 was ploughed to pieces, only a scatter of burnt bone and bronze fragments, and a comb-tooth, radiating from a square depression of a few millimeters deep survived to signal the former emplacement of an Anglo-Saxon cremation. Mound 17, to the north, was quite a different experience, for here fortune had decreed that we should encounter the second intact wealthy burial to be found at Sutton Hoo in modern times. Although no ship-burial, it was not lacking in interest, either as a mortuary ritual of a special kind or as a key episode in the development of the cemetery.

Two grave-pits lay west–east, parallel and side by side (pl. 10.9: fig. 10.2). In the northernmost of the two was the fully-articulated remains of a horse or pony, surviving both as sand-stain (mainly the belly and neck) and as bone (pl. 10.11). There were no grave goods, but some kind of organic furnishing was implied by traces of as yet unidentified detritus. The more southerly grave was that of a young person of high status—the so-called "Sutton Hoo prince" (pl. 10.10). The body of a young man lay in a coffin that was originally cylindrical in shape, recalling a tree-trunk, and held together with curved iron clamps. Beside him lay a sword with a bronze buckle inlaid with garnets and two sword pyramids. By his ear was a strike-a-light purse. Outside the coffin to the north was a comb set on end, an iron-bound bucket, a cauldron with a pottery vessel inside, and at the east end a bronze drinking bowl over four animal ribs—lamb or pork chops. The persistent staining observed around the latter area may have been due to the decay products of the meat, or to some cloth or leather container—such as a haversack. At the west end, a complex of metal objects and traces of leather was lifted in a block and is being dissected in the British Museum; enough has now been seen to identify the complex as belonging to a bridle or bridles or caparison. We should eventually be able to see this ornamented harness reconstructed; it has an iron snaffle bit and gilt-bronze axe-shaped pendants, circular gilt-bronze strap-distributors and many small copper-alloy pendants which seem to have hung from breast-straps or brow-bands. Above the bridle was the stain of a circular wooden tub, and beneath the coffin lay two spears and a shield.

The excavation of this grave was greatly enhanced by the expertise of colleagues from the British Museum Conservation Laboratory, whose job was to save the finds from deterioration by getting them out, at the same time as mine was to resolve the stratigraphic sequence by keeping them in. It can be confidently reported that both objectives succeeded. The finds arrived intact in the Museum, and the ritual and sequence of the burial can be written with some precision. A rectangular pit 3.4 by 1.7m and some 1.36m deep, was abandoned for a few hours under rain. The pit was then furnished. After the spears, the shield was placed flat with the boss uppermost. On the rim of the shield, was put the iron-bound bucket, next to it the cauldron, and next to that the haversack. At the west end, the bridle was deposited. Only then did the coffin arrive. Presumably destined for the empty south side, it ended up, no doubt due to the cumbersome mechanics of its installation, in the center, where it settled canted up on top of the shield boss. In the tilted coffin, the body rolled southwards on top of the sword. The coffin was now in place, but the assemblage was not complete. The comb, disturbed from the coffin roof by backfilling, or thrown by a mourner, must have slipped down the north side of the curved coffin until it assumed the vertical position in which it was found. The backfilling then proceeded. After some 30 centimeters of earth had already filled the grave, a wooden tub was placed at the west end. If such a tub can be associated with feeding a horse, then it may have been at this moment that the horse was dispatched to join his master. About the mound that was thrown over the two burials we know little, but that it was modest; there was no quarry ditch or quarry pits. The scraping of topsoil had been reduced on discovery to a barely detectable swelling some 14m in diameter.

A PROVISIONAL MODEL

Although there had been some trimming and a great deal of discussion, the area completed in 1992 was essentially that proposed in 1986. It is important to realize that the sample proposed was that deemed necessary to answer the question; we stopped because the work had been finished, not because we had run out of money or interest. Sutton Hoo is not merely the first British excavation to follow a published research design, but one of the few to stop because it was completed. That is not to say that knowledge of the Sutton Hoo cemetery is complete or ever will be, or even that it is yet possible to appreciate the full significance of what has been found. The analysis on which the post-excavation teams at the British Museum and the University of York are now embarked would certainly be pointless if the full story could already be told. The prudent interim therefore halts here. But it is no more than human wish to inspect the summary plan of the burial ground assembled in figure 10.2, to wonder what the story may turn out to be, and whether the research procedure so publicized and exposed in so many media, will turn out to have been valid.

Two assertions on behalf of the excavation sample might be made with reasonable security. First that the cemetery is generally late—late sixth to eighth century—and of uniformly high status. There are no convincing burials, whether cremation or inhumation, of conventional fifth–sixth century type. This is no "folk cemetery" which developed extravagant burial styles in its later phases, but a "separated" cemetery, reserved for the elite, where to gain entry you must either belong to the aristocracy or be co-opted into their ideological drama. At a superficial level, the evidence offers endorsement to the suggestion that Sutton Hoo was the burial ground of "kings," who can now be shown to have been dynastic (honoring children), militantly pagan and claiming the right over life and death. It will I believe be accepted that cremation under mound, ship burial and human sacrifice which are all new to the ritual repertoire of East Anglia, are intended to convey pagan rather than Christian ideological signals. The burial rites, moreover find their parallels in Scandinavia (we need say nothing of the finds whose implications are far less specific). So, if we believe (in line with modern theories of material culture) that burial, and perhaps most particularly burial at this level of status, is a deliberate statement made by intelligent humans at a moment of crisis, then the signals which emanate from Sutton Hoo are specific, the cry of a people at once pagan, autonomous, maritime and concerned to conserve an ancestral allegiance with the Scandinavian heartlands and their politics, across the North Sea. In this interpretation, the context in which such signals become necessary can only be where the protagonists are threatened by their converse: Christianity, the adoption of which reaches beyond the tonsure and the church to fealty to the Franks and their imperial echoes. Sutton Hoo is therefore a theater in which the longest running theme is the defiant pagan politics of an arriviste monarchy.[29]

Very much more difficult will be the task of ordering the burials encountered into a coherent sequence of events, to chronicle the history of
how such rituals and attitudes became adopted, when and why. It must be
said at once that the evidence for the sequence in which the burials were
celebrated is very poor and unlikely to improve greatly. We have a stratigraphic hint that Mound 6 was constructed after Mound 5. We may expect a sequence of radiocarbon dates from the British Museum's
laboratory which may distinguish episodes more than fifty years apart.
And it can be hazarded, although with more than usual rashness, that
Mound 17 will turn out to be datable from its metalwork to the mid or
late sixth century. Such fragile and equivocal data, even when we have
them, will hardly support a historical sequence; but a sequence there obviously was. A most tentative, almost recreational attempt follows
here—the final part of my model (fig. 10.9).

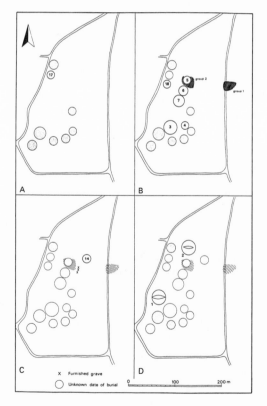

Fig. 10.9. The Development of the Anglo-Saxon Burial Ground:
A Preliminary Model.

Mound 17 was a rich burial, but not especially so, and might not be out of place at the high status end of those "folk cemeteries" that abound in East Anglia, such as Spong Hill, or at neighboring Snape.[30] Its position on the crest of the riverward slope adds to the impression that it might be among the earliest graves, a young member of an aristocratic family whose new separate cemetery this was to be. In a second phase, and in a severe change of mood, Mound 5 was erected on the highest part of the promontory. The honored person was cremated and his memory exacted, and subsequently continued to exact, the right of human tribute. These are signs which may be connectable with the assumption of kingship, and kingship in a pagan context. Similar sacrificial rituals were practiced around a tree on the eastern periphery. Cremation was adopted in subsequent high-ranking burials all along the spine of the cemetery, Mounds 6, 7, 3 and 4, each one on this interpretation endorsing, or at least not contradicting, the pagan and probably Scandinavian manifesto initiated by Mound 5.

In a third phase, two new burial rites are introduced: coffin burial in rather plain graves for children or adolescents, and a chamber-grave under a mound for a woman. These, like Mound 17 in the putative "phase 1," have nothing specifically Scandinavian about them, and they are being said to sit in the sequence where they do simply by virtue of their position in the cemetery. In a fourth and final phase, with the most extravagant and defiant non-Christian gesture of all, two ship-burials are added: that to the north (Mound 2) has a chamber grave beneath the ship under the mound; while that to the west (Mound 1) has a chamber constructed within a ship in a trench under a mound.

As a final and illicit indulgence, (and because if I do not, then others will) it would be highly diverting, if wholly unscientific, to place this sequence in a framework of early English history and even furnish it with some of the characters involved. We could surmise how the family which chose the site were, or became, the Wuffingas, successful landowners who claimed kingship under Wuffa and began to contrive the ideological apparatus to secure its continuance without the assistance of the font, the Bishops or the Franks. While Wuffa lay implacably beneath Mound 5, the men of Kent succumbed to both Christianity and the domination of Frankia. Wuffa's successors were cremated, giving a nod to their political mentors across the North Sea. Other members of the family, such as the children and at least one woman, were honored, but not used to signal the exotic political affinities of the kingdom. In a final lured twilight, Raedwald or Sigeberht, Eorpwald or Ecgric, the last champions of an independent East Anglia, set out in ships laden with newly-contrived regalia, to bring the bad news to the gods. In an episode lasting less than a century, perhaps much less, a peculiar political experiment had flared and failed.

Sutton Hoo is an intriguing site and has not become less so after the intensive scientific scrutiny of the last nine years. It remains a constant temptation to the story teller and I am aware of succumbing. This sequence of events is the weakest of my offerings and the most vulnerable to the rigors of future analysis. At present the story is little more than the stuff of dreams, which I share with the reader, more out of camaraderie than conviction. But the readers of this book will be dreamers too, otherwise they would never have picked it up.

ACKNOWLEDGEMENTS

The Sutton Hoo Research project has benefited greatly from the friendship and advice of the Sutton Hoo Research Committee, and from the supportive management of the Sutton Hoo Research Trust (at various times Christopher Brooke, John Evans, Michael Robbins, Paul Ashbee, David Attenborough, Martin Biddle, Rupert Bruce-Mitford, Barry Cunliffe, Catherine Hills, John Hurst, Ian Longworth, Henry Loyn, David Phillipson, Robert Pretty, David Pretty, Phillip Rahtz, Michael Tite, Keith Wade, Leslie Webster, Martin Welch, Stanley West, David Wilson, Ted Wright). To these must be added Angela Evans, who was seconded from the British Museum for successive seasons and who has the responsibility for the curation of the early medieval finds, all of which (thanks to the Pretty family) are destined for the national collection. John Knight steered us through the legal thickets which beset us. The local landowners (Anne Tranmer, John Miller and Peter Waring) gave the project their support. Our principal sponsors were the Society of Antiquaries of London, the British Museum and the British Broadcasting Corporation. The project team numbered many hundreds of students, volunteers, professionals and volunteer-professionals from Universities and Units in many countries, but the nucleus was provided by Madeleine Hummler, Andrew Copp, Jenny Glazebrook, Cathy Royle and Linda Peacock of the University of York, and Annette Roe, Justin Garner-Lahire and Gigi Signorelli of the Società Lombarda d'Archeologia. Post-excavation work is being carried out at the Department of Archaeology, University of York, King's Manor, York, UK, to which any correspondence should be addressed.

NOTES

[1] *Ipswich Journal* 24, Nov. 1860.

[2] R. Hoppitt, "Sutton Hoo 1860," *Proc. of the Suffolk Inst. of Archaeol.* 36(1) (1985), 41–42.

[3] R. L. S. Bruce-Mitford, *Aspects of Anglo-Saxon Archaeology. Sutton Hoo and Other Discoveries* (London, 1974), 114–40.

[4] Ibid., 166.

[5] See, T. D. Kendrick, "The Gold Ornaments," "The Large Hanging-Bowl," "The Archaeology of the Jewellery," *Antiquity* 14 (March 1940), 28–39. The March 1940 issue of *Antiquity,* edited by O. G. S. Crawford and R. Austin, was devoted entirely to Sutton Hoo.

[6] R. L. S. Bruce-Mitford, *The Sutton Hoo Ship Burial,* vol. 1 (London, 1975); R. L. S. Bruce-Mitford, *The Sutton Hoo Ship Burial,* vol. 2 (London, 1978); R. L. S. Bruce-Mitford, *The Sutton Hoo Ship Burial,* vol. 3 (London, 1983).

[7] Bruce-Mitford, *Sutton Hoo Ship Burial,* vol. 1, pp.11, 57.

[8] See further, I. Longworth and I. A. Kinnes, *Sutton Hoo Excavations 1966, 1968–70,* British Museum Occasional Paper 23 (London, 1980).

[9] Bruce-Mitford, *Sutton Hoo Ship Burial,* vol. 1, 11; Longworth and Kinnes, *Sutton Hoo Excavations.*

[10] H. M. Chadwick, "Who Was He?" *Antiquity* 14 (March 1940), 76–87.

[11] Bruce-Mitford, *Sutton Hoo Ship Burial,* vol. 1.

[12] M. O. H. Carver, "Research Design," *Bul. of the Sutton Hoo Research Com.* 4 (1986).

[13] J. Hines, *The Scandinavian Character of Anglian England in the pre-Viking Period,* B.A.R. Brit. ser. 124 (Oxford, 1984).

[14] M. O. H. Carver, "Pre-Viking Traffic in the North Sea," in S. McGrail, ed., *Maritime Celts, Frisians and Saxons,* C.B.A. Research Rep. 71 (1990), 117–25; B. Myhre, "Chieftain's Graves and Chiefdom Territories in South Norway in the Migration Period," *Studien zur Sachsenforschung* 6 (1987), 169–87.

[15] Following H. W. Böhme, "Das Ende der Römerherrschaft in Britannien und die angelsächsische Besiedlung Englands im 5. Jahrhundert," *Jahrbuch des Römisch-Germanischen Zentralmuseums Mainz* 33 (1986), 469–574.

[16] M. O. H. Carver, "Kingship and Material Culture in Early Anglo-Saxon East Anglia," in S. Bassett, ed., *The Origins of Anglo-Saxon Kingdoms* (London & New York, 1989), 141–58.

[17] Ibid.

[18] J. Newman, "The Late Roman and Anglo-Saxon Settlement Pattern in the Sandlings of Suffolk," in M. O. H. Carver, ed., *The Age of Sutton Hoo* (Woodbridge & Rochester, 1992), 25–38.

[19] See further *Bul. of the Sutton Hoo Research Com.* 1 (1983).

[20] M. Carver, "Ideology and Allegiance in Early East Anglia," in R. Farrell and C. Neuman de Vegvar, eds., *Sutton Hoo: Fifty Years After,* American Early Medieval Studies 2 (Oxford, OH, 1992), 173–92.

[21] *Bul. of the Sutton Hoo Research Com.* (1986).

[22] Ibid. For the principles see, M. O. H. Carver, "Digging for Data: Archaeological Approaches to Data Definition, Acquisition and Analysis," in R. Francovich and D. Manacorda (a.c.d.) *Lo Scavo archaeologico: dalla diagnosi all' edizione* (Florence, 1990), 45–120.

[23] B. Hope-Taylor, *Yeavering: An Anglo-British Centre of Early Northumbria* (London, 1977).

[24] *Bul. of the Sutton Hoo Research Com.* 5 (1988), 4.

[25] Bruce-Mitford, *Sutton Hoo Ship Burial,* vol. 1, 115–23.

[26] *Bul. of the Sutton Hoo Research Com.* 6 (1989), 7–13, 21–23.

[27] M. Müller-Wille, *Das Bootkammergrab von Haithabu,* Berichte über die Ausgrabungen in Haithabu 8 (1976).

[28] Longworth and Kinnes, *Sutton Hoo Excavations.*

[29] Carver, "Ideology and Allegiance."

[30] W. Filmer-Sankey, "Snape Anglo-Saxon Cemetery: the Current State of Knowledge," in Carver, *Age of Sutton Hoo,* 39–51.

Table 10.1. Sutton Hoo: Inventory of AngloSaxon Burials, 1992

Mounds, Unexcavated and Conserved for Future Study

Mounds 8, 9, 10 [possibly robbed], 11 [attempted robbing 1982: INT 17], 12, 15, 16.

Mounds, or Former Mounds, Excavated to Date

Mound 1: [*Burial* 1] INHUMATION W–E in chamber in ship in trench; with sword, shield, helmet, regalia, silverware, lyre, drinking horns, clothing, buckets, cauldron etc.

INTACT. Excavated 1939, 1965–71 (INT 5–10); published Bruce-Mitford 1975, 1978, 1983.

DATED: ca. 625 A.D. (grave goods)

MOUND 2: [*Burial 2*] INHUMATION W–E in chamber under ship; originally with sword, shield, belt-buckle (?), silver buckle, drinking-horns, tub (?), iron-bound bucket, cauldron (?), bronze bowl, blue glass jar, silver-mounted box, silver-mounted cup, 5 knives in sheaths, textiles.

ROBBED OR EXCAVATED without record, possibly in 1860 (INT 1). Excavated 1938 (INT 3; Bruce-Mitford 1975). Excavated 1986–9 (INT 26, 41).

DATED: late sixth/early seventh century (grave-goods)

MOUND 3: [*Burial 3*] CREMATION on oak tray or dug-out boat; with lime-stone plaque, bone-facings (for box?), bronze ewer-lid, francisca, comb, textile, pottery sherds (?), horse (cremated).

ROBBED or EXCAVATED without record (nineteenth century?). Excavated 1938 (INT 2; Bruce-Mitford 1975).

DATED: late sixth/early seventh century (grave-goods)

MOUND 4: [*Burial 4*] CREMATION in bronze bowl (fragments), with playing piece, textile, horse (cremated).

ROBBED or EXCAVATED without record (nineteenth century ?). Excavated 1938 (INT 4; Bruce-Mitford 1975).

DATED: late sixth/early seventh century (grave-goods)

MOUND 5: [*Burial 5*] CREMATION in bronze bowl (fragments), with composite playing pieces, iron shears, silver-mounted cup, comb, knife in sheath, ivory fragment, glass fragments, textiles, animal bone—possibly dog (cremated).

ROBBED or EXCAVATED without record (twice). Excavated 1970 (INT 12; Longworth and Kinnes 1980), 1988 (INT 41).

SURROUNDED by "satellite burials" of Group 2 (see below).

DATED: late sixth/early seventh century (grave-goods)

MOUND 6: [*Burial 6*] CREMATION in bronze bowl (fragments), with copper-alloy sword-pyramid, bone comb (fragments), textiles.

ROBBED or EXCAVATED without record (nineteenth century?). Excavated 1989–91 (INT 44).

DATED: late sixth/early seventh century (grave-goods); stratigraphically later than Mound 5.

MOUND 7: [*Burial 7*] CREMATION in bronze bowl (fragments), with reticella bead, bone gaming-counters, silver-gilt fragment, iron knife, textiles, animal bone.

ROBBED OR EXCAVATED without record (nineteenth century?). Excavated 1990–1 (INT 44)

DATED: late sixth/early seventh century (grave-goods)

MOUND 13: Unidentified burial rite.

    ROBBED or EXCAVATED without record (nineteenth century?). Mound sectioned 1991–2. Burial unidentified (INT 55).

    UNDATED

MOUND 14: [*Burial 8*] INHUMATION (possible female) in chamber, with silver-mounted cup (?), silver buckle, silver chain, bronze fittings for box (?), bronze pins, bronze chateleine, bronze girdle hangers, bronze bowl (?), textiles.

    ROBBED or EXCAVATED without record (nineteenth century?). Excavated 1991 (INT 50).

    DATED: late sixth/early seventh century (grave-goods)

MOUND 17: [*Burial 9*] INHUMATION W–E in iron-clamped wooden coffin, with (in coffin) sword, bronze buckle inlaid with garnets, two silver(?) sword pyramids, bronze-fitting, iron dagger, strike-a-light purse (containing garnet and millefiori fragments and buckle); (outside coffin, within grave pit) two spears, shield, bucket, cauldron, pottery vessel, "haversack"(?) containing animal ribs and flanged bronze bowl; comb, harness for horse (including gilt-bronze discs, axe-shaped pendants with animal ornament, an iron snaffle bit, leather straps), wooden tub.

Associated with [*Burial 10*] INHUMATION of HORSE, adjacent and parallel. Unfurnished.

    INTACT: Excavated 1991 (INT 48).

    DATED: sixth/seventh century (grave-goods)

MOUND 18: [*Burial 11*] CREMATION in bronze bowl (fragments), with textiles and bone comb (teeth only)

    PLOUGHED AWAY. Excavated 1966, 1989 (INT 11, 48)

    DATED: Anglo-Saxon (comb)

[MOUND 19—shown not to have existed during excavation in 1991 (INT 55).]

MOUND 20: [*Burial 12*] INHUMATION NW–SE in wooden coffin of child, with iron spear-head, bronze buckle and bronze pin.

    INTACT. Excavated 1987 (INT 41).

    DATED: Anglo-Saxon (grave-goods)

Burials without Evidence for Mounds

CREMATIONS

Burial 13 [INT 11, Aiii]: Unurned cremation. Undated.

Burial 14 [INT 11, Aiv]: Cremation in pottery vessel. Sixth–seventh century (?)

FURNISHED INHUMATIONS

Burial 15 [INT 50, F54]: W–E, extended on back, in coffin, with two bronze buckles and dagger/knife in sheath.

Burial 16 [INT 50, F58]: W–E, extended on back, in coffin with bronze needle-case(?) having leather stopper, bronze ring-headed pin and glass ring-beads, and iron rod, chain or coffin-fitting.

SATELLITE BURIALS
GROUP 1: On Eastern Periphery

INT 32

Burial 17 [F9(254)]: N–S, flexed on back. DATED: 540–700 A.D. (c 14)

Burial 18 [F39(101,245,246)]: W–E, extended on back in coffin.

Burial 19 [F40(102,247)]: E–W, extended, prone, with hands tied behind back (?)

Burial 20 [F106(248,249)]: NW–SE, extended, on back, in coffin/tree trunk, with animal joint(?). Under cairn.

Burial 21 [F108(251)]: W–E, extended, on back, without head.

Burial 22 [F109(252)]: W–E, extended, on back; above *Burial 21* and with head of F251 in lap. DATED: 680–820 A.D. (c 14-accelerator)

Burial 23 [F137/1]: E–W, MALE, extended, on back, with broken neck.

Burial 24 [F137/2]: Prob. MALE, crouching; beneath *Burial 23.*

Burial 25 [F146(258)]: SE–NW, prob. MALE, extended, prone, with wrists and ankles "tied."

Burial 26 [F154(259)]: W–E, extended, on back, above *Burial 25.*

Burial 27 [F161(260,261)]: W–E, on side, in "ploughing position," with ard and rod. Prob. MALE.

Burial 28 [F163(262)]: W–E, kneeling, top of head missing.

Burial 29 [F166(263)]: W–E, extended, on back, hands "tied" and stretched above the head.

Burial 30 [F173(264)]: W–E, MALE, extended, on back, wrist over wrist.

Burial 31 [F231(237)]: N–S, extended.

Burial 32 [F227/1(238)]: W–E, extended, prone.

Burial 33 [F227/2(239)]: W–E, extended, prone, lying with *Burial 32.*

Burial 34 [F235(240)]: W–E, flexed, in square coffin, chest or barrel.

INT 52

Burial 35 [F4(34)]: W–E, extended, on back, head detached and placed looking north on right arm.

Burial 36 [F37(71)]: NW–SE, tightly crouched, lying on right side, head facing north

Burial 37 [F25(72)]: NW–SE, flexed at knees, lying on back.

Burial 38 [F35(75)]: NW–SE, lying on back, knees bent back to shoulders.

Burial 39 [F36 (74)]: NW–SE, kneeling, face down, left arm behind back.

GROUP 2: Associated with Mound 5

INT 41

Burial 40 [F81(152)]: W–E, prob. MALE, flexed, on side in "sleeping" position, with head detached and rotated.

Burial 41 [F82(507,509,510)]: S–N, flexed, on side; with organic stains (=additional human limbs?). Cuts quarry pit F508.

Burial 42 [F86/1(148)]: N–S, MALE, extended, on back, with head detached and lying with neck uppermost.

Burial 43 [F86/2(149)]: N–S, prob. FEMALE, extended, prone on top of *Burial 42* with human limbs/jaw.

Burial 44 [F124(542)]: NW–SE, extended, on back.

Burial 45 [F154(55) = INT 12, grave 3]: W–E, prob. MALE, prone.

Burial 46 [F424(499)]: NW–SE, flexed, on side. Cuts quarry pit F130.

Burial 47 [F435]: Body piece, possibly part of a long-bone. Grave cuts quarry pit F133.

Burial 48 [F486(555)]: S–N, slightly flexed, on side, head detached and placed below knee.

Burial 49 [F517(524,525)]: NW–SE, extended, on back, head wrenched out of alignment, with organic "scarf" around neck. Cuts quarry pit F129, which contained bone fragments of large mammal.

Burial 50 [F588=INT 12, grave 1]: S–N, flexed on side.

Burial 51 [F590=INT 12, grave 2]: W–E, extended, on back.

INT 44

Burial 52 [F215(216)]: NW–SE, extended, on back, lower left leg broken, head detached and turned through 180 degrees.

INT 48

Burial 53 [F349(351)]: N–S, extended, prone, under plank, right arm extended above head; with organic stains; within quarry pit F287.

INT 50

Burial 54 [F141(162)]: S–N, flexed, on side, in "sleeping" position, without head. Cuts quarry pit F30.

Burial 55 [F341(379)]: E–W, bent over backwards, or truncated. Cut by later cow-burial F342).

GROUP 3: Isolated Grave near Mound 17

Burial 56 [INT 11, pit 1]: E–W, skull only, detached and facing foot end, with glass bead and bronze fitting. (Longworth and Kinnes, *Sutton Hoo Excavations*) DATED: 670–830 A.D. (c 14).

Pl. 10.1. The Sutton Hoo burial mounds (foreground: to the left of the wood) with the River Deben and the North Sea (photo after Carver, *Age of Sutton Hoo,* pl. 23A).

Pl. 10.2. The Sutton Hoo site in 1983, looking west. The "zip fasteners" are anti-glider ditches cut during the Second World War (photo after Carver, *Age of Sutton Hoo,* pl. 23B).

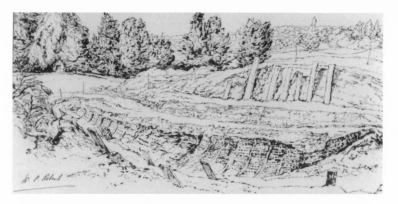

Pl. 10.3. Charcoal sketch by W. P. Robins of Mound 1 under excavation.

Pl. 10.4. Sutton Hoo: the excavated sample (photo after Carver, *Age of Sutton Hoo,* pl. 25).

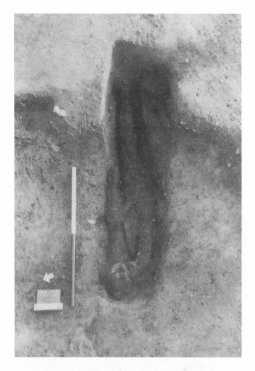

Pl. 10.5. "Satellite" burials: (top) Mound 5, Group 2, and (bottom) Eastern Cemetery, Group 1 (photo after Carver, *Age of Sutton Hoo,* pl. 26).

Pl. 10.6. Mound 2: the chamber and later trenches (photo after Carver, *Age of Sutton Hoo*, pl. 27).

Pl. 10.7. Mound 2 and Mound 5 (foreground) under excavation. Mound 20 can be seen at bottom, right of excavated area (photo after Carver, *Age of Sutton Hoo*, pl. 28).

Pl. 10.8. Mound 14 under excavation (photo after Carver, *Age of Sutton Hoo*, pl. 29).

Pl. 10.9. Mound 17: the two burials (photo after Carver, *Age of Sutton Hoo,* pl. 30).

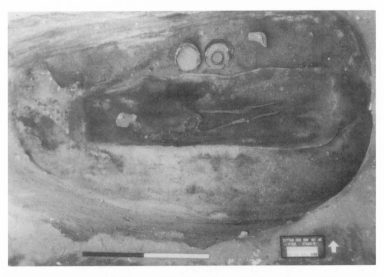

Pl. 10.10. Mound 17: the "prince's" burial (photo after Carver, *Age of Sutton Hoo,* pl. 31).

Pl. 10.11. The horse burial beneath Mound 17 (photo after Carver, *Age of Sutton Hoo,* pl. 32).

CHAPTER 11

Beowulf and Sutton Hoo
The Odd Couple

ROBERTA FRANK

Nineteen thirty-nine was special. It saw the end of the Spanish Civil War and the beginning of World War II. Hollywood's creative energy peaked and in a few miraculous months produced *Ninotchka, The Wizard of Oz, Mr. Smith Goes to Washington, Stagecoach, Goodbye, Mr. Chips, Dark Victory, Wuthering Heights, Goné With the Wind,* and Bugs Bunny. The uranium atom was split, the New York World's Fair opened, John Steinbeck published *The Grapes of Wrath,* and Joe DiMaggio was named most valuable player in the American League. It was also fifty years ago that the first ship rivet in Mound 1 at Sutton Hoo was uncovered, on 11 May 1939.

One of my colleagues used to tell his *Beowulf* students the story of the well-intentioned stranger who, late one night, seeing a man on hands and knees beneath a streetlight searching for something, offered assistance. "Are you sure this is the spot?" he asked. "No," came the answer, "but this is where the light is." Sutton Hoo in 1939 lit up a bit of Dark Age Britain; *Beowulf* responded, like a moth to a flame; and nothing has been the same since. The glorious evidence dug up from Mound 1 was at once asked to illuminate our unique poem, and *Beowulf,* to articulate the burial deposit. The mutual affinity of *Beowulf* and Sutton Hoo was, in the first flush of discovery, inevitably exaggerated. Scholars today who caution that "*Beowulf* has no necessary direct connection with Sutton Hoo,"[1] or that the link between the two "has almost certainly been made too specific,"[2] are in no danger of being hounded out of the profession. But their carefully phrased warnings came too late: it is not nice to tell a couple on the eve of their golden anniversary that they have little in common, and besides, it is no longer true. Even if our rumbling poem and silent mound did not have much to say to each other fifty years ago, they do now. A lot of hard work, energy, and stubbornness went into making this marriage stick. And in Auden's words: "Like everything which is not the involuntary result of fleeting emotion but the creation of time and will, any marriage, happy or unhappy, is infinitely more interesting and significant than any romance, however passionate."[3]

The story of how *Beowulf* and Sutton Hoo got together, what they came finally to mean to each other, and what the long-term effects of their union were bears an uncanny resemblance to the plot of a Greek New Comedy and, indeed, of most comedy down to our own day. The young couple had much to overcome: a certain difference in age (three and a half centuries, if you believe some people); the usual in-law problems (Vendel, Valsgärde, Suffolk and Uppland, Wuffings and Wylfings became inextricably, even incestuously, involved with each other). These and other obstacles to the marriage had to be removed by supporting players, stock characters of stage and scholarship like the *miles gloriosus*, the parasite, the lovable curmudgeon, and the bemused tyrant. The more complicated their maneuvers, the more absurd the gimmick that ensured a happy ending, the better the comedy.

The story of how *Beowulf* and Sutton Hoo met is well known. According to the received version, they first came face to face in a court of law. It was on a Monday, 14 August 1939. In the village hall of Sutton, some two miles away from the discovery, an inquest was being held to find out whether or not the grave goods were treasure trove.[4] What happened next was described in 1948 by Sune Lindqvist, a professor at Uppsala: "Much surprise was occasioned by the news of the Coroner's Inquest—something unfamiliar to the Swedes—at which the legal title to the find was decided with the help of the passages in *Beowulf* describing the passing of Scyld and the lavish furnishing of *Beowulf*'s memorial mound."[5] Lindqvist then quoted the relevant lines, concluding, "At all events it is obvious that the *rapprochement* that was at once made between the Sutton Hoo burial and the substance of *Beowulf* was fully warranted, and rich with possibilities. Everything seems to show that these two documents complement one another admirably. Both become the clearer by the comparison."[6] In other words, it was love at first sight. Charles Wrenn, who like Lindqvist had not been present at the inquest, spelled out in 1959 what Lindqvist had only hinted at, that *Beowulf* had been read aloud to an appreciative jury. The court decision, he reported, "was reached after the jurymen had listened to an exposition of the account of the ship-passing of Scyld Scefing in *Beowulf* with its astonishing parallels to the Sutton Hoo ship-cenotaph: and the matter was clinched by the reading of the story of the final disposal of the Dragon's hoard in lines 3156–68."[7] Wrenn repeated his story in another 1959 essay, concluding with a complaint that "though this public citation of *Beowulf* and its parallels with Sutton Hoo in a court of law might be thought to have drawn the first attention to the light which the one might throw upon the other, it was not till 1948 that an outstanding scholar [Lindqvist] took especial pains to emphasize the fundamental importance of the new finds for the study of the poem."[8]

If in 1939 the recitation of *Beowulf* in the village hall of Sutton did not make as big a splash as Wrenn would have wished, it may be because it never happened. For it was not until 1948, when Lindqvist penned his piece, that anyone imagined that the words of the poem had been declaimed to the Sutton jury. The court deposition of Charles Phillips, the site archaeologist, simply stated, "There is contemporary literary evidence that the burial of chieftains among the northern nations in the Dark Ages was the occasion of celebrations and feasting, which lasted for several days, and nothing can be more certain than the public character of the Sutton Hoo burial."[9] Quotations from *Beowulf* did, however, form part of an editorial in the *East Anglian Daily Times* on 17 August 1939. And two days earlier, 15 August, the London *Times,* having reported the inquest decision along with Phillips's statement about "contemporary literary evidence," concluded that "the nature of the objects found reminds one . . . very strongly of the passage in 'Beowulf' in which jewels and treasures from different lands are piled round the dead king's body in the centre of a ship" (p. 9, col. 2). Reports of the excavation in *The Antiquaries Journal* and in *Antiquity* for 1940 include citations from *Beowulf,* with both Phillips and Hector Munro Chadwick quoting the poet's account of Scyld Scefing's funeral as "an interesting parallel."[10] In January 1947, in the first of many issues of *The Sutton Hoo Ship-Burial: A Provisional Guide,* put out by the British Museum, Rupert Bruce-Mitford, then Assistant Keeper in the Department of British Antiquities, quoted the usual passages from *Beowulf* and noted that "these literary accounts make it plain that the Sutton Hoo treasures were not buried in secret. They also make it plain that those who buried the treasure had no intention of recovering them later. It was these considerations which led the Suffolk jurors, in accordance with English law, to find that the gold and silver in the ship were not Treasure Trove."[11] Lindqvist's imaginative reconstruction the very next year of a courthouse drama, in which portions of *Beowulf* were read aloud to the jury, and Wrenn's repeated statements in the decade following that *Beowulf* "clinched" the Sutton Hoo case, go beyond the evidence of any of the published accounts available to them. Like so much in this torrid love story, the oft-recited tale of how the young couple first met rests on nothing more solid than "a conspiracy of romantic hopes";[12] the yearned-for hard facts melt, like popsicles, at our touch.

It is important to recall that *Beowulf,* though relatively young, and clean-cut when hitched to Sutton Hoo, had a past. What the poem faced after 1939 was not unlike the gropings and assignations it knew in the second half of the nineteenth century. The first scholarly edition of the poem, by John Mitchell Kemble (a great Anglo-Saxonist and Fanny's brother), published in two volumes between 1835 and 1837, was accompanied by an English translation that made the poem accessible to a wider public.[13] Among the first antiquaries to cite from Kemble's edition was William J. Thoms, the English translator and annotator of Jens Worsaae's *The Primeval Antiquities of Denmark.* He noted in 1849 that the figure most often found perched on Germanic helmets was the boar, "and it is to this custom that reference is made in *Beowulf* where the poet speaks of the boar of gold, the boar hard as iron."[14] In 1852 Charles Roach Smith, in the second volume of his *Collectanea antiqua, etchings and notices of ancient remains illustrative of the habits, customs, and history of past ages,* cited various passages from Kemble's *Beowulf* relevant to the ornamented swords, runic hilts, decorated ale cups, mail shirts, shields, and other objects that had been excavated from Saxon cemeteries. He, like Thoms, was particularly struck by the parallel between Beowulf's boar-crested helmet and the one found at Benty Grange; after quoting the relevant Old English lines, he concluded, "Nothing can be more satisfactory than the explanation of the hog upon the Saxon helmet found in Derbyshire presented by these citations from ... *Beowulf.*"[15] *Beowulf* is similarly exploited in John Yonge Ackerman's *Remains of Pagan Saxondom* (1855)[16] and in Roach Smith's 1856 introduction to *Inventorium sepulchrale: An account of some antiquities dug up at Gilton, Kingston, Sibertswold, Barfriston, Beakesbourne, Chartham, and Crundale in the County of Kent from A.D. 1757 to A.D. 1773 by the Rev. Bryan Faussett of Heppington.*[17] (This was the Faussett who boasted of digging up twenty-eight graves in one day, and nine barrows before breakfast.)[18] The excerpts from *Beowulf* in *Ten Year's Diggings in Celtic and Saxon Grave Hills in the Counties of Derby, Stafford, and York from 1848 to 1858 with Notices of Some Former Discoveries,*

Hitherto Unpublished, and Remarks on the Crania and Pottery from the Mounds, published in 1861 by Thomas Bateman, came secondhand from Smith's *Collectanea,* but Bateman also describes one Dano-Norwegian burial custom not yet encountered in England: "Sometimes the bodies were placed in the small ships or boats of the period, which were dragged on shore and then buried under a barrow within view of the ocean. It is with interments of this late and peculiar description that the greatest variety of curious and rare objects is found."[19] The very next year, 1862, the first ship burial on English soil was dug up at Snape in Suffolk, only a few miles from Sutton Hoo. The coupling of objects mentioned in *Beowulf* with those excavated from Anglo-Saxon cemeteries continued unabated into the twentieth century: in 1923 the official British Museum *Guide* directed visitors curious about the ring-sword supposedly mentioned in *Beowulf* to the "top of Case 49 for specimens from Faversham and Gilton, Kent."[20] Sutton Hoo was not *Beowulf*'s first suitor, just the richest.

In the 1930s *Beowulf* was sought after by social historians as well as by archaeologists. H. M. Chadwick, in 1940 one of the first to suggest that *Beowulf* and Sutton Hoo could do a lot for each other, had long criticized his colleagues for their reluctance to make use of archaeological and legendary material.[21] In 1935, Ritchie Girvan took up the challenge; his *Beowulf and the Seventh Century* attempted to show how closely the poem reflected the social and political realities of its time.[22] Even J. R. R. Tolkien, that most literary of Anglo-Saxonists, admonished readers of his 1936 essay, "*Beowulf*: the Monsters and the Critics," that "*Beowulf* is a historical document of the first order for the study of the mood and thought of the period, and one perhaps too little used by historians,"[23] Major studies between 1936 and 1939 by Swedish and Norwegian archaeologists express a similar optimism, praising *Beowulf* for its accurate portrayal of the material life of the age: "It can be shown from archaeological evidence," note the authors of one book, "that the poem has preserved accurately many details of the Scandinavian society to which the tradition originally belonged, as has been mentioned several times in this survey, the descriptions in *Beowulf* can often be illustrated directly by the Scandinavian antiquities of the period."[24] To have foreign wooers was undoubtedly a feather in *Beowulf*'s cap and an incentive to Englishmen to bring the poem home.

The exciting news from Sutton Hoo kept students of *Beowulf* busy for years composing supplements, appendices, and addenda to earlier work. Even a historical novel like Gisela Reichel's 1962 *Hakon's Song:*

A Story about the Writer of the Beowulf Poem seemed incomplete to the author without a postscript on Sutton Hoo.[25] Frederick Klaeber in the 1941 supplement to his edition of the poem had time only to note cautiously that "a burial ship apparently dating from the 7th century has been dug up in East Suffolk."[26] The upbeat mood of Wrenn's 1959 supplement to R. W. Chamber's *Beowulf* is more typical. It is not so much a critical overview as a eulogy, an epithalamium in honor of the new couple in town. Here are his opening words:

> By far the greatest single event in *Beowulf* studies in the period under review was the excavating of the East Anglian king's ship-cenotaph with its treasures almost intact in the summer of 1939. Indeed this may well seem the most important happening since the Icelander Jón Grímur Thorkelin made his transcripts of the *Beowulf* MS. And from them published the first edition of the poem. For by the recognition of the significance of the Sutton Hoo finds has come about the illumination in a truly revolutionary manner of the whole background of the poem—historical, archaeological and folkloristic—as well as to some extent the means towards the reassessment of the problem of its genesis. By study of the actual parallels from the Sutton Hoo treasures . . . has been established a historical basis in reality for that loving connoisseurship of material art which used to astonish the critics of this "Dark Age" poem. The swords and helmets, the royal standards, the precious drinking-bowls of *Beowulf* and its harp, have become suddenly vitally related to actual history. The seemingly ambivalent relationships of pagan Germanic and Christian elements in *Beowulf* have become natural and intelligible through their material parallels at Sutton Hoo. The so puzzling and basic position of the Swedes and the Geats of southern Sweden in the poem has become convincingly historical. *Beowulf* is seen, as a result of the Sutton Hoo finds . . . , to be the product of a civilization of the highest then known cultivation, centuries in advance of the rest of Western Europe. The funeral departure of Scyld Scefing . . . , the hoard of ancient treasures in the dragon's mound . . . , and the account of Beowulf's own funeral rites, all these now may be seen to contain memories of factual traditions not far from living recollection when the poem was composed.[27]

Wrenn covers all the bases. Sutton Hoo was, is, and will be the answer to *Beowulf*'s dreams and prayers. No red-blooded poem or Englishman could want more. But when we look back, from the perspective of this golden anniversary, to see what a half-century of togetherness with Sutton Hoo has actually done for *Beowulf,* it is hard not to be disappointed.

Happy relationships are supposed to make you look younger. Life with Sutton Hoo, however, did nothing to retard the aging of *Beowulf*; indeed, it had the opposite effect. The discovery at once lent support to the traditional dating of the poem, thought in 1939 to have been composed in the late seventh or very early eighth century. In the 1920s, Liebermann, Cook, and Lawrence had dated *Beowulf* to 675–725 and decided it was Northumbrian.[28] The poem aged a bit more in the 1930s, when Girvan proposed 700 as the latest possible date and raised the possibility of East Anglian origins.[29] A seventh-century East Anglian ship burial and a seventh-century East Anglian *Beowulf* was a match made in heaven. In her 1945 lectures, written even before the objects of Sutton Hoo could be viewed, Elizabeth Martin-Clarke noted the perfect convergence: "It is of remarkable interest that scholars . . . do ascribe *Beowulf* to a non-West-Saxon area and allocate its production to a period of time not later than the middle of the eighth century and probably as early as, if not earlier than, the middle of the seventh century."[30] Bruce-Mitford in 1947 saw the poem as just a bit younger than the burial: "It is generally accepted that *Beowulf* was composed in England about the year A.D. 700, that is, some forty-five years after the burial of the Sutton Hoo ship" (at that time thought to have occurred between 650–670).[31] Lindqvist in 1948 did not hesitate to place the poem in East Anglia and its composition in 700, within living memory of those who had witnessed the construction of Mound 1.[32]

Sutton Hoo has, over the years, been not so much a brake on successive attempts to rejuvenate its younger partner as a yo-yo string; it lets *Beowulf* fall forward, naturally, propelled by the gravity of the moment, before yanking the poem back, into its grasp again. Wrenn, for example, started out in 1950 with a firm date of ca. 700 but, three years later, moved to a somewhat less firm date of "before 750."[33] In between, Dorothy Whitelock had singlehandedly advanced the terminus ad quem of *Beowulf* from 700 to 825, halting before the Viking incursions of mid-century.[34] Wrenn fought against her late dating of *Beowulf* with Sutton Hoo as his chief weapon, arguing in 1959, for example, that "the seemingly vivid memories of the Sutton Hoo ship-burial which lie behind the accounts of the passing of Scyld Scefing and of the hero's own funeral rites in the poem, would point rather to an earlier date for its composition."[35] And again: "The Sutton Hoo discoveries . . . have furnished new evidence bearing on the date and genesis of *Beowulf,* clearing away obstacles to the early dating of the poem."[36] It is now generally acknowledged that neither an East Anglian origin for *Beowulf* nor a date of composition anywhere near the date of the burial is demonstrable, but so strong are the bonds between the poem and its "significant other" that, though frayed, they seem unable to be severed.

A number of studies published over the last twenty-five years have explored a possible late-ninth or tenth-century date for the poem.[37] But the yo-yo trick, that silent "Come back, little *Beowulf*" flick of the wrist, is still at work. "There is a close link," insists Hilda Ellis Davidson in 1968, "between objects and funeral practices as described in *Beowulf* and archaeological evidence from the sixth and seventh centuries A.D. . . . Links with the royal ship burial of Sutton Hoo are particularly detailed and impressive . . . There are no allusions in the poem to objects or practices which must be dated later than the seventh century."[38] Eric John, arguing in 1973 against an early-tenth-century date, is also convinced that "the archaeological evidence certainly suggests a much earlier date, nearer the traditional date."[39] "Aspects of the poem's 'archaeology,'" Patrick Wormald confirms in 1978, ". . . point towards an earlier rather than a post-Viking date."[40] "In an English context," states John Hines in 1984, "the archaeological horizon of *Beowulf* reflects the late 6th and 7th centuries with a striking consistency." For it is, he explains, "material of the later sixth and seventh centuries that corresponds most closely to the objects mentioned in the poem."[41]

Back in 1957, before any of these claims were made, Rosemary Cramp observed wisely if too optimistically that "today one would hesitate even more than Stjerna did [in 1912] to rely on archaeological evidence for dating *Beowulf*; gaps in the material evidence after the cessation of heathen burials are still too immense."[42] Despite her warning, archaeology is still being used, subtly, to age *Beowulf*. The corselet or coat of mail found at Sutton Hoo (and matched by chain mail in Swedish seventh- and eighth-century boat graves) shows, we are told, how accurately the *Beowulf* poet described his warriors' byrnies, the iron circles "'hard and hand-locked,' ringing as the wearer walked (322–23) and acting as a 'woven breast-net' against attack (551–53)."[43] The accuracy of this description has, of course, no bearing on the date of the poem, and not only because chain mail, like pattern-welded sword blades, continued in use into the tenth century. *Beowulf* is, above all, a work of the imagination. A poet who tells us in loving if bloody detail precisely what happens when dragon fangs wrap themselves around a warrior's neck was certainly able to represent the sounds and texture of a mail coat without having handled one himself. For the material culture of *Beowulf* is the conventional apparatus of heroic poetry. Old Norse skalds from the tenth to thirteenth centuries allude in terms almost identical to those of the *Beowulf* poet to the clattering, interlocked rings of byrnies they call "ring-woven," "ring-sark," "iron-sark," and "ring-shirt."[44] The so-called archaeological horizon of *Beowulf* is remarkably wide, stretching from late Roman times to the Norman Conquest. No linguistic, historical, or archaeological fact compels us to anchor *Beowulf* within reach of Sutton Hoo. If we do so it is more from our emotional commitment to their association than from hard evidence.

It is also because a grateful *Beowulf* is loath to leave Sutton Hoo's side. Mound 1 has served the poem well and faithfully these fifty years. It is largely thanks to the ship burial that the poet's golden hero remains in the mind's eye, not as a shapeless hulk, cloaked Grendel-like in mist, but as a well-turned-out knight in shining armor. From the top of his head to the tips of his spears he is heavy metal. The *Beowulf* whose footsteps we hear departing Denmark—the poet says, with deliberate metrical weighting, *"guðrinc goldwlanc græsmoldan træd"* (the gold-adorned warrior trod the greensward, line 1881)—cannot be traveling lightly: our imagination puts a crested helmet with garnet-eyed boar images on his head, a pair of clasps with garnet and glass cloisonné on his shoulders, on his arm a shield shining gilt bronze, at his waist a great gold buckle, a gold-framed purse, a gold and jeweled sword pommel above a gold-embossed scabbard, and spilling all over him a splendid confusion of golden hinges, clasps, mounts, and ornamental studs. Sutton Hoo casts light on *Beowulf* because our memory lets its "things" do duty for the poet's words. When the shape of an item, such as the helmet or harp, changes, the poem graciously adjusts. The revised helmet with its new lifesaving features was an easy substitution. More embarrassing was the 1970 transformation of the harp into a Germanic round lyre, for *Beowulf* scholars had already made much of the 1948 reconstruction.[45] Lexicography, however, came swiftly to the rescue, murmuring that it was the word, not the thing, that we had earlier got wrong: the *hearpe* that once in Heorot sung was not what we now think of as a harp but was, instead, a "lyre."[46]

Sutton Hoo's power over *Beowulf* can be traced in the Old English dictionaries produced over the last fifty years. Entries for words that name objects in the burial deposit have become progressively more precise, and not always to the advantage of the poetry. One term apparently "solved" with Sutton Hoo's help is the notorious *wala* (MS *walan*), the feature that the *Beowulf* poet focuses on when describing a helmet given to his hero. This *wala* is "wound about with wires" that go "around the roof of the helmet" (lines 1030–34). In 1898 *wala* was defined as "some part of a helmet"; in 1912, as "guard, bulge, a part of the helmet"; in 1931, as "ridge, rib, comb" (of helmet).[47] In 1952 Bruce-Mitford, on the basis of the first reconstruction of the Sutton Hoo helmet, confirmed what Knut Stjerna in 1912 and Elizabeth Martin-Clarke in 1945 had suggested with regard to a detached comb found with a helmet in Boat Grave 1 at Vendel. The *wala* was the nose-to-nape band of the late Roman parade helmet, the thick tubular iron crest or comb running up over the crown.[48] The Sutton Hoo helmet crest, he declared, "has enabled the meaning of the unique word *wala* to be established precisely for the first time."[49] Typical post-Sutton Hoo dictionary entries gloss *wala* as "metal ridge on top of helmet, like that on Sutton Hoo helmet at *Beowulf* 1031," and as "ridge or comb inlaid with wires running on top of helmet from front to back," with the definition referring the reader to Rupert Bruce-Mitford's 1952 statement.[50] These definitions of *wala* give a special sense to its use in *Beowulf*, a sense that fits the immediate context. Elsewhere in Old English, when the word occurs in charter bounds it apparently means "ridge (of land); when the term refers, four times, to man-made objects it seems to have the general sense "raised band or strip."[51] In three of these four occurrences, including *Beowulf*, *wala* is found in conjunction with the word *wir* (Mod. E. "wire," OE "metal ornament, thread"), and in all four, *wala* appears to refer to some kind of raised ornamentation, whether the decorative ribbing on the walls of a Roman building or, in an Old Testament gloss, the ornamental brass work that Hiram of Tyre designed for Solomon, specifically the two rows of striated ornamentation about the edge of a cast bronze piece. Giving *wala* in *Beowulf* a special meaning, defining it as the comb on a Sutton Hoo type helmet, is not wrong, but it has the unfortunate effect of ironing out the figurative language. If the Old English poet had wanted to use a technical term, the gloss word *camb,* "comb" of a helmet, was ready and waiting,[52] but he used *wala,* instead, in a generalizing, metaphorical way, as part of his overall architectural imagery. In conjunction with the other shelter words in the passage, *wala* suggests a vault, an overhanging, protecting roof that shielded the man within from the showers raining down upon him.[53] The Sutton Hoo helmet gives us an idea of what such a protuberance may have looked like; the poem explores its essence.

Perhaps the quickest way to gauge the influence of Sutton Hoo on *Beowulf* is to pick up any post-1939 translation of the poem, such as the excellent one by Howell D. Chickering that many of us assign year after year to our students.[54] Most noticeable is a drastic increase in the gold and silver content of the verse. In line 37, in a passage describing burial treasure from far-off lands, the translator's words "bright gold and silver" and "gems" are an interpretation of the Old English term *frætwa*, meaning "ornaments, treasure, armor." The translation fits Sutton Hoo with its forty-five individual pieces of gold jewelry (forty-five not counting the coins and blank ingots) and its sixteen pieces of late antique silver, but it is alien to *Beowulf*, which never once mentions the lesser metal. In line 2761 of the poem, the Old English words *fyrnmanna fatu*, "cups of ancient men," have been similarly transmuted into "golden beakers" (as have *bunan*, "cups," in line 2775), while the descriptive phrase in line 2762, *hyrstum behrorene*, "deprived of adornments," is refined into "its garnets broken." Garnets, like silver, are never mentioned in *Beowulf*, but the Sutton Hoo burial deposit contains four thousand of them, estimated to represent a year's gem-cutting for a workshop of seventeen men.[55] Apparently, as far as students of *Beowulf* are concerned, the riches of Sutton Hoo belong equally to its long-term partner, their poem.

The presence of Sutton Hoo in translations of *Beowulf* is largely unconscious, the result of years of seeing each in the other. The same subtle interaction may have affected the Old English text of the poem. Before 1939, the last two words of line 3157a read on *[h]liðe* (on a hill, cliff); now, in almost all editions of the poem, they are *on hoe* (on a promontory). Although *hoh* is the Old English word from which modern Hoo (as in Sutton) developed, it was in the year before the excavation that the manuscript page was photographed under ultraviolet light, producing the new reading.[56] Klaeber, in his 1941 supplementary notes, rejected *hoe* because, he argued, "the noun *hoh* in the sense of 'promontory' occurs nowhere else in Old English poetry,"[57] and Holthausen in 1948, reluctant to alter his edition, convinced himself that the photographs showed *liðe* rather than *hoe*.[58] But many more editors, beginning in 1940, were delighted with the change, and Wrenn explains why: "If my reading of lines 3156–8 is correct, *Beowulf*, it may be worth noticing, was given his funeral barrow on just such a headland as has given us the name Sutton Hoo."[59] And although a number of the 1938 ultraviolet readings have been ignored, challenged, or modified in the last half-century, there has not since 1948 been a whisper of discontent with *hoe*. The silence is surprising. Not only is the meaning "promontory" otherwise restricted to prose, as Klaeber noted, but the form *hoe* rather than *ho* should have raised, if not a hue and cry, at least a few scholarly eyebrows: the dative singular ending -*oe* does not occur in prose until the reign of Edgar in the late tenth century, and is never found in verse.[60] Yet *hoe* sits still, lofty and solitary, in our editions, and we nod approvingly. Burying *Beowulf* on a hoo is a good thing, since it allows Sutton Hoo once again to shed its lovely light over our poem.

"But what light," asked Michael Wallace-Hadrill, "does *Beowulf* cast upon Sutton Hoo?" "Not very much," was his answer.[61] What the poem has shed, and that liberally, upon the ship burial seems to have been its Scandinavian, regal, and pagan color. From the start, the apparent Swedish connections of Sutton Hoo recalled the geography of *Beowulf,* the poet's almost exclusive concern with one corner of Scandinavia. By 1948, the East Anglian royal line of the Wuffings had been found to include two names similar to two in *Beowulf*: English Wuffings became Wylfings, who although not Swedish were vaguely Baltic, while Wehha of the East Anglian king list became Weohstan, father of Wiglaf and kinsman of Beowulf, not Swedish perhaps, but at least near neighbors. The goal of these onomastic mergers was to suggest that *Beowulf* was composed in honor of the Sutton Hoo Wuffings, "who were in origin Swedes," said Lindqvist, "a branch of the Royal House of Uppsala and descendants of Wiglaf."[62] So because there is a Swedish element at Sutton Hoo and in *Beowulf,* there is a Swedish element in the East Anglian genealogies, and because there is a Swedish element in the East Anglian genealogies, there is a Swedish element in Sutton Hoo and *Beowulf.* The argument is perfectly circular and apparently irresistible, since it is still widely accepted as fact.[63] The first step—dyeing Sutton Hoo Nordic blonde—was taken by Rupert Bruce-Mitford in the 1940s and repeated by him in every decade thereafter: "It may be taken as certain," he wrote in 1949, "that in the Sutton Hoo grave we meet pure Scandinavian elements in the East Anglian milieu, as we meet them in *Beowulf.*"[64] And again: "It is the unique nature of the Swedish connection revealed at Sutton Hoo that seems to open up the possibility of a direct connection between the poem and the burial."[65]

Yet this "Swedish connection," though much invoked, is still unproven. There are parallels between the burial deposits at Sutton Hoo, Vendel and Valsgärde, but the usual biological explanation, the positing of a common royal ancestor, is at the very least contestable. It is far from certain that the treasures of Sutton Hoo are heirlooms, handed down from father to son like Weohstan's helmet, mail coat, and sword in *Beowulf.* Similarities between the East Anglian and East Scandinavian material may have more to do with the mobility of Dark Age artisans, a shared North Sea/Baltic trade in luxury items, and the desire of two wealthy fringe groups to adopt locally all the status symbols of the Franks. The Sutton Hoo articles crying out for a link with Sweden are few, chiefly the shield (and here there are suggestive Langobardic analogues) and, to a lesser extent, the helmet.[66] *Beowulf,* with its Danish, Swedish, and Geatish cast of characters and its focus on the shores of the Kattegat, is far more exclusively Scandinavian. The garnet- and gold-work of the ship burial hint at a Kentish pedigree;[67] the Coptic dish, the ten silver bowls, the Greek-inscribed spoons, the silver ladle, and the Anastasius Dish are east Mediterranean in origin; the combs are from Saxony; the great cauldron, the chain, the hanging bowls, the millefiori inlays, the naturalistic stag, even the singular dinner bell discovered in 1970 point to the Romano-British world; while the thirty-seven Merovingian gold coins and the congruence of the gold buckle and purse-lid designs with known Frankish objects recall East Anglia's powerful overseas neighbor.[68] The objects of Sutton Hoo, even those most often called barbaric, belong less to the *Beowulf* poet's retrospective Germania than to a European maritime culture that had for centuries imitated Roman ways.

Beowulf tells of treasure-bestowing pagan kings, and once the unparalleled richness of Mound 1 was known, scholars wasted no time in declaring the burial "royal" and "pagan." H. M. Chadwick in 1940 declared it "impossible to believe that in the times with which we are concerned a treasure of such amount and value can have belonged to anyone except a king," and he cited in support the passage in *Beowulf* in which the hero on his return home presents to his king all the treasures he had been given in Denmark.[69] The bronze stag now topping Sutton Hoo's ceremonial whetstone called to mind the Danish royal hall in *Beowulf,* Heorot or "hart," so named, suggests one writer, possibly thinking of the whetstone, because of the "stags' heads . . . displayed over the door."[70] Another scholar is so eager to have the iron stand of Sutton Hoo resemble the golden standards of *Beowulf*'s kings that he invents for the former a gold-embroidered banner, concluding, "Indeed the royal standard— though of course the gold embroidery of the Sutton Hoo exemplar has left no trace— . . . is a marked feature alike at Sutton Hoo and in *Beowulf.*"[71] (Unfortunately for this parallel, the one thing we can be sure about in connection with the iron stand of Mound 1 is that there never were any gold threads associated with it.)[72] The splendor of the burial deposit at Sutton Hoo is unmatched in the sixth and seventh century North and may well indicate the grave of a king, though it is salutary to recall that the graves at Vendel and Valsgärde were once interpreted as royal, but are now regarded as the tombs of great landowners.[73] But if a king, how big a king? Without other royal graves to compare with Mound 1, we have no way to judge the relative status and wealth of the man commemorated,[74] or his religion. Because the poet of *Beowulf* tells of the doings and deaths of noble heathen, his accounts of cremations, auguries, buried gold, and funeral boats have been used to color Sutton Hoo pagan. We keep trying to find in Mound 1 the heathen remains that the nineteenth century long sought in the words of *Beowulf*, with a similar lack of success. For although the Christian objects buried at Sutton Hoo do not prove that the deceased was Christian, there is nothing in the deposit that could not have been owned by a Christian. The desire to uncover leafy pagan beliefs at Sutton Hoo seems to be behind the notion that the Sutton Hoo harp was shattered at the graveside in an act of ritual destruction.[75] Numismatists, weighing the possible supernatural uses to which the gold coins and blanks might have been put, attribute their own paganizing imagination to the poet's audience: "Perhaps," suggests one, "the first hearers of *Beowulf* envisaged ghostly oarsmen taking over the conduct of Scyld's funeral ship once it was out of sight of land."[76] Another writer, identifying the iron stand with Scyld's golden banner, confidently reports that "the standard of the Wuffings was placed in the howe of Sutton Hoo to accompany its dweller as he sailed into the realm of the dead."[77] Sutton Hoo is so malleable, so full of possibilities, that *Beowulf*, the speaking partner, is able to shape the mound in its own image. What resistance could a poor little rich dig offer? There was no other role model on the horizon, no other mirror to look in and be seen, no other constant guide and helpmate. Like any marriage, that of *Beowulf* and Sutton Hoo has limited, for better or worse, the couple's options, preventing each from wandering wherever curiosity and natural inclination led.

By the late 1950s, *Beowulf* and Sutton Hoo were so inseparable that, in study after study, the appearance of one inevitably and automatically evoked the other. If *Beowulf* came on stage first, Sutton Hoo was swiftly brought in to illustrate how closely seventh-century reality resembled what the poet depicted; if Sutton Hoo performed first, *Beowulf* followed close behind to give voice to the former's dumb evidence. And just as, after year's of living together, husband and wife or man and dog start to look and sound alike, so now—fifty years down the road—the two at moments seem to merge, to become interchangeable. Because the Danish king in *Beowulf* picks at a stringed instrument, we are informed that the king buried at Sutton Hoo was an accomplished performer on the harp;[78] because the golden standard of Beowulf's dragon kicked around for some time before ending up in his den, we are asked to believe that the iron stand at Sutton Hoo was "already ancient when buried."[79] Men boast over mead cups in *Beowulf,* and we are quickly assured that the impressive drinking horns of Mound 1 were "intended for just such occasions."[80] And when Beowulf dies, we are consoled with the thought that "his grave must have been much like the ship burial discovered in our own generation at Sutton Hoo"[81] (give or take a few rivets, I suppose). In plotting the *Beowulf*/Sutton Hoo story, a half-century of scholarship has lingered over scenes of discovery and reconciliation, of harmony and consonance, destining the pair to live happily ever after. For, as Byron's *Don Juan* says:

> All tragedies are finished by death,
> All comedies are ended by a marriage. (canto 3, stanza 9)

The only sour note in all this sweetness comes from after-dinner speakers who imagine themselves called upon, even at this late hour, to lament, as if they were dealing with a realistic novel, the triumph of arbitrary plot over probability, of pictorial convenience over consistency of characterization. Such killjoys may even try to tell you that a temporary separation, perhaps a creative divorce, would be productive for both parties. But don't worry. Neither *Beowulf* nor Sutton Hoo is about to throw over fifty years of shared learning and experience, at least not until a more likely prospect comes along.

NOTES

[1] R. T. Farrell, *Beowulf, Swedes and Geats, Saga-Book of the Viking Society* 18 (1972), 281.

[2] E. G. Stanley, "The Date of *Beowulf:* Some Doubts and No Conclusions," in C. Chase, ed., *The Dating of Beowulf* (Toronto, 1981), 197–211, at p. 205.

[3] W. H. Auden, *A Certain World: A Commonplace Book* (New York, 1970), 248.

[4] The definitive account is R. L. S. Bruce-Mitford, *The Sutton Hoo Ship Burial,* with contributions by P. Ashbee et al., 3 vols. in 4 (London, 1975–83), vol. 1, 718–31.

[5] S. Lindqvist, "Sutton Hoo och *Beowulf,*" *Fornvännen* 43 (1948), 94–110; English translation by R. L. S. Bruce-Mitford, "Sutton Hoo and *Beowulf,*" *Antiquity* 22 (1948), 131–40, at p. 131.

⁶ Lindqvist, "Sutton Hoo and *Beowulf*," 140.

⁷ C. L. Wrenn, "Sutton Hoo and *Beowulf*," *Mélanges de linguistique et de philologie: Fernand Mossé in memoriam,"* (Paris, 1959), 495–507; reprinted in *An Anthology of Beowulf Criticism,* comp. L. E. Nicholson (Notre Dame, IN, 1963), 313.

⁸ C. L. Wrenn, "Recent Work on *Beowulf* to 1958: Chapter 1, Sutton Hoo and *Beowulf*," in R. W. Chambers, *Beowulf: An Introduction to the Study of the Poem,* 3rd ed. (Cambridge, 1959; repr. 1963), 510.

⁹ C. W. Phillips, cited in Bruce-Mitford, *The Sutton Hoo Ship Burial,* vol. 1, 722.

¹⁰ C. W. Phillips, "The Excavation of the Sutton Hoo Ship Burial," *Antiquaries J.* 20 (1940), 149–202, at p. 182; and H. M. Chadwick, "Who Was He?" *Antiquity* 14 (1940), 76–87, at p. 87.

¹¹ R. L. S. Bruce-Mitford, *The Sutton Hoo Ship Burial: A Provisional Guide* (London, 1947), 41.

¹² The phrase is from Eric Stanley's preliminary statement (1979) to the Toronto conference on the date of *Beowulf* (20–23 April 1980).

¹³ J. M. Kemble, *The Anglo-Saxon Poems of Beowulf, The Travellers Song, and the Battle of Finnesburh* (London, 1833 [100 copies]; 2nd ed., vol. 1, 1835); vol. 2, *A Translation of the Anglo-Saxon Poem of "Beowulf," with a Copious Glossary, Preface, and Philological Notes* (London, 1837).

¹⁴ W. J. Thoms, *The Primeval Antiquities of Denmark. Translated and Applied to the Illustration of Similar Remains in England* (London, 1849), cited in T. Bateman, *Ten Years' Diggings . . .* (London, 1861; repr. 1978), 32–33. Three years earlier, Thoms had introduced the term "folklore" into the English language, replacing with "a good Saxon compound" what had previously been called "popular antiquities" or "popular literature" (*Athenaeum,* no. 982 [22 August 1846], 862).

¹⁵ C. R. Smith, *Collectanea antiqua . . .* (London, 1852), vol. 2, 241. I am deeply grateful to E. G. Stanley who, with fortitude and humor, tracked down this volume for me at the Bodleian Library, where it had languished misshelved and unread for over a century.

¹⁶ J. Y. Ackerman, *Remains of Pagan Saxondom* (London, 1855), xvff.

¹⁷ C. R. Smith, "Introduction," *Inventorium sepulchrale: an Account . . . by the Rev. Bryan Faussett of Heppington* (London, 1856), xxxv.

¹⁸ Faussett excavated about seven hundred graves in all. See C. J. Arnold, *An Archaeology of the Early Anglo-Saxon Kingdoms* (London, 1988), 3.

¹⁹ Bateman, *Ten Year's Diggings,* x. Boat burial had been mentioned in Scandinavian literature since the late seventeenth century. M. Müller-Wille, "Boat Graves in Northern Europe," *Int. J. of Nautical Archaeol. and Underwater*

Exploration 3.2 (1974), 187–204, estimates about 300 locations with more than 420 boat graves. In 1874, T. Wright, *The Celt, the Roman, and the Saxon: A History of the Early Inhabitants of Britain* (London, 1874), 465–504, was still citing the *Collectanea* and included the usual excerpts (now nine in number) from *Beowulf.*

[20] *The British Museum Guide to Anglo-Saxon Antiquities* (1923), 48.

[21] See esp. H. M. Chadwick, *The Origin of the English Nation* (Cambridge, 1907), and *idem, The Heroic Age* (Cambridge, 1912). He was impressed, too, with the relevance to Old English verse of what was being dug up in Scandinavia: "The evidence of these deposits then fully bears out the statements of the poems. So numerous were the articles found that it is possible to reconstruct from them with certainty the whole dress and equipment of the warriors of those days" (*The Origin,* 187).

[22] R. Girvan, *Beowulf and the Seventh Century* (London, 1935; 2nd ed., with a new chapter by R. L. S. Bruce-Mitford, 1971).

[23] J. R. R. Tolkien, "*Beowulf:* The Monsters and the Critics," *P.B.A.* 22 (1936), 245–95, as reprinted in *An Anthology of Beowulf Criticism,* comp. Nicholson, 51–103, at 69.

[24] H. Shetelig and H. Falk, *Scandinavian Archaeology,* trans. E. V. Gordon (Oxford, 1937), 265.

[25] G. Reichel, *Hakon's Lied: Ein Roman um den Schreiber des Beowulf-Epos* (Leipzig, 1962), Sutton Hoo postscript, 261–64.

[26] F. Klaeber, *Beowulf and the Fight at Finnsburg* (Boston, 1922; London, 1923; 3rd ed. with supplement, 1941), 453.

[27] C. L. Wrenn, "Recent Work on *Beowulf,*" 508.

[28] F. Liebermann, "Ort und Zeit der Beowulfdichtung," in *Nachrichten von der königl. Gesellschaft der Wissenschaften zu Göttingen,* phil.-hist. Klasse (1920), 253–76; A. S. Cook, "The Possible Begetter of the Old English *Beowulf* and *Widsith,*" *Trans. of the Connecticut Acad. of Arts and Sciences* 25 (1922), 281–346; and W. W. Lawrence, *Beowulf and the Epic Tradition* (Cambridge, MA, 1930), 244–91.

[29] Girvan, *Beowulf and the Seventh Century.*

[30] E. Martin-Clarke, *Culture in Early Anglo-Saxon England* (Baltimore, 1947), 56.

[31] Bruce-Mitford, *The Sutton Hoo Ship-Burial: A Provisional Guide,* 39.

[32] Lindqvist, "Sutton Hoo and *Beowulf,*" 131.

[33] J. R. Clark Hall, trans., *Beowulf and the Finnesburg Fragment,* rev. ed. with notes and intro. by C. L. Wrenn (London, 1950); C. L. Wrenn, ed., *Beowulf with the Finnesburg Fragment* (London, 1953), 32–37.

[34] D. Whitelock, *The Audience of Beowulf* (Oxford, 1951), 25.

[35] Wrenn, "Sutton Hoo and *Beowulf,*" in *An Anthology of Beowulf Criticism,* comp. Nicholson, 328.

[36] Wrenn, "Sutton Hoo and *Beowulf,*" in Chambers, *Beowulf,* 523.

[37] See C. Chase, "Opinions on the Date of *Beowulf,* 1815–1980," in Chase, *The Dating of Beowulf,* 5–7, and articles in the volume by Kiernan, Goffart, Murray, Page, Frank, and Stanley.

[38] H. Ellis Davidson, "Archaeology and *Beowulf,*" in G. N. Garmonsway and J. Simpson, eds., *Beowulf and its Analogues* (London, 1968), 359.

[39] E. John, "*Beowulf* and the Margins of Literacy," *Bul. of the John Rylands University Library of Manchester* 56 (1973–74), 388–422, at p. 392.

[40] P. Wormald, "Bede, *Beowulf,* and the Conversion of the Anglo-Saxon Aristocracy," in R. T. Farrell, ed., *Bede and Anglo-Saxon England: Papers in Honour of the 1300th Anniversary of the Birth of Bede . . . ,* B.A.R. Brit. ser. 46 (Oxford, 1978), 32–95, at p. 94.

[41] John Hines, *The Scandinavian Character of Anglian England in the Pre-Viking Period,* B.A.R. Brit. ser. 124 (Oxford, 1984), 296–97.

[42] R. Cramp, "*Beowulf* and Archaeology," *M.A.* 1 (1957), 57–77, reprinted in D. K. Fry, ed., *The Beowulf Poet: A Collection of Critical Essays* (Englewood Cliffs, N.J., 1968), 117.

[43] Ellis Davidson, "Archaeology and *Beowulf,*" 353.

[44] See F. Jónsson, *Lexicon poeticum antiquae linguae septentrionalis . . . af Sveinbjörn Egilsson,* 2nd ed. (Copenhagen, 1931; repr. 1966), s.v. *hringofinn, hringkofl, hringserkr, jarnserkr, hringskyrta,* etc.

[45] See J. B. Bessinger, "*Beowulf* and the Harp at Sutton Hoo," *University of Toronto Quarterly* 27 (1957), 148–68. The current reconstruction of the *hearpe* is explained in R. and M. Bruce-Mitford, "The Sutton Hoo Lyre, *Beowulf,* and the Origins of the Frame Harp," *Antiquity* 44 (1970), 7–13, reprinted in R. L. S. Bruce-Mitford, *Aspects of Anglo-Saxon Archaeology* (London, 1974), 188–97.

[46] *Hearpe,* "Lyre," quickly found its way into textbook glossaries; it appeared the very next year, e.g. F. G. Cassidy and R. N. Ringler, eds., *Bright's Old English Grammar and Reader* (New York, 1971), 434.

[47] See s.v. wal, *wala,* and *walu,* respectively in J. Bosworth and T. N. Toller, *An Anglo-Saxon Dictionary . . .* (1882–98; repr. Oxford, 1983); C. W. M. Grein, *Sprachschatz der angelsächsischen Dichter* (Cassel, 1861–64; rev. ed. by J. Köhler, with the help of F. Holthausen, Heidelberg, 1912–14); J. R. Clark Hall, *A Concise Anglo-Saxon Dictionary for the Use of Students* (London, 1894; 3rd ed., rev. and enlarged, 1931).

[48] See note 21 in Bruce-Mitford's appendix on "The Sutton Hoo Ship-Burial," in *A History of the Anglo-Saxons,* R. H. Hodgkin, 2 vols. (Oxford, 1935; 3rd ed., 1952), vol. 2, 752–54, reprinted as chapter 9, "A Note on the Word *Wala* in

Beowulf," in Bruce-Mitford, *Aspects of Anglo-Saxon Archaeology,* 210–13. Also K. Stjerna, *Essays on Questions Connected with the Old English Poem of "Beowulf,"* trans. and ed. by J. R. Clark Hall (Coventry, 1912), 14; and Martin-Clarke, *Culture in Early Anglo-Saxon England,* 63 and 76.

[49] Bruce-Mitford, "The Sutton Hoo Helmet," *British Museum Quarterly* 36 (Autumn 1972), 120, reprinted in Bruce-Mitford, *Aspects of Anglo-Saxon Archaeology,* 204.

[50] H. D. Merritt, supplement to *A Concise Anglo-Saxon Dictionary,* J. R. Clark Hall, 4th ed. (Cambridge, 1960), s.v. *walu;* and A. Campbell, *Enlarged Addenda and Corrigenda to the Supplement by T. Northcote Toller to an Anglo-Saxon Dictionary Based on the Manuscript Collections of Joseph Bosworth* (Oxford, 1972), s.v. *wala.*

[51] See examples and discussion in H. Meritt, "Three Studies in Old English," *American J. of Philology* 62 (1941), 334–38. Outside of *Beowulf, wala* occurs in verse only as the second element of a compound: *weallwalan wirum (Ruin,* line 20). Unless otherwise stated, editions and abbreviations used are those cited in *A Microfiche Concordance to Old English: The Lists of Texts and Index of Editions,* ed. R. L. Venezky and A. diPaolo Healey, Publications of the *Dictionary of Old English* I (Toronto, 1980).

[52] See *Fascicle C* of *The Dictionary of Old English,* ed. A. C. Amos and A. diPaolo Healey et al. (Toronto, 1988), s.v. *camb* 2b.

[53] In lines 1030–34, e.g., the poet has the *wala,* said to provide *heafodbeorg* (head protection) around the helmet's *hrof* (roof), deflecting swords described as *scurheard* (shower-hard); cf. *scurbeorg* (roof), *Ruin,* line 5.

[54] H. D. Chickering, *Beowulf: A Dual Language Edition* (New York, 1977).

[55] See E. James, *The Franks* (Oxford, 1988), 204, following B. Arrhenius, *Merovingian Garnet Jewellery: Emergence and Social Implications* (Stockholm, 1985).

[56] A. H. Smith, "The Photography of Manuscripts," *London Medieval Studies* 1 (1938), 179–207. Smith gives *lide* (visual) but *hoe* (photograph). The upper part of what looks like *d* in the manuscript disappears under ultraviolet light. The photographs read *hleo* before *on hoe,* but both J. C. Pope (*The Rhythm of Beowulf,* [New Haven, 1942], 232–34) and N. Davis (in *Beowulf,* ed. J. Zupitza, 2nd ed., E.E.T.S. 245 [London, 1959], xi) reject *hleo* in favor of the "almost inevitable" *hlæw.*

[57] Klaeber, *Beowulf and the Fight at Finnsburg,* 459.

[58] F. Holthausen, *Beowulf nebst dem Finnsburg-Bruchstück,* 2 vols. (Heidelberg, 1905–06; 8th ed. 1948), 126.

[59] Wrenn, "Sutton Hoo and *Beowulf*" in Chambers, *Beowulf,* 514. The first editor to accept *hoe* as the MS reading is E. von Schaubert, 15th rev. ed. (Pader-

born, 1940) of M. Heyne, ed., *Beowulf. Mit ausführlichem Glossar* (Paderborn, 1863).

[60] The earlist *hoe* spelling in the Toronto *Microfiche Concordance* is the place-name *on Wirtroneshoe* in a Somerset charter from 973 (Sawyer 791 [Birch 1294], 8); the spelling *(fram micle) hohe* occurs two years earlier, in a 971 charter from County Lincoln (Sawyer 782 [Birch 1270], 5). Under the year 654, *Chronicle A* (tenth century) spells the East Anglian place-name *æt Icanho; Chronicle E* (twelfth century), under the year 653, has *æt Icanhoe.* Of the fifty-four OE spellings ending in *-oe* only one, *Noe* (Noah), a foreign proper name, occurs in verse. I am indebted to the late A. C. Amos, coeditor of the *Dictionary of Old English,* for a list of these spellings.

[61] J. M. Wallace-Hadrill, "The Grave of Kings," *Studi Medievali,* 3rd ser., 1, (1960), 177–94, reprinted with additions in J. M. Wallace-Hadrill, *Early Medieval History* (Oxford, 1975), 41.

[62] Lindqvist, "Sutton Hoo and *Beowulf,*" 140. In the same volume of *Fornvännen,* B. Nerman, "Sutton Hoo: en svensk kunga-eller hövdinggrav," 65–93, argued that the man commemorated was a Swede. Two years earlier, H. Maryon, "The Sutton Hoo Shield," *Antiquity* 20 (1946), 21–30, suggested that all the treasures, jewelry included, were Swedish imports. The question posed by N. E. Lee's title, "The Sutton Hoo Ship Built in Sweden?" (*Antiquity* 31 [1957], 40–41), was answered in the affirmative. N. K. Chadwick, "The Monsters and *Beowulf,*" in P. Clemoes, ed., *The Anglo-Saxons: Studies in Some Aspects of Their History and Culture Presented to Bruce Dickens* (London, 1959), 202, observed, tentatively, that just as *Wehha* was a possible diminutive for *Weohstan,* "*Wuffa* is a possible Anglo-Saxon diminutive for Beo-wulf." Cf. R. L. S. Bruce-Mitford, *The Sutton Hoo Ship-Burial: A Handbook* (British Museum, 1968), 70: "The most likely explanation [for the Swedish pieces at Sutton Hoo] seems to be that the dynasty of the Wulfings was Swedish in its origin, and that probably Wehha, said to be the first of the family to rule over the Angles in Britain, was a Swede." J. L. N. O'Laughlin, "Sutton Hoo—the Evidence of the Documents," *M.A.* 8 (1964), 1–19, held that the Wufffings/Wylfings were Geats, who had won in battle against the Swedes the heirlooms buried at Sutton Hoo. See Farrell, "*Beowulf,* Swedes, and Geats," 273, on the weaknesses of both these opposed solutions.

[63] See, e.g. J. M. Wallace-Hadrill, *Bede's "Ecclesiastical History of the English People": A Historical Commentary* (Oxford, 1988), 190 (lines 13–19; II, 15): "Wuffing connections with their homeland, Sweden, seem to have been less active than those they enjoyed with Francia." J. Campbell in J. Campbell et al., eds., *The Anglo-Saxons* (Oxford & Ithaca, 1982), 67, is more tentative: "Wuffa, perhaps the Swedish founder of the line . . ." H. Mayr-Harting, *The Coming of*

Christianity to Anglo-Saxon England (London, 1972), 17, follows O'Louglin rather than Lindqvist: his Wuffings are Geats.

[64] R. L. S. Bruce-Mitford, "The Sutton Hoo Ship Burial: Recent Theories and Comments on General Interpretation," *Proc. of the Suffolk Inst. of Archaeol. and Natural Hist.* 25 (1949), 1–78, reprinted in *Aspects of Anglo-Saxon Archaeology,* 52. On the Swedish question, see esp. pp. 43–72.

[65] R. L. S. Bruce-Mitford, "Sutton Hoo and the Background to the Poem," added chapter in Girvan, *Beowulf and the Seventh Century* (2nd ed., 1971), 85–98, reprinted as "Sutton Hoo and the Background to *Beowulf,*" in Bruce-Mitford, *Aspects of Anglo-Saxon Archaeology,* 259. Bruce-Mitford still regards the Swedish connection as dominant: see "The Sutton Hoo Ship-Burial: Some Foreign Connections," in *Settimane di studio del Centro italiano sull'alto medioeve* 32: *Angli e Sassoni al di qua e al di là del mare* 1 (Spoleto, 1986), 195–207.

[66] Bruce-Mitford, *The Sutton Hoo Ship-Burial,* vol. 2, 91–99 and 205–25; and J. Werner, "Ein langobardischer Schild von Ischl an der Alz," *Bayerische Vorgeschichtsblätter* 18 (1952), 45–58. Doubts concerning the overriding influence of eastern Sweden are expressed by Werner, "Das Schiffsgrab von Sutton Hoo: Forschungsgeschichte und Informationsstand zwischen 1939 und 1980," *Germania* 60 (1982), 193–228; and by D. M. Wilson, "Sweden—England," in J. P. Lamm and H-A Nordström, eds., *Vendel Period Studies* (Stockholm, 1983), 163–66.

[67] M. O. H. Carver, "Sutton Hoo in Context," in *Angli e Sassoni,* 77–123, at pp.106–07.

[68] On the gold buckle as reliquary, see Werner, "Das Schiffsgrab von Sutton Hoo," 198–201; contra Bruce-Mitford, "The Sutton Hoo Ship-Burial: Some Foreign Connections," 80–87. On the combs, see Bruce-Mitford, *The Sutton Hoo Ship-Burial,* vol. 3, 827–30. I am much indebted to I. Wood for a preview of his article concerning the Merovingian presence in Mound 1; see "The Franks and Sutton Hoo," in I. Wood and N. Lund, eds., *People and Places in Northern Europe, 500–1600: Essays in Honour of Peter Hayes Sawyer,* (Woodbridge, 1991), 1–14.

[69] H. M. Chadwick, "Who Was He?" 77.

[70] M. Wood, *In Search of the Dark Ages* (London, 1981), 69. Also, W. A. Chaney, *The Cult of Kingship in Anglo-Saxon England: The Transition from Paganism to Christianity* (Berkeley, 1970), 132.

[71] Wrenn, "Sutton Hoo and Beowulf," *An Anthology of Beowulf Criticism,* comp. Nicholson, 316–17.

[72] Bruce-Mitford, "Sutton Hoo and the Background to the Poem, " in Girvan, *Beowulf and the Seventh Century* (2nd ed., 1971), 93, reprinted in Bruce-Mitford, *Aspects of Anglo-Saxon Archaeology,* 257.

[73] See B. Ambrosiani, "Background to the Boat-Graves of the Mälaren Valley," in Lamm and Nordström, *Vendel Period Studies,* 17–18.

[74] This point was made in 1960 by Wallace-Hadrill, "The Graves of the Kings," esp. 41–47.

[75] Chaney, *Cult of Kingship,* 98.

[76] P. Grierson, "The Purpose of the Sutton Hoo Coins," *Antiquity* 44 (1970), 14–18, at p. 17, cited in E. G. Stanley, "Some Doubts and No Conclusions," in Chase, *Dating of Beowulf,* 204.

[77] Chaney, *Cult of Kingship,* 144.

[78] C. L. Wrenn, *A Study of Old English Literature* (London, 1967), 140.

[79] Wrenn, "Sutton Hoo and Beowulf," in *An Anthology of Beowulf Criticism,* comp. Nicholson, 318; in his chapter of the same name in Chambers, *Beowulf,* 520, Wrenn assigns the standard "in all probability" an early sixth-century date.

[80] Ellis Davidson, "Archaeology and *Beowulf,* 352.

[81] K. Rexroth, "Classics Revisited—IV: *Beowulf,*" *Saturday Review* 10 April 1965, 27, reprinted in Fry, *The Beowulf Poet: A Collection of Critical Essays,* 169.

CHAPTER 12

Children, Death and the Afterlife in Anglo-Saxon England

SALLY CRAWFORD

INTRODUCTION

Childhood studies have developed apace since Ariès published his seminal work *L'Enfant et la vie familiale sous l'ancien regime* (Paris, 1960), but the history of Anglo-Saxon childhood has received relatively little attention.[1] This is not perhaps surprising; the evidence is scarce and difficult to interpret, but children are a part of Anglo-Saxon society, and archaeologists and historians alike do make references to the existence of children in this period. The subject may appear too obvious to require study, but what do we really know about the nature of Anglo-Saxon childhood and attitudes towards children? The lack of a critical assessment of the history of Anglo-Saxon childhood has led to assertions being made which are based on assumption rather than fact.[2] It may be a difficult and inconclusive task, but it is surely worth the effort now to try to wring from the evidence some possible models of Anglo-Saxon childhood to set against present assumptions. This paper will examine only one aspect of childhood: the attitude of parents towards child mortality. Given the nature of the evidence and the state of our understanding of Anglo-Saxon childhood, what follows is not intended to provide answers but to raise questions that should, perhaps, have been asked before now.

Mortality rates dominate all interpretations of past parental attitudes towards children. According to Ariès, high infant mortality will force parents to take little interest in the welfare of their offspring because such fragile life is not worth the emotional investment of love and care. Equally, they will favor large families, in the hope that one or two of their children will survive. Ariès's thesis has much to recommend it, although more recent social historians would argue that natural parental love should be given a greater role. In either case, the psychological upheaval of coping with the death of a child will be dramatic, and may lead to apparently callous and contradictory behavior. As an example, rural Chinese parents today, living in a society with very high infant mortality rates, believe that, if a child falls ill or dies, it is because the evil spirit within it is deliberately thwarting the hopes of the parents. Thus any guilt engendered by apparently careless or callous behavior on the part of the parent (most peasant farmers have neither the time to care for sick children nor the money to spare for medicine) is offset by the excuse that the child died deliberately, prompted by its evil spirit.[3] Different societies will adopt different attitudes to cope with the fragility of infant life, to enable parents to bear the emotional pain of losing a vulnerable infant. The social and spiritual consequences of this mortality rate have a major impact on any society, and are reflected in the wider sphere of attitudes towards the afterlife, and attitudes towards children in general, and it may be that echoes of this impact are to be detected in documentary and archaeological sources from the Anglo-Saxon period.

It is impossible to reconstruct infant and child mortality rates from the Anglo-Saxon period, but given that this was a pre-industrial society without the benefits of modern medical knowledge, the mortality rate must have been high. Surviving documentary evidence from the later Anglo-Saxon period suggests that the vulnerability of a child's[4] life in this period of primitive medicine was accepted as a commonplace. Infant mortality was understood as a typical hazard of childhood. In the prognostications on a child's birth, written in the tenth century,[5] there are numerous dire predictions. These predictions are derivative, but they are written in the vernacular and must have seemed to be relevant to Anglo-Saxon society to the scribe at least. They would make chilling reading for any pregnant mother hoping to divine the future of her baby. A child born on the fifth night of the moon will die young; a child born on the eighth night will die immediately. If it is born on the fifteenth night it will die immediately, and again, instant death on the twentieth. These prognostications must have been guaranteed a level of accuracy sufficient to make them worth the labor and expense of writing them down.

The documentary sources for the Anglo-Saxon period would indicate that adults did not take a callous attitude towards the possibility of losing their children. The Reverend Oswald Cockayne's monumental work *Leechdoms, Wortcunning and Starcraft of Early England* (1884–86) remains the only comprehensive collection of Anglo-Saxon medicine and charms. It includes a transcription of Bald's *Leechbook*,[6] a medical text written late in the Anglo-Saxon period, but containing a number of remedies that seem to originate in a pagan past,[7] and the earliest medical book in the vernacular. This, and the other remedies deriving from Greek and Latin origins, provide an instructive manual revealing how important the business of childbirth was perceived to be, and also, incidentally, revealing how little the doctors of the day could do to alter infant mortality statistics. Cockayne's work contains twelve surviving Anglo-Saxon remedies dealing with the problems of difficult pregnancy, stillbirth and miscarriage. The majority are concerned with encouraging the baby, dead or alive, to be expelled from the womb at the proper time, and involve the use of drinks made from fieldmore, fleabane, pennyroyal, dittany and wolf's milk, all of which are variously recommended for stomach-ache, snakebite and arrow-wounds: a group of remedies, in other words, classed as useful for expelling dangerous substances out of the body.

There are also a number of remedies, no doubt equally efficacious, that rely heavily on chants and magic:

> let the woman who cannot bring forth her child, take milk from a cow of one colour in her hand, then sip it up with her mouth, and then go to running water and spit the milk into it, and then scoop up with the same hand a mouthful of water . . . and then let her go into a different house from the one she came out of.[8]

Perhaps the gymnastics involved in this remedy would have been enough to induce birth in a heavily pregnant woman. Certainly the doctors giving their advice are confident of success, even to excess:

> in order that a woman may give birth quickly, take seed of coriander, 11 grains or 13, knit them with a thread on a clean linen cloth; let then a person who is a virgin, boy or girl, take them and hold this at the left thigh, near the genitals, and as soon as the birth is over, take away the medicine, in case part of the insides follow after it.[9]

In spite of this assurance, such remedies can have done little to improve the chances of an infant living, rather than dying. The only response to disease was to resort to a mixture of "medicine" (herbal remedies that may have had some medical validity) and "magic". What responses would there have been when these remedies failed and the child died?

PAGANS AND INFANTS IN THE BURIAL RITUAL

In the pagan period, the only reconstructable evidence about infants derives from excavated cemeteries. Unfortunately, infants are badly underrepresented in the skeletal record from cemetery sites.[10] In a database containing over 1,000 aged skeletons from early Anglo-Saxon cemetery sites, less than 6% of burials are aged under three years of age[11] (sixty-one out of 1271 burials), and only 11% are under five years of age (130 out of 1271 burials) of those skeletons to which it is possible to assign an age. This peculiarity has not passed unnoticed by archaeologists. At Buckland, Dover,[12] a cemetery in use in successive phases from the mid-fifth to the mid-eighth centuries, extending from the pagan well into the Christian period, has few infant burials. The excavator comments:

> There was evidently some reason, which operated during both the pagan and Christian periods, why infants under five years of age were not buried with other children, adolescents and mature adults. In the whole cemetery, there was only one child under 5, the girl in grave 21, and this burial was exceptional, because the head was placed at the east end of the grave. There must have been some very special reason which permitted departure from tradition in this sole instance . . . Comparison may be made with the Polhill cemetery, where there are no infant burials, but there were sixteen children under five years of age, out of a total of 125 burials. At Lyminge, out of 44 burials, there were only two children between 2 and 6 years, and one between 6–12 months. . . . The evidence therefore varies at different cemeteries in the same county.[13]

This raises two questions: why were infants not buried in the ordinary cemetery, and what happened to their bodies after death? We must also consider the significance of the bodies that were included in the adult cemetery.

There are three plausible explanations for the dearth of infants in pagan Anglo-Saxon cemeteries.

1. Infant bones are fragile and decompose rapidly, thus they may not be readily identifiable in the archaeological record. However, even if the bones have completely disintegrated, it should be possible to identify grave cuts, particularly on those sites where excavators have been able to identify post-holes. Comparable sites from other periods do not yield such universally low numbers of infants. At the Roman site

of Owlesbury, Hampshire,[14] 34.8% of the burials were of under-fives: at Norwich,[15] the late Anglo-Saxon site contained 45% of infant burials, of those burials to which it was possible to assign an age: at Raunds,[16] a 20% level of infant mortality is represented in the excavated area, while at Winchester, of the 250 graves excavated in the cathedral area, 27.2% were of children under two years of age.[17]

There are exceptions to the general "rule" that pagan Anglo-Saxon sites contain low numbers of infant burials. The late pagan site of Lechlade, Gloucs., contains forty-four burials of children aged six years or less, making up 20% of the cemetery population of which twenty-five burials are of infants under three years of age.[18] Of these forty-four infants, thirteen are in double burials with adult females, males or older juveniles. Taking Anglo-Saxon cemeteries generally, of those infants that have been recovered, about 17% are included in double burials (twenty-two out of 130 infant burials), compared to the rest of the aged population, of which 9% are buried in double or multiple graves (ninety-five out of 1141 burials). The double infant burials may represent the only infant burials within a site. At Nassington, Northants.,[19] for example, out of over forty burials, only two infants were found, in the form of a skull buried by the hand of female burial 31, and another skull in the crook of the arm of female burial A.

The higher representation of infants in double burials is probably connected with the high mortality rate of infants. If two deaths coincided, it may have been a matter of convenience to bury the bodies together, and this would be particularly likely where mothers and their sickly children died after childbirth. Equally, if disease attacked a community, weak infants might be expected to die with their carers.

2. Infants were buried more shallowly than adults, and their graves have disappeared over time. This might be an inadvertent consequence of the difficulty of digging a deep, small grave. Alternatively, dead infants may have been of so little consequence that a shallow grave was considered sufficient for their resting place. Of course, infants if they were buried shallowly, would have been more prone to excavation by scavenging wolves and dogs. There are a number of implications in the idea of the Anglo-Saxons accepting the possibility that the infant they buried carelessly on the Tuesday[20] was missing or thrown up from its grave on the Wednesday after a night-raid by hungry animals. I will return to this later.

3. Perhaps infants were not, as a rule, buried in adult cemeteries at all. Other methods may have been used to dispose of the quantity of dead infants that must have been cluttering up the Anglo-Saxon world. It is possible that infants were assigned their own space, away from the usual burial ground. There is no archaeological evidence for such juvenile apartheid, but to postulate its existence is to add another dimension to the question of Anglo-Saxon attitudes towards dead infants.

The infants buried within the normal cemetery are distinguished by a lack of grave goods in comparison to other age groups. At Lechlade, a late sixth/seventh century site, with an unusually high number of infants, twenty-three are buried without grave goods: a further six are buried with only beads, while the remaining fifteen are given slightly more luxurious burial. At Alton, Hants.,[21] where again there is a relatively high proportion of infants, (eight out of fifty inhumations)—six of the infants were buried without grave goods, while of the remaining two, one was buried with a bone bead, and one, a four-year old, was buried with a bead and a knife. This pattern is in keeping with that for other sites.[22] It must be stressed that in the majority of excavated sites, no infants have been found at all. Compared to infants, much higher levels of deposition of grave goods occur with other age groups. Never buried with weapons,[23] only rarely buried with more than a bead, buckle or pot, infants represent the "poorest" members of the community. If grave goods are a representation of status in life, then infants had little value to society, and certainly no status in death. If grave goods within Anglo-Saxon cemeteries represent any form of belief in an afterlife, then infants were clearly expected to arrive in the new life as helpless and useless as they left it. Having said that, there are some extraordinary exceptions to this rule, whose wealth of grave goods sets them apart from infants, children and adults alike. At Finglesham, for example, there are no burials of infants under eighteen months, but there are nineteen burials of infants aged between eighteen months and five years. Of these infants, twelve are buried with no grave goods, six are buried with only one or two items, but three girls are buried with expensive necklaces. The most spectacular is grave 7, of a girl aged between two and five years, who is buried with a wheel-thrown bottle, a Roman flagon, a knife, chatelaine and pouch, and an elaborate necklace including a gold solidus of Sigebert II/III.[24]

Infants within the cemetery record tend to be accorded unique or unusual burial ritual. Many of them are buried with other bodies.

They tend to be given noticeably few grave goods, or a spectacular excess. They may be marked by some other means: at Holborough, Kent, the seventh-century cemetery contains exclusively W–E burials, except for one infant, buried N–S. At Apple Down, West Sussex, structure 32 consists of four post-holes arranged at each corner of a square, with a fifth post-hole in the center of the structure containing the cremated remains of an infant or child. While this is not the only post-hole structure at the site, it is noticeable that this feature has drawn particular comment as "the most striking example" of a post-hole burial.[25] Cremation is the most expensive and technically difficult form of disposal of a dead body.

Cemeteries whose use borders the transitional period between the arrival of Christianity and the abandonment of these sites for church graveyards show a particularly high level of what may be described as "uneasiness" about infant burials. The case of Lechlade has been mentioned, where, within the context of Anglo-Saxon cemeteries, a surprisingly high number of infants are buried in the cemetery. This may not reflect deliberate intention on the part of the burying community; it may yet be demonstrated that the low number of infant burials within pagan cemeteries may have more to do with modern excavation techniques than with any Anglo-Saxon burial practice. Stronger evidence for deliberate activity directed towards children and infants is visible in the attributes of their burial. At Marina Drive, Dunstable, Bedfordshire,[26] the cemetery did not come into use until shortly before the coming of Christianity in the late sixth century. It produced a number of grave goods which may be confidently defined as "amuletic". These included two beaver teeth, three cowrie shells, one faceted crystal, one ox rib and one quartz crystal. Apart from a bag of human teeth, these were the only "amulets" within the cemetery, and they were all found with children between the ages of one and six years. Within the Anglo-Saxon burial ritual, amulets are by no means exclusively buried with infants and children, but it is not uncommon for infants to be buried with such items, and Marina Drive offers the most striking example of this tendency. Whatever it was about an individual's death that motivated the buriers to include amulets amongst the grave goods, infants often qualified for the distinction.

At Winnall II,[27] the excavators note that this post-Conversion site contains a number of burials marked by having stones buried over their bodies, which, it is speculated, may represent attempts to lay ghosts. These possibly "revenant" burials include the juveniles in graves 9, 18, 24b and 33, of which the occupants are aged four years, eighteen months, eight years and eleven years respectively. Not all children are buried with stones over their bodies, and some adults are, but a very high proportion of the children (four out of nine) receive this treatment. At Lechlade, the body in grave 140, aged about nine to ten, was buried with stone blocks over the head, by the pelvis and over the knee: the burial dates to the late seventh or early eighth century, right at the end of the site's use for burial. The undatable burial 177, of a two to three year old, was buried with a stone between the right arm and chest and over the feet. Other methods of burial associated with preventing the dead from walking are also found at Lechlade. Grave 74 is of a nine to ten year old, buried prone, with its head at knee-level to one side of the body. The other two prone burials are of a female aged over forty and a fourteen–fifteen year old. Again, what we are seeing is not a ritual aimed exclusively at infants and children, but a ritual provoked by some condition of life or death that children and infants are more likely to fulfill than adults.

Later documentary evidence sheds little light on any interpretation of these or the other pagan burial rituals, but in the Scandinavian *Njal's Saga*,[28] Hrafnkell piles up a cairn over the boy whom he is forced to kill in fulfillment of his vow; in the sagas generally only murdered men are covered with stones or turf, or witches or wizards who have been stoned to death for their crimes. It is dangerous to use late Scandinavian sources to elucidate pagan Anglo-Saxon material, but it provides an interesting context for attitudes towards the dead that might lead to such behavior.[29] Graves marked by stones over the bodies might indicate an exceptional or threatening death, or perhaps exceptional or threatening times, such as a period of religious conversion.

The evidence from the pagan cemeteries would indicate that, on the whole, infants must have been afforded a fairly casual burial. Either they were not included in the adult cemetery at all, and their fate leaves no archaeological trace, or they were buried shallowly within the pagan cemetery, and their graves have been lost over time, or a few are included within the pagan cemetery but tend to be marked out in some way, either by inclusion with adults, or by some unusual feature of the burial. Towards the end of the use of the pagan cemeteries, at a time when Christianity must have been influencing ideas about burial and the afterlife, there is a suggestion that infant burials begin to receive greater emphasis. Why should the archaeological record indicate greater worry about the infant afterlife in the Conversion period?

EARLY CHRISTIAN ATTITUDES TOWARD
INFANTS AND THE AFTERLIFE

The church taught that adults and babies too, unless they were baptized, would not reach heaven.[30] This meant, effectively, that all infants, not just those that died in peculiar or threatening circumstances, had the potential to hold a grievance against the living if they died before baptism. The idea that the dead could have malign intentions towards the living, and that even dead infants could be susceptible to this behavior, might not seem obvious and needs some illustration. I have already suggested examples from the pagan archaeological record where infants are given unusual treatment in death, but no actual intention to "lay" a ghost can be deduced from this, although there is a strong temptation to interpret the presence of amulets and stones in graves in this way. A persuasive case might be made for the dramatic Worthy Park burial 38,[31] which illustrates that the emphasis in cases of violent death was on the infant, rather than the adult burial. In this example, the grave contains a woman with a newly-born child lying head down between her thighs, its feet still apparently enclosed within the woman's pelvic girdle, as if the infant and mother had died at the moment of childbirth. The infant's body is covered by a layer of chalk. The fact that there is no chalk over the mother suggests that it was the infant, not the adult, whose death presented a particular problem and whose burial deserved special treatment.

This burial poses problems of interpretation, in that the foetus must have been visible to the buriers. Its articulated feet bones appear to lie undisturbed in the pelvic girdle, rather than to have fallen through after decomposition, as would have been the case if the infant had been lying on top of the body of the woman. This suggests that the foetus may have been expelled after the woman had died. This is not beyond the bounds of possibility. Parikh asserts that when the body of a pregnant woman decomposes, the foetus may be expelled after about 48–72 hours.[32] This gives an interesting insight into pagan Anglo-Saxon burial practice: the woman would seem to have been dead for at least two days before her burial. The horrifying expulsion of her still-born child after the mother's death might be sufficient cause to explain the peculiar circumstances of this burial.

What might an Anglo-Saxon have to fear from a dead infant? The only texts relating to infant burials are both mysterious and sinister, and typically ambiguous. In one, a charm from the *Lacnunga,*[33] a late Anglo-Saxon text, there are hints that a dead infant could in some way influence or prevent birth. A woman who has miscarriages is to take a bit of her own child's grave and wrap it in black wool and sell it to the trader and then say: "I sell it, I have sold it, this black wool and these grains of sorrow." The other reference to superstitious attitudes towards infants appears in Ælfric's *Lives of the Saints,* where he reminds his audience of those "witless women" who draw their infants through the earth at crossroads and so commit them to the devil.[34] The meaning is obscure but unpleasant, and the subsequent text suggests that the infants actually perish during this procedure, and are the devil's in death. Ælfric, in his homilies, terrorizes his listeners with tales of ghosts and the terrible fates of those who die in sin.[35] Characteristic of the tales that he felt his audience would be prepared to accept is the story of a child monk who missed his parents so much that he ran away from the monastery.[36] He died the instant he arrived at his parents' house. Whenever they tried to bury him, the next day his body was found thrown out of the grave, until Benedict intervened with a consecrated wafer to lay on his breast. The audience is clearly supposed to be shocked by the idea that the child would not stay in the grave; in other words, it is not a phenomenon to which listeners were accustomed, but nonetheless, it cannot have been felt to be so implausible that it could not possibly happen. One might argue that these Anglo-Saxons, fed on a diet of extraordinary and exotic miracle stories, would be gullible enough to swallow any tale, but we must question whether they would accept a story that they believed to be utterly beyond the bounds of probability. Ælfric thought his audience would accept the concept that the earth, under these miraculous circumstances, would reject an unholy body, and the popularity of the story in other contexts testifies that the idea was tolerated in other European societies at this time too.[37]

Paul Barber,[38] in his work on traditional European beliefs in revenantism (the belief that the dead may return to life), draws attention to the particular susceptibility of infants to have a malign existence after death in the popular imagination. He offers two plausible suggestions as to why this should be. In the first place, he demonstrates the link between disease and the phenomenon of revenants. The popular belief in large parts of Europe is that when there is an outbreak of hauntings—of corpses coming to life, taking life from the living, and turning the newly-dead into revenants—the culprit is always the first person who died. His victims are his nearest friends and relatives, those with whom he was most regularly in contact. This superstition, Barber deduces, arose out of the attempt by the ignorant to explain the introduction of fatal infectious disease into the community. Naturally, infants are the most vulnerable to disease, and thus are most likely to die under these sinister circumstances. A similar story is found in an Anglo-Saxon context, although here its circumstances are so interpreted that the infectious child, drawing its carer to death, is given miraculous significance. The story, related by Bede, concerns a monastic child called Esica:

> who, because of his age, being yet really an infant, was brought up in the house of the virgins to learn his lessons there. This child being taken with the aforesaid plague, when he came to his last moment, cried out three times upon one of the virgins consecrated to Christ, speaking to her, as if she were present, by her own name, "Eadgyth, Eadgyth, Eadgyth", and therewith ending the temporal life entered into life eternal. But that virgin which he called at his death, straightway in the place where she was, being there taken with the same sickness, the very same day that she was called was taken out of this life, and followed him that called her to the kingdom of heaven.[39]

Arguably, such episodes in hagiography or ecclesiastical literature are to be seen as commonplaces of the genre, but this is not a reason to dismiss such evidence. There must be some root of truth in this kind of tale for it to have sustained the "willing suspension of disbelief" in the listeners. Equally, our modern understanding of infections enables us to give a scientific explanation to this kind of incident, and it is clear that an infectious child may well pass on its infections to its carers. Adults are, on the whole, less likely to succumb to disease, so the Esica/Eadgyth case cannot have been particularly common, but nevertheless, it must have occurred. Modern interpreters can explain the phenomenon by suggesting infection, and by supposing that Eadgyth had formed some bond with the child, probably by acting as its carer/surrogate mother. She was absent at the time of the child's death; small wonder that Esica should call on her in his last moments. In Bede's time, a different, and in this case mystical, explanation was sought.

The scavenging dogs around a cemetery also play a part in the European story of revenantism. Barber cites numerous examples from European folklore in which the action of dogs and wolves grubbing out fresh corpses was reinterpreted as an attack by the animals on revenants attempting to rise from the dead. Dogs thus became the traditional enemies of vampires. One is reminded inexorably of Ælfric's child who would not stay in his grave until an "amulet" was placed on his chest. Wolves and dogs certainly inhabited the Anglo-Saxon countryside, and the early cemeteries, on the periphery of settlements, must have been targets. It is a commonplace amongst archaeologists that infants were buried more shallowly than adults (and therefore fail to survive in the archaeological record), and thus one could suppose that they were the most convenient prey for dogs and other scavengers. The discovery of an empty infant grave so shortly after the death of the child could easily give rise to extreme fears and superstitions.

Could the introduction of Christianity have put an end to these superstitions, or, as the late pagan cemeteries indicate, could it indeed have heightened the superstition? I have already suggested that Christianity placed all those who were not baptized in a vulnerable position, and it is not unlikely that the rite of baptism may have been regarded by the new converts as a further charm against the spirits of dead infants. The teachings of the church throughout the Anglo-Saxon period emphasized that children, even though they had no understanding, had to be baptized, although there seems to have been some resistance to this idea. Even at the end of the Anglo-Saxon period, Ælfric feels obliged to reiterate the idea that infants had to be baptized, though they could not understand the ritual. The subject arises, for example, in the Sermon on the Lord's Epiphany, on the Second Sunday in Lent, and on the Sacrifice on Easter-Day. Ælfric is one of a long line of ecclesiastics attempting to preach this message. Augustine's eighth question to Gregory, according to Bede's account, was about baptism, including the question as to how soon after birth an infant could be baptized, particularly if it was in danger of dying. Gregory replied that it could be baptized the very hour it was born, even though it lacked understanding.[40]

The lawcodes reiterate the necessity to baptize the infant at all costs, and impose severe penalties for failure to do so. Ine's second law states that a "a child is to be baptized within 30 days: if it is not, 30 shillings compensation."[41] The fine itself is not exceptionally heavy compared to other fines for other crimes, but the second part of this law is rather different: "if however it dies without being baptized, he shall pay as compensation all he possesses." To fail to baptize the child was not a serious offense, but to allow a child to die unbaptized was. The law indicates that many parents were reluctant to baptize their apparently healthy infants:

perhaps there was an unintentional correlation in their perception between death and baptism. The "Northumbrian priest's law" reinforces the haste to baptize—"each child shall be baptized within 9 days: if not 6 oras."[42] Guthlac, the model child of model Christian parents was, we are informed, baptized after eight days,[43] and Bede (H.E. ii, 24) notes that the very first Northumbrian to receive baptism was Eanflaed, the newly born daughter of Edwin. Other children of Edwin's died apparently at the moment of baptism—they were still wearing the chrism.

It may be that the references to baptism in the surviving documentary evidence represent no more than the continuation of an ecclesiastical debate that had no relevance to the actual state of affairs. After all, by the time Ælfric was writing, England had been Christian for some centuries, and baptism of infants ought to have been a matter of course. However, a late account from Cornwall, written about 1200, suggests that even notably pious Christian parents could fail in this duty.[44] The manuscript concerns the life of Peter of Cornwall and Launceston, and describes the events occurring to his pious family. One family member, Ailsi (a corruption of the Anglo-Saxon name Aethelsige), had visions through the medium of his dead fourth son, Paganus, so called, we are told, because "he was a long time a pagan, living twelve years before he was baptized."[45] We are given no reason why Paganus was not baptized by his parents, although his name may indicate that he was unusual in this respect. Within the same family, we are told of a child who died at the same time as her grandfather: "she had died in a state of innocence, immediately after baptism, and still dressed in white."[46] Why should Paganus have remained unbaptized all through childhood while other children in his family were baptized almost at birth? Perhaps the circumstances of the granddaughter's death provide the key. Baptism was for sickly children, used as a last-minute resort to save the child's life or to ensure its smooth entry into heaven. A lively child had no need of baptism.

This view is exemplified in the attitude of one of the new converts to Christianity who came to Wilfrid on one of his missionary journeys into the countryside. The woman:

> held in her bosom the body of her first-born child, wrapped in rags and hidden from sight; she uncovered the face of the corpse for the bishop to confirm it among the rest, hoping thus to be able to bring it back to life.[47]

The bishop discovering the ruse, would have refused to baptize the child, but, after some persuasion, he did so. The woman's expectations were confirmed—the child was revived, and she hastened away with it. Subsequent events showed that the woman remained a heathen even after this demonstration of Christian power.

Baptism is not an archaeologically identifiable rite, but burials in excavated Christian Anglo-Saxon graveyards may throw light on the question of Anglo-Saxon attitudes towards infants and their Christian afterlife. One peculiarity of infant burials is that they tend to be clustered under the eaves-drips of the church, possibly because the water dripping from the holy roof might be thought to "double-bless" the infants. Such clusters are noticeable at Raunds, Whithorn, Jarrow and Winchester. Indeed, for Hartlepool, the presence of a cluster of infant burials has been used to locate the probable site of the lost church.[48] It must be stressed that the habit of burying infants under the eaves-drips is by no means unique to the Anglo-Saxons: Pliny notes that it was customary to bury the bodies of very young infants "*in subgrundariis*,"[49] and this was interpreted by Fulgentius (*Sermones Antiqui* 7) as referring to infants who had not been alive more than forty days.[50] This pattern of burial is common in churches from all periods throughout western Europe.

It is certain that a higher percentage of infants are recovered from Christian than pagan cemeteries in an Anglo-Saxon context, and while the sudden enthusiasm for burying infants in the adult cemetery undoubtedly represents the control the Christians exercised over the customs of the converted, it may also represent the augmentation of pagan superstitions about children who died suddenly and inexplicably, by the additional fear over what would befall the soul of an unbaptized child. Under such circumstances, a place under the holy roof within holy ground must have offered an ideal burial site. That this special area for infants was seen to have peculiar properties is reinforced by the "children's cemetery" at Whithorn.[51] In the earliest phase of the cemetery, the corner under the eaves-drips was exclusively for infants, according to custom.[52] Towards the end of the eighth century, a period of difficulty for the Christians at Whithorn, this exclusive infant cemetery is also used for the burial of older children up to twelve years of age. The reason for the change in the function of this space is open to speculation, but a possible answer might be that, as Christianity was placed under strain, and the fate of those who died unexpectedly appeared less certain, the population using the cemetery may have felt that it was just as well to give older children the benefit of this holy space too. Fears that his might not be enough to keep the spirits of the dead quiet are hinted at in the spread of cremated human bones that seal the last phase of the "children's cemetery." Cremation, of course, was a pagan practice, and the last resort of those trying to rid themselves of revenants.[53] Amongst the thirty-seven skeletons in the "children's graveyard," two are buried with amber beads—remarkable amulets within the context of a "Christian" burial site.

CONCLUSION

There are clear signs within the pagan period that the burial of infants was often seen to involve peculiar rituals such as burial contrary to the prevailing orientation, burial with stones over the body, or burial with amuletic artifacts. That such treatment is not exclusive to infants suggests that it has more to do with the manner of death than with any specific age-related rituals, but that a high proportion of infants are buried with such peculiarities implies that infants were particularly susceptible to the kind of deaths that would lead to this behavior. Infant death is characterized by often being unexpected and inexplicable, as the Anglo-Saxon prognostications illustrate.

The advent of Christianity may not have resulted in a decline in the superstitious treatment of infant burials: rather, late pagan cemetery sites are characterized by a spate of peculiar or more frequent infant burials, such as occur at Marina Drive and Lechlade, and these peculiarities may even be extended to include older children, as at Winnall II or the apparently Christian site of Whithorn. Later documentary evidence suggests that, far from alleviating fears about the spiritual fate of infants who died under mysterious circumstances, Christianity, with its emphasis on the necessity for baptism, increased anxieties about infants. There are hints that baptism might have been popularly misunderstood as applying particularly to infants on the brink of death, acting either as a cure or an assurance that the spirit of the dead infant would sleep quietly. The fact that the spirit of Paganus, who, although of Christian family, was not baptized until his twelfth year (it is tempting to speculate that this took place just before he sickened and died, though of course the evidence does not support such a tempting speculation), returned to haunt the living in the form of benign visitations, indicates the force of belief that the spirit of the unbaptized dead child would be unlikely to rest. Superstitions towards infants, common in many pre-industrial societies, and arising out of the high infant mortality rates, would appear to have been present throughout the pagan period, and to have continued in some form into the Christian period too.

ACKNOWLEDGMENTS

I am grateful to Corpus Christi College, Oxford and to the British Academy for supporting my research.

NOTES

[1] For useful material on the history of Anglo-Saxon childhood see M. S. Kuefler, "A Wryed Existence: Attitudes toward Children in Anglo-Saxon England," *J. of Social Hist.* 24 (4) (Summer, 1991), 823–34, for an analysis of the written sources; and S. E. E. Crawford, "Age Differentiation and Related Social Status: a Study of Early Anglo-Saxon Childhood," unpublished D.Phil. thesis, Oxford, 1991, for an analysis of the archaeological evidence.

[2] This is particularly apparent among archaeologists when it comes to defining the difference between a "child" and an "adult" within the cemetery ritual. See S. E. E. Crawford, "When do Anglo-Saxon Children Count?" *J. of Theoretical Archaeol.* 2 (1991), 17–24.

[3] I am grateful to P. Hase for these observations on attitudes towards children in rural China.

[4] The word "infant" is used in this paper to mean children of five years old and under. The word "child" is used to mean juveniles too young to be considered adults in the Anglo-Saxon community, up to twelve or fourteen years of age. See Crawford, "When do Anglo-Saxon Children Count?"

[5] O. Cockayne, *Leechdoms, Wortcunning and Starcraft of Early England,* 3 vols. (London, 1864–66), vol. 3, 184.

[6] Ibid., vol. 2.

[7] M. L. Cameron, "Bald's 'Leechbook'; its Sources and Their Use in its Compilation," *A.S.E.* 12 (1983), 153–82.

[8] From *Lacnunga* 104 (Cockayne, *Leechdoms,* vol. 3, 69): "Se man se þe maege bearn afedan nime þonne anes bleos cu meoluc on hyre handae 7 gesupe þonne mid hyre muþe 7 gange þonne to yrnendum waetere 7 spere þaes in þa meolc 7 hlade þonne mid þaere ylcan hand. þaes waeteres muð fulre . . . 7 þonne ga heo in oþer hus oþer heo ut ofeode."

[9] From the Anglo-Saxon translation of the remedy in the *Herbarium Apuleii* (Cockayne, *Leechdoms,* vol. 1, 219): "Wið þaet hreadlice cennan maege genim þysse ylcan coliandran saed endlufon corn oððe þreottyne cnyte mid anum ðraede on anum claenan linenan claþe mine ðonne an man þe sy maegðhades man . cnapa oððe maegden 7 healde aet þam wynstran þea neah þam gewealde 7 sona swa eall sea geeacnung gedon bea do sona laecedom aweg þy laes þaes innoðes dael þaes aefter filige."

[10] Statistics are drawn from a database of thirteen excavated cemetery sites (Crawford, "Age Differentiation"). These sites have been chosen because children are present in the cemetery population. Many Anglo-Saxon cemetery sites, particularly those that have been partially or badly excavated, contain no infants or children at all, and so the statistics quoted in this paper are, on a national scale, over-generous to children.

[11] The ages are taken as the maximum possible age for that skeleton at the time of death according to the excavator's report. Children who have been given a wider age range, for example, four to eight years of age, have been excluded from the "five and under" category. Given the accuracy of ageing infants from skeletal material (see Crawford, "Age Differentiation"), this method of grouping is most likely to represent true infants.

[12] V. I. Evison, *Dover: The Buckland Anglo-Saxon Cemetery,* English Heritage Archaeol. Rep. 3 (London, 1987).

[13] Ibid., 146. In the published catalogue, Grave 21 is described as a "6–12" year old. In Table XLIX (p. 200), five graves containing bodies described as "0–6" years old are given—this list does not include grave 21. Of these five burials, one (grave 20) seems to me to be a dubious infant given the adult-related grave goods included in the grave. Of the remaining four, the only positive "infant" is the "0–6" year old lying, unborn, in its mother's pelvis. There is obviously some conflict here between the excavator's comments and the information given in the grave catalogue.

[14] J. Collis, "Owlesbury (Hants) and the Problem of Burials on Rural Settlements," in R. Reece, ed., *Burial in the Roman World,* C.B.A. Research Rep. 22 (London, 1977), 26–35.

[15] B. Ayres, *Excavation within the North-East Bailey of Norwich Castle, 1979,* East Anglian Archaeol. Rep. 28 (Gressenhall, 1985).

[16] A. Boddington, "Raunds, Northamptonshire: Analysis of a Country Churchyard," *World Archaeol.* 18.3 (1987), 411–25.

[17] B. Kølbye-Biddle, "A Cathedral Cemetery: Problems in Excavation and Interpretation," *World Archaeol.* 17.1 (1975), 87–108.

[18] I am grateful to the Oxford Archaeological Unit for access to the site record ahead of publication.

[19] E. T. Leeds and R. J. C. Atkinson, "An Anglo-Saxon Cemetery at Nassington, Northants," *Antiquaries J.* 24 (1944), 100–29.

[20] According to the Prognostics, pregnant mothers were most likely to die on this day (Cockayne, *Leechdoms,* vol. 3, 147).

[21] V. I. Evison, *An Anglo-Saxon Cemetery at Alton, Hampshire,* Hampshire Field Club and Archaeol. Soc. Monograph 4 (Southampton, 1988).

[22] For the entire database population to which it was possible to assign an age, 73% were buried with grave goods (931 out of 1,271 burials). Of those aged five or under, 41% were buried with grave goods (fifty-four out of 130 burials). Of the total population, 17% were buried with only one grave good (210 out of 1,271 burials), while 27% were buried with five or more grave goods (339 out of 1,271 burials). Of those aged five or under, 22% (twenty-nine out of 130 burials) were buried with only one grave good, while only 4% were buried with five or more grave goods (five out of 130 burials).

[23] I have not classified knives as weapons, since they are frequently buried with infants, children and women as well as adult males, so would seem to qualify as useful tools for both sexes, rather than functioning as weapons. Of spears, shields and swords, none have been found in the burials of children whose maximum possible age does not exceed five, with the exception of one spear mentioned in the Oxford Archaeological Unit's pre-publication records of the Didcot and Berinsfield cemeteries. The spear ascribed to the infant here is more likely to have belonged to the adult with whom the infant was buried, and by whose head the spear rests. I know of no indisputable cases where an infant is buried with a spear, and the weight of evidence would suggest that any such burial, were it discovered, would be extremely unusual in the cemetery ritual and therefore outside of any normal mortuary behavior.

[24] I am grateful to Sonia Hawkes for access to unpublished material from the Finglesham excavation.

[25] Remarked upon by D. Wilson, *Anglo-Saxon Paganism* (London & New York, 1992), 57.

[26] C. L. Matthews, "The Anglo-Saxon Cemetery at Marina Drive, Dunstable," *Bedfordshire Archaeol. J.* 6 (1962), 23–26.

[27] A. L. Meaney and S. C. Hawkes, *Two Anglo-Saxon Cemeteries at Winnall,* Soc. for Medieval Archaeol. Monograph Series 4 (London, 1970).

[28] M. Magnusson and H. Palsson, trans., *Njal's Saga* (Baltimore, 1960).

[29] It should be noted that there is a strong tradition of superstitious attitudes towards children in Scandinavian sources. See particularly J. Pentikainen, *The Nordic Dead Child Tradition* (Helsinki, 1968), for a summary.

[30] See, for example, Gregory's reply to Augustine's question on the issue of infant baptism (B. Colgrave and R. Mynors, *Bede's Ecclesiastical History of the English People* [Oxford, 1969] i, 27—hereafter *H.E.*).

[31] S. C. Hawkes and C. Wells, "An Anglo-Saxon Obstetric Calamity from Kingsworthy, Hampshire," *Medical and Biological Illustration* 25 (1975), 47–51.

[32] C. K. Parikh, *Parikh's Text Book of Medical Jurisprudence and Toxicology* (Bombay, 1979), 159.

[33] Cockayne, *Leechdoms,* vol. 3, 67.

[34] W. W. Skeat, *Ælfric's 'Lives of the Saints,'* 2 vols., E.E.T.S. 76, 82, 94, 114 (London, 1881), 375. "Eac sum gewitlease wif farað to wega gelaetum and teoð heora cild þurh ða eorðan an swa deofle betaecað hi sylfe, and heora bearn. sume hi acwellað heora cild aerðam þe hi acennade beon oððe aefter acennednysse. þaet hi cuðe ne beon ne heora manfulla forligr amelded ne wurðe ac heora yfel is egeslec. and endleaslic morð þaer losað þaet cild laðlice haeðen and seo arleasa modor. butan heo hit aefre gebete." ("Likewise some witless women go to cross-roads and draw their children through the earth and thus commit themselves and their children to the devil. Some of them kill their children before they are born, or after birth, that they may not be discovered nor their wicked adultery be betrayed. Then the child perishes, a loathsome heathen, and the wicked mother, unless she do penance for it.")

[35] B. Thorpe, *The Homilies of Ælfric,* vol. 2 (London, 1884–86).

[36] Ibid., 175.

[37] The story was originally told by St. Gregory in his Dialogues (Dialogue II (24)), and was also repeated in the Irish collection *De Cura pro mortuis (Die irische Kanonensammlung,* [Collectio Canonum Hibernensis], ed. F. W. H. Wasserschleben, 2nd ed. [Lepzig, 1885], Bk. iv, chap. 3, p. 43). I am most grateful to E. O'Brien for drawing my attention to these references.

[38] *Vampires, Burial and Death: Folklore and Reality* (New Haven, 1988).

[39] *H.E.* iv,8. "Erat in eodem monasterio puer trium circiter non amplius annorum, Aesica nomine, qui propter infantilem adhuc aetatem in virginum Deo dedicatarum solebat cella nutriri ibique meditari. Hic praefata pestilentia tactus, ubi ad extrema pervenit, clamavit tertio unam de consecratis Christo virginibus, proprio eam nomine quasi praesentum alloquens 'Eadgyd, Eadgyd, Eadgyd', et sic terminans temporalem vitam intravit aeternum. At virgo illa, quam moriens vocobat, mox in loco quo erat eadem adtacta infirmitate, ipso, quo vocitata est, die de hac luce subtracta et illum, qui se vocavit, ad regnum caeleste secuta est."

[40] *H.E.* i, 27.

[41] F. L. Attenborough, *The Laws of the Earliest English Kings* (Cambridge, 1922), 37.

[42] B. Thorpe, *Ancient Laws and Institutes of England* (London, 1840), x, 417.

[43] B. Colgrave, *Felix's Life of St. Guthlac* (Cambridge, 1956), 76.

[44] P. Hull and R. Sharpe, "Peter of Cornwall and Launceston," *Cornish Studies* 13 (1986 for 1985), 5–53.

[45] Ibid., 27.

[46] Ibid.

[47] B. Colgrave, *The Life of Bishop Wilfrid by Eddius Stephanus* (Cambridge, 1927), 38.

[48] Suggested by R. Daniels in his paper, "The Anglo-Saxon Monastery at Hartlepool, England," presented to the First International Conference of Medieval Archaeology, York 1992.

[49] *Naturalis Historia* 7.16.72.

[50] In D. J. Watts, "Infant Burials and Romano-British Christianity," *Archael. J.* 146 (1989), 372–83.

[51] P. Hill, *Whithorn 3: Excavations 1988–90, Interim Report* (Whithorn, 1989–90). I am grateful to the excavator, Peter Hill, for drawing my attention to this interesting feature of the Whithorn cemetery and for his comments on the burials.

[52] Peter Hill has pointed out that the Northumbrian group of burials, including these children, has a higher rate of perinatal mortality than other phases of the cemetery use. He suggests that this Northumbrian group shows that infants have been excluded from the thirteenth to fifteenth century phase, perhaps because unbaptized children were excluded from the later phases.

[53] Barber, *Vampires,* 75.

CHAPTER 13

An Anglo-Saxon "Cunning Woman" from Bidford-on-Avon

TANIA M. DICKINSON

In the course of the last two decades, it has become increasingly accepted that Early Saxon burials must be studied within an explicit theoretical framework.[1] Yet, by its nature, excavation sometimes yields unusual material which requires, at least initially, empirical examination of both its immediate context and wider parallels in order to promote more general interpretation. While this paper is essentially an archaeological anecdote, its broader remit is to enhance the agenda for studying Anglo-Saxon burials and society. Its subject is a single female grave, grave HB2, which was found in 1971 at the extreme northern edge of the well-known mixed (inhumation and cremation) cemetery at Bidford-on-Avon, Warwickshire. Development work on the site in recent decades has added over twenty burials to the 200-plus recovered earlier in the twentieth century,[2] but their *ad hoc* discovery has unfortunately militated against prompt publication. So this paper also offers partial recompense for the delay, by highlighting what has proved to be one of the most interesting burials. Through her jewelry the woman in HB2 had links with "Anglian" England and post-Roman western Britain, while her burial assemblage may give us a glimpse of ritual and superstition within ordinary Anglo-Saxon communities.

HB2 was situated some 50m north of the 1922–23 excavations. The grave (fig.13.1) was orientated south–west to north–east and measured 2.02m in length, 1.20m in width and 0.22m in depth. It contained the skeleton of a young adult female lying extended on her back with her head turned to the right. The objects which were found on the body can be separated, initially, into three assemblages: (1) fastenings for clothing

HB 2

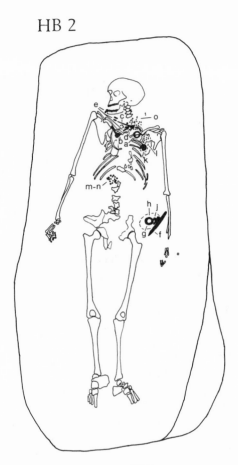

Fig. 13.1. Plan of Bidford-on-Avon grave HB2.

at the neckline; (2) a series of beads, pendants and allied items in the upper body area; and (3) objects from and/or with a bag, suspended by the left hip. Their identification, reconstruction and cultural context will be explored in turn, leading to an overall assessment of the date and significance of the burial.

FASTENINGS FROM THE CLOTHING

Two brooches fastened a bast-fiber dress at the shoulders—a small-long at the right (fig.13.2 b) and a penannular at the left (fig. 13.2 a). A woolen

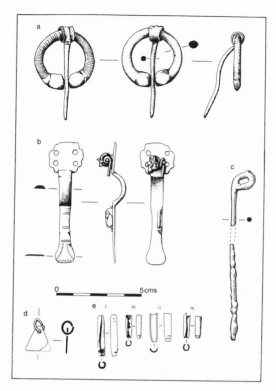

Fig. 13.2. Grave goods from HB2.

garment (?shawl) was gripped tightly under the neck by a simple iron pin (fig. 13.2 c). Neither of the brooches is closely datable. The small-long brooch belongs with types derivative (in Leeds' pre-war classificatory terms) from the "Cross Potent" form (subtype b or ci), though it also compares with examples of the "Cross Pattié" form.[3] It can currently be dated no more closely than to Hines's "Anglian English Migration Period," that is late fifth to late sixth century.[4] The penannular brooch occasioned my writing a paper redefining the entire group to which it belongs.[5] Such penannulars, now known as Type G1, are *the* characteristic metal-type of early post-Roman (late fourth to sixth centuries) western Britain: a particular abundance comes from the Rahtzian sites of Cannington and Cadbury Congresbury. At present, it would seem that those found in Anglo-Saxon burials, as here, were not made locally, but acquired individually from western sources, through the mechanism of exchange—familial or less personal—is unknown. My proposal that those brooches found in Anglo-Saxon contexts differed in formal details from those in "Celtic" contexts still holds interest, but two additions to my published corpus have weakened the statistical correlation (viz. Capton, Devon; St. Ewe, nr. Polmassick, Cornwall.)[6]

BEADS, PENDANTS AND OTHER ITEMS
FROM THE UPPER BODY

Glass and amber beads were found in two groups, fifteen just right of the lower vertebrae (four of amber, fig. 13.5 n, apparently lying centrally to a cluster of blue glass annular beads, fig. 13.4 m) and thirty-nine scattered about the neck and left shoulder. The latter consisted of sixteen amber beads (fig. 13.5 o,i–iv), mostly smaller than those by the vertebrae, while the glass beads were also small, including annular beads in plain red (fig. 13.5 o,v), green (fig. 13.5 o,vi) and yellow (fig. 13.5 o,vii), globular drawn and crimped beads, three with remnant gold foil (fig. 13.5 o,viii–ix), and fifteen minute green annular beads (fig. 13.5 o,x). If strung together, these would have given a minimum span of 142mm, sufficient to have hung between the two brooches. It is not clear, however, that the other beads came from this string or even from a second festoon, for they would give a minimum span of only 88mm. Arguably, given their location high on the waist, they ornamented a cord or textile belt: bead-belts have been proposed for the fifth-century "Princess's" grave at Zweeloo, Netherlands[7] and the sixth-century grave 48 at Andover Portway East, Hants.[8]

Several of the glass bead-types are Roman in origin, but continued in use through the Saxon period.[9] Amber beads in quantity, often associated, as here, with metal-in-glass beads, appear in the Upper Thames region, however, to be mainly a sixth-century feature.[10]

I come now to the most complicated part of the assemblage. A damaged triangular "spangle" on a ring (fig. 13.2 d) and four narrow copper alloy tubes (fig. 13.2 e) were found in the area of the neck and jaw, while a disc-shaped pendant (fig. 13.4 k) and twelve miniature bucket pendants (fig. 13.4 l) were found *underneath* the left shoulder blade, the latter towards the top of the shoulder, the former partly below the ribs. The "spangle" may simply have been part of the string of beads suspended from the brooches or adorned the pin, to which it was closest, for both contexts are typical for these little bits of metal which would have glinted and tinkled.[11] The costume jewelry may then have consisted of two brooches, bead-necklet, pin and perhaps a bead-belt. But the other items, I believe, belonged to a separate object, worn around the neck, which, like the bag-collection at the thigh, had a different role.

The four cylinders varied in length between 23mm and 11mm, and in diameter between 3mm and 5mm; one (fig. 13.2 e,i) had one end pinched together and all probably contained traces of leather. They should be compared not with metal beads, but with lace tags. Although most lace-tags come from seventh-century contexts, often from shoes, earlier instances are known, as at Sleaford grave 123, Lincs.[12] and Morning Thorpe grave 86, Norfolk, where also they were found with miniature bucket pendants.[13]

The twelve miniature bucket pendants from HB2 were made from three pieces of sheet metal each, a coiled strip for the wall, a disc for the base and a curved strip for the handle. They contained remains of spun animal-fiber thread, in one case lying flat across the base, and they were surrounded by a dark brown substance. This last had twill-weave cloth and leather lying in the same plane, with the buckets in contact with the textile surface. Soil from beneath the buckets contained bast fibers. At the time of excavation, they were thought to have been threaded on a strap, although they did not lie in a single row.

Miniature bucket pendants have entered the literature on Early Saxon England only relatively recently[14] and over twenty finds can now be catalogued. The majority are identical in proportions and construction to the Bidford examples. An unassociated set from Holywell Row, Suff. (Cambridge University Museum of Archaeology and Anthropology Z.7165e) and finds from two graves at Morning Thorpe, Norf. (92 and 415),[15] have two cut-out rectangular suspension loops at the top of the wall; an example from Eastry Updown grave 15, Kent, has a wire suspension loop.[16]

Bucket pendants occur most frequently either in ones or twos or in sets of seven to twelve, but occasionally there are up to twenty. They are placed either at the hip or, more commonly, at the neck or chest. In the former case, only one or two are involved, hung or carried with other items from the girdle (e.g. Sleaford grave 124/125, Lincs.;[17] Morning Thorpe grave 86, Norf.;[18] probably Nassington grave 31, Northants.[19]). In the latter case, the buckets may be associated with beads, forming part of a necklet. The single bucket from Eastry Updown made a centerpiece for a string of beads and wire rings, while larger sets could be strung between a pair of brooches, as seems to be the case at Nassington grave I,[20] or even form a separate festoon, as at Bergh Apton grave 34, Norf.,[21] and

West Heslerton grave 2F 13, N. Yorks. (where the buckets may have been on a cabled thread and the beads on a separate thread of coarse bast fiber).[22]

But the Bidford buckets are unlikely to have been part of the bead necklet, for they were away from the main cluster of beads, underneath the shoulder blade, and they were associated with leather. There are fortunately three other cases, all from sites in North and East Yorkshire, which prompt an alternative interpretation. In Driffield I, grave 22, seven buckets were found with "a quantity of dark matter resembling decayed leather" immediately underneath the chin. They were set on their ends in a row, apparently fastened together by a thin flat piece of bronze.[23] In fact, the latter was two rectilinear staples of the kind usually found as repairs for wooden vessels and could not have functioned as proposed. Maybe the contiguous bucket handles gave the impression of a single connecting band: the bucket pendants from Morning Thorpe grave 92, Norf., were also found upright and in a row, but in this case no organic material was observed and they were with the brooches and beads.[24] At the neighboring Driffield site of Cheesecake Hill, in grave 6, twenty buckets were found close together, erect and possibly upside down. They edged a crescentic or semicircular object made of (?covered by) thin sheet bronze, near to the upper edge of which lay a rod-like iron object, though it is hard to believe that this last item, given its form, was functionally related to the buckets.[25] Despite their vagueness, these reports suggest that miniature buckets could be mounted on a leather and/or metal object—a strap or, in the case of Cheesecake Hill, something like a bib or even a modern child's purse, hung round the neck. That bucket pendants were sewn, probably on leather, seems to be confirmed by conservation work currently being undertaken on one of several further grave finds from West Heslerton.[26]

The best explanation of the Bidford case, then, is that the buckets were either contained within a cloth-lined bag or were sewn on to the cloth exterior of a leather bag, bib or, less likely, strap. The four lace-tags thus become intelligible as the terminals of two pairs of leather thongs which fastened the bag or bib round the neck, allowing it to hang loosely over the chest. Since the buckets were found underneath the shoulder, it must be assumed that either the bag was put there deliberately or that in the course of burial it swung over the shoulder. If the bast fibers beneath the buckets come from the same garment as those on the small-long brooch, that is from the dress, then it must be further assumed that the bag also became caught up in its folds.

What might this object have been for? In England bucket pendants are found primarily in Anglian cultural contexts of the sixth century; the only certain exception is the later seventh-century find from Eastry Updown. Despite an apparent chronological gap, they would seem to be derived from comparable pendants found widely over Europe, especially central and eastern Europe, during the Late Roman Iron Age.[27]

It is widely assumed that these bucket pendants are amuletic and symbolic as much as ornamental. In England, though not on the Continent, they are the perquisite of women and (sometimes) girls. A simple iconographic explanation equates miniature buckets with full-size ones, and in turn to drink; they might then symbolize the role of alcohol socially and perhaps ritually (as a means of prophetic communication) and women's role within this.[28] If so, their occasional association with children, as at Driffield I, grave 22 and perhaps Eastry Updown grave 15, requires a special explanation (ascribed status?).

Such an interpretation might be endorsed by the fact that below the miniature buckets, either in the bag or sewn outside but lower down, was a convex disc pendant with central circular opening and triangular suspension hole (fig. 13.4 k). Such pendants can occur as ornaments on the vertical supports of "bronze"-bound wooden buckets (e.g. Higham, Kent; Haslingfield, Camb; Berinsfield grave 149, Oxon:[29] the pendants on the buckets from Fetcham, Surrey, and Rainham, Essex, are different in form, while those from Chesssell Down unassociated 28, Isle of Wight, should be compared with a different type of object altogether[30]). Disc pendants also occur separately, for example in a late fifth- or early sixth-century grave at Leagrave, Beds., and the sixth-century graves 3 and 22 at Chessell Down. Most are simply stamped and gilded or tinned, but that in Chessell Down grave 3, over twice the size of the rest, has a bar above the suspension loop decorated with crude zoomorphic terminals (not spirals, *pace* Arnold).[31] It compares with a pendant found at the hip of the skeleton in Petersfinger grave 19, Wilts.,[32] which not only has outward-facing animals crouching above the suspension loop, but a solid center bordered by Salin's Style I. In turn again, this is linked formally with much more substantial, quoit-shaped pendants from Cambridge and from Sweden and Finland (where they are taken to be belt-fittings).[33] So, while these discs could be suspended on buckets, they could also serve, variously, as ornamental claps on belts or as pendants from belts or even perhaps from necklets. In the last two cases their use might have been secondary and it is a moot point whether they retained any "bucket" connotation from a primary role, though the Bidford case raises that possibility. Either way, these disc pendants might have had an amuletic value, although Meaney does not include them in her lists.[34]

One objection to this interpretation is the presence of textile fragments *inside* the Bidford miniature buckets. I have noticed three other instances of this phenomenon: a single thread is visible within one of the buckets from Driffield I, grave 22, E. Yorks. (Hull Museum); fragments occur in all the buckets from Lakeneath, Suff. (Cambridge University Museum of Archaeology and Anthropology, 97.45), and quite distinctly rolled wads of material are in the unassociated set from Holywell Row, Suff. Textile may have been present in the buckets from West Heslerton grave 2F 13, and significant amounts of solder (more than would have been used in their construction?) have been positively identified.[35] On the Continent, a single specimen from a necklet from Bargensdorf, Mecklenburg, is said to have contained a kind of incense,[36] while wood occurred in an example from the Nydam bog deposit, although this might have been post-depositional.[37]

It is difficult to see how textile or other inclusions relate to buckets used as containers for drinks. A more pertinent analogy might be with seventh-century "thread boxes," which contain scraps of fabric or herbs and which are now regarded as items with symbolic and magical rather than utilitarian purpose.[38] While this may reinforce the interpretation of miniature buckets as amuletic, it suggests that the ideology which surrounded them was highly complex and unlikely to be easily explained. Nonetheless, the cloth and leather object with its ?bucket-pendant and miniature buckets emerges as a highly charged item, which may have conferred or represented specific magical or symbolic functions, and which by its very emblematic appearance may have signified a special role or status for its wearer.

OBJECTS FROM/WITH A BAG BY THE LEFT HIP

Between the left side of the pelvis and the lower left arm was "what looked like decayed leather." Centrally placed above this were two rings, one of heavy cast copper alloy, the other, smaller, of iron bearing remains of a twill-weave textile in animal fiber (fig. 13.3 g). The rings may have been inside a textile and (?) leather bag or suspended from or by it, or perhaps, given their position, acted as closures for its mouth. To the left of the rings there was an antler cone (fig. 13.3 j), which might also have been within the bag or suspended, and a small, worn, bronze disc-headed stud (fig. 13.3 h) which is more likely to have been within a bag.

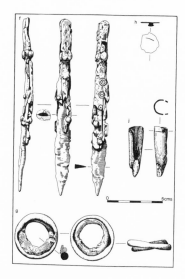

Fig. 13.3. Grave goods from HB2.

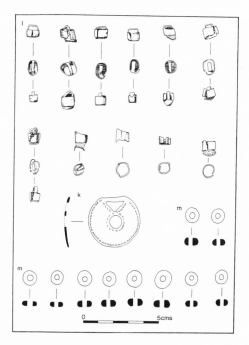

Fig. 13.4. Grave goods from HB2.

Such collections of objects hung from the girdle, with or without a bag, are an established feature of female graves throughout the Germanic world.[39] Their contents commonly seem to lack utilitarian purpose and regularly include particular types of material,[40] notably sets of rings,[41] old or fragmentary items, like the stud,[42] and something of animal substance.

The antler cone from HB2, which falls into the last category, is unparalleled. At first sight it might be compared with pyramidal or cylindrical bone pendants known from Migration Period Europe and, to a lesser extent, from England, which Werner argued were fertility amulets.[43] But those are not only different in shape but also perforated at their narrow not broad end. Could the Bidford cone symbolize a drinking horn, an object type which is otherwise apparently not represented among the stock of Anglo-Saxon amulets?[44] And, if so, does it reinforce the possible drinking symbolism of the miniature buckets and disc pendant? Or does it simply provide, through its material, a prophylactic or allusion to fertility or immortality?[45]

Finally, lying by the left side of the bag at the hip, but, given its length (156mm), probably suspended independently from the belt, was a knife (fig. 13.3 f). The iron blade and tang are quite unremarkable in form and size, being typical of this most common artifact from Anglo-Saxon graves. But attached to it and extending both beyond the tip of the tang and halfway down the blade was a bone handle: it was made from two strips of equine or bovine long bone, fastened together by four iron rivets, and was decorated with double bull's-eyes. The resultant proportions are unusual: in the hand it feels more like a scalpel than a traditional dinner or kitchen knife. It is like neither straightforwardly long-handled knives (e.g. those typical of late fourth-/early fifth century Lower Saxony,[46] or two from Sutton Hoo,[47]) nor like the specialized broad-tanged/stubby-bladed "Stanley" knife of tenth-century date from Canterbury.[48] I have found only one satisfactory parallel—from a sixth century burial at Pewsey, Wilts. (grave 27);[49] but while it matches the particular proportions, decoration and construction of the Bidford knife exactly, it does not advance understanding of the specific function or context of such knives.

CONCLUSION

Despite their number, the objects in Bidford grave HB2 are neither particularly sensitive chronologically nor obviously indicative of wealth: for example, the jewelry seems modest and there are no accessory vessels. The small-long brooch, amber beads, miniature bucket pendants and disc pendant together point to deposition probably within the first three-quarters of the sixth century.

Yet individually the objects have occasioned a substantial amount of comment, with a high proportion being identified as "amuletic," "symbolic" or rare in the corpus of Anglo-Saxon grave goods. Meaney has explored at some length the significance of bag-collections such as that found by the left hip of HB2.[50] The odd mixture of amulets and "junk" may be both the stock-in-trade and sign of women possessed of special powers. "Cunning women," as she calls them, would have practiced primarily beneficent magic, healing, protecting and divining the future. On the basis that graves with large bag-collections occur often only once per cemetery,[51] such women would have been special within their community, or at least their honoring in death was special.

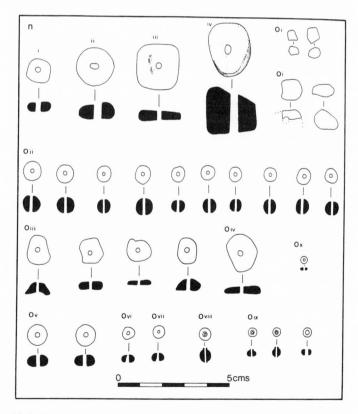

Fig. 13.5. Grave goods from HB2.

I would contend that grave HB2 at Bidford-on-Avon also represents such a "cunning woman." Indeed, the nature of her possessions adds strength to the argument, for it does not rest solely upon having an "amulet-bag." In particular, the amuletic and "badge-like" bib with its bucket pendants independently suggests that this was the grave of someone with special powers. Even the unusual "scalpel-like" knife might have been designed for specific uses associated with her craft. Discussion has thus not simply added another example to those advanced by Meaney, but materially bolstered her hypothesis. There is now a strong case for burials which may represent "cunning women" to be investigated on a systematic and contextual, rather than anecdotal, basis, and for themes alluded to here, notably the connection between women and drinking rituals, to be explored more fully.

ACKNOWLEDGMENTS

I am most grateful to Bill Ford (excavator), Helen MacClagan (Warwick Museum) and Sue Hirst (project director) for permission to publish grave HB2 ahead of the definitive site report. The following provided specialist help in identifying organic remains: Mark Norman, Leonard Willkinson, Gordon Hillman, Barbara Noddle and Robert Janaway. Sue Hirst drew figure 13.1 and Howard Mason drew the finds. The late Hayo Vierck generously supplied the references to bucket pendants from Bargensdorf and Nydam, and Dominic Powlesland and Sonia Hawkes have given me permission to refer to discoveries from their excavations at respectively West Heslerton and Eastry Updown.

NOTES

[1] This paper was originally written for Professor Philip Rahtz's *Festschrift*. Its opening paragraphs, which naturally contained personal allusions, have been rewritten by the author in a vein more suited to the present publication.

[2] J. Humphreys, J. W. Ryland, E. A. B. Barnard, F. C. Wellstood,and T. G. Barnett, "An Anglo-Saxon Cemetery at Bidford-on-Avon, Warwickshire," *Archaeologlia* 73 (1922–23), 89–116; J. Humphreys, J. W. Ryland, E. A. B. Barnard, F. C. Wellstood, and T. G. Barnett, "An Anglo-Saxon Cemetery at Bidford-on-Avon, Warwickshire: Second Report on the Excavations," *Archaeologia* 74 (1923–24), 271–88.

[3] E. T. Leeds, "The Distribution of the Angles and Saxons Archaeologically Considered," *Archaeologia* 91 (1945), 1–106, at pp. 22, 94.

[4] J. Hines, *The Scandinavian Character of Anglian England in the pre-Viking Period,* B.A.R. Brit. ser. 124 (Oxford, 1984), 10–13.

[5] T. M. Dickinson, "Fowler's Type G Penannular Brooches Reconsidered," *M.A.* 26 (1982), 41–68.

[6] Capton, Devon: M. Todd, "A Romano-Celtic Silver Brooch from Capton, near Dartmouth," *Proc. Devon Archaeol. Soc.* 41 (1983), 130–32; St. Ewe: R. Penhallurick, pers. comm.

[7] W. A. van Es and J. Ypey, "Das Grab der 'Prinzessin' von Zweeloo und seine Bedeutung im Rahmen des Gräberfeldes," in H-J. Hässler, ed., *Studien zur Sachsenforschung* 1, Festschrift für A. Genrich (Hildesheim, 1977), 97–126, at p. 123.

[8] A. M. Cook and M. W. Dacre, *Excavations at Portway, Andover,* Oxford University Com. Archaeol. Monograph 4 (Oxford, 1985), 37, 81.

[9] G. C. Boon, "Gold in Glass Beads from the Ancient World," *Brittania* 7 (1977), 193–207; C. M. Guido, *The Glass Beads of the Prehistoric and Roman Periods in Britain and Ireland* (London, 1978).

[10] T. M. Dickinson, "The Anglo-Saxon Burial Sites of the Upper Thames Region, and their Bearing on the History of Wessex, c. A.D. 400–700," unpub. D. Phil. thesis, University of Oxford, 1976.

[11] A. L. Meaney, *Anglo-Saxon Amulets and Curing Stones,* B.A.R. Brit. ser. 96 (Oxford, 1981), 189–90.

[12] T. M. Dickinson, *Cuddesdon and Dorchester-on-Thames, Oxfordshire: Two Early Saxon "Princely" Sites in Wessex,* B.A.R. Brit. ser. 1 (Oxford, 1974), 7–9.

[13] B. Green, A. Rogerson, and S. M. White, *The Anglo-Saxon Cemetery at Morning Thorpe, Norfolk I and II,* East Anglian Archaeol. Rep. 36 (Gressenhall, 1987), 59, fig. 322Giii.

[14] Meaney, *Anglo-Saxon Amulets,* 166–68; Hines, *Scandinavian Character of Anglian England,* 13, 306, Map 1.3.

[15] Green, Rogerson and White, *Anglo-Saxon Cemetery at Morning Thorpe,* figs. 326A and 456C.

[16] S. C. Hawkes, pers. comm.

[17] G. W. Thomas, "On Excavations in an Anglo-Saxon Cemetery at Sleaford in Lincolnshire," *Archaeologia* 50 (1887), 383–406, at 396.

[18] Green, Rogerson and White, *Anglo-Saxon Cemetery at Morning Thorpe,* 59.

[19] E. T. Leeds and R. J. C. Atkinson, "An Anglo-Saxon Cemetery at Nassington, Northants," *Antiquaries J.* 24 (1944), 100–29, at p. 110.

[20] Ibid., 113, 125, fig. 6.

[21] B. Green and A. Rogerson, *The Anglo-Saxon Cemetery at Bergh Apton, Norfolk I: Catalogue,* East Anglian Archaeol. Rep. 7 (Gressenhall, 1978), 27, figs. 30, 83Gi.

[22] D. Powlesland, pers. comm.

[23] J. R. Mortimer, *Forty Years' Researches in British and Saxon Burial Mounds of East Yorkshire* (London, 1905), 281, pl. CI, Fig. 802.

[24] Green, Rogerson and White, *Anglo-Saxon Cemetery at Morning Thorpe,* 61.

[25] Ibid., 291–92, pl. CXII, Fig. 873.

[26] D. Powlesland, pers. comm.

[27] Cf. K. Raddatz, *Das Thorsbjerger Moorfund: Gürtelteile und Körperschmuck,* Offa-Bücher 13 (Neumunster, 1957), 139; K. Godlowski, *The Chronology of the Late Roman and Early Migration Periods in Central Europe* (Krakow, 1970), 24, 39–40, 57, 84, pls. I,32, II,9, III,25, V,14, VII,22, IX,19; H. Schach-Dorges, *Die Bodenfunde des 3. bis 6. Jahrhunderts nach Chr. zwischen unterer Elbe und Oder,* Offa-Bücher 23 (Neumunster, 1970), 84, who cites only one example later than the fourth century; Meaney *Anglo-Saxon Amulets,* 167; Hines, *Scandinavian Character of Anglian England,* 13, relates them specifically to cultural contacts with southern Denmark and Schleswig-Holstein in the Migration Period.

[28] Meaney, *Anglo-Saxon Amulets,* 168; cf. M. J. Enright, "Lady with a Mead Cup: Ritual, Group Cohesion and Hierarchy in the Germanic Warband," *Frümittelalterliche Studien* 22 (1988), 170–203.

[29] Cf. C. J. Arnold, *The Anglo-Saxon Cemeteries of the Isle of Wight* (London, 1982), 59, where, however, the various formal types of discs and their contexts are confused.

[30] Discussed by Hines, *Scandinavian Character of Anglian England,* 226, 337.

[31] Arnold, *Anglo-Saxon Cemeteries of the Isle of Wight,* 20.

[32] E. T. Leeds and H. de S. Shortt, *An Anglo-Saxon Cemetery at Petersfinger, near Salisbury, Wilts.* (Salisbury, 1953), 13, pl. VI.

[33] A. Erä-Esko, *Germanic Animal Art of Salin's Style I in Finland* (Helsinki, 1965), 60, 68, 72, fig. 50, pl. IX,32.

[34] Meaney, *Anglo-Saxon Amulets.*

[35] D. Powlesland, pers. comm.

[36] W. Karbe, "Der Germanenfriedhof von Bargensdorf," *Zeitschrift Mecklenburg* 31 (1936), 8–10, at p. 9.

[37] C. Engelhardt, *Nydam Mosefund* (Copenhagen, 1865), 19.

[38] Meaney, *Anglo-Saxon Amulets,* 184–89.

[39] Dickinson, "Anglo-Saxon Burial Sites," 227–43; D. Brown, "The Significance of the Londesborough Ring Brooch," *Antiquaries J.* 57 (1977), 96–99; J. N. L. Myres, "Amulets or Small Change?" *Antiquaries J.* 58 (1978), 352; Meaney, *Anglo-Saxon Amulets,* 247–62.

[40] Meaney, *Anglo-Saxon Amulets,* 249–53.

[41] Ibid., 176–78.

[42] Ibid., 222–28.

[43] J. Werner, "Herkuleskeule und Donar-Amulett," *Jahrbuch des Römisch-Germanischen Museums Mainz* 11 (1964), 176–97; Meaney, *Anglo-Saxon Amulets,* 162–64.

[44] Meaney, *Anglo-Saxon Amulets,* 139.

[45] Ibid., 142.

[46] H. W. Böhme, *Germanische Grabfunde des 4. bis 5. Jahrhunderts zwischen Unterer Elbe und Loire: Studien zur Chronologie und Bevökerungsgeschichte* (Munich, 1974), 128.

[47] R. L. S. Bruce-Mitford, *The Sutton Hoo Ship Burial,* vol. 3.ii (London, 1983), 883–85.

[48] J. Graham-Campbell, "An Anglo-Scandinavian Ornamented Knife from Canterbury, Kent," *M.A.* 22 (1978), 130–33.

[49] K. Annable, pers. comm.

[50] Meaney, *Anglo-Saxon Amulets,* 249–62.

[51] Ibid., 249.

CHAPTER 14

Questioning the Monuments
Approaches to Anglo-Saxon Sculpture through Gender Studies

CAROL FARR

WHY GENDER STUDIES?

"Gender studies" represents a range of approaches based on acknowledgement of the social construction of gender, that is, a society's ideal of the masculine and feminine as opposed to strictly biological differences of the sexes.[1] Of what use can this approach be to modern understanding of Anglo-Saxon sculpture? After all, most of these monuments survive as rough fragments, often decorated with interlace patterns and vinescroll rather than human figures. Rarely are they connected with sites and circumstances of patronage permitting us more than some elusive shred of evidence to reveal their early medieval nature. Moreover, nearly all of them suffered uprooting from their original contexts centuries ago, and few examples can even be dated on any evidence beyond stylistic comparisons. How could gender studies possibly be of help in understanding works presenting such limited iconography and which are so alienated from their early medieval historic, social and physical context? Perhaps art historians and archaeologists should recognize the limitations and be content with recording and cataloguing the surviving fragments? These classification studies underpin the construction of stylistic and iconographic relations which may in turn allow ordering them within a chronological framework and creating other groupings, for example, "schools" or regional types.[2] Furthermore, could not those who desire understanding of the monuments' significance pursue their meaning exclusively in patristic and Anglo-Saxon exegetical texts, since the sculptures' most obvious contexts are ecclesiastic, probably most often monastic?

"No" to all the above questions can be supported on several levels, embracing critical and conceptual operations of argument and epistemology as well as considering the historic context and nature of the physical material. While questions of chronology and sorting out stylistic and iconographic relations remain important, gender studies, as well as other theoretical approaches, are valuable to the modern understanding of Anglo-Saxon sculpture precisely because it is so sparse of iconography and autonomous from early medieval contexts. Nearly all questions that seek classes of knowledge make assumptions, usually unstated. For example, questions on chronology may easily inhere a need for consistent, step-by-step developments, achieved in even phases at sites that in fact may have differed considerably in their production and use of stone sculpted monuments. Although gender studies or gender theory makes its own assumptions, discussed *infra,* it can open a critical window upon assumptions of continuities and point toward recognition of the often artificial network of connections twentieth-century scholars create to link surviving objects and texts.

Gender theory is also helpful because of the expectations of late-twentieth-century archaeology and art history. In the first half of this century both served the needs of collections and connoisseurs for curatorship and valuation (mainly by attribution and aesthetic judgement), but today education of a wider public about the uses and value, material and nonmaterial, of material culture for individuals and society determines most of the concerns of museum exhibitions, publications and university courses. The social questions brought forth by gender studies can broaden the doorway of interest and relevance, while simultaneously illuminating the differences of modern and past societies. This widening of the questions does not mean an increasing generalization, an oversimplification, but instead that the questions are directed at historically situated social contexts in which the sculpture was produced and viewed.

Seeing works of Anglo-Saxon sculpture as participants in a past society can lend a self-critical sharpening of questions about meanings of human figures carved on the monuments. Modern scholars are left with texts known during the early Middle Ages as their most informative interpretative source. Responses to questions of meaning, to be valid as attempts to understand meaning created in early medieval contexts, have to recognize that the texts construct ideals and ideology, and to a lesser degree provide straightforward information about experiences and perceptions of audiences. Gender studies concern the construction of ideals and as such orient thinking toward their recognition and analysis. Moreover, the relationship between a text and a work of art, even contemporary ones, is seldom direct. For example, a single text cannot operate as a kind of decoding system for a work of art. It is unlikely that an early medieval viewer ever stood next to a stone cross with a copy of one of Bede's exegetical works in hand to interpret the figures and scenes. Any viewer would have received verbal interpretative material within a larger system of belief, which included sermons, prayers, the rituals of the liturgy in its annular cycle, and, for monastic viewers, contemplative, private reading. Audiences perceived a visual image or monument's meaning within a cumulative mental and physical environment of written and oral texts, rituals of the liturgy and other images and objects.[3] Furthermore, the modern scholar's one-to-one equivalency of interpretations read in a patristic or early medieval text with a supposedly intended meaning of a visual image assumes a continuity between text and image in an homogenous context and, therefore, should be recognized as artificial. Even orthodox religious environments could vary from place to place and time to time: the culture of late seventh-century Jarrow was not identical with that of a later royal ecclesiastic center such as Repton.[4] Self-critical as well as precise questioning is crucial to the further understanding of the sculpture. Theoretical frameworks and approaches, such as gender theory or gender studies, encourage the modern scholar's awareness of assumed continuities and, if properly used, actually require recognition of simplistic connections modern academic audiences often create amongst the surviving objects and texts.

Moreover, on the historical level, some important questions relating to gender need consideration. Firstly, royal and aristocratic women were of acknowledged importance in the creation of the contexts—a christianized society, monasteries and pastoral efforts—within which the sculpted monuments were made and viewed. While one need look no farther than Bede's *Historia ecclesiastica* for accounts of Æthelthryth, Hieu and Hild, the names of many others are known from hagiography, charters and other manuscript sources.[5] How did these highly connected women fit into a world that was being shaped by a religion which on the one hand extended a universal ideal but simultaneously was intolerant of variant traditions and which constructed females as incapable of the same level of spiritual authority and experience as males? The gender construct was seen as deriving from divine authority, laid down in its essentials in Genesis in the Bible. It was articulated into its orthodox Christian form in the authoritative texts of the Church Fathers, based in part upon the highly prestigious writings of ancient Greek and Roman authors. Christian constructs of women as spiritually chaotic and concupiscent temptresses, for whom marriage was the primary social relationship, coexisted with what would seem to be conflicting secular aristocratic feminine ideals. These secular ideals seem to have accorded high-born women higher status than did Mediterranean, Christian constructs, allowing them a network of influence based upon their natural kinship over that of marriage. Moreover the negative origin myth was absent. The tension between Christian and secular ideals of kinship in Anglo-Saxon society, and the need for negotiation between the two, has already been noted. Following this observation, it seems likely that ideals of male and female also were negotiated over the period of christianization of Anglo-Saxon society.[6] Ecclesiastic centers and monasteries probably were the most important places for the writing of texts and creation of images and monuments which could have served this agenda within their general monastic and pastoral missions. Sculpted stone crosses and shrines, as public monuments, may have participated in this process of negotiation by presenting images of holiness which in turn could have been reinterpreted according to the needs of patrons and audience.

IMAGES OF WOMEN ON ANGLO-SAXON SCULPTURE

Asking about the situation of aristocratic women and the possible functions of sculpted monuments within christianization brings up another set of questions. Namely, why are there so few images of women on the sculpted monuments? Non-Marian female figures on surviving pre-Viking examples probably number fewer than ten. Nearly all of these come from sites for which we have no evidence of female or double monasteries or of female patrons, while major sites such as Whitby and Gloucester, for which evidence of double monastic communities is definite, have no surviving sculpted images of women.

It would seem logical to look to the negative constructs of patristic and early medieval exegesis to explain the scarcity of female imagery. In particular, the asceticism of the early Church, beginning with the writings of Paul, saw males as essentially rational and spiritual, females as irrational and physical. Monastic asceticism, therefore, saw the female in terms of the physical body, that which is to be denied or negated and from which spiritual wisdom is barricaded.[7] For this reason, exegesis—written by monastic, priestly males—can be seen as determining the exclusion of non-Marian female images from most sculpted monuments.

On the other hand, to accomplish the christianization of society as well as to express its own doctrines, the Church needed to promote universal ideals and to include more diverse audiences than monastic or ecclesiastic males. Such inclusive, egalitarian ideals exist alongside the negative female constructs in biblical and exegetical texts.[8] While these Christian texts remain an important element to our understanding of the sculpted figural images, they cannot tell the whole story by themselves.

Furthermore, it would be dangerous to assume that the ideals expressed in any text belonged to an homogeneous society of "Anglo-Saxons." One could take a cue from Michel Foucault's work on "discursive formations" and his criticism of continuity to question the assumption that gender has a continuity in the discourses of Anglo-Saxon society as they survive in the present.[9] In fact, the construct of gender was most likely discontinuous, more accurately described as constructs of gender. Probably a single, stable concept of male and female never existed, but instead gender would have been constructed as multiple, complex ideals that coexisted, shifted and changed over time. Joan Cadden, in her work on medical treatises and other writings on medieval sex differences, has pointed out the lack of theoretically or systematically determined late antique and early medieval concepts of male and female. Early medieval medical descriptions of male and female were often contradictory and not reconciled within a single text, and collections of diverse explanation, information and prescriptions seem to have been readily accepted.[10] Furthermore, material culture itself, such as burials and their furnishings, resists simple typologies and categorizations, especially categorization by gender.[11] It is important to think carefully about the difference that social classes, historic periods and other contexts can bring to bear on the construct of gender, which is not absolute but determined by social and historic processes.

The social context of monasteries was aristocratic, often royal, and their material culture reflects this high status: monastic and aristocratic secular sites sometimes appear identical.[12] Abbess Hild's double monastery—or community of male and female religious—was one of the most important centers of the pre-Viking period. Through the kinship relations of its abbesses it had royal connections and was the site of royal burials. Its role as an ecclesiastical training center and its prestige as the site of the synod of 664 indicate its influence and importance. The site of Hild's monastery, which Bede states was called Streanaeshalch, is now generally believed to have been at Whitby, although the relics of King Edwin described in the *Historia ecclesiastica* may have resided at a site near

York, now thought to be Strensall, a small town to the north of the city.[13] Even though its textual documentation may be relatively good for the period, Whitby presents two difficulties. Firstly, the site has never been satisfactorily excavated. Some question exists as to where the Anglo-Saxon monastery was sited: was it beneath the remains of the twelfth-century monastery, or was it somewhere nearby? Documentation of the finds from the first excavation, done in the 1920s, is poor, making as well as leaving much work to be done to build any accurate idea of what the early medieval buildings and burials were like.[14] Secondly, the sculpted material found so far at Whitby includes very little figural imagery, making it resistant to many traditional art historical methodologies.[15] A carved cross shaft survives at Hackness, one of Whitby's daughter communities, but this work presents considerable difficulties, discussed below. Nonetheless, Whitby and Hackness remain extremely important sites because of their documentation as double or women's monastic communities with royal connections. If properly excavated, their seventh- through mid-ninth-century remains could provide valuable material for the study of early Anglo-Saxon monastic spaces, especially those of women's communities, as recently explored for other, mostly later sites by Roberta Gilchrist.[16] They might also prove informative in connection with the material of high-status secular sites, shedding light on the material culture of royal and aristocratic females in the early Anglo-Saxon period to complement the historic and archaeological material of the later period.[17]

THE HACKNESS 1 CROSS SHAFT

The fragmentary cross shaft now known as Hackness 1 (pl. 14.1) was created and viewed within the late eighth- to ninth-century community of nuns, and probably brothers, at Hackness.[18] It is the only known early Anglo-Saxon sculpted stone monument which may present a non-Marian female image and bear an inscription of an Anglo-Saxon female name. Found as two fragments in 1848 in one of the outbuildings of Hackness Hall, its original position is unknown. It is usually dated from the late eighth century to the early ninth century, mainly on stylistic grounds, although the shaft's inscriptions could date from the late seventh or early eighth century with ornament and portrait being carved in a later phase.[19] If this dating is correct, the surviving monument post-dates the seventh-century context as described by Bede. The presence of its early medieval female audience is documented, and its concern with an

Pl. 14.1. Hackness 1, Cross Shaft, Face A, Fragments a, b (photo, author).

Anglo-Saxon holywoman can be considered probable because of its inscriptions. The faces of the shaft, as now reassembled are:[20]

Face A (pl. 14.1): The top fragment (a) bears a panel with a reverse S vinescroll over a square panel with a portrait. It is thought to represent a woman because the figure seems to have long hair and because two of the four inscriptions on the fragments mention the name "Oedilburga". On the base or bottom fragment (b), the tails, hind and forelegs of a pair of confronted profile animals are carved, below which is a pair of scrolls resembling an ionic capital.

Face B: On the top fragment (a), a Latin inscription reconstructed by Higgitt and Page as OEDILBURGA BEATA [AD S]EMPER and translated, OEDILBURGA BLESSED FOREVER . . . . A panel of plant scroll is below. On the bottom fragment (b), there is an inscription in cryptic characters resembling Ogham, with a panel of interlace below. The cryptic inscription has not been satisfactorily deciphered.

Face C: Fragment *a* is decorated with an upper panel of interlace; below this a fragment of a panel of letters that appear runic in form, followed by three and a half lines of hahal runes and three Latin capitals, ORA. The runic inscriptions have not been convincingly reconstructed and translated. No identifiable carving survives on the bottom fragment.

Face D: Higgitt and Page have reconstructed and translated the fragmentary words inscribed in Roman capitals on (*a*) as SEMPER, MEMORES, MATER AMANTISSIMA: . . . FOR EVER . . . MINDFUL . . . MOST LOVING MOTHER; the panel below has an S-shaped vinescroll. The bottom fragment has part of a panel with an inscription reconstructed and translated as RELIGIOSA ABBATISSA OEDILBURGA ORATE: RELIGIOUS ABBESS, OEDILBURGA, PRAY FOR

Besides their damaged state and the difficulty of the runic and cryptic inscriptions, study of the Hackness 1 stones is complicated by several questions. Firstly, their material—two separate pieces of poor quality local sandstone—separates them from the three other, smaller, possibly contemporary or older carved fragments from Hackness, which are made of much better sandstone, probably brought from near Whitby. The quality of the stone accounts for the lumpy effect and awkwardness of some of the carving and inscriptions.[21] Why was this conspicuous and probably fine monument made from such poor stone? Could choice of local stone have been determined by later organization of production, assuming that the shaft's inscriptions and surviving carvings are contemporaneous? Would the stone surface have been covered with painted stucco or plaster? Moreover, does the portrait represent the "Oedilburga" of the inscriptions? Other names may have been inscribed on the missing parts of the shaft, especially in view of the second person plural imperative, *orate,* of the inscription on face D of the bottom fragment. Also, it is possible that reconstruction of a static, unified monument would be erroneous. Could the lower stone have been a separate memorial stone? Other carved stones that possibly originated as grave markers, grave covers, or parts of a composite shrine (among other possible functions) survive at Hackness.[22] Could the lower stone have been added to an existing cross-shaft? Were parts of the stone recarved? One or several reworkings could explain the varying depths of relief from panel to panel. James Lang, moreover, has pointed out the resemblance of the inscriptions and their placement to those on late seventh and early eighth-century stone monuments at Whitby, in contrast to the deeply carved vinescroll and interlace panels, which are unlike any stone sculpture surviving from Whitby and would indicate a late eighth- or early ninth-century date. This inconsistency, combined with the possible intrusion of the final line of the inscription of fragment (a), face B, could indicate creation of the monument in two phases: first, it was a plain inscribed shaft, like those at Whitby, and later, around 800, the decorative panels were added.[23] The inscriptions, however, cannot be dated with certainty as several of their features are exceptional amongst pre-Viking monuments.[24] The modern viewer perhaps sees the remains of a mutable ensemble of carvings and inscriptions surviving from more than one period.

While these "discontinuities" complicate any vision of the shaft as a static unity, they are in themselves informative and signal to the thoughtful modern viewer the need for a self-critical approach that can cope with the shaft's apparent dynamics and ambiguities. But how much is known of the context at Hackness from the seventh through early ninth centuries? Bede tells of Hild's founding of Hackness in 680, the year of her death. His account of Begu, nun of Hackness, and her vision of Hild's ascent into heaven gives a glimpse of the community at prayer, venerating the dead abbess, and emphasizes its position in the hierarchy of the larger community centered at Streanaeshalch.[25] Otherwise no documentary evidence is known to survive until the eleventh century. Historians generally assume that Viking raiders wiped out the monastic community at Hackness as they did Whitby, probably about 867–869, although it seems its two churches, dedicated to St. Peter and St. Mary, became parish churches, possibly after the monastery came to an end.[26] By the 1060s, it was not included within the parochial embrace of the church of St. Mary at Whitby, which apparently was the major pastoral center for the later liberty of Whitby Strand, but by that date, Hackness had three churches, indicating its pastoral importance.[27] This is much more than is known today about most of the sites of early Anglo-Saxon sculpture, but a gap in historical documentation still exists for the later eighth and ninth centuries when possibly the inscriptions and probably the portrait, vine-scroll, and other decoration were carved.

The monument itself, however, is an important survival of this context. Its inscriptions suggest some important connections. The "Oedilburga" mentioned in three of them could have been Ethelburga, abbess of Lyminge, whose marriage to Edwin of Northumbria not only made her a relative of Hild of Whitby but also had brought about the conversion of King Edwin and the Northumbrians.[28] King Edwin's relics were almost certainly located within Whitby's larger monastic community, where they would have been tangible and important reminders of its royal, dynastic connections.[29] The Hackness cross shaft, therefore, may have stood within Whitby's surviving eighth- and ninth-century spiritual and political network. The Latin inscriptions could have served to affirm the connections, as well as to offer powers of intercession to monastic and lay audiences.

The runic and cryptic inscriptions must have had a significance for the audience, although modern epigraphers and experts on ogham and runic inscriptions despair of reading them and consider their obscurity exceptional.[30] Because these inscriptions are difficult or impossible for modern scholars to decode, they are usually assumed to indicate the presence of a small, highly learned, most likely clerical audience within the community at Hackness, or that their deliberate obscurity was meant to exclude all but God from their readership.[31] A clerical audience would mean a male audience. One wonders if the inscriptions would necessarily exclude most of the community and, considering that the Latin inscriptions may address Oedilburga as intercessor, the holywoman herself. Modern scholarship assumes, probably correctly, an ecclesiastic context for highly developed literacy, but evidence exists, especially from Irish, Pictish and Scandinavian contexts, for the use of coded systems such as *hahal* runes and ogham in high-status lay contexts.[32] Undoubtedly such inscriptions spoke of authority and prestige in a general way to those unable to read them, but most often messages inscribed on the stone monuments seem to address a reader, even requiring prayer from reader and listener.[33] Why would the Hackness 1 cross shaft, which seems to address either a human audience or the community's intercessor with its Latin inscriptions, exclude most or all of that audience or community with an accompanying and exceptionally obscure inscription? Does the cryptic inscription represent an assertion of a hierarchy of spiritual authority and/or learnedness within the community which may have excluded women from its apex? These are important questions, but at this point they are all but impossible to answer with any confidence.

The shaft's decoration and portrait could also have participated in the construction of aristocratic and ecclesiastic ideals. Lang has pointed out the resemblance of the combination, on face C, of inscription and carved interlace with Whitby Cross 21, suggesting production by one hand.[34] Could the likeness have served as a reminder to the Hackness community, or anyone who had been to the monastery at Whitby, of its position within an important monastic family? The sensitively carved plant scrolls with the carefully oriented planes of their backgrounds may also speak of high status in their fine quality, as well as their classicism emulated from the court culture of Charlemagne and the Mercians, ultimately an ideological style expressing alignment with centralized Christian authority. These are, again, difficult questions to answer because, as Cramp has pointed out, for the surviving examples of sculpture, artistic and political networks do not coincide neatly.[35]

THE HACKNESS 1 PORTRAIT

The badly damaged portrait image, moreover, seems to construct its (probably) female subject along the same, conventional lines as images of apostles, evangelists and male saints carved on cross shafts dated to the late eighth and early ninth century. It resembles portraits on some other cross shafts in its frontality and enclosure within a simple panel space, although without the enclosing architectural frame of columns, capitals and arch found at Otley (pl. 14.2).[36] Most surviving portrait busts on cross shafts are placed within arched panels, but square panels without interior arches occur on cross shafts at Hoddom and Ilkley (pl. 14.3), where zooanthropomorphic evangelists are represented.[37] This type resembles examples in manuscript art, particularly the evangelist portraits in the Book of Cerne.[38] Of the examples of sculpted relief portrait busts where the lower part of the panels survive, nearly all the figures hold books, while examples at Eyam and Bakewell hold objects

Pl. 14.2. Otley 1, Cross, Face C3 (photo, author).

Pl. 14.3. Ilkley, Cross Shaft (photo, S. M. Alexander).

usually identified as horns or musical instruments.[39] Although the Hackness panel's lower part has been badly damaged, it seems probable that this figure, too, held a book. A veiled, apparently female figure holding a book survives at Breedon (pl. 14.4), and another possible female example of this type may be seen in the very damaged relief portrait head on the Collingham shaft.[40] In a more specific image at Bradbourne in the Peak District (pl. 14.5), a bird perches on the shoulder of a book-bearing male, perhaps identifying the figure as St. Gregory or another exegete inspired by the Holy Spirit.[41] None of the surviving portrait busts are accompanied by identifying inscriptions. The stone relief busts, however, almost certainly are based on the author and evangelist portrait tradition of book art and, therefore, probably refer to the divine authority of orthodox texts, an association which the image of Christ on the Rothbury 1 cross shaft, discussed below, touches upon.[42] The reference to divine authority is probably the reason why female figures, including the Virgin, are rarely depicted holding books in the manner of evangelists or other authors in early medieval art.[43] Whether or not the portrait figure on the Hackness 1 shaft held a book, it seems to have represented a kind of mnemonic or memorial image of a holy person, in the manner of portraits of the powerful and holy innate to the culture of Christianity from its birth within the Roman Empire.[44] The vocabulary of the inscriptions, with references to the eternal, venerated holywoman ("Oedilburga blessed forever"), who is the head of a spiritual family ("most loving mother"), and whose name is called upon as an intercessory figure ("religious abbess, Oedilburga, pray for . . .") is closely tied to the memorialization of the long-dead as well as to Bede's praise of founding abbesses.[45] Taken together, the inscriptions and portrait, assuming they refer to the same person, could represent promotion of the spiritual authority of the community, expressing the intercessory powers of Hackness's venerable abbesses and possibly a spiritual family history of holywomen.

Does the Hackness shaft promote the holiness and authority of an abbess as a sanctity undistinguished from and equal to that of the evangelists and church fathers? It seems unlikely, although impossible to say for sure, that the late eighth- and ninth-century community at Hackness would have accorded Oedilburga or any other holywoman such status. Could the Hackness portrait, as a memorial or iconic image, have represented an elaboration on the idea of the evangelist portrait, as the Breedon relief bust may have? One may think of the variations in other sculpted examples, that is the relief busts holding horns or what appear to

Pl. 14.4. Breedon Wall Panel (photo, author).

Pl. 14.5. Bradbourne, Cross Shaft (photo, author).

be musical instruments, which probably depict musicians of earthly and heavenly liturgy. Could portrait images depict women as reciters or performers of texts rather than as authors?

While Aldhelm wrote of virgin saints as athletes and victors, the image of holywomen as members of the heavenly chorus of virgins had been established in Anglo-Latin literature by the time of Bede, who created an image of Abbess Æthelthryth as a harpist singing to Christ, the bridegroom.[46] The category of virgin saints appears in litanic prayers in late eighth- and early ninth-century manuscripts from Ireland and Anglo-Saxon England, including the Stowe Missal and Book of Cerne.[47] In the Benedictional of Æthelwold, dated 963–84, St. Æthelthryth and six of the figures in the Choir of Virgins, including Æthelthryth and Mary Magdalene, hold books.[48] In eleventh-century Anglo-Saxon art, female saints holding books sometimes accompany the Virgin, for example in the canon tables of two early eleventh-century gospel books at Cambridge, and the virgins in the choirs of saints within the frame of the incipit of the Gospel of John in the Grimbald Gospels, also early eleventh-century, hold books.[49] All of these tenth- and eleventh-century examples are full-length figures, not portrait busts.[50] The choirs of virgins in later examples are participants in a heavenly or apocalyptic liturgy, thus they are part of the body of righteous who are eternal witnesses of God.[51] Books can be indicators of testimony to divine truth, as seen in Crucifixion images of the later Anglo-Saxon period, where St. John holds or writes in a book or scroll. In at least two of these scenes, in the Arundel Psalter and the Weingarten Gospels, the Virgin Mary also holds a book.[52] In the Weingarten Gospels, she witnesses further by touching Christ's wound. Aldhelm and Ælfric knew of the patristic tradition which privileged John and Mary as witnesses because of their virginity, and it is probably as reminders of their position at the head of the litany of virgins that they are so often depicted beneath the cross in the frontispieces of eleventh-century Anglo-Saxon manuscripts. As virgin witnesses next to the most important virgin human, Christ, they are the greatest intercessors.[53]

Does a portrait of a woman holding a book or at least a female portrait resembling the evangelist or author type depict a virgin mother abbess who has a place in the choir of virgins, an intercessor? While the evidence upon which this suggestion is based comes from wide-ranging sources, some of them not exactly close to late eighth-century Hackness, the veiled portrait bust at Breedon, Bede's image of Æthelthryth, and the later Anglo-Saxon full-length female figures holding books could point to development of images of virgin witnesses and intercessors, based on the author portrait tradition, over the eighth century and continuing in later Anglo-Saxon art under influences from the Continent. Even if the inscriptions of Hackness 1 predate the portrait, the monument could represent an accretion of textual and visual responses to needs for construction of a holy virgin mother abbess and intercessor.[54] Such a series of responses could be seen as growing from diverse constructs and ideals, reinterpreted and adapted by makers and audience.

DIVERSE IDEALS AT ROTHBURY, ST. ANDREW AT AUCKLAND, AND RUTHWELL

Other examples of images of women carved on early Anglo-Saxon stone monuments seem to express a range of constructs and ideals for female sanctity. Besides the Hackness portrait and inscriptions, non-Marian female figures survive in examples from Rothbury and St. Andrew at Auckland, as well as at Ruthwell.[55]

Jane Hawkes has recently interpreted one of the scenes on the Rothbury 1 cross shaft fragment as the Raising of Lazarus, identifying the female figure who turns away from the miracle as Martha, the sister of Lazarus.[56] In the account of the miracle in the Gospel of John (11:1–44), Christ, aware of Lazarus's illness, waits until the brother's death before returning to Bethany. When he arrives, Martha proclaims her faith that her brother would not have died had Jesus been present. In the ensuing dialogue, she further proclaims her faith in the final resurrection of the dead and, prompted by Jesus' statement, "I am resurrection and life . . . no one who is alive and has faith shall ever die," her belief that he is the Son of God. During the actual miracle of the raising of Lazarus, Jesus weeps silently but prays aloud to God the Father, explaining that he speaks only that those present would believe that "you did send me." Hawkes points out Martha's visual prominence in the sculpted scene and relates this feature to Augustine's commentary in which he interprets Martha as the faith necessary for salvation and eternal life.[57] Hawkes relates Martha's reception of Christ's words confirming eternal life through faith in the Word to the portrait of Christ on the opposite side of the cross shaft, depicting him pointing a prominent finger to the gospel book he holds. The pointing finger reappears in the Lazarus scene, touching the eyebrow of "sleeping" Lazarus; reception of the word brings life and salvation to the faithful. Hawkes explains Martha's position turned away from Christ as resulting from the confined vertical space of the top of the shaft and the pose of the figure's probable Early Christian model.

Placing the scene in the context of Northumbrian ecclesiastic and monastic culture, one may find further reasons for her backturned pose.

Bede refers to the story briefly in his exegesis on the Song of Songs.[58] There he emphasizes Christ's silence during the story, alluding to the idea that he did not prove faith in salvation through "vision of the eyes" or "something heard with the ears": faith and salvation operate on a spiritual level. Martha turns away possibly because the relief's subject is not the miracle itself but faith in the salvation that is the deeper meaning of the resurrection of Lazarus. Martha is shown to possess the inner spiritual wisdom and rationality of faith. She receives the Word on a non-material, interior level, not through physically sensing the miracle. The image may then depict a female figure as a receiver of spiritual wisdom.

The cross shaft at St. Andrew, Auckland, dated late eighth century, has long been considered to present a female figure, usually interpreted as Ecclesia, in the panel above the Crucifixion scene.[59] Judith Calvert has argued that this figure in fact represents an angel, but she has reinterpreted the Crucifixion scene as the martyrdom of St. Andrew. The two damaged figures over the arms of the cross carved in the panel below depict Stratocles and Maximilla, brother and wife of the proconsul who ordered Andrew's martyrdom. Converts of Andrew, they removed his body from the cross.[60] Calvert's interpretation is convincing and means that a female witness to Andrew's martyrdom is portrayed on the stone cross at Auckland. Maximilla would then represent a female witness to spiritual truth, a woman, like Martha, possessing spiritual rationality.

Non-Marian images on the shaft and panel below the head of Ruthwell Cross, taken together, seem to construct holy women as triumphant and prominent participants in monasticism, but there the images locate them below the authority of a male, sacerdotal ideal.[61] The panel placed at the top of the cross shaft showing two women facing each other may depict Martha and Mary as "Worthy Women" in a way that refers to the image of Mary Magdalene below as well to depictions of the Visitation. The associations construct them as humble virgins, playing as well upon negative Christian female constructs of the chaotic and concupiscent woman, referred to in the ambiguously double-sided image of Mary Magdalene anointing the feet of Christ. It is quite possible that the "Worthy Women" panel was understood by its early medieval audience to have been connected with the image of Mary Magdalene below as a kind of qualifier. Mary Magdalene the *meretrix* (prostitute) reverses into *merita* (worthy woman or lady) by the virtues of humility and chastity. The paired female figures, however, are qualified by the male pairs of the healing of the man born blind and Paul and Anthony in the desert which display the superior sanctity of miracles and priesthood.

CONCLUSION: FRAGMENTING THE MONOLITH

There seems to be no indication amongst the surviving images and inscriptions from the Hackness shaft of the venerated abbess's subordination to sacerdotal ideals exclusive to constructs of male holiness. This would disrupt any assumed unified gender construct shared with the Ruthwell cross, where images acknowledging the holiness and importance of ecclesiastical women are placed alongside a gendered imagery which subordinates them. But Ruthwell's images of women probably belong to an earlier period or at least predate the portrait and ornamental carving of the Hackness shaft. Is the difference due to chronological context in addition to the context of art traditions and/or ecclesiastic agendas active in each place? One could point to the Sandbach cross shafts, works roughly contemporary with Hackness in which empanelled images of single full-length figures are presented alongside more complex narrative scenes.[62] These are surviving examples which show that varied subjects, like earlier ones at Ruthwell, could be combined on one monument with single figures in a late eighth- to early ninth-century context. The need to construct ideals of sanctity and to relate sanctity to theologically relevant and socially understandable issues such as the ontology of gender and how such concepts order human society determines both invention of new kinds of images and the use of visual and textual traditions on public monuments such as carved stone crosses. The examples discussed here are all fragments that survived by chance, and the fact that modern understanding of them will never be complete has to be acknowledged. Broader questions, like those relating to gender ideals, can help make other questions of political and artistic networks evoke richer responses from the monuments.

NOTES

[1] See, for example, M. Foucault, *Herculine Barbin: Being the Recently Discovered Memoirs of a Nineteenth Century French Hermaphrodite,* R. McDougall, trans. (New York, 1980); M. W. Conkey and J. D. Spector, "Archaeology and the Study of Gender," in M. B. Schiffer, ed., *Advances in Archaeological Method and Theory 7* (New York, 1984), 1–38; J. K. Conway, S. C. Bourque, and J. W. Scott, *Learning about Women: Gender, Politics, and Power*

(Ann Arbor, 1989); E. Showalter, *Speaking of Gender* (New York, 1989); M. W. Conkey and J. M. Gero, "Tensions, Pluralities, and Engendering Archaeology: An Introduction to Women and Prehistory," in J. M. Gero and M. W. Conkey, eds., *Engendering Archaeology: Women and Prehistory* (Oxford, 1991), 3–30; K. S. Lesick "Re-engendering Gender: Some Theoretical and Methodological Concerns on a Burgeoning Archaeological Pursuit," and R. Gilchrist, "Ambivalent Bodies: Gender and Medieval Archaeology," in J. Moore and E. Scott, eds., *Invisible People and Processes: Writing Gender and Childhood into European Archaeology* (London, 1997), 31–41 and 42–58.

[2] For the methodological model, see R. J. Cramp, "General Introduction to the Series," in R. Cramp, *Corpus of Anglo-Saxon Stone Sculpture,* vol. 1, *County Durham and Northumberland* (Oxford, 1984), ix–l; or R. Cramp and R. N. Bailey, *Corpus of Anglo-Saxon Stone Sculpture,* vol. 2, *Cumberland, Westmorland and Lancashire North-of-the-Sands* (Oxford, 1988), ix–l. (Hereafter *Corpus 1, Corpus 2.*)

[3] A good discussion of this verbal and visual matrix in Anglo-Saxon England and early medieval Ireland is É. Ó. Carragáin, *The City of Rome and the World of Bede,* Jarrow Lecture 1994 (Jarrow, 1995); another good example, although centred on the trumeau in the Abbey of Sainte-Mairie at Souillac: M. Camille, "Mouths and Meanings: Towards an Anti-Iconography of Medieval Art," in B. Cassidy, ed., *Iconography at the Crossroads: Papers from the Colloquium Sponsored by the Index of Christian Art, Princeton University, 23–24 March 1990* (Princeton, 1993), 43–57.

[4] On Jarrow, see R. J. Cramp, "Jarrow Church," *Archaeol. J.* 133 (1976), 220–28; M. B. Parkes, *The Scriptorium of Monkwearmouth and Jarrow,* Jarrow Lecture 1982 (Jarrow, 1982); on Repton, H. M. Taylor and J. Taylor, *Anglo-Saxon Architecture,* vol. 2 (Cambridge, 1965) 510–16; D. Hinton, *Archaeology, Economy and Society: England from the Fifth to the Fifteenth Century* (London, 1998), 47–52, 54, 55, 60, 70, 94; M. Biddle and B. Kjølbye Biddle, "The Repton Stone," *A.S.E.* 14 (1985) 233–92; P. Stafford, *The East Midlands in the Early Middle Ages* (Leicester, 1985), 55–56, 101–02, 106–08, 110–11.

[5] Æthelthryth, Hieu and Hild in Bede, *Historia Ecclesiastica* iii.8, 24, 25, iv,19, 20, 23, v.24, trans. B. Colgrave, ed. J. McClure and R. Collins (Oxford, 1969), 151, 154, 202–07, 210–14, 292 [hereafter *H.E.*]; Ælfflæd in Eddius, *The Life of Bishop Wilfrid* XLII, LX, ed. and trans. B. Colgrave (Cambridge, 1927), 88–89, 128–133; Osric's 675 charter for Berta, the Frankish founding abbess of Bath, and her successor, the Anglo-Saxon Beorngyth, S 51, see P. Sims-Williams, *Religion and Literature in Western England, 600–800* (Cambridge, 1990), 56–57, 111–12, 120; on the late seventh- and early eighth-century St. Mildburg, abbess of Wenlock, her sister Mildthryth, abbess of Minster-in-Thanet,

ibid., 42, 48–50, 98, 110–11, 118–19, 122, 243–44; D. Rollason, *The Mildrith Legend: A Study in Early Medieval Hagiography in England* (Leicester, 1982), and on the abbesses of Gloucester: Cyneburg, Eadburg, and Eafe, Sims-Williams, *Religion and Literature,* pp. 122–25.

⁶ S. Hollis, *Anglo-Saxon Women and the Church: Sharing a Common Fate* (Woodbridge, 1992), 5–13, 15–45; see also the criticisms of C. Lees and G. Overing, "Birthing Bishops and Fathering Poets: Bede, Hild, and the Relations of Cultural Production," *Exemplaria* 6 (1994) 35–65; and B. Sawyer, review of Hollis, Anglo-Saxon Women, in *J. of Ecclesiastical Hist.* 45 (1994) 119–21; on the tension between aristocratic and monastic concepts of family, see H. Mayr-Harting, *Bede, the Rule of Saint Benedict, and Social Class,* Jarrow Lecture 1975 (Jarrow, 1976).

⁷ M. Harlow, "Female into Male, Won't Go! Gender and Early Christian Asceticism," in Moore and Scott, *Invisible People,* 169–177. Harlow (p. 171), cites I Corinthians 11:3–7.

⁸ See D. B. Martin, *The Corinthian Body* (New Haven, 1995), 32, 94–96, 232–33, on Paul's use of the body image to invert status or social hierarchies while preserving the subordination of women as lower points on the spectrum of a construct described as a single gender which was male. On the "one-sex" model of the ancient world, which constructed women as imperfect men, see T. Lacquer, *Making Sex: Body and Gender from the Greeks to Freud* (Cambridge, MA, 1990), 5–6.

⁹ M. Foucault, *The Archaeology of Knowledge,* trans. A. M. Sheridan Smith (London, 1972; repr., 1992), 3–71.

¹⁰ J. Cadden, *Meanings of Sex Difference in the Middle Ages: Medicine, Science, and Culture* (Cambridge, 1993), 47–53.

¹¹ For example, the difficulty of associating types of burial goods with male or female individuals; see S. J. Lucy, "Housewives, Warriors and Slaves? Sex and Gender in Anglo-Saxon Burials," in Moore and Scott, *Invisible People,* 150–68.

¹² For example, Glastonbury Tor, Tintagel, Burrow Hill, Brandon; see Hinton, *Archaeology,* 15, 57.

¹³ P. Rahtz, "Anglo-Saxon and Later Whitby," in L. R. Hoey, ed., *Yorkshire Monasticism: Archaeology, Art and Architecture, from the Seventh to Sixteenth Centuries* (Leeds, 1995), 1–11, at pp. 1–2; L. A. S. Butler, "Church Dedications and the Cults of Anglo-Saxon Saints in England," in L. A. S. Butler and R. K. Morris, eds., *The Anglo-Saxon Church: Papers on History, Architecture, and Archaeology in Honour of Dr. H. M. Taylor* (London, 1986), 44–50, at pp. 49–50; R. J. Cramp, "A Reconsideration of the Monastic Site of Whitby," in R. M. Spearman and J. Higgitt, eds., *The Age of Migrating Ideas: Early Medieval Art in Northern Britain and Ireland* (Edinburgh & Stroud, 1992), 64–73, at pp. 64–65.

[14] R. J. Cramp, "Analysis of the Finds Register and Location Plan of Whitby Abbey," in D. Wilson, ed., *The Archaeology of Anglo-Saxon England* (London, 1976), 453–58; Rahtz, "Anglo-Saxon," 5–9; M. Johnson, "The Saxon Monastery at Whitby: Past, Present, Future," in M. Carver, ed., *In Search of Cult: Archaeological Investigations in Honour of Philip Rahtz,* (Woodbridge & Rochester, 1993), 85–89. See also J. Hawkes's contribution in this volume.

[15] See Hawkes, in this volume.

[16] R. Gilchrist, *Gender and Material Culture: the Archaeology of Religious Women* (London, 1994); see also discussion of historical and literary material for the Anglo-Saxon periods by Hollis, *Anglo-Saxon Women,* especially 75–150, 243–300.

[17] See P. Stafford, *Queen Emma and Queen Edith: Queenship and Women's Power in Eleventh-Century England* (Oxford, 1997), 65–96, 97–161, especially 143–159; also, Hollis's discussion of textual material covering the earlier period, in *Anglo-Saxon Women,* 65–74, 151–242.

[18] A. H. Thompson, "The Monastic Settlement at Hackness," *Yorkshire Archaeol. J.* 27 (1924), 388–405, at pp. 388–89, points out Bede's use of the phrase *dormitorium sororum* and masculine plural nominative *isti* instead of the feminine plural (*istae*), implying the presence of men, in *H.E.* iv,23.

[19] J. Lang, *Corpus of Anglo-Saxon Stone Sculpture,* vol. 3, *York and Eastern Yorkshire* (Oxford, 1991), 140 (hereafter *Corpus* 3). The complications are discussed *infra*.

[20] The following description and reconstructions of the inscriptions are based on J. Higgitt and R. I. Page, "Hackness," in *Corpus* 3, 136–39, and illustrations 454–470. See also R. Page, *An Introduction to English Runes* (London, 1973), 64, 66; P. Grosjean, "Un fragment d'obituaire anglo-saxon du VIIIe siècle, naguère conservé à Munich, Appendix I: l'inscription latine de Hackness," *Analecta Bollandiana* 79 (1961), 340–43.

[21] Higgitt, Page, and Lang, in *Corpus* 3, 135, 138, 139, 141–42; Lang dated Hackness 2 ("part of a grave marker") as late seventh to eighth century, based on comparisons of its incised cross with the free-standing crosses from Whitby, and 3 ("part of grave-cover or impost") late seventh to early eighth century, on comparisons of the animal ornament with that of the Franks Casket, Book of Durrow, Cologne *Collectio Canonum,* and a carved stone fragment from Monkwearmouth (9A). Lang dates Hackness 4, "architectural fragment (?)" or part of a composite shrine, as "eighth century," based on Winterbotham's comparisons with ninth-century metalwork from Whitby and Little Howe, North Riding. See J. J. Winterbotham, "An Anglo-Saxon Carved Stone from Hackness, North Yorkshire," *Antiquaries J.* 62 (1982), 357–58.

[22] *Corpus* 3, 141–42.

[23] Ibid., 139.

[24] Higgitt, in *Corpus* 3, 138.

[25] Bede, *H.E.* iv,23, 213–14.

[26] Thompson, "The Monastic Settlement," 389; J. J. Winterbotham, *Hackness in the Middle Ages* (Hackness, 1985), 4, 9–10; A. Thacker, "Monks, Preaching and Pastoral Care in Early Anglo-Saxon England," in J. Blair and R. Sharpe, eds., *Pastoral Care Before the Parish* (Leicester, 1992), 137–70, at pp. 143–45, on Whitby's eleventh-century role as "the administrative centre of a major estate."

[27] Thacker, "Monks," 144, 145.

[28] Higgitt, in *Corpus* 3, 138–39; Grosjean, "Un fragment," 341; Winterbotham, 8.

[29] Rahtz, "Anglo-Saxon and Later Whitby," 1–2; Butler, "Church Dedications," 49–50. See also R. K. Morris, *Churches in the Landscape* (London, 1989), 124, on the head of King Edwin placed in the chapel of St. Gregory, in St. Peter's, York, in Bede, *H.E.* ii,20.

[30] See the comments of Higgitt and Page, in *Corpus* 3, 136–39. The recently published reconstruction and translation of the cryptic inscription (R. Sermon, "The Use of Computers in the Decipherment of the Hackness Cross Cryptic Inscriptions," in J. Huggett and N. Ryan, eds., *Computer Applications and Qualitative Methods in Archaeology* 1994, B.A.R. Int. ser. 600 [Oxford, 1995], 253–57) cannot be supported as accurate and are based on a flawed methodology: cf. the discussions of D. McManus, "Ogam: Archaizing, Orthography, and the Authenticity of the Manuscript Key to the Alphabet," *Ériu* 37 (1986), 1–31; D. McManus, *A Guide to Ogham* (Maynooth, 1991); C. Swift, *Ogham Stones and the Earliest Irish Christians* (Maynooth, 1997), 49–128.

[31] J. Higgitt, "Words and Crosses: The Inscribed Stone Cross in Early Medieval Britain and Ireland," in J. Higgitt, ed., *Early Medieval Sculpture in Britain and Ireland*, B.A.R. Brit. ser. 152 (Oxford, 1986), 125–50, at pp. 133, 146; Page, *Introduction*, 64, 66.

[32] Swift, *Ogham Stones*, 42-48; McManus, *Guide*, 54-61; K. Forsyth, "The Inscriptions on the Dupplin Cross," in C. Bourke, ed., *From the Isles of the North: Early Medieval Art in Ireland and Britain* (Belfast, 1995), 237–44, at p. 237; R. Page, *Introduction*, 61–64, 66–68. See also J. Jesch, *Women in the Viking Age* (Woodbridge & Rochester, 1991), 42–74.

[33] Higgitt, "Words and Crosses," 146; see also E. Okasha, " The Commissioners, Makers and Owners of Anglo-Saxon Inscriptions," *A.S.S.A.H.* 7 (Oxford, 1994), 71–77, at pp. 72, 73.

[34] *Corpus* 3, 140.

[35] Cramp, "A Reconsideration," 68–70.

[36] *Corpus* 3, 140; R. Cramp, "The Position of the Otley Crosses in English Sculpture of the Eighth to Ninth Centuries," in V. Milajcik, ed., *Kolloquium über spätantike und frühmittelalterliche Skulptur II* (Mainz, 1970), 55–63, at pp. 58–61; I. N. Wood, "Anglo-Saxon Otley: An Archiepiscopal Estate and Its Crosses in a Northumbrian Context," *Northern Hist.* 23 (1987), 20–38, at pp. 26–37. Examples of portrait busts are more numerous than any other type of human figure in early Anglo-Saxon sculpture. In addition to those mentioned here, they occur on most of the Peak District crosses, as well as on shaft fragments from Halton (Lancashire), Rugby and Easby.

[37] For the Hoddom cross shaft, Cramp, "Position of the Otley Crosses," 59, 62, and Tafel 47.1; on Ilkley, R. Cramp, "The Evangelist Symbols and Their Parallels in Anglo-Saxon Sculpture," in R. Farrell, ed., *Bede and Anglo-Saxon England: Papers in Honour of the 1300th Anniversary of the Birth of Bede, Given at Cornell University in 1973 and 1974,* B.A.R. Brit ser. 46 (Oxford, 1978), 118–30, at p. 126.

[38] M. P. Brown, *The Book of Cerne: Prayer, Patronage, and Power* (London, 1996), 73–103.

[39] R. Cramp, "Schools of Mercian Sculpture," in *Mercian Studies,* ed. A. Dornier (Leicester, 1977), 191–233, at pp. 218–219.

[40] Cramp, "Schools of Mercian Sculpture," 210; M. Clayton, *The Cult of the Virgin Mary in Anglo-Saxon England* (Cambridge, 1990), 152–53; on the Collingham cross shafts, Cramp, "Position of the Otley Crosses," 61, and Tafel 47.2. The Breedon bust could represent a veiled male, because the hand appears to be in a gesture of blessing and the hand holding the book is veiled. These features could indicate depiction of a priestly figure, although, again, no images of veiled priests are known to survive from early Anglo-Saxon England. On the other hand, the bust could be compared with the veiled female figure, who holds a cross and censer—both of which are liturgical objects—and is labeled "Sca Maria," at the incipit of the mass for Christmas Eve in the Gellone Sacramentary (Paris, Bibl. Nat., lat. 12168, f.1), a late eighth-century liturgical manuscript attributed to northern France; see J. J. G. Alexander, *The Decorated Letter* (New York, 1978), pl. 4, 46–47. See also Robert Deshman's discussion of depictions of the Virgin as a symbolic altar, R. Deshman, *The Benedictional of Aethelwold* (Princeton, 1995), 17.

[41] G. LeBlanc-Smith, "Three Pre-Norman Crosses in Derbyshire," *The Reliquary,* n.s. 10 (1904) 194–204; G. F. Browne, "Bradbourne Cross, Derbyshire," *Archaeol. J.* 45 (1888), 7–11.

[42] On evangelist portraits and symbols, see P. Bloch, "Evangelisten," *Reallexikon zur deutschen Kunstgeschichte* 6 (Stuttgart, 1973), 448–68; U. Nilgen, "Evangelisten," *Lexikon der christlichen Ikonographie* 1 (Rome, 1968) 696–713;

P. Underwood, "The Fountain of Life in the Manuscripts of the Gospels," *Dumbarton Oaks Papers* 5 (Washington, D.C., 1950), 41–138; on the Rothbury cross shaft, see J. Hawkes, "The Rothbury Cross: An Iconographic Bricolage," *Gesta* 35.1 (1996), 77–94, at pp. 80–81.

[43] The Virgin is shown holding a book on a Carolingian ivory of the Metz school (the Brunswick Casket where the book rests beneath her hand on a lectern), but it probably is meant to refer to her reading of the psalms and thus her piety; Clayton, *Cult of the Virgin Mary,* 160–61, 171; Deshman, *Benedictional of Aethelwold,* fig. 1 (Brunswick Casket). See the discussion below of images of female saints who hold books in tenth- and eleventh-century Anglo-Saxon art.

[44] See R. Cormack, *Painting the Soul: Icons, Death Masks and Shrouds* (London, 1997), 64–88; A. Grabar, *Christian Iconography: A Study of Its Origins* (London & Henley, 1980), 60–86.

[45] Higgitt, in *Corpus* 3, 138–39.

[46]*H.E.* iv,20.

[47] In the Stowe Missal, in the Mass *apostolorum et martirum et sanctorum et sanctatarum virguinum,* ff 38–38v, and in the Book of Cerne (Cambridge, University Library, MS Ll.1.10), in the prayer *Oratio matutinalis* (number 7), f.45b. See G. F. Warner, ed., *The Stowe Missal: MS. D.II.3 in the Library of the Royal Irish Academy, Dublin,* Henry Bradshaw Society 31, 32 (Woodbridge & Rochester, 1989), 19; A. B. Kuypers, ed., *The Prayer Book of Aedelualod the Bishop Commonly Called the Book of Cerne* (Cambridge, 1902), 91; also J. Hennig, "Studies in Early Western Devotion to the Choirs of Saints," *Studia Patristica* 8 (1963), 239–47.

[48] London, B.L., Add. 49598, ff 1, 2.

[49] Cambridge, Pembroke College 301, f. 2v, dated about 1020; Cambridge, Trinity College B.10.4, f. 12v, the Trinity Gospels, first quarter of the eleventh century; see E. Temple, *Anglo-Saxon Manuscripts 900–1066* (London, 1976), 83–84 (Cambridge, Trinity College B.10.4, Trinity Gospels), 91–92, fig. 233 (Cambridge, Pembroke College 301), 86–88 (London, B.L., Add. 34890, f. 115); also Clayton, *Cult of the Virgin Mary,* 160–61, 171; Deshman, *Benedictional of Aethelwold,* 146, 150–51, pls. 1, 2, 8, 28.

[50] A number of eighth- and ninth-century full-length sculpted relief male figures survive, usually shown in architectural settings on the sides of shrines or on slabs: for example, the Hedda Stone at Peterborough, the sarcophagus fragments at Breedon, and panels from Fletton, Castor, and Breedon. None of the surviving early full-length figures holding books can be identified as female.

[51] Deshman, *Benedictional of Aethelwold,* 98; J. O'Reilly, "St. John as a Figure of the Contemplative Life: Text and Image in the Art of the Anglo-Saxon Benedictine Reform," in N. Ramsay, M. Sparks, and T. Tatton-Brown, eds., *St.*

Dunstan: His Life, Times and Cult (Woodbridge & Rochester, 1992), 165–85, at pp. 179–80.

[52] London, B.L., Arundel 60, f.12v (Arundel Psalter), and New York, Pierpont Morgan Library, MS 709, f.1v (Weingarten *or* Judith of Flanders Gospels).

[53] B. Raw, *Anglo-Saxon Crucifixion Iconography and the Art of the Monastic Revival* (Cambridge, 1990), 96–101.

[54] See also the discussion of Bede's gendering of authorship, in Lees and Overing, "Birthing Bishops."

[55] Important examples of Marian iconography survive at Ruthwell, Hovingham, Dewsbury, Wirksworth, and Sandbach. Although extremely relevant to constructs of gender and of sanctity in general, images of the Virgin Mary present theological complexities that are beyond the scope of this discussion of holywomen. On the Marian iconography of Ruthwell, see É. Ó. Carragáin, *City of Rome,* 30–36, 73–80; É. Ó. Carragáin, "Liturgical Innovations Associated with Pope Sergius and the Iconography of the Ruthwell and Bewcastle Crosses," in Farrell, *Bede and Anglo-Saxon England,* 131–147; É. Ó. Carragáin, "The Ruthwell Crucifixion Poem in its Iconographic and Liturgical Contexts," *Peritia* 6–7 (1987–88), 1–71; and the discussion in his forthcoming book in the British Library Studies in Medieval Culture series. For Hovingham, Sandbach, and Wirksworth, see J. Hawkes, "Mary and the Cycle of Resurrection: the Iconography of the Hovingham Panel," in Spearman and Higgitt, *Age of Migrating Ideas,* 254–60; J. Hawkes, "The Wirksworth Slab: An Iconography of *Humilitas*," *Peritia* 9 (1995), 246–89, and, "A Question of Judgement: The Iconographic Programme at Sandbach, Cheshire," in Bourke, *From the Isles of the North,* 213–19.

[56] Shaft fragment 1bC, dated first half of the ninth century; see *Corpus* 1, 217–221, pl. 213, 1215; Hawkes, "The Rothbury Cross," 85–87; J. Hawkes, "The Miracle Scene on the Rothbury Cross Shaft," *Archaeologia Aeliana,* series 5, 17 (1989) 207–11.

[57] Augustine, Tractate XLIX in *Joannis Evangelium,* XI, 1–54, ed. J.-P. Migne, *Patrologia Latina* 35, 1756–57, cited in Hawkes, "The Rothbury Cross," 93.

[58] Bede, *In Cantica Canticorum,* ed. D. Hurst, *C.C.S.L.* 119B, (Turnhout, 1983), 289: "Credo ad speciem genarum eius esse referendum quod exultavit in spiritu parvulorum fidei congratulans, quod dolebat super duritia cordis infidelium, quod resuscitarus Lazarum gaudebat propter discipulos ut crederent, quod flentes sorores sive amicos eius intuens flevit et turbavit semet ipsum, quod imminente passione *coepit contristari et maestus esse,* quod nullum risui vel supervacuis verbis tempus indulgebat, quod non secundum visionem oculorum iudicavit neque secundum auditum aurium arguebat, quod sicut ovis ad occisionem ductus est et quasi agnus coram tondente sic non apervit os suum."

[59] B. Kurth, "Ecclesia and an Angel on the Andrew Auckland Cross," *J. of the Warburg and Courtauld Institutes* 6 (1943), 213–14; Cramp, Corpus 1, 37.

[60] J. Calvert, "The Iconography of the St. Andrew Auckland Cross," *Art Bul.* 66.4 (1984), 543–55, at pp. 546–48.

[61] See C. A. Farr, "Worthy Women on the Ruthwell Cross: Woman as Sign in Early Anglo-Saxon Monasticism," in C. E. Karkov, M. Ryan and R. Farrell, eds., *The Insular Tradition* (Albany, 1997), 45–61.

[62] See Hawkes, "A Question of Judgement."

CHAPTER 15

Statements in Stone
Anglo-Saxon Sculpture, Whitby
and the Christianization of the North

JANE HAWKES

It is the purpose of this paper to consider, in general terms, the role of Anglo-Saxon sculpture and its figural iconography in the process of christianizing the north of England, and more specifically, the ways in which sculpture from the ecclesiastical site at Whitby and its satellites could be viewed within these perameters.

ANGLO-SAXON SCULPTURE

The sculpture produced in Anglo-Saxon England during the so-called "Anglian" (pre-Viking) period has been viewed in a number of ways by modern scholars. Most popular have been the stylistic analyses which have been used to date the material and to establish groups of related sculptures.[1] More recent has been the interest in the iconography of the carvings; studies of this type have provided insights into the wider cultural contacts and theological milieux of the centers responsible for the production of the material.[2] However, in the process of uncovering this type of information and exposing the potentially esoteric nature of Anglo-Saxon ecclesiastical culture, there has been a tendency to obscure the more visually obvious, and perhaps primary purpose lying behind the use of the stone sculpture during the early period of christianization in the north of Anglo-Saxon England.

The documentary evidence for the early use of stone in Anglo-Saxon England indicates that where it was first utilized—by Wilfrid, at Ripon (Yorkshire), and Hexham (Northumberland), and by Benedict Biscop and Ceolfrid at Wearmouth and Jarrow (Tyne and Wear) in the latter half of the seventh century—it was employed deliberately, and at some considerable expense, to proclaim loudly and clearly the existence and standing of those ecclesiastical centers from the moment of their inception.[3] Wilfrid's church at Hexham, for instance, is described by his contemporary biographer, "Eddius Stephanus," in terms of the depth of its foundations, its crypts "of wonderfully dressed stone," its columns, side aisles, walls "of notable length and height," its passages and spiral stairs. So impressive was it in this biographer's opinion that there was not a church outside Italy ("this side of the Alps") "built on such a scale."[4]

Parts of these stone structures have survived—in the crypts at Hexham and Ripon, and in the standing fabric of the churches at Jarrow and Monkwearmouth (pl. 15.1). Considered alongside the grandiose Romanesque and Gothic structures of the later Middle Ages, the remains of these buildings may well appear unimpressive, or "primitive," to the eye of subsequent (later medieval and modern) viewers. Nevertheless, in terms of their Anglo-Saxon setting it is hard to overestimate their impact. Being multi-storied and built of stone they would have stood out impressively in a landscape otherwise filled with settlements composed largely of single-storied structures of wood, thatch, wattle and daub.

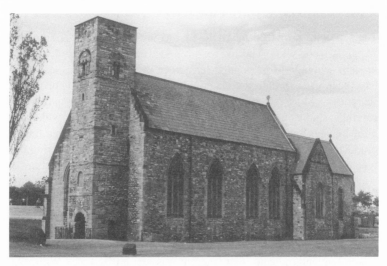

Pl. 15.1. The Church of St. Peter, Monkwermouth, Late Seventh Century (photo, author).

Furthermore, the appearance of these early churches was enhanced by carved ornament; sculpture was inextricably linked to the statements made by these stone buildings. It was employed in the decoration of the architectural features and furniture inside and out; it was used to mark the graves of the dead inhabitants of the ecclesiastical communities; and it was used in the construction and decoration of the large-scale monuments—the monolithic crosses set up in the Northumbrian countryside from the first half of the eighth century onwards, probably initially under the patronage of ecclesiastical centers like Wearmouth-Jarrow and Hexham.[5]

There is, moreover, a growing body of evidence to suggest that much of this sculpture, particularly the crosses, was originally brightly painted and sometimes set with paste glass and metal fittings.[6] Treated in this manner many details, including inscriptions, which are not now visible could have been much clearer. More importantly, although the monuments and their carvings are striking enough in their present restrained monotone, they would have been truly eye-catching in their original glittering polychrome.

The impressive nature of stone sculpture in the Early Christian North of Anglo-Saxon England was not, however, simply a matter of visual effect; it seems it was also a relatively rare phenomenon. For instance, of the approximately 230 pieces of carved stone associated with pre-Viking contexts north of the Tees, nearly 180 come from just five sites: Lindisfarne, Hartlepool, Hexham, Wearmouth and Jarrow. Most of the remainder have emerged from centers related to these sites, such as the Lindisfarne dependency at Norham. This strongly implies that even when factors such as the vagaries of survival are taken into consideration, stone carving was not a very widespread activity in the region between the later seventh and ninth centuries. Thus, even in their current, often fragmentary state, it is possible to appreciate the deliberate nature of the investment made by certain early ecclesiastical centers—an investment in the labor and materials involved in quarrying, transporting, carving and decorating the monuments. By its very existence (without even considering the carved details) we can assume that stone was employed in the north of Anglo-Saxon England with the intention of impressing those who viewed it.

THE ICONOGRAPHY OF ANGLO-SAXON SCULPTURE

These intentions become even more apparent when the decoration itself is considered—particularly the figural iconography—although academic

Pl. 15.2. The Crucifixion Panel on the "Spital Cross," from Hexham, Mid-Eighth Century (photo, Department of Archaeology, University of Durham, photographer T. Middlemass).

concerns can sometimes obscure this. Taking the Crucifixion panel on the "Spital Cross" at Hexham as an example (pl. 15.2), a modern academic audience might appreciate the fact that, dated to the mid-eighth century, it represents a rare and early example of the Crucifixion in Anglo-Saxon art. The only other surviving contemporary version of the

Pl. 15.3. The Crucifixion Miniature in the Durham Gospels, ca. 700
(photo, The Dean and Chapter of Durham).

scene is that found in the Durham Gospel fragment (Durham, Cathedral Library A.II.17, f.383v), dated to ca. 700 (pl. 15.3).[7]

Alternatively, such an audience might appreciate the fact that the carved image presents a depiction of the Crucified which is unusual in Christian art, generally, at the time, in that he is depicted wearing a loincloth. Between the fourth and later eighth and ninth centuries, it was more common to illustrate Christ wearing a long robe, as indeed he is in the Durham Gospel fragment.[8]

Again, a modern academic viewer might value the (not unrelated) fact that the iconography of the Hexham Crucifixion panel indicates that those responsible for its production had access to a model-type of early (probably fourth-century) date and of Western Mediterranean origin. This is suggested both in the way Christ's head is slightly turned to the side and in the use of the loincloth, as opposed to the longer robe favored in iconographic types originating in the Eastern Mediterranean. A comparison of the scenes depicted on the Hexham panel and a fourth-century ivory panel from Italy, now in the British Museum (pl. 15.4), and those featured in the Durham Gospel miniature and the sixth-century Rabula Gospel Book, indicate the distinct iconographic sources lying ultimately behind the Anglo-Saxon images.[9]

Yet another concern of the modern academic viewing the Hexham panel might be its theological references. The way the crucifix fills and quarters the field refers the onlooker to the universal nature of the Crucifixion and the salvation available through it.[10] Here, this reference is extended by the inclusion in the scene of Longinus (the blind spear-bearer cured by the blood of the crucified Christ). His presence is not simply a matter of narrative necessity; it also signifies the miraculous nature of the salvation offered by the blood of Christ, available to each individual Christian (metaphorically blinded by sin) at the daily celebration of the Eucharist.[11] Reference to the Eucharist is probably also indicated by the fact that Christ is shown in this panel flanked by two figures (Longinus and Stephaton, the sponge-bearer). Recent work on images of Christ in the art of Early Christian Northumbria has demonstrated that Christ flanked by two figures was a motif commonly employed to signify eucharistic concerns.[12]

Whatever the specific interest(s) of the modern academic art historian, however, the Hexham Crucifixion panel is not just an image which illustrates the widespread cultural contacts of the Northumbrian (or, in this case, Wilfridian) church; nor does it function solely to illuminate the complex and esoteric nature of northern Christianity in the first half of

Pl. 15.4. Ivory Plaque Depicting the Crucifixion, Italy, Fourth Century (photo, courtesy of the British Museum).

the eighth century. In its own time, being carved on a stone cross-shaft, it would also have been a clear pointer to the existence of the Christian church in the region and all that that institution stood for: learning, faith and salvation, yes; but also its widespread power and authority derived, not so much from human might, but rather from divine right. In the way the panel is presented and arranged is a statement that those responsible for its production are a power to be reckoned with. The image is, significantly, set at the base of the shaft—Christ Crucified stands at the eye-level of anyone kneeling before the monument. And, the image is arranged, not in a narrative manner (as on the British Museum ivory), but in an iconic and hierarchical manner. By means of the presentation and arrangement of the panel, those who commissioned and designed it ensured that Christ, his salvation, and the role of the church in that salvation, were placed directly before those who viewed it. The church after all, was the medium by which salvation was to be transmitted to humanity; the church was the dispenser of the sacraments through which salvation was to be made possible. Its authority, legitimacy, indeed its very existence, derived from the Being (Christ) displayed so prominently on the cross-shaft.

Thus, however art historians choose to read the stone monuments, or the images carved on them, it should be borne in mind that Anglo-Saxon sculpture was the product of ecclesiastical centers that were using stone to proclaim their socio-economic status, as much as the religion they advocated, and the figural decoration of those monuments was integral to that agenda in many cases.

ANGLO-SAXON WHITBY AND ITS STONEWORK

The ecclesiastical center at Whitby (Yorkshire) seems to have been no exception to this in its use of sculpture. Documentary evidence provides ample indication of the extremely prestigious status of the foundation in the seventh and early eighth century. It was established on land donated by Oswin after his victory over the Mercians in 655. Its first abbess, Hild, a princess of the Deiran blood-royal, was related to most of the rulers of Northumbria of the time, as was her niece and eventual successor, Ælfflæd. Under these women, the monastery served as the burial place for the Northumbrian royal family, and was selected to host the celebrated Synod of 664; twenty years later, in 685, Ælfflæd was negotiating the return from exile of her half-brother, Aldfrith, to rule the kingdom after the death of Ecgfrith at Nechtansmere.[13] Such events provide an unequivocal testament to the very high socio-political status of Whitby in the North from the time of its foundation.

Within this context a "propagandistic" use of stone might not be unexpected, and indeed, the archaeological evidence does indicate the presence of stone structures on the site during the pre-Viking period. While the details of the initial excavation report need to be treated with caution, the sculpture which has survived from the site confirms the presence of such buildings, and indicates that they were embellished in a manner comparable to those set up by Wilfrid and Benedict Biscop.[14]

Two halves of an L-shaped stone (pl. 15.5), identified as the remains of a lintel, have survived from Whitby, along with a baluster shaft (pl. 15.6), very like those found in such numbers at the Wearmouth-Jarrow complex and related centers. There was also a moulded string-course, a stone arch and an inscribed architectural slab.[15] Furthermore, if consideration of the use of stone at Whitby is extended to include its satellites (fig. 15.1), we find that at Lythe, a Whitby cell established just across the bay from the "mother house," a jamb-stone has survived along with a stone gable-finial, while at the Hackness cell there is an impost decorated

Pl. 15.5. Lintel from Whitby, Late Seventh/Early Eighth Century (photo, Department of Archaeology, University of Durham, photographer T. Middlemass).

Pl. 15.6. Baluster Shaft from Whitby, Late Seventh/Early Eighth Century (photo, Department of Archaeology, University of Durham, photographer T. Middlemass).

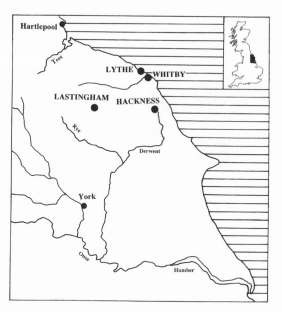

Fig.15.1. Map of Whitby and its Satellites in the Late Seventh/Early Eighth
Century (Nyree Finlay).

with zoomorphic interlace. At Lastingam, the site of another (more celebrated) Whitby cell, described by Bede as having a stone church in the
early eighth century, there is another gable finial and decorated stone
jamb. All these pieces have been dated to the later decades of the seventh
and early part of the eighth century.[16]

   Together these remains suggest that, overall, the Whitby complex,
like the newly established "Roman" sites of Ripon-Hexham and Wearmouth-Jarrow, was declaring itself visually in stone from a period fairly
soon after its establishment. Indeed, it may have been "selling" itself
quite literally through its stone. Geological surveys suggest that not only
did the stone for the sculpture at Lythe, Hackness and Lastingham come
from the quarries at Whitby, but so too did the stone for carvings found at
numerous sites throughout north and east Yorkshire (at, for example,
Kirkdale, Stonegrave, Hovingham, Middleton, Sinnington, Amotherby,
Sherburn, Filey and Londesborough, to name just a few).[17] Evidence
such as this would seem to confirm the general impression that Whitby,
in keeping with its royal status, was enhancing its prestige through the
medium of stone.

Despite this, however, it has to be said that in their decoration, the Whitby carvings of the seventh and eighth centuries bear very little comparison to the more elaborate work of the other ecclesiastical centers where stone-work played such an important role. At first sight there is nothing to compare with the grandiose crosses and complex figural iconography employed at Wearmouth-Jarrow or Hexham in the eighth century. There are, nevertheless, some indications that symbolic statements were being made through the more "simplified" motifs chosen to decorate the Whitby monuments.

The eighth-century cross-head originally inset with bright metal or glass from Lastingham, for instance, displays a floriated sun-burst motif at its center (pl. 15.7). This distinctive design is found elsewhere at the center of an early cross-head at Hexham (pl. 15.8), where a more elaborate version has also survived in an architectural panel.[18] There is some debate as to whether this latter (architectural) piece is of Anglo-Saxon manufacture, or a piece of Roman carving reused in Wilfrid's church. But, whatever its date of production, it seems to have featured in an Anglo-Saxon context. Furthermore, it closely parallels a similar panel set in the gable over the entrance to the seventh-century Baptistery at Poitiers.[19] With such a notable parallel the motif at Hexham presumably contributed to the up-market continental appearance of Wilfrid's founda-

Pl. 15.7. Cross-Head from Lastingham, Eighth Century (photo, author).

Pl.15.8. Cross-head from Hexham, Eighth Century (photo, Department of Archaeology, University of Durham, photographer T. Middlemass).

tion. Its reproduction in the decoration of subsequent pieces of clearly Anglo-Saxon manufacture, the cross-heads at Hexham and Lastingham, may well reflect this perception, but being placed at the center of a cross-head, the motif in this specific context may also have been employed symbolically as a complex reference to Christ: as a sunburst it functions as an aniconic reference to Christ as the Sun; in its (potential) cross-shape it provides a reference to the Crucifixion; and in its floriate aspect it may refer to the "fruitful" nature of Christ and his sacraments, a powerful concept celebrated by many writers of the early church.[20]

Whether this set of references is valid, the point remains that the use of this motif at Lastingham represents a rare instance of relative elaboration, both in the form of monument (a monumental free-standing cross), and in the type of decoration associated with stone artifacts from the Whitby complex in the seventh and eighth centuries. Even in the ninth century, when more elaborate pieces were being produced (such as a carved cross at Hackness and a figured slab from Whitby), they were still an unusual phenomenon in the context of Whitby scultpure.[21] By far the most popular monuments surviving at this center were plain crosses and grave-markers, some of which are incised with commemorative inscriptions (pl. 15.9).

Given the status of Whitby and its contact (evident from the baluster shaft) with centers that did favor very elaborate decorative sculptural monuments at an early date, this might be considered surprising. In terms of cultural contacts, however, although Whitby was a royal center and in touch with sculptural developments at Wearmouth-Jarrow, the primary affiliation of the center does seem to have been Lindisfarne; its first abbess, Hild, was very much the protégé of Aidan and the Lindisfarne community. The earliest sculpture which has survived from that center was, like that at Whitby, much more restrained in its decorative impulses than the more elaborate pieces which have emerged from Hexham and Wearmouth-Jarrow.[22]

Furthermore, and perhaps of more relevance, in the eighth century both Lindisfarne and Whitby, and the related center at Hartlepool, do seem to have had a distinct taste for a specific type of monument: those of a funerary or commemorative nature. At Lindisfarne and Hartlepool it is the so-called "pillow" or "name stones" which form the largest single group of carvings.[23] Few of these have been found at Whitby,[24] but the predominant interest there was still in things commemorative. It is an interest reflected in the extraordinarily large number of funerary crosses which have survived. Being finely dressed on only one side, it would seem that many of these were designed to stand against a wall, possibly in the *porticus* which are cited in the documentary sources as the important places of burial in the monastery.[25]

Moreover, the other non-architectural stones which have survived at Whitby and its satellites reinforce this apparent interest in commemoration. One function of the ninth-century shaft from Hackness, for instance, seems to have been to commemorate (or venerate) one Œdilburga,[26]

Pl. 15.9. Funerary Cross from Whitby, Eighth Century (Photo: Department of Archaeology, University of Durham. Photographer T. Middlemass).

while the ninth-century slab carved with animal ornament from Whitby was originally part of an elaborate shrine. It is not insignificant that this was incised on the inside with a simple outline cross, in much the same manner as the wooden reliquary coffin made for Cuthbert at Lindisfarne in 698;[27] the design of this cross is not unlike those of the "plain" crosses erected as visible grave-markers at Whitby. Overall, the use of stone at the Whitby complex implies a strong interest in commemorating the dead throughout the pre-Viking period.

As far as the generally restrained appearance of most of the funerary monuments is concerned, it should be remembered that they might originally have been painted, which would have enhanced them somewhat. More importantly, their relative plainness may have more to do with modern perceptions than any contemporary consideration of them in their original setting. Cramp has suggested that these monuments reflect contact with Continental Merovingian fashions of the seventh century, while more recently Bailey has argued that the Whitby funerary crosses represent the earliest form of the free-standing cross, which, during the course of the eighth century, was to become such an elaborate monument type.[28] In their initial stages, therefore, these crosses, simple though they are in their decorative repertoire, probably represented a fairly innovative design concept in stone grave-markers.

Furthermore, it has been suggested by Higgitt that the commemorative inscriptions found on some of these crosses range in date from the late seventh to ninth centuries.[29] While this may be so, the design of the cross on which the epitaphs occur was not subject to any great change, implying that the funerary crosses continued to be produced at Whitby over a considerable period of time; its form, established at an early date, was reproduced over and over by succeeding generations, almost as a "trade-mark." Alternatively, Lang has suggested that the crosses are all much of a date, but the inscriptions, originally painted on, were "touched up" and made more permanent by being incised as they wore out.[30]

Whichever explanation is preferred, the use of stone at Whitby suggests a strong interest in commemorating the dead, and this interest was maintained for as long as the center flourished during the pre-Viking period. Given that this was the burial place of kings, queens and royal abbesses, this is, perhaps, not a surprising observation. But the fact that so much stone is used in the pursuit of this activity, and that it continued for such an extended period of time; the fact that a significant percentage of the means at Whitby's disposal was employed, deliberately and consistently, over such a period to make the graves of the dead visible and permanent in the eyes of the living, is significant. It suggests that the center was not simply constructing itself as a permanent feature of the landscape (geographically as well as politically), but was establishing itself as a focus of public veneration of the dead, perhaps as a pilgrimage center.

ACKNOWLEDGEMENTS

Thanks are due to Richard Bailey and Catherine Karkov, and above all, to Jim Lang for their comments and criticisms in the preparation of this paper, delivered at the Third International Medieval Congress held at Leeds in 1996.

NOTES

[1] Stylistic studies concerned with establishing chronologies of Anglo-Saxon sculpture include those by W. G. Collingwood, "Anglian and Anglo-Danish Sculpture in the West Riding, with Addenda to the North and East Ridings and York, and a General Review of the Early Christian Monuments of Yorkshire," *Yorkshire Archaeol. J.* 23 (1914–15), 129–299; *idem, Northumbrian Crosses of the Pre-Norman Age* (London, 1927; repr. Lampeter, 1989); *idem,* "A Pedigree of Anglian Crosses," *Antiquity* 6 (1932) 35–54; J. Brønsted, *Early English Ornament,* trans. A. F. Major (London & Copenhagen, 1924); A. W. Clapham, *English Romanesque Architecture before the Conquest* (Oxford, 1930); E. Kitzinger, "Anglo-Saxon Vine-Scroll Ornament," *Antiquity* 10 (1936), 61–71; G. B. Brown, *The Arts in Early England,* vol 6.2, ed. E. H. Sexton (London, 1937); and T. D. Kendrick, *Anglo-Saxon Art to A.D. 900* (London, 1938); *idem, Late Saxon and Viking Art* (London, 1949). Studies which have sought to establish groups of related sculptures include: R. Cramp, Early Northumbrian Sculpture, *Jarrow Lecture* (Jarrow, 1965); *idem,* "Schools of Mercian Sculpture," in A. Dornier, ed., *Mercian Studies* (Leicester, 1977), 191–233; *idem, Corpus of Anglo-Saxon Stone Sculpture 1: County Durham and Northumberland,* 2 vols. (Oxford, 1984), xlvii–xlviii (hereafter *Corpus* 1); R. N. Bailey, "The Chronology of Viking-Age Sculpture in Northumbria," in J. Lang, ed., *Anglo-Saxon and Viking Age Sculpture and its Context,* B.A.R. Brit. ser. 49 (Oxford, 1978), 173–203; J. Lang, "Continuity and Innovation in Anglo-Scandinavian Sculpture," ibid., 145–72.

[2] Such studies include those by B. Kurth, "Ecclesia and an Angel on the Andrew Auckland Cross," *J. of the Warburg and Courtauld Institutes* 6 (1943), 213–14; *idem,* "The Iconography of the Wirksworth Slab," *Burlington Mag.* 86 (1945), 114–121; É. Ó. Carragáin, "Liturgical Innovations Associated with Pope Sergius and the Iconography of the Ruthwell and Bewcastle Crosses," in R. T. Farrell, ed., *Bede and Anglo-Saxon England: Papers in Honour of the 1300th Anniversary of the Birth of Bede . . . ,* B.A.R. Brit. ser. 46 (Oxford, 1978), 131–147; *idem,* "Christ over the Beasts and the Agnus Dei: Two Multivalent Panels on the Ruthwell and Bewcastle Crosses," in P. E. Szarmach and V. D. Oggins, eds., *Sources of Anglo-Saxon Culture* (Kalamazoo, MI, 1986), 377–403; *idem,* "The Ruthwell Cross and Irish High Crosses: Some Points of Comparison and Con-

trast," in M. Ryan, ed., *Ireland and Insular Art* A.D. *500–1200* (Dublin, 1987), 111–128; *idem,* "A Liturgical Interpretation of the Bewcastle Cross," in M. Stokes and T. L. Burton, eds., *Medieval Literature and Antiquities: Studies in Honour of Basil Cottle* (Cambridge, 1987), 15–42; *idem,* "The Ruthwell Cucifixion Poem and its Iconographic and Liturgical Contexts," *Peritia* 6–7 (1987–88), 1–71; *idem,* "Seeing, Reading, Singing the Ruthwell Cross: Vernacular Poem, Old English Liturgy and Implied Audience," *Medieval Europe 1992: Art and Symbolism, pre-printed papers* 7, (York, 1992), 91–96; E. Coatsworth, "The Iconography of the Crucifixion in pre-Conquest Sculpture in England," unpub. Ph. D. thesis, University of Durham, 2 vols, 1979); I. Wood, "Anglo-Saxon Otley: An Archiepiscopal Estate and its Crosses in a Northumbrian Context," *Northern Hist.* 23 (1987), 20–38; J. Hawkes, "Mary and the Cycle of Resurrection: The Iconography of the Hovingham Panel," in R. M. Spearman and J. Higgitt, eds., *The Age of Migrating Ideas: Early Medieval Art in Northern Britain and Ireland* (Edinburgh, 1993), 254–260; *idem,* "The Wirksworth Slab: An Iconography of Humilitas," *Peritia* 8 (1995), 1–32; *idem,* "The Rothbury Cross: An Iconographic Bricolage," *Gesta* 35 (1996) 77–94; cf. R. N. Bailey, *England's Earliest Sculptors* (Toronto, 1996).

³ For Ripon and Hexham see the accounts in B.Colgrave, ed., *The Life of Bishop Wilfrid by Eddius Stephanus* (Cambridge, 1927), XVII, XXII, pp. 34–37, 44–47; for Wearmouth-Jarrow see Bede, *Historiam Abbatum* (5–7) in C. Plummer, ed., *Venerabilis Baedae Historium ecclesiasticam gentis Anglorum,* 2 vols in 1 (Oxford, 1896), 368–71.

⁴ ". . . cuius profunditatem in terra cum domibus mire politis lapidibus fundatam et super terram multiplicem domum columnis variis et porticibus multis suffultam mirabileque longitudine et altitudine murorum ornatam et liniarum variis anfractibus viarum, aliquando sursum, aliquando deorsum per cocleas circumductam, non est meae parvitatis hoc sermone explicare, quod sanctus pontifex noster, a spiritu Dei doctus, opera facere excogitavit, neque enim ullam domum aliam citra Alpes montes talem aedificatam audivimus." Colgrave, *Life of Wilfrid,* XXII, p. 46.

⁵ For a summary of the carved stone architectural features, furniture, grave-markers and crosses associated with Hexham, Wearmouth and Jarrow, see Cramp, *Corpus* 1, 174–93, 122–34, 106–22; for Ripon, see Collingwood, *Northumbrian Crosses,* 95–98, 109–112.

⁶ For a summary see Bailey, *Earliest Sculptors,* 5–11.

⁷ See Cramp, *Corpus,* 1 (no.2), 176–77, pl.173,914–17, for discussion of the Hexham cross; and J. J. G. Alexander, *Insular manuscripts 6th to the 9th Century* (London, 1978), 40–42 (no.10), for discussion of the Durham Gospel miniature. Other images of the Crucifixion depicting Christ wearing a loincloth that have

survived in pre-Viking contexts in Anglo-Saxon England, such as those carved on the cross-head of the Rothbury cross (Northumberland) and the base of the Ruthwell cross (Dumfriesshire), date to the last decades of the eighth century, and the mid ninth century (see Hawkes, "The Rothbury Cross," 77–80; Coatsworth, "Iconography of the Crucifixion," 175–200; R. N. Bailey and R. Cramp, *Corpus of Anglo-Saxon Stone Sculpture*, vol. 2, *Cumbria, Westmorland and Lancashire-north-of-the-Sands* (Oxford, 1988; hereafter *Corpus* 2), 19–22.

[8] See Coatsworth, "Iconography of the Crucifixion," 253–58 for summary of the early use of the loincloth in Crucifixion iconography; cf. G. Schiller, *Iconography of Christian Art*, vol 2, trans. J. Seligman (London, 1972), pls. 323, 326, 350, 354–56; and J. Hawkes, *Anglo-Saxon Sandbach: A Study in Iconography*, forthcoming English Heritage monograph.

[9] See Schiller, *Iconography*, pl. 327 for the Rabula Gospels miniature.

[10] Ibid., 92–93; Coatsworth, "Iconography of the Crucifixion," 24–27, 67–68; and Hawkes, *Anglo-Saxon Sandbach*.

[11] Schiller, *Iconography*, 93–94; Coatsworth, "Iconography of the Crucifixion," 66–85.

[12] Ó. Carragáin, "Christ over the Beasts."

[13] See, for example, B. Colgrave and R. A. B. Mynors, eds., *Bede's Ecclesiastical History of the English People* (Oxford, 1969; repr.1991), iii,23–24, iv,23, pp. 286–95, 404–15 (hereafter *H.E.*); and Bede's prose life of St. Cuthbert, in B. Colgrave, ed., *Two Lives of St Cuthbert* (Cambridge, 1940), XXIV, pp. 234–39; the anonymous life of St Cuthbert, in ibid., VI, pp. 102–05; and Eddius Stephanus, in Colgrave, *Life of Wilfrid*, LX, pp. 130–33; cf. C. Fell, "Hild, Abbess of Strenaeshalch," in H. Bekker-Nielsen, P. Foote, J. H. Jørgensen and T. Nyberg, eds., *Hagiography and Medieval Literature: A Symposium* (Odense, 1981), 76–99; and C. Karkov, "Whitby, Jarrow and the Commemoration of Death in Northumbria," in J. Hawkes and S. Mills, eds., *Northumbria's Golden Age* (Stroud, 1998), 114–23.

[14] C. R. Peers and C. A. R. Radford, "The Saxon Monastery at Whitby," *Archaeologia* 89 (1943), 27–88; cf. P. Rahtz, "Whitby," *Yorkshire Archaeol. J.* 40 (1958), 604–18; *idem*, "The Building Plan of the Anglo-Saxon Monastery of Whitby Abbey," in D. M.Wilson, ed., *The Archaeology of Anglo-Saxon England* (London, 1976), 459–62; R. Cramp, "Anglo-Saxon Monasteries of the North," *Scottish Archaeol. Forum* 5 (1973), 104–24; *idem*, "Monastic Sites," in Wilson, *Archaeology*, 201–52; *idem*, "Analysis of the Finds Register and Location Plan of Whitby Abbey," in ibid, 453–57; *idem*, "A Reconsideration of the Monastic Site of Whitby," in Spearman and Higgitt, *Age of Migrating Ideas*, 64–73; A. White, "Finds from the Anglian Monastery at Whitby," *Yorkshire Archaeol. J.* 56 (1984), 33–40; and J. Lang, *Corpus of Anglo-Saxon Stone Sculpture 6: Northern Yorkshire* (Oxford, forthcoming) (hereafter *Corpus* 6).

[15] For the stone architectural remains from Whitby see Cramp, "Reconsideration," and Lang, *Corpus* 6; cf. Cramp, *Corpus* 1, 120–21.28–29 for the baluster shafts from Wearmouth-Jarrow.

[16] For discussion of the pieces from Lythe see Lang, *Corpus* 6; for those from Hackness and Lastingham, see J. Lang, *Corpus of Anglo-Saxon Stone Sculpture 3. York and Eastern Yorkshire* (Oxford, 1991) nos. 3, 4: 141–42, ills 471–77; nos. 8, 9: 171–72; ills 605–613. For Bede's reference to the stone church at Lastingham see *H.E.* ill. 23, pp. 286–89.

[17] See J. R. Senior, "Regional Geology," in Lang, *Corpus* 3, 11–15.

[18] Cramp, *Corpus* 1 nos. 8, 22: 179–80, 186, pls. 172,910–13, 182,972.

[19] J. Hubert, J. Porcher and W. F. Volbach, *Europe of the Invasions* (New York, 1969), fig.48.

[20] E.g. Bede, "Homily on Luke 1.39-55," trans. in L. T. Martin and D. Hurst, *Bede the Venerable: Homilies on the Gospels,* vol.1, *Advent to Lent* (Kalamazoo, 1991), 30–43, esp. 32–34.

[21] For the Hackness cross see Lang, *Corpus* 3, no.1: 135–141, ills. 454–63, 466; for the figured slab from Whitby see Peers and Radford, "Whitby," pl.XX.

[22] For a summary of the Lindisfarne sculpture, see Cramp, *Corpus* 1, 194–208 .

[23] For Hartlepool, see ibid., 97–101; for discussion of the name stones, see E. Okasha, *Hand-list of Anglo-Saxon non-Runic Inscriptions* (Cambridge, 1971), 75–79; idem., "The Inscribed Stones from Hartlepool," in Hawkes and Mills, *Golden Age,* 113–25.

[24] Okasha, *Hand-list,* 124–25.

[25] Over forty-one fragments are listed from Whitby in Lang, *Corpus* 6; for reference to the *porticus* at Whitby see Bede, *H.E.* iii,24, p. 293; for recent discussion of *porticus* in Anglo-Saxon context see É. Ó. Carragáin "The Term *Porticus* and *Imitatio Romae* in early Anglo-Saxon England," in H. Conrad O'Brien, A.M. D'Arcy and J. Scattergood, eds., *Text and Gloss: Studies in Insular Learning and Literature Presented to Joseph Donovan Pheifer* (Dublin, 1999), 13–34.

[26] Lang, *Corpus* 3, 136–37.

[27] R. N. Bailey, "St. Cuthbert's Relics: Some Neglected Evidence," in G. Bonner, D. Rollason and C. Stancliffe, eds., *St. Cuthbert, his Cult and his Community to A.D. 1200* (Woodbridge, 1987), 231–46; J. M. Cronyn and C. V. Horie, "The Anglo-Saxon Coffin: Further Investigations," in ibid., 247–56.

[28] Cramp, "Reconsideration"; Bailey, *Earliest Sculptors,* 50–52.

[29] J. Higgitt, "Monasteries and Inscriptions in Early Northumbria, the Evidence of Whitby," in C. Bourke, ed., *From the Isles of the North* (Belfast, 1995), 229–36.

[30] J. Lang, pers. comm.

CHAPTER 16

Women's Costume in the Tenth and Eleventh Centuries and Textile Production in Anglo-Saxon England

GALE R. OWEN-CROCKER

WOMEN'S COSTUME IN THE TENTH AND ELEVENTH CENTURIES

The Literary Evidence

The tenth-century Benedictine Reform brought with it an intellectual revival. English scholars were composing in their own language and were also glossing or translating into English some of the numerous Latin texts in circulation. In an enthusiasm for learning, and what seems to have been an urge to conserve material already in existence, texts were copied and recopied. Many manuscripts from the late Anglo-Saxon period survive today and not only give us some specific information about dress in England, but also provide us with a vocabulary of Old English garment names recorded as glosses to Latin texts.

Ælfric, the best-known scholar of his day, has left us evidence that fabrics and jewels were being imported regularly into England. In the *Colloquy,* a Latin work composed about the year 1000 for the instruction of boys in a monastic school, Ælfric creates the character of the *Mercator,* or merchant, who traffics in *Purpurum et sericum, pretiosas gemmas et aurum, uaris uestes et pigmenta . . .* [1] (Purple and silk, precious gems and gold, colored [or various] garments and dyes . . .).

In general, the Old English prose and poetry best known as literary texts do not give us much information about dress. The tenth-century poem, *Judith,* for instance, gives us a very traditional portrait of a lady, *torhtan mægð,* "bright maiden," *ælfscinu,* "beautiful as a fairy," and *wundenlocc,* "with braided hair,"[2] which is very vague. Our key evidence

423

tends to come from lesser-known works, many of them written with practical purpose such as instructive or legal documents. We are fortunate in having copies of the wills of some wealthy Anglo-Saxon ladies who bequeathed clothes. In particular, the wills of Wynflæd[3] and Æthelgifu[4] enumerate garments.

The Anglo-Latin glosses which survive in many manuscripts are of limited value for our purpose. They give us many garment-names,[5] but these terms are definable only by the Latin words they gloss. Some of these Old English garment terms do not survive in any other context. (This is why we do not know if some of the garment-names belonged exclusively to women's costume or men's.) Many of the lemmata concerned with dress derive ultimately from glosses to Aldhelm's description of clothing in *De Laudibus Virginitatis.*[6] Some of the others can be traced back to the *Etymologiae* of Isidore of Seville.[7]

An interesting source of information is the *Indicia Monasterialia,* a catalogue of sign-language by means of which silent monks might indicate their needs.[8] When an item of clothing was required, the explicit instructions given for miming can indicate to us the shape of the garment. Most of the garments referred to in this text are monastic, but there is one revealing reference to a woman's fillet (p. 435, below). Less explicitly, the relatively large numbers of Old English texts and translations surviving from the period contain numerous passing references to clothing, which, although not precise descriptions, do contribute to our corpus of information.

The Evidence of Art

With the era of the Benedictine Reform, pictorial representations of women appear with some frequency for the first time in the Anglo-Saxon period. Many of these, it must be stated, are somewhat removed from everyday life since they represent mythological, allegorical or biblical subjects. Often, details of attitude or costume are recognizably stylized, in the manner of the Winchester School, as, for example the hunched shoulder and fluttering drapery of the weeping Virgin figure in the late tenth-century London, B. L. Harley 2904 (fig. 16.1). There is reason to believe, however, that at least some artists, particularly the early eleventh-century illuminators of the Old English Hexateuch, London, B. L. Cotton Claudius Biv (figs. 16.2–16.4), were influenced by life as well as by other drawings,[9] and from their work we can deduce features of costume. The same is true of the Bayeux "Tapestry." although only three women appear in it. (figs. 16.5–16.7). (The technique of the "Tapestry" is discussed below.)

We have near-contemporary "portraits" of royal ladies whose costume may be compared with that of figures in other works: Cnut's queen, Ælfgifu (Emma), appears in a drawing probably made in 1031[10] in a Winchester manuscript, London, B. L. Stowe 944 (fig. 16.8), and in a Flemish or northern French manuscript, London, B. L. Add. 33241, made the following decade (fig. 16.9). Edith, wife of Edward the Confessor, is seen in the Bayeux "Tapestry" (fig. 16.5). In the medium of sculpture, there are some female figures on small ivory carvings but, of the larger stone sculptures extant from the period, those of southern England, executed in the Winchester Style, have no detailed female figures. Sculptures of the Viking-influenced north, very different in style and subject matter, of which the most famous is the Gosforth (Cumbria) Cross,[11] depict women in the trailing gown of Scandinavian tradition.

Archaeological Evidence

The great silver disc brooches which first appeared in the ninth century continued to be made in the tenth and eleventh, and it is from the latest example in the series that we learn that such brooches could be worn by women: the brooch from Sutton, Isle of Ely,[12] bears on its reverse an inscription naming the female owner Ædvwen.[13] The brooch, which is decorated in the Anglo-Scandinavian Ringerike Style, is artistically inferior to the masterpieces of the ninth century. The later Kings School, Canterbury, brooch[14] is also less impressive, suggesting a deterioration in this type of jewelry, perhaps because the upper classes were no longer wearing such things and what are preserved are the possessions of a lower social class.[15] Most of the brooches we have from this period are made of base metal. There are exceptions, such as the gold and enamel brooch set with pearls from Dowgate Hill, London (now in the British Museum), but on the whole gold and silver are rare finds. It has been thought that this reflects a genuine shortage of precious metals in secular hands, especially for use in jewelry. Economic reasons for such a shortage have been suggested;[16] or piety may have decreed that gold and silver were confined to religious pieces.[17] However, C. R. Dodwell has demonstrated from documentary sources that magnificent treasures of silver and gold were in the hands of the Church at the Conquest,[18] articles which, probably, had been in secular use previously. It is apparent, both from the wills of seculars and from the records of gifts given by seculars to religious foundations, that costly jewelry was certainly in existence and that this jewelry was probably gold.[19] We must draw the conclusion that it existed, but has not survived.

Circular brooches were the general rule. Nummular (coin) brooches seem to have been very common. There are a few disc brooches from this period with animals on them[20] and a small number of enameled brooches, including a rare non-circular brooch from Winchester[21] and another in the Ashmolean Museum[22] which were probably made in this country but copy a type made in the Rhineland and North Germany.

Disc-headed pins seem to have disappeared by the tenth century, although plain straight pins continued in use and ring-headed ones were quite common. We have an elaborate decorated pin made of silver from the Trewhiddle hoard (deposited ca. 872–5),[23] but we do not know how this luxury object was used. (It may have been ecclesiastical.) Strap ends continued in use, also the small objects which archaeologists have called "dress hooks". A pair of these hooked tags, found at the knees of a skeleton of indeterminate sex in Winchester Cathedral (fig. 16.10), has been assumed to be fasteners for gartering, but this seems implausible and impractical. In at least two instances hooked tags seem to have secured money bags,[24] and it is uncertain whether any of these hooks were directly associated with clothing. Finger rings, both plain and decorated, seem to have continued in popularity.

Still within the realm of archaeological evidence, we may learn something about late Anglo-Saxon textiles from the vestments of St. Cuthbert, recovered when the reliquary coffin of the saint was opened in 1827. The fabrics recovered included imported silks and native embroideries. The silks, even in their present fragmentary state, give us some idea of the wares which the merchants Ælfric knew of were bringing to England, some of which doubtless were worn by wealthy seculars. The embroideries demonstrate the kind of technique which might have decorated the fillets, cuffs and borders of secular garments. (The textiles are discussed in detail below.)

Color in Art and Reality

Many of the pictures in Anglo-Saxon manuscripts are line-drawings executed in brown or colored inks. Others are painted in a gloriously rich variety of shades. It would be wise, however, not to interpret too literally the coloring of garments shown in late Anglo-Saxon art. The embroiderers of the Bayeux "Tapestry" might color a horse green with two terracotta legs! The effect is not incongruous in context, for one responds to the tonal contrast rather than to the degree of realism in the shades; but this means that when a woman is depicted in the Bayeux "Tapestry" wearing a brown robe with pendant sleeves lined in blue (fig. 16.6), we cannot take it as proven that the Anglo-Saxons literally lined their sleeves with a contrasting color. The variety of shade conveys the difference between the outer and inner surfaces of the sleeve as it does the outer and inner legs of the horse.

Similarly, the painters of Anglo-Saxon illuminations may not have been concerned with literal depictions of dress colors. Manuscript illuminations, like the embroidered pictures, were executed in bold outline which was subsequently "colored in" rather as a child fills in a coloring book, and with the same disregard for consistency. If we consider a scene from the "Tapestry" in which a cask of wine is carried by wagon (Scene 37), we can see that the barrel hoops, wheel spokes and harness are colored inconsistently. How much reliance can we place, therefore, on the contrasting girdles and stockings of the accompanying figures?

A painter may sometimes have misunderstood the outline (perhaps because it was made for him by another artist, or because he copied it from a model he did not understand) and introduced an unwarranted change of color. There is an example of this in an illumination in London, B. L. Harley 2908, f.123v which led the costume historian Planché to conclude that women's costume included a single mitten.[25] I feel that the painter has misunderstood the drawing: the figure makes a traditional gesture in which the upraised hand is covered by the robe. In coloring the hand area blue, the painter has created a false impression of a mitten. Similarly, the areas of decoration on cuffs, hems and, sometimes, on the skirts of women in illustrations may be authentic—we have literary evidence for the first two kinds of ornament—or they could be artistic flourishes.

Provided we avoid the kind of naivety which led one costume historian to believe that Anglo-Saxon men habitually dyed their hair and beards blue because they are painted blue in London, B. L. Cotton Claudius Biv, the richness of color in late Anglo-Saxon art can tell us much about the taste of the people. The polychrome jewelry of early centuries has testified to their love of bright color; the dyed threads in the Bayeux "Tapestry" and the Cuthbert embroideries demonstrate something of the range of fabric colors available. There are eight colors detectable in the Bayeux "Tapestry": a terracotta red, three shades of green, two shades of blue and two of yellow. In the Cuthbert embroideries there are shades of reds, greens and fawns, plus brown, pink, blue and white as well as gold. The richest fabric we know of was called *godweb* in English, *purpura* in Latin. A thick, silken cloth, made in various colors as well as purple (below, p. 455), it was a luxury cloth suitable for liturgical use, but could also be owned by wealthy English seculars. In her late tenth-century will, a woman named Æthelgifu bequeathed *iii godwebbenan cyrtlas* as well as other garments of various shades: *hire rotostan cyrtel* ("her brightest kirtle"), *minne blæwenan cyrtel* ("my blue kirtle") and *oðera hire dunnan cyrtla* ("others of her brownish kirtles").[26] The *dunnan,* "brownish" garments were perhaps made of undyed wool.[27] The dun-colored garments were also prized, however, for in the same century a woman named Wynflæd saw fit to bequeath *hyre bestan dunnan tunecan* ("her best brownish tunic") as well as *hyre blacena tunecena* ("[one] of her black tunics").[28] As I have suggested elsewhere,[29] the darker garments bequeathed by this lady may have been for religious use. Indeed, it was expected that women should wear sober clothing on religious occasions: *Wif moton under brunum hrægle to husle gan*[30] ("women must attend Eucharist in a dark garment").

Cloaks

There are numerous cloak names documented from the late Anglo-Saxon period, of which the most common are: *basing, hacele, hwitel, loða, mentel, rift, sciccels and wæfels.* In most cases the sources of the word are glosses, but literary evidence proves that the *hacele* and *mentel* could be worn by women (although both words were also applied to men's garments): in an account of the martyrdom of St. Pelagia a *hacele* is worn by a woman[31] (apparently as a penitential garment, although this is not a usual association) and in Wynflæd's will a *mentel* (one of at least two Wynflæd owned, apparently) is bequeathed to the testatrix's granddaughter and a *mentelpreon* (a "cloak-pin" or "cloak-brooch") to her daughter. The granddaughter, recipient of *hyre beteran mentel,* is also to receive a fastener: *hyre ealdan gewiredan preon* ("her old wire [?filigree] brooch" or "pin").[32] Another woman, Wulfwaru, bequeathed to a church something which might have been a garment. She referred to the object as a *hrycg-hrægl* ("back-garment"),[33] an unusual word which could, conceivably, mean "cloak" (although, in another Anglo-Saxon will, Bishop Alfwold bequeathed *i hrigchrægl* and *i sethrægl,* "one back-garment and one seat-cloth,"[34] a context which makes the *hrycg-hrægl* sound more like a cover for furniture than an article of clothing).

A cloak arranged symmetrically over both shoulders with an opening at the front, which could be pulled over the head to form a hood, which was in use in the eighth and ninth centuries, is still found, but in a minority of illustrations. A cloak like this can be seen on the figure of a woman journeying by foot in a scene from London, B. L. Cotton Claudius Biv (fig. 16.2). A garment draped as loosely as this would seem to require some fastener at the neck or chest, as can be seen in a late tenth-century drawing in a manuscript of Prudentius' allegorical poem *Psychomachia*. In isolation the drawing would not offer strong evidence, since firstly the set of drawings (like the other three Anglo-Saxon *Psychomachia* cycles) is known to be based on a fifth-century continental original[35] and secondly the artist was illustrating a Latin text. However, in this case, the artist was required to illustrate, among numerous other details, the appearance of the personified *Superbia* ("Pride"). The Latin text specified that her garments included a *palla* (a "garment" or "cloak") gathered *a pectore nodum* ("in a knot at the breast").[36] The artist chose to picture her in a hooded cloak, clasped by a central brooch (fig. 16.11). It is a practical-looking arrangement, and, since we know that large disc brooches were fashionable at this time, probably consistent with contemporary dress.

A garment which could be either a small cloak or a shawl or scarf, is wound round the head of the personified *Luna* (the Moon) as illustrated in the early eleventh-century London, B. L. Cotton Tiberius Bv (fig. 16.12). There is no visible brooch or pin, however, and the arrangement of the garment, which has one narrow end or corner hanging below the arm, seems improbable (or, at best, insecure). The swirling garment represents the moon's rays (as the sun's rays are depicted round the head of *Sol* in the same figure) and the artist may have been as indifferent to realism on this point as he was in the harnessing of the beasts which draw the couple's chariots.

A fragmentary sculpture of the Madonna from Sutton-on-Derwent, Humberside,[37] bears the remains of a row of tassels which may have ornamented the garment. The sculpture is characteristically Viking in style and the tassels are a feature which do not occur in Anglo-Saxon work, although fringed and tasseled cloaks are common on Roman sculptures of Germanic figures (fig. 16.13), so they may have been a traditional decoration.

The Sleeveless Overgarment, With and Without Hood

Women are very often depicted in a loose, sleeveless garment which hangs from the shoulders, and which would cover the arms if they hung down. When the arms were raised (the position in most illustrations) the garment hung down between them as far as the knees, in a point or curve. It was fuller and longer at the back. This cloak was worn over a longer garment, and in some cases artists seem to depict another, knee-length robe between the two. At the wrists the tight sleeves of an inner garment are always visible, and sometimes the looser sleeves of a gown may also be seen between the cloak and the tight sleeves. The costume can be seen on the allegorical figure of *Philosophia* in Cambridge, Trinity College, 0.3.7, a Canterbury manuscript of Boethius dating to ca. 970 (fig. 16.14). Some drawings suggest that this garment was hooded, as for example on f.8 (fig. 16.15) of London, B. L. Harley 603, a Canterbury psalter of the early eleventh century (a copy of the early ninth-century Utrecht Psalter). Others suggest that a separate hood or wimple was worn over it. The distinction is not always very clear-cut in line drawings, which at this time often had numerous "fussy" lines depicting swirls and folds, but it is more obvious in painted pictures and in one scene from the Bayeux "Tapestry" where different colors are used for the headdress and cloak.

The shoulders of female figures are normally covered by the headdress, but one must assume that the cloak (if not hooded) was of a rectangular or oval shape, with an aperture for the head which was concealed by the headdress. The draping of the garment would be dependent upon the position of the hole. As the garment was longer at the back than the front, it seems that the aperture was not central.

Germanic *men* on Roman sculptures are depicted in a short cloak of the poncho type, which was probably made of animal skin, and derived its shape from the natural dimensions of the beast. Men evidently continued to wear fur jerkins.[38] However, there is no evidence of continuity between these and the cloth garment worn by women in late Anglo-Saxon illustrations. Indeed it seems likely that the garment was introduced and popularized through Christian art. In Anglo-Saxon art the Virgin was generally depicted in this costume, and it is also found on allegorical figures such as *Philosophia* in Cambridge, Trinity College 0.3.7 (fig. 16.14) and in the sumptuous illustration of St. Etheldreda (fig. 16.17) in the Benedictional of St. Æthelwold (a Winchester manuscript of ca. 971–84), where it appears to be confined at the waist by a broad sash. The use of the garment in these very stylized and derivative illuminations might lead to the suspicion that this *pallium*-like cloak was simply copied from imported manuscripts and not actually part of the Anglo-Saxon woman's wardrobe. (The garment does not appear on Anglo-Viking carvings.) However, there is some evidence that it was worn in the eleventh century, for it appears in London, B. L. Cotton Claudius Biv (fig. 16.3), and also in the Bayeux "Tapestry", possibly on Queen Edith (fig. 16.5) and more clearly, on the enigmatic figure labeled "Ælfgive" (fig. 16.7). The latter, since she is named, was presumably, like Edith, of high rank[39] and the garment, therefore, an aristocratic one. (It is not worn by the anonymous woman who leads her child from a burning house in a later scene [47] in the "Tapestry" fig. 16.6). It may have developed in importance only after the reign of Cnut (who died in 1035) for his queen is pictured in London, B. L. Stowe 944 wearing only a simple shoulder covering over her sleeved gown (fig. 16.8).

The Sleeved Gown

Many female figures appear in long, sleeved gowns. The necklines of these garments are concealed by the headdress, but the gowns seem to be tailored, unlike the sleeveless overgarments (above) which hang loosely from the shoulders. Until the early eleventh century the sleeves are depicted as either straight or only slightly flared at the lower end and often turned back to form a cuff (fig. 16.8). The sleeve often reaches only to the forearm (or falls back when the arm is raised) and sometimes leaves exposed the tighter sleeve of an undergarment (fig. 16.19, left hand). London, B. L. Cotton Claudius Biv contains several depictions of women in straight sleeves which, when hanging down, conceal the hands completely (fig. 16.4). This, apparently a device for keeping the hands warm, does not seem to be illustrated anywhere else in Anglo-Saxon art although it was a recognized feature of Roman costume—the Latin word *manica* originally signified a sleeve of this kind (later "glove"). Strips of simple ornament drawn at the sleeve ends by the Claudius artist suggest that embroidered or braided borders decorated the sleeves.

Wider sleeves may have been coming into fashion in the 1030s since the figure of the Virgin in London, B. L. Stowe 944 wears fairly wide sleeves (fig. 16.20) although Ælfgifu, Cnut's queen, in the same drawing has only slightly flared cuffs (fig. 16.8). Later in the eleventh century the sleeves were to flare into exaggerated points. Ælfgifu, now Cnut's widow, wears such sleeves in a portrait of her in London, B. L. Add. 33241, executed in the 1040s (fig. 16.9), but this is Flemish or northern French work and may predate the fashion in England. It is found in a drawing of the Crucifixion in the Gospels belonging to Judith, Countess of Flanders (New York, Pierpont Morgan Library 709) which is no earlier than the 1050s.[40] Both the Virgin and a small figure probably representing Judith herself wear gowns with long pointed sleeves with contrasting cuffs (figs. 16.21, 16.22). Similar sleeves are worn by the woman fleeing the burning building in the Bayeux "Tapestry" (fig. 16.6).

Many of the gowns are ankle-length. Some have a pronounced hem, or border of contrasting color at the bottom of the skirt (figs. 16.2, 16.7, 16.14, 16.17, 16.21). In some cases, an area of fullness at the feet suggests that the garment might have trailed on the ground. (Figs. 16.6, 16.14. The feet, unnaturally tiny, are always visible in these drawings, but the hem of the skirt sometimes looks as if it has been kicked up.) Decoration is occasionally suggested on the skirts of these gowns. Figures in Carolingian and Ottonian illumination sometimes wear gowns with elaborate front and border decoration, depicted colorfully with a series of circles or other ornamental devices (see figs. 16.23, 16.24); but these details do not appear on the drawings of women normally assigned to English artists. (The borders of men's tunics occasionally have simple decoration.)

The arms of female figures are almost always covered in illustrations. (The mythological figure of *Luna,* figure 16.12, is a rare exception.) In some cases it appears that the wide-sleeved garment was worn beneath the draped one, while close-fitting inner sleeves indicate yet another garment beneath. There are several instances where an artist has drawn a woman with a wide sleeve on one arm, and the other arm holding up the material of a *pallium* (e.g. fig. 16.19). Possibly the artist, in confusion, has drawn an impossible hybrid, but perhaps the costume could look like this if one garment were worn over the other.

When one tries to assign a name to the sleeved gown, one must recognize that this is the garment which seems to have been worn by secular women on most occasions, that it could be brightly colored and might have decoration at the wrists and elsewhere. If we consider the wills of wealthy ladies in the late Anglo-Saxon period, we find that the garment mentioned most often is the *cyrtel.* The *cyrtel* could be made in various colors, possibly in various fabrics, and it was valuable enough to be bequeathed. Despite the fact that the word *cyrtel* seems to have originally signified a short garment (it derives from Latin *curtus,* "short"), and continued to be used of the short tunic worn by men, it seems likely that its meaning had become extended, and that by this time it was used of a woman's gown.

The Girdle and Sash

In some illustrations the gown hangs loose, in others it appears to be pouched at the hip, as if over a concealed girdle. Some figures wearing the draped outer garment appear to have a broad, self-colored sash at the waist. A diagonal line suggests that the sash may be wrapped round twice or arranged with a twist in it (fig. 16.19). A rather different impression is given by the painting of Judith of Flanders (fig. 16.22) which, unlike most pictures of women, is a true profile. A tight belt is visible at the front of her gown, cinching the fabric to show off her waist, but it does not seem to continue round the back. The only parallel known to this author is on the earlier Genoels-Elderen Diptych (fig. 16.25), which may be Northumbrian work.

There are never any pendant girdle ends or any signs of a buckle, nor are there any tools or personal ornaments hanging from the girdle or sash.

The Undergarment

The sleeves of an undergarment are often visible at the wrist. They are colored white in painted pictures, suggesting linen material. The sleeves usually have a wrinkled appearance, perhaps because they were rather long, but perhaps because they were deliberately pleated for a decorative effect. The undergarments of the Viking Age women buried at Birka, Sweden, were pleated in this way, by the *plissé* technique in which the fabric was drawn together with needle and thread, soaked and stretched, thereby creating tight pleats, which were not, however, permanent, and would wash out. The Birka garments are now believed to have been imported into Sweden, probably from Kiev, certainly from a Slavonic area,[41] which makes it less likely that they were also known in England, but the parallel is still worth noting.

Hair and Headgear

Almost all illustrations of women from this period depict them in headdresses which cover the head and neck. In crowd scenes women are usually distinguished from men by their covered heads. There are, however, examples of bare-headed women in the illustrated Prudentius manuscripts: in London, B. L. Cotton Cleopatra Cviii, for example, the personified Vice *Avaritia* has an uncovered head and loose hair. This suggests that such an appearance was considered undesirable as was to be expected in a Christian society which followed St. Paul's dictum that women should cover their heads (I Corinthians, ii:5–6). The costume historian James Laver has stated that in the Anglo-Saxon period "young girls wore their hair long and loose over their shoulders, with a band to keep it from being too unruly. In the privacy of their homes women of all classes wore their hair the same way."[42] These suggestions seem plausible enough, but in fact there is little to confirm them in Anglo-Saxon art. Apart from the personified vices mentioned above, women's heads are depicted as covered, indoors and out. Headbands were certainly worn, but in conjunction with a cloth headdress, not in isolation (see below). Artists certainly did not distinguish between maiden and matron: they depicted the astrological sign *Virgo* as a woman wearing the usual headdress (see London, B. L. Arundel 60, f.5 and London, B. L. Cotton Tiberius Bv, f.7) and in London, B. L. Cotton Claudius Biv, where the artist, who, following the text, must have been aware that he was depicting unmarried girls likewise pictured them with covered heads (e.g. fig. 16.3).

The headcloth concealed hair, neck and shoulders. This garment perhaps owed its existence to the dissemination of Byzantine art through Christian Europe, although its origin lies, probably, further east—a similar headdress appears on a carving of the Virgin on a sixth-century Syrio-Palestinian ivory panel[43] (although this could be a wrap-around head cloth), but it seems to have appeared on Byzantine mosaics as early as the fifth century (Sta. Maria Maggiore, Rome, on the triumphal arch).[44] It was not, at this stage, the only women's headgear depicted, but it continued to be shown during the centuries when Byzantine art was at its most spectacular and influential (the ninth to thirteenth).[45]

There is some variation in the way this headdress is depicted by Anglo-Saxon artists, but this may be a matter of personal style. Some females (often biblical figures) appear to wear very loose headdresses with many folds; others have a closer-fitting version. Normally these hoods are drawn without any decoration, but there are exceptions in a group of female figures in London, Lambeth Palace Library 200 f.68v (fig. 16.26), a late tenth-century manuscript of Aldhelm's *De Virginitate*. The figures probably represent the nuns of Barking to whom this work was dedicated. Three of the ladies appear to have embroidered, possibly jeweled, headdresses. In one case there is just a simple ornament at the forehead, in the others there is a medial line and one has decoration on either side of the line.[46] There are what appear to be patterned headdresses on two female busts in the frame of an illumination in the Bury St. Edmunds Psalter (Rome, Vatican Bibliotheca Apostolica Reg. lat. 12), a Canterbury manuscript from the second quarter of the eleventh century (fig. 16.27). Usually the headdress reaches to just below the shoulders, but sometimes it seems to hang lower, combining the functions of headdress and cloak.

There are numerous documented Old English names for headgear, but the word *wimpel*[47] stands out when we seek a name for the typical headdress, for the garment shown in Anglo-Saxon illustrations closely resembles the article known as a wimple in later medieval times[48] and which has survived into our own day among some orders of nuns. Another significant term is *cuffie*, or *cuffia*, to which the modern "coif" is related. The term may also be connected to Old English *cufle* or *cugele*, "a monk's cowl," which suggests that the *cuffie* was hood-like. The word certainly referred to a garment of some value, since it appears as a bequest in Wynflæd's will.[49] Alternative headdress names are *hæt, hod* and *hufe*.

A fillet was considered a characteristic feature of the secular (married) woman's appearance, as we may deduce from the *Indicia Monasterialia*. The sign-language to be used in indicating a woman gives us some idea of the appearance of the fillet: *Gewylces ungehadodes wifes tacen is þæt þu [strice] mid foreweardum fingrum þin forwearde heafod fram þam anum earan to þon oþrum on bindan tacne.*[50] ("The sign for any unconsecrated woman is that you [indicate] with your forefingers your forehead from one ear to the other in a sign of a *binde.*") Both documentary and art evidence suggest that the fillet was worn in conjunction with a headdress of fabric rather than by itself. Wynflæd bequeathed two fillets in her will; one bequest, to a woman who was probably a secular, consisted of *cuffian and bindan,*[51] the other to Ceolthryth, a woman who seems to have been attached to a convent, was of *hyre betsð haliryft and hyre betstan bindan* ("her best holy veil and her best fillet").[52] Fillets are illustrated only rarely, but two types are represented: Queen Ælfgifu in the "portrait" in London, B. L. Stowe 944 (fig. 16.8), wears a decorated band across her forehead, under her hood. Two streamers ending in decorated tags emerge from her hood at the back, suggesting that, in this case, the fillet consisted of a narrow piece of fabric, embroidered or brocaded, possibly jeweled, and of considerable length. It probably resembled the narrow band worn by the allegorical *Pompa* in Prudentius illustrations (fig. 16.19), where it was presumably an indication of worldly vanity. In shape, although not in the manner of wearing, this band may have resembled the ecclesiastical stole.

The other kind of fillet is seen in various illuminations in the illustrated Hexateuch, London, B. L. Cotton Claudius Biv (fig. 16.3). This headband, which appears to be a continuous circlet, is worn outside the hood, like earlier headbands on the Grand Camée de France (fig. 16.28), and the Halberstadt Diptych (fig. 16.29). Such a band could have been made of cloth or leather; it could, possibly, have been solid metal, or, more likely, richly brocaded or embroidered with gold on a base of braided textile. We have three late Anglo-Saxon wills in which gold bands are bequeathed (they are called *bænd* or *bend*),[53] and although the contexts do not make it certain that these bands are for the head, this seems probable since the Old English word *bend* is found elsewhere glossing Latin *diadema* and *nimbus*.[54] They were all bequeathed for their bullion value; in each case the testator wished the bands to be divided up.

A group of women in the illuminated psalter, London, B. L. Harley 603 (fig. 16.15) seem to have projections under their hoods which could belong to some kind of caps or hats. It is tempting to identify this projection with the *scyfel,* a word found in glosses translating Latin *mafors* ("a woman's veil")[55] and *maforte* ("headdress"),[56] for among its cognates is Icelandic *skupla, skypill,* "a woman's hood hiding or shading her face."[57] The modern "shovel" as in "shovel-hat" may also be related.

Some female figures in illuminations wear a scarf or veil which is arranged in various ways. The dancing figure of *Luxuria* in the London, B. L. Add. 24199 Prudentius wears the scarf over her head (fig. 16.18). It crosses over her chest, passes under her arms and hands and forward over her right arm. A similar scarf is worn turban-style on some ivory carvings depicting the Virgin (fig. 16.30); one end of the garment encircles the neck, falling forward onto the shoulder. The scarf or veil is worn (fig. 16.31) by a woman in a group of female figures addressed by the poet in an illustration to Aldhelm's poems in London, Lambeth Palace Library 200. Again, the woman probably represents a nun of Barking so this additional headgear may represent the holy veil.

Possibly the scarf could also be worn wrapped around a hat, since a figure in the eleventh-century Paris Psalter, wearing what appears to be a round hat, carries a scarf.[58] (There is a scarf wrapped around a hat in this way in a ninth-century Carolingian illumination.)[59]

A veil which is squarish, rather than long, is held by an angel over the head of Queen Ælfgifu in the Stowe manuscript miniature. Queens seem to have worn a distinctive headdress, possibly a veil of this kind, in conjunction with a crown, since the monks' gesture representing "the King's wife" implies it: *Cyninges wifes tacen is þæt þu strece onbutan heofod, and sete syððan þine hand bufon þin heofod.*[60] ("The sign of the King's wife is that you extend [your hand] about your head, and afterwards set your hand above your head.") Queens on the Lady Gunhild's Cross, an ivory carving, ca. 1075,[61] and in the Stuttgart Psalter (fig. 16.24), wear veils under their crowns. The Stuttgart Psalter (e.g. on f.58r) also shows the veil being worn by itself, decorated at the front and hanging down at the back, leaving the neck exposed, but this is not a fashion, so far, found in English art.

Several documented Old English words appear to mean "veil": *rift* is used very often of nun's clothing, and came to stand for the religious life as we speak of "taking the veil" today;[62] Wynflæd, who was apparently a secular, bequeathed a *rift*,[63] but she may have owned it because she was a vowess, one of the pious women, often widows, who chose to live the religious life although they were not professed nuns.[64] To Wynflæd the *rift* differed from the *cuffie*. She seems to have bequeathed the former to a religious and the latter to a secular.[65] The word *wrigels*, sometimes signifying the wrapping of a corpse, could also be used of the holy veil.[66] *Orel*, although it is found mostly in glossaries rather than literary texts, could also have been used with religious significance.[67] Probably the veil could be worn in conjunction with a fillet, in view of Wynflæd's bequest of her best holy veil and her best fillet to Ceolthryth.[68]

In Anglo-Saxon art, women's hair is almost always hidden except for the occasional suggestion at the forehead. A unique exception, a depiction of the Virgin on an ivory book-cover (fig. 16.30), shows what appears to be a plait of hair over the crown, suggesting that women in the late Anglo-Saxon period were wearing their hair up. It would be practical, with the very loose-looking headdresses of the age, to have a plait or firm mound of hair to which to pin the wimple, hood or veil. Pins are never shown in illustrations, but several names for them appear in glossaries. Some of these, readily comprehensible compounds like *feax-preon*[69] ("hairpin") and *hær-nædl*[70] ("hair-needle"), may have been nonce-words, but we also find *cæfing*,[71] *up-legen*[72] and *þrawing-spinel*,[73] the latter apparently a pin for curling the hair.

The Leggings

In all Anglo-Saxon art women's legs are normally concealed by the skirts which fall to their feet. However, in London, B. L. Add. 24199, the Vice *Superbia* is shown on horseback, and enough of the leg is revealed to demonstrate that a strip of cloth is wound round from mid-calf to ankle in parallel bands, with two ends or strings hanging over the foot (fig. 16.11). Although the evidence is limited, it is possible that these bands were in general use; similar leggings are a very common component of male costume and there is much linguistic evidence of them. Three of the documented words are compounds of obvious meaning: *hosebend*[74] "hose band," *sceanc-bend*[75] "leg band," and *sceanc-gegirela*[76] "leg-ornament." *Wining*[77] was evidently a word in common use for a binding round the lower legs and the word *nostle*, which seems to have been a more general word for "band" or "fillet" could also be used of a leg band.[78]

The Footwear

Women in illustrations wear flat-soled ankle shoes, which, in painted pictures, are normally colored black. They are quite plain, except for a strip running down the front of the foot which is sometimes shown on the rare occasions when a foot is not in profile. In many of the illustrations the toes of the shoes are pointed, but not exaggeratedly so. There are hardly any variations in the depictions of women's footwear, apart from the slight stylistic differences between artists. A rare exception is the line drawing in London, Lambeth Palace Library 200 (f.68v) representing Aldhelm and (probably) the nuns of Barking; here, one woman wears ankle shoes which are left uncolored by the artist. Dots down the front perhaps represent laces. Two women wear low shoes or slippers with decorative projections at the instep. All the pictures that we have of women, even when they are illustrating narrative, are formal in pose and stylized in execution; the ankle shoe (*scoh*)[79] was the appropriate footwear in this context. Yet linguistic evidence and archaeological finds confirm that several different types of footwear were in existence. It seems likely that, according to situation, women might also have available to them various designs of ankleshoe (fig. 16.32), slippers (*stæppe-scoh,*[80] *slipe-scoh,*[81] *swiftlere*[82] see fig. 16.34), sandals (*crinc,*[83] *calc,*[84] *rifeling*[85]), raw hide shoes (*hemming, rifeling* see fig. 16.35)[86] and boots (see fig. 16.33).

The "Woman's Outfit"

The will of a woman named Wulfwaru includes the bequest to her elder daughter of "one woman's outfit, complete" (*anes wifscrudes*).[87] Unlike Wynflæd and Æthelgifu, Wulfwaru did not enumerate individual garments in her will, simply leaving to her younger daughter all the remaining female clothing . . . *ic geann ealles þæs wifscrudes þe þer to lafe bið.*[88] Nevertheless the bequest of "one woman's outfit, complete" suggests that the garments could be conceived as a costume, the individual pieces perhaps matching in fabric, color or trimming.

Elaborate Dress

Dodwell has shown that sumptuous textiles existed in great numbers in Anglo-Saxon England, textiles which dazzled the Normans who refer to them.[89] These fabrics included imported silks, often patterned; fabrics embroidered with gold, not only as an ornament for the edge of a piece of material, but sometimes so heavily decorated with gold as to appear encrusted with it; fabrics adorned with pearls and other jewels; fur-trimmed robes. Most of the evidence for the existence of these textiles concerns their use as religious vestments, but there is every reason to believe that royal and wealthy seculars also possessed such magnificent apparel. As Dodwell points out, the fact that the religious vocation of King Edgar's daughter Edith was said to be tested by jeweled robes and cloaks interwoven with gold is significant: "there is no reason to think that . . . her attire and tastes were different from those of her predecessors or successors."[90] More specifically, Matilda, William the Conqueror's queen, bequeathed one of her own cloaks to be used as a cope. The garment is described as being "of gold" (*ex auro*).[91] Matilda is known to have used English embroideresses[92] and if the gold work on this cloak was embroidered, it was probably English work.

Anglo-Saxon artists rarely suggest opulent fabrics, particularly for garments. We occasionally find what look like embroidered, even jeweled cuffs (figs. 16.4, 16.9) and very rarely a suggestion of ornament on a headdress (figs. 16.26, 16.27). Pattern on the skirts of the gown is found only occasionally, for example, exceptionally ornate, on the Virgin figure in a late tenth-century psalter, London, B. L. Harley 2904 (fig. 16.1), and, less elaborate, on a Virgin in a psalter dated to ca. 1060, London, B. L. Arundel 60.[93] Generally, such ornament is rather unsystematic, highlighting the knees of the figures and the hems of the gowns, but not giving a clear picture of overall decoration. An artist wishing to suggest elaborate dress was more likely to do so by adding an extra layer to the woman's garments, indicated by color contrast. For example, the figure of the Virgin in a richly decorated miniature, which was made after 966, in London, B. L. Cotton Vespasian Aviii (The New Minster Charter) wears a hood or wimple to her shoulders, a cloak which descends to the ankles at the back but only to the waist at the front, revealing a knee-length garment with tight sleeves and an ankle-length one below it. This proliferation of garments may not have been realistic.

Viking Costume

Female figures on Anglo-Viking sculptures are dressed in the Scandinavian iconographical tradition. There are profile figures on the Gosforth, Cumbria, Cross[94] and on a hogback tombstone from Sockburn, Co. Durham[95] and a full-face figure on a Sockburn cross shaft[96] which show that the unbelted gown trailing at the back in a "train" and surmounted by a short cloak or shawl, pointed at the back, was the costume which represented women in Anglo-Viking as well as in Swedish art (figs. 16.36, 16.37). We do not know how far the sculptors were guided by tradition, or to what extent these carvings represent what Viking women were actually wearing in England in the tenth century. The knotted pony-tail hairstyle is shown on the Gosforth Cross, and the hair on the Sockburn cross shaft figure is shown drawn back from the face, probably representing the same style. Two hogbacks from Lowther, Cumbria, show the hair worn in two plaits or tails, on either side of the face.[97]

Viking women in England almost certainly changed their style of dress towards the end of our period. The traditional tortoise brooches, worn in pairs at the shoulders, as earlier Anglo-Saxon women had worn brooches, have not been found in Viking York. Women seem to have adopted the single circular brooch, for the latest in our corpus of great silver disc brooches, the eleventh-century example from Sutton, Isle of Ely with a woman's name on it, is decorated according to Scandinavian taste.[98] The lack of head-covering which must have once distinguished Viking women from Anglo-Saxon, probably gave way to covered heads. A tenth-century hood made of silk and with linen ties was excavated from the Coppergate site in York (figs. 16.38–16.39), and fragments of two others have been found elsewhere in York and Lincoln (fig. 16.40). The silk was imported, but the caps were almost certainly made in this country. If so, they probably followed an established pattern for hoods, which were normally made of linen. The Coppergate hood could have fitted an adult or a child; it could be fastened so that it framed the face or tied at the nape of the neck.[99]

TEXTILE PRODUCTION

Archaeological Evidence

Excavation has produced two kinds of evidence: fragments of cloth, which, on analysis, can tell us something about the way the fabric was made; and pieces of equipment which had been used in the spinning and weaving processes.

Anglo-Saxon pagan and conversion period cemeteries have produced numerous small fragments of cloth, usually attached to metal, and more often from female burials than male. Textiles have been found among the king's effects in the Sutton Hoo ship burial, preserved by the presence of much metal.[100] Pieces of fabric have been recovered in other circumstances, usually where the ground has been waterlogged, such as from medieval rubbish pits. The excavation of later urban sites, such as Anglian and Anglo-Viking York, Winchester and the City of London has produced numerous small pieces. The textile remains from burials have the advantage that they are roughly datable from the associated grave goods, can be assigned to male or female owners and, from their position, give us some indication of function. The remains, however, consist of very tiny fragments. Pieces of cloth from urban sites are sometimes larger but are without context and sometimes have not been dated very closely.

With regard to textile tools, again both graves and settlement sites give us information. Pagan women were probably often buried with their spinning equipment and it is common to find in women's graves large beads which could have acted as whorls, or fly-wheels, for spindles. Spindles themselves were probably made of wood in most instances, and have not survived, but an iron example with a bone whorl on it was found in a grave at Wingham, Kent.[101]

Excavation of Anglo-Saxon settlement sites, particularly early villages,[102] has very often produced finds of the rings (usually clay but sometimes stone) which are known as "loom weights" and are characteristic of a piece of machinery which has been called "the warp-weighted loom" (fig. 16.41). These loom weights, together with tools such as combs, beaters and pickers, testify to a great deal of cloth-making in Anglo-Saxon settlements.

Finds of textile tools may be interpreted in the light of established knowledge of crafts in later medieval and modern times: hand spinning is an unchanging technique still practiced in some parts of the world; the warp-weighted loom was used by various peoples, and continued to be utilized until recent times in remote areas of Scandinavia. There is a collection of modern examples in the National Folk Museum in Oslo. Marta Hoffmann, the museum curator, has studied and examined the techniques of weaving with this loom, and the tools associated with it, enabling us to reconstruct how cloth was woven in the Dark Ages.[103] Tablet weaving, which produced flexible braids, is now enjoying a limited revival, and equipment may be bought from craft shops.

Literary Evidence

It has been claimed[104] that the warp-weighted loom is referred to in Aldhelm's Latin riddle *De Lorica,* and in the Old English translations of it, the Leiden Riddle and *The Exeter Book* Riddle 35. In describing obliquely a coat of mail the author asserts that although the object he describes is a garment, it was not woven on a loom:

> . . . Licia nulla trahunt nec garrula fila resultant . . .
> Nec radiis carpor duro nec pectine pulsor . . .[105]

Translated and augmented in the Old English:

> . . . Wundene me ne beod wefle, ne ic wearp hafu
> ne purh preata gepræcu præd me ne hlimmed
> ne æt me hrutende hrisil scriped
> ne mec ohwonan sceal amas cnyssan . . .[106]

(. . . Wefts are not interlaced for me, neither have I a warp, nor does thread resound for me through the force of strokes, nor does the whirring shuttle move through me, nor shall weavers' tools beat me from anywhere . . .)[107]

If the warp-weighted loom is indeed referred to here (and this is by no means certain, although the words *purh preata gepræcu* have been taken to signify the "shedding" operation of this loom), the poem confirms that this equipment was very familiar to Anglo-Saxons. At the least it is interesting to find a male scholar so familiar with the intricacies of the woman's craft of weaving. References to looms have also been claimed for Riddles 56 and 70 ("Web in the Loom" and "Shuttle," respectively) though with less certainty.[108]

Several glossaries contain numerous Latin words to do with the textile industry, with their Old English equivalents,[109] and we have a list of the textile equipment considered necessary for a large eleventh-century estate to own in *Gerefa,* a treatise on the responsibility of a steward:

He sceal . . . habban . . . fela towtola: flexlinan, spinl, reol, gearnwindan, stodlan, lorgas, presse, pihten, timplean, wifte, wefle, wulcambe, cip, amb, crancstæf, sceaðele, seamsticcan, scearra, nædle, slic.[110]

(He must . . . have . . . many textile implements: flaxcoil (?distaff), spindle, reel, yarn winder, ?uprights, beams, ?presses, ?some kind of comb, ?temple [the modern name for a piece of wood used to keep the width of the weaving constant], weft, weft [again ?warp intended], wool combs, ?some mechanism for turning the beam, ?beater, weaver's stick [?picker or beater or turning handle for the bean], ?shuttle, seamsticks, shears, needle, bobbin.)

Several of these terms are of uncertain meaning; interestingly, however, there is no mention of loom weights, unless this is what is meant by *presse*. Possibly the author expected the estate workers to use some other kind of loom, a vertical two-beam loom, or possibly, by this date, a horizontal treadle one (below, p. 446).

Spinning

Spinning was women's work, and for all but high-ranking women, must have been a constant occupation. Spinning was carried out by hand, for the spinning wheel had not yet been invented. The process of preparing the fibers for weaving was complex. A fleece, or wool (OE *flæþ, flis, wull,* or *wull-flys*) would be washed and combed with a wool comb (OE *camb, bannuc-camb, pihtene* or *wull-camb*). Flax fibers to be made into linen (OE *fleax, lin, linen* or *twin*) would be beaten and combed with a hackle or flax comb. The fibers were then wound onto a distaff (?*fleax-lin, wull-mod*), and attached to the stick-like spindle (*in-spinn, spinel*). On the spindle was a whorl (?*hweorfa*), which acted as a fly wheel. The whorl would be a pottery or wood disc, or a large bead could be used. The spinner flicked the whorl, which continued to revolve. The fibers were pulled from the distaff and twisted together into a thread. When the spun yarn (*gearn*) became so long that the spindle and whorl touched the ground and ceased to revolve, the spinner wound the spun thread (*þræd*) onto the spindle and started again.

The spinner could choose the direction of spinning by flicking the whorl either to the right or to the left, producing either Z-spun or S-spun threads (figs. 16.42, 16.43). Z-spinning was the more common in Anglo-Saxon times, but twills in the two types of thread, Z-spun (warp) and S-spun (weft) are often found in the same fragment of textile. It is possible for a weaver to produce patterns, including checks, by combining Z- and S-spun threads, effects which the Anglo-Saxons achieved.[111] Thread could be spun loosely or tightly. Sometimes more than one thread would be twisted together to make two- or more ply. The finished threads would be used in weaving on the loom to make fabric for clothing, bedding, hangings and bags; for braiding or plaiting into belts, cuffs and edgings, or for sewing thread.

Winding

The spindle with thread wound round it could possibly be used directly as a bobbin but this is unlikely; it might have been convenient to wind the thread into measurable lengths, in skeins, in which case a special skeinwinding reel could be employed, together with a swift, which wound the thread from the skeins into convenient balls. (Both types of object were deposited in the ninth-century ship burial at Oseberg, Norway.)[112] These are possible referents for the Old English words *reol* and *gearnwinde,* which are listed in *Gerefa* as *towtola* ("textile implements").

Tablet Weaving

The ingenious method of braiding known to modern exponents as tablet weaving was used to make belts, cuffs, ornamental braids to be stitched on to garments and, significantly, for the integral borders of textiles woven on the large warp-weighted loom (see below). The small (about 4.5 cm) tablets were probably made of thin pieces of wood or of hide in Anglo-Saxon times. They were usually square with a hole in each of the four corners, although triangular, three-hole tablets also existed and some tablet weaving used only two holes (either being made on two-hole tablets or on only half the holes of normal, square tablets).

In order to weave a braid (fig. 16.44), the weaver passed a separate warp thread through each hole in each tablet; individual threads entered the holes from either right or left according to the desired pattern. The tablets were placed in a pack and the ends of the warp threads secured. (It was simple for the weaver to tie one end to her belt.)

The weaver required a bobbin of weft thread and a small beating tool. To weave, she would pass the weft through the shed (the gap between the upper and lower warp threads). To change the shed, she turned the tablets one quarter, thus changing the relative positions of the holes. The weft thread was then passed back through the new shed.

Numerous turns of the tablets naturally over-twisted the warp threads. It was possible to untwist them by reversing the direction of turning, although this required care if a pattern was involved. Modern Scandinavian exponents achieve this simply by turning the weaving upside down!

Tablet weaving produces a braid which is thick and flexible and which can be patterned on both sides, the weft being concealed except at the edges. Undecorated braids can consist of a series of warp twists lying in the same direction (fig. 16.45) or (and this is a common variation, especially on the edges of braids) a series of chevrons, consisting of alternate Z and S twists, which gives the effect of a plait (fig. 16.46). This can be achieved by threading alternate tablets differently. It is possible to produce geometric patterns, either running continuously or in a series of blocks: two fragmentary braids found at Fonaby, Lincolnshire, had un-patterned chevron borders of unequal width, framing a diagonally pat-terned center area worked partly on two, partly on four, holes of the tablets. There are scraps of similar braids from Mucking, Essex,[113] Bergh Apton, Norfolk[114] and Portway, Hampshire.[115]

The most skilled weavers probably produced imaginative designs which were influenced by changes in fashion such as we find in illumi-nated manuscripts (one might look particularly at the borders of full-page illuminations for an insight into designs from the seventh century onwards), but there was probably a strong traditional element too, and, among the early settlers and the rustic population throughout our period, custom may have established patterns which were peculiar to families or regions. Unfortunately, the surviving examples recovered so far have been too few and small to test this hypothesis.

Braids were certainly made in bright colors, and color-contrast was used to embellish the woven pattern. The narrower braid from Fonaby, about 2 cm. wide, had blue or green in the central part, bordered by red, with a blue edging to the wider border. A Mucking, Essex, braid had blue, and possibly yellow, threads, bordered by red. The end of a linen braid, found attached to a strap end at Cambridge, and probably part of a belt, was worked in three colors, which were still identifiable in 1951 as white, pale blue-green and indigo (pl. 16.1).[116]

Tablet-woven braids could be embellished further by needlework. There is as yet only slight evidence from Anglo-Saxon England, but Mi-gration Age graves in Norway have produced examples on which needle-work decoration has been worked, in blocks, on untwisted warp threads at the center of the braid. This created a swastika pattern in red, blue and yellow on a braid from Øvre Berge,[117] and a series of stylized animals worked in animal hair (probably goat) from Snartemo (Grave 2)[118] and Evebø.[119] (The Anglo-Saxons may also have made use of goat hair.)[120] The most luxurious effect was achieved by decorating in gold thread, which could be achieved by brocading during the weaving process or by embroidering with a needle on the woven cloth. Goldwork was probably used for edging sleeves or hems. It was exploited effectively on the head-bands worn by wealthy, probably royal ladies in sixth-century Kent. Analysis of the remains of those headbands shows that they were deco-rated in simple geometric patterns, which occasionally incorporated crosses (fig. 16.47).[121] In the pagan period the decoration was carried out with strips of solid gold, beaten flat. In the Christian period the gold used for embroidery was a metal strip spun round a fiber core.[122]

Weaving

All weaving and spinning seem to have been women's work in Anglo-Saxon England, a fact that became incorporated into the English language: we still call unmarried women "spinsters." In Old English literature women who bring together peoples in friendship or dynastic marriage are called "peaceweavers." They continued to be female tasks until men began to operate the horizontal loom (which was not used in Europe before ca. 1000 A.D.), despite the fact that weaving, particularly on the warp-weighted loom, could be heavy work.

It is certain that the Anglo-Saxons made use of the warp-weighted loom,[123] not just because the non-perishable loom weights are common archaeological finds, but also because pieces of cloth from Anglo-Saxon context have been found to incorporate the tablet-woven starting border characteristic of this type of loom.

The loom consisted of two uprights (?*stodlan*) and a horizontal beam (*lorh, uma* or *web-beam*) to which the warp threads (*wearp*) were fastened. This could be achieved by means of the starting border, which was made by setting up the tablets with their warp threads through the holes, passing a weft thread through the warp in the usual way, then winding it round a number of pegs set wide apart before passing it back through the tablets. As this action was repeated, a tablet-woven braid with a series of long weft loops at one side would be created. The completed braid would be sewn through holes in the horizontal beam at the top of the large loom, when the loops, hanging vertically, would become the warp for the loom weaving. The ornamental edge could be incorporated into the finished blanket or garment.

The loom normally rested against a wall, or roof beam, so that the uprights were tilted. A bar (the shed rod) was fixed between them. Half the warp threads were pulled forward in front of the shed rod. The rest were allowed to hang straight down behind it. This division of the warp threads created a natural shed, that is, the space through which weft threads (*ab, aweb, wefta,* or *weft*) passed. (This natural shed is characteristic of the warp-weighted loom; the shed must be made mechanically on other looms.) The lower ends of the warp threads were tied, in bunches, to the loom weights, in such a way that there was equal weight on the back and front threads.

Attached to the uprights were brackets supporting the heddle rod. This was the movable part of the loom. The warp threads which were hanging free at the back of the loom were attached by threads, or leashes

(?*hefeld*) to the heddle rod. By moving this rod away from the loom, the weaver could pull the back threads forward, thus "changing the shed." A plain weave (tabby) would require one heddle rod; a simple 2x2 twill, and more complex twills, three (see below, pp. 449–452).

Weaving by this method was a strenuous task. The weaver had to stand up, rather than sit; she might climb on a bench to reach the top. Rather than crouch uncomfortably at the bottom, she might wind completed cloth onto the beam at the top of the loom. This was relatively simple if the beam was made to revolve by means of a handle (a sophistication known to the Romans; the Anglo-Saxons may have used it too ?*crancstæf*); otherwise the alternative was to lift the heavy beam and laboriously wind the cloth onto it.

A single weaver would have been constantly on the move and weaving was probably carried out by two workers. Judging by the size of surviving modern looms, the heddle rod was too wide and heavy to be lifted easily by one woman; she would have to lift one side of the rod into its new position, then walk to the other side of the loom to repeat the operation with the other side of the rod. The movement of passing the weft through the shed between the warps was similarly difficult for one weaver alone. She might have used a shuttle (*hrisl, ?sceaðel*), but this was not the flying shuttle of modern times, for the warp-weighted loom has no conveniently placed bar for a shuttle to run along. Anglo-Saxon weavers may have used, as modern Scandinavian women have done, a loose bobbin of threads which could be thrown into the shed and plucked out the other side. Two weavers could pass the bobbin to each other.

The threads of a loom may cling together and can be straightened by means of bone or wooden pickers, pointed at each end. After the weft had been passed through the warp several times the fabric would still resemble loose netting, and the weft would be deliberately made wavy, to prevent it pulling too tight and narrowing the cloth. (The use of a thicker warp thread at each end would strengthen the sides, important if a blanket or cloak was being made.) The threads had to be compressed by beating with a beater, an awkward task with the warp-weighted loom since weaving starts at the top and threads must be beaten upwards. Modern beaters are wooden, and sword-shaped. No wooden examples have survived from Anglo-Saxon times but some metal ones have, from graves of wealthy, sixth-century Kentish/Frankish women. It is interesting to speculate whether their resemblance to weapons had a ritual significance: the weaving sword may have symbolized woman's role as peacemaker, just as the battle sword symbolized man's function as war maker.[124]

The warp-weighted loom was not capable of weaving bales of cloth to be cut up. The length of the finished fabric was dependent on the height of the loom, plus the amount that could be wound up onto the beam. Probably the weaver set out to make a garment- or blanket-length, and measured her warp threads accordingly. A braided closing border could be added to the end of the cloth. This was done by attaching tablets to the last threads in the weft direction. The warp threads of the large loom passed through the shed of the tablets before being cut off.

Probably most women could weave, and, in the early centuries of our period, the more utilitarian cloths were produced by the women of a family, as needed. The warp-weighted loom is easily dismantled, and in recent times in Scandinavia the components would be stored in a barn; when a blanket or garment was needed the loom could be set up against the kitchen wall for the time required to weave it, perhaps a few days. (The collapsible nature of the equipment is emphasized by the fact that in the languages of northern Europe the loom was not referred to as a unit, but in terms of its parts: uprights, beams, rods.) The Anglo-Saxons, however, did not have the cozy all-purpose farm-house kitchen or the small family unit of modern Scandinavia. Excavation of Anglo-Saxon villages shows that the main hall provided a nucleus, while *grubenhäuser* (huts with sunken floors, or hollows under the floors), housed crafts and industry. As far as we can tell, a *grubenhaus* catered only for one occupation, and where evidence of looms has been found, we seem to have vestiges of buildings catering specifically for weaving. Loom weights have been found within *grubenhäuser* on many sites. One, at Old Erringham, Sussex,[125] and a more substantial building at Upton, Northamptonshire,[126] each had evidence of two looms and were probably weaving sheds. The settlement at West Stow, Suffolk, where archaeologists found loom weights in three *grubenhäuser* as well as other weaving equipment, such as combs, may have been producing enough cloth to supply other settlements.[127] As Anglo-Saxon society changed, and large estates, both secular and ecclesiastical, arose, weaving certainly became more organized and a specialized task. In some households the skilled workers were slaves—Wynflæd mentioned two such women in her will (*ane crencestran and ane semestran*, "a woman-weaver and a seamstress").[128]

It is possible that the Anglo-Saxons knew some other loom from earliest times, but since archaeological evidence cannot testify to this there is no certainty. The strongest indication of some other loom is the presence of 2x1 twill fabrics from pre-eighth-century burials, as well as from later urban sites. These uncommon, "three-shed twills" *could* have been woven on the warp-weighted loom, but are unlikely to have been, since the "over two, under one" progression (fig. 16.48) does not utilize the natural shed. It is possible, even probable, that the early examples were imports (see p. 451), but the later ones, for example, from the City of London, may not have been. In any case, the Anglo-Saxon settlers may have copied a two-beam loom from their Romano-British neighbors. The warp-weighted loom continued to be used throughout the period—there are loom weights from late occupation sites—but it is possible that a two-beam loom co-existed, and gradually superseded it. The decline of loom weights in York from the tenth century suggests that the two-beam loom supplanted it at that time, and the use of a distinctive tool—a single ended pin beater—indicates that the two-beam loom was in use at a manorial estate at Goltho, Lincolnshire, in the tenth century.[129]

A two-beam loom[130] consists, basically, of uprights and two parallel beams at top and bottom. The loom is vertical, not tilted like the warp-weighted loom. The loom may be set up by winding the warp thread in a continuous spiral round the two beams. The weaving is compacted with a toothed beater (*?pihten*)[131] rather than a sword-shaped one. After weaving, the cloth is removed by cutting the warp threads or sliding them off the beams. Thus, the finished product is a flat piece of cloth with cut or looped warp threads at top and bottom, rather than a braided border. Alternatively, it is possible to weave a cylindrical piece of cloth, by winding the warp threads both around the beams and around a stick or cord laid parallel to them. If, at the end of the weaving, the stick or cord is left in place, the result is a cylinder of cloth; if it is removed, the cloth can be laid out flat. This cylindrical weaving was certainly known in Iron Age Denmark, for the *peplos*-type gown from Huldremose (pl. 16.2) was woven this way. The method might, perhaps have been known to the Anglo-Saxons, who wore a similar gown in the fifth and sixth centuries, but fragments of tablet weave on their brooches suggest that their version of the *peplos* was often woven with a starting border and, hence, on the warp-weighted loom. Ultimately the two-beam loom was to give way to the horizontal, treadle-operated loom, which was already, it seems, in York by the late eleventh century.[132] A man's tool, it heralded a cultural change: faster weaving, the beginning of mass production and industrialization.

Types of Weave

The simplest weave is tabby, or plain weave (fig. 16.49), in which the weft thread passes over one, under one, of the warps (fig. 16.50). Finds vary from coarse quality, like sacking, to very fine fabrics which belonged to garments. Tabby is easily woven, but particularly simple on the warp-weighted loom with its natural shed. Another common weave to have survived is, however, the 2x2 twill, which has a pattern of diagonal lines (figs. 16.51, 16.52). Again, various qualities of cloth have been analyzed, but we can safely say that this was the material frequently used for the *peplos*-type gown.

Patterned twills are rarer and were certainly luxury fabrics. Their geometric patterns were the result of skilled weaving, using three heddle rods and the shed rod in a complex sequence. The characteristic appearance of the fabric is a series of asymmetrical diamonds or lozenges (fig. 16.53). In English these are called, by modern experts, broken diamond or lozenge twills; the Norwegian name *ringvend* "ring-weave" is equally descriptive.[133]

The early Anglo-Saxon examples include some exceptionally rich deposits, such as Sutton Hoo, Suffolk and Broomfield, Essex. There are later examples from occupation sites, including Viking York and London.

The English patterned twills belong to a considerable corpus of similar high quality fabrics known from north-west Europe, most of them from Scandinavia and Iceland, and belonging to the tenth century. The Viking Age examples from Birka, Sweden, where they were found in more than forty graves, have received considerable attention.[134]

These twills probably evolved specially for the warp-weighted loom and some Scandinavian examples had clearly been woven on it; but the Birka twills were of such consistently high quality that it was thought they were the work of skilled professional weavers[135] whose expertise was greater and more standardized than could be found locally.[136] The Scandinavian contexts are consistent with the probability that this luxury cloth was traded on the international market: Birka was a busy trading port, so was Kaupang in Norway. The various find spots in Norway (mostly coastal) suggest trading. The Norwegian contexts include the mid-ninth-century burial at Oseberg of a queen who had the wealth and taste to command the most prestigious goods available.[137]

Geijer suggested that these luxury patterned twills should be identified with the *pallium fresonicum* or "Frisian cloth" well-known to historians.[138] According to Charlemagne's biographer the Monk of St. Gall, the Frankish Emperor sent some of this cloth to Haroun-al-Rashid, in the ninth century.[139] It is generally accepted that the role of the Frisians who gave their name to the cloth was that of traders rather than manufacturers. Various possible non-Frisian European sources have been discussed[140] but Geijer has made the well-supported suggestion that the cloth was manufactured in Syria and exported to the West.[141] The sixth- and seventh-century examples from England could well have been imported through trade with Frisia. On the other hand, these Anglo-Saxon examples are the earliest in north-west Europe, and it is quite possible that they were made in England, or Ireland, and exported from there to Scandinavia. This is not to deny that diamond twill was woven in Syria and that this could also be traded to Europe. Anne Stine Ingstad has found three varieties of this twill among the fabrics from the Oseberg ship, a royal woman's tomb: one of mohair and of such fine quality that she believes it to be Syrian; another, typical of finds from burials in north-west Europe, possibly imported from the British Isles. The third, she believes, was probably woven in the queen's own workshops, a suggestion which, if it is correct, means that skilled professional weavers could have been working in Scandinavia, employed by a wealthy patron.[142]

It would be pleasant to think that the Anglo-Saxons were the first European professional weavers of diamond twills; but the weave itself was known much earlier to the Germanic people; a mantle from Gerum, Sweden, dating from the Bronze Age, is the earliest known example, and a piece of checkered cloth from Karlby, Denmark, belongs to the same era.[143] There are a number of examples from the western territories of the Roman Empire including Britain.[144] The weave may be depicted on several surviving pieces of art: there are incised diamond patterns on the clothing of two women depicted on sculptures from Mainz (fig. 16.54) and there is a similar effect on the trousers of a male figure ("a Parthian prisoner") depicted on a Roman clay lamp found at Corfu.[145]

Three end twill (fig. 16.55), which has a 2x1 pattern on one side, 1x2 on the other, is also uncommon. This fabric, while much rarer than broken diamond twill, sometimes occurs in sixth- and seventh-century burials which also contain broken diamond twill. This cloth, too, occurred in the rich Broomfield and Sutton Hoo deposits, and at least one other example (from Lakenheath) is of very high quality. The particularly interesting feature of this cloth is that it is unlikely to have been woven on the warp-weighted loom, since the "over two under one" progression (fig. 16.48) does not make use of the natural shed which is an advantage this loom has over others. It has therefore been suggested that this cloth was imported with (again) Syria as the suggested place of origin.[146] Wild, however, has recently pointed out the relatively large number of textiles from the Roman era which have been found in Germanic areas—Denmark,

north and south Germany—and also in Britain.[147] This may imply that
the barbarians of western Europe were making the cloth themselves. The
Anglo-Saxons, therefore, might have learned the art either from their
continental kin or from their Roman neighbors in Britain, from whom
they may have copied the two-beam loom.

Fibers

The vast majority of textile fragments found in Anglo-Saxon context[148]
are of sheep's wool (*wull*). The fleece type is, on the whole, what Ryder
calls "generalized medium," and this was doubtless produced in England.[149] Very fine wool, such as was found in the Sutton Hoo ship burial[150] was probably imported. Finds of vegetable fiber are less common.
This may reflect the rather more luxurious role of linen (*lin, linen* or
twin), something we can deduce from Bede's anecdote of St. Etheldreda,
who chose wool to mortify the flesh, but is more likely to be an accident
of survival, that the woolen garments were more likely to be in contact
with metal, which preserved them, than the linen ones, that iron is kinder
to wool than linen[151] (and most brooch pins are iron) and that while wool
may survive in waterlogged deposits, linen may not. The finds may reflect geographical or cultural conditions too, wool being fairly quickly
turned into garments, given a supply of pasture and sheep, whereas linen
production takes several months and considerable organization.

Whereas the woolen fibers have been found in the various twill
weaves and, less commonly, tabby, the fibers which have been identified
as linen have more frequently been woven into tabby cloth.[152] Probably
these fragments sometimes came from shrouds, particularly when they
were preserved on the *outsides* of brooches or buckles. (This is much less
common than preservation on the *back* of a brooch.) In the case of two
Fonaby grave groups, however, the relationship of tabby weaves on the
front of brooches to other fabrics suggested that the tabbies belonged to
head-veils which were overlaid, in the brooch area, by cloaks. These
Fonaby tabbies seem to have been wool, but they suggest that the other
tabbies on the fronts of brooches, whether linen or wool, could also have
been from veils.

Finds from Finglesham, Kent[153] of linen threads on the backs of
buckles from male graves suggest that there, in the seventh century, men
were wearing linen shirts or tunics which must have been belted, but usually fibers from the backs of buckles have been found to be wool. An example is the now well-known belt suite decorated in so-called Quoit

Brooch style, found at Mucking Grave in 117, where the metal preserved a "sandwich" of linen, leather belt and woolen garment.[154] This belt suite must have been worn by a man in a position of authority in the fifth century.

Silk, which must always have been expensive and luxurious, seems to have been imported into England from almost the earliest days of Anglo-Saxon Christianity, for use as ecclesiastical vestments. Our earliest authenticated example of silk (thread on a fragment of flax, tabby-woven cloth, perhaps a silk stripe, or decoration on the linen), was found inside a small seventh-century reliquary in a child's grave at Updown, Kent. The textile fragment was probably a holy relic, snipped from an ecclesiastical vestment, perhaps associated with one of the first missionaries.[155] Crowfoot has identified what was probably a silk-covered button from a grave and smith's hoard found at Tattersall Thorpe, Lincolnshire. This was late seventh- or eighth-century.[156]

We can learn something about the nature of imported silks from the remains of precious cloths presented at various times to the shrine of the Northumbrian saint, Cuthbert, and preserved in his reliquary coffin.[157] The tenth- or eleventh-century "Rider" silk, a cloth probably of Persian origin, and named from the falconer figure incorporated in its design, was printed in gold. The seventh-century "Nature Goddess" silk, and a cloth ornamented with peacocks and griffins, had their multicolored designs woven in. Fawn-colored tissued taffetas had probably been used as linings for vestments. These taffetas had probably been woven as early as the seventh century, although we do not know when they were imported and made into garments.

Fragments from the grave of the last Anglo-Saxon king, Edward the Confessor, show that the body was shrouded in a golden-colored silk with a self-colored pattern woven in a "damask" technique. The design, of roundels with confronting birds and conventional plants between, is typically Byzantine.[158] The silk was not, probably, made as a shroud; it may have been a garment which the king wore in his lifetime. It had perhaps been a coronation gift. It has been suggested that this particular silk did not come to England through commercial channels, but directly from the east to the king.[159] As such, it must have been unusually opulent, and we are fortunate to have first-hand evidence of the finest fabrics in England in 1066.

Certainly the importation of silk by personal gift was the rule rather than the exception in the seventh, eighth and ninth centuries. We have documentary evidence of silks being presented to English churches as early as the seventh and eighth.[160] Individual pilgrims were able to purchase silks abroad for their churches (where they were used as altar cloths and hangings) or for their own use. Theodred, a tenth-century Bishop of London bequeathed in his will two such vestments: *min wite massehakele . . . and . . . þere gewele massehakele þe ic on Pauie bouhte* ("my white cope . . . and . . . the yellow cope which I bought in Pavia").[161] Pavia, capitol of Lombardy in northern Italy, and on the pilgrims' route from England to Rome, was an important trading center for eastern fabrics.[162]

By the tenth and eleventh centuries professional merchants were bringing luxury textiles to England, as attested by Ælfric (see p. 423). Silk garments were certainly available to seculars at this time, although the rich and royal may have had them before. The Monk of St. Gall tells us that Carolingian courtiers wore silk (from Pavia) in the ninth century.[163]

Certainly the imported silk found a ready market. It was still much in demand for ecclesiastical purposes, and wealthy seculars were probably using silk for hangings and cushions as well as clothing.[164] According to a post-Conquest source, King Edgar gave silk to Kenneth, King of the Scots, in 975.[165] Silk being exchanged between royalty is not surprising; but archaeological finds are demonstrating that silk was also worn by those in humbler circumstances. From York, a complete silk cap has been recovered (figs. 16.38, 16.39)[166] and the remains of others have been found in London,[167] Lincoln (fig. 16.40)[168] and York. From Milk Street, London, there are the remains of a silk ribbon, 9mm wide, dyed red and blue, and two silken cords, one probably yellow, the other red.[169]

Although there is documentary and archaeological evidence of many silk textiles in late Anglo-Saxon England, we should not underestimate the value of these fabrics. Dodwell interprets a remark of Bede's about the worth of some textiles to imply that the price of one silk "would have kept one and a half families for life."[170] Against this, there is the evidence that London families of the tenth century could afford to throw away silk ribbons. There is of course a difference in scale; a silken robe, elaborately patterned and perhaps encrusted with embroidery, would be a luxury for the highest in the land; a cap ribbon was a woman's trinket; but both had been laboriously extracted from the silk worm, dyed, woven and imported from the east, with all the dangers and expenses that the journey entailed. If prosperous Londoners could be so blasé about silk cords and ribbons, these things must have become fairly commonplace.

The silks discussed so far were imported already woven, but it is evident that silken thread was also imported. The finest Anglo-Saxon embroidery is carried out in silk thread. It is certain that this embroidery work is English, not imported, for there is documentary evidence about English embroideresses as well as the indisputably English St. Cuthbert embroideries which prefigure the English Winchester Style of art as well as carrying an "inscription" stating that they were made to the orders of an English queen for an English bishop.[171] Silk threads for sewing and embroidery would consist of relatively small quantities, but if the English were actually weaving silk themselves (and the English design of the late eighth- or early ninth-century "David silk" now in Maaseik, Belgium,[172] suggests that they may have been) this means that considerable amounts of silken thread were coming into the country.

The Anglo-Saxons used the words *seoluc* and *side* for silk, but they also used the word *godweb* for very luxurious cloth. The meaning behind this compound word is not, simply "good cloth" but "a godly or divine cloth." It was used to translate Latin *purpura,* which, literally, means "purple" or "purple cloth." Dodwell, however, has suggested that the Anglo-Saxons did not use the terms *godweb* and *purpura* for the purple-dyed silk which was a not uncommon luxury at the time, but reserved them for some very special material. Dodwell demonstrates that this material might be of various colors, not just purple: English churches owned vestments of red, white, green and black *purpura*. Some descriptions imply that there was more than one color in it. Essentially *godweb/purpura* was thick and iridescent; Dodwell argues convincingly that this material was shot-silk taffeta.[173]

The Finishing Processes

The processes by which linen and woolen fabrics were "finished" were to become major industries in the later Middle Ages: as early as the twelfth century the Lower Brook Street area of Winchester had become a center for fulling and dyeing,[174] and there were no doubt similar urban concentrations in other towns. The finishing processes for wool included fulling—scouring, beating and bleaching the cloth—teasing, in which the nap of the cloth was raised with teasels, and shearing the raised surface, a procedure which might be repeated several times.[175] We do not know how early these processes became popular. The verb *tæsan* "to tease wool" and the noun *fullere* "a fuller" are old English words; but the fact is, that of the many fragments of textile from the Anglo-Saxon period, there are very few examples, early or late, which have been teaseled. The rare examples from Anglo-Saxon graves are mostly from sites where there had been continuity of occupation since Roman times, and where the Anglo-Saxons almost certainly learned the process from the Romano-Britons.[176] Whether the art was lost, or whether it continued to be used in some areas is, so far, uncertain; certainly no tubs or other vessels for fulling, or for dyeing, have been found. However, the finishing processes would produce a thick, felted cloth, the luxury feature of which was the finished surface. Such processes would have been inappropriate for the diamond- or lozenge-patterned twills which were the most luxurious products of the warp-weighted loom, for the woven geometric patterns which had taken great skill to achieve would have been obscured by the finishing. This fact does not completely rule out fulling—there is a Romano-British diamond twill from Verulamium which had been finished in this way[177]—but the weave and the finishing are not really compatible.

Almost certainly the conception of a luxury woolen fabric changed over the Anglo-Saxon period, and this may have been associated with a change of loom. It seems likely that, together with absorbing other southern European influences, the Anglo-Saxons came to demote the warp-weighted loom to the more mundane proposes, while another kind of loom and elaborate finishing came to be the rule for fine clothes. Yet the patterned twills continued to be made in late Saxon times (and beyond). They have been found, for example, in eleventh-century context in the City of London.[178] This type of cloth, and the loom on which it was originally woven, continued to be popular among the Scandinavian peoples. Broken diamond twill, as already stated, has been found in Viking Age Scandinavia, and it has also been found in Viking York.[179]

Linen, also, was subject to finishing processes such as bleaching and smoothing. Glass linen smoothers have been found in urban context in late Anglo-Saxon and Anglo-Scandinavian towns.[180]

Although the Anglo-Saxons' enjoyment of bright colors is evident in their polychrome jewelry and their paintings, it is likely that the lower classes did not possess clothes which were dyed. There was, at this time, great variety in the natural colors of fleeces, with brown, black, white and gray sheep.[181] It was possible to weave checked or striped material by using contrasting wools,[182] and subtle effects may have been created by exploiting threads which had been woven in different directions. It is a fact that a majority of the woven fabrics from our period which have been scientifically examined have not been found to be dyed; the vats and furnaces which would have been necessary for dyeing have not, so far, been identified.

Artificially colored clothes were probably the prerogative of the wealthy, and highly prized. Æthelgifu's will, with its mention of her blue kirtle as well as her brightest and her brownish kirtles (see above, p. 428) gives us a glimpse of the possibilities. A few continental examples, far better preserved than anything from England, widen the picture: the sixth-century Merovingian lady wearing a ring inscribed "Arnegund", with her violet colored tunic under a red gown;[183] the Oseberg queen in an embroidered and appliquéd gown of red, with a red dress over it; and her attendant in an appliquéd gown of blue.[184]

Aldhelm wrote of clothes being brightly colored using the Latin terms *coccinea* and *iacintina* to describe the shades, which later Anglo-Saxons glossed *wealrœd* (or *weolcrœd*) and *hœwen* or *wœden,* respectively. Bede confirms that the Anglo-Saxons made a dye from shellfish[185] (OE *wealc,* "a whelk, cockle"). Undoubtedly vegetable dyes were a major source of color. These were certainly made locally, but as Ælfric's *Mercator* testifies, dyestuffs were also regularly imported (see above, p. 423, and n.1). The pigments in just a few relevant textiles give us some idea of the sources. The Sutton Hoo textiles were dyed blue with woad, yellow with weld and, possibly, red with madder.[186] The Oseberg queen's attendant's blue outfit was probably dyed with woad, a plant almost certainly available to the Anglo-Saxons. The queen herself was in red garments which had been dyed with madder, but we should note that they were almost certainly imported from the east. A piece of red and blue braid from London may also have been made of threads dyed abroad, as it was silk. A piece of silken cord from London had been dyed, probably yellow, with weld. A poncho or coat from Rønbjerg, Denmark, was colored yellowish-red from alder bark.[187]

In ancient (classical) times it seems to have been normal to dye an entire fleece or a hank of linen.[188] In the medieval period textile workers might dye an entire garment after weaving (as was the case with the Oseberg queen's costume) or they could dye some or all of the spun yarn before weaving (as, apparently, in the case of the Rønbjerg garment). The latter method would have been used if a colored pattern was to be woven in, as for example, in a striped cloth, of which there are surviving fragments from Broomfield and, possibly, Fonaby.[189]

The embroidery threads from the St. Cuthbert embroideries and the Bayeux "Tapestry" demonstrate the very large range of colors and shades available.

Embroidery

English women were to become famous in the later Middle Ages for their embroidery, which was known as *opus anglicanum*—"English work." Their particular claim to fame was in the making of orphreys, the ornaments embroidered, often in gold, on ecclesiastical vestments.[190] The traditions of embroidery, however, certainly went back to long before the Conquest. The association of women with embroidery was apparently proverbial.[191] It was probably practiced as a domestic craft at all levels of society, and the finest work involving gold was considered suitable for great ladies. The craft was carried out on such a scale that professional embroideresses were needed, and these seem to have included both slaves and freewomen.[192]

From the pagan period there survive only a few fragments of what were probably fairly unpretentious pieces of embroidery in wool. From Alfriston, Sussex, there is evidence of a belt which may have been embroidered in a geometric design. The textile was found on the inner sides of iron tabs which were found with the belt equipment, and was described as being of a delicate quadrangular pattern.[193] There is an oxidized scrap of what may have been a leaf scroll in stem and satin stitches on a piece of checked cloth from Worthy Park, Hampshire,[194] and from Kempston, Bedfordshire, the remains of an interlace design in red, blue and yellow worked on a lozenge twill fabric which may have been dark brown.[195]

There are three well-known examples of embroidery which are generally accepted as late Anglo-Saxon work,[196] and although two are ecclesiastical (the Maaseik embroideries[197] and the matching stole and maniple of St. Cuthbert)[198] and the other (the Bayeux "Tapestry")[199] a hanging, not a garment, they give us first hand testimony of the type and quality of late Anglo-Saxon embroidery.

The earliest, but least well preserved, of the three are the embroideries now stitched into the composite vestments known as the *casula* of Saints Harlindis and Relindis, kept at Maaseik, Belgium. The embroideries have been falsely attributed to the saints (who seem to have flourished in the early eighth century), but recent research has demonstrated, on stylistic grounds, that they are southern English work of the late eighth or early ninth century. They seem to have been taken to the Continent soon after manufacture.

The embroidery is worked on a linen backcloth in silk threads of red, beige, green, yellow, light blue and dark blue and in "spun gold" threads. The designs were outlined in silk, then filled with gold threads which were attached by surface couching. A polychrome background worked in split stitch and stem stitch, in silk, completely covered the backcloth. Three designs are extant: continuous arcading which contains and encloses areas of densely-packed ornament of zoomorphic, geometric, stem and foliate kinds; roundels containing birds and animals in profile; and four monograms, two with geometric, two with stem and leaf ornament. Large pearls, or beads, were once attached to the embroideries, edging the arcades and roundels, but these were not original and may have been added after the embroideries reached the Frankish Empire, although the work may have been carried out as early as the ninth century.

The St. Cuthbert vestments were among the treasures found in the saint's coffin in Durham Cathedral when it was opened in 1827. The needlework can be dated by the embroidered words recording that they were made by the orders of Ælfflæd, for Bishop Frithestan: *Ælfflæd fieri precepit. Pio episcipo Fridestano.* Frithestan was Bishop of Winchester; Ælfflæd was step-mother to King Athelstan. The vestments must have been made in southern England about the second decade of the tenth century and probably presented to the saint's shrine by Athelstan on his visit north in 934.

The embroidery, carried out on a background of silk, consists of figures of prophets and ecclesiastics and decorative motifs outlined, in split stitch, in dark brown or green. Hands, faces, costume and other items are filled with a variety of other colors. Spun gold is used for haloes and other details. The iconography of the Cuthbert embroideries is biblical and ecclesiastical, but the techniques employed here could equally well be applied to the clothing worn by wealthy seculars. Dodwell seems to suggest that the golden bands bequeathed by various seculars were woven fillets embroidered with gold, and that the headband worn by Cnut's queen, and the stole flaunted by the allegorical figure of *Pompa* in Anglo-Saxon drawings were bejeweled, golden embroideries of this kind.[200]

The so-called "Tapestry" (it is actually embroidered), which was probably made in the decade following the Norman Conquest, while probably made for Bishop Odo of Bayeux, and conceived on the grand scale (it is about 70m long) is not executed in the grand manner—it does not have the silk and gold of ecclesiastical vestments; instead the stitches are made in wool on a linen background. Outlines are worked in stem stitch, usually in a dark color, although paler shades are sometimes used to convey skin tones. Stem stitch is also used for lettering and to suggest folds in costume. Figures, animals and objects are "filled in" in couching stitch. A range of shades of blues, yellows, reds and green is used. Apart from the main panel which depicts the narrative, the "Tapestry" has upper and lower borders, the content of which sometimes reflects the subject matter in the central panel, sometimes consists of plant or animal ornament. The style is sometimes rather formal, almost heraldic; elsewhere very informal, even frivolous. The St. Cuthbert embroideries, too, contain ornament supplementary to the figure work: one can recognize the acanthus leaf which was to become a major motif of Winchester Style art. It seems highly likely that the Anglo-Saxons, loving animal and plant ornament as they did, would decorate their clothes with embroidered motifs of this kind, and also with the sort of geometric motifs we find in manuscript illuminations. This point is demonstrated by the decoration on the vestments of ecclesiastics pictured in illuminated manuscripts. Dodwell points out that the acanthus leaf is embroidered on the vestment in several cases and cites many documented references to plants, beasts and religious scenes being portrayed on vestments; seed pearls or other jewels were stitched on to provide additional splendor.[201]

If work like this was being carried out on ecclesiastical garments it surely had a parallel in the secular world. Scandinavian evidence supports this suggestion. The ninth-century garments of the Oseberg queen and her attendant were decorated with needlework: the queen's fine, tabby-woven undergown, which was made of wool, was embellished with appliqué work in silk, embroidery in rings and embroidered seams. Her attendant's gown also had appliqué work in a tabby-woven wool. The appliquéd shapes represented, among other things, animal heads. Appliqué work and embroidery have also been found on the fronts of women's undergowns at Birka.[202] Perhaps most significant is the stem stitch embroidery on a man's garment from Mammen, Denmark, for there was clearly English influence on this rich, late tenth-century burial, evident both from the Anglo-Scandinavian Jellinge Style ornament on an axe and in the embroidered motifs themselves. The garment, which was possibly a cape, was made of 2x1 twill, and was said to have been decorated with gold pailettes when it was found, although these are now lost. The embroidered motifs themselves included stems and acanthus leaves, stylized beasts (lion or deer) in profile and human masks.[203]

If we want some idea of the kinds of motifs that would be used to decorate English clothing, clearly we can look to manuscript illumination for inspiration. We might also look to metalwork; in particular the Trewhiddle Style, which features lively, attractive little animals (very secular in their friskiness) would have adapted well to needlework, and is, indeed, reflected in the ecclesiastical embroideries at Maaseik.

It is disappointing that the artists depicting secular figures give us so little indication of this kind of decoration. There are only very stylized indications of ornament at the cuffs (usually dots or circles) and, less often, at the hems of garments and rare, faint suggestions of floral ornament on the skirts. The decoration on the garment of the Virgin in London, B. L. Harley 2904 (fig. 16.1), bands round King Edward's shins in the "Tapestry" and the triple circles on King Edgar's costume in London, B. L. Cotton Tiberius Aiii suggest something more elaborate, but are surely just a modest indication of what was actually worn.

NOTES

[1] G. N. Garmonsway, ed., *Aelfric's Colloquy* (London, 1939), 33, lines 159–60.

[2] *Judith* lines 43, 14, 103, in G. P. Krapp and E. V. K. Dobbie, eds., *Beowulf and Judith,* A.S.P.R., 4 (London & New York, 1953), 100, 99, 103.

[3] D. Whitelock, ed., *Anglo-Saxon Wills* (Cambridge, 1930), No. III. The bequests of items of dress are discussed in detail in G. R. Owen, "Wynflæd's Wardrobe," *A.S.E.* 8 (1979), 195–222.

[4] D. Whitelock, N. Ker and Lord Rennell, *The Will of Æthelgifu* (Oxford, 1968).

[5] G. R. Owen-Crocker, *Dress in Anglo-Saxon England* (Manchester, 1986), 203–08.

[6] Ibid., 88. Aldhelm, *De Virginitate,* LXIII; R. Ehwald, *Aldhelmi Opera,* M.G.H., Auctores Antiquissimi, 15 (Berlin, 1919), 138, lines 2–5.

[7] W. M. Lindsay, ed., *Isidori Hispalensis Episcopi Etymologiarum sive Originum,* 2 vols (Oxford, 1911). Isidor lists and defines Latin garment names. Sometimes he gives unusual interpretations of well-known words, for example his definition of *palla* (XIX, 25, 2); cf. A. Souter, *A Glossary of Later Latin to 600 A.D.* (Oxford, 1949), 283.

[8] F. Kluge, "Zur Geschichte der Zeichensprache angelsächsische Indicia Monasterialia," *Internationale Zeitschrift für Allgemeine Sprachwissenschaft,* 2 (1885), 116–37.

[9] C. R. Dodwell and P. Clemoes, *The Old English Illustrated Hexateuch,* E.E.M.F. 18 (Copenhagen, 1974), 66.

[10] The dates of the English illuminated manuscripts given here are from E. Temple, *Anglo-Saxon Manuscripts 900–1066,* A Survey of Manuscripts Illuminated in the British Isles, 2, ed. J. J. G. Alexander (London, 1976).

[11]R. N. Bailey and R. J. Cramp, *Cumberland, Westmorland and Lancashire North-of-the-Sands* vol. 2, *Corpus of Anglo-Saxon Stone Sculpture,* (London, 1988), 100–04, ills. 288–308 (hereafter *Corpus* 2).

[12] D. M. Wilson, *Anglo-Saxon Ornamental Metalwork 700–1100 in the British Museum* (London, 1964), 174–77 and pls. XXXI, XXXII.

[13] R. I. Page, "Appendix A," in ibid., 86–88.

[14] Wilson, *Anglo-Saxon Ornamental Metalwork,* 124–27.

[15] D. A. Hinton, "Late Anglo-Saxon Metalwork: An Assessment," *A.S.E.* 4 (1975), 171–80, at p. 179.

[16] M. Dolley, "The Nummular Brooch from Sulgrave," in P. Clemoes and K. Hughes, eds., *England Before the Conquest: Studies in Primary Sources Presented to Dorothy Whitelock* (Cambridge, 1971), 333–49, at p. 346. Dolley blames, at least in part, over-valuation of the silver coinage, preventing ordinary individuals from being able to afford to wear gold and silver.

[17] Hinton ("Late-Anglo-Saxon Metalwork," 179–80,) points out that many of the surviving artifacts, even secular ones, have religious emblems upon them. He suggests that although there was considerable wealth in private hands it was no longer fashionable for the aristocracy to "vaunt" it by "rich display."

[18] C. R. Dodwell, *Anglo-Saxon Art. A New Perspective* (Manchester & Ithaca, 1982), esp. Chapter 7. Dodwell (p. 215) enumerates the following uses of gold and silver: ". . . large-scale effigies . . . textile coverings of tombs and altars, on costumes and vestments, in jewellery, weapons, ships, domestic plate, household furnishings, reliquaries, book-bindings, church vessels and altars . . ."

[19] Ibid., 188–89.

[20] N. Smedley and E. Owles, "Some Anglo-Saxon 'Animal' Brooches," *Proc. of the Suffolk Inst. of Archaeol. and Natural Hist.* 30 (1965), 166–74; D. A. Hinton in M. Biddle, ed., *Object and Economy in Medieval,* Winchester Studies 7, 2 vols. (Oxford, 1990), vol. 2, 636–39.

[21] No. 2031, Hinton, in ibid. The brooch is about 25 mm. long and is rectangular with lobed corners.

[22] D. A. Hinton, *A Catalogue of the Anglo-Saxon Ornamental Metalwork 700–1100 in the Department of Antiquities, Ashmolean Museum* (Oxford, 1974), No. 35.

[23] Wilson, *Anglo-Saxon Ornamental Metalwork,* 7 and pl. XXXVI.

[24] From Tetney, Lincolnshire and from a hoard found in Rome, Italy: J. Graham-Campbell and E. Okasha, "A Pair of Inscribed Anglo-Saxon Hooked Tags from the Rome (Forum) 1883 Hoard," *A.S.E.* 20 (1991), 221–29, esp. 223.

[25] J. R. Planché, *History of British Costume* (London, 1847), 38, fig. This drawing is probably, in fact, continental, see G. R. Owen, "Anglo-Saxon Costume," unpub. doctoral diss., University of Newcastle upon Tyne, 1976, vol. 1, 6–7.

[26] Whitelock, Ker and Rennel, *Will of Æthelgifu,* 13, lines 47–49.

[27] Ibid., 82.

[28] Whitelock, *Anglo-Saxon Wills,* 14, lines 10, 14.

[29] Owen, "Wynflæd's Wardrobe," 203–04.

[30] *Confessionale Pseudo-Egberti, in* B. Thorpe, ed., *Ancient Laws and Institutes of England* (London, 1840), II, 162.

[31] G. Herzfeld, *An Old English Martyrology,* E.E.T.S., o.s. 116 (London, 1900), 192, line 1.

[32] Whitelock, *Anglo-Saxon Wills,* 14, lines 11–12..

[33] Ibid., 62, line 21.

[34] A. S. Napier and W. H. Stevenson, *The Crawford Collection of Early Charters and Documents* (Oxford, 1895), 23, line 22.

[35] H. Woodruff, *The Illustrated Manuscripts of Prudentius* (Cambridge, MA, 1930), 21; Temple, *Anglo-Saxon Manuscripts,* nos. 48–51.

[36] H. J. Thomson, trans., *Prudentius,* Loeb Classical Library, 2 vols. (London, 1949–53), vol. 1, 292, line 187.

[37] Collingwood, "A Cross-fragment at Sutton-on-Derwent," *Yorkshire Archaeol. J.* 29 (1927–29), 238–40, plate opposite p. 238, a.

[38] G. R. Owen-Crocker, "The Search for Anglo-Saxon Skin Garments and the Documentary Evidence," in E. Cameron, ed., *Leather and Fur: Aspects of Early Medieval Trade and Technology* (London, 1998), 27–43.

[39] J. B. McNulty, ("The Lady Aelfgyva in the Bayeux Tapestry," *Speculum* 55 (1980), 659–68), suggests the woman is Ælfgifu of Northampton, King Cnut's "other" wife. (His queen was Emma of Normandy, also called Ælfgifu.)

[40] The small figure at the foot of the cross is usually (though not universally) interpreted as Judith of Flanders (1032–94). The manuscript is dated to *post* 1051, but the Crucifixion is considered an addition to the manuscript and may be "a good deal later"; C. R. Dodwell, *The Pictorial Arts of the West 800–1200* (New Haven & London, 1993), 114 including caption to fig. 103, 145 n.101.

[41] A. Geijer, "The Textile Finds from Birka," in N. B. Harte and K. G. Ponting, eds., *Cloth and Clothing in Medieval Europe: Essays in Memory of Professor E. M. Carus-Wilson* (London, 1983), 80–90, at pp. 87–88.

[42] J. Laver, *Costume (The Arts of Man)* (London, 1963), 26.

[43] D. Talbot-Rice, *Byzantine Art,* revised and expanded (Harmondsworth, 1968), fig. 12.

[44] Ibid., fig. 108, lower.

[45] See the Virgin Hodeghetria, a tenth-century piece in the Victoria and Albert Museum, Talbot-Rice, *Byzantine Art,* fig. 419.

⁴⁶ Unfortunately the figures are only minor ones in the group (see Temple, *Anglo-Saxon Manuscripts,* Ill. 132). The most decorated headdress seems to belong to the costume with the only decorated sleeve that is shown and the distinctive light-colored ankle shoes.

⁴⁷ The word is recorded in glosses only: to *ricinum,* (T. Wright and R. P. Wülcker, eds., *Anglo-Saxon and Old English Vocabularies,* 2nd ed. [London, 1884], 107, 37, *anabola,* (ibid., 125, 8), *cyclade* (*veste*) (L. Goossens, ed., *The Old English Glosses of MS. Brussels, Royal Library, 1650, Aldhelm's "De laudibus virginitatis,"* [Brussels, 1974], 419, line 4172), and *mafortibus* (W. S. Logeman, "De Consuetudine Monachorum," *Anglia* 13 [1891], 365–454, at p. 37 [where the lemma is no longer legible]; Goossens, *Old English Glosses,* 480, line 5210).

⁴⁸ Chaucer's Prioress wore a "wympul" which was "pynched" (probably pleated), *The Canterbury Tales, The General Prologue,* line 151, in F. Robinson, ed., *The Works of Geoffrey Chaucer,* 2nd ed. (London, 1957), 18. The author of the thirteenth-century *Ancrene Wisse* considered wimples extravagant and worldly, warning his readers that they should veil, not wimple, themselves. J. R. R. Tolkien, ed., *Ancrene Wisse,* E.E.T.S., o.s. 249 (London, 1962), 215, line 25. *O.E.D.* "wimple: a garment of linen or silk, formerly worn by women, so folded as to envelop the head, chin, sides of the face and neck."

⁴⁹ Whitelock, *Anglo-Saxon Wills,* 14, line 17.

⁵⁰ Kluge, "Zur Geschichte der Zeichensprache," 129, para. 127.

⁵¹ Whitelock, *Anglo-Saxon Wills,* 14, line 17.

⁵² Ibid., lines 15–16.

⁵³ Byrhtric and Ælfswith bequeathed *healfne bænde gyldene,* Whitelock, *Anglo-Saxon Wills,* 28, lines 4–5; Wulfwaru left a *bend* worth twenty mancuses, ibid., 64, lines 20–21; Æthelgifu bequeathed to a relative five mancuses [of gold] which were to be cut from her *bend,* Whitelock, Ker and Remel, *Will of Æthelgifu,* 13.

⁵⁴ Among a group of glosses on the subject of head-coverings and head ornaments, we find *diadema, bend agimmed and gesmiðed* and *nimbus, mid goldgesiwud bend,* Wright and Wülcker, *Anglo-Saxon and Old English Vocabularies,* 152, 25–26.

⁵⁵ Ibid., 268, 6.

⁵⁶ W. M. Lindsay, ed., *The Corpus Glossary* (Cambridge, 1921), 110, line 9: Wright and Wülcker, *Anglo-Saxon and Old English Vocabularies,* 442, 21.

⁵⁷ J. Bosworth and H. N. Toller, eds., *An Anglo-Saxon Dictionary* and *Supplement* with enlarged corrigenda and Addenda by A. Campbell, 2 vols. (London, 1972), 846.

⁵⁸ Paris, Bibliothèque Nationale Fonds Latin 8824, f.3; B. Colgrave, ed., *The Paris Psalter,* E.E.M.F. 8 (Copenhagen, 1958).

[59] Vienna, Nationalbibliothek Cod. 2687; A. Goldsmidt, *Die deutsche Buch-malerei,* 2 vols. (Florence & New York, 1928), vol. 1, pl. 62.

[60] Kluge, "Zur Geschichte der Zeichensprache," 128, para. 119.

[61] J. Beckwith, *Ivory Carvings in Early Medieval England* (London, 1972), 58–59, pl. 84.

[62] *H.E.* iv, 19; J. Schipper, ed., *Konig Alfreds Übersetzung von Bedas Kirchengeschichte,* Bibliothek der angelsächsischen Prosa, eds. C. W. M. Grein, R. P. Wülcker and H. Hecht, 4 (Leipzig,1899), 442, line 2501.

[63] Whitelock, *Anglo-Saxon Wills,* 14, line 15.

[64] J. L. André, "Widows and Vowesses," *Archaeol. J.* 49 (1892), 69–82.

[65] Owen, "Wynflæd's Wardrobe," 199.

[66] R. Morris, ed., *The Blickling Homilies of the Tenth Century,* E.E.T.S., o.s. 58, 63, 73 (London, 1874–80), 61, line 16; U. Lindelöf, ed., *Rituale Ecclesiae Dunelmensis, The Durham Collectar,* Surtees Society 140 (Durham, 1927), 106.

[67] W. W. Skeat, ed., *Aelfric's Lives of the Saints,* 3 vols., E.E.T.S., o.s. 76, 82, 94, 114 (London, 1881–1900), I, 172, line 36.

[68] Whitelock, *Anglo-Saxon Wills,* 14, lines 15–16.

[69] Wright and Wülcker, *Anglo-Saxon and Old English Vocabularies,* 107, 38.

[70] A. S. Napier, ed., *Old English Glosses,* Anecdota Oxoniensia, Medieval and Modern Series, 11 (Oxford, 1900), 33, line 1200; K. W. Bouterwek, ed., *Screadunga* (Elberfeld, 1858), 435.

[71] F. Kluge, "Angelsächsische Glossen," *Anglia* 8 (1885), 448–52, at p. 450; Napier, *Old English Glosses,* 124, line 4821; 146, line 389; Wright and Wülcker, *Anglo-Saxon and Old English Vocabularies,* 107, 28; 223, 16.

[72] Ibid., 107, 38; 223, 16.

[73] Napier, *Old English Glosses,* 33, line 1200; Goossens, *Old English Glosses,* 439, line 4528; 479, line 5207.

[74] Napier, *Old English Glosses,* 124, line 4822.

[75] Wright and Wülcker, *Anglo-Saxon and Old English Vocabularies,* 152, line 39.

[76] Ibid., 467, line 29.

[77] Kluge, "Zur Geschichte der Zeichensprache," 127, para. 103; Wright and Wülcker, *Anglo-Saxon and Old English Vocabularies,* 125, 14 and 16; 234, 22.

[78] Ibid., 153, line 3; F. Holthausen, "Die Leidener Glossen," *Englische Studien,* 50 (1916–17), 327–40, at p. 330, line 110.

[79] The occurrences of the word in its various forms are numerous; representative examples are: glossing *calciamentum,* Wright and Wülcker, *Anglo-Saxon and Old English Vocabularies,* 327, 31; Luke, 3: 16, W. W. Skeat, ed., *The Holy Gospels in Anglo-Saxon, Northumbrian and Old Mercian Versions* (Cambridge,

1871–87), 41; *Colloquium,* Garmonsway, *Aelfric's Colloquy,* 35, line 171. Glossing *calcarium,* Wright and Wülcker, *Anglo-Saxon and Old English Vocabularies,* 283, 18; *calceos,* ibid., 197, 13; *caliga,* ibid., 362, 38; *fico,* ibid., 125, 24; *galliculae,* ibid., 414, 31.

[80] Lindsay, *Corpus Glossary,* 171, line 708; Wright and Wülcker, *Anglo-Saxon and Old English Vocabularies,* 277, line 30.

[81] Ibid., 277 line 29 (earlier *slebescoh,* Lindsay, *Corpus Glossary,* 165, line 394).

[82] Ibid., 125, 26; Garmonsway, *Aelfric's Colloquy,* 35, line 171.

[83] E. Steinmayer, "Lateinische und altenglische Glossen," *Zeitschrift für deutsches Alterthum* 33 (1889), 242–51, at p. 250, line 2.

[84] Mark 6: 9, Skeat, *Holy Gospels,* 42.

[85] Glossing *obstrigelli,* Wright and Wülcker, *Anglo-Saxon and Old English Vocabularies,* 125, 33. (*Obstrigellus,* "a shoe sole, sandal fastened to the feet by straps.")

[86] Owen-Crocker, *Dress in Anglo-Saxon England,* chapter IV, note 61.

[87] Whitelock, *Anglo-Saxon Wills,* 64, line 11.

[88] Ibid., lines 12–13.

[89] Dodwell, *Anglo-Saxon Art,* 170–87.

[90] Ibid., 179 citing Goscelin, *La Legende de Ste Edith.* See A. Wilmart, ed., "La Légende de Ste. Édith en prose et vers par le moine Goscelin," *Analecta Bollandiana* 56 (1938), 4–101, 265–307, at p. 44.

[91] Dodwell, *Anglo-Saxon Art,* 179–80, citing L. Musset, ed., *Les actes de Guillaume le Conquérant et de la reine Mathilde pour les abbayes caennaises, Mémoires de la Societé des Antiquaires de Normandie* 37 (1967), No. 16, 112–13.

[92] Dodwell, *Anglo-Saxon Art,* 179–80; *Domesday Book,* I, 74b.

[93] In both cases the garments of Christ and St. John are similarly patterned.

[94] *Corpus* 2, 100–04, ills. 288–308.

[95] R. Cramp, *Corpus of Anglo-Saxon Stone Sculpture in England,* vol. 1, *County Durham and Northumberland* (Oxford, 1984), no. 15, p. 141, pl.138,741.

[96] Ibid., no. 3A, p. 136, pl. 130,710.

[97] W. G. Collingwood, "The Lowther Hogbacks," *Trans. of the Cumberland and Westmorland Antiquarian and Archaeol. Soc.* 7 (1907), 152–64, at pp. 153, 160, pl. and fig. opposite pp. 152, 160.

[98] Wilson, *Anglo-Saxon Ornamental Metalwork,* pls XXXI, XXXII.

[99] P. Walton, "A Silk cap from Coppergate," *Interim [Bulletin of the York Archaeological Trust]* 7.2 (1980), 3–5; A. Muthesius, "The Silk Fragment from 5 Coppergate," in A. MacGregor, *Anglo-Scandinavian Finds from Lloyds Bank, Pavement and Other Sites,* in P. V. Addyman, ed., The Archaeology of York 7.3 (London, 1982) 132–36. The assumption that this is a woman's garment is, admittedly, subjective.

[100] The definitive publication by E. Crowfoot appears in the third volume of *The Sutton Hoo Ship Burial,* ed. R. L. S. Bruce-Mitford (London, 1983), although there have been many references to the Sutton Hoo textiles in Crowfoot's earlier publications.

[101] J. Y. Akerman, "Notes of Antiquarian Researches in the Summer and Autumn of 1854," *Archaoelogia* 36 (1855), 175–86, at p. 178.

[102] There is a general discussion and a gazetteer of sites in P. Rahtz, "Buildings and Rural Settlement," and "Gazetteer of Anglo-Saxon Domestic Settlement Sites," in D. Wilson, ed., *The Archaeology of Anglo-Saxon England* (London, 1976), 49–98. 405–45.

[103] M. Hoffmann, *The Warp-weighted Loom: Studies in the History and Technology of an Ancient Implement,* Studia Norvegica 14 (Oslo, 1964).

[104] E. Von Erhardt-Siebold, "The Old English Loom Riddles," in T. A. Kirby and H. B. Woolf, eds., *Malone Anniversary Studies, Philologica* (Baltimore, 1949) 9–17; J. Gerritsen, "þurh þreata geþræcu," *English Studies* 35 (1954), "Notes and News," 259–62; cf. R. W. Zandvoort, "The Leiden Riddle," *English and Germanic Studies* 3 (1949–50), 42–56. E. Crowfoot has observed to me that the riddle as translated here could refer to any pre-treadle loom not just the warp-weighted.

[105] R. Ehwald, *Aldhelmi Opera,* M.G.H., Auctores Antiquissimi 15, (Berlin, 1919), 111–12.

[106] The Exeter Book version. Both Old English texts are printed in A. H. Smith, ed., *Three Northumbrian Poems,* corrected edition (London, 1968).

[107] Zandvoort's version, which is basically Onion's translation with slight alterations. Gerritsen would render *þreata geþracu as* "the crowded many." I have substituted "tools" for Zandvoort's "reeds" since the weaver's reed belonged to the horizontal treadle loom.

[108] Von Erhard-Siebold, "Old English Loom Riddles."

[109] Wright and Wülcker, *Anglo-Saxon and Old English Vocabularies,* 186, 29 (intermittently)—188, 13; 262, 5–33; 293, 36–294, 25; 328, 19–25.

[110] F. Liebermann, *Die Gesetze der Angelsachsen,* 3 vols. (Halle, 1898–1916), vol. 1, 455.

[111] M. Hald, *Ancient Danish Textiles from Bogs and Burials,* trans. J. Olsen, English edition, *Publications of the National Museum of Denmark, Archaeological-Historical Series* 21 (Copenhagen, 1980), figs. 68, 73, 74, 76, gives third-century Danish examples, but E. Crowfoot informs me that it is now believed that these fabrics were dyed, although all trace of the dye has disappeared. The English examples are mostly replaced textiles (i.e. the organic material is replaced by rust, though the pattern remains).

[112] Hoffmann, *Warp-weighted Loom,* 291–94, figs. 122, 124. This was, of course, the burial of a wealthy woman, and these weaving tools may have been rare luxuries.

[113] E. Crowfoot, "The Textiles," in A. M. Cook, *The Anglo-Saxon Cemetery at Fonaby, Lincolnshire,* Occasional Papers in Lincolnshire History and Archaeology 6 (1981), 89–100, at 98–99.

[114] E. Crowfoot, "The Textiles," in B. Green and A. Rogerson, *The Anglo-Saxon Cemetery at Bergh Apton, Norfolk,* East Anglian Archaeol. Rep. 7 (Gressenhall, 1978), 98–106, at pp. 101, 106.

[115] E. Crowfoot in A. M. Cook and M. W. Dacre, *Excavations at Portway, Andover, 1974–5,* Oxford University Com. for Archaeol. Monograph 4 (1985), 99–102.

[116] G. M. Crowfoot, "Textiles of the Saxon Period in the Museum of Archaeology and Ethnology," *Proc. of the Cambridge Antiquarian Soc.* 44 (1951), 26–32, at pp. 28–30.

[117] B. Hougen, *Snartemofunnene, Norske Oldfunn* 7 (Oslo, 1935), pl. XVII, pp. 77–79, 115.

[118] Ibid., 68–69, 114.

[119] H. Dedekam, *To tekstilfund fra folkvandringstidan,* Bergen Museum Arbok (Bergen, 1924–5), pl. III–IV.

[120] E. Crowfoot, "The Textiles," in Cook, *Anglo-Saxon Cemetery at Fonaby,* 96. Crowfoot informs me that the recorded examples from Fonaby, now lost, were small and doubtful. They may have been deteriorated silk. The short, coarse hairs of the goat are not well suited to needlework (except for imported mohair).

[121] E. Crowfoot and S. C. Hawkes, "Early Anglo-Saxon Gold Braids," *M.A.* 11 (1967), 42–86, figs. 13, 14.

[122] Silk in the St. Cuthbert relics (E. Plenderleith, "The Stole and Maniples: the Technique," in C. F. Battiscombe, ed., *The Relics of St. Cuthbert* [Oxford, 1956], 375–96), cow-tail hair in the embroideries and tablet-woven braid from Maaseik (M. Budny and D. Tweddle, "The Maaseik Embroideries," *A.S.E.* 13 [1984], 65–96, at p. 76). The core of examples from the ninth- to tenth-century burials from Cathedral Green, Winchester, is now missing, but was probably silk. An inferior piece of spun gold from a fourteenth-century grave on the same site had a core of wool. (See E. Crowfoot, "Textiles," in Biddle, ed., *Object and Economy in Medieval Winchester,* vol. 2, 467–88, nos. 1009–55).

[123] Hoffmann, *Warp-weighted Loom.*

[124] The relationship between battle sword and sword-shaped beater may be closer than mere similarity of proportions: a weaving beater found in a female grave at Spong Hill, Norfolk, had originally been a pattern-welded sword, which was ground down for its new function. See B. Gilmour, Appendix II: "X-Radiographs of Two Objects: the Weaving Batten (24/3), and Sword (40/5)," in C. Hills, K. Penn and R. Rickett, *The Anglo-Saxon Cemetery at Spong Hill, North Elmham,* East Anglian Archaeol. Rep. 21 (Dereham, 1984), 160–63.

[125] Reconstructed in the Weald and Downland Open Air Museum near Chichester, Sussex. "Sussex: Old Erringham," *M.A.* 9 (1965), 175.

[126] D. A. Jackson, D. W. Harding and J. N. L. Myres, "The Iron Age and Anglo-Saxon Site at Upton, Northants," *Antiquaries J.* 49 (1969), 202–21, at pp. 206–10.

[127] S. E. West, "The Anglo-Saxon Village of West Stow," *M.A.* 13 (1969), 1–20, at p. 5.

[128] Whitelock, *Anglo-Saxon Wills*, p. 10, line 30.

[129] P. Walton Rogers, *Textile Production at 16–22 Coppergate*, in P. V. Addyman, ed., The Archaeology of York 17.11 (London, 1997), 1753, 1824.

[130] Hald, *Ancient Danish Textiles*, 203–18.

[131] Walton Rogers, *Textile Production*, 1824.

[132] A well worn piece of equipment, believed to be a heddle cradle, testifies to this. Ibid., 1815.

[133] Personal communication from M. Hoffmann, Norse Folkesmuseum, Oslo. This resemblance to rings and, hence, to chain mail, may have given rise to the name *haberget*, a term well documented from England and France in the twelfth and thirteenth centuries (cf. the word *hauberk*, "a mailcoat"); E. M. Carus-Wilson, "Haberget: A Medieval Textile Conundrum," *M.A.* 13 (1969), 148–66. Diamond twills of this later period are much coarser than our examples and were probably woven on a horizontal treadle loom. Geijer, "Textile Finds from Birka," 85–86.

[134] See A. Geijer, *Birka* III, *Die Textilfunde aus den Gräbern* (Uppsala, 1938); Geijer, "Textile Finds from Birka"; I. Hägg, "Viking Women's Dress at Birka: A Reconstruction by Archaeological Methods," in Harte and Ponting, *Cloth and Clothing in Medieval Europe*, 316–50.

[135] Hoffmann, *Warp-weighted Loom*, 229, 235.

[136] Ibid., 238, 239, 249.

[137] A. S. Ingstad, "The Functional Textiles from the Oseberg Ship," in L. B. Jørgensen and K. Tidow, eds., *Textilsymposium Neumünster,* 85–96, at pp. 90–91.

[138] Geijer, *Birka*, 41–43.

[139] *Gesta*, II, para. 9; G. H. Pertz, M.G.H., *Scriptores* 7, 2 (Berlin, 1829), 752, line 41.

[140] Notably H. Pirenne, "Draps de frise ou draps de Flandre?" *Vierteljahrschrift für Social- und Wirtschaftsgeschichte* 7 (1909), 308–15.

[141] A. Geijer, "Var järnålderns 'frisiska kläde' tillverkat i Syrien?" ["The *pallium fresonicum* of the Viking Age, was it manufactured in Syria?"], *Fornvännen* 60 (1965), 112–32 [English summary pp. 130–32], 130–32. Geijer cited a fragment of this weave of proven Syrian origin.

[142] Ingstad, "Functional Textiles," 88–91.

143 J. P. Wild, *Textile Manufacture in the Northern Roman Provinces* (Cambridge, 1970), 48: Hald, *Ancient Danish Textiles*, 44–47.

144 Wild, *Textile Manufacture*, 48–49, 98–100, 116.

145 H. B.Walters, *Catalogue of the Greek and Roman Lamps in the British Museum* (London, 1914), 74, no. 497.

146 Hoffmann, *Warp-weighted Loom*, 251–52.

147 J. P. Wild, "Some New Light on Roman Textiles," in Jørgensen and Tidow, *Textilsymposium Neumünster*, 10–22, at pp. 12–13.

148 The Manchester Medieval Textiles Project, directed by Elizabeth Coatsworth and Gale Owen-Crocker, is currently compiling a computerized catalogue of medieval textiles of the British Isles. As of December 1997 there were about 3,000 items (all fragments) listed from the Anglo-Saxon period.

149 M. L. Ryder, "European Wool Types from the Iron Age to the Middle Ages," in Jørgensen and Tidow, *Textilsymposium Neumünster*, 224–38, at pp. 226–27.

150 E. Crowfoot, "The Textiles," in Bruce-Mitford, *The Sutton Hoo Ship Burial*, vol. 3, 409–79, at pp. 440–42, 456–57.

151 R. C. Janaway, "Corrosion Preserved Textile Evidence: Mechanism, Bias, and Interpretation," *Evidence Preserved in Corrosion Products: New Fields in Artefact Studies*, Occasional Papers 8 (1989), 21–29.

152 There are cases of linen in more complicated weaves, for example the broken diamond twill used for pillows at Sutton Hoo.

153 Unpublished information from E. Crowfoot and S. Hawkes.

154 The buckle suite is described in V. Evison, *The Fifth Century Invasions South of the Thames* (London, 1965), 242–43. Unpublished information on the textiles from E. Crowfoot and W. T. Jones.

155 S. Hawkes, "The Archaeology of Conversion: Cemeteries," in J. Campbell, et al., eds., *The Anglo-Saxons* (Oxford, 1982), 48–49, at p. 49; unpublished information from E. Crowfoot and S. Hawkes.

156 Unpublished information from E. Crowfoot. The site is published in D. A. Hinton, with a contribution by R. White, "A Smith's Hoard from Tattershall Thorpe, Lincolnshire: A Synopsis," *A.S.E.* 22 (1993), 147–66. The silk is mentioned with no additional information at p. 159 n.26. It is described as a "cut circle of unpatterned cloth" in E. Crowfoot, F. Pritchard and K. Staniland, *Textiles and Clothing c. 1150–c. 1450*, Medieval Finds from Excavations in London 4 (London, 1992), 83.

157 G. Brett, "The 'Rider' Silk," in Battiscombe, *The Relics of St. Cuthbert* (Oxford, 1956), 470–83; J. F. Flanagan, "The Figured-Silks," ibid., 484–525. They may have been vestments, but, as E. Crowfoot has pointed out to me, as there is no trace of sewing on the three big silks, they may have been large wrappings, not garments.

[158] Dodwell, *Anglo-Saxon Art,* 162–65 and pl. 39; unpublished information from Linda Woolley, Department of Textiles and Dress, Victoria and Albert Museum, London.

[159] K. Cigaar, "England and Byzantium on the Eve of the Norman Conquest," *Anglo-Norman Studies 5, Proceedings of the Battle Conference, 1982,* ed. R. A. Brown (Woodbridge & Totowa, 1982), 78–90, at p. 90.

[160] Lull to York, M. Tangl, ed., *S. Bonafatii et Lulli Epistolae,* M.G.H., *Epistolae* 4, *Epistolae Selectae,* I (Berlin, 1916), No. 125, p. 263, lines 5–6; Wilfrid to Ripon, B. Colgrave, ed., *Eddius Life of St. Wilfrid—The Life of Bishop Wilfrid by Eddius Stephanus* (Cambridge, 1927), 120.

[161] Whitelock, *Anglo-Saxon Wills,* 4, lines 25–29.

[162] Dodwell, *Anglo-Saxon Art,* 151.

[163] Pertz, M.G.H., *Scriptores 7,* 760, line 41.

[164] Hangings and cushions in ecclesiastical context are illustrated in Dodwell, *Anglo-Saxon Art,* pls. 19, 20, and hangings in secular context, pls. 33–35. Dodwell discusses textiles as wall hangings and room dividers in secular context, p. 132.

[165] The thirteenth-century chronicler Roger of Wendover; H. O. Coxe, ed., *Rogeri de Wendover Chronica sive Flores Historiarum,* 4 vols. (London, 1841–42), vol. 1, 416.

[166] P. Walton, "A Silk Cap from Coppergate," 3–5; P. Walton, *Textiles, Cordage and Raw Fibre from 16–22 Coppergate,* in P. V. Addyman, ed., The Archaeology of York 17.5 (London, 1989), 360–69, 375–77. Other silk fragments have been excavated from York, including what may be the remains of more caps and ribbons, two originally dyed red. I am grateful to P. Walton Rogers for showing me these finds.

[167] F. Pritchard, "Textiles from Recent Excavations in the City of London," in Jørgensen and Tidow, *Textilsymposium Neumünster,* 193–203, at p. 197.

[168] Walton, "Silk Cap," 3–4.

[169] Pritchard, "Textiles from Recent Excavations," 197. Most of the Milk Street finds were from pits.

[170] Dodwell, *Anglo-Saxon Art,* 145.

[171] R. Freyhan, "The Place of the Stole and Maniples in Anglo-Saxon Art of the Tenth Century," in Battiscombe, *The Relics of St. Cuthbert,* 409–32. See above, p. 459.

[172] Budny and Tweddle, "The Maaseik Embroideries," 72–73.

[173] Dodwell, *Anglo-Saxon Art,* 145–50. Interestingly, the term "scarlet," which appeared in European languages in the eleventh century, was also originally applied to a kind of cloth and only later confined to the bright red color, J. H. Munro, "The Medieval Scarlet and the Economics of Sartorial Splendour," in Harte and Ponting, *Cloth and Clothing in Medieval Europe,* 13–70.

[174] D. Keene, "The Textile Industry," in Biddle, *Object and Economy in Medieval Winchester,* vol. 1, 200–14, at p. 201.

[175] R. Patterson, "Spinning and Weaving," in C. Singer, E. J. Holmyard, A. R. Hall, and J. Williams, eds., *A History of Technology,* 5 vols. (Oxford, 1956–70), 191–220.

[176] E. Crowfoot, "The Textiles," in Cook, *Anglo-Saxon Cemetery at Fonaby,* 96, 108, note 2. The unpublished examples are from Mucking (three cases, one Roman, two Anglo-Saxon) and Stretton-on-Fosse (four cases). There have been two possible cases from Fonaby. Penelope Walton Rogers has identified a small number of napped (teasled) fabrics from Anglian cemeteries, such as West Heslerton, N. Yorkshire. They probably derived from cloaks and belonged to prosperous individuals. Walton Rogers, *Textile Production,* 1774.

[177] Wild, *Textile Manufacture,* 84.

[178] Pritchard, "Textiles from Recent Excavations," 195.

[179] J. Hedges, "Textiles," in MacGregor, *Anglo-Saxon Finds from Lloyds Bank,* 102–27.

[180] Thetford, London, Winchester and York; Walton Rogers, *Textile Production,* 1777–78.

[181] Ryder, "European Wool Types," 229.

[182] Cf. Broomfield Barrow, E. Crowfoot, "The Textiles," in Bruce-Mitford, *Sutton Hoo Ship Burial,* vol. 3, 468, 470–71.

[183] J. Werner, "Frankish Royal Tombs in the Cathedrals of Cologne and St. Denis," *Antiquity* 38 (1964), 201–16, at p. 212.

[184] Ingstad, "Functional Textiles," 94.

[185] *H.E.* i, chap. 1; Colgrave and Mynors, 14.

[186] M. C. Whiting, Appendix to E. Crowfoot, "The Textiles," in Bruce-Mitford, *Sutton Hoo Ship Burial,* vol. 3, 465.

[187] K. H. Nielsen, "The Rønbjerg Garment in Tunic-form," in Jørgensen and Tidow, *Textilsymposium Neumünster,* 44–62, at p. 58 note 10.

[188] Wild, *Textile Manufacture,* 80.

[189] E. Crowfoot, "The Textiles," in Cook, *Anglo-Saxon Cemetery at Fonaby,* 96, 108 note 1.

[190] A. G. L. Christie, *English Medieval Embroidery* (Oxford, 1938).

[191] *Fæmne æt hyre bordan geriseð* "It is fitting that a woman should be at her embroidery" (or, possibly, "at her table." Cf. Bosworth and Toller, *Dictionary,* 116 *borde* and Bosworth and Toller, *Supplement,* 101 *borda* II) A.S.P.R., 3, 159, line 63.

[192] Dodwell, *Anglo-Saxon Art,* 70, 72.

[193] Grave 20. A. F. Griffith and L. F. Salzman, "An Anglo-Saxon Cemetery at Alfriston, Sussex," *Sussex Archaeol. Collections* 66 (1914), 16–53, at pp. 34–35, 39–40, 44–45, and information from Lewes Museum.

[194] Grave 75, found on the blade of a knife; a male grave. Unpublished information from E. Crowfoot and S. Hawkes.

[195] Unpublished information from E. Crowfoot. The box and its contents are discussed in A. Meaney, *Anglo-Saxon Amulets and Curing Stones,* B.A.R. Brit. ser. 96 (Oxford, 1981), 184.

[196] Budny and Tweddle, "Maaseik Embroideries," 86–87, identify two minor pieces: some fragments of gold embroidery, perhaps ninth-century, among the relics of St. Ambrose in Milan and a simply-embroidered pouch from York, dating to the second half of the tenth century. A study of Anglo-Saxon embroideries is currently being undertaken by Elizabeth Coatsworth.

[197] Budny and Tweddle, "Maaseik Embroideries."

[198] Plenderleith, "Stole and Maniples"; C. Hohler, "The Stole and Maniples: The Iconography," in Battiscombe, *Relics of St. Cuthbert,* 396–408; Freyhan, "Place of the Stole and Maniples."

[199] F. M. Stenton, *The Bayeux Tapestry,* 2nd ed. (London, 1965); D. M. Wilson, *The Bayeux Tapestry* (London, 1985); but the costume shows up well in the illustrations in two (undated) publications available from the Bayeux Tapestry Museum in Normandy, France, both entitled *Tapisserie de Bayeux.* One is identified as "Heimdal," the other is a reduced reproduction of the whole Tapestry "Dessin de Roland Lefranc."

[200] Dodwell, *Anglo-Saxon Art,* 175. In the subsequent paragraph gold hems, cuffs and other gold embroideries are discussed.

[201] Ibid., 183, 185. The acanthus leaf is illustrated in pls. 49, 50 and color pl. D.

[202] Ingstad, "Functional Textiles," 92, 94. Ingstad refers to the reconstruction of the Birka costume in I. Hägg, *Kvinnodräkten i Birka. Livplaggens rekonstruktion pa grundval av det arkeologiska materialet, Aun,* 2 (1974), which I have not seen but Hägg, "Viking Women's Dress," 328, 334, identifies as part of the Birka costume a tunic ornamented at the front with tablet woven bands decorated with silver, mounted on silk. This was worn over the shirt and under the *peplos*-type garment (called "skirt" by Hägg following Geijer, *Birka III*).

[203] Hald, *Ancient Danish Textiles,* 103–04, 281–82, figs. 90–92, 294. A striking replica of the Mammen clothing has been made, but it should be noted that while this is authentic as regards yarn types, weaving techniques and the vivid red and blue coloring, the style of the costume is unknown and the reconstruction is based on the image of Cnut in London, B. L. Stowe 944; E. Munksgaard, "Kopien af dragten fra Mammengravern," in M. Iverson, ed., *Mammen: grav, kunst og samfund i vikingetid,* Jysk Arkaeologisk Selskab 28 (1991), 151–54.

Fig. 16.1 The Virgin from London, B. L.
Harley 2904

Fig. 16.2–16.4. Figures from London, B. L. Cotton Claudius Biv

Fig. 16.5. Queen Edith
from the Bayeux
"Tapestry"

Fig. 16.6–16.7. Figures from the Bayeux
"Tapestry"

Fig. 16.8. Queen Emma from
London, B. L. Stowe 944

Fig. 16.9. Queen Emma from
London, B. L. Add. 33241

Fig. 16.10.
Hooked Tag
from Winchester

Fig. 16.11. *Supurbia* from the
Psychomachia

Fig. 16.12. *Luna* from
London, B. L. Cotton
Tiberius Bv

Fig. 16.13. Figure on the Portonaccio
Sarcophagus

Fig. 16.14. *Philosophia* from
Cambridge, Trinity College 0.3.7

Fig. 16.15. Figure from London, B. L. Harley 603

Fig. 16.16. Figure from the Adamklissi Monument

Fig. 16.17. Etheldreda from London, B. L. Add. 49598

Fig. 16.18. *Luxuria* from the *Psychomachia*

Fig. 16.19. *Pompa* from the *Psychomachia*

Fig. 16.20. The Virgin from London, B. L. Stowe 944

Fig. 16.21. The Virgin from the
Gospels of Judith of Flanders

Fig. 16.22. Judith from the Gospel
of Judith of Flanders

Fig. 16.23–16.24. Figures from the
Stuttgart Psalter

Fig. 16.25. Figures from the
Genoels-Elderen Diptych

Fig. 16.26. Heads of Figures from London, Lambeth Palace Library 200

Fig. 16.27. Figure from the Bury Psalter

Fig. 16.28. Figure on the *Grand Camée de France*

Fig. 16.29. Figures from the Halberstadt Diptych

Fig. 16.30. The Virgin from an Ivory Book-Cover

Fig. 16.31. Figure from London, Lambeth Palace Library 200

Fig. 16.32. Shoe Mounted on Bone Skate

Fig. 16.34. Child's Slipper

Fig. 16.33. Boot

Fig. 16.35. Modern Irish "Pampoodie," a Raw Hide Shoe

Fig. 16.36. Viking Figure from Oland (drawn by John Hines)

Fig. 16.37. Figure on a Picture Stone from Gotland

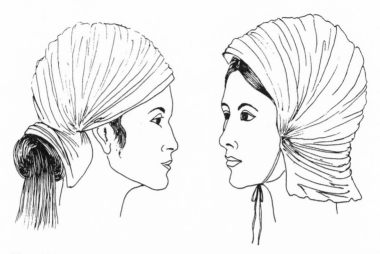

Fig. 16.38–16.39. The Coppergate Cap (adapted from drawings by Penelope Walton Rogers)

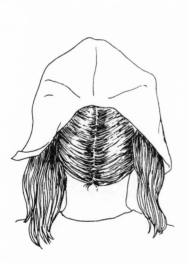

Fig. 16.40. The Lincoln Cap (after a drawing by Anna Muthesius)

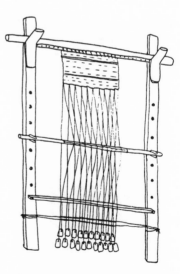

Fig. 16.41. Warp-Weighted Loom

Fig. 16.42. Z-Spinning   Fig. 16.43. S-Spinning

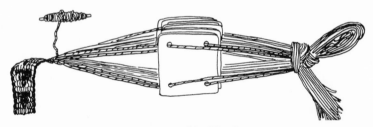

Fig. 16.44. Tablet Weaving

Fig. 16.45. Plain Tablet Twists   Fig. 16.46. Chevron Tablet Twists

Fig. 16.47. Reproduction of a
Kentish Fillet

Fig. 16.48. 2x1 Twill

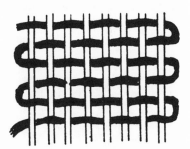

Fig. 16.49–16.50. Tabby

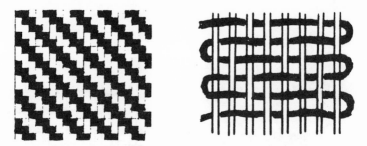

Fig. 16.51–16.52. 2x2 Twill

Fig. 16.53. Typical Diamond
Twill (adviser: P. Walton Rogers)

Fig. 16.54. "Trouser Suit" on Girl
from Mainz

Fig. 16.55. 2x1 Twill

Plate 16.1. Girdle End with Textile from St. John's, Cambridge (photo, after Owen-Crocker, *Dress in Anglo-Saxon England,* pl. VI)

Plate 16.2. *Peplos*-Type Gown from Huldremose (photo, after Owen-Crocker, *Dress in Anglo-Saxon England,* pl. I)

Index